UNIVERSITY CASEBOOK SERIES

2015 CASE SUPPLEMENT AND
STATUTORY APPENDIX

COPYRIGHT

CASES AND MATERIALS

EIGHTH EDITION

ROBERT A. GORMAN
Kenneth W. Gemmill Professor of Law Emeritus
University of Pennsylvania

JANE C. GINSBURG
Morton L. Janklow Professor of
Literary and Artistic Property Law
Columbia University School of Law

R. ANTHONY REESE
Chancellor's Professor of Law
University of California, Irvine

SUPPLEMENT

by

JANE C. GINSBURG
R. ANTHONY REESE

FOUNDATION PRESS

© 2012 THOMSON REUTERS/FOUNDATION PRESS
© 2013 by LEG, Inc. d/b/a West Academic Publishing
© 2014 LEG, Inc. d/b/a West Academic
© 2015 LEG, Inc. d/b/a West Academic
    444 Cedar Street, Suite 700
    St. Paul, MN 55101
    1-877-888-1330

Printed in the United States of America

ISBN: 978-1-63459-491-2

TABLE OF CONTENTS

TABLE OF CASES

The principal cases are in bold type.

UNIVERSITY CASEBOOK SERIES®

2015 CASE SUPPLEMENT AND
STATUTORY APPENDIX

COPYRIGHT

CASES AND MATERIALS

EIGHTH EDITION

CHAPTER 2

COPYRIGHTABLE SUBJECT MATTER

A. IN GENERAL

1. ORIGINAL WORKS OF AUTHORSHIP

a. WHAT IS AUTHORSHIP?

Page 82. Insert before Questions:

The COMPENDIUM OF THE U.S. COPYRIGHT OFFICE PRACTICES (3d ed. 2014) states that the Office will not register "works that lack human authorship." Section 313.2 of the Compendium further specifies:

> [T]he Copyright Act protects "original works of *authorship*." 17 U.S.C. § 102(a) (emphasis added). To qualify as a work of "authorship" a work must be created by a human being. See *Burrow-Giles Lithographic Co.*, 111 U.S. at 58. Works that do not satisfy this requirement are not copyrightable.
>
> The Office will not register works produced by nature, animals, or plants. Likewise, the Office cannot register a work purportedly created by divine or supernatural beings, although the Office may register a work where the application or the deposit copy(ies) state that the work was inspired by a divine spirit.
>
> Examples:
> - A photograph taken by a monkey.
> - A mural painted by an elephant.
> - A claim based on the appearance of actual animal skin.
> - A claim based on driftwood that has been shaped and smoothed by the ocean.
> - A claim based on cut marks, defects, and other qualities found in natural stone.
> - An application for a song naming the Holy Spirit as the author of the work.
>
> Similarly, the Office will not register works produced by a machine or mere mechanical process that operates randomly or automatically without any creative input or intervention from a human author.
>
> Examples:
> - Reducing or enlarging the size of a preexisting work of authorship.

- Making changes to a preexisting work of authorship that are dictated by manufacturing or materials requirements.

- Converting a work from analog to digital format, such as transferring a motion picture from VHS to DVD.

- Declicking or reducing the noise in a preexisting sound recording or converting a sound recording from monaural to stereo sound.

- Transposing a song from B major to C major.

- Medical imaging produced by x-rays, ultrasounds, magnetic resonance imaging, or other diagnostic equipment.

- A claim based on a mechanical weaving process that randomly produces irregular shapes in the fabric without any discernible pattern.

Do you agree that all of the above examples lack human authorship? With which examples might you take issue with, and why? How much, and what kind, of human intervention would contribute sufficient human authorship to these examples? The first example given in the Compendium would appear to cover the photo below, which was taken by a macaque who stole photographer David Slater's camera and pressed buttons that resulted in a number of photographs. Samuel Gibbs, *Monkey business: macaque selfie can't be copyrighted, say US and UK*, THE GUARDIAN, Aug. 22, 2014, at http://www.theguardian.com/technology /2014/aug/22/monkey-business-macaque-selfie-cant-be-copyrighted-say-us-and-uk.

How would the Compendium approach treat the products of Ginny Fisher's New Orleans business called Puppy Picasso? Customers bring their dogs to Fisher, who "tapes a piece of canvas—16 by 20, 24 by 36 or

36 by 48 inches—to the floor, puts paint all over the fenced-in canvas and leads the animal around with treats to direct where she wants it to go," as shown in the pictures below. Lorena O'Neil, *Painting With Puppies*, OZY, Aug. 21, 2014 (http://www.ozy.com/good-sht/painting-with-puppies/32721.article). Are the canvases copyrightable?

Page 83. Add new Questions 5, 6, and 7:

5. The Compendium states that "the Office cannot register a work purportedly created by divine or supernatural beings, although the Office may register a work where the application or the deposit copy(ies) state that the work was inspired by a divine spirit." Why does the attribution of authorship change the outcome? Suppose the work were a critical edition of a musical composition or literary work, or a restoration of an artwork, in which the editor or restorer sought to present the work in the purity of its creation by the original (perhaps long-dead) author: Is the editor or restorer an "author" if she endeavors to eliminate all trace of authorship by anyone other than the initial author?

6. Kim Seng Co packages and sells Vietnamese food. Its package of rice stick noodles appears on the left below. Kim Seng has sued its competitor J & A, alleging that J & A committed copyright infringement in producing its package of rice stick noodles, which appears on the right below. The photograph on each package depicts a traditional Vietnamese dish—a bowl filled with rice sticks topped with egg rolls, grilled meat, and assorted garnishes. Because Kim Seng did not obtain a transfer of copyright from the photographer of the image on its package, Kim Seng bases its claim of copyright on its creation of the "food sculpture" arranging the elements shown in the photograph, of which the photographer then created a two-dimensional representation. Is the "bowl of food sculpture" an original work of authorship? *See Kim Seng Co. v. J & A Importers, Inc.,* 810 F.Supp.2d 1046 (C.D.Cal. 2011).

Kim Seng Package   **J & A Package**

7. Teller, a magician, has long performed a magic trick called "Shadows." The routine

> consists of a spotlight trained on a vase containing a single rose. The light falls in such a manner that the shadow of the rose is projected onto a white screen positioned some distance behind it. Teller then enters the otherwise still scene, picks up a large knife, and proceeds to use the knife to dramatically sever the leaves and petals of the rose's shadow on the screen slowly, one-by-one, whereupon the corresponding leaves of the real rose sitting in the vase fall to the ground, breaking from the stem at the point where Teller cut the shadow.

The scene closes with Teller pricking his thumb with the knife, and holding his hand in front of the canvas. A silhouette of a trail of blood appears, trickling down the canvas just below the shadow of Teller's hand. Teller then wipes his hand across the "blood" shadow, leaving a crimson streak upon the canvas

Teller has brought an infringement action against Dogge, a Dutch magician who has posted to YouTube a video of a very similar routine, and has offered to disclose the secret of the trick. Teller asserts that "Shadows" is a dramatic work; Dogge responds that it is a mere magic trick not protectable by copyright. How should the court rule? *See Teller v. Dogge*, 8 F.Supp.3d 1228 (D. Nev. 2014).

Garcia v. Google, Inc., 786 F.3d 733 (9th Cir. 2015, en banc). Mark Basseley (aka Youssef) hired Ms. Garcia to perform in what he described to her as a "desert epic" film in the vein of *The Son of the Sheik*. Unbeknownst to her, after filming her performance, he then dubbed over the dialogue, added other scenes, and uploaded a trailer for the film to YouTube as *Innocence of Muslims*, an anti-Muslim propaganda film. Garcia subsequently received death threats and, asserting copyright ownership of her five-second performance, demanded that YouTube remove the trailer. A panel of the Ninth Circuit held that Garcia was the author and copyright owner of her performance, and granted a preliminary injunction barring YouTube from showing the film. The Ninth Circuit vacated that judgment and an en banc panel held the district court did not abuse its discretion in holding that Garcia was not likely to succeed on the merits of her copyright claim.

The central question is whether the law and facts clearly favor Garcia's claim to a copyright in her five-second acting performance as it appears in *Innocence of Muslims*. The answer is no. . . .

Under the Copyright Act, "[c]opyright protection subsists . . . in original works of authorship fixed in any tangible medium of expression . . . [including] motion pictures." 17 U.S.C. § 102(a). That fixation must be done "by or under the authority of the author." 17 U.S.C. § 101. Benchmarked against this statutory standard, the law does not clearly favor Garcia's position.

The statute purposefully left "works of authorship" undefined to provide for some flexibility. See 1 Nimmer on Copyright § 2.03. Nevertheless, several other provisions provide useful guidance. An audiovisual work is one that consists of "a series of related images which are intrinsically intended to be shown" by machines or other electronic equipment, plus "accompanying sounds." 17 U.S.C. § 101. In turn, a "motion picture" is an "audiovisual work[ ] consisting of a series of related images which, when shown in succession, impart an impression of motion, together with accompanying sounds, if any." *Id.* These two definitions embody the work here: *Innocence of Muslims* is an audiovisual work that is categorized as a motion picture and is derivative of the [film's] script. Garcia is the author of none of this and makes no copyright claim to the film or to the script.

Instead, Garcia claims that her five-second performance itself merits copyright protection. In the face of this statutory scheme, it comes as no surprise that during this litigation, the Copyright Office found that Garcia's performance was not a copyrightable work when it rejected her copyright application. The Copyright Office explained that its "longstanding practices do not allow a copyright claim by an individual actor or actress in his or her performance contained within a motion picture." Thus, "[f]or copyright registration purposes, a motion picture is a single integrated work. . . . Assuming Ms. Garcia's contribution was limited to her acting performance, we cannot register her performance apart from the motion picture."

We credit this expert opinion of the Copyright Office—the office charged with administration and enforcement of the copyright laws and registration. The Copyright Office's well-reasoned position "reflects a 'body of experience and informed judgment to which courts and litigants may properly resort for guidance.'" [Citation.]

In analyzing whether the law clearly favors Garcia, *Aalmuhammed v. Lee*, 202 F.3d 1227 (9th Cir. 2000), provides a useful foundation. There, we examined the meaning of "work" as the first step in analyzing joint authorship of the movie *Malcolm X*. The Copyright Act provides that when a work is "prepared by two or more authors with the intention that their contributions be merged into inseparable or interdependent parts of a unitary *whole*," the work becomes a "joint work" with two or more authors. 17 U.S.C. § 101 (emphasis added). Garcia unequivocally disclaims joint authorship of the film.

In *Aalmuhammed*, we concluded that defining a "work" based upon "some minimal level of creativity or originality . . . would be too broad and indeterminate to be useful." 202 F.3d at 1233 (internal quotation marks omitted). Our animating concern was that this definition of "work" would fragment copyright protection for the unitary film *Malcolm X* into many little pieces:

> So many people might qualify as an "author" if the question were limited to whether they made a substantial creative contribution that that test would not distinguish one from another. Everyone from the producer and director to casting director, costumer, hairstylist, and "best boy" gets listed in the movie credits because all of their creative contributions really do matter.

Id.

Garcia's theory of copyright law would result in the legal morass we warned against in *Aalmuhammed*—splintering a movie into many different "works," even in the absence of an independent fixation. Simply put, as Google claimed, it "make[s] Swiss cheese of copyrights."

Take, for example, films with a large cast—the proverbial "cast of thousands"—such as *Ben-Hur* or *Lord of the Rings*. The silent epic *Ben-Hur* advertised a cast of 125,000 people. In the

Lord of the Rings trilogy, 20,000 extras tramped around Middle-Earth alongside Frodo Baggins (played by Elijah Wood). Treating every acting performance as an independent work would not only be a logistical and financial nightmare, it would turn cast of thousands into a new mantra: copyright of thousands.

. . .

The reality is that contracts and the work-made-for-hire doctrine govern much of the big-budget Hollywood performance and production world. Absent these formalities, courts have looked to implied licenses. Indeed, the district court found that Garcia granted Youssef just such an implied license to incorporate her performance into the film. But these legal niceties do not necessarily dictate whether something is protected by copyright, and licensing has its limitations. As filmmakers warn, low-budget films rarely use licenses. Even if filmmakers diligently obtain licenses for everyone on set, the contracts are not a panacea. Third-party content distributors, like YouTube and Netflix, won't have easy access to the licenses; litigants may dispute their terms and scope; and actors and other content contributors can terminate licenses after thirty five years. See 17 U.S.C. § 203(a)(3). Untangling the complex, difficult-to-access, and often phantom chain of title to tens, hundreds, or even thousands of standalone copyrights is a task that could tie the distribution chain in knots. And filming group scenes like a public parade, or the 1963 March on Washington, would pose a huge burden if each of the thousands of marchers could claim an independent copyright.

The Second Circuit has reached a similar conclusion with respect to a film *director's* claim of single authorship of his inseparable contributions to the audiovisual work. In 16 Casa Duse LLC v. Merkin, ___ F.3d ___, 2015 WL 3937947 (2d Cir. June 28, 2015), the court, citing *Garcia*, observed,

Filmmaking is a collaborative process typically involving artistic contributions from large numbers of people, including—in addition to producers, directors, and screenwriters—actors, designers, cinematographers, camera operators, and a host of skilled technical contributors. If copyright subsisted separately in each of their contributions to the completed film, the copyright in the film itself, which is recognized by statute as a work of authorship, could be undermined by any number of individual claims. These various contributors may make original artistic expressions, which are arguably fixed in the medium of film footage. But while originality and fixation are necessary prerequisites to obtaining copyright protection, see 17 U.S.C. § 102(a), they are not alone sufficient: Authors are not entitled to copyright protection except for the "works of authorship" they create and fix. [Citation.] Our conclusion in the present case does not suggest that motion picture directors such as Merkin may never achieve copyright protection for their creative efforts. The director of a film may, of course, be the sole or joint author of that film, such that she or he can secure copyright protection for the work. And authors of freestanding works that are incorporated into a film, such as dance performances or songs, may copyright these "separate and independent work[s]." 17 U.S.C. § 101 (defining "collective work"). But a director's contribution to an integrated "work of authorship" such as a film is not itself a "work of authorship" subject to its own copyright protection.

QUESTIONS

1. Is there a difference between an actor's performance and the appearance of a member of the public in a march or demonstration?

2. Does the Ninth Circuit decline to recognize Ms. Garcia's performance as a work of authorship because of the dreaded consequences?

3. As we will see, *infra* Chapter 3.A and B, the Copyright Act provides a variety of solutions to the problems of multiple authorship. If a contribution to a motion picture or other work involving multiple participants meets minimum standards of originality, creativity and substantiality (see *infra* subsection 2.A.1.b), is it appropriate for a court to reject the contributor's claim to be the author of that contribution? See *Garcia v. Google*, 786 F.3d 727, ___ (Kozinski, J., dissenting): "When dealing with material created during production of a film or other composite work, the absence of a contract always complicates things. Without a contract the parties are left with whatever rights the copyright law gives them. It's not our job to take away from performers rights Congress gave them."

4. Why would Garcia "unequivocally disclaim[ ] joint authorship of the film"? See *infra*, Chapter 3.A.3 (Ownership of Joint Works).

2. FIXATION IN TANGIBLE FORM

Page 94. Add a new Question 6:

6. Is a "drawing created on a chalkboard or a sculpture created out of moldable clay" sufficiently "fixed" to qualify for copyright protection, given that the work can easily be altered? *See FireSabre Consulting LLC v. Sheehy*, 2013 WL 5420977 (S.D.N.Y. 2013).

Page 99. Add after the PROBLEM:

QUESTION

In October 2010, singer-songwriter Carol Daggs performed three of her original songs at the Organixsoul showcase at the City Place Inn & Suites in Springfield Massachusetts. Tony Bass, producer of the cable public access program *City Beat TV* was recording the showcase, including Daggs's performance. Daggs contends she was never informed that the showcase was being recorded; Bass contends that before she began performing she was aware that he was recording the show. After her performance, Daggs approached Bass, introduced herself, and requested a courtesy copy of her set. Bass, who alleges he identified himself as producer of *City Beat TV*, promptly sent her a DVD of her performance at no charge. Daggs contends that Bass never informed her that her set would be broadcast on TV and never asked for her permission to do so. In November 2010, Daggs's performance was broadcast on the *City Beat TV* show on a public access cable channel in Springfield. Daggs later sued Bass for, among other claims, violating 17 U.S.C. § 1101. Bass has moved to dismiss Daggs's complaint for failure to state a claim, arguing that Daggs implicitly licensed his acts. Daggs has moved for summary judgment on her § 1101 claim. How should the court rule? See *Daggs v. Bass*, 104 U.S.P.Q.2d 1767 (D.Mass. 2012).

C. FACTS AND COMPILATIONS

2. COMPILATIONS

Page 132. Add at the end of Question 1:

In 2012 the Copyright Office issued a policy statement announcing that "unless a compilation of materials results [in] a work of authorship that falls within one or more of the eight categories of authorship listed in section 102(a) of title 17, the Office will refuse registration in such a claim. Thus, the Office will not register a work in which the claim is in a "compilation of ideas," or a "selection and arrangement of handtools" or a "compilation of rocks." Neither ideas, handtools, nor rocks may be protected by copyright (although an expression of an idea, a drawing of a handtool or a photograph of rock may be copyrightable)." 77 Fed.Reg. 37,605, 37,607 (June 22, 2012). Is this a proper interpretation of the statute? Under this approach, would the arrangement of furniture be copyrightable? Or the selection and arrangement of a series of yoga poses? See *Bikram's Yoga College of India, L.P. v. Evolation Yoga, LLC*, 105 U.S.P.Q.2d 1162 (C.D.Cal. 2012).

Page 150. Add at the end of Question 3:

See also U.S. Copyright Office, *Registration of Claims to Copyright*, 77 Fed.Reg. 37,605 (2012).

4. MAPS

Page 164. Add new Question 4:

4.   The Nielsen Co., famed for its television ratings, produces "designated market area" [DMA] maps, which divide the United States into approximately 210 TV market regions. A DMA region consists of all counties whose largest viewing share is given to stations of the same market area. Nielsen draws the boundaries for its DMA regions each year by grouping counties together according to its own estimates, projections, and ratings of television program audiences. In part, Nielsen uses data collected from "Local People Meters" and/or "measurement diaries." Local People Meters are electronic devices that constantly monitor the viewing behavior of residents in the 25 largest DMA regions to measure stations tuned to and viewers' behavior. Measurement diaries, used in smaller markets, are paper records distributed to a random sample of households. Truck Ads sells advertising appearing on the sides of trucks and mobile billboards. Its website displays a "designated market area" map allegedly copied from Nielsen's. In response to Nielsen's copyright infringement suit, Truck Ads asserts that Nielsen's DMA maps are not copyrightable because they merely depict facts and/or because any expression is necessarily merged with the idea of depicting a television DMA. How should the court rule? See *Nielsen Co. v. Truck Ads, LLC*, 102 U.S.P.Q.2d 1020 (N.D.Ill. 2011).

D. DERIVATIVE WORKS

Page 167. Insert before QUESTIONS:

———

Section 103(b) specifies that the "copyright in a . . . derivative work extends only to the material contributed by the author of such work, as distinguished from the preexisting material employed in the work, and does not imply any copyright in the preexisting material." In **Cooley v. Penguin Group**, 31 F.Supp.3d 599 (S.D.N.Y. 2014), the Southern District of New York recently applied this principle to an infringement claim concerning photographs of a sculpture. National Geographic commissioned the sculptor, Cooley, to create the sculptures, and also commissioned the photographer, Psihoyos, to produce photos of the sculptures which would then illustrate an article in its magazine. National Geographic's agreements with Cooley and Psihoyos provided that National Geographic would own the copyright in both the sculpture and the photos, but that after the photos appeared in the magazine, National Geographic would return the copyright in the sculpture to Cooley and the copyright in the photos to Psihoyos, which it did. When Cooley later discovered that Psihoyos was licensing the photos of the sculptues to other publishers, he sued Psihoyos and the publishers, alleging that this use of Psihoyos's photos infinged on Cooley's copyrights in his sculptures.

> . . . The remaining question on this point is the extent, if any, to which Psihoyos's copyright in the photographs—not the sculptures—gave him the right to license and otherwise deal with the photographs as he has since May 1997 and gives him such rights going forward. . . .

> The Court assumes that Psihoyos's photographs reflect some element of originality. It thus assumes that Psihoyos owns valid copyrights in the photographs. But that does not mean that Psihoyos's copyrights in the photographs give him the unrestricted right to use and license them as he wishes without regard to Cooley's copyrights in the sculptures those photographs depict.

> As an initial matter, the fact that Psihoyos is assumed to own valid copyrights in the photographs is the beginning, not the end, of the analysis. The Copyright Act grants the author of a derivative work copyright protection only in whatever increment of original expression the author contributes, but does not disturb the ownership of the copyright or the rights of its holder in respect of the underlying work. In other words, "[t]he copyright in [the derivative] work is independent of, and does not affect or enlarge the scope, duration, ownership, or subsistence of, any copyright protection in the pre-existing material," even where the new and pre-existing material are "inseparably intertwined." The copyright in a derivative work thus does not confer the unfettered—let alone exclusive—right to reproduce the derivative work in a manner that would infringe rights of the holder of the copyright in the underlying work absent a license to reproduce or otherwise use the underlying work.

In light of these principles, Psihoyos's copyrights in his photographs are essentially immaterial here. They give him rights only to the extent that he may exercise them without infringing Cooley's copyrights in the sculptures. As his original contributions to the photographs are inextricably intertwined with Cooley's sculp-tures, Psihoyos's ability to exploit his own rights to the photographs without Cooley's consent is virtually nonexistent. If he reproduces an image of a Cooley sculpture, he reproduces also the sculpture, which infringes Cooley's rights if done without Cooley's authorization. Indeed, Psihoyos does not even dispute that his photographs are substantially similar to Cooley's sculptures—the point of taking them after all was to reproduce them accurately, if in but two dimensions—thus, conceding infringement absent some affirmative defense.

Page 184. Add a new Question 4:

4. Consider a textbook that contains problems that teachers assign students to solve. Is a "solutions manual" that consists solely of the answers to the problems in that textbook a copyrightable derivative work? Does it matter if the answers consist of a key to multiple choice questions? *See Pearson Education, Inc. v. Ishayev*, 963 F.Supp.2d 239 (S.D.N.Y. 2013).

E. COMPUTER PROGRAMS

Page 206. Insert after QUESTIONS:

Oracle America v. Google, Inc.
750 F.3d 1339 (Fed. Cir. 2014).

■ O'MALLEY, CIRCUIT JUDGE.

This copyright dispute involves 37 packages of computer source code. The parties have often referred to these groups of computer programs, individually or collectively, as "application programming interfaces," or API packages, but it is their content, not their name, that matters. The predecessor of Oracle America, Inc. ("Oracle") wrote these and other API packages in the Java programming language, and Oracle licenses them on various terms for others to use. Many software developers use the Java language, as well as Oracle's API packages, to write applications (commonly referred to as "apps") for desktop and laptop computers, tablets, smartphones, and other devices.

. . .

There are 37 Java API packages at issue in this appeal, three of which are the core packages identified by the district court. These packages contain thousands of individual elements, including classes, subclasses, methods, and interfaces.

Every package consists of two types of source code—what the parties call (1) declaring code; and (2) implementing code. Declaring code is the expression that identifies the prewritten function and is sometimes referred to as the "declaration" or "header." As the district court explained, the "main point is that this header line of code introduces the method body and specifies very precisely the inputs, name and other functionality." The expressions used by the programmer from the declaring code command the computer to execute the associated implementing code, which gives the computer the step-by-step instructions for carrying out the declared function.

. . .

With respect to the 37 packages at issue, "Google believed Java application programmers would want to find the same 37 sets of functionalities in the new Android system callable by the same names as used in Java." To achieve this result, Google copied the declaring source code from the 37 Java API packages verbatim, inserting that code into parts of its Android software. In doing so, Google copied the elaborately organized taxonomy of all the names of methods, classes, interfaces, and packages—the "overall system of organized names—covering 37 packages, with over six hundred classes, with over six thousand methods." The parties and district court referred to this taxonomy of expressions as the "structure, sequence, and organization" or "SSO" of the 37 packages. It is undisputed, however, that Google wrote its own implementing code, except with respect to: (1) the rangeCheck function, which consisted of nine lines of code; and (2) eight decompiled security files.

As to rangeCheck, the court found that the Sun engineer who wrote it later worked for Google and contributed two files he created containing the rangeCheck function—"Timsort.java" and "ComparableTimsort"—to the Android platform. In doing so, the nine-line rangeCheck function was copied directly into Android. . . .

Google released the Android platform in 2007, and the first Android phones went on sale the following year. Although it is undisputed that certain Android software contains copies of the 37 API packages' declaring code at issue, neither the district court nor the parties specify in which programs those copies appear. Oracle indicated at oral argument, however, that all Android phones contain copies of the accused portions of the Android software. Android smartphones "rapidly grew in popularity and now comprise a large share of the United States market." Google provides the Android platform free of charge to smartphone manufacturers and receives revenue when customers use particular functions on the Android phone. Although Android uses the Java programming language, it is undisputed that Android is not generally Java compatible. As Oracle explains, "Google ultimately designed Android to be incompatible with the Java platform, so that apps written for one will not work on the other."

. . .

At this stage, it is undisputed that the declaring code and the structure and organization of the Java API packages are original. The testimony at trial revealed that designing the Java API packages was a creative process and that the Sun/Oracle developers had a vast range of options for the structure and organization. In its copyrightability decision, the district court specifically found that the API packages are both creative and original, and Google concedes on appeal that the originality requirements are met. The court found, however, that neither the declaring code nor the SSO was entitled to copyright protection under the Copyright Act.

Although the parties agree that Oracle's API packages meet the originality requirement under Section 102(a), they disagree as to the proper interpretation and application of Section 102(b). For its part, Google suggests that there is a two-step copyrightability analysis, wherein Section 102(a) grants copyright protection to original works, while Section 102(b) takes it away if the work has a functional component. To the contrary, however, Congress emphasized that Section 102(b) "in no way enlarges or contracts the scope of copyright protection" and that its "purpose is to restate . . . that the basic dichotomy between expression and idea remains unchanged." *Feist*, 499 U.S. at 356 (quoting H.R. Rep. No. 1476, 94th Cong., 2d Sess. 54). "Section 102(b) does not extinguish the protection accorded a particular expression of an idea merely because that expression is embodied in a method of operation." *Mitel, Inc. v. Iqtel, Inc.*, 124 F.3d 1366, 1372 (10th Cir. 1997). Section 102(a) and 102(b) are to be considered collectively so that certain expressions are subject to greater scrutiny. *Id.* In assessing copyrightability, the district court is required to ferret out apparent expressive aspects of a work and then separate protectable expression from "unprotectable ideas, facts, processes, and methods of operation." *See Atari*, 975 F.2d at 839.

Of course, as with many things, in defining this task, the devil is in the details. Circuit courts have struggled with, and disagree over, the tests to be employed when attempting to draw the line between what is protectable expression and what is not. *Compare Whelan Assocs., Inc. v. Jaslow Dental Lab., Inc.*, 797 F.2d 1222, 1236 (3d Cir. 1986) (everything not necessary to the purpose or function of a work is expression), *with Lotus*, 49 F.3d at 815 (methods of operation are means by which a user operates something and any words used to effectuate that operation are unprotected expression). When assessing whether the non-literal elements of a computer program constitute protectable expression, the Ninth Circuit has endorsed an "abstraction-filtration-comparison" test formulated by the Second Circuit and expressly adopted by several other circuits. *Sega Enters. Ltd. v. Accolade, Inc.*, 977 F.2d 1510, 1525 (9th Cir. 1992) ("In our view, in light of the essentially utilitarian nature of computer programs, the Second Circuit's approach is an appropriate one."). This test rejects the notion that anything that performs a function is necessarily uncopyrightable. *See Mitel*, 124 F.3d at 1372 (rejecting the *Lotus* court's formulation, and concluding that, "although an element of a work may be characterized as a method of operation, that element may nevertheless contain expression that is eligible for copyright protection."). And it also rejects as flawed the *Whelan* assumption that, once any separable idea can be identified in a computer program everything else must be protectable expression, on grounds that more than one idea may be embodied in any particular program. *Altai*, 982 F.2d at 705–06.

Thus, this test eschews bright line approaches and requires a more nuanced assessment of the particular program at issue in order to determine what expression is protectable and infringed. As the Second Circuit explains, this test has three steps. In the abstraction step, the court "first break[s] down the allegedly infringed program into its constituent structural parts." *Id.* at 706. In the filtration step, the court "sift[s] out all non-protectable material," including ideas and "expression that is necessarily incidental to those ideas." *Id.* In the final step, the court compares the remaining creative expression with the allegedly infringing program.

. . .

2. The Structure, Sequence, and Organization of the API Packages

The district court found that the SSO of the Java API packages is creative and original, but nevertheless held that it is a "system or method of operation . . . and, therefore, cannot be copyrighted" under 17 U.S.C. § 102(b). *Copyrightability Decision*, 872 F. Supp. 2d at 976–77. In reaching this conclusion, the district court seems to have relied upon language contained in a First Circuit decision: *Lotus Development Corp. v. Borland International, Inc.*, 49 F.3d 807 (1st Cir. 1995), *aff'd without opinion by equally divided court* (1996).

In *Lotus*, it was undisputed that the defendant copied the menu command hierarchy and interface from Lotus 1–2–3, a computer spreadsheet program "that enables users to perform accounting functions electronically on a computer." 49 F.3d at 809. The menu command hierarchy referred to a series of commands—such as "Copy," "Print," and "Quit"—which were arranged into more than 50 menus and submenus. *Id.* Although the defendant did not copy any Lotus source code, it copied the menu command hierarchy into its rival program. The question before the court was "whether a computer menu command hierarchy is copyrightable subject matter." *Id.*

Although it accepted the district court's finding that Lotus developers made some expressive choices in selecting and arranging the command terms, the First Circuit found that the command hierarchy was not copyrightable because, among other things, it was a "method of operation" under Section 102(b). In reaching this conclusion, the court defined a "method of operation" as "the means by which a person operates something, whether it be a car, a food processor, or a computer." *Id.* at 815.[10]

Because the Lotus menu command hierarchy provided "the means by which users control and operate Lotus 1–2–3," it was deemed unprotectable. *Id.* For example, if users wanted to copy material, they would use the "Copy" command and the command terms would tell the computer what to do. According to the *Lotus* court, the "fact that Lotus developers could have designed the Lotus menu command hierarchy differently is immaterial to the question of whether it is a 'method of operation.' " *Id.* at 816. (noting that "our initial inquiry is not whether the Lotus menu command hierarchy incorporates any expression"). The court further indicated that, "[i]f specific words are essential to operating something, then they are part of a 'method of operation' and, as such, are unprotectable." *Id.*

On appeal, Oracle argues that the district court's reliance on *Lotus* is misplaced because it is distinguishable on its facts and is inconsistent with Ninth Circuit law. We agree. First, while the defendant in *Lotus* did

---

[10]   The *Lotus* majority cited no authority for this definition of "method of operation."

not copy any of the underlying code, Google concedes that it copied portions of Oracle's declaring source code verbatim. Second, the *Lotus* court found that the commands at issue there (copy, print, etc.) were not creative, but it is undisputed here that the declaring code and the structure and organization of the API packages are both creative and original. Finally, while the court in *Lotus* found the commands at issue were "essential to operating" the system, it is undisputed that—other than perhaps as to the three core packages—Google did not need to copy the structure, sequence, and organization of the Java API packages to write programs in the Java language.

More importantly, however, the Ninth Circuit has not adopted the court's "method of operation" reasoning in *Lotus*, and we conclude that it is inconsistent with binding precedent. Specifically, we find that *Lotus* is inconsistent with Ninth Circuit case law recognizing that the structure, sequence, and organization of a computer program is eligible for copyright protection where it qualifies as an expression of an idea, rather than the idea itself. *See Johnson Controls*, 886 F.2d at 1175–76. And, while the court in *Lotus* held "that expression that is part of a 'method of operation' cannot be copyrighted," 49 F.3d at 818, this court—applying Ninth Circuit law—reached the exact opposite conclusion, finding that copyright protects "the expression of [a] process or method," *Atari*, 975 F.2d at 839.

We find, moreover, that the hard and fast rule set down in *Lotus* and employed by the district court here—i.e., that elements which perform a function can never be copyrightable—is at odds with the Ninth Circuit's endorsement of the abstraction-filtration-comparison analysis discussed earlier. As the Tenth Circuit concluded in expressly rejecting the *Lotus* "method of operation" analysis, in favor of the Second Circuit's abstraction-filtration-comparison test, "although an element of a work may be characterized as a method of operation, that element may nevertheless contain expression that is eligible for copyright protection." *Mitel*, 124 F.3d at 1372. Specifically, the court found that Section 102(b) "does not extinguish the protection accorded a particular expression of an idea merely because that expression is embodied in a method of operation at a higher level of abstraction." *Id.*

Other courts agree that components of a program that can be characterized as a "method of operation" may nevertheless be copyrightable. For example, the Third Circuit rejected a defendant's argument that operating system programs are "per se" uncopyrightable because an operating system is a "method of operation" for a computer. *Apple Computer, Inc. v. Franklin Computer Corp.*, 714 F.2d 1240, 1250–52 (3d Cir. 1983). The court distinguished between the "method which instructs the computer to perform its operating functions" and "the instructions themselves," and found that the instructions were copyrightable. *Id.* at 1250–51. In its analysis, the court noted: "[t]hat the words of a program are used ultimately in the implementation of a process should in no way affect their copyrightability." *Id.* at 1252 (quoting CONTU Report at 21). The court focused "on whether the idea is capable of various modes of expression" and indicated that, "[i]f other programs can be written or created which perform the same function as [i]n Apple's operating system program, then that program is an expression of the idea and hence copyrightable." *Id.* at 1253. Notably, no other circuit has adopted the First Circuit's "method of operation" analysis.

Courts have likewise found that classifying a work as a "system" does not preclude copyright for the particular expression of that system. *See Toro Co. v. R & R Prods. Co.*, 787 F.2d 1208, 1212 (8th Cir. 1986) (rejecting the district court's decision that "appellant's parts numbering system is not copyrightable because it is a 'system' " and indicating that Section 102(b) does not preclude protection for the "particular expression" of that system); *see also Am. Dental Ass'n v. Delta Dental Plans Ass'n*, 126 F.3d 977, 980 (7th Cir. 1997) ("A dictionary cannot be called a 'system' just because new novels are written using words, all of which appear in the dictionary. Nor is word-processing software a 'system' just because it has a command structure for producing paragraphs.").

Here, the district court recognized that the SSO "resembles a taxonomy," but found that "it is nevertheless a command structure, a system or method of operation—a long hierarchy of over six thousand commands to carry out pre-assigned functions." *Copyrightability Decision*, 872 F. Supp. 2d at 999–1000.[12] In other words, the court concluded that, although the SSO is expressive, it is not copyrightable because it is also functional. The problem with the district court's approach is that computer programs are by definition functional—they are all designed to accomplish some task. Indeed, the statutory definition of "computer program" acknowledges that they function "to bring about a certain result." See 17 U.S.C. § 101 (defining a "computer program" as "a set of statements or instructions to be used directly or indirectly in a computer in order to bring about a certain result"). If we were to accept the district court's suggestion that a computer program is uncopyrightable simply because it "carr[ies] out pre-assigned functions," no computer program is protectable. That result contradicts Congress's express intent to provide copyright protection to computer programs, as well as binding Ninth Circuit case law finding computer programs copyrightable, despite their utilitarian or functional purpose. Though the trial court did add the caveat that it "does not hold that the structure, sequence and organization of all computer programs may be stolen," *Copyrightability Decision*, 872 F. Supp. 2d at 1002, it is hard to see how its method of operation analysis could lead to any other conclusion.

While it does not appear that the Ninth Circuit has addressed the precise issue, we conclude that a set of commands to instruct a computer to carry out desired operations may contain expression that is eligible for copyright protection. *See Mitel*, 124 F.3d at 1372. We agree with Oracle that, under Ninth Circuit law, an original work—even one that serves a function—is entitled to copyright protection as long as the author had multiple ways to express the underlying idea. Section 102(b) does not, as Google seems to suggest, automatically deny copyright protection to elements of a computer program that are functional. Instead, as noted, Section 102(b) codifies the idea/expression dichotomy and the legislative history confirms that, among other things, Section 102(b) was "intended to make clear that the expression adopted by the programmer is the

---

[12] This analogy by the district court is meaningful because taxonomies, in varying forms, have generally been deemed copyrightable. See, e.g., Practice Mgmt. Info. Corp. v. Am. Med. Ass'n, 121 F.3d 516, 517–20 (9th Cir. 1997); Am. Dental, 126 F.3d at 978–81.

copyrightable element in a computer program." H.R. Rep. No. 1476, 94th Cong., 2d Sess. 54. Therefore, even if an element directs a computer to perform operations, the court must nevertheless determine whether it contains any separable expression entitled to protection.

On appeal, Oracle does not—and concedes that it cannot—claim copyright in the idea of organizing functions of a computer program or in the "package-class-method" organizational structure in the abstract. Instead, Oracle claims copyright protection only in its particular way of naming and organizing each of the 37 Java API packages. Oracle recognizes, for example, that it "cannot copyright the idea of programs that open an internet connection," but "it can copyright the precise strings of code used to do so, at least so long as 'other language is available' to achieve the same function." Appellant Reply Br. 13–14 (citation omitted). Thus, Oracle concedes that Google and others could employ the Java language—much like anyone could employ the English language to write a paragraph without violating the copyrights of other English language writers. And, that Google may employ the "package-class-method" structure much like authors can employ the same rules of grammar chosen by other authors without fear of infringement. What Oracle contends is that, beyond that point, Google, like any author, is not permitted to employ the precise phrasing or precise structure chosen by Oracle to flesh out the substance of its packages—the details and arrangement of the prose.

As the district court acknowledged, Google could have structured Android differently and could have chosen different ways to express and implement the functionality that it copied. Specifically, the court found that "the very same functionality could have been offered in Android without duplicating the exact command structure used in Java." *Copyrightability Decision*, 872 F. Supp. 2d at 976. The court further explained that Google could have offered the same functions in Android by "rearranging the various methods under different groupings among the various classes and packages." *Id.* The evidence showed, moreover, that Google designed many of its own API packages from scratch, and, thus, could have designed its own corresponding 37 API packages if it wanted to do so.

Given the court's findings that the SSO is original and creative, and that the declaring code could have been written and organized in any number of ways and still have achieved the same functions, we conclude that Section 102(b) does not bar the packages from copyright protection just because they also perform functions.

QUESTION

In *Lotus*, Borland could have written (and in later versions of Quattro Pro, largely did write) the menu commands without adopting Lotus' hierarchy. But Lotus users who switched to Borland's spreadsheet could not have "imported" their macros; they would have had to rewrite them to perform the same shortcuts on the rival spreadsheet. *Oracle v. Google* presented no similar end-user programming concerns. Can *Lotus* be limited to those facts, or are the First Circuit and Federal Circuit (anticipating the Ninth Circuit) in irreconcilable conflict regarding the interpretation of "method of operation"?

F. PICTORIAL, GRAPHIC AND SCULPTURAL WORKS

2. THE PROBLEM OF APPLIED ART

c. WHAT IS A "USEFUL ARTICLE"?

Page 228. Insert at line 9 of first paragraph:

It is important to distinguish the utility of the work as a depiction from the other useful purposes to which the depiction might be put. For example, in **Home Legend LLC v. Mannington Mills, Inc.**, 784 F.3d 1404 (11th Cir. 2015), the declaratory judgment plaintiff Home Legend copied Mannington Mills' "Glazed Maple" floor covering design depicting "stained and apparently time-worn maple planks." The design appeared on "décor paper" laminated onto floor boards that are not in fact planks sawn from tree trunks, but rather consist of compacted wood fibre and resin. Mannington Mills' design team created the décor paper to emulate the appearance of actual boards after "twenty or thirty years, including the effects 'age and wear and patina' might have on the planks." Home Legend contended successfully before the district court that the floor boards were "useful articles" from which the design-bearing décor paper was inseparable because the design "had the function of hiding wear to the floor." The Eleventh Circuit reversed, declining to rule that such a purpose would make the work functional as a matter of copyright law:

> [E]ven if placing an otherwise copyrightable two-dimensional design on a product serves the secondary function of hiding wear or other imperfections in the product, that is not enough to invalidate the copyright protection for the design. Hanging an Ansel Adams print over an unsightly water stain on a living room wall might make the print "functional" in the same way the district court found the Glazed Maple design to be, but it would have no effect on the copyright in the work itself.

d. SEPARABILITY

Page 248. Insert following *Pivot Point*:

Varsity Brands, Inc. v. Star Athletica, LLC, 110 U.S.P.Q.2d 1150 (W.D.Tenn. 2014). In this controversy concerning cheerleading uniforms, the court surveyed Circuit authority subsequent to *Pivot Point*:

> The Fifth Circuit declined to apply the Seventh Circuit's aesthetic influence test to garment design in *Galiano* [*v. Harrah's Operating Co., Inc.*, 416 F.3d 411 (5th Cir. 2005)]. In *Galiano*, the plaintiff was the founder and owner of a clothing design company that produced uniforms for Harrah's casinos, who applied for and received copyright protection for her sketches of a costume collection. After the expiration of a consulting agreement with Harrah's, she sued Harrah's for continuing to use and order the uniforms she had designed. The court looked to the marketability test proposed in Nimmer on Copyright: "[C]onceptual severability exists where there is any substantial likelihood that even if the article had no utilitarian use it would still be marketable to some significant segment of the community simply because of its aesthetic qualities."

Galiano, 416 F.3d at 419; Nimmer, § 2.08[B][3], at 2–99. The court adopted the marketability test for garment design only, and noted that the test has the benefits of being a "more determinate rule" that provides necessary clarity for the conceptual severability analysis. *Galiano*, 416 F.3d at 421. Turning to the uniforms at issue in *Galiano*, the court concluded that the plaintiff had made no showing that its designs were marketable independent of their utilitarian function as casino uniforms.

The Fourth Circuit recently applied *Pivot Point* in *Universal Furniture Int'l, Inc. v. Collezione Europa USA, Inc.*, 618 F.3d 417 (4th Cir. 2010) (per curiam), a case involving competing furniture companies. Universal Furniture produced two collections of furniture that incorporated decorative carvings on the furniture; Collezione imitated these designs and produced similar furniture at lower cost. The Fourth Circuit held that the decorative elements (as opposed to the shape) of Universal Furniture's designs could receive copyright protection. The court reasoned that the furniture compilations were "superfluous nonfunctional adornments for which the shape of the furniture (which is not copyrightable) serves as the vehicle. . . . [T]he designs are 'wholly unnecessary' to the furniture's utilitarian function." *Id.* at 434. Turning to the *Pivot Point* aesthetic influence test, the court recognized that Universal Furniture's designer "was influenced by function in designing [the] decorative elements. After all, . . . 'furniture has got to function.' " *Id.* Nevertheless, the court held that the designer's artistic judgment was sufficiently independent because "his objective in compiling these decorative elements onto the basic shapes of the furniture was not to improve the furniture's utility but to 'give [the pieces] a pretty face.' " *Id.* The court further noted that the conceptual separability test provided in § 101 is conjunctive, but that as applied to decorations on furniture, the test presented a "metaphysical quandary"[,] namely that "[t]he elements serve no purpose divorced from the furniture—they become designs in space." *Id.* However, because the designs were original and conceptually severable from utilitarian aspects of the furniture, the court concluded that the decorative features were entitled to copyright protection.

Two cases from the Second Circuit also bear mentioning. In *Chosun [Int'l, Inc. v. Chrisha Creations, Ltd.*, 413 F.3d 324 (2d Cir. 2005)], the court considered whether elements of a plush sculpted animal costume could be separable from the overall design of the costume and thus eligible for protection under the Copyright Act. 413 F.3d at 329. The court vacated the district court's dismissal of the plaintiff's copyright claims, noting that "when a component of a useful article can actually be removed from the original item and separately sold, without adversely impacting the article's functionality, that physically separable design element may be copyrighted." *Id.* This supports *Galiano*'s marketability test by incorporating a consideration of whether a design element could be separately marketed into the issue of conceptual severability.

The Second Circuit directly addressed garment design in *Jovani* [*Fashion, Ltd. v. Fiesta Fashions*, 500 F.Appx. 42, 44 (2d Cir. 2012)], where the plaintiff appealed the dismissal of its copyright claim alleging that the defendant infringed a registered copyright for the design of a prom dress. 500 F.App'x at 43. The plaintiff argued that the "arrangement of decorative sequins and crystals on the dress bodice; horizontal satin ruching at the dress waist; and layers of tulle on the skirt" qualified as conceptually separable dress elements worthy of copyright protection. The court held that physical separability was impossible, as the "removal of these items would certainly adversely affect the garment's ability to function as a prom dress, a garment specifically meant to cover the body in an attractive way for a special occasion." *Id.* at 44. Similarly, the court held that conceptual severability was also impossible: "the artistic judgment exercised in applying sequins and crystals to the dress's bodice and in using ruched satin at the waist and layers of tulle in the skirt does not invoke in the viewer a concept other than that of clothing." *Id.* at 45. Instead, the decorative elements on the dress were used to enhance the functionality of the dress for a special occasion, merging the aesthetic with the functional in an attractive way for that special occasion. *Id.* Although the prom dresses at issue undoubtedly had artistic elements:

> the decorative choices . . . merge with those that decide how (and how much) to cover the body. Thus, a jeweled bodice covers the upper torso at the same time that it draws attention to it; a ruched waist covers the wearer's midsection while giving it definition; and a short tulle skirt conceals the wearer's legs while giving glimpses of them.

Id. The court concluded that because it was impossible to separate the aesthetic design from the functional effect of that design, copyright protection could not extend to cover plaintiff's dresses.

It is obvious that there is considerable disagreement regarding the proper standard to apply when considering whether elements of protectable PGS works are separable from their utilitarian function.

As to the cheerleader uniforms at issue, Varsity contended the designs on its uniforms were "separable" because "a blank cheerleading silhouette 'covers the body to the same degree, wicks away moisture, and withstands the rigors of cheerleading movements at least as much as, if not more than, a garment that has a design on the front of it.'" The court, however, determined that designs that evoke the uniforms' cheerleading function were necessary to the purpose of the uniforms:

> Put another way, a cheerleading uniform loses its utilitarian function as a cheerleading uniform when it lacks all design and is merely a blank canvas. An examination of the blank cheerleading silhouettes that Varsity submitted illustrates this

point. (Without the kind of ornamentation familiar to sports (or cheerleading) fans, the silhouette no longer evokes the utilitarian concept of a cheerleading uniform, a garment that is worn by a certain group of people in a specific context. [Varsity's argument] ignores the fact that the utilitarian function of a cheerleading uniform is not merely to clothe the body; it is to clothe the body in a way that evokes the concept of cheerleading. Artistic judgment and design are undeniably important in this context, but they are not separable from the utilitarian function of the resulting garment.

Has the court confused utilitarian function with the function of conveying information? (Recall that the latter utility does not make an article "useful" within the meaning of the statutory definition.)

Page 250. Add new Questions 5–8:

5.   Gotham Garage builds and sells full-scale, drivable Batmobile replica cars, as shown in the photo from the firm's website on the next page. DC Comics, copyright owner of the Batman comics, alleges that Gotham Garage's cars infringe its copyright in the comic book images of the Batmobile. Garage, invoking section 113(b), urges that a drivable car is a useful article, and cannot infringe its depiction. How should the court rule? *See DC Comics v. Towle*, 101 U.S.P.Q.2d 1551 (C.D.Cal. 2012).

     6.   Design Ideas designs and manufactures home and office furnishings, including the items below, left, which hold tea candles. Subsequently, Yankee Candle Co. began selling the tealight candle holders pictured below, right. Design Ideas brought suit alleging copyright infringement of their design, but Yankee Candle argues that the holders are useful articles not entitled to protection. Are any of the candle holders' elements separable under the tests considered by the *Pivot Point* court? *See Design Ideas, Ltd. v. Yankee Candle Co., Inc.*, 889 F.Supp.2d 1119 (C.D.Ill. 2012).

7.   Jovani Fashion designed and sold the prom dress pictured below, left. Subsequently, Fiesta Fashions manufactured and sold the dress pictured below, right. Jovani brought suit, alleging copyright infringement, but are any of the elements separable under the tests considered by the *Pivot Point* court? See *Jovani Fashion, Ltd. v. Fiesta Fashions*, 500 Fed.Appx. 42 (2d Cir. 2012).

8.   Inhale, Inc. manufactures and sells various smoking products, including the hookah water container pictured below:

What elements of the water container are separable and thus entitled to copyright protection, if any? *See Inhale, Inc. v. Starbuzz Tobacco, Inc.*, 755 F.3d 1038 (9th Cir. 2014).

G. ARCHITECTURAL WORKS

Page 262. Add a new Question 4 and the following case note:

4.   Aretha Architect designed a suburban home. Without Aretha's authorization, Boris Builder created a brochure depicting the façade of the Aretha home and substantially copying its floorplans. Boris' clients, however, substantially modified the floorplans to their individual requirements when they built their homes, although they left the façade largely intact. In response to Aretha's copyright infringement action, Boris claims that the "architectural work" necessarily consists of the arrangement of the interior space, which he ultimately did not copy. Aretha replies that the façade suffices to constitute the architectural work. How should the court rule? *See Axelrod & Cherveny, Architects, P.C. v. T & S Builders Inc.*, 943 F.Supp.2d 357 (E.D.N.Y. 2013).

Scholz Design, Inc. v. Sard Custom Homes, LLC, 691 F.3d 182 (2d Cir. 2012). Scholz drew architectural plans for three homes in 1989. In 1992 he licensed the plans to a builder, Sard Custom Homes, for a three-year period, which was renewed for another three years. The builder, however, retained a copy of the plans, which it ultimately put on its website. In 2010 Scholz sued for copyright infringement of its rights in the pictorial, graphic or sculptural work embodied in the plans. The district court treated the plans as architectural works and denied protection on the ground that they lacked detail sufficient to permit the building to be built from the plans. The Second Circuit reversed:

> The district court apparently was of the view that, because the drawings were architectural, something more was required for their copyright protection. It is black-letter law, however, that courts accept as protected "any work which by the most generous standard may arguably be said to evince creativity." 1–2 Melville B. Nimmer & David Nimmer, Nimmer on Copyright § 2.08 (2012). . . .

> We see no reason why Scholz's drawings depicting the appearance of houses it had designed should be treated differently from any other pictorial work for copyright purposes. Andrew Wyeth and Edward Hopper were famous for their paintings of houses, and Claude Monet for paintings of the Houses of Parliament and of Rouen Cathedral. None of these depictions of buildings were sufficiently detailed to guide construction of the buildings depicted, but that would surely not justify denying them copyright protection. If an exact copy of Scholz's drawings was made by the defendant, as alleged, and as appears to be the case based on the evidence submitted with the complaint, that would appear to constitute infringement.

> . . .

> C.   *The Architectural Works Copyright Protection Act*

> We think that the district court's ruling likely stemmed from a misunderstanding regarding the relationship both before and after enactment of the AWCPA between the scope of protection for pictorial works such as these drawings under the Copyright Act, and that afforded architectural works under the Copyright Act.

> While we think this to be a straightforward case of infringement, the district court did not. The defendants contended, and the district court agreed, that because the drawings at issue were "architectural drawings," something more was required of them for copyright protection than would be required for any other "pictorial, graphic, or sculptural work" under section 102(a)(5). Indeed, architectural works are currently afforded special status under the law. That special status is, however, irrelevant for purposes of this case because Scholz is not alleging infringement under the AWCPA, but under the pre-existing protection of the Copyright Act for pictorial works. The fact that Scholz's drawings might or might not be protected under the AWCPA, depending on various factors, does not deprive them of the protection they have as pictorial works regardless of those factors.

> Prior to the enactment of the AWCPA, while architectural structures themselves did not receive copyright protection, architectural plans, blueprints, and technical drawings, as well as original, creative sketches of the type at issue here, were indeed covered under the Copyright Act's protection of "pictorial, graphic, and sculptural works." 17 U.S.C. § 102(a)(5).

Scholz contends that the drawings are protected under section 102(a)(5), and not under section 102(a)(8), which, as part of the AWCPA, added protection for "architectural works." According to Scholz, the AWCPA is therefore inapplicable. We agree. The AWCPA did not affect the copyright protection that section 102(a)(5) has long extended to architectural plans, drawings, and blueprints.

H. CHARACTERS

Page 267. Delete Question 5.

Page 271. Add the following new principal case after the QUESTION following *Gaiman v. McFarlane*:

Klinger v. Conan Doyle Estate, Ltd.

755 F.3d 496 (7th Cir. 2014).

■ POSNER, CIRCUIT JUDGE.

Arthur Conan Doyle published his first Sherlock Holmes story in 1887 and his last in 1927. There were 56 stories in all, plus 4 novels. The final 10 stories were published between 1923 and 1927. As a result of statutory extensions of copyright protection culminating in the 1998 Copyright Term Extension Act, the American copyrights on those final stories (copyrights owned by Doyle's estate, the appellant) will not expire until 95 years after the date of original publication—between 2018 to 2022, depending on the original publication date of each story. The copyrights on the other 46 stories and the 4 novels, all being works published before 1923, have expired . . .

Once the copyright on a work expires, the work becomes a part of the public domain and can be copied and sold without need to obtain a license from the holder of the expired copyright. Leslie Klinger, the appellee in this case, co-edited an anthology called *A Study in Sherlock: Stories Inspired by the Sherlock Holmes Canon* (2011)—"canon" referring to the 60 stories and novels written by Arthur Conan Doyle, as opposed to later works, by other writers, featuring characters who had appeared in the canonical works. Klinger's anthology consisted of stories written by modern authors but inspired by, and in most instances depicting, the genius detective Sherlock Holmes and his awed sidekick Dr. Watson. Klinger didn't think he needed a license from the Doyle estate to publish these stories, since the copyrights on most of the works in the "canon" had expired. But the estate told Random House, which had agreed to publish Klinger's book, that it would have to pay the estate $5000 for a copyright license. Random House bowed to the demand, obtained the license, and published the book.

Klinger and his co-editor decided to create a sequel to *A Study in Sherlock,* to be called *In the Company of Sherlock Holmes.* They entered into negotiations with Pegasus Books for the publication of the book and W.W. Norton & Company for distribution of it to booksellers. Although the editors hadn't finished the book, the companies could estimate its likely commercial success from the success of its predecessor, and thus decide in advance whether to publish and distribute it. But the Doyle estate learned of the project and told Pegasus, as it had told Random House, that Pegasus would have to obtain a license from the estate in order to be legally authorized to publish the new book. The estate didn't threaten to sue Pegasus for copyright infringement if the publisher didn't obtain a license, but did threaten to prevent distribution of the book. It did not mince words. It told Pegasus: "If you proceed instead to bring out *Study in Sherlock II* [the original title of *In the Company of Sherlock Holmes*] unlicensed, do not expect to see it offered for sale by Amazon, Barnes & Noble, and similar retailers. We work with those compan[ies] routinely to weed out unlicensed uses of Sherlock Holmes from their offerings, and will not hesitate to do so with your book as well." There was also a latent threat to sue Pegasus for copyright infringement if it published Klinger's book without a license, and to sue Internet service providers who distributed it. Pegasus yielded to the threat, as Random House had done, and refused to publish *In the Company of Sherlock Holmes* unless and until Klinger obtained a license from the Doyle estate.

Instead of obtaining a license, Klinger sued the estate, seeking a declaratory judgment that he is free to use material in the 50 Sherlock Holmes stories and novels that are no longer under copyright, though he may use nothing in the 10 stories still under copyright that has sufficient originality to be copyrightable—which means: at least a tiny bit of originality, *Feist Publications, Inc. v. Rural Telephone Service Co.,* 499 U.S. 340, 345 (1991).

The estate defaulted by failing to appear or to respond to Klinger's complaint, but that didn't end the case. Klinger wanted his declaratory judgment. The district judge gave him leave to file a motion for summary judgment, and he did so, and the Doyle estate responded in a brief that made the same arguments for enlarged copyright protection that it makes in this appeal. The judge granted Klinger's motion for summary judgment and issued the declaratory judgment Klinger had asked for, thus precipitating the estate's appeal.

The appeal challenges the judgment on two alternative grounds. The first is that the district court had no subject-matter jurisdiction because there is no actual case or controversy between the parties. The second ground is that if there is jurisdiction, the estate is entitled to judgment on the merits, because, it argues, copyright on a "complex" character in a story, such as Sherlock Holmes or Dr. Watson, whose full complexity is not revealed until a later story, remains under copyright until the later story falls into the public domain. The estate argues that the fact that early stories in which Holmes or Watson appeared are already in the public domain does not permit their less than fully "complexified" characters in the early stories to be copied even though the stories themselves are in the public domain.

[The court concluded that] the [district] judge was right to assert (and retain) jurisdiction over the case, and we come to the merits, where the issue as we said is whether copyright protection of a fictional character can be extended beyond the expiration of the copyright on it because the author altered the character in a subsequent work. In such a case, the Doyle estate contends, the original character cannot lawfully be copied without a license from the writer until the copyright on the later work, in which that character appears in a different form, expires.

We cannot find any basis in statute or case law for extending a copyright beyond its expiration. When a story falls into the public domain, story elements—including characters covered by the expired copyright—become fair game for follow-on authors, as held in *Silverman v. CBS Inc.,* 870 F.2d 40, 49–51 (2d Cir. 1989), a case much like this one. At issue was the right to copy fictional characters (Amos and Andy) who had appeared in copyrighted radio scripts. The copyrights covered the characters because they were original. As in this case the characters also appeared in subsequent radio scripts that remained under copyright, though the copyrights on the original scripts in which the characters had appeared had expired. The court ruled that "a copyright affords protection only for original works of authorship and, consequently, copyrights in derivative works secure protection only for the incremental additions of originality contributed by the authors of the derivative works." *Id.* at 49. The copyrights on the derivative works, corresponding to the copyrights on the ten last Sherlock Holmes stories, were not extended by virtue of the incremental additions of originality in the derivative works.

And so it is in our case. The ten Holmes-Watson stories in which copyright persists are derivative from the earlier stories, so only original elements added in the later stories remain protected. The "freedom to make new works based on public domain materials ends where the resulting derivative work comes into conflict with a valid copyright," *Warner Bros. Entertainment, Inc. v. X One X Productions,* 644 F.3d 584, 596 (8th Cir. 2011)—as Klinger acknowledges. But there is no such conflict in this case.

Lacking any ground known to American law for asserting post-expiration copyright protection of Holmes and Watson in pre-1923 stories and novels going back to 1887, the estate argues that creativity will be discouraged if we don't allow such an extension. It may take a long time for an author to perfect a character or other expressive element that first appeared in his early work. If he loses copyright on the original character, his incentive to improve the character in future work may be diminished because he'll be competing with copiers, such as the authors whom Klinger wishes to anthologize. Of course this point has no application to the present case, Arthur Conan Doyle having died 84 years ago. More important, extending copyright protection is a two-edged sword from the standpoint of inducing creativity, as it would reduce the incentive of subsequent authors to create derivative works (such as new versions of popular fictional characters like Holmes and Watson) by shrinking the public domain. For the longer the copyright term is, the less public-domain material there will be and so the greater will be the cost of authorship, because authors will have to obtain licenses from copyright holders for more material—as illustrated by the estate's demand in this case for a license fee from Pegasus.

Most copyrighted works include some, and often a great deal of, public domain material—words, phrases, data, entire sentences, quoted material, and so forth. The smaller the public domain, the more work is involved in the creation of a new work. The defendant's proposed rule would also encourage authors to continue to write stories involving old characters in an effort to prolong copyright protection, rather than encouraging them to create stories with entirely new characters. The effect would be to discourage creativity.

The estate offers the hypothetical example of a mural that is first sketched and only later completed by being carefully painted. If the sketch is allowed to enter the public domain, there to be improved by creative copiers, the mural artist will have a diminished incentive to perfect his mural. True; but other artists will have a greater incentive to improve it, or to create other works inspired by it, because they won't have to pay a license fee to do so provided that the copyright on the original work has expired.

The estate asks us to distinguish between "flat" and "round" fictional characters, potentially a sharper distinction than the other one it urges (as we noted at the beginning of this opinion), which is between simple and complex. Repeatedly at the oral argument the estate's lawyer dramatized the concept of a "round" character by describing large circles with his arms. And the additional details about Holmes and Watson in the ten late stories do indeed make for a more "rounded," in the sense of a fuller, portrayal of these characters. In much the same way we learn things about Sir John Falstaff in *Henry IV, Part 2,* in *Henry V* (though he doesn't actually appear in that play but is merely discussed in it), and in *The Merry Wives of Windsor,* that were not remarked in his first appearance, in *Henry IV, Part 1.* Notice also that *Henry V,* in which Falstaff is reported as dying, precedes *The Merry Wives,* in which he is very much alive. Likewise the ten last Sherlock Holmes stories all are set before 1914, which was the last year in which the other stories were set. One of the ten, *The Adventure of the Veiled Lodger* (published in 1927), is set in 1896. Thus a more rounded Holmes or Watson (or Falstaff) is found in a later work depicting a younger person. We don't see how that can justify extending the expired copyright on the flatter character. A contemporary example is the six *Star Wars* movies: Episodes IV, V, and VI were produced before I, II, and III. The Doyle estate would presumably argue that the copyrights on the characters as portrayed in IV, V, and VI will not expire until the copyrights on I, II, and III expire.

The estate defines "flat" characters oddly, as ones completely and finally described in the first works in which they appear. Flat characters thus don't evolve. Round characters do; Holmes and Watson, the estate argues, were not fully rounded off until the last story written by Doyle. What this has to do with copyright law eludes us. There are the early Holmes and Watson stories, and the late ones, and features of Holmes and Watson are depicted in the late stories that are not found in the early ones (though as we noted in the preceding paragraph some of those features are retrofitted to the earlier depictions). Only in the late stories for example do we learn that Holmes's attitude toward dogs has changed—he has grown to like them—and that Watson has been married twice. These additional features, being (we may assume) "original" in the generous sense that the word bears in copyright law, are protected by the unexpired copyrights on the late stories. But Klinger wants just to copy the Holmes and the Watson of the early stores, the stories no longer under copyright. The Doyle estate tells us that "no workable standard exists to protect the Ten Stories' incremental character development apart from protecting the completed characters." But that would be true only if the early and the late Holmes, and the early and the late Watson, were indistinguishable—and in that case there would be no incremental originality to justify copyright protection of the "rounded" characters (more precisely the features that makes them "rounder," as distinct from the features they share with their earlier embodiments) in the later works.

It's not unusual for an author to use the same character in successive works, yet with differences resulting, in the simplest case, just from aging. In Shakespeare's two *Henry IV* plays, the Henry who later becomes Henry V is the Prince of Wales, hence Crown Prince of England; in *Henry V* he is the King of England. Were *Henry IV* in the public domain and *Henry V* under copyright, Henry Prince of Wales could be copied without Shakespeare's permission but not Henry V. Could the Doyle estate doubt this? Could it think Holmes a more complex and altered character than Henry?

The more vague, the less "complete," a character, the less likely it is to qualify for copyright protection. An author "could not copyright a character described merely as an unexpectedly knowledgeable old wino," but could copyright "a character that has a specific name and a specific appearance. Cogliostro's age, obviously phony title ('Count'), what he knows and says, his name, and his faintly Mosaic facial features combine to create a distinctive character. No more is required for a character copyright." *Gaiman v. McFarlane,* 360 F.3d 644, 660 (7th Cir. 2004); see also *Nichols v. Universal Pictures Corp.,* 45 F.2d 119, 121 (2d Cir. 1930) (L. Hand, J.). From the outset of the series of Arthur Conan Doyle stories and novels that began in 1887 Holmes and Watson were distinctive characters and therefore copyrightable. They were "incomplete" only in the sense that Doyle might want to (and later did) add additional features to their portrayals. The resulting somewhat altered characters were derivative works, the additional features of which that were added in the ten late stories being protected by the copyrights on those stories. The alterations do not revive the expired copyrights on the original characters.

We can imagine the Doyle estate being concerned that a modern author might write a story in which Sherlock Holmes was disparaged (perhaps by being depicted as a drug dealer—he was of course a cocaine user—or as an idiot detective like Inspector Clouseau of the *Pink Panther* movies), and that someone who read the story might be deterred from reading Doyle's Sherlock Holmes stories because he would realize that he couldn't read them without puzzling confusedly over the "true" character of Sherlock Holmes. The analogy would be to trademark dilution, as if a hot-dog stand advertised itself as "The Rolls-Royce Hot-Dog Stand." No one would be confused as to origin—Rolls-Royce obviously would not be the owner. Its concern would be that its brand would be diminished by being linked in people's involuntary imagination to a hot-dog stand; when they thought "Rolls-Royce," they would see the car and the hot-dog stand—an anomalous juxtaposition of high and low. There is no comparable doctrine of copyright law; parodies or burlesques of copyrighted works may or may not be deemed infringing, depending on circumstances, but there is no copyright infringement of a story or character that is not under copyright. Anyway it appears that the Doyle estate is concerned not with specific alterations in the depiction of Holmes or Watson in Holmes-Watson stories written by authors other than Arthur Conan Doyle, but with *any* such story that is published without payment to the estate of a licensing fee.

With the net effect on creativity of extending the copyright protection of literary characters to the extraordinary lengths urged by the estate so uncertain, and no legal grounds suggested for extending copyright protection beyond the limits fixed by Congress, the estate's appeal borders on the quixotic. The spectre of perpetual, or at least nearly perpetual, copyright (perpetual copyright would violate the copyright clause of the Constitution, Art. I, § 8, cl. 8, which authorizes copyright protection only for "limited Times") looms, once one realizes that the Doyle estate is seeking 135 years (1887–2022) of copyright protection for the character of Sherlock Holmes as depicted in the first Sherlock Holmes story.

AFFIRMED.

J. GOVERNMENT WORKS AND OTHER PUBLIC POLICY ISSUES

1. GOVERNMENT WORKS

Page 294. Add a new Question 8:

8. The *Banks v. Manchester* decision, discussed at length in *Veeck*, resolved the copyright status of judicial opinions. What about documents drafted by attorneys and filed in court during the litigation that leads to those opinions—complaints, answers, memoranda of support, appellate briefs, etc.? If an online legal research service such as Westlaw or LEXIS copies such litigation documents at the courthouse and makes them available online to subscribers just as it does with judicial opinions, is the service committing copyright infringement? *See White v. West Publ'g Corp.*, 29 F.Supp.3d 396 (S.D.N.Y. 2014).

CHAPTER 3

OWNERSHIP

A. INITIAL OWNERSHIP

2. AUTHORSHIP AS AN ECONOMIC CONCEPT: WORKS MADE FOR HIRE

a. EMPLOYEE-CREATED WORKS

Page 324. In the first paragraph, replace the citation for *Molinelli-Freytes* with "792 F.Supp.2d 164 (D.P.R. 2010)".

b. SPECIALLY ORDERED OR COMMISSIONED WORKS

Page 327. Add to end of Note "If a Work is 'Specially Ordered of Commissioned' Within § 101(2), at What Point in the Parties' Relationship Must a Contract Making it a 'Work for Hire' Be Executed?":

In *Zenova Corp. v. Mobile Methodology LLC*, 997 F.Supp.2d 207 (E.D.N.Y. 2014), Mobile Methodology commissioned web design services from Zenova. The parties' written contract provided, *inter alia*, that Zenova was "producing this project as 'works for hire' " for Mobile Methodology, and that "[u]pon full payment of all invoices due, copyright and all rights to page designs, web development source code, and graphic source files" would belong to Mobile Methodology. The contract further provided that: "To be valid, this agreement must be signed within 30 days of the date signed by [Zenova], and be accompanied by an initial deposit." Mobile Methodology failed to sign the contract within the stated period. Applying the common law of contracts, the court determined that timely signature was a prerequisite to the contract's formation, and that as a result, "the parties had no legally enforceable work for hire agreement."

3. AUTHORSHIP AS AN INTELLECTUAL CONCEPT: JOINT WORKS

Page 341. Insert before QUESTIONS:

Postscript: In January 2012, following further court decisions in his favor, Gaiman reached a settlement with McFarlane in their dispute over Medieval Spawn (and another character, "heavenly warrior Angela"), agreeing to equal ownership of Spawn #9 and #26 and to payment to Gaiman of a share of the profits attributable to two more characters determined to have been derivative of Medieval Spawn and Angela.

B. TRANSFER OF COPYRIGHT OWNERSHIP

1. DIVISIBILITY AND FORMAL REQUIREMENTS

Page 350. Add at the end of Question 1:

See *Baisden v. I'm Ready Productions, Inc.*, 693 F.3d 491 (5th Cir. 2012) ("[W]e have never held that an implied license could not arise in other circumstances where the totality of the parties' conduct supported such an outcome.").

Page 352. In the first paragraph, replace the *Righthaven* citation with "791 F.Supp.2d 968 (D.Nev. 2011)".

Page 352. Add at the end of Question 7:

See *Associated Press v. Meltwater U.S. Holdings, Inc.*, 931 F.Supp.2d 537 (S.D.N.Y. 2013) (posting of AP news articles online by AP licensees without using metatag indicating that the articles should not be accessed by web crawling programs did not constitute implied license to defendant news monitoring service to copy the posted articles).

Page 352. Add a new Question 8:

8.   Section 204 requires a writing signed by "the owner of the rights conveyed or such owner's duly authorized agent." Is a writing signed by someone who has apparent or ostensible authority from the author sufficient? (Ostensible authority "is such as a principal, intentionally or by want of ordinary care, causes or allows a third person to believe the agent to possess." Calif. Civ. Code § 2317.) For example, if a movie studio sends an email with proposed terms for buying the movie rights in a novel to the novelist's lawyer, and the lawyer responds in a signed email, "Done—thanks!," does the lawyer's email satisfy § 204 if the movie studio reasonably believed that the lawyer was the novelist's agent? See *MVP Entm't, Inc. v. Frost*, 149 Cal.Rptr.3d 162 (Cal.Ct.App. 2012).

2. SCOPE OF GRANT

Page 369. Add after Questions following *Rosetta Books*:

HarperCollins Publishers LLC v. Open Road Integrated Media, LLP

7 F.Supp.3d 363 (S.D.N.Y. 2014).

Buchwald, J.

Plaintiff HarperCollins Publishers LLC ("HarperCollins") brings this action against defendant Open Road Integrated Media, LLP ("Open Road"), alleging willful infringement of HarperCollins' rights under federal copyright law to the well-known children's novel *Julie of the Wolves*. Open Road, a digital publisher who has issued an e-book version of *Julie of the Wolves*, counters that the operative contract, signed in 1971, does not convey exclusive electronic publication rights to HarperCollins. Now pending before the Court are the parties' cross-motions for summary judgment. For the reasons stated herein, this Court grants plaintiff's motion and denies defendant's motion.

BACKGROUND

I. Factual Allegations

The present dispute arises out of a publishing agreement (hereafter the "contract" or the "agreement") executed on April 13, 1971 by the author Jean George and the publishing house Harper & Row, plaintiff's predecessor in interest, which, broadly speaking, gave plaintiff the right to publish George's children's novel *Julie of the Wolves*. The novel was first published in hardcover format by Harper & Row in 1972. It won the Newbury Medal in 1973 for the most distinguished contribution to children's literature and was a finalist for the 1973 National Book Award. Between 1972 and December 2011, HarperCollins sold more than 3.8 million units of the novel in hardcover and paperback, among other formats. Then and in the years since, *Julie of the Wolves* has been considered a celebrated title in children's literature.

By the 1971 contract, Ms. George conveyed publishing rights to HarperCollins to publish *Julie of the Wolves* in exchange for a $2,000 advance and royalty payments of between ten and fifteen percent, depending on number of copies sold. The contract contemplated the sale of paperback editions ("cheap edition") but did not specify the royalty rate for paperbacks, instead indicating that the publisher would pay a paperback royalty "to be mutually agreed."

The contract contains several clauses critical to the outcome of this suit. Paragraph 1 of the agreement grants to HarperCollins "the exclusive right to publish" *Julie of the Wolves* "in book form" in the English language and within specified territory. In addition to this broad grant language, the contract provided in a paragraph entitled "Disposition of Subsidiary Rights" that "[i]t is understood and agreed that the Publisher shall have the exclusive right to sell, lease or make other disposition of the subsidiary rights in which he has an interest under the terms of clause (subject to the 'consultation' provision in 7f) 19 and 20."

Paragraph 20, in turn, makes the following provision:

Anything to the contrary herein notwithstanding, the Publisher shall grant no license without the prior written consent of the Author with respect to the following rights in the work: *use thereof in storage and retrieval and information systems, and/or whether through computer, computer-stored, mechanical or other electronic means now known or hereafter invented* and ephemeral screen flashing or reproduction thereof, whether by print-out, phot[o] reproduction or photo copy, including punch cards, microfilm, magnetic tapes or like processes attaining similar results, and net proceeds thereof shall be divided 50% to the Author and 50% to the Publisher. However, such license shall not be deemed keeping the work in print once the work has gone out of print in all editions." (emphasis added)

This clause was inserted at the request of Ms. George's literary agency, Curtis Brown, which negotiated the contract on the author's behalf. The language of Paragraph 20 was drafted by Curtis Brown in 1967 and was apparently standard in contracts negotiated by Curtis Brown with American publishers. In fact, identical language was included in at least six contracts between Ms. George and Harper & Row that predate the operative contract in the instant matter. In eight subsequent contracts between Ms. George and HarperCollins, the words "and/or" were deleted, such that the relevant language read "use thereof in storage and retrieval systems, whether through computer, mechanical, or other electronic means now known or hereafter invented . . . ."

In addition to these critical clauses, the contract also contained other paragraphs pertinent to this action, including Paragraph 19, which gave the Publisher the right "to reprint the said Work in whole or in part in the form of excerpts, digests and selections in one or more issues of a newspaper, magazine, book or anthology," with revenues generally divided evenly between author and publisher. Contract ¶ 19. The contract also contained a "Reserved Rights" clause that reserved to the author "[a]ll rights in the Work now existing, or which may hereafter come into existence, not specifically herein granted," including motion picture rights. Contract ¶ 14. The contract provided for a New York choice of law. Contract ¶ 27.

In the decades that followed, the parties apparently coordinated with regard to the use of the work by third parties in electronic formats. Repeatedly in recent years, HarperCollins forwarded requests to Ms. George "[p]er our agreement," to use text from *Julie of the Wolves* in CD-Roms, online teaching materials, online examination materials and the like, including in August 1998 a request to include *Julie of the Wolves* in a test of an early e-book reading device. The record before us indicates that Ms. George generally agreed to these requests, sometimes after negotiating a more favorable royalty. The parties disagree, however, on the implication to be taken from these communications regarding third-party uses. HarperCollins asserts that this course of performance was undertaken pursuant to the requirements of Paragraph 20. Open Road contends that these uses fell under the "permissions" provision set forth in Paragraph 19; and further notes that Ms. George unilaterally granted electronic rights to the Work without HarperCollins's involvement (but apparently also without HarperCollins knowledge or consent).

The events immediately precipitating this lawsuit began in 2010, nearly forty years after the execution of the operative contract, at which point the publishing world featured an e-book market. E-book technology enables the full text of a book to be presented in digital form, to be read on a computer or portable electronic device, such as a dedicated e-book reader, a smart phone, or a pad/tablet. Defendant Open Road is an e-book publisher and multimedia content company established in 2009.

In 2010, Open Road approached Ms. George's literary agent Curtis Brown with a proposal to publish an e-book edition of *Julie of the Wolves* in exchange for a 50% royalty to Ms. George. Preferring initially to pursue an e-book publication with her longtime publisher HarperCollins, Ms. George authorized her agent to contact HarperCollins and suggest the e-book publication, with the proviso that HarperCollins match Open Road's 50% royalty offer. HarperCollins expressed interest in electronic publication; however, they counter-offered only a 25% royalty. Dissatisfied with that offer and expressing her belief that she—not HarperCollins—owned the e-book rights, Ms. George instead contracted in April 2011 with Open Road to publish *Julie of the Wolves* as an e-book. Before doing so, Ms. George entered an agreement with Open Road, by which the electronic publisher agreed to indemnify Ms. George in the event HarperCollins asserted a claim against the author. Open Road subsequently distributed *Julie of the Wolves* as an e-book via a number of distribution channels; between October 2011 and March 2012, approximately 1,600 such e-book copies were sold.

Plaintiff HarperCollins filed suit against Open Road on December 23, 2011 . . .

. . .

Based on a plain reading of the contractual language, we hold that the 1971 contract grants HarperCollins the exclusive right to license third parties to publish e-book versions of *Julie of the Wolves*. This determination follows from the contract as a whole, and chiefly from Paragraphs 1, 20 and 23.

A. Paragraph 1

Paragraph 1 conveyed to HarperCollins "the exclusive right to publish [*Julie of the Wolves*] . . . in book form." Relying heavily on prior precedent from this district, Open Road argues that this language cannot possibly extend to e-book publication rights. *See Random House, Inc. v. Rosetta Books LLC*, 150 F.Supp.2d 613, 620 (S.D.N.Y. 2001). However, the operative contract here differs significantly from its counterpart in *Rosetta Books*, which was held to be limited to paper book publication. In the instant case, the governing grant conveys the right "to publish . . . in book form," whereas in *Rosetta Books*, the grant was one "to print, publish and sell." As was explicitly argued in the earlier case, the inclusion of the word "print" has a limiting effect and a strong connotation of paper copy. The word "print" is absent from the 1971 contract governing here, thereby distinguishing the case at bar from *Rosetta Books*.

Nonetheless, given that we must interpret the contract as a whole, we need not reach the issue of whether Paragraph 1 standing alone is sufficient to convey e-book publication rights. [Citation.] With that precept in mind, we turn next to evaluate Paragraph 20, which, by explicitly granting HarperCollins certain rights associated with use by "electronic means," created a critical distinction from *Rosetta Books*, whose contract made no mention of electronic exploitation at all.

B. Paragraph 20

Paragraph 20, supported by the grant provision in Paragraph 23, enables HarperCollins to issue licenses, subject to the author's permission, to use the work in "in storage and retrieval and information systems, and/or whether through computer, computer-stored, mechanical or other electronic means now known or hereafter invented." This language, encompassing as it does the forward-looking reference to technologies "now known or hereafter invented," is sufficiently broad to draw within its ambit e-book publication. Although no commercial market for e-books existed at the time of its drafting, e-book technology comprises a later-invented version of the very "computer, computer-stored, mechanical or other electronic means" provided by Paragraph 20.

In light of precedent indicating that broad grant language will extend to later-invented uses, e-book publication "may reasonably be said to fall within the medium as described in the license." *Bartsch*, 391 F.2d at 155. Our conclusion that e-books constitute a permissible new use follows both from the expansive contractual language and from the lens through which the Second Circuit directs us to construe it. The applicable Second Circuit precedent cautions courts not to limit new uses to those that "fall within the unambiguous core meaning of the term" provided by the contract. *Id.* Rather, the e-book format constitutes a permissible extension of "book form" via "storage and retrieval and information systems, and/or whether through computer, computer-stored, mechanical or other electronic means" just as the television broadcast of a movie and the videocassette constituted a lawful extension of the motion picture form in *Bartsch* and *Boosey*, respectively.

When considered in comparison to contracts in similar cases, the contractual language here is as broad as that previously found to be sufficient to encompass a later-developed new use. The *Bourne* contract conveyed the "right to record such music mechanically in any and all other motion pictures to be produced. . . ." [Citation.] In *Boosey*, the grant language provided rights "to record [the composition] in any manner, medium or form" for use "in [a] motion picture." [Citation.] In *Bartsch*, the contract granted the right "to copyright, vend, license and exhibit such motion picture photoplays throughout the world; together with the further sole and exclusive rights by mechanical and/or electrical means to record, reproduce and transmit sound"—a conveyance that appears rather similar in scope to Ms. George's grant to HarperCollins of the "exclusive right to publish [*Julie of the Wolves*] in book form." [Citation]; Contract ¶ 1. Notably, none of the contracts in *Bartsch*, *Bourne*, or *Boosey* included any reference to rights in future technologies that exists in the contract here.

By specifically providing for anticipated electronic means that might be "hereafter invented," the 1971 contract's grant language becomes greater in breadth, at least with respect to new uses, than the analogous contracts in Second Circuit new use precedent, which were themselves found sufficiently broad to encompass an electronic new use. Interpreting similar forward-looking contractual language in a new use context, another court in this district drew the same conclusion. *See Reinhardt v. Wal-Mart Stores, Inc.,* 547 F.Supp.2d 346, 354–55 (S.D.N.Y. 2008). In *Reinhardt*, a 1984 recording agreement wherein "records" were defined as "all forms of reproduction including pre-recorded tapes and discs and electronic video recordings, *now or hereafter known*" was construed to authorize later-invented digital and internet-enabled uses. *Id.* (emphasis added). Relying, as we do here, on the Second Circuit standards set forth in *Boosey*, the district court in *Reinhardt* explained that "[t]he phrase 'now or hereafter known,' when referring to forms of reproduction, reveals that future technologies are covered by the agreement" and that the language "creates an expansive rather than a restrictive conveyance of rights." [Citation.] The language of Paragraph 20—"now known or hereafter invented"—tracks its analog in *Reinhardt* rather closely and results in a similarly expansive conveyance of rights with regard to future technologies.

. . .

QUESTION

Do you find the court's distinguishing of *Rosetta Books* persuasive? Why do you suppose the author's literary agents would have requested the insertion of the highlighted language in Paragraph 20?

Page 380. Add to end of Note before QUESTIONS:

In August 2011, the Second Circuit overturned the district court's certification of the class, finding that the named plaintiffs failed to adequately represent the interests of all class members. In particular, the court ruled that the interests of the named plaintiffs, who had registered at least some of the disputed works either before their infringement (Category A plaintiffs) or before the initiation of the infringement action (Category B), and who consequently would have been entitled to actual or (for Category A) statutory damages, conflicted with the interests of the far larger number of class members whose works were never registered (Category C). "Because the Settlement capped recovery and administrative costs at $18 million, named plaintiffs . . . cannot have had an interest in maximizing compensation for every category. Any improvement in the compensation of, for example, Category C claims would result in a commensurate decrease in the recovery available for Category A and B claims. Further, given that Categories A and B amount to approximately 1% of the total number of claims, named plaintiffs would receive a greater share of a given amount of compensation allocated to Categories A and B, compared to what they would receive if that compensation were spread over the far greater quantity of Category C claims. Named plaintiffs' natural inclination would therefore be to favor their more lucrative Category A and B claims." *See In re Literary Works in Electronic Databases Copyright Litigation*, 654 F.3d 242 (2d Cir. 2011).

Page 382. Add at the end of the first full paragraph:

Another situation that comes within the Copyright Act's provisions on transfers "by operation of law" involves corporate dissolution. Consider a small corporation, owned by the company's founder as sole shareholder, that purchases copyrights in musical works from the songwriter who created those works. If the corporation later dissolves (perhaps for failure to file required reports with the incorporating state), what happens to ownership of the copyrights that the songwriter transferred to the corporation? If the incorporating state's law provides that the dissolved corporation's assets shall be distributed to the corporation's shareholder(s), will the transfer of ownership of the copyrights from the corporation to the sole shareholder be valid under 201(d)(1) and 204(a) as occurring "by operation of law"? *See Gomba Music, Inc. v. Avant*, 62 F.Supp.3d 632 (E.D.Mich. 2014).

CHAPTER 4

DURATION AND RENEWAL, AND TERMINATION OF TRANSFERS

A. DURATION AND RENEWAL

1. THE POLICY DEBATE

Page 409. Replace Note at top of page with the following:

Extension of copyright (or "neighboring rights") term in Europe has continued. The European Directive 2011/77/UE of September 27, 2011 amended the term of protection in "related rights" in sound recordings from 50 years from first publication to 70 years from first publication or first "making available" (anticipating dissemination by digital streaming rather than distribution of physical phonorecords). The Directive includes two provisions designed to ensure that performers (and not merely record producers) benefit from the term extension. First, if at the end of 50 years, the sound recording is no longer offered for sale or made available by wired or wireless means, the performer may terminate her assignment of rights to the producer. The producer, however, is accorded one year following the performer's notification to put the recording back on sale or make it available; rights revert to the performers only if the producer fails to put the recording back into commerce. As we shall see in comparison with the U.S. reversion right (*infra* section C of this Chapter in the main casebook), the Directive seems to invert the application of reversion rights. In U.S. copyright law (going back to the British Statute of Anne in this regard), rights revert to authors in order to enable them to participate in their works' success, particularly when their publishing contracts did not anticipate significant sales. While U.S. authors may reclaim rights in all works coming within the scope of the reversion right, one may suppose that the principal works at issue will be the ones that have done well. By contrast, the Directive's one-year grace period granted to record producers would seem to ensure that performers retrieve rights only in recordings without commercial value, since valuable works either would still be in commerce or would be placed back in commerce upon the performer's notifying the producer of her intent to terminate her grant of rights.

The Directive's second performer-oriented measure, however, does aim to provide performers a continuing interest in works currently in commerce. The Directive identifies two classes of performers, non-featured performers who received a one-time payment for their contributions, and featured artists who receive royalties. The first group of performers enjoys, during the last twenty years of the sound recording's duration of protection, a non-transferable right to an annual remuneration equivalent to 20% of the producer's revenue from the exclusive rights of distribution, reproduction and making available of sound recordings. Featured artists whose contracts provide for royalties will be entitled to a "clean slate" during the last twenty years, because the Directive provides that "neither advance payments nor any contractually defined deductions shall be deducted from the payments made to the performer following the 50th year . . . " In other words, for the last 20 years, whether or not a sound recording has "made back its advance," the featured performer will be entitled to the contractually-provided royalty rate. (The Directive does not, however, ensure that the royalty rate will be non-trivial.) While the Directive goes into effect November 1, 2013, its text is not entirely clear regarding the application of the performers' royalty provisions to contracts concluded before the effective date.

2. COPYRIGHT DURATION UNDER THE 1976 ACT, AS AMENDED IN 1998

a. WORKS CREATED OR UNPUBLISHED AFTER 1977

Page 411. Immediately before the start of Section A.2.b., add the following note:

When Congress first extended federal copyright protection to sound recordings, it did so only prospectively, covering recordings fixed on or after February 15, 1972. Section 301(c) of the 1976 Act carried that decision forward and effectively limits federal copyright protection for sound recordings to those fixed on or after February 15, 1972. As a result, sound recordings made prior to February 15, 1972—commonly referred to as "pre-1972" recordings—are protected, if at all, by state statutes and court decisions that vary from state to state, and whatever protection those laws afford can continue until 2067.

In 2009, Congress directed the Copyright Office to study the desirability of extending federal copyright to pre-1972 sound recordings, and specifically to look at the effect that doing so would have on preservation, public access, and the economic interests of rightsholders. The Copyright Office issued its report in December 2011 (available at http://www.copyright.gov/docs/sound/pre-72–report.pdf) and recommended bringing pre-1972 sound recordings into federal copyright protection. The report argued that this "will improve the certainty and consistency of copyright law, will likely encourage more preservation and access activities, and should not result in any appreciable harm to the economic interests of right holders." Federalizing protection for pre-1972 sound recordings would mean, the report observed, that all of the rights and limitations in the Copyright Act that apply currently to federally protected sound recordings would apply to the newly federally protected pre-1972 works, as would any future rights or limitations that Congress enacted.

With respect to the mechanics of federalization, the report recommended that the initial owner of the federal copyright in a pre-1972 sound recording should be the person who owns the corresponding state law rights in the recording "at the moment before the legislation federalizing protection goes into effect." And the report recommended a general term of federal protection of 95 years from publication or, if the recording had not been published prior to federalization, 120 years from fixation, though protection for all pre-1972 recordings would end on February 15, 2067 (as with state protection under the current provisions of section 301(c)) and transitional provisions would provide certain minimum terms of protection.

No legislation implementing the report's recommendations has yet been introduced.

b.   1976 ACT TREATMENT OF WORKS FIRST PUBLISHED UNDER THE 1909 ACT

Page 416. Add at the end of the carryover paragraph:

A recent Second Circuit decision (involving the comic book *Ghost Rider*) held that an author's agreement to transfer "forever all rights of any kind and nature in and to" the copyrighted work to the grantee was ambiguous as to the parties' intent to convey renewal rights. *Gary Friedrich Enterprises, LLC v. Marvel Characters, Inc.*, 716 F.3d 302 (2d Cir. 2013).

Page 420. At the end of the second paragraph, replace the citation with the following:

See, e.g., Roger Miller Music, Inc. v. Sony/ATV Publishing, LLC, 672 F.3d 434 (6th Cir. 2012) (author's assignee filed for copyright renewals in January and April 1992; author died in October 1992; renewal copyrights vested in assignee, and not in author's surviving spouse, on January 1, 1993).

c.   WORKS IN THE PUBLIC DOMAIN PRIOR TO JANUARY 1, 1978 AND RESTORATION OF COPYRIGHTS IN FOREIGN WORKS

Page 423. Add Questions to the end of Note on "Works in the Public Domain prior to January 1, 1978 and Restoration of Copyrights in Foreign Works":

QUESTIONS

1.   Nora Novelist resides and published a work of fiction in a country with which the U.S. did not then have copyright relations. During that time, Trudy Translator published an unauthorized translation in the United States. When Nora's State joins the Berne Convention, will Nora have a successful infringement claim in the U.S. against Trudy's translation?

2.   A few years after Nora's state joins the Berne Convention, the publisher of Trudy's translation decides to publish the translation in electronic book ('eBook') form. He considers that his reliance interest in the translation extends to an eBook version of the translation, meaning that he will only have to pay Nora 'reasonable compensation,' but cannot be enjoined from disseminating the eBook version. Nora Novelist contends that the eBook is a new derivative work as to which the publisher is not a reliance party. Who should prevail? See *Peter Mayer Pub'rs. Inc. v. Shilovskaya*, 11 F.Supp.3d 421 (S.D.N.Y. 2014).

Pages 424–437. Replace the *Luck's Music Library* opinion and the circuit court opinion in *Golan v. Holder*, and the QUESTIONS that follow them, with the following:

Golan v. Holder

132 S.Ct. 873 (2012).

■ JUSTICE GINSBURG delivered the opinion of the Court.

The Berne Convention for the Protection of Literary and Artistic Works (Berne Convention or Berne), which took effect in 1886, is the principal accord governing international copyright relations. Latecomer to the international copyright regime launched by Berne, the United States joined the Convention in 1989. To perfect U.S. implementation of Berne, and as part of our response to the Uruguay Round of multilateral trade negotiations, Congress, in 1994, gave works enjoying copyright protection abroad the same full term of protection available to U.S. works. Congress did so in § 514 of the Uruguay Round Agreements Act (URAA), which grants copyright protection to preexisting works of Berne member countries, protected in their country of origin, but lacking protection in the United States for any of three reasons: The United States did not protect works from the country of origin at the time of publication; the United States did not protect sound recordings fixed before 1972; or the author had failed to comply with U.S. statutory formalities (formalities Congress no longer requires as prerequisites to copyright protection).

The URAA accords no protection to a foreign work after its full copyright term has expired, causing it to fall into the public domain, whether under the laws of the country of origin or of this country. Works encompassed by § 514 are granted the protection they would have enjoyed had the United States maintained copyright relations with the author's country or removed formalities incompatible with Berne. Foreign authors, however, gain no credit for the protection they lacked in years prior to § 514's enactment. They therefore enjoy fewer total years of exclusivity than do their U.S. counterparts. As a consequence of the barriers to U.S. copyright protection prior to the enactment of § 514, foreign works "restored" to protection by the measure had entered the public domain in this country. To cushion the impact of their placement in protected status, Congress included in § 514 ameliorating accommodations for parties who had exploited affected works before the URAA was enacted.

Petitioners include orchestra conductors, musicians, publishers, and others who formerly enjoyed free access to works § 514 removed from the public domain. They maintain that the Constitution's Copyright and Patent Clause, Art. I, § 8, cl. 8, and First Amendment both decree the invalidity of § 514. Under those prescriptions of our highest law, petitioners assert, a work that has entered the public domain, for whatever reason, must forever remain there.

In accord with the judgment of the Tenth Circuit, we conclude that § 514 does not transgress constitutional limitations on Congress' authority. Neither the Copyright and Patent Clause nor the First

Amendment, we hold, makes the public domain, in any and all cases, a territory that works may never exit.

I

A

Members of the Berne Union agree to treat authors from other member countries as well as they treat their own. Berne Convention, Sept. 9, 1886, as revised at Stockholm on July 14, 1967, Art. 1, 5(1), 828 U.N.T.S. 221, 225, 231–233. Nationals of a member country, as well as any author who publishes in one of Berne's 164 member states, thus enjoy copyright protection in nations across the globe. Each country, moreover, must afford at least the minimum level of protection specified by Berne. The copyright term must span the author's lifetime, plus at least 50 additional years, whether or not the author has complied with a member state's legal formalities. And, as relevant here, a work must be protected abroad unless its copyright term has expired in either the country where protection is claimed or the country of origin. Art. 18(1)–(2).[1]

A different system of transnational copyright protection long prevailed in this country. Until 1891, foreign works were categorically excluded from Copyright Act protection. Throughout most of the 20th century, the only eligible foreign authors were those whose countries granted reciprocal rights to U.S. authors and whose works were printed in the United States. See Act of Mar. 3, 1891, § 3, 13, 26 Stat. 1107, 1110; Patry, The United States and International Copyright Law, 40 Houston L. Rev. 749, 750 (2003).[2] For domestic and foreign authors alike, protection hinged on compliance with notice, registration, and renewal formalities.

The United States became party to Berne's multilateral, formality-free copyright regime in 1989. Initially, Congress adopted a "minimalist approach" to compliance with the Convention. H. R. Rep. No. 100–609, p. 7 (1988) (hereinafter BCIA House Report). The Berne Convention Implementation Act of 1988 (BCIA), 102 Stat. 2853, made "only those changes to American copyright law that [were] clearly required under the

---

[1]   Article 18 of the Berne Convention provides:

"(1) This Convention shall apply to all works which, at the moment of its coming into force, have not yet fallen into the public domain in the country of origin through the expiry of the term of protection.

"(2) If, however, through the expiry of the term of protection which was previously granted, a work has fallen into the public domain of the country where protection is claimed, that work shall not be protected anew.

"(3) The application of this principle shall be subject to any provisions contained in special conventions to that effect existing or to be concluded between countries of the Union. In the absence of such provisions, the respective countries shall determine, each in so far as it is concerned, the conditions of application of this principle.

"(4) The preceding provisions shall also apply in the case of new accessions to the Union and to cases in which protection is extended by the application of Article 7 or by the abandonment of reservations."

[2]   As noted by the Government's amici, the United States excluded foreign works from copyright not to swell the number of unprotected works available to the consuming public, but to favor domestic publishing interests that escaped paying royalties to foreign authors. This free-riding, according to Senator Jonathan Chace, champion of the 1891 Act, made the United States "the Barbary coast of literature" and its people "the buccaneers of books." S. Rep. No. 622, 50th Cong., 1st Sess., p. 2 (1888).

treaty's provisions," BCIA House Report, at 7. Despite Berne's instruction that member countries—including "new accessions to the Union"—protect foreign works under copyright in the country of origin, Art. 18(1) and (4), the BCIA accorded no protection for "any work that is in the public domain in the United States," § 12, 102 Stat. 2860. Protection of future foreign works, the BCIA indicated, satisfied Article 18. See § 2(3), 102 Stat. 2853 ("The amendments made by this Act, together with the law as it exists on the date of the enactment of this Act, satisfy the obligations of the United States in adhering to the Berne Convention. . . ."). Congress indicated, however, that it had not definitively rejected "retroactive" protection for preexisting foreign works; instead it had punted on this issue of Berne's implementation, deferring consideration until "a more thorough examination of Constitutional, commercial, and consumer considerations is possible." BCIA House Report, at 51, 52.

The minimalist approach essayed by the United States did not sit well with other Berne members. While negotiations were ongoing over the North American Free Trade Agreement (NAFTA), Mexican authorities complained about the United States' refusal to grant protection, in accord with Article 18, to Mexican works that remained under copyright domestically. The Register of Copyrights also reported "questions" from Turkey, Egypt, and Austria. Thailand and Russia balked at protecting U.S. works, copyrighted here but in those countries' public domains, until the United States reciprocated with respect to their authors' works.

Berne, however, did not provide a potent enforcement mechanism. The Convention contemplates dispute resolution before the International Court of Justice. But it specifies no sanctions for noncompliance and allows parties, at any time, to declare themselves "not . . . bound" by the Convention's dispute resolution provision. Unsurprisingly, no enforcement actions were launched before 1994. Although "several Berne Union Members disagreed with [our] interpretation of Article 18," the USTR told Congress, the Berne Convention did "not provide a meaningful dispute resolution process." [General Agreement on Tariffs and Trade (GATT): Intellectual Property Provisions, Joint Hearing before the Subcommittee on Intellectual Property and Judicial Administration of the House Committee on the Judiciary and the Subcommittee on Patents, Copyrights and Trademarks of the Senate Committee on the Judiciary, 103d Cong., 2d Sess., p. 137 (1994) (URAA Joint Hearing)] (statement of [Ira S. Shapiro, General Counsel, Office of the U. S. Trade Representative (USTR)]). This shortcoming left Congress "free to adopt a minimalist approach and evade Article 18." Karp, Final Report, Berne Article 18 Study on Retroactive United States Copyright Protection for Berne and other Works, 20 Colum.–VLA J. L. & Arts 157, 172 (1996).

The landscape changed in 1994. The Uruguay round of multilateral trade negotiations produced the World Trade Organization (WTO) and the Agreement on Trade-Related Aspects of Intellectual Property Rights (TRIPS). The United States joined both. TRIPS mandates, on pain of WTO enforcement, implementation of Berne's first 21 articles. TRIPS, Art. 9.1, 33 I. L. M. 1197, 1201 (requiring adherence to all but the "moral rights" provisions of Article 6*bis*). The WTO gave teeth to the

Convention's requirements: Noncompliance with a WTO ruling could subject member countries to tariffs or cross-sector retaliation. The specter of WTO enforcement proceedings bolstered the credibility of our trading partners' threats to challenge the United States for inadequate compliance with Article 18. See URAA Joint Hearing 137 (statement of Shapiro, USTR) ("It is likely that other WTO members would challenge the current U.S. implementation of Berne Article 18 under [WTO] procedures.").[8]

Congress' response to the Uruguay agreements put to rest any questions concerning U.S. compliance with Article 18. Section 514 of the URAA, 108 Stat. 4976 (codified at 17 U.S.C. § 104A), extended copyright to works that garnered protection in their countries of origin, but had no right to exclusivity in the United States for any of three reasons: lack of copyright relations between the country of origin and the United States at the time of publication; lack of subject-matter protection for sound recordings fixed before 1972; and failure to comply with U.S. statutory formalities (e.g., failure to provide notice of copyright status, or to register and renew a copyright). See § 104A(h)(6)(B)–(C).

Works that have fallen into the public domain after the expiration of a full copyright term—either in the United States or the country of origin—receive no further protection under § 514.[12] Copyrights "restored"[13] under URAA § 514 "subsist for the remainder of the term of copyright that the work would have otherwise been granted . . . if the work never entered the public domain." § 104A(a)(1)(B). Prospectively, restoration places foreign works on an equal footing with their U.S. counterparts; assuming a foreign and domestic author died the same day, their works will enter the public domain simultaneously. Restored works, however, receive no compensatory time for the period of exclusivity they would have enjoyed before § 514's enactment, had they been protected at the outset in the United States. Their total term, therefore, falls short of that available to similarly situated U.S. works.

The URAA's disturbance of the public domain hardly escaped Congress' attention. Section 514 imposed no liability for any use of foreign works occurring before restoration. In addition, anyone remained free to copy and use restored works for one year following § 514's enactment. See 17 U.S.C. § 104A(h)(2)(A). Concerns about § 514's compatibility with the Fifth Amendment's Takings Clause led Congress

---

[8] Proponents of prompt congressional action urged that avoiding a trade enforcement proceeding—potentially the WTO's first—would be instrumental in preserving the United States' "reputation as a world leader in the copyright field." URAA Joint Hearing 241 (statement of Eric Smith, International Intellectual Property Alliance (IIPA)). In this regard, U.S. negotiators reported that widespread perception of U.S. noncompliance was undermining our leverage in copyright negotiations. Unimpeachable adherence to Berne, Congress was told, would help ensure enhanced foreign protection, and hence profitable dissemination, for existing and future U.S. works.

[12] Title 17 U.S. C. § 104A(h)(6)(B) defines a "restored work" to exclude an original work of authorship" that is "in the public domain in its source country through expiration of [its] term of protection." This provision tracks Berne's denial of protection for any work that has "fallen into the public domain in the country of origin through the expiry of the term of protection." Art. 18(1).

[13] Restoration is a misnomer insofar as it implies that all works protected under § 104A previously enjoyed protection. Each work in the public domain because of lack of national eligibility or subject-matter protection, and many that failed to comply with formalities, never enjoyed U.S. copyright protection.

to include additional protections for "reliance parties"—those who had, before the URAA's enactment, used or acquired a foreign work then in the public domain. See § 104A(h)(3)–(4). Reliance parties may continue to exploit a restored work until the owner of the restored copyright gives notice of intent to enforce—either by filing with the U.S. Copyright Office within two years of restoration, or by actually notifying the reliance party. § 104A(c), (d)(2)(A)(i), and (B)(i). After that, reliance parties may continue to exploit existing copies for a grace period of one year. § 104A(d)(2)(A)(ii), and (B)(ii). Finally, anyone who, before the URAA's enactment, created a "derivative work" based on a restored work may indefinitely exploit the derivation upon payment to the copyright holder of "reasonable compensation," to be set by a district judge if the parties cannot agree. § 104A(d)(3).

B

In 2001, petitioners filed this lawsuit challenging § 514. They maintain that Congress, when it passed the URAA, exceeded its authority under the Copyright Clause and transgressed First Amendment limitations. The District Court granted the Attorney General's motion for summary judgment. *Golan v. Gonzales,* 2005 WL 914754 (D. Colo. 2005). In rejecting petitioners' Copyright Clause argument, the court stated that Congress "has historically demonstrated little compunction about removing copyrightable materials from the public domain." *Id.* at *14. The court next declined to part from "the settled rule that private censorship via copyright enforcement does not implicate First Amendment concerns." *Id.* at *17.

The Court of Appeals for the Tenth Circuit affirmed in part. *Golan v. Gonzales,* 501 F.3d 1179 (2007). The public domain, it agreed, was not a "threshold that Congress" was powerless to "traverse in both directions." *Id.* at 1187 (internal quotations marks omitted). But § 514, as the Court of Appeals read our decision in *Eldred* v. *Ashcroft,* 537 U.S. 186 (2003), required further First Amendment inspection. The measure " 'altered the traditional contours of copyright protection,' " the court said—specifically, the "bedrock principle" that once works enter the public domain, they do not leave. *Ibid.* (quoting *Eldred*). The case was remanded with an instruction to the District Court to address the First Amendment claim in light of the Tenth Circuit's opinion.

On remand, the District Court's starting premise was uncontested: Section 514 does not regulate speech on the basis of its content; therefore the law would be upheld if "narrowly tailored to serve a significant government interest." Summary judgment was due petitioners, the court concluded, because § 514's constriction of the public domain was not justified by any of the asserted federal interests: compliance with Berne, securing greater protection for U.S. authors abroad, or remediation of the inequitable treatment suffered by foreign authors whose works lacked protection in the United States.

The Tenth Circuit reversed. Deferring to Congress' predictive judgments in matters relating to foreign affairs, the appellate court held that § 514 survived First Amendment scrutiny. Specifically, the court determined that the law was narrowly tailored to fit the important government aim of protecting U.S. copyright holders' interests abroad.

We granted certiorari to consider petitioners' challenge to § 514 under both the Copyright Clause and the First Amendment, and now affirm.

II

We first address petitioners' argument that Congress lacked authority, under the Copyright Clause, to enact § 514. The Constitution states that "Congress shall have Power . . . [t]o promote the Progress of Science . . . by securing for limited Times to Authors . . . the exclusive Right to their . . . Writings." Art. I, § 8, cl. 8. Petitioners find in this grant of authority an impenetrable barrier to the extension of copyright protection to authors whose writings, for whatever reason, are in the public domain. We see no such barrier in the text of the Copyright Clause, historical practice, or our precedents.

A

The text of the Copyright Clause does not exclude application of copyright protection to works in the public domain. Petitioners' contrary argument relies primarily on the Constitution's confinement of a copyright's lifespan to a "limited Tim[e]." "Removing works from the public domain," they contend, "violates the 'limited [t]imes' restriction by turning a fixed and predictable period into one that can be reset or resurrected at any time, even after it expires."

Our decision in *Eldred* is largely dispositive of petitioners' limited-time argument. There we addressed the question whether Congress violated the Copyright Clause when it extended, by 20 years, the terms of existing copyrights. Ruling that Congress acted within constitutional bounds, we declined to infer from the text of the Copyright Clause "the command that a time prescription, once set, becomes forever 'fixed' or 'inalterable.' " "The word 'limited,' " we observed, "does not convey a meaning so constricted." Rather, the term is best understood to mean "confine[d] within certain bounds," "restrain[ed]," or "circumscribed." The construction petitioners tender closely resembles the definition rejected in *Eldred* and is similarly infirm.

The terms afforded works restored by § 514 are no less "limited" than those the CTEA lengthened. In light of *Eldred,* petitioners do not here contend that the term Congress has granted U.S. authors—their lifetimes, plus 70 years—is unlimited. Nor do petitioners explain why terms of the same duration, as applied to foreign works, are not equally "circumscribed" and "confined." Indeed, as earlier noted, the copyrights of restored foreign works typically last for fewer years than those of their domestic counterparts.

The difference, petitioners say, is that the limited time had already passed for works in the public domain. What was that limited term for foreign works once excluded from U.S. copyright protection? Exactly "zero," petitioners respond. Brief for Petitioners 22 (works in question "received a specific term of protection . . . sometimes expressly set to zero"; "at the end of that period," they "entered the public domain"); Tr. of Oral Arg. 52 (by "refusing to provide any protection for a work," Congress "set[s] the term at zero," and thereby "tell[s] us when the end has come"). We find scant sense in this argument, for surely a "limited time" of exclusivity must begin before it may end.

Carried to its logical conclusion, petitioners persist, the Government's position would allow Congress to institute a second "limited" term after the first expires, a third after that, and so on. Thus, as long as Congress legislated in installments, perpetual copyright terms would be achievable. As in *Eldred,* the hypothetical legislative misbehavior petitioners posit is far afield from the case before us. In aligning the United States with other nations bound by the Berne Convention, and thereby according equitable treatment to once disfavored foreign authors, Congress can hardly be charged with a design to move stealthily toward a regime of perpetual copyrights.

B

Historical practice corroborates our reading of the Copyright Clause to permit full U.S. compliance with Berne. Undoubtedly, federal copyright legislation generally has not affected works in the public domain. Section 514's disturbance of that domain, petitioners argue, distinguishes their suit from Eldred's. In adopting the CTEA, petitioners note, Congress acted in accord with "an unbroken congressional practice" of granting pre-expiration term extensions. No comparable practice, they maintain, supports § 514.

On occasion, however, Congress has seen fit to protect works once freely available. Notably, the Copyright Act of 1790 granted protection to many works previously in the public domain. Act of May 31, 1790 (1790 Act), § 1, 1 Stat. 124 (covering "any map, chart, book, or books already printed within these United States"). Before the Act launched a uniform national system, three States provided no statutory copyright protection at all. Of those that did afford some protection, seven failed to protect maps; eight did not cover previously published books; and all ten denied protection to works that failed to comply with formalities. The First Congress, it thus appears, did not view the public domain as inviolate. As we have recognized, the "construction placed upon the Constitution by [the drafters of] the first [copyright] act of 1790 and the act of 1802 . . . men who were contemporary with [the Constitution's] formation, many of whom were members of the convention which framed it, is of itself entitled to very great weight." *Burrow-Giles Lithographic Co. v. Sarony,* 111 U.S. 53, 57.[21]

Subsequent actions confirm that Congress has not understood the Copyright Clause to preclude protection for existing works. Several private bills [in 1849, 1874, and 1898] restored the copyrights of works that previously had been in the public domain. . . . These bills were unchallenged in court.

Analogous patent statutes, however, were upheld in litigation. In 1808, Congress passed a private bill restoring patent protection to Oliver Evans' flour mill. When Evans sued for infringement, first Chief Justice Marshall in the Circuit Court, *Evans v. Jordan,* 8 F.Cas. 872 (No. 4,564)

---

[21] The parties debate the extent to which the First Congress removed works from the public domain. We have held, however, that at least some works protected by the 1790 Act previously lacked protection. In *Wheaton v. Peters,* 33 U.S. 591 (1834), the Court ruled that before enactment of the 1790 Act, common-law copyright protection expired upon first publication. Thus published works covered by the 1790 Act previously would have been in the public domain unless protected by state statute. Had the founding generation perceived the constitutional boundary petitioners advance today, the First Congress could have designed a prospective scheme that left the public domain undisturbed.

(Va. 1813), and then Justice Bushrod Washington for this Court, *Evans v. Jordan,* 13 U.S. 199 (1815), upheld the restored patent's validity. After the patent's expiration, the Court said, "a general right to use [Evans'] discovery was not so vested in the public" as to allow the defendant to continue using the machinery, which he had constructed between the patent's expiration and the bill's passage. *Id.,* at 202. See also *Blanchard v. Sprague,* 3 F.Cas. 648, 650 (No. 1,518) (C.C.D. Mass. 1839) (Story, J.) ("I never have entertained any doubt of the constitutional authority of congress" to "give a patent for an invention, which . . . was in public use and enjoyed by the community at the time of the passage of the act.").

This Court again upheld Congress' restoration of an invention to protected status in *McClurg v. Kingsland,* 42 U.S. 202 (1843). There we enforced an 1839 amendment that recognized a patent on an invention despite its prior use by the inventor's employer. Absent such dispensation, the employer's use would have rendered the invention unpatentable, and therefore open to exploitation without the inventor's leave.

Congress has also passed generally applicable legislation granting patents and copyrights to inventions and works that had lost protection. An 1832 statute authorized a new patent for any inventor whose failure, "by inadvertence, accident, or mistake," to comply with statutory formalities rendered the original patent "invalid or inoperative." An 1893 measure similarly allowed authors who had not timely deposited their work to receive "all the rights and privileges" the Copyright Act affords, if they made the required deposit by March 1, 1893. And in 1919 and 1941, Congress authorized the President to issue proclamations granting protection to foreign works that had fallen into the public domain during World Wars I and II.

. . .

Installing a federal copyright system and ameliorating the interruptions of global war, it is true, presented Congress with extraordinary situations. Yet the TRIPS accord, leading the United States to comply in full measure with Berne, was also a signal event. Given the authority we hold Congress has, we will not second-guess the political choice Congress made between leaving the public domain untouched and embracing Berne unstintingly.

C

Petitioners' ultimate argument as to the Copyright and Patent Clause concerns its initial words. Congress is empowered to "promote the Progress of Science and useful Arts" by enacting systems of copyright and patent protection. U.S. Const., Art. I, § 8, cl. 8. Perhaps counterintuitively for the contemporary reader, Congress' copyright authority is tied to the progress of science; its patent authority, to the progress of the useful arts.

The "Progress of Science," petitioners acknowledge, refers broadly to "the creation and spread of knowledge and learning." They nevertheless argue that federal legislation cannot serve the Clause's aim unless the legislation "spur[s] the creation of . . . new works." Because § 514 deals solely with works already created, petitioners urge, it "provides no plausible incentive to create new works" and is therefore invalid.

The creation of at least one new work, however, is not the sole way Congress may promote knowledge and learning. In *Eldred,* we rejected an argument nearly identical to the one petitioners rehearse. . . .

Even were we writing on a clean slate, petitioners' argument would be unavailing. Nothing in the text of the Copyright Clause confines the "Progress of Science" exclusively to "incentives for creation." Evidence from the founding, moreover, suggests that inducing *dissemination*—as opposed to creation—was viewed as an appropriate means to promote science. See *Nachbar, Constructing Copyright's Mythology, 6 Green Bag 2d 37,* 44 (2002) ("The scope of copyright protection existing at the time of the framing," trained as it was on "publication, not creation," "is inconsistent with claims that copyright must promote creative activity in order to be valid." (internal quotation marks omitted)). Until 1976, in fact, Congress made "federal copyright contingent on publication[,] [thereby] providing incentives not primarily for creation," but for dissemination. [Perlmutter, Participation in the International Copyright System as a Means to Promote the Progress of Science and Useful Arts, 36 Loyola (LA) L. Rev. 323, 334 n.5 (2002)]. Our decisions correspondingly recognize that "copyright supplies the economic incentive to create *and disseminate* ideas." *Harper & Row, Publishers, Inc. v. Nation Enterprises,* 471 U.S. 539, 558 (1985) (emphasis added).

Considered against this backdrop, § 514 falls comfortably within Congress' authority under the Copyright Clause. Congress rationally could have concluded that adherence to Berne "promotes the diffusion of knowledge". A well-functioning international copyright system would likely encourage the dissemination of existing and future works. Full compliance with Berne, Congress had reason to believe, would expand the foreign markets available to U.S. authors and invigorate protection against piracy of U.S. works abroad, thereby benefitting copyright intensive industries stateside and inducing greater investment in the creative process.

The provision of incentives for the creation of new works is surely an essential means to advance the spread of knowledge and learning. We hold, however, that it is not the sole means Congress may use "[t]o promote the Progress of Science." See Perlmutter, *supra,* at 332 (United States would "lose all flexibility" were the provision of incentives to create the exclusive way to promote the progress of science).[28] Congress determined that exemplary adherence to Berne would serve the objectives of the Copyright Clause. We have no warrant to reject the rational judgment Congress made.

---

[28] The dissent suggests that the "utilitarian view of copyrigh[t]" embraced by Jefferson, Madison, and our case law sets us apart from continental Europe and inhibits us from harmonizing our copyright laws with those of countries in the civil-law tradition. For persuasive refutation of that suggestion, see Austin, Does the Copyright Clause Mandate Isolationism? 26 Colum. J. L. & Arts 17, 59 (2002) (cautioning against "an isolationist reading of the Copyright Clause that is in tension with . . . America's international copyright relations over the last hundred or so years").

III

A

We next explain why the First Amendment does not inhibit the restoration authorized by § 514. To do so, we first recapitulate the relevant part of our pathmarking decision in *Eldred*. . . .

[In *Eldred*,] we recognized that some restriction on expression is the inherent and intended effect of every grant of copyright. Noting that the "Copyright Clause and the First Amendment were adopted close in time," 537 U.S., at 219, we observed that the Framers regarded copyright protection not simply as a limit on the manner in which expressive works may be used. They also saw copyright as an "engine of free expression[:] By establishing a marketable right to the use of one's expression, copyright supplies the economic incentive to create and disseminate ideas." . . .

We then described the "traditional contours" of copyright protection, i.e., the "idea/expression dichotomy" and the "fair use" defense.[29] . . .

Given the "speech-protective purposes and safeguards" embraced by copyright law, we concluded in *Eldred* that there was no call for the heightened review petitioners sought in that case. We reach the same conclusion here. Section 514 leaves undisturbed the "idea/expression" distinction and the "fair use" defense. Moreover, Congress adopted measures to ease the transition from a national scheme to an international copyright regime: It deferred the date from which enforcement runs, and it cushioned the impact of restoration on "reliance parties" who exploited foreign works denied protection before § 514 took effect. . . .

B

Petitioners attempt to distinguish their challenge from the one turned away in *Eldred*. First Amendment interests of a higher order are at stake here, petitioners say, because they—unlike their counterparts in *Eldred*—enjoyed "vested rights" in works that had already entered the public domain. The limited rights they retain under copyright law's "built-in safeguards" are, in their view, no substitute for the unlimited use they enjoyed before § 514's enactment. Nor, petitioners urge, does § 514's "unprecedented" foray into the public domain possess the historical pedigree that supported the term extension at issue in *Eldred*.

However spun, these contentions depend on an argument we considered and rejected above, namely, that the Constitution renders the public domain largely untouchable by Congress. Petitioners here attempt to achieve under the banner of the First Amendment what they could not win under the Copyright Clause: On their view of the Copyright Clause, the public domain is inviolable; as they read the First Amendment, the public domain is policed through heightened judicial scrutiny of Congress' means and ends. As we have already shown, the text of the Copyright Clause and the historical record scarcely establish that "once a work enters the public domain," Congress cannot permit anyone—"not even the creator—[to] copyright it". And nothing in the historical record,

---

[29] On the initial appeal in this case, the Tenth Circuit gave an unconfined reading to our reference in *Eldred* to "traditional contours of copyright." 501 F. 3d, at 1187–1196. That reading was incorrect, as we here clarify.

congressional practice, or our own jurisprudence warrants exceptional First Amendment solicitude for copyrighted works that were once in the public domain. Neither this challenge nor that raised in *Eldred,* we stress, allege Congress transgressed a generally applicable First Amendment prohibition; we are not faced, for example, with copyright protection that hinges on the author's viewpoint.

The Tenth Circuit's initial opinion determined that petitioners marshaled a stronger First Amendment challenge than did their predecessors in *Eldred,* who never "possessed unfettered access to any of the works at issue." 501 F. 3d, at 1193. See also id., at 1194 ("[O]nce the works at issue became free for anyone to copy, [petitioners] had vested First Amendment interests in the expressions, [thus] § 514's interference with [petitioners'] rights is subject to First Amendment scrutiny."). As petitioners put it in this Court, Congress impermissibly revoked their right to exploit foreign works that "belonged to them" once the works were in the public domain.

To copyright lawyers, the "vested rights" formulation might sound exactly backwards: Rights typically vest at the *outset* of copyright protection, in an author or rightholder. See, e.g., 17 U.S. C. § 201(a). Once the term of protection ends, the works do not revest in any rightholder. Instead, the works simply lapse into the public domain. Anyone has free access to the public domain, but no one, after the copyright term has expired, acquires ownership rights in the once-protected works.

Congress recurrently adjusts copyright law to protect categories of works once outside the law's compass. For example, Congress broke new ground when it extended copyright protection to foreign works in 1891, to dramatic works in 1856, to photographs and photographic negatives in 1865, to motion pictures in 1912, to fixed sound recordings in 1972, and to architectural works in 1990. And on several occasions, as recounted above, Congress protected works previously in the public domain, hence freely usable by the public. If Congress could grant protection to these works without hazarding heightened First Amendment scrutiny, then what free speech principle disarms it from protecting works prematurely cast into the public domain for reasons antithetical to the Berne Convention.

Section 514, we add, does not impose a blanket prohibition on public access. Petitioners protest that fair use and the idea/expression dichotomy "are plainly inadequate to protect the speech and expression rights that Section 514 took from petitioners, or . . . the public"—that is, "the unrestricted right to perform, copy, teach and distribute the *entire* work, for any reason." "Playing a few bars of a Shostakovich symphony," petitioners observe, "is no substitute for performing the entire work."[34]

But Congress has not put petitioners in this bind. The question here, as in *Eldred,* is whether would-be users must pay for their desired use of the author's expression, or else limit their exploitation to "fair use" of that work. Prokofiev's Peter and the Wolf could once be performed free of charge; after § 514 the right to perform it must be obtained in the marketplace. This is the same marketplace, of course, that exists for the music of Prokofiev's U.S. contemporaries: works of Copland and

---

[34] Because Shostakovich was a pre-1973 Russian composer, his works were not protected in the United States.

Bernstein, for example, that enjoy copyright protection, but nevertheless appear regularly in the programs of U.S. concertgoers.

Before we joined Berne, domestic works and some foreign works were protected under U.S. statutes and bilateral international agreements, while other foreign works were available at an artificially low (because royalty-free) cost. By fully implementing Berne, Congress ensured that most works, whether foreign or domestic, would be governed by the same legal regime. The phenomenon to which Congress responded is not new: Distortions of the same order occurred with greater frequency—and to the detriment of both foreign and domestic authors— when, before 1891, foreign works were excluded entirely from U.S. copyright protection. *See Kampelman, The United States and International Copyright*, 41 Am. J. Int'l L. 406, 413 (1947) ("American readers were less inclined to read the novels of Cooper or Hawthorne for a dollar when they could buy a novel of Scott or Dickens for a quarter."). Section 514 continued the trend toward a harmonized copyright regime by placing foreign works in the position they would have occupied if the current regime had been in effect when those works were created and first published. Authors once deprived of protection are spared the continuing effects of that initial deprivation; § 514 gives them nothing more than the benefit of their labors during whatever time remains before the normal copyright term expires.

. . .

IV

Congress determined that U.S. interests were best served by our full participation in the dominant system of international copyright protection. Those interests include ensuring exemplary compliance with our international obligations, securing greater protection for U.S. authors abroad, and remedying unequal treatment of foreign authors. The judgment § 514 expresses lies well within the ken of the political branches. It is our obligation, of course, to determine whether the action Congress took, wise or not, encounters any constitutional shoal. For the reasons stated, we are satisfied it does not. The judgment of the Court of Appeals for the Tenth Circuit is therefore

Affirmed.

JUSTICE KAGAN took no part in the consideration or decision of this case.

■ JUSTICE BREYER, with whom JUSTICE ALITO joins, dissenting.

In order "[t]o promote the Progress of Science" (by which term the Founders meant "learning" or "knowledge"), the Constitution's Copyright Clause grants Congress the power to "secur[e] for limited Times to Authors . . . the exclusive Right to their . . . Writings." This "exclusive Right" allows its holder to charge a fee to those who wish to use a copyrighted work, and the ability to charge that fee encourages the production of new material. In this sense, a copyright is, in Macaulay's words, a "tax on readers for the purpose of giving a bounty to writers"— a bounty designed to encourage new production. As the Court said in *Eldred*, " '[t]he economic philosophy behind the [Copyright] [C]lause . . . is the conviction that encouragement of individual effort by personal gain is the best way to advance public welfare through the talents of authors and inventors.' " . . .

The statute before us, however, does not encourage anyone to produce a single new work. By definition, it bestows monetary rewards only on owners of old works—works that have already been created and already are in the American public domain. At the same time, the statute inhibits the dissemination of those works, foreign works published abroad after 1923, of which there are many millions, including films, works of art, innumerable photographs, and, of course, books—books that (in the absence of the statute) would assume their rightful places in computer-accessible databases, spreading knowledge throughout the world. In my view, the Copyright Clause does not authorize Congress to enact this statute. And I consequently dissent.

I

The possibility of eliciting new production is, and always has been, an essential precondition for American copyright protection. The Constitution's words, "exclusive Right," "limited Times," "Progress of Science," viewed through the lens of history underscore the legal significance of what the Court in *Eldred* referred to as the "economic philosophy behind the Copyright Clause." That philosophy understands copyright's grants of limited monopoly privileges to authors as private benefits that are conferred for a public reason—to elicit new creation.

Yet, as the Founders recognized, monopoly is a two-edged sword. On the one hand, it can encourage production of new works. In the absence of copyright protection, anyone might freely copy the products of an author's creative labor, appropriating the benefits without incurring the nonrepeatable costs of creation, thereby deterring authors from exerting themselves in the first place. On the other hand, copyright tends to restrict the dissemination (and use) of works once produced either because the absence of competition translates directly into higher consumer prices or because the need to secure copying permission sometimes imposes administrative costs that make it difficult for potential users of a copyrighted work to find its owner and strike a bargain. Consequently, the original British copyright statute, the Constitution's Framers, and our case law all have recognized copyright's resulting and necessary call for balance.

At the time the Framers wrote the Constitution, they were well aware of Britain's 18th-century copyright statute, the Statute of Anne, (1710) . . . It bore the title: "An Act for the Encouragement of Learning, by vesting the Copies of printed Books in the Authors or Purchasers of such Copies, during the Times therein mentioned." And it granted authors (not publishers) and their assignees the "sole Right and Liberty of printing" their works for limited periods of time *in order to encourage them* "to compose *and write useful* Books." 8 Anne, ch. 19, § 1 (emphasis added). . . .

Many early colonial copyright statutes, patterned after the Statute of Anne, also stated that copyright's objective was to encourage authors to produce new works and thereby improve learning. . . .

At least, that was the predominant view expressed to, or by, the Founders. . . .

This utilitarian view of copyrights and patents, embraced by Jefferson and Madison, stands in contrast to the "natural rights" view underlying much of continental European copyright law—a view that the

English booksellers promoted in an effort to limit their losses following the enactment of the Statute of Anne and that in part motivated the enactment of some of the colonial statutes. Premised on the idea that an author or inventor has an inherent right to the fruits of his labor, it mythically stems from a legendary 6th-century statement of King Diarmed " 'to every cow her calf, and accordingly to every book its copy.' " A. Birrell, Seven Lectures on the Law and History of Copyright in Books 42 (1899). That view, though perhaps reflected in the Court's opinion, runs contrary to the more utilitarian views that influenced the writing of our own Constitution's Copyright Clause. . . .

This utilitarian understanding of the Copyright Clause has long been reflected in the Court's case law. . . .

Congress has expressed similar views in congressional Reports on copyright legislation. Thus, for example, an 1892 House Report states:

> "The object to be attained and the reason for the constitutional grant of power are imbedded in the grant itself. They are 'to promote the progress of science and the useful arts.' . . . [The Clause says] nothing . . . about any desire or purpose to secure to the author or inventor his 'natural right to his property.' " H.R. Rep. No. 1494, 52d Cong., 1st Sess., 2.

Similarly, the congressional authors of the landmark 1909 Copyright Act wrote:

> "The Constitution . . . provides that Congress shall have the power to grant [copyrights] . . . [n]ot primarily for the benefit of the author . . . but because the policy is believed to be for the benefit of the great body of people, *in that it will stimulate writing and invention,* to give some bonus to authors and inventors." H. R. Rep. No. 2222, 60th Cong., 2d Sess., 7 (1909).

And they went on to say:

> "Congress must consider . . . two questions: First, how much will the legislation stimulate the producer and so benefit the public; and, second, how much will the monopoly granted be detrimental to the public? The granting of such exclusive rights, under the proper terms and conditions, confers a benefit upon the public that outweighs the evils of the temporary monopoly." *Ibid.*

The upshot is that text, history, and precedent demonstrate that the Copyright Clause places great value on the power of copyright to elicit new production. Congress in particular cases may determine that copyright's ability to do so outweighs any concomitant high prices, administrative costs, and restrictions on dissemination. And when it does so, we must respect its judgment. *See Eldred,* 537 U.S., at 222. But does the Clause empower Congress to enact a statute that withdraws works from the public domain, brings about higher prices and costs, and in doing so seriously restricts dissemination, particularly to those who need it for scholarly, educational, or cultural purposes—all *without providing any additional incentive* for the production of new material? That is the question before us. And, as I have said, I believe the answer is no. Congress in this statute has exceeded what are, under any plausible reading of the Copyright Clause, its permissible limits.

II

[T]he Act covers vast numbers of works. The first category includes works published in countries that had copyright relations with the United States [between 1923 and 1989], such as most of Western Europe and Latin America, Australia, and Japan, whose authors did not satisfy American copyright formalities, perhaps because the author, who may not have sought an American copyright, published the book abroad without proper American notice, or perhaps because the author obtained a valid American copyright but failed to renew it.

The second category (works that entered the public domain due to a lack of copyright relations) includes, among others, all works published in Russia and other countries of the former Soviet Union before May 1973 (when the U.S.S.R. joined the Universal Copyright Convention (UCC)), all works published in the People's Republic of China before March 1992 (when bilateral copyright relations between the People's Republic and the United States were first established), all South Korean works published before October 1987 (when South Korea joined the UCC), and all Egyptian and Turkish works published before March 1989 (when the United States joined Berne).

The third category covers all sound recordings from eligible foreign countries published after [*sic*] February 15, 1972. The practical significance of federal copyright restoration to this category of works is less clear, since these works received, and continued to receive, copyright protection under state law.

Apparently there are no precise figures about the number of works the Act affects, but in 1996 the then-Register of Copyrights, Marybeth Peters, thought that they "probably number in the millions." The Year in Review: Accomplishments and Objectives of the U.S. Copyright Office, 7 Ford. Intellectual Property Media & Entertainment L. J. 25, 31 (1996).

A

The provision before us takes works from the public domain, at least as of January 1, 1996. It then restricts the dissemination of those works in two ways.

First, "restored copyright" holders can now charge fees for works that consumers previously used for free. . . .

Second, and at least as important, the statute creates administrative costs, such as the costs of determining whether a work is the subject of a "restored copyright," searching for a "restored copyright" holder, and negotiating a fee.

. . .

B

I recognize that ordinary copyright protection also comes accompanied with dissemination-restricting royalty charges and administrative costs. But here the restrictions work special harm. For one thing, the foreign location of restored works means higher than ordinary administrative costs. For another, the statute's technical requirements make it very difficult to establish whether a work has had its copyright restored by the statute. . . .

Worst of all, "restored copyright" protection removes material from the public domain. In doing so, it reverses the payment expectations of those who used, or intended to use, works that they thought belonged to them. Were Congress to act similarly with respect to well-established property rights, the problem would be obvious. This statute analogously restricts, and thereby diminishes, Americans' preexisting freedom to use formerly public domain material in their expressive activities.

Thus, while the majority correctly observes that the dissemination-restricting harms of copyright normally present problems appropriate for legislation to resolve, the question is whether the Copyright Clause permits Congress seriously to exacerbate such a problem by taking works out of the public domain without a countervailing benefit. This question is appropriate for judicial resolution. Indeed, unlike *Eldred* where the Court had to decide a complicated line-drawing question—when is a copyright term too long—here an easily administrable standard is available—a standard that would require works that have already fallen into the public domain to stay there.

The several, just mentioned features of the present statute are important, for they distinguish it from other copyright laws. By removing material from the public domain, the statute, in literal terms, "abridges" a preexisting freedom to speak. In practical terms, members of the public might well have decided what to say, as well as when and how to say it, in part by reviewing with a view to repeating, expression that they reasonably believed was, or would be, freely available. Given these speech implications, it is not surprising that Congress has long sought to protect public domain material when revising the copyright laws. . . .

Moreover, whereas forward-looking copyright laws tend to benefit those whose identities are not yet known (the writer who has not yet written a book, the musician who has not yet composed a song), when a copyright law is primarily backward looking the risk is greater that Congress is trying to help known beneficiaries at the expense of badly organized unknown users who find it difficult to argue and present their case to Congress. In *Eldred*, I thought this problem was severe. And in light of the fact that Congress, with one minor exception, heard testimony only from the representatives of existing copyright holders, who hoped that passage of the statute would enable them to benefit from reciprocal treatment of American authors abroad, I cannot say that even here the problem, while much diminished, was nonexistent.

Taken together, these speech-related harms (e.g., restricting use of previously available material; reversing payment expectations; rewarding rent-seekers at the public's expense) at least show the presence of a First Amendment interest. And that is enough. For present purposes, I need not decide whether the harms to that interest show a violation of the First Amendment. I need only point to the importance of interpreting the Constitution as a single document—a document that we should not read as setting the Copyright Clause and the First Amendment at cross-purposes. Nor need I advocate the application here of strict or specially heightened review. I need only find that the First Amendment interest is important enough to require courts to scrutinize with some care the reasons claimed to justify the Act in order to determine whether they constitute reasonable copyright-related justifications for the serious harms, including speech-related harms, which the Act seems likely to impose.

C

1

This statute does not serve copyright's traditional public ends, namely the creation of monetary awards that "motivate the creative activity of authors," *Sony*, 464 U. S., at 429, "encourag[e] individual effort," *Mazer*, 347 U. S., at 219, and thereby "serve the cause of promoting broad public availability of literature, music, and the other arts," *Twentieth Century Music*, 422 U. S., at 156. . . .

[The majority finds past instances of Congress' restoration of protection for expired copyrights or patents.] [P]ast congressional practice . . . mostly suggests that Congress may provide new or increased protection both to newly created and to previously created works [or consists of] private bills, statutes retroactively granting protection in wartime, or the like [and] designed to provide special exceptions for . . . equitable reasons. In fact, Congressional practice . . . consists of a virtually unbroken string of legislation preventing the withdrawal of works from the public domain. See, e.g., Berne Convention Implementation Act of 1988, § 12, 102 Stat. 2860 (the Act "does not provide copyright protection for any work that is in the public domain in the United States"); Copyright Act of 1976, Tit. I, § 101, 90 Stat. 2573 (declining to extend copyright protection to any work that is in the public domain prior to the Act taking effect); Copyright Act of 1909, § 7, 35 Stat. 1077 ("[N]o copyright shall subsist in the original text of any work which is in the public domain, or in any work which was published in this country or any foreign country prior to the going into effect of this Act and has not been already copyrighted in the United States"); Act to Amend the Several Acts Respecting Copy Rights § 16, 4 Stat. 439 (the Act "shall not extend to any copyright heretofore secured, the term of which has already expired"); see also H. R. Rep. No. 1742, 87th Cong., 2d Sess., 3 (1962) (expressing concern that because "it is not possible to revive expired terms of copyright, it seems to the committee to be desirable to suspend further expiration of copyright for a period long enough to enable the working out of remaining obstacles to the overall revision of the copyright law").

2

The majority makes several other arguments. First, it argues that the Clause does not require the "creation of at least one new work," but may instead "promote the Progress of Science" in other ways. And it specifically mentions the "dissemination of existing and future works" as determinative here. The industry experts to whom the majority refers argue that copyright protection of already existing works can help, say, music publishers or film distributers raise prices, produce extra profits and consequently lead them to publish or distribute works they might otherwise have ignored. But ordinarily a copyright—since it is *a monopoly* on *copying—restricts* dissemination of a work once produced compared to a competitive market. And simply making the industry richer does not mean that the industry, when it makes an ordinary *forward-looking* economic calculus, will distribute works not previously distributed. The industry experts might mean that temporary extra profits will lead them to invest in the development of a market, say, by advertising. But this kind of argument, which can be made by distributers of all sorts of goods, ranging from kiwi fruit to Swedish furniture, has little if anything to do with the nonrepeatable costs of initial creation, which is the special concern of copyright protection.

Moreover, the argument proves too much. . . . It is the kind of argument that could justify a legislature's withdrawing from the public domain the works, say, of Hawthorne or of Swift or for that matter the King James Bible in order to encourage further publication of those works; and, it could even more easily justify similar action in the case of lesser known early works, perhaps those of the Venerable Bede. The Court has not, to my knowledge, previously accepted such a rationale—a rationale well removed from the special economic circumstances that surround the nonrepeatable costs of the initial creation of a "Writing." And I fear that doing so would read the Copyright Clause as if it were a blank check made out in favor of those who are not themselves creators.

. . . [T]he copyright holders' representatives who appeared before Congress testified that withdrawing [preexisting foreign] works from the American public domain would permit foreign copyright owners to charge American consumers more for their products; and that, as a result, the United States would be able to persuade foreign countries to allow American holders of preexisting copyrights to charge foreign customers more money for their products.

This argument, whatever its intrinsic merits, is an argument that directly concerns a private benefit: how to obtain more money from the sales of existing products. It is not an argument about a public benefit, such as how to promote or to protect the creative process.

Third, the majority points out that the statute "gives [authors] nothing more than the benefit of their labors during whatever time remains before the normal copyright term expires." But insofar as it suggests that copyright should in general help authors obtain greater monetary rewards than needed to elicit new works, it rests upon primarily European, but not American, copyright concepts.

Fourth, the majority argues that this statutory provision is necessary to fulfill our Berne Convention obligations. The Treaty, in Article 18, says that the "Convention shall apply to all works which, at the moment of its coming into force [i.e., 1989 in the case of the United States] have not yet fallen into the public domain in the country of origin through the expiry of the term of protection" The majority and Government say that this means we must protect the foreign works at issue here. And since the Berne Convention, taken as a whole, provides incentives for the creation of new works, I am willing to speculate, for argument's sake, that the statute might indirectly encourage production of new works by making the United States' place in the international copyright regime more secure.

Still, I cannot find this argument sufficient to save the statute. For one thing, this is a dilemma of the Government's own making. The United States obtained the benefits of Berne for many years despite its failure to enact a statute implementing Article 18. . . . [In negotiating TRIPS,] the Government, although it successfully secured reservations protecting other special features of American copyright law, made no effort to secure a reservation permitting the United States to keep some or all restored works in the American public domain. Indeed, it made no effort to do so despite the fact that Article 18 explicitly authorizes countries to negotiate exceptions to the Article's retroactivity principle. See Art. 18(3) ("The application of [the retroactivity] principle *shall be subject to any provisions contained in special conventions to that effect* existing or to be concluded between countries of the Union" (emphasis added)).

For another thing, the Convention does not require Congress to enact a statute that causes so much damage to public domain material. Article 18(3) also states that "the respective countries shall determine, each in so far as it is concerned, *the conditions of application of this principle."* (Emphasis added.) Congress could have alleviated many of the costs that the statute imposes by, for example, creating forms of compulsory licensing . . .

To say this is not to criticize the Convention or our joining it. Rather, it is to argue that the other branches of Government should have tried to *follow* the Convention and in particular its provisions offering compliance flexibility. The fact that the statute has significant First Amendment costs is relevant in this respect, for that Amendment ordinarily requires courts to evaluate less restrictive, alternative possibilities. Doing so here, reveals that neither Congress nor the Executive took advantage of less-restrictive methods of compliance that the Convention itself provides. And that fact means that the Convention cannot provide the statute with a constitutionally sufficient justification that is otherwise lacking.

III

The fact that, by withdrawing material from the public domain, the statute inhibits an important preexisting flow of information is sufficient, when combined with the other features of the statute that I have discussed, to convince me that the Copyright Clause, interpreted in the light of the First Amendment, does not authorize Congress to enact this statute.

I respectfully dissent from the Court's contrary conclusion.

QUESTIONS

1.   Does it make sense to defer to Congress' judgment if copyright lobbyists substantially influenced that judgment?

2.   Should a court show equal deference to Congress when it restores expired copyrights as when it extends existing viable ones? Why or why not?

3.   Section 104A, and the *Golan* decision, involve restoration of copyright only in works of foreign origin. Loss of copyright for failure to comply with formalities before 1989, though, also affected works of U.S. authors: if Book *A* was published in 1950 without proper copyright notice, it failed to secure federal copyright and fell into the public domain immediately. Given the Supreme Court's views in *Golan* and *Eldred* of the scope of Congress' copyright power, could Congress constitutionally restore copyright protection to U.S.-origin works such as Book *A* that fell into the public domain because of noncompliance with required formalities? Or would the fact that the Berne Convention does not require a member nation to apply its provisions retroactively (or at all) to its own nationals make such a restoration constitutionally infirm?

4. If Congress does have the power to restore copyright in U.S.-origin works such as Book *A* in Question 3, for how long a period of time can the restored copyright last? Consider that the copyright in Book *B*, also published in 1950 but with proper copyright notice (and properly renewed in 1978), will enjoy 95 years of copyright and expire in 2045. If Congress passes a domestic restoration act effective in 2015, must it take the same approach as in Section 104A and restore the copyright in Book *A* beginning in 2015 and ending 31 years later in 2045—that is, only for the remainder of the term that Book *A* would have had if copyright had been properly secured in the first place? Or would concerns about parity between Books *A* and *B* allow Congress to grant Book *A* a copyright that begins in 2015 and lasts for a full 95–year term, until 2110?

B. RENEWALS AND DERIVATIVE WORKS

Page 448. Add new Question 2 following *Russell v. Price* and renumber existing question as Question 1:

2. Arthur Conan Doyle published four Sherlock Holmes novels and 56 short stories. Ten of the stories remain under copyright, having been first published after 1922. The fifty previous works are in the public domain. Suppose you wish to write a new Sherlock Holmes detective story. Do the subsisting copyrights bar your endeavor in whole or in part? *See Klinger v. Conan Doyle Estate*, 755 F.3d 496 (7th Cir. 2014).

C. TERMINATION OF TRANSFERS

1. IN GENERAL

Pages 454–472. Replace the *Siegel v. Warner Bros. Entertainment Inc.* opinion and subsequent questions with the following opinion:

Scorpio Music S.A. v. Willis

102 U.S.P.Q.2d 1606 (S.D. Cal. 2012).

■ MOSKOWITZ, CHIEF JUDGE.

Defendant Victor Willis ("Willis" or "Defendant") has filed a motion to dismiss Plaintiffs' Complaint. On March 20, 2012, the Court held oral argument on the motion. For the reasons discussed below, Defendant's motion is **GRANTED.**

I. *FACTUAL BACKGROUND*

Defendant Victor Willis is the original lead singer of the Village People. This lawsuit concerns Willis's attempt to terminate his post-1977 grants to Can't Stop Music of his copyright interests in 33 musical compositions ("Compositions"), including the hit songs, "YMCA," "In the Navy," and "Go West."

Plaintiff Scorpio Music S.A. ("Scorpio") is a French corporation engaged in the business of publishing and otherwise commercially exploiting musical compositions. Plaintiff Can't Stop Productions, Inc.,

("CSP") is the exclusive sub-publisher and administrator in the United States of musical compositions published and owned by Scorpio Music. Can't Stop Music ("CSM") is a division of Plaintiff Can't Stop Productions, Inc.

Plaintiffs allege that between 1977 and 1979, they hired Willis to translate the lyrics of and/or create new lyrics for certain musical compositions which were owned and published in France by Scorpio. Copyright registrations for the 33 Compositions at issue credit Willis as being one of several writers. By way of Adaptation Agreements, Willis transferred his copyright interests in the subject Compositions to CSM, and CSM thereupon assigned to Scorpio its rights in the lyrics. The Adaptation Agreements provided that Willis would receive a set percentage (12%–20%, depending on the composition) of CSM's gross receipts from exploitation of the Compositions.

In January 2011, Willis served on Plaintiffs a "Notice of Termination of Post-1977 Grants of Copyright on Certain Works of Victor Willis" with respect to his interests in the 33 Compositions.

On July 14, 2011, Plaintiffs commenced this lawsuit. Plaintiffs challenge the validity of the termination and seek a declaratory judgment that Willis has no right, title, or interest in the copyrights to the Compositions, requiring Willis to withdraw the notice of termination, and enjoining Willis from making any claims to the copyrights in the Compositions. In the event that Willis is found to have a right to terminate, Plaintiffs seek a declaration that (1) Willis's reversion of rights be limited to "the same percentage ownership as he receives as compensation relating to the Compositions and as set forth in the Adaptation Agreements"; and (2) Willis be enjoined from terminating any licenses issued or derivative works authorized, by Plaintiffs, which existed prior to the termination of the copyright assignment.

II. *DISCUSSION*

A. *Validity of the Notice of Termination*

Plaintiffs' main argument is that Willis's notice of termination is not valid because Willis is the only author who served a notice of termination. According to Plaintiffs, under 17 U.S.C. § 203(a)(1), a majority of all of the authors who transferred their copyright interests in a joint work, whether their transfers were part of the same transaction or separate transactions, must join in a termination for it to be valid. Willis and Amicus Songwriters' Guild of America ("SGA"), on the other hand, contend that since Willis was the only person who executed the grants of his copyright interests in the Compositions, he alone has the ability to terminate those grants. The Court agrees with Willis and SGA.

Because the transfers of copyright at issue in this case occurred after January 1, 1978, the Copyright Act of 1976 ("Act") governs. The Act provides authors and their statutory successors with the ability to terminate a transfer of copyright or license by serving advance notice under specified time limits and conditions.

. . . The issue before the Court is whether, in a case where joint authors of a work transfer their respective copyright interests through separate agreements, a single author may alone terminate his separate grant of his copyright interest in the joint work or whether a majority of all the authors is necessary to terminate that grant. Upon consideration of the language and purpose of 17 U.S.C. § 203 in conjunction with the law governing the rights of joint authors, the Court concludes that a joint author who separately transfers his copyright interest may unilaterally terminate that grant.

When interpreting a statute, we start with the "plain meaning" of the statute's text. As explained by the Supreme Court, "courts must presume that a legislature says in a statute what it means and means in a statute what it says there." *Conn. Nat'l Bank v. Germain,* 503 U.S. 249, 253–54 (1992). However, "we do more than view word or sub-sections in isolation. We derive meaning from context, and this requires reading the relevant statutory provisions as a whole." *Hanford Downwinders Coal., Inc. v. Dowdle,* 71 F.3d 1469, 1475 (9th Cir. 1995).

Section 203(a)(1) provides, "In the case of a grant executed by one author, termination of the grant may be effected by that author." Section 203(a)(1) goes on to provide, "In the case of a grant executed by two or more authors of a joint work, termination of the grant may be effected by a majority of the authors who executed it." When referring to a grant executed by two or more authors of a joint work, section 203(a)(1) refers to a "grant" in the singular, not "grants." Thus, under the plain meaning of the statute, if two or more joint authors join in a grant of their copyright interests, a majority of the authors is necessary to terminate the grant. If, however, a single joint author enters into a grant of his copyright interest, that author alone can terminate his grant.

The Court's reading of section 203(a)(1) harmonizes with the law governing the rights of joint authors, both as it existed at the time of the passage of the Act and as it exists today. As recognized in the House Report accompanying the passage of the Copyright Act of 1976, "Under the bill, as under the present law, coowners of a copyright would be treated generally as tenants in common, with each coowner having an independent right to use of [sic] license the use of a work, subject to a duty of accounting to the other coowners for any profit." H.R.Rep. No. 94–1476, at 121 (1976). Then, as now, each co-owner of a joint work becomes a holder of an undivided interest in the whole. Thus, "[i]n the absence of an agreement to the contrary, one joint owner may always transfer his interest in the joint work to a third party, subject only to the general requirements of a valid transfer of copyright." *Nimmer on Copyright* § 6.11 (2011) ("*Nimmer*").

Congress was aware that a single joint author may grant his interest in the joint work separately from his co-authors or may join in a grant with one or more of his co-authors. Knowing this, Congress legislated that *"[i]n the case* of a grant executed by two or more authors of a joint work," a majority of the authors who executed the grant is necessary for termination. 17 U.S.C. § 203(a)(1) (Emphasis added.) In other words, *when* two or more authors of a joint work execute a joint grant, a majority of the authors who executed the grant is necessary to terminate the grant. Section 203(a)(1) certainly does not *require* that a joint author enter into a joint grant with one or more of his co-authors. Nor does the statute provide that where two or more joint authors enter into separate *grants,* a majority of those authors is needed to terminate any one of those *grants.*

Plaintiffs argue that the term "grant" as used in section 203(a)(1) refers collectively to all transfers by joint authors, even if the transfers were separate transactions. This argument is not persuasive. Nowhere does the statute indicate that the term "grant" has a special meaning and encompasses all transfers of interest by joint authors, regardless of whether the joint authors individually transferred their interests through different instruments at different times.[2]

Furthermore, it makes sense to interpret the term "grant" to refer to a *single* transaction whereby the rights of one or more joint authors [were] transferred, because the time for terminating a grant is calculated from the date of execution of the grant. Under Plaintiffs' interpretation, in the case of separate transfers by joint authors, there would be uncertainty regarding the date of execution, which could become a moving target. For example, if joint authors A, B, C, and D each separately transferred their interests, with an interval of several years between each transfer, would the "date of execution" keep changing as each author transfers his/her interest? If so, it could be many years after A's transfer that the "grant" is considered "executed."

Finally, it would be contrary to the purpose of the Act to require a majority of all joint authors who had, at various times, transferred their copyright interests in a joint work to terminate the legally permissible *separate* grant by one joint author of his undivided copyright interest in the work. The purpose of the Act was to "safeguard[ ] authors against unremunerative transfers" and address "the unequal bargaining position of authors, resulting in part from the impossibility of determining a work's value until it has been exploited." H.R.Rep. No. 94–1476, at 124 (1976). Under Plaintiffs' interpretation, it would be more difficult to terminate an individual grant than it would be to make it in the first place.

Plaintiffs attempt to support their position by pointing to the law governing pre-1978 grants. Grants executed prior to January 1, 1978 are terminable by each executing joint author (to the extent of the particular author's interest), even if a majority of the executing joint authors do not join in the termination. 17 U.S.C. § 304(c)(1). As discussed in *Nimmer,* § 11.03, it appears that Congress treated pre-1978 grants differently because if a grantor of renewal rights failed to survive until such rights vested, the renewal rights would pass to the grantor's successors and the original grantee would take nothing. Accordingly, "[b]ecause joint-author grants of renewal rights thus terminate individually by operation of law upon an author's death, it was thought 'inappropriate' to require anything more than individual termination via the termination provisions." *Id.* The stricter requirement for termination of post-1977 grants begs the question of whether a "grant" may encompass separate transfers of interest by joint authors and does not shed any light on the matter before the Court.

Plaintiffs attempt to support their position by relying on language in *Sweet Music, Inc. v. Melrose Music Corp.,* 189 F.Supp. 655 (S.D.Cal. 1960), where the court explained that it did not make a difference to the outcome of the case that plaintiff joined in the same assignment agreement as the deceased co-author as opposed to having executed a

---

[2]   In this case, it also appears that at least some of the joint authors granted their copyright interests to Scorpio, not CSM, as Willis did. Thus, Plaintiffs would include under the umbrella of a "grant," separate transactions where copyright interests were transferred to related but different entities.

separate assignment. However, *Sweet Music* concerned the enforceability of an assignment of renewal interests by one author where a co-author, who also assigned his renewal interests, died prior to renewal. *Sweet Music* did not concern the termination of grants under the Copyright Act of 1976 and does not shed light on the issue before the Court.

The Court concludes that because Willis granted his copyright interests in the Compositions separately from the other co-authors, Willis may, under 17 U.S.C. § 203, unilaterally terminate his grants. Thus, Plaintiffs' declaratory relief claim fails to the extent it is based on the inability of Willis to terminate his grants of copyright. To be clear, Willis's termination affects only the copyright interests that he previously transferred (his undivided interest in the joint work). The copyright interests transferred by the other co-authors will not be affected by Willis's termination.

B. *Writer for Hire*

In their Complaint, Plaintiffs allege that Willis has no rights in the copyrights at issue because he was a "writer for hire" who rendered his services as an employee of CSM. At oral argument, counsel for Plaintiffs represented that they were withdrawing this claim.

C. *Percentage of Copyright Interest*

In the event Willis is found to have a right to terminate his grants of copyright interest in the Compositions, Plaintiffs seek a declaration that Willis "be limited to the same percentage ownership as he receives as compensation relating to the Compositions and as set forth in the Agreements." However, Plaintiffs' claim is not supported by the law.

Upon termination, Willis would get back what he transferred—his undivided interest in the whole. See 17 U.S.C. § 203(b) (explaining that upon the effective date of termination, "all rights under this title that were covered by the terminated grants revert to the author. . . .") Absent a different agreement among the joint authors (of which there is no evidence in this case), the joint authors shared equally in the ownership of the joint work, even if their respective contributions to the joint work were not equal. *Nimmer,* § 6.08. Thus, if Willis was one of three joint authors of a musical composition, Willis would have a 1/3 undivided copyright interest in the composition. If Willis granted his copyright interest in the composition to CSM and then later terminated that grant, Willis would get back his 1/3 undivided copyright interest, regardless of what percentage royalty he was paid during CSM's ownership of the copyright interest.

Plaintiffs do not claim that the royalty percentages, which ranged from 12 to 20%, were based on the percentage of Willis's copyright interests, and it does not appear that this was the case. For example, Willis is one of three authors listed on the copyright registration for "YMCA." Assuming the three authors were actually joint authors, Willis has a 1/3 undivided interest in the copyright. However, the Adaptation Agreement pertaining to YMCA provides for a 20% royalty.

Plaintiffs do not cite any legal authority supporting the proposition that upon termination of his grants, Willis does not get back the percentage of copyright interest he granted, but, rather, is limited to a percentage of ownership equal to the royalty percentage. The Court concludes that Plaintiffs' position lacks merit and dismisses Plaintiffs' declaratory relief claim on this issue.

It appears that there is a dispute between Plaintiffs and Willis, with respect to some or all of the Compositions, regarding the percentage of copyright interest Willis originally held, granted, and wants back. At oral argument, counsel for Willis indicated that Willis contends that Henri Belolo, one of the individuals listed as an author on the copyright registrations for some or all of the Compositions, was not actually a joint author. If Willis is correct, his undivided interest in the Compositions is larger than it appears. For example, Willis would have a 1/2 undivided interest in YMCA instead of a 1/3 undivided interest.

The Complaint makes a passing reference to the dispute regarding authorship. The Complaint states that upon information and belief, Willis claims the right to recapture at least half of the copyrights in each of the Compositions. The Complaint also states that Willis "ignores the existence of other people listed as writers of the Compositions to claim that he, alone, wrote all of their lyrics." However, the Complaint does not seek a declaration regarding the determination of the issue of authorship and the percentage of copyright interest Willis granted and is entitled to receive back.

It is necessary for Plaintiffs to know what percentage of the copyright interest Willis is entitled to receive back, because, among other things, it will affect Plaintiffs' duty to account to Willis and the other joint author(s). Therefore, the Court will allow Plaintiffs to amend their Complaint to seek declaratory relief on this issue.

D.   *Statute of Limitations*

In the Complaint, Plaintiffs allege that Willis's claim to the copyright in the Compositions is somehow time-barred.

To the extent Plaintiffs argue that Willis is time-barred from arguing that a "co-author" listed on a copyright registration is not actually a joint author, this argument is premature. As already discussed, Plaintiffs have not yet sought a declaration regarding the percentage of Willis's copyright interest in each of the Compositions. To the extent Plaintiffs argue that Willis is time-barred from claiming that the percentage of his copyright interests exceeds the royalty percentages set forth in the Adaptation Agreements, the Court rejects Plaintiffs' argument. For the reasons discussed above, Plaintiffs' claim that the percentage of copyright interest recoverable by Willis is capped by the royalty percentage has no legal basis, and Plaintiffs have not explained why Willis should be time-barred from asserting his rights under the law.

E.   *Termination of Existing Licenses and Derivative Works*

Plaintiffs also seek a declaration that Willis is precluded from terminating any licenses issued or derivative works authorized by Plaintiffs prior to the termination of the copyright assignment. Willis does not dispute that existing derivative works may continue to be exploited under existing licenses under the terms of the grants and the existing licenses. *See* 17 U.S.C. § 203(b)(1). Therefore, it does not appear that there is a controversy in this regard. If Plaintiffs can point to facts showing that there is a controversy regarding utilization of derivative works prepared prior to the termination of the grants, Plaintiffs may amend their Complaint to include these facts.

III. *CONCLUSION*

For the reasons discussed above, Willis's motion to dismiss is **GRANTED.** Plaintiffs' Complaint is **DISMISSED** for failure to state a claim. The Court grants Plaintiffs leave to file an amended complaint within 30 days of the entry of this Order. If Plaintiffs do not file an amended complaint, this case shall be closed.

[In March 2015, a jury resolved the dispute over the percentage of Willis's copyright interest in some of the musical compositions at issue in the case. For 24 of those compositions, the parties disputed whether Henri Belolo was a coauthor with Willis and Jacques Morali (with each owning a one-third interest in the copyright on the composition), or whether Willis and Morali were the only co-authors (with each owning a one-half interest). For 13 of the compositions, including "YMCA", the jury found that Willis had established that Belolo was *not* a co-author. As a result, Willis owned, and could reclaim through his termination, fifty-percent of the copyright interest in those 13 musical works. (For the other 11 compositions, including "In the Navy," the jury found Willis had not met his burden to establish that Belolo was not a co-author.) *See Scorpio Music (Black Scorpio) S.A. v. Willis*, 2015 WL 1387729 (S.D.Cal.2015).]

QUESTIONS

1. Assume that a joint work is created by three co-authors and each co-author separately grants all of his rights in the work to Publisher. If one of the co-authors separately terminates his grant to Publisher, but the other co-authors do not, can Publisher continue to exploit the joint work? What rights, if any, can the terminating co-author exploit when the termination takes effect? (Recall the difference between exclusive and nonexclusive licenses with respect to joint works.)

2. An author wrote 15 books featuring the same main character, publishing one book a year for 15 years. The author then granted to a film studio the movie rights in all 15 works. At the proper time, the author's successors effectively terminate the author's transfer as to the first 10 works, but fail to terminate the studio's rights in the last 5 works (because they neglected to list those works in the termination notice). After the termination, would the studio remain free to use only those aspects of the character that appear for the first time in the five unterminated works? Or would the unterminated transfer of rights in the 5 later works implicitly include the right to use the aspects of the character that were originally copyrighted in the first 10 works but that appear again in the 5 later works? *See Burroughs v. Metro-Goldwyn-Mayer, Inc.*, 683 F.2d 610 (2d Cir. 1982).

2. SCOPE OF THE TERMINATION RIGHT

Page 485. Add a new Section C.2.d. before the start of Section 3:

d. TERMINATION AND SAME-SEX MARRIAGE

Section 203(a)(2)(A) provides that if a deceased author has left a widow or widower, that survivor will own either all, or 50%, of the dead author's termination interest. How does this provision apply to an author's same-sex spouse? Consider the situation of Alex Author.

In 1980, Alex wrote a literary work entitled *Novel* and assigned the copyright in it to Entertainment Conglomerate (EC), which published *Novel* to great acclaim that same year. On May 17, 2004, Massachusetts became the first U.S. state to allow same-sex couples to marry, and Alex married Sam Spouse, his same-sex partner of many years, in Massachusetts in June 2004. If Alex had died in 2005, would Sam have owned Alex's interest in terminating the 1980 transfer to EC?

Section 101 defines the author's widow or widower as "the author's surviving spouse under the law of the author's domicile at the time of his or her death," and Sam meets that definition and therefore would seem to own all or 50% of Alex's termination interest. But section 3 of the so-called Defense of Marriage Act (DOMA), adopted in 1996, provided that "[i]n determining the meaning of any Act of Congress, . . . the word "spouse" refers *only to a person of the opposite sex* who is a husband or wife." 1 U.S.C. § 7. This provision dictated that the Copyright Act's definition of "widow" or "widower" would not extend to Sam, and Sam would not own any share of Alex's termination interest under § 203(a)(2)(A). In June 2013, the Supreme Court ruled that section 3 of DOMA was unconstitutional, *U.S. v. Windsor*, 570 U.S. ___, 133 S.Ct. 2675 (2013), so an author's surviving same-sex spouse like Sam should then have qualified as a widow or widower for purposes of § 203(a)(2)(A).

The elimination of section 3 of DOMA did not resolve all relevant issues regarding termination by same-sex surviving spouses. Consider the following example involving additional facts about Alex Author and Sam Spouse:

> In 2014, Alex and Sam moved to Florida, which did not allow same-sex marriage and did not recognize same-sex marriages performed in other states. If Alex died later that year, would Sam own any of Alex's termination interest under § 203(a)(2)(A)? (Recall that the Copyright Act defines the author's widow or widower as "the author's surviving spouse *under the law of the author's domicile at the time of his or her death*.")

The Supreme Court's decision in *Obergefell v. Hodges*, ___ U.S. ___, 135 S.Ct. 2584 (Jun. 26, 2015), should now answer this question. In that decision, the Court not only ruled that "same-sex couples may exercise the fundamental right to marry in all States," but also held that "there is no lawful basis for a State to refuse to recognize a lawful same-sex marriage performed in another State on the ground of its same-sex character." *Id.* (slip op. at 28). As a result, Sam should be recognized as Alex's surviving spouse in any state to which the couple moves.

Does the *Obergefell* opinion also resolve international issues facing authors with same-sex spouses? What if Alex and Sam relocate to Italy and Alex dies domiciled there? Recall that the Copyright Act defines Alex's widow or widower as his "surviving spouse under the law of the author's domicile at the time of his or her death." Italy does not recognize marriages of same-sex couples, and *Obergefell*'s marriage-recognition holding obviously does not affect Italian law. Thus, under these facts, the statute would not seem to recognize Sam as Alex's widower entitled to terminate Alex's copyright transfers. Is the Copyright Act's definition, as applied to Alex and Sam, constitutional after *Obergefell*?

Bills currently pending in both the House and Senate to amend the Copyright Act would end the disparate treatment of same-sex spouses of authors who die while domiciled abroad. Copyright and Marriage Equality Act, H.R. 238, 114th Cong. (2015); S. 23, 114th Cong. (2015). These bills would amend the Copyright Act's definition of " 'widow' or 'widower' " to read:

> An individual is the "widow" or "widower" of an author if the courts of the State in which the individual and the author were married (or, if the individual and the author were not married in any State but were validly married in another jurisdiction, the courts of any State) would find that the individual and the author were validly married at the time of the author's death, whether or not the spouse has later remarried.

Id. § 2(a).

The language in these bills covering couples "not married in any State" would also appear to recognize marriages entered into by same-sex couples in foreign countries that allow such couples to marry, regardless of where the author is domiciled at death. Without that amendment, how will the current statute apply if, for example, an Italian author and her same-sex partner travel outside Italy, get married, and return to live in Italy? When the Italian author dies, will her same-sex spouse be entitled to exercise her U.S. termination right?

For more on these questions, see, e.g., Brad A. Greenberg, *DOMA's Ghost and Copyright Reversionary Interests*, 108 N.W. L. Rev. Colloquy 391 (2014); R. Anthony Reese, *Be Careful Where You Live When You Die: Termination of Transfers and Marriage Inequality*, ___ IP THEORY ___ (forthcoming 2015).

Even after the Supreme Court's decisions, questions regarding termination by same-sex spouses of deceased authors may remain. Consider the following alternative scenario involving Alex and Sam. In this scenario, Alex died in 2005, survived by Sam and by an adult daughter, Daphne. In 2007, Daphne served a termination notice on Publisher terminating Alex's 1980 assignment to publisher and stating an effective date of July 1, 2015. May Publisher now challenge the termination as invalid, arguing that under the *Windsor* and *Obergefell* decisions, Daphne owns only 50% of Alex's termination interest? If Daphne's termination notice was effective, may Sam now claim ownership of 50% of the rights that revert in July 2015?

CHAPTER 5

FORMALITIES

B. PUBLICATION AND NOTICE BEFORE THE 1976 ACT

Page 504. Add the following squib before the QUESTIONS:

Warner Bros. Entertainment, Inc. v. X One X Productions, 644 F.3d 584 (8th Cir. 2011). The plaintiff owns the copyright in the classic films *The Wizard of Oz* and *Gone With the Wind*. When those films were made and originally released, publicity materials—such as movie posters, lobby cards, still photographs, and press books—showing the costumed actors posed on the film sets were distributed to theaters and printed in newspapers and magazines. "The images in these publicity materials were not drawn from the film footage that was used in the films; rather, they were created independently by still photographers and artists before or during production of the films." The defendant reproduced images, in whole or in part, from these publicity materials, and when the plaintiff sued for infringement, the court considered whether the materials were copyrighted:

> Whether a work entered the public domain prior to January 1, 1978, the effective date of the 1976 Copyright Act, must be determined according to copyright law as it existed before that date, under the 1909 Copyright Act. *See Brown v. Tabb,* 714 F.2d 1088, 1090–91 (11th Cir. 1983). Under the 1909 Copyright Act, one who created an artistic work held a common law copyright in that work until "publication" occurred. If the publication complied with the notice requirements of the 1909 Copyright Act, the common law copyright was replaced with a federal statutory copyright, but a publication without the prescribed notice resulted in the forfeiture of any copyright. In other words, the general rule under the 1909 Copyright Act is that a work published in the United States without the statutorily required copyright notice fell into the public domain, "precluding forever any subsequent copyright protection of the published work." *Twin Books Corp. v. Walt Disney Co.,* 83 F.3d 1162, 1165–66 (9th Cir. 1996).

> Warner Bros. concedes that the publicity materials now copied by [defendants] were distributed to theaters without the statutorily required notice, but it nevertheless contends that these materials were not injected into the public domain because their distribution was a "limited publication." As distinguished from a "general publication" that results in injection into the public domain, a limited publication is one that occurs "under conditions which exclude the presumption that [the work] was intended to be dedicated to the public." *Am. Tobacco Co. v. Werckmeister,* 207 U.S. 284, 299 (1907). Courts developed the doctrine of limited publication "[t]o lessen the sometimes harsh effect of the rule that publication destroyed common law rights." *Brown,* 714 F.2d at 1091. Warner Bros.

contends that the conditions for a limited publication were satisfied for the movie posters and lobby cards for *The Wizard of Oz* and *Gone with the Wind* because those materials were not distributed directly to the general public, but rather were leased solely to theaters under an agreement (the "National Screen Agreement") that required the materials to be returned or destroyed after the theater stopped running the subject film.

We have held that a publication is general, rather than limited, if the rights-holder demonstrated an express or implied intent to abandon his right to control distribution and reproduction of his work, as determined objectively from "the implications of his outward actions to the reasonable outsider." *Nucor Corp. v. Tenn. Forging Steel Serv., Inc.,* 476 F.2d 386, 390 n. 7 (8th Cir. 1973). There is a dearth of Eighth Circuit case law applying this test, and the parties argue this issue under a framework developed by the Ninth Circuit and adopted by several other circuits defining a limited publication as a distribution (1) to a definitely selected class of persons, (2) for a limited purpose, (3) without the right of reproduction, distribution, or sale. *See White v. Kimmell,* 193 F.2d 744, 746–47 (9th Cir. 1952). We agree that this test may help to focus the analysis.

Based on the record, any reasonable jury would have to conclude that the "return or destroy" provisions of the National Screen Agreement did not effectively preclude redistribution or sale of the images in the publicity materials made available to theaters for *The Wizard of Oz* and *Gone with the Wind.* For example, Leith Adams, Warner Bros.'s expert, conceded that theaters could "buy by the thousands" handouts and promotional flyers to pass out to the general public. At least some of these handouts and flyers included images of the characters. "Exploitation books" associated with *The Wizard of Oz* and *Gone with the Wind* allowed theaters to select promotional giveaway or sale items for the public, ranging from color-tinted publicity photographs to matchbooks to spare-tire covers. No evidence suggests that theaters were expected to recover these items from the public and return or destroy them. Adams also conceded that in addition to movie posters and lobby cards for the theaters' own premises, theaters could obtain movie posters expressly constructed for posting on telephone poles throughout the theater's local area. When asked if these movie posters generally were returned or destroyed, Adams responded, "I don't think so but I don't know." We also note that Loew's initially took steps to obtain a federally registered copyright in some of the still photographs used in publicity materials for *The Wizard of Oz,* suggesting that Loew's did not expect the National Screen Agreement to preserve its copyrights in such materials.

As an additional matter, publicity material images for the films were distributed directly to the general public through newspapers and magazines. . . . Here, the record includes publicity photographs for *The Wizard of Oz* that appeared in

McCall's magazine, *The Saturday Evening Post,* the *St. Louis Post-Dispatch,* and the *Chicago Herald and Examiner* before the film was released. It also includes publicity photographs for *Gone with the Wind* that appeared in the *Atlanta Constitution* and the *Atlanta Journal,* and other published material indicating that *Gone with the Wind* publicity photographs appeared in several magazines in the United States before the film was released. Obviously, in each case, the rights-holder granted the right of "reproduction, distribution [and] sale" of the subject publicity photographs to each respective newspaper and magazine. *White,* 193 F.2d at 747. At least one court has held that distribution of promotional photographs to theaters, even under an effective condition that the photographs be returned, is not sufficient to demonstrate a limited publication where the photographs are also distributed for use by newspapers and magazines. *See Milton H. Greene Archives, Inc. v. BPI Commc'ns, Inc.,* 378 F.Supp.2d 1189, 1198–99 (C.D.Cal. 2005), *aff'd,* 320 Fed.Appx. 572 (9th Cir. 2009) (unpublished per curiam).[6]

Given the undisputed evidence regarding handouts, flyers, giveaway and sale items, and movie posters for telephone poles distributed under the National Screen Agreement (in apparent contravention of its "return or destroy" provisions), as well as the widespread distribution of many publicity images to newspapers and magazines, the only possible "implications of [Loew's] outward actions to the reasonable outsider" is that Loew's intended to abandon the right to control reproduction, distribution, and sale of the images in the publicity materials. In terms of the Ninth Circuit test, the publicity materials simply were not distributed to a definitely selected class of persons without the right of reproduction, distribution, or sale. To the contrary, the purpose of the distribution of all of these publicity materials was to reach as much of the public as possible. The studio itself happily estimated at the time that over 90 million people would see the advertising campaign for *The Wizard of Oz.* In practical terms, "courts have hesitated to find general publication if to do so would divest the common law right to profit from one's own work," [*Burke v. National Broad. Co.,* 598 F.2d 688, 691 (1st. Cir. 1979)], but here it appears Loew's viewed the publicity materials as a tool to maximize profit from the copyrighted films, not as an independent source of revenue. Therefore, we conclude that the publicity materials for *The*

---

[6] Warner Bros. argues that the distribution to newspapers and magazines is irrelevant in this case because [defendant] extracts images only from restored movie posters and lobby cards, not from newspapers and magazines. Experts for both parties agreed, however, that the materials provided to theaters, on the one hand, and the materials provided to newspapers and magazines, on the other, were drawn from a single, comprehensive set of publicity images created for the sole purpose of promoting each film. Both avenues of distribution would be relevant to a reasonable outsider trying to discern Loew's intent to place limits on reproduction, distribution, and sale when it put these publicity materials in others' hands without copyright notice.

Wizard of Oz and *Gone with the Wind* . . . are in the public domain.[7]

D. DEPOSIT AND REGISTRATION

2. REGISTRATION

a. PROCEDURE

Page 515. Insert after carryover paragraph:

A registration obtained through knowing misrepresentation of copyright ownership is subject to invalidation, but amendments to the copyright act require referral of the issue to the Register of Copyrights. As explained in **DeliverMed Holdings v. Schaltenbrand**, 734 F.3d 616 (7th Cir. 2013):

> Although we have no problem upholding the trial court's ultimate factual finding, we asked the parties to file supplemental briefing on whether the district court made a legal error when invalidating DeliverMed's copyright registration. Among other innovations, the most recent amendments to the Copyright Act instituted a new procedure for courts confronted with a registration allegedly obtained by knowing misstatements in an application. *See generally* Prioritizing Resources and Organization for Intellectual Property Act of 2008 ("PRO IP Act"), Pub. L. No. 110–403, § 101, 122 Stat. 4256, 4257–58. Recall that the Copyright Act provides for the invalidation of registrations where the registrant knowingly misrepresented information in his application and "the inaccuracy of the information, if known, would have caused the Register of Copyrights to refuse registration." 17 U.S.C. § 411(b)(1)(A)–(B). Instead of relying solely on the court's own assessment of the Register's response to an inaccuracy, the statute obligates courts to obtain an opinion from the Register on the matter:
>
>> In any case in which inaccurate information . . . is alleged, the court shall request the Register of Copyrights to advise the court whether the inaccurate information, if known, would have caused the Register of Copyrights to refuse registration.
>
> 17 U.S.C. § 411(b)(2). In one of the few instances in which it was called upon to deliver its opinion to a federal court, the Register described the purpose of this mechanism:

---

[7] Warner Bros. also argued in district court that the publicity materials are protected by the film copyrights as derivative works of the films. Under the 1909 Copyright Act, what came to be known as "derivative works" were defined as "[c]ompilations or abridgements, adaptations, arrangements, dramatizations, translations, or other versions of works in the public domain or of copyrighted works. . . . " 17 U.S.C. § 7 (repealed effective 1978). Here, it is undisputed that the publicity materials were not based on film footage used in the copyrighted films, but rather on still photographs and artists' renderings created independently from the film footage. Because they were not adapted or otherwise created from the films, the publicity materials cannot be "derivative works" of the films.

17 U.S.C. § 411(b)(2) was amended to ensure that no court holds that a certificate is invalid due to what it considers to be a misstatement on an application without first obtaining the input of the Register as to whether the application was properly filed or, in the words of § 411(b)(2), "whether the inaccurate information, if known, would have caused the Register of Copyrights to refuse registration."

Response of the Register of Copyrights to Request Pursuant to 17 U.S.C. § 411(b)(2) at 10–11, *Olem Shoe Corp. v. Wash. Shoe Co.*, No. 1:09–cv–23494 (S.D. Fla. Oct. 14, 2010); *see also* United States Copyright Office, Annual Report of the Register of Copyrights: Fiscal Year Ending September 30, 2009, 34 (2009) *available at* http://www.copyright.gov/reports/annual/2009/ar2009.pdf ("The [PRO IP] Act . . . amended section 411 . . . by adding subsection (b) to create a new procedure . . . that requires courts to seek the advice of the Copyright Office on issues that may involve fraud on the Copyright Office.").

In this case, the parties did not ask the district court to consult the Register before invalidating DeliverMed's registration. Instead, the court relied upon its own speculation that "had the application contained truthful information as to . . . the facts supporting DeliverMed's claim to ownership, the Copyright Office would have rejected DeliverMed's application." The district court's reasoning seems consistent with the Register's practice. *See* 37 C.F.R. § 202.3(c) ("An application for copyright registration may be submitted by . . . the owner of any exclusive right in a work, or the duly authorized agent of any such . . . owner"); U.S. Copyright Office, Compendium II: Copyright Office Practices, § 606.03 (1988) ("The Copyright Office will refuse to register a claim when it has knowledge that the applicant is not authorized to submit the claim."). But under section 411(b)(2), a court still must request a response from the Register before coming to a conclusion as to the materiality of a particular misrepresentation. By granting a declaratory judgment invalidating DeliverMed's copyright registration without following the statutorily mandated procedure, the district court made a legal error.

Page 515. Add at the end of the paragraph beginning "A related issue, receiving sparse but contradictory treatment from courts . . .":

Airframe Systems v. L-3 Communications, 658 F.3d 100 (1st Cir. 2011) (plaintiff demonstrated copying of unregistered version of computer source code; summary judgment for defendant affirmed because plaintiff did not demonstrate substantial similarity of copying relative to a registered version of the source code).

Page 518. Add to end of carryover paragraph:

Two Circuits have upheld the Copyright Office's authority to permit group registrations of collective works without listing the names of each author of the component works, so long as the registrant is a copyright owner of those works. See *Alaska Stock, LLC v. Houghton Mifflin Harcourt Pub'g Co.*, 747 F.3d 673 (9th Cir. 2014); *Metropolitan Regional*

Information Systems, Inc. v. American Home Realty Network, Inc., 722 F.3d 591 (4th Cir. 2013). As the Ninth Circuit explained:

> We are not performing a mere verbal, abstract task when we construe the Copyright Act. We are affecting the fortunes of people, many of whose fortunes are small. The stock agencies through their trade association worked out what they should do to register images with the Register of Copyrights, the Copyright Office established a clear procedure and the stock agencies followed it. The Copyright Office has maintained its procedure for *three* decades, spanning multiple administrations. The livelihoods of photographers and stock agencies have long been founded on their compliance with the Register's reasonable interpretation of the statute. Their reliance upon a reasonable and longstanding administrative interpretation should be honored. Denying the fruits of reliance by citizens on a longstanding administrative practice reasonably construing a statute is unjust.

b.   EFFECT OF REGISTRATION

Page 519. Add after the first sentence of the second full paragraph:

Courts frequently defer to the Copyright Office's assessments of originality or, in the case of pictorial, graphic or sculptural works, of separability of aesthetic from functional elements. See, e.g., *Design Ideas, Ltd. v. Yankee Candle Co., Inc.*, 889 F.Supp.2d 1119 (C.D.Ill. 2012) (deferring to Copyright Office refusal to register sailboat-shaped tealight holders as insufficiently creative and non-separable useful articles).

Page 522. Add before QUESTIONS:

The First and Second Circuits have declined to decide between the "registration" and "application" approaches to compliance with section 411, see *Alicea v. Machete Music*, 744 F.3d 773 (1st Cir. 2014); *Psihoyos v. John Wiley & Sons*, 748 F.3d 120 (2d Cir. 2014). In *Psihoyos*, plaintiff photographer filed his action within three years of the defendant's alleged infringing publication, but failed not only to obtain a registration for the work with the Copyright Office, but even to file an application for registration before initiating suit. The Second Circuit affirmed the district court's exercise of discretion denying the plaintiff leave to amend its complaint to allege subsequent compliance with section 411 when Psihoyos submitted the applications after discovery had closed and the defendant had filed its summary judgment brief.

Suppose a copyright plaintiff filed suit in a jurisdiction that follows the "registration" approach, and filed an application for copyright registration before the limitations period expired, but the registration did not issue until after limitations period expired. Should the court dismiss the action?

Page 523. Add to end of Question 3:

Cf. *Alaska Stock, LLC v. Houghton Mifflin Harcourt Pub'g Co.*, 747 F.3d 673 (9th Cir. 2014) (upholding effect of group registration on component works when all are owned by the registrant).

CHAPTER 6

EXCLUSIVE RIGHTS UNDER COPYRIGHT

A. THE RIGHT TO REPRODUCE THE WORK IN COPIES & PHONORECORDS UNDER § 106(1)

1. THE RIGHT TO MAKE COPIES

a. WHAT IS A "COPY"?

Page 555. Add before QUESTIONS:

Applying *Cablevision* to other time-shifting technologies, other courts have also identified the user as the sole "maker" of the copy. Dish Network, a satellite TV transmission service which retransmits television programming under license, offers its customers the Hopper, a set-top box with both digital video recording and video-on-demand capabilities. Dish's "PrimeTime Anytime" ("PTAT") feature allows subscribers to set a single timer on the Hopper to record and store on the Hopper all primetime programming on any of the four major broadcast networks each night of the week. In **In re AutoHop Litigation (Dish Network v. American Broadcasting Cos., Inc.)**, 2013 U.S. Dist. LEXIS 143492 (S.D.N.Y. 2013), the court stated that

> the pivotal factor in this Circuit for direct liability [for infringement of the reproduction right] is initiation of the act of copying rather than the selection of offerings for possible copying or the creation of the technological structure . . . DISH has no control over which programs will be shown on those networks or in what order, just as it has no control over which of its subscribers choose to copy those programs. The DISH subscriber must decide if he or she wants to use the PTAT feature and the subscriber must "enable" PTAT before the Hopper will record any programs. The DISH subscriber selects which of the networks' primetime offerings to record and which nights he or she wants to record and, once the subscriber enables the PTAT, the recordings are saved on the subscriber's personal hard drive on the Hopper, rather than at DISH headquarters. The subscribers also decide whether their copies reside on their individual Hopper devices from two to eight days, and can decide if they want to keep certain programs longer."

Similarly, the Ninth Circuit in *Fox v. Dish Network*, 747 F.3d 1060 (9th Cir. 2014) stated that "operating a system used to make copies at the user's command does not mean that the system operator, rather than the user, caused copies to be made. Here, Dish's program creates the copy only in response to the user's command. Therefore, the district court did not err in concluding that the user, not Dish, makes the copy."

Does the same conclusion regarding who engages in the allegedly infringing act apply when the automated service enables customers to obtain performances (rather than copies) of works? See *American Broadcasting Cos., Inc. v. Aereo, Inc.*, 573 U.S. ___, 134 S.Ct. 2498 (2014), *infra* this Supplement, page 142.

b.   PROVING INFRINGEMENT

ii.   *Proof of Copying*

Page 567. Add after *Price* (before note on Circumstantial Proof of Copying):

QUESTION

How probable must a "reasonable possibility of access" be? Does it suffice that the defendant could have seen plaintiff's work, and that the defendant failed to provide a satisfactory explanation of how it came to create its allegedly infringing work? See *Building Graphics, Inc. v. Lennar Corp.*, 708 F.3d 573 (4th Cir. 2013).

Page 576. Add at the bottom of the page:

QUESTION

William Faulkner's 1950 novel *Requiem for a Nun* includes the lines, "The past is never dead. It's not even past." Woody Allen's 2011 film *Midnight in Paris*, which won the Academy Award for Best Original Screenplay, features actor Owen Wilson playing a writer who, while on vacation in Paris, finds himself travelling back in time to the 1920s each night at midnight. At one point, Wilson's character says to his fiancé, " 'The past is not dead! Actually, it's not even past.' You know who said that? Faulkner. And he was right. And I met him, too. I ran into him at a dinner party." Faulkner's estate, which owns the copyright in *Requiem for a Nun*, has sued the film's distributor for copyright infringement. How should the court rule? See *Faulkner Literary Rights, LLC v. Sony Pictures Classics, Inc.*, 953 F.Supp.2d 701 (N.D.Miss. 2013).

iii.   *Proving that Copying Infringed*

Page 583. Add before *Nichols v. Universal Pictures Corp.*:

Blehm v. Jacobs

702 F.3d 1193 (10th Cir. 2012).

■ MATHESON, CIRCUIT JUDGE.

Appellant Gary Blehm brought this copyright infringement action against brothers Albert and John Jacobs and the Life is Good Company (collectively "Life is Good"). . . .

I. BACKGROUND

A. *Factual Background*

1. *Development and Distribution of Mr. Blehm's Copyrighted Works*

Mr. Blehm is a commercial artist who lives in Colorado Springs, Colorado. In the late 1980s, he developed characters called "Penmen." According to Mr. Blehm, each Penman is "a deceptively-simple looking figure" that "engage[s] in a variety of activities pulled directly from [his] colorful life experiences." The Penmen have "round heads, disproportionately large half-moon smiles, four fingers, large feet, disproportionately long legs, and a message of unbridled optimism." Below is an example of a Penman.

The Penmen are a product of Mr. Blehm's commercial art training. Through his training, Mr. Blehm learned how to "add a slight bend to a figure's limb to show weight bearing into it" and how, as he puts it, to apply negative space. Eventually, Mr. Blehm developed rules and guidelines for drawing each Penman. These rules and guidelines include a specific shape for each Penman's head, specific length and height requirements for each character, rules on fluidity and perspective, and the "Penmen parallel curve," which Mr. Blehm employs to "create eye-pleasing shapes within the negative space."

Between 1989 and 1993, Mr. Blehm developed six posters featuring Penmen and registered them with the U.S. Copyright Office (the "copyrighted works"). Each poster contains hundreds of black-and-white Penmen in a variety of poses. [In 1990, Blehm began selling posters nationally through distributors.] . . .

After experiencing success with the posters, Mr. Blehm expanded the Penmen line. He began making Penmen t-shirts. He developed a Penmen comic strip, which eventually was printed in newspapers with a combined circulation of over five million. Mr. Blehm also created a Penmen book, which is sold nationally.

2. *The Jacobs Brothers, Life is Good, and the Development of "Jake"*

Starting in 1989, the Jacobs brothers designed and sold t-shirts "infused with a positive undertone as a reflection of their beliefs." The brothers sold t-shirts in areas around Boston, including Harvard Square, not far from the Harvard Coop. During the 1993 holiday season, the Jacobses sold t-shirts from carts in the Cambridgeside Galleria and the Emerald Square Mall, both of which had Prints Plus stores that sold Mr. Blehm's posters.

According to the Jacobses, around April 1994 John Jacobs drew a sketch of a figure with a red face, wide smile, sunglasses, and a beret.

The figure was enclosed in two circles. John hung the sketch on the wall of the brothers' apartment.

The Jacobses recall hosting a party in August 1994 at their apartment and soliciting feedback on the sketch from their friends. After a friend stated that the figure in the sketch "really has life figured out," John Jacobs wrote "Life is good" under the image. They named the image "Jake," a spinoff of their last name.

The Jacobses soon made and sold t-shirts featuring Jake at street fairs and to retailers. As demand for the shirts increased, John Jacobs added a torso, arms, and feet to the Jake head. Jake was portrayed engaging in simple activities, such as biking, hiking, golfing, and playing soccer. Below is an example of an early Jake image.

The Jacobses incorporated Life is Good in 1997 with the "overarching themes of optimism, simplicity, humor, and humility." In 2003, they hired Joseph Burke and William Gillis to help design shirts. Depictions of Jake have increased in complexity over the years—from Jake engaging in simple poses to Jake engaging in actions and wearing clothes.

The Jacobses, Mr. Burke, and Mr. Gillis contend they had never heard of the Penmen before Mr. Blehm's lawsuit.

   . . .

II. DISCUSSION

   . . .

Mr. Blehm argues that the district court erred in granting summary judgment to Life is Good on the basis that the legally protectable elements of his copyrighted works are not substantially similar to the accused Jake images. . . .

After a de novo review of the substantial similarity between the protectable elements of the Penmen and the accused Life is Good images, we affirm the district court's ruling that the copyrighted and accused works are not substantially similar. . . .

A. *Substantial Similarity*

   . . .

a. *Legally Protectable Elements: The Idea/Expression Distinction*

. . . [L]egal protection does not extend to all aspects of a copyrighted work. . . . Section 102(b) provides, "In no case does copyright protection . . . extend to any idea . . . [or] concept . . . regardless of the form in which it is described, explained, illustrated, or embodied in such work." This provision enshrines the "fundamental tenet" that copyright "protection extends only to the author's original expression and not to the ideas embodied in that expression." *Gates Rubber Co.*, 9 F.3d at 836.

Thus, courts comparing works must first distill the protectable elements of the copyrighted work—i.e., determine what aspects constitute protectable expression. . . .

. . .

2. *Comparing the Penmen and Jake Images*

Mr. Blehm asserts that the district court's substantial similarity analysis excluded protected expression from the Penmen and focused on differences between the Penmen and Jake images rather than similarities. When his works' expression is considered and compared to the Jake images for similarities, Mr. Blehm argues, a reasonable jury could determine that Life is Good unlawfully appropriated protectable expression by taking material of substance and value.

The district court viewed the Penmen as "simple" stick figures and explained that any similarities between them and the Jake images "result[ ]from common themes and general concepts such as the idea of a person skateboarding, playing [F]risbee, playing a musical instrument, holding a birthday cake, roasting a marshmallow over a campfire, or holding his hand in a peace sign." These themes, the court noted, are unprotected ideas. It further explained that no copyright protection extends to Penmen poses that flow from the described activities, or to anatomical similarities between the Penmen and Jake images.

After parsing out these elements, the district court concluded that "the remaining original expression [of the Penmen] that is subject to protection is thin." It determined that the Penmen and Jake images are different "with respect to color, the orientation of the body, the relation of the body to the head, expression, clothing and other features," and that any similarities "flow from considerations external to the Plaintiff's creativity, such as common themes and natural poses."

The district court was correct that Mr. Blehm has no copyright over the idea of a cartoon figure holding a birthday cake, catching a Frisbee, skateboarding, or engaging in various other everyday activities. Nor can the Jake images infringe on the Penmen because the figures share the idea of using common anatomical features such as arms, legs, faces, and fingers, which are not protectable elements. Mr. Blehm's copyright also does not protect Penmen poses that are attributable to an associated activity, such as reclining while taking a bath or lounging in an inner tube. These everyday activities, common anatomical features, and natural poses are ideas that belong to the public domain; Mr. Blehm does not own these elements.

Although we do not consider these unprotected elements in our substantial similarity analysis, we acknowledge that Mr. Blehm's works do contain some protectable expression. The Penmen at first glance might be considered simple stick figures, but they are more nuanced than a child's rudimentary doodling. For example, the prototypical Penman has a rounded, half-moon smile that takes up a substantial portion of the face. Mr. Blehm has chosen to omit any other facial features on the Penmen. Each figure is filled in black, except for the white half-moon smile, and each Penman's head is detached, hovering above the body.

Many of the Penmen stand facing the viewer, flashing the half-moon smile.

Mr. Blehm also drew the Penmen according to his own rules and guidelines. The figure's head might be perceived as slightly disproportional to the body. Its arms and legs are thin, long, and disproportionate to the torso, which is relatively short. Mr. Blehm also chose to give the Penmen four fingers—each about as thick as their arms and legs—on each hand, as well as feet that are disproportionately long and thick compared with the rest of the body.

Thus, each Penman reflects particular stylistic choices Mr. Blehm has made. It is likely that these stylistic choices contributed substantially to the success of his copyrighted works. Although some may discount Mr. Blehm's drawings as simple stick figures, we are mindful that each Penman follows a seemingly uniform standard to achieve a unique expression. We also are cognizant that under the law of copyright, "even a modicum of creativity may suffice for a work to be protected." *Universal Athletic Sales Co. v. Salkeld*, 511 F.2d 904, 908 (3d Cir. 1975). Mr. Blehm's works easily clear that threshold.

Having identified protectable expression in Mr. Blehm's drawings, we must determine whether that expression is substantially similar to the allegedly infringing Life is Good images. Life is Good is not entitled to summary judgment unless its Jake figures are so dissimilar from the protectable elements of the Penmen that no reasonable jury could find for Mr. Blehm on the question of substantial similarity.

To show substantial similarity, Mr. Blehm provided the district court with an exhibit juxtaposing 67 individual Penmen with a corresponding, allegedly infringing Jake image. We have reviewed these images and agree with the district court's grant of summary judgment in favor of Life is Good. We now address two of Mr. Blehm's proposed comparisons, which he highlights in his appellate brief, and explain why the Life is Good images are so dissimilar from the protectable elements of Mr. Blehm's images that no reasonable jury could find in his favor.

a.   ***The Peace Sign Images***

The first example in Mr. Blehm's exhibit juxtaposes a Penman and Jake image standing and displaying the peace sign. Because we must separate unprotected ideas from expression, our analysis does not consider that both drawings share the idea of a cartoon figure making a common hand gesture. But we do consider whether the Jake image is substantially similar to Mr. Blehm's expression of this idea.

Mr. Blehm urges us to find certain similarities between the images. He notes that both have round heads. But Mr. Blehm has no copyright protection in general human features. Further, the figures' heads are not similarly round. Jake's head is more oval and somewhat misshapen, whereas the Penman's head is circular and uniform.

Mr. Blehm suggests that the figures have similar proportions, such as the size of the figures' heads, arms, legs, and feet compared with their bodies. A close review of the figures, however, yields the opposite conclusion. Jake's head is very large compared with the body, while the Penman's head is relatively proportional. The Penman's arms and legs are long and disproportionate to its truncated torso. Jake, on the other hand, has more proportional limbs compared with his torso. The figures' feet are distinctly different: the Penman's are thick, long, and roll-shaped, but Jake's are shorter and triangular.

Nevertheless, there are some similarities between the Penman and Jake. Both have black-line bodies, four fingers, and large half-moon smiles, and their feet are pointed outward. But even these similarities have important differences, or are not protectable expression. For example, Jake's fingers appear stubbier. The choice to display the figures' feet outward also naturally flows from the common idea of drawing a two-dimensional stick figure and is thus unprotected.

The figures' smiles thus seem to be the crux of this litigation. The Penman and Jake both face the viewer with disproportionately large half-moon smiles. A smile can be drawn in various ways. Here, they share a crescent shape, but the idea of a crescent-shaped smile is unprotected. Rather, the expression of the smiles must be substantially similar and important to the overall work.

The Penman's smile is all white, as is Jake's. The smiles on both figures take up a large portion of the head. But the Penman's smile is rounded on the tips, whereas the tips of Jake's smile are sharper angled. Jake's smile, by virtue of the size of his head, is much larger compared with his body than is the Penman's. And although both smiles are white, the Penman's is set on an all-black head, making it appear different from Jake's, which is the *outline* of a smile on a white head with black sunglasses.

Indeed, Mr. Blehm's decision to omit eyes and other facial features on the Penman makes the figure susceptible to an interpretation that the Penman is not smiling at all. One interpretation is that the white space on the head is not a smile, but is the Penman's face with no features. The black above the half-moon shape can be perceived as hair swooping down over the Penman's forehead. Thus, the Penman's lack of facial features make it susceptible to different interpretations. The Jake figure is not susceptible to similar confusion.

Any similarity between smiles also is insubstantial in light of other differences between the figures. Jake's head is attached to the body, and his head is white and has black sunglasses. The Penman's head is detached and is black with no eyes. Jake sports a beret, and his whole figure is displayed on a color background, whereas the Penman has no headwear and is portrayed against a plain white background. The Jake image's arms are positioned differently from the Penman, with Jake's left arm curved, rather than sharp and angular. Mr. Blehm also chose a unique feature for the Penman's peace-sign expression—white space in the figure's hand—that the Jake image does not share.

We conclude that no reasonable juror could determine that the Jake figure is substantially similar to the *protected, expressive* choices Mr. Blehm used for the Penman figure.

[The court's analysis of images of Penman and Jake each trying to catch a frisbee between his legs is omitted.]

Mr. Blehm urges that we should focus on the images' similarities, not their differences. He is correct that "[t]he touchstone of the [substantial similarity] analysis is the overall similarities rather than the minute differences between the two works." *Country Kids*, 77 F.3d at 1288 (quotations omitted). But this does not mean we merely look at the images, notice they are similar because they are cartoon figures with big smiles engaging in like activities, and end our substantial similarity analysis in Mr. Blehm's favor. Mr. Blehm's copyright protection lies in the *particular way* he chose to express these works. And we must be careful not to grant Mr. Blehm a monopoly over all figures featuring black lines representing the human form. Our analysis cannot be so generous as to sweep in all manner of stick figures as potentially infringing on his works.

As Nimmer explains, the substantial similarity inquiry is a problem of "line drawing." 4 Nimmer § 13.03[A]. Truer words could not have been spoken about this case. We have focused on the unique expression in Mr. Blehm's Penmen. Other than the half-moon smile—a feature among the figures that is similar, but not substantially so—we see insubstantial similarity in expression between the Penmen and Jake.

Copying alone is not infringement. The infringement determination depends on what is copied. Assuming Life is Good copied Penmen images when it produced Jake images, our substantial similarity analysis shows it copied ideas rather than expression, which would make Life is Good a copier but not an infringer under copyright law.

III. CONCLUSION

For the foregoing reasons, we affirm the district court's grant of summary judgment in favor of Life is Good.

QUESTION

Blehm submitted to the court a chart comparing 67 images of Penman and Jake that Blehm asserts showed substantial similarity. The first two pages of that chart appear below. The appeals court stated that it had reviewed these images and concluded that they "are so dissimilar as to protectable expression that the substantial similarity question need not go to a jury." Do you agree?

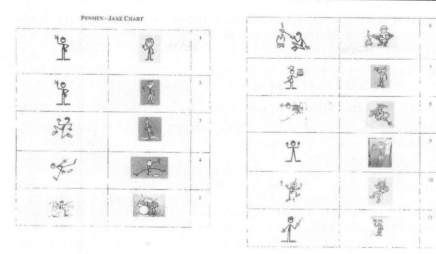

PENMEN - JAKE CHART

Page 600. Add a new Question 8 after the carryover paragraph:

8. RMLS, a real estate listing service, claims copyright in the following listing for a property available for sale:

Public Remarks: Lakefront living at it's [sic] finest! Southern views from either of your 2 decks or patio, Full finished basement w/ceramic tile & infloor heat, & many more upgrades. Sandy lakeshore, yard w/minimal maintenance, perfect for that getaway you've been looking for

Bath Description: Main Floor Full Bath, Upper Level 3/4 Bath, 3/4 Basement

Roof: Asphalt Shingles, Pitched, Age 8 Years or Less

Amenities-Unit: Deck, Patio, Dock, Balcony, Kitchen Window, Vaulted Ceiling(s), Tiled Floors, Walk-In Closet, Washer/Dryer Hookup, Security System

Special Search: Main Floor Laundry, All Living Facilities on One Level

RMLS has discovered the following listing for the same property on NeighborCity, a competing property listing website:

Property Description: Lakefront living at it's [sic] finest! Southern views from either of your 2 decks or patio, Full finished basement w/ceramic tile & infloor heat, & many more upgrades. Sandy lakeshore, yard w/minimal maintenance, perfect for that getaway you've been looking for

Roof: Asphalt Shingles, Pitched, Age 8 Years or Less

Exterior Features: Balcony, Deck, Dock, Patio

Interior Features: Kitchen Window, Security System, Tiled Floors, Vaulted Ceiling(s), Walk-in Closet, Washer/Dryer Hookup, Main Floor Full Bath, 3/4 Basement, All Living Facilities on One Level.

RMLS has sued NeighborCity for infringement. How should the court rule? See *Regional Multiple Listing Service of Minnesota, Inc. v. American Home Realty Network, Inc.*, 104 U.S.P.Q.2d 1195 (D.Minn. 2012).

Page 600. In the first full paragraph, replace the citation for *Goldberg* with "787 F.Supp.2d 1013 (N.D.Cal. 2011)".

Page 618. Add the following new cases before the *Steinberg* opinion:

Despite Judge Learned Hand's warning against dissection of plot and character into their component banal elements, the same court's later decision in *Computer Associates v. Altai* illustrates judicial willingness to apply a "filtration" analysis at least in connection with technological subject matter. The following decisions, from different circuits, apply a filtration analysis to photographs and to motion picture characters. The courts were not endeavoring to isolate and eliminate trite and unprotectable traits, but to ascertain whether infringement occurred when the attributes captured in the source copies were not created by the plaintiff or were in the public domain. As you read the opinions, consider whether in this context, notwithstanding the anti-dissection principle, filtering is justified (or necessary).

Harney v. Sony Pictures Television, Inc.

704 F.3d 173 (1st Cir. 2013).

■ LIPEZ, CIRCUIT JUDGE.

On a sunny April day in 2007, freelancer Donald Harney snapped a photograph ("the Photo") of a blond girl in a pink coat riding piggyback on her father's shoulders as they emerged from a Palm Sunday service in the Beacon Hill section of Boston. Just over a year later, the pair in the Photo became a national media sensation. The father, soon-to-be revealed as a German citizen who had assumed the name Clark Rockefeller, had abducted his daughter during a parental visit and was being sought by law enforcement authorities. Harney's father-daughter photo was used in an FBI "Wanted" poster, and the image was widely distributed in the media as the abduction saga unfolded. Appellee Sony Pictures Television, Inc. ("Sony") later produced a made-for-television movie based on Gerhartsreiter's identity deception. Sony depicted the Photo in that movie using an image that was similar in pose and composition to Harney's original, but different in a number of details. [The photos at issue are reproduced at the end of this opinion.]

Harney subsequently filed this infringement action, alleging that appellees' use of his photograph without permission violated federal copyright law. Appellees moved for summary judgment. Concluding that no reasonable jury could find "substantial similarity" between Sony's recreated photo and Harney's original, the district court held that Sony had not violated Harney's exclusive rights to his work. After careful review, we affirm the grant of summary judgment for appellees.

I.

. . .

Harney spotted Gerhartsreiter and his daughter, Reigh, on the morning of April 1, 2007 while on assignment for the *Beacon Hills Times*, a neighborhood newspaper that had asked Harney to take photos of people in and around Beacon Hill. A professional photographer for more than two decades, Harney approached Gerhartsreiter and his daughter as they left a service at the Church of the Advent and obtained permission to photograph them for the newspaper. The Photo was published on the front page of the paper later that month, with the caption, "Parishioners Clark and Reigh 'Snooks' Rockefeller of Pinckney Street celebrated Palm Sunday at the Church of the Advent on March 31 [sic]."

In July 2008, Gerhartsreiter abducted his daughter during a custodial visit. Without Harney's knowledge or consent, a portion of the Photo was placed on an FBI "Wanted" poster that was distributed nationwide. Harney states that he did not object to this use of the photograph because he did not want to impede the search for the missing child.

The Photo of the seemingly happy father and child became the iconic image of the bizarre saga of Gerhartsreiter, a "professional" imposter who had been passing himself off as a member of the high profile Rockefeller family and whose previous false identities included descendant of British royalty, Wall Street investment advisor and rocket scientist. He also was wanted for questioning in connection with a twenty-year-old homicide in California. Public interest in the story remained high long after Reigh was safely returned to her mother, and interest likewise remained high in Harney's photograph because of its prominent role in the manhunt. Harney licensed the Photo for use in multiple media outlets, including *Vanity Fair* magazine. In 2010, Sony completed and released a made-for-television movie titled *Who is Clark Rockefeller?*, which was distributed to cable stations by appellee A & E Television Networks, LLC. The ninety-minute docudrama was based on Gerhartsreiter's life, "retell[ing] in dramatic fashion Clark Rockefeller's story and the search for Clark and Reigh."

To depict the role that the Photo played in the abduction events, Sony recreated it using the actors who were cast in the roles of Clark and Reigh. The new photo ("the Image") was displayed for a total of about forty-two seconds in five scenes demonstrating the Photo's use during the manhunt in three different contexts: (1) as the image in the Wanted poster, (2) in a law enforcement briefing room, and (3) in television news reports about the abduction. The Image also appears, for less than one second, in one of the twenty-two television commercials publicizing the movie.

The Photo and the Image share several important features. Both show a young blond girl wearing a long pink coat and light-colored tights riding piggyback on a man's shoulders. The pair are smiling in both photographs, and they are looking straight at the camera at roughly the same angle. Although Gerhartsreiter and Reigh are closer to the camera in the Photo than the actors are in the Image, both pictures show only the father's upper body. In both, the father is holding papers in his left arm with the text of the first page facing the camera.

Some of the differences are minor. Reigh's coat is a darker pink than the coat worn by the child actor, and its buttons are placed higher on the garment. Although both men are wearing jackets and ties, Gerhartsreiter's jacket is a dark tweed while the actor's is a solid tan.

Several of the distinctions, however, are more significant. The background behind Gerhartsreiter and Reigh consists of a leafless tree, the church spire, and a bright blue sky. In the Image, nearly all of the background consists of dark leaves on the branches of a tree, with bits of white-grey sky peeking through in spots. The papers in Gerhartsreiter's hand are easily identifiable as the program for the service at the Church of the Advent, while the writing on the front of the papers in the actor's hand is not legible. Its text, however, plainly does not resemble the program held by Gerhartsreiter. Reigh is holding up a palm leaf in her left hand, but both of the child actor's hands are by her sides, resting on her legs.

Shortly after answering Harney's complaint, which was filed in July 2010, appellees moved for summary judgment on the ground that the Image was not "substantially similar" to the Photo . . . [The district court granted summary judgment and Harney appealed.]

II.

. . .

[I]t is permissible to mimic the non-copyrightable elements of a copyrighted work. Copyright protection "extend[s] only to those components of a work that are original to the author," and a work that is sufficiently "original" to be copyrighted may nonetheless contain unoriginal elements. [*Feist Publ'ns, Inc. v. Rural Tel. Serv. Co.*, 499 U.S. 340, 348 (1991).] The Supreme Court recently confirmed that "every idea, theory, and fact in a copyrighted work becomes instantly available for public exploitation at the moment of publication." *Golan v. Holder*, ___ U.S. ___, 132 S.Ct. 873, 890 (2012) (quoting *Eldred v. Ashcroft*, 537 U.S. 186, 219 (2003)) (internal quotation mark omitted). Hence, assessing substantial similarity requires close consideration of which aspects of the plaintiff's work are protectible and whether the defendant's copying substantially appropriated those protected elements.

We have thus described the inquiry into substantial similarity as embracing two different types of scrutiny. The court initially "dissect[s]" the earlier work to "separat[e] its original expressive elements from its unprotected content." *Coquico*, 562 F.3d at 68. The two works must then be compared holistically to determine if they are "substantially similar," but giving weight only to the *protected* aspects of the plaintiff's work as determined through the dissection. We have explained that two works are substantially similar if " 'the ordinary observer, unless he set out to detect the disparities, would be disposed to overlook them, and regard their aesthetic appeal as the same.' " *Concrete Mach. Co. v. Classic Lawn Ornaments, Inc.*, 843 F.2d 600, 607 (1st Cir. 1988) (quoting *Peter Pan Fabrics, Inc. v. Martin Weiner Corp.*, 274 F.2d 487, 489 (2d Cir. 1960) (Learned Hand, J.))). This assessment, of course, must be informed by the dissection analysis.

Although the dissection analysis typically is performed by the court as a matter of law, the determination of substantial similarity is ordinarily assigned to the fact finder. Faced with a motion for summary judgment, however, a court may be asked both to dissect a protected work and to determine whether a reasonable jury could conclude that "an ordinary observer" examining the two works would see the defendant's version as a wrongful appropriation of the plaintiff's protected expression. We have cautioned that "the court should not lose sight of the forest for the trees" when making these determinations. *Coquico*, 562 F.3d at 68. The court must "be careful not to over-dissect the plaintiff's work, causing it to ignore the plaintiff's protectable expression." *Situation Mgmt. Sys., Inc. v. ASP. Consulting LLC*, 560 F.3d 53, 59 (1st Cir. 2009). Likewise, in making the holistic assessment, the court "should take pains not to focus too intently on particular unprotected elements at the expense of a work's overall protected expression." *Coquico*, 562 F.3d at 68; *see also CMM Cable Rep, Inc. v. Ocean Coast Props., Inc.*, 97 F.3d 1504, 1515 (1st Cir. 1996) (recognizing "the potential 'danger . . . that courts . . . will so "dissect" the work as to classify all its elements as unprotectable . . . [thereby possibly] blind[ing it] to the expressiveness of their ensemble'" (alterations in original) (quoting Jane C. Ginsburg, *Four Reasons and a Paradox: The Manifest Superiority of Copyright over Sui Generis Protection of Computer Software*, 94 Colum. L. Rev. 2259, 2561 (1994))).

Applying these principles to news photography, which seeks to accurately document people and events, can be especially challenging. "[A]rtists [ordinarily] have no copyright in the 'reality of [their] subject matter,'" [citation omitted], and the news photographer's stock-in-trade is depicting "reality." Yet "the photographer's original conception of his subject" is copyrightable. *Kisch v. Ammirati & Puris Inc.*, 657 F. Supp. 380, 382 (S.D.N.Y. 1987) (internal quotation marks omitted). Courts have recognized originality in the photographer's selection of, inter alia, lighting, timing, positioning, angle, and focus. *See, e.g., Leigh*, 212 F.3d at 1215; *Mannion v. Coors Brewing Co.*, 377 F. Supp. 2d 444, 450–51 n.37 (S.D.N.Y. 2005); *Kisch*, 657 F. Supp. at 382. Photographers make choices about one or more of those elements even when they take pictures of fleeting, on-the-spot events. Additional factors are relevant when the photographer does not simply take her subject "as is," but arranges or otherwise creates the content by, for example, posing her subjects or suggesting facial expressions.

Although the comparison is not perfect, the division between protected and unprotected elements of a photograph could be likened to the separation drawn by copyright law between protected expression and unprotected ideas. Where the photographer is uninvolved in creating his subject, that subject matter—whether a person, a building, a landscape or something else—is equivalent to an idea that the law insists be freely available to everyone. The choices made by the photographer to generate a particular image depicting that subject matter, however, ordinarily transform "the idea" of the subject into a protectible expressive work.

Alternatively, subject matter that the photographer did not create could be viewed as "facts" that, like ideas, are not entitled to copyright protection. The Supreme Court has observed that "[t]he most fundamental axiom of copyright law is that '[n]o author may copyright his ideas or the facts he narrates.'" *Feist Publ'ns*, 499 U.S. at 344–45 (quoting *Harper & Row, Publishers, Inc. v. Nation Enters.*, 471 U.S. 539, 556 (1985)) (alteration in original). The exclusion of facts from copyright protection arises from the constitutional requirement of "originality"—"[t]he sine qua non of copyright." . . . A photograph that consists of public-domain subject matter may thus be protected from copying because it involves creative expression, but with the protection limited to the work's original elements.

In sum, in reviewing a grant of summary judgment for the defendant based on the absence of substantial similarity, where neither the subject matter of the earlier work nor its arrangement are attributable to the photographer, as is the case here, we first must look closely to identify the expressive choices in the plaintiff's work that qualify as original. After performing that dissection, we must consider whether any reasonable jury focusing solely on those original elements could find that the defendant's work is substantially similar to the plaintiff's. Summary judgment is " 'appropriate only when a rational fact finder, correctly applying the pertinent legal standards, would be compelled to conclude that no substantial similarity exists between the copyrighted work and the allegedly infringing work.' " [Citations omitted.]

III.

It is undisputed both that Harney owns a valid copyright in the Photo and that Sony copied the Photo. The sole contested element of Harney's infringement claim is whether the Image "can fairly be regarded as appropriating the original expression of the earlier (protected) work" to such an extent that the Image and the Photo are properly described as "substantially similar." *Coquico*, 562 F.3d at 67. Sony emphasizes that it copied "only the bare minimum of the elements needed to conjure up the original" for the purpose of depicting the Photo's prominent role in Gerhartsreiter's story. The company argues that the only similarity between the two works is "essentially the [unprotectible] idea of a young girl atop her father's shoulders," with "the other details in the Photo either . . . significantly altered or omitted entirely." With the unprotectible elements excluded, Sony asserts, "there is no substantial similarity in the respective expressions . . . , and therefore no infringement."

Unsurprisingly, Harney sees a much closer relationship between the two works. He asserts that the Photo "captivated the public's imagination" because of "its haunting depiction of the lie that was Clark Rockefeller's life," and he argues that "[t]he works are substantially similar because Sony took the expressive heart from Harney's Photograph." He notes Sony's admission that it intended to replicate the Photo and points out that Sony copied "numerous elements" of his image, including "the angle from which the picture was taken, the pose, the wardrobe, and even the color and type of Reigh's coat and the paper Rockefeller has clenched to his chest in his right hand." Harney maintains that the alterations Sony made to "details around the periphery" of his image "do not change the core similarity between the works" and, "most importantly, the alterations made no change to what these works express about the Rockefeller story." Therefore, he states, "a reasonable juror could find that the works are substantially similar."

The parties thus agree that the two photographs bear a resemblance. Indeed, Sony sought to create just such an impression of similarity. The question before us is whether the equivalence between the works can support a copyright infringement claim.

. . .

B. The District Court's Ruling

In performing the dissection analysis required by our precedent, the district court observed that Harney did not prearrange the subject matter of the Photo:

> Harney captured a moment in time of a father and daughter passing through Beacon Hill. The Rockefellers were not models. Harney did not select their clothes, give them a church program and palm leaf as props, or ask them to pose. Those aspects of the Rockefellers' appearance are factual realities that exist independently of any photo. They are not Harney's original expression, and they are not copyrightable elements of his photograph.

The court acknowledged Harney's "significant creative input" in combining various elements—Gerhartsreiter and Reigh in the foreground, holding the program and palm leaf, and the church in the background—to "evok[e] the essence of Beacon Hill on Palm Sunday." The court also observed that "[t]he lighting in the photograph highlights the church and the young daughter and displays the long shadows of early spring." The court noted, however, that the Image did not share Harney's expressive elements, pointing in particular to elimination of the palm leaf and church.

The court thus concluded that the only common element of the two photographs for which Harney could take credit was "the position of the individuals relative to the boundaries of the photo, although in the original Clark Rockefeller's face is closer to the camera and less of his body is visible." It concluded that "[t]his limited sharing" did not infringe Harney's copyright. It explained:

> The message conveyed by the Sony Images is the factual information about the Rockefellers' appearance. There is nothing suggestive of Beacon Hill or a religious context. The positioning of the Rockefellers in the middle of the frame, visible from mid-chest upward, is an element of minimal originality and an insufficient basis, without more, to find substantial similarity.

C. Dissection

We note at the outset of our discussion that Harney undisputedly produced an original, expressive work. Indeed, it is possible to identify multiple ideas creatively expressed through the Photo's combination of images. The district court noted one: "the essence of Beacon Hill on Palm Sunday." In addition, the piggyback pose of the smiling father and child as they exited church on a bright sunny day—the Photo's dominant image—suggests the idea of close family ties and, in particular, father-daughter bonding. Over time, as Harney argues, the Photo also came to represent a specific father-daughter story and the deception at its foundation.

These ideas are expressed with artistic flair: the framing of Gerhartsreiter and Reigh against the backdrop of the church reflects a distinctive aesthetic sensibility, and Harney's artistry also is reflected in the shadows and vibrant colors in the Photo—perhaps the result of his use of an electronic flash and professional editing software. Positioning the pair in the middle of the frame as they look straight into the camera, and at a close distance, also involves aesthetic judgments that contribute to the impact of the photograph.

Inescapably, however, Harney's creation consists primarily of subject matter—"facts"—that he had no role in creating, including the central element of the Photo: the daughter riding piggyback on her father's shoulders. Harney nonetheless asserts that there are "no unprotectable elements that ordinary observers should exclude from their analysis" of substantial similarity. He argues that, rather than separating out the "independently existing facts" contained in the Photo, the district court should have focused on the photograph's unique expression of the Rockefeller saga. He claims that the court's dissection analysis "failed to cut fine[ly] enough, throwing out the work's expressive content with the bathwater of 'independently existing facts.' " Under a "proper dissection," he argues, "the fact finder should be allowed to consider the similarities in the pose of the Rockefellers because Sony copied the pose for its expressiveness, not [its] factual value." Simply stated, Harney's view appears to be that ordinary dissection analysis is inapposite because Sony copied the Photo's expression of "the Rockefeller Story" and not simply the factual content of his photograph.

For multiple reasons, we are unpersuaded that this is an appropriate way to evaluate Harney's infringement claim. First, Harney's argument leaves no room for the dissection analysis that our precedent prescribes. The premise of the dissection analysis is that protectible expression is sometimes constructed from components that are free for the taking. The Supreme Court has noted that "facts themselves do not become original through association," *Feist Publ'ns*, 499 U.S. at 349, confirming the need to identify the unprotected elements in a protected work so that only *unlawful* copying is penalized. Although the Supreme Court made its observation in a very different context—determining the copyright protection available for telephone directory white pages—the same principle is inherent in the proposition, accepted as applicable to photography, that artists may not copyright the "reality of [their] subject matter." [Citations omitted.] We therefore reject Harney's assertion that we should not catalog the protectible and unprotectible elements of the Photo.

A second problem with Harney's argument is that he seeks to enlarge the scope of his copyright protection by attributing to the Photo an idea—Gerhartsreiter's deception—that is not discernible from the image itself and did not originate with him. The idea of the deception, of course, is not itself protectible. The Photo of the smiling pair may be understood as an expression of that idea only when we take into account the subsequent events that revealed the falsity underlying the specific father-daughter relationship that Harney randomly documented. Indeed, expanding a photograph's copyright protection based on later events appears to be what Harney has in mind when he asserts that "we cannot penalize authors who are fortunate enough to have once obscure works suddenly become important due to their relevance to changing circumstances." Harney warns that rejecting copyright protection for photographs whose significance the photographer "could not have foreseen . . . when he snapped the shutter [would cause] every stock photograph ever taken [to] enter[ ] the public domain."

We have sympathy for Harney's concern about the protection afforded to spontaneous photography, which by its nature consists primarily of "[i]ndependently existing facts." Indeed, assuring copyright protection for fleeting images of newsworthy persons or events encourages freelance photographers to continue creating new images, advancing the goal of the Constitution's copyright clause "to promote the Progress of . . . useful Arts," U.S. Const., art. I, § 8, cl.8. We disagree, however, that application of the ordinary dissection analysis will deny copyright protection for such works. As described above, Harney created an original protectible image. His photograph may not be reproduced in its entirety without his permission unless the copier is able to prove fair use. Nor may the original components noted above, including the particular juxtaposition of the father-daughter and the church, be freely copied if an ordinary observer would view the resulting image as "substantially similar" to his original.

Certainly, the *value* of an image can change over time along with observers' attitudes toward its subject matter. Photographs of celebrities as children or unusual images of notable buildings later demolished may become of wide interest decades after they were taken. Likewise, the actual identity of the father and child in Harney's photograph became important only after Reigh's abduction. While Harney should benefit from the added interest in his photograph, as he did through the payments from *Vanity Fair* and other publications, such newfound interest does not change the originality *vel non* of the individual components of the work. It does not, in other words, change Harney's creative contributions to the Photo. Moreover, recalibrating a work's originality based on a new idea of what it expresses would undermine the distinction that remains between ideas and expression in visual works. In short, we do not see how subsequent events can fortuitously transform unoriginal elements of a visual work into protectible subject matter.

For similar reasons, we also reject the argument that failing to classify the piggyback pose of Clark and Reigh as a protectible aspect of the Photo is an instance of "los[ing] sight of the forest for the trees." *Coquico*, 562 F.3d at 68. Harney describes this central image of the photograph as its "expressive heart." Yet, as we have explained, any expression of the Gerhartsreiter story seen in the Photo is attributable not to the photograph itself but to unrelated news events that associated the Photo with the new idea of deception. That new association did not, however, change the character of the Photo's unprotectible factual components.

Hence, we agree with the district court's application of the dissection analysis and its recitation of the unprotected and protected elements of the Photo. Harney may not claim exclusive rights to the piggyback pose of Gerhartsreiter and Reigh, their clothing, the items they carried, or the Church of the Advent shown with bright blue sky behind it. However, the framing of Gerhartsreiter and Reigh against the background of the church and blue sky, with each holding a symbol of Palm Sunday, creates a distinctive, original image. Harney's creativity is further reflected in the tones of the Photo: the bright colors alongside the prominent shadows. Finally, the placement of the father and daughter in the center of the frame, with only parts of their bodies depicted, is composition both notable and protectible.

We thus turn to consider whether the Image unlawfully appropriated an impermissible portion of the plaintiff's "original expressive elements," *Coquico*, 562 F.3d at 68.

D. Substantial Similarity

Harney's difficulty in alleging infringement is that almost none of the protectible aspects of the Photo are replicated in the Image. Without the Palm Sunday symbols, and without the church in the background—or any identifiable location—the Sony photograph does not recreate the original combination of father-daughter, Beacon Hill and Palm Sunday. Although the two photographs appear similar upon a first glance, that impression of similarity is due largely to the piggyback pose that was not Harney's creation and is arguably so common that it would not be protected even if Harney had placed Gerhartsreiter and Reigh in that position. Significantly, the two photographs are notably different in lighting and coloring, giving them aesthetically dissimilar impacts. Harney's features vivid colors and distinct shadows, while the Image is washed out and is far less attractive or evocative.

The Image does copy the placement of Gerhartsreiter and Reigh in the frame—which was Harney's choice and thus an element of original composition. We agree with the district court, however, that locating the subject of a photograph in the middle of a frame is "an element of minimal originality and an insufficient basis, without more, to find substantial similarity."

. . .

We recognize that Sony's Image and Harney's Photo are similar, as Sony intended. But as we have explained, the question of infringement is governed not merely by whether the copy mimics the plaintiff's work, but also, more importantly, by whether the similarity arises from protected elements of the original.

Sony copied little of Harney's original work—only the placement of Gerhartsreiter and Reigh in the photograph—and no jury could conclude that the similarity resulting solely from that copying is substantial. Moreover, given the differences in background, lighting and religious detail, a reasonable jury comparing the entirety of the two works could not conclude that the ordinary observer would "regard their aesthetic appeal as the same." *Peter Pan Fabrics*, 274 F.2d at 489. . . .

Harney Photo

Sony Image

Warner Bros. Entertainment, Inc. v.
X One X Productions

644 F.3d 584 (8th Cir. 2011).

■ GRUENDER, CIRCUIT JUDGE.

A.V.E.L.A., Inc., X One X Productions, and Art-Nostalgia.com, Inc. (collectively, "AVELA") appeal a permanent injunction prohibiting them from licensing certain images extracted from publicity materials for the films *Gone with the Wind* and *The Wizard of Oz,* as well as several animated short films featuring the cat-and-mouse duo "Tom & Jerry." The district court issued the permanent injunction after granting summary judgment in favor of Warner Bros. Entertainment, Inc., Warner Bros. Consumer Products, Inc., and Turner Entertainment Co. (collectively, "Warner Bros.") on their claim that the extracted images infringe copyrights for the films. For the reasons discussed below, we affirm in part, reverse in part, and remand for appropriate modification of the permanent injunction.

I. BACKGROUND

Warner Bros. asserts ownership of registered copyrights to the 1939 Metro-Goldwyn-Mayer ("MGM") films *The Wizard of Oz* and *Gone with the Wind.* Before the films were completed and copyrighted, publicity materials featuring images of the actors in costume posed on the film sets were distributed to theaters and published in newspapers and magazines. The images in these publicity materials were not drawn from the film footage that was used in the films; rather, they were created independently by still photographers and artists before or during production of the films. The publicity materials, such as movie posters, lobby cards, still photographs, and press books, were distributed by the original rights-holder, MGM's parent company Loew's, Inc., and did not comply with the copyright notice requirements of the 1909 Copyright Act,

17 U.S.C. §§ 1 *et seq.* (1976) (superseded effective 1978). Warner Bros. also asserts ownership of registered copyrights to various animated Tom & Jerry short films that debuted between 1940 and 1957. Movie posters and lobby cards for these short films also were distributed without the requisite copyright notice. As a result, Warner Bros. concedes that it has no registered federal copyrights in the publicity materials themselves.[2]

AVELA has acquired restored versions of the movie posters and lobby cards for *The Wizard of Oz, Gone with the Wind,* and several Tom & Jerry short films. From these publicity materials, AVELA has extracted the images of famous characters from the films, including Dorothy, Tin Man, Cowardly Lion, and Scarecrow from *The Wizard of Oz;* Scarlett O'Hara and Rhett Butler from *Gone with the Wind;* and the eponymous Tom and Jerry. AVELA licenses the extracted images for use on items such as shirts, lunch boxes, music box lids, and playing cards, and as models for three-dimensional figurines such as statuettes, busts, figurines inside water globes, and action figures. In many cases, AVELA has modified the images, such as by adding a character's signature phrase from the movie to an image modeled on that character's publicity photograph. In other cases, AVELA has combined images extracted from different items of publicity material into a single product. In one example, a publicity photograph of Dorothy posed with Scarecrow serves as the model for a statuette and another publicity photograph of the "yellow brick road" serves as the model for the base of that same statuette.

Warner Bros. sued AVELA, claiming that such use of the extracted images infringes the copyrights for the films. Warner Bros. also asserted claims of, *inter alia,* trademark infringement and unfair competition. AVELA contended that the distribution of the publicity materials without copyright notice had injected them into the public domain, thus precluding any restrictions on their use. On cross-motions for summary judgment, the district court granted summary judgment to Warner Bros. on the copyright infringement claim and denied summary judgment to both parties on the trademark infringement and unfair competition claims.

The district court's analysis did not require it to determine expressly whether the publicity materials had reached the public domain. Instead, the district court held that, even if the images were extracted from public domain materials, AVELA's practice of modifying the extracted images for placement on retail products constituted infringement of the film copyrights. Warner Bros. averred that it would not assert the copyrights against unaltered reproductions of individual items of publicity material, eliminating any need to resolve whether the publicity materials were in the public domain.

Based on the finding of copyright infringement, the district court separately entered a permanent injunction against all use of the publicity material images, except for exact duplication of individual items of publicity material. AVELA appeals the entry of the permanent injunction.

---

[2] Some of the still photographs for *The Wizard of Oz* and a few of the movie posters for the Tom & Jerry films complied with copyright notice provisions, but those copyrights were not timely renewed.

II. DISCUSSION

[As noted *supra*, Chapter 5, page 71, this Supplement, the court concluded that the publicity materials for the films had entered the public domain under the 1909 Act by being published without the requisite copyright notice.]

C. Copyright Infringement and the Right to Make Use of Public Domain Materials

The elements of copyright infringement are (1) ownership of a valid copyright and (2) copying of original elements of the copyrighted work. As discussed above, Warner Bros. has established ownership of valid copyrights in the movies and animated shorts. Copying can be shown either by (1) direct evidence of copying, or (2) access to the copyrighted material and substantial similarity between the AVELA work and the copyrighted work. There is no dispute that AVELA had access to the films in question, each of which has a long history of popularity. *See, e.g., Metro-Goldwyn-Mayer, Inc. v. Am. Honda Motor Co.,* 900 F.Supp. 1287, 1297 (C.D.Cal. 1995) ("[T]he sheer worldwide popularity and distribution of the Bond films allows the Court to indulge a presumption of access."). In addition, there is no dispute that the images in the AVELA works are substantially similar to the images in the copyrighted films, as they are in fact images of the same people in the same costumes (or, in the case of Tom and Jerry, of the same cartoon characters). The only remaining question is whether AVELA has appropriated "original elements" of the films or solely elements that are in the public domain.

Warner Bros. does not challenge the products that are exact reproductions of an entire item of publicity material. Instead, Warner Bros. contends that AVELA has extracted images from the public domain materials and used them in new ways that infringe the copyrights in the associated films. AVELA admits that it has used the images in new ways (and indeed has applied for its own copyrights for such derivative works), but it counters that there is no limitation on the public's right to modify or make new works from public domain materials.

AVELA is correct that, as a general proposition, the public is not limited solely to making exact replicas of public domain materials, but rather is free to use public domain materials in new ways (*i.e.,* to make derivative works by adding to and recombining elements of the public domain materials). "[W]here a work has gone into the public domain, it *does* in fact follow that any individual is entitled to develop this work in new ways." *Pannonia Farms, Inc. v. USA Cable,* 2004 WL 1276842, at *9 & n. 20 (S.D.N.Y. June 8, 2004) (rejecting the theory that the plaintiff's copyrights in nine original Sherlock Holmes stories gave the plaintiff the exclusive right to make derivative works featuring the Holmes and Dr. Watson characters because fifty-plus earlier stories already had reached the public domain). Nevertheless, this freedom to make new works based on public domain materials ends where the resulting derivative work comes into conflict with a valid copyright.

For example, in *Silverman v. CBS Inc.,* 870 F.2d 40 (2d Cir. 1989), a number of pre-1948 Amos 'n' Andy radio scripts had entered the public domain. However, CBS held valid copyrights in a number of post-1948 radio scripts and, arguably, in a later television series. In 1981, Silverman began developing a Broadway musical version of Amos 'n'

Andy, and CBS alleged that his script infringed its copyrights. Like AVELA here, Silverman argued that because the pre-1948 Amos 'n' Andy scripts were in the public domain, he was free to make any derivative work he wished featuring the Amos 'n' Andy characters. The court disagreed, holding that derivative works based on the public domain scripts still would infringe to the extent they used "any further delineation of the characters contained in the post-1948 radio scripts and the television scripts and programs, if it is ultimately determined that these last items remain protected by valid copyrights." *Id.* at 50; *see also Pannonia Farms,* 2004 WL 1276842, at *9 (noting that although the characters of Sherlock Holmes and Dr. Watson were in the public domain based on fifty-plus public domain original stories, a new work that incorporated "character traits newly introduced" by the nine later original stories still under copyright would infringe those copyrights).

In other words, if material related to certain characters is in the public domain, but later works covered by copyright add new aspects to those characters, a work developed from the public domain material infringes the copyrights in the later works to the extent that it incorporates aspects of the characters developed solely in those later works. Therefore, we must determine (1) the apparent scope of the copyrights in the later works (here, the films), (2) the scope of the material dedicated to the public in the publicity materials, which correspondingly limits the scope of the film copyrights, and (3) the scope into which each of AVELA's images falls. If an AVELA work falls solely within the scope of the material dedicated to the public, there can be no infringement liability under the film copyrights. On the other hand, if some portion of an AVELA work falls outside the scope of the material dedicated to the public, but within the scope of the film copyrights, AVELA is liable for infringement.

1. The Scope of the Film Copyrights

It is clear that when cartoons or movies are copyrighted, a component of that copyright protection extends to the characters themselves, to the extent that such characters are sufficiently distinctive. *See, e.g., Gaiman v. McFarlane,* 360 F.3d 644, 661 (7th Cir. 2004) ("[A] stock character, once he was drawn and named and given speech [in a comic book series] . . . became sufficiently distinctive to be copyrightable."); *Olson v. Nat'l Broad. Co., Inc.,* 855 F.2d 1446, 1452 (9th Cir. 1988) (holding that "copyright protection may be afforded to characters visually depicted in a television series or in a movie" for "characters who are especially distinctive"); *Metro-Goldwyn-Mayer,* 900 F.Supp. at 1296 (holding that plaintiffs' copyrighted James Bond films established a copyright in the character of James Bond). The district court thoroughly and accurately applied this principle to the instant case, and the parties do not contest the district court's analysis. We agree with the district court's conclusion that Dorothy, Tin Man, Cowardly Lion, and Scarecrow from *The Wizard of Oz,* Scarlett O'Hara and Rhett Butler from *Gone with the Wind,* and Tom and Jerry each exhibit "consistent, widely identifiable traits" in the films that are sufficiently distinctive to merit character protection under the respective film copyrights. *See Rice v. Fox Broad. Co.,* 330 F.3d 1170, 1175 (9th Cir. 2003).

AVELA correctly points out that the scope of copyright protection for the characters in the films *The Wizard of Oz* and *Gone with the Wind* is limited to the increments of character expression in the films that go beyond the character expression in the books on which they were based. *See Silverman,* 870 F.2d at 49 ("[C]opyrights in derivative works secure protection only for the incremental additions of originality contributed by the authors of the derivative works."). While true, this has little practical effect in the instant case, as a book's description of a character generally anticipates very little of the expression of the character in film:

> The reason is the difference between literary and graphic expression. The description of a character in prose leaves much to the imagination, even when the description is detailed—as in Dashiell Hammett's description of Sam Spade's physical appearance in the first paragraph of The Maltese Falcon. "Samuel Spade's jaw was long and bony, his chin a jutting v under the more flexible v of his mouth. His nostrils curved back to make another, smaller, v. His yellow-grey eyes were horizontal. The v motif was picked up again by thickish brows rising outward from twin creases above a hooked nose, and his pale brown hair grew down—from high flat temples—in a point on his forehead. He looked rather pleasantly like a blond satan." Even after all this, one hardly knows what Sam Spade looked like. But everyone knows what Humphrey Bogart looked like.

Gaiman, 360 F.3d at 660–61.

The film actors' portrayals of the characters at issue here appear to rely upon elements of expression far beyond the dialogue and descriptions in the books. AVELA has identified no instance in which the distinctive mannerisms, facial expressions, voice, or speech patterns of a film character are anticipated in the corresponding book by a literary description that evokes, to any significant extent, what the actor portrayed. Put more simply, there is no evidence that one would be able to visualize the distinctive details of, for example, Clark Gable's performance *before* watching the movie *Gone with the Wind,* even if one had read the book beforehand. At the very least, the scope of the film copyrights covers all visual depictions of the film characters at issue, except for any aspects of the characters that were injected into the public domain by the publicity materials.

2.   The Scope of the Material Dedicated to the Public

AVELA contends that the injection of the publicity materials into the public domain simultaneously injected the film characters themselves into the public domain. To the extent that copyright-eligible aspects of a character are injected into the public domain, the character protection under the corresponding film copyrights must be limited accordingly.

As an initial matter, we reject AVELA's contention that the publicity materials placed the entirety of the film characters at issue into the public domain. The isolated still *images* included in the publicity materials cannot anticipate the full range of distinctive speech, movement, demeanor, and other personality traits that combine to establish a copyrightable character. *See, e.g., Gaiman,* 360 F.3d at 660 (holding that the character's "age, obviously phony title ('Count'), what he knows and says, [and] his name" combine with his visual appearance "to create a distinctive character"); *Metro-Goldwyn-Mayer,* 900 F.Supp.

at 1296 (citing "various character traits that are specific to Bond—i.e. his cold-bloodedness; his overt sexuality; his love of martinis 'shaken, not stirred;' his marksmanship; his 'license to kill' and use of guns; his physical strength; [and] his sophistication," rather than his visual appearance alone, as establishing the copyrightability of the character); *cf. Walker v. Viacom Int'l, Inc.*, 2008 WL 2050964, at *5–6 (N.D.Cal. May 13, 2008) (holding that a copyrighted cartoon consisting of "four small and largely uninformative black and white panels" that conveyed "little to no information about [the character's] personality or character traits" was insufficient to establish copyright protection of the character). Nevertheless, the publicity materials could have placed some aspects of each character's visual appearance into the public domain.

A situation somewhat similar to the one we face was presented in *Siegel v. Warner Bros. Entm't Inc.*, 542 F.Supp.2d 1098 (C.D.Cal. 2008). The defendants owned the copyright in two promotional announcements for Superman comics, published before the first Superman comic book was issued. The black-and-white promotional announcements each included an image of the protagonist "wearing some type of costume" and "holding aloft a car." *Id.* at 1126. The defendants argued that their copyright in the promotional announcements gave them rights over the entirety of the Superman character as later developed (and copyrighted separately) in the comic book. The court disagreed, stating:

> [N]othing concerning the Superman storyline (that is, the literary elements contained in Action Comics, Vol. 1) is on display in the ads; thus, Superman's name, his alter ego, his compatriots, his origins, his mission to serve as a champion of the oppressed, or his heroic abilities in general, do not remain within defendants sole possession to exploit. *Instead the only copyrightable elements left [to defendants] arise from the pictorial illustration in the announcements, which is fairly limited.*

Id. (emphasis added). As a result, the scope of the promotional announcements encompassed only the limited character of "a person with extraordinary strength who wears a black and white leotard and cape." *Id.* Despite the earlier publication of the promotional announcements, the copyright in the later comic book nevertheless encompassed the fully developed character with "Superman's distinctive blue leotard (complete with its inverted triangular crest across the chest with a red 'S' on a yellow background), a red cape and boots, and his superhuman ability to leap tall buildings, repel bullets, and run faster than a locomotive, none of which is apparent from the announcement." *Id.* Importantly, the scope of the character copyrighted through the promotional announcements was viewed on the strict basis of what was clearly visible in the announcements, not through the additional perspective of the later, more developed work.

In the instant case, the only "copyrightable elements" in the publicity materials (albeit injected into the public domain, rather than registered for copyright) are even more limited than in *Siegel*. While the promotional announcements in *Siegel* at least showed proto-Superman holding a car over his head, establishing a distinguishing characteristic of "extraordinary strength," the publicity materials here reveal nothing of each film character's signature traits or mannerisms. At most, the publicity materials could have injected some of the purely visual characteristics of each film character into the public domain, akin to the character in "a black and white leotard and cape." *Id.*

Because we must rely solely on visual characteristics, the individuals shown in the publicity materials establish "characters" for copyright purposes only if they display "consistent, widely identifiable" visual characteristics. The *Walker* case is instructive in this regard. There, the plaintiff asserted his copyright in a comic strip entitled "Mr. Bob Spongee, The Unemployed Sponge" against the producers of the animated television series "SpongeBob SquarePants." 2008 WL 2050964 at *1. The plaintiff had created sponge dolls based on his comic strip and placed advertisements in a newspaper. Because these materials revealed "little to no information about Mr. Bob Spongee's personality or character traits," *id.* at *5, the court could look only to his visual appearance for distinctiveness. The court held that in such a situation, a consistent visual appearance throughout the materials was a prerequisite for character protection. Because of variations in the sponge's clothing, color, eye and nose shape, and hair among the comic strip, dolls, and advertisements, the plaintiff's copyright did not create *any* character protection.[8]

Therefore, we must determine if any individual is depicted with consistent, distinctive visual characteristics throughout the various publicity materials. If so, those consistent visual characteristics define the "copyrightable elements" of that film character, *Siegel,* 542 F.Supp.2d at 1126, which were injected into the public domain by the publicity materials. If not, then there are no visual aspects of the film character in the public domain, apart from the publicity material images themselves.

With respect to the cartoon characters Tom and Jerry, we note that on the spectrum of character copyrightability, the category of cartoon characters often is cited as the paradigm of distinctiveness. The record indicates that the Tom & Jerry publicity materials consist of just one public domain movie poster for each copyrighted short film, and the visual characteristics of Tom and Jerry in the first poster, for *Puss Gets the Boot* (released in 1940), are quite different from the characters popularly recognized as Tom and Jerry today. In addition, the first poster by itself reveals no distinctive character or visual traits, but only visual characteristics typical to cats and mice. As a result, the first poster is essentially a generic cat-and-mouse cartoon drawing that cannot establish independently copyrightable characters.

Meanwhile, the copyrighted short film that immediately followed the first poster revealed Tom and Jerry's character traits and signature antagonistic relationship. With the benefit of these strong character traits, the first short film *was* sufficient to establish the copyrightable elements of the Tom and Jerry characters as depicted therein. In such a situation, each subsequent movie poster could inject into the public domain only the increments of expression, if any, that the movie poster

---

[8] Of course, the presence of distinctive qualities apart from visual appearance can diminish or even negate the need for consistent visual appearance. *See, e.g., Metro-Goldwyn-Mayer,* 900 F.Supp. at 1296 (holding that variations in the visual appearance of James Bond did not negate character protection in light of his many distinctive and consistently displayed character traits; the fact that "many actors can play Bond is a testament to the fact that Bond is a unique character whose specific qualities remain constant despite the change in actors").

itself added to the already-copyrighted characters from previously released Tom & Jerry films. *See Russell v. Price,* 612 F.2d 1123, 1128 (9th Cir. 1979) ("[A]lthough the derivative work may enter the public domain, the matter contained therein which derives from a work still covered by statutory copyright is not dedicated to the public."). Because they "derive[ ] from a work still covered by statutory copyright," the underlying characters of Tom and Jerry are not in the public domain until the copyrights in the Tom & Jerry short films begin to expire.

In contrast to Tom & Jerry, the record is clear that a veritable blitz of publicity materials for *Gone with the Wind* and *The Wizard of Oz* was distributed prior to the publication of each film. However, with respect to *Gone with the Wind,* the publicity material images are far from the cartoon-character end of the spectrum of character copyrightability. There is nothing consistent and distinctive about the publicity material images of Vivian Leigh as Scarlett O'Hara and Clark Gable as Rhett Butler. They certainly lack any cartoonishly unique physical attributes, and neither one is shown in a consistent, unique outfit and hairstyle. As a result, the district court correctly held that the publicity material images for *Gone with the Wind* are no more than "pictures of the actors in costume." Indeed, if the publicity material images from *Gone with the Wind* were sufficient to inject all visual depictions of the characters Scarlett O'Hara and Rhett Butler into the public domain, then almost *any* image of Vivian Leigh or Clark Gable would be sufficient to do so as well. Therefore, the only images in the public domain are the precise images in the publicity materials for *Gone with the Wind.*

The characters in *The Wizard of Oz* lie closer to the cartoon-character end of the spectrum. There are many stylized aspects to the visual appearances of Scarecrow, Tin Man, and Cowardly Lion, and they perhaps might be considered as live-action representations of cartoon characters. Dorothy, while not so thoroughly stylized, wears a somewhat distinctive costume and hairstyle. However, a close examination of the record reveals that these potentially distinctive visual features do not appear in a consistent fashion throughout the publicity materials. For example, in the publicity materials, Judy Garland as Dorothy sometimes wears a red dress and bow and black slippers, rather than the distinctive blue dress and bow and ruby slippers of the film, and her hairstyle also varies. From image to image, Scarecrow's costume color ranges from yellow to blue to black, Cowardly Lion's from light yellow to very dark brown, and Tin Man's from shiny silver to a dull blue-gray.[9] Moreover, there are publicity material images in which other stylized elements of the characters' costumes and faces are significantly different from the look used in the film. For example, in some images Tin Man's face appears metallic, and in others it appears flesh-colored. If the publicity material images for *The Wizard of Oz* were held to establish the visual elements of copyrightable characters, their scope would encompass almost any character who wears a scarecrow or lion costume, and a wide range of little girl and silver robotic costumes as well, creating an unacceptable result:

---

[9]   The record shows that these extreme color variations resulted from the practice of using artists to hand-color still photographs originally taken in black-and-white (because color photography was relatively new and expensive). The coloration artists often were left to their own discretion in choosing colors for each photograph.

> If a drunken old bum were a copyrightable character, so would
> be a drunken suburban housewife, a gesticulating Frenchman,
> a fire-breathing dragon, a talking cat, a Prussian officer who
> wears a monocle and clicks his heels, a masked magician, and,
> in Learned Hand's memorable paraphrase of *Twelfth Night,* "a
> riotous knight who kept wassail to the discomfort of the
> household, or a vain and foppish steward who became amorous
> of his mistress." *Nichols v. Universal Pictures Corp.,* 45 F.2d
> 119, 121 (2d Cir. 1930). It would be difficult to write successful
> works of fiction without negotiating for dozens or hundreds of
> copyright licenses, even though such stereotyped characters are
> the products not of the creative imagination but of simple
> observation of the human comedy.

Gaiman, 360 F.3d at 660. While the overly broad characters would be in
the public domain rather than copyrighted in the instant case, the
analysis of the copyrightability of a character must be the same in either
case.

We conclude that the characters' visual appearances in the publicity
materials for *The Wizard of Oz* do not present the requisite consistency
to establish any "copyrightable elements" of the film characters' visual
appearances. Therefore, once again, the only images in the public domain
are the precise images in the publicity materials for *The Wizard of Oz.*

3. AVELA's Use of the Public Domain Images

We held above that no visual aspects of the film characters in *Gone
with the Wind* and *The Wizard of Oz* are in the public domain, apart from
the images in the publicity materials themselves. Therefore, any visual
representation that is recognizable as a copyrightable character from one
of these films, other than a faithful copy of a public domain image, has
copied "original elements" from the corresponding film. We must examine
the AVELA products based on *The Wizard of Oz* and *Gone with the Wind*
to determine which ones display "increments of expression," *Silverman,*
870 F.2d at 50, of the film characters beyond the "pictures of the actors
in costume" in the publicity materials. The AVELA products in the record
can be analyzed in three categories.

The first category comprises AVELA products that each reproduce
one image from an item of publicity material as an identical two-
dimensional image. While Warner Bros. does not challenge the
reproduction of movie "posters as posters (or lobby cards as lobby cards),"
it does challenge the reproduction of a single image drawn from a movie
poster or lobby card on T-shirts, lunch boxes, music box lids, or playing
cards, for example. We read the district court's permanent injunction to
follow Warner Bros.'s distinction, forbidding all uses except the
reproduction of items of publicity material "in their entirety." However,
no reasonable jury could find that merely printing a public domain image
on a new type of surface (such as a T-shirt or playing card), instead of the
original surface (movie poster paper or lobby card paper), adds an
increment of expression of the film character to the image.[10] Similarly,
Warner Bros. presents no reasoned argument as to why the reproduction

---

[10]   This principle would not apply if the new surface itself is independently evocative of the
film character. For example, reproducing a publicity image of Judy Garland as Dorothy on a
ruby slipper might well infringe the film copyright for *The Wizard of Oz.*

of one smaller contiguous portion of an image from an item of publicity material, rather than the entirety of the image from that item, would add an increment of expression of the film character. As a result, products that reproduce in two dimensions any one portion of an image from any one item of publicity material, without more, do not infringe Warner Bros.'s copyright. For products in this category, we reverse the grant of summary judgment to Warner Bros. with respect to *The Wizard of Oz* and *Gone with the Wind* and direct the entry of summary judgment for AVELA. We also vacate the permanent injunction to the extent it applies to products in this category.

The second category comprises AVELA products that each juxtapose an image extracted from an item of publicity material with another image extracted from elsewhere in the publicity materials, or with a printed phrase from the book underlying the subject film, to create a new composite work. Even if we assume that each composite work is composed entirely of faithful extracts from public domain materials, the new arrangement of the extracts in the composite work is a new increment of expression that evokes the film character in a way the individual items of public domain material did not. For example, the printed phrase "There is no place like home" from the book *The Wizard of Oz* and a publicity material image of Judy Garland as Dorothy, viewed side by side in uncombined form, are still two separate works, one literary and one a picture of an actor in costume. In contrast, a T-shirt printed with the phrase "There's no place like home" along with the same image of Judy Garland as Dorothy is a new single work that evokes the film character of Dorothy much more strongly than the two separate works.[11] Because "the increments of expression added [to the public domain materials] by the films are protectable," one making a new work from public domain materials infringes "if he copies these protectable increments." *Silverman,* 870 F.2d at 50. Like the juxtaposition of an image and a phrase, a composite work combining two or more separate public-domain images (such as Judy Garland as Dorothy combined with an image of the Emerald City) also adds a new increment of expression of the film character that was not present in the separate images. Accordingly, products combining extracts from the public domain materials in a new arrangement infringe the copyright in the corresponding film. We affirm the district court's grant of summary judgment to Warner Bros. with respect to *The Wizard of Oz* and *Gone with the Wind* and the permanent injunction for this category of products.

The third category comprises AVELA products that each extend an image extracted from an item of publicity material into three dimensions (such as statuettes inside water globes, figurines, action figures, and busts). Many of these products also include a juxtaposition of multiple extracts from the public domain materials, and such composite works infringe for the reasons explained in the preceding paragraph. Even where the product extends a single two-dimensional public domain image

---

[11] Many of the phrases drawn from the underlying books are modified to some degree in the corresponding films, such as contracting "There is" to "There's" in the cited example. The parties dispute whether such modified phrases are original to the films, and thus within the scope of the film copyrights, or still recognizable as phrases drawn from the books, and thus outside the scope of the film copyrights. We need not resolve that question because we hold that, even if the phrases taken alone are outside the scope of the film copyrights, the juxtaposition of the phrases with images from the publicity materials is an infringement of the film copyrights.

into three dimensions, a three-dimensional rendering must add new visual details regarding depth to the underlying two-dimensional image. (As a simple illustration, it is impossible to determine the length of someone's nose from a picture if they are looking directly at the camera.) Of course, even more visual details must be added if the two-dimensional image is transformed into a fully realized figure, as most three-dimensional AVELA products are. (Otherwise, for example, the back of each figurine character would be blank.) Much of this visual information is available in the feature-length films, there the characters are observable from a multitude of viewing angles.

In depositions, the AVELA licensees who developed the action figures, figurines, water globes, and busts made no pretense that they were not guided by their knowledge of the films. Instead, they indicated that, while each three-dimensional design began with an image from the public domain photo stills and movie posters, the goal was to create a product recognizable as the film character. The only reasonable inference is that the details added to establish perspective and full realization were chosen to be consistent with the film characters. As a result, the addition of visual details to each two-dimensional public domain image to create the three-dimensional product makes impermissible use of the "further delineation of the characters contained in" the feature-length films. *See Silverman,* 870 F.2d at 50. Accordingly, we also affirm the district court's grant of summary judgment to Warner Bros. with respect to *The Wizard of Oz* and *Gone with the Wind* and the permanent injunction for this category of products.

We also held above that the characters of Tom and Jerry are not in the public domain. In addition, because the characters achieved copyright protection through the short films before all but the first movie poster entered the public domain, and the later movie posters necessarily exhibit those characters, even the use of any movie poster but the first requires Warner Bros.'s authorization. Warner Bros. has granted such authorization to the extent it has averred that it will not challenge the reproduction of movie "posters as posters (or lobby cards as lobby cards)."

Therefore, AVELA may use the first Tom & Jerry poster, for the short film *Puss Gets the Boot,* in the fashion described above for the publicity materials for *Gone with the Wind* and *The Wizard of Oz.* . . . With respect to all later Tom & Jerry posters, AVELA is authorized to make faithful reproductions, but not to reproduce those movie poster images on other products or to make derivative works based on Tom and Jerry. . . .

iv. Applying the Analytical Framework: Review Questions

Page 635. Add the following new Question 7:

7. Consider the lyrics of the two songs printed below. Assuming that Kanye West had access to Vince P's song, are there sufficient probative similarities for a court to find that West copied that song? Would an audience find sufficient substantial similarities of protected expression to conclude that West's song infringes? See *Peters v. West,* 692 F.3d 629 (7th Cir. 2012).

Stronger *Vince P*	*Stronger* *Kanye West*
Chorus (2x)	Chorus:
What don't kill me make me stronger	N-N-N—now th-th-that don't kill me
The more I blow up the more you wronger	Can only make me stronger
You copped my CD you can feel my hunger	I need you to hurry up now
The wait is over couldn't wait no longer	Cause I can't wait much longer
	I know I got to be right now
	Cause I can't get much wronger
	Man, I've been waitin' all night now
	That's how long I've been on ya
Verse 1:	Verse 1:
I came from the bottom of the bottom	I need you right now
To make it to the bottom	I need you right now
A & R's back then should have signed	Let's get lost tonight
Said I wasn't gangsta said I couldn't	You could be my black Kate Moss
Vince P why don't you stick to making	Play secretary I'm the boss tonight
You know what how bout I rap on my beats	And you don't give a f* * * what they all say right?
Make my own tracks stack my own stacks	Awesome, the Christian in Christian
I'm hot you a loser and that's a fact	Damn they don't make 'em like this anymore
I'm bout to take you back when emcees was real	I ask, cause I'm not sure
Didn't care where you from or if you had a deal	Do anybody make real sh*t anymore?
Fist fights no guns no body packing steel	Bow in the presence of greatness
Family reunions food on the grill	Cause right now thou has forsaken us
This ain't my barbeque but can I get a	You should be honored by my lateness
I'm still real hungry and I just ate	That I would even show up to this fake sh*t
This ain't my barbeque but can I get a	So go ahead go nuts go ape sh*t
I'm still real hungry and I just ate	Especially in my Pastelle or my Bape
	Act like you can't tell who make this
Chorus (2x) [as before]	New gospel homey take six, and take this, haters
Verse 2:	Chorus [as before]
I ain't from Europe but I wear Lacoste	
And every day I hustle like Rick Ross	Verse 2:
Trying to get a model chick like Kate Moss	I need you right now

Then trade her to another team like

I'm the chosen one cause I got the force

And I'm the unsigned hype but I'm not in

All these dudes in Chicago tried to diss me

Cause on the low they girls they kiss me

And when I'm on the road you know they miss me

Check out my MySpace check the Bentley

I'm moving on up like George and Weezy

And money on my mind like Little Weezy

I'm the brand new kick pusher music distributor

And make crazy rhymes like I'm related to Luda

You can find me at the Croc Lounge

Or at the Funky Buddha

Catch a plane from O'Hare straight to Burmuda

Check my lex diamonds call me Lex

Don't like guns but my beats are ruggas

Can't you feel how these horns going right through you

Can't you feel how these horns going right through you

I'm Vince P and I'm going to the top

And I won't stop till I get to the top

You know my rhymes is hot and you know my beats is hot

You know Vince P is going going to the top

Chorus (2x) [as before]

I need you right now

me likey

I don't know if you got a man or not,

If you made plans or not

If God put me in your plans or not

I'm trippin' this drink got me sayin' a lot

But I know that God put you in front of me

So how the h*ll could you front on me

There's a thousand you's there's only one of me

I'm trippin', I'm caught up in the moment right?

This is Louis Vuitton Don night

So we gon' do everything that Kan like

Heard they'd do anything for a Klondike

Well I'd do anything for a blonde d*ke

And she'll do anything for the limelight

And we'll do anything when the time's right

ugh, baby you're makin' it (harder, better, faster, stronger)

Chorus [as before]

Verse 3:

I need you right now

I need you right now

You know how long I've been on ya?

Since Prince was on Apollonia

Since O.J. had Isotoners

Don't act like I never told ya (x6)

Baby you're making it (harder, better, faster, stronger)

Chorus [as before]

2. THE RIGHT TO MAKE PHONORECORDS

b. MUSICAL COMPOSITIONS: THE COMPULSORY LICENSE UNDER § 115

Page 640.   Add to end of first full paragraph:

In July 2012 the Court of Appeals for the District of Columbia Circuit held ruled that Copyright Royalty Board judges are not "inferior officers," and that the statutory provision limiting the Librarian of Congress' ability to remove CRB judges therefore violated the constitution's "appointments clause." The Court nonetheless salvaged the statute and the CRB by "severing" and invalidating only the restriction on the Librarian's removal power. Intercollegiate Broadcasting System, Inc. v. Copyright Royalty Board, 684 F.3d. 1332, 103 U.S.P.Q.2d 1337 (D.C. Cir. 2012).

c. REPRODUCTION RIGHTS IN SOUND RECORDINGS

Page 646. Add after the end of the carryover paragraph:

Not all courts have treated the substantial similarity analysis as irrelevant to determining whether a defendant's sampling infringes on the plaintiff's copyrighted sound recording. *See TufAmerica, Inc. v. WB Music Corp.*, 113 U.S.P.Q.2d 1076 (S.D.N.Y. 2014). The plaintiff in that case claimed that the defendant's recording "Run This Town" (featuring Jay-Z, Rihanna, and Kanye West) used a sample from the plaintiffs recording "Hook & Sling Part I" 42 times. The court described the sample (consisting of the lead vocalist shouting the word "Oh!") as lasting a "fraction of a second" and as appearing in the defendants' recording at most "only in the background and in such a way as to be audible and aurally intelligible only to the most attentive and capable listener." The plaintiff brought a common-law infringement claim in a pre-1972 sound recording, but the court stated that the elements of that claim "are substantially the same as" those of a federal copyright infringement claim. On the defendants' motion to dismiss, the court engaged in a full analysis of substantial similarity and concluded that the works "bear no substantial similarity to one another" and therefore dismissed the complaint.

B. THE RIGHT TO PREPARE DERIVATIVE WORKS UNDER § 106(2)

3. MORAL RIGHTS

Page 677. Add to end of paragraph of citations to post-*Dastar* decisions:

Logan Developers, Inc. v. Heritage Bldgs, Inc., 108 U.S.P.Q.2d 1523 (E.D.N.C. 2013) (*Dastar* forecloses false designation claim based on blueprints allegedly copied from protected building designs) ("There is no allegation in the complaint that Heritage obtained Logan's physical copies of the [building] design, placed its mark on the specific physical document, made no other alterations to the document, and offered the document itself for sale. Under *Dastar*, that is what is required to make out a § 43(a) false designation of origin Lanham Act claim.").

a. FEDERAL LAW PROTECTION OF MORAL RIGHTS

i. What is a "Work of Visual Art"?

Page 681. Add after paragraph on *Martin v. City of Indianapolis*:

In **Cohen v. G&M Realty**, 988 F.Supp.2d 212 (S.D.N.Y. 2013), graffiti artists failed in their invocation of VARA to obtain a preliminary injunction "to prevent the destruction of their paintings that adorned the exterior of the buildings owned by the defendants, which are scheduled for demolition. The . . . buildings, located in Long Island City, had become the repository of the largest collection of exterior aerosol art (often also referred to as 'graffiti art') in the United States, and had consequently become a significant tourist attraction—commonly known as 5 Pointz." The court found that while the site in general was well-known, as were some of the artists, few of the 24 wall paintings at issue presented sufficiently serious questions going to the merits to make them a fair ground for litigation as to whether they had achieved "recognized stature."

When it came to whether any of the 24 works were of "recognized stature," much of the testimony did not differentiate between these discrete words, and by and large assumed that if the work had artistic merit it was ipso facto of recognized stature. Thus, one of the plaintiffs, Danielle Mastrion, whose portrait of "Kool Herc" is among the 24, considered all of them to be of recognized stature because they satisfied factors such as "technical ability, composition, color, line work, detail and also the artist's credentials." And Joe Conzo, Jr., a documentary photographer, who described himself as one of the "forefathers" of the hip-hop culture reflected in the works at 5Pointz, essentially agreed, describing the works in general as "innovative" and "colorful," and in some cases, "pioneering." He believed that each of the 24 paintings was deserving of VARA protection because of the common elements of their "details" and "hard work."

. . .

The focus of whether any of plaintiffs' 24 paintings were not only works of stature, but had also achieved the requisite recognition to bring them within the embrace of VARA, centered on the testimony of each party's proffered art expert. The defendants' expert, Erin Thompson, an art history professor of impeccable academic credentials, took a restrictive view of both the concept of "stature" and "recognition." In her opinion, while "quality is certainly one of the factors in the stature" of a work of art, "stature is recognizing not particular qualities of objects, but the way these qualities are valued by the public." And while she recognized that being "innovative" and possessing "uniqueness" are additional factors bearing upon a work's stature, ultimately to qualify as such a work, it should be at a level where scholars agree that it is "changing the history of art."

As for the concept of "recognition," Professor Thompson's inquiry focused on ascertaining whether any of 24 works had been mentioned in academic publications or on the Internet. She found that for 19 of the 24, "there were no dissertations, no journal articles, no other scholarly mentions of the work," and there were no Google results for either the name of the work or the artist: "no one at all had seen fit to put on the Internet the name of that work." Of the other five, three were mentioned "by the artists themselves or on the 5Pointz web site," and "two of the remaining works each have one mention a piece on a street art web site, on a blog, or an artist's blog." . . .

Although acknowledging that the art at 5Pointz had indeed achieved widespread recognition as a tourist attraction, Professor Thompson believed that this would not satisfy VARA recognition unless the visitors came "to see a particular work of art." If so, this would qualify as the requisite statutory recognition even in the absence of any academic recognition. As she acknowledged in response to the court's questioning:

> THE COURT: So am I correct in understanding that recognition . . . is somewhat an expansive concept? You can have academic recognition. You can have practical recognition by people flocking to see something. Even if it's not in any book, it would all be under the umbrella of this concept of recognition, right?
>
> THOMPSON: Correct.

Thompson acknowledged that an aerosol artist's work, although a "sub-culture" of the art world, could be of recognized stature if there were a "consensus of the scholarly community and the art community," even if painted on the exterior of a building. She gave as an example the work of the internationally recognized aerosol artist Banksy, who had been mentioned "in something like a hundred and thirty dissertations and more than 1500 scholarly articles," and whose recent work, completed on October 31, 2013, generated more than 400,000 Google results after only two weeks. . . .

Plaintiffs' expert, Daniel Simmons, Jr., the head of the Rush Philanthropic Arts Foundation and the owner of two well-known New York City art galleries, agreed with Thompson that aerosol art can achieve recognized stature and gave credible testimony as to both stature and recognition. Simmons, a visual artist in his own right, has received many awards for his life-long commitment to art education. He has also amassed a personal collection of mostly contemporary art which he valued at $5 million . . .

As for stature, Simmons' focus was, not surprisingly, also on the work's quality, such as "design, color, shape, form" and characteristics of "symmetry" and "innovation." He believed that all 24 works qualified as "real artworks." . . .

As for recognition, Simmons opined that it means "there's enough people that know what [the work] looks like, and feels like and what it's trying to impart; that it would be, to me, if it was missing from the canon of art history, that it would be a loss." He testified that if a work of art "was exhibited in galleries, and museums, and in places where large number of people could see it, that would be recognized stature;" thus, "it would have to be significant public exposure." . . .

Simmons had no knowledge of whether the 5Pointz artists or their works were the subject of any academic works, but he believed that "everything is in flux from the old ways of doing things, and the way things are publicized and the way the media looks at things." The thrust of his testimony regarding recognition for the 5Pointz artwork of [particular named plaintiffs], and the other celebrated 5Pointz aerosol artists was that people are drawn to see their works because of the artists' reputations and the uniqueness of 5Pointz as an internationally recognized place to view the works at one location.

. . .

At the end of his testimony, when asked by plaintiffs' counsel "what impact would the loss of the works of visual [art] have on the art world and Hip Hop community," Simmons responded: "I think New York City as a whole would be diminished. It's a major tourist attraction for Long Island City. Its part of the development of Long Island City. Just like, pretty much . . . MoMa being there, it's a drawing point for artists and art lovers to come from all over the world to see."

In Simmons' opinion, 5Pointz and its extraordinary aerosol art had become "[p]art of the urban landscape," and "should be preserved, if possible."

. . .

The Court regrettably had no authority under VARA to preserve 5Pointz as a tourist site. That authority is vested in state or local authorities, and since 5Pointz had become such a scenic attraction, the City probably could have exercised its power of eminent domain to acquire the site outright. It chose not to. Although the Court was taken by the breadth and visual impact of 5Pointz, its authority under VARA is consequently limited to determining whether a particular work of visual art that was destroyed was one of "recognized stature," and if so, what monetary damages the creator of each work is entitled to.

The evidence adduced at the preliminary injunction hearing leads the Court to conclude that at least some of the 24 works, which plaintiffs contend were of recognized stature, . . . present "sufficiently serious questions going to the merits to make them a fair ground for litigation." [Citation] The final resolution of whether any do indeed qualify as such works of art is best left for a fuller exploration of the merits after the case has been properly prepared for trial, rather than at the preliminary injunction stage. Since VARA does not define "recognized stature," the court ultimately will have to decide whether to embrace the strictures of the academic views espoused by the defendants or the more expansive ones suggested by the plaintiffs. . . .

C. THE RIGHT TO DISTRIBUTE COPIES AND PHONORECORDS UNDER § 106(3)

1. THE PURPOSE AND APPLICATION OF THE DISTRIBUTION RIGHT

Page 714. Add before the discussion of *Capitol Records v. Thomas*:

If a defendant has sent a paying customer an email containing a hyperlink to an online location where an infringing copy of the plaintiff's work is located, has the defendant infringed on the plaintiff's distribution right? Can the plaintiff prevail in an infringement suit against the defendant alleging direct infringement without showing that the defendant posted the infringing copy at the linked-to location? *See Pearson Education, Inc. v. Ishayev*, 963 F.Supp.2d 239 (S.D.N.Y. 2013).

2. THE FIRST SALE DOCTRINE (EXHAUSTION OF THE DISTRIBUTION RIGHT) AND ITS EXCEPTIONS

Page 716. Add after Section 109(a):

Section 109(a) codifies the "first sale doctrine," under which the copyright owner's distribution right in a particular copy of the work is "exhausted" after its first sale. Often traced to the Supreme Court's decision in *Bobbs-Merrill Co. v. Straus*, discussed in *Vernor v. Autodesk, Inc.*, immediately following, the doctrine's roots in fact extend back to the mid-18th century, to the Lord Chancellor's decision in *Pope v. Curl*, 2 Atk. 342 (Ch. 1741). Alexander Pope obtained an injunction against the unauthorized publication of his letters by Edmund Curl, notwithstanding Curl's defense that he had lawfully obtained the letters from their owners, who, as the owners, were entitled to publish them. Lord Chancellor Hardwicke acknowledged that Curl's sources lawfully owned the paper upon which Pope's words appeared. But unpublished letters, the court continued, entail two different kinds of property, the property in the paper, belonging to the recipient of the letter, and the property in the right to publish the words, which remains with the writer. Copyright concerns the incorporeal "work" and the corresponding rights to reproduce and distribute (and, today, adapt, and publicly perform and display), not the physical object in which the work is fixed. The chattel rights of the owner of the physical property are limited to that material object; acquisition of the chattel does not bring with it the right to make copies, etc. This principle is codified at section 202 of the U.S. Copyright Act, discussed, *supra* Chapter 1.F in the main casebook. While the property rights are distinct, they occasionally overlap or conflict. See, e.g., *CCNV v. Reid, supra* Chapter 3.A.2 in the main casebook (commissioning party owned the sculpture but not the copyright; artist permitted access to sculpture in order to exercise his copyright).

The first sale doctrine regulates the rights of the copyright and chattel owners by establishing that once authorized copies have been lawfully distributed, the property rights of the chattel owner in the physical object prevail. The doctrine turns on the distinction between the "work" and the "copy". Accordingly, the chattel owner may dispose of her physical object (but she may not make further copies, for that conduct would invade the incorporeal property rights in the work). Because the chattel rights in the copy include the right to resell it, the first sale doctrine underpins the development of a secondary market for used copies. In this view of the first sale doctrine, the used book (etc.) market is a *consequence* of the distinction between the two kinds of property rights. Other views of the doctrine, expressed in some of the following materials, suggest that the *purpose* of the first sale doctrine is to foster secondary markets. What difference does it make?

Page 731. At the bottom of the page, add the following:

Capitol Records LLC v. ReDigi, Inc., 934 F.Supp.2d 640 (S.D.N.Y. 2013). ReDigi operates what it calls the "world's first pre-owned digital marketplace" at www.redigi.com. The following description of ReDigi's operations is paraphrased from the company's own documents:

> After signing up for a ReDigi account, downloading and installing ReDigi's Music Manager software, and logging in, a user can upload an eligible music file from the user's computer to the user's Cloud Locker in ReDigi's cloud-based storage system. A user's Cloud Locker consists of file pointers that associate particular eligible files with a particular user's account and indicate in which Cloud Locker those files are stored. Only the user associated with a particular Cloud Locker has access to its contents. The user can listen to an uploaded file by logging in to the user's account and streaming the file from the Cloud Locker to an internet-connected device.

> Only files originally and legally downloaded from iTunes are eligible for upload; music tracks copied from CDs or downloaded from other online venders or file sharers, or obtained from any other source, are not eligible. Music Manager analyzes each file that a user seeks to upload to determine that it was legally downloaded by the user from iTunes; even after Music Manager allows a file to be uploaded, it conducts additional and more intensive analysis to confirm eligibility, including verifying that the file was not modified or tampered with.

> Music Manager continuously runs in the background on a user's computer. When an eligible file is uploaded to user's Cloud Locker, all copies of that file are deleted from the user's computer, and from attached synchronization and storage devices. If any storage or synchronization device is connected to the user's computer after the upload, Music Manager automatically searches such devices for copies of any eligible file previously uploaded; if a copy is detected, the user is prompted to authorize the deletion of the copy, and if the user fails to do so, the user's ReDigi account is suspended.

> A user can offer an uploaded eligible file for resale to other ReDigi users. ReDigi earns a transaction fee from each sale.

When one ReDigi user sells a file to another ReDigi user, the file pointer associating the file with the Cloud Locker of the selling user is modified to associate the file with the Cloud Locker of the purchasing user; the file itself remains in the same location in the ReDigi cloud and is not copied. After the sale, the selling user no longer has any access to the file sold.

If a user downloads a file from his Cloud Locker, the file is deleted from the Cloud Locker.

Capitol Records charged ReDigi with infringement of the reproduction and distribution rights. ReDigi contended that its system offered the digital equivalent of the used record market, and accordingly should benefit from the first sale doctrine. The district court disagreed and granted summary judgment for Capitol Records. Relying in part on *London-Sire*, it held that ReDigi reproduced the files on its servers and distributed copies to its customers. The court found no statutory basis for a digital first sale doctrine; rather the text of the statute clearly precluded the doctrine's application to dematerialized copies. The court declined ReDigi's invitation to craft such an exception:

> [T]he first sale doctrine does not protect ReDigi's distribution of Capitol's copyrighted works. This is because, as an unlawful reproduction, a digital music file sold on ReDigi is not "lawfully made under this title." 17 U.S.C. § 109(a). Moreover, the statute protects only distribution by "the owner of a particular copy or phonorecord . . . of that copy or phonorecord." Here, a ReDigi user owns the phonorecord that was created when she purchased and downloaded a song from iTunes to her hard disk. But to sell that song on ReDigi, she must produce a new phonorecord on the ReDigi server. Because it is therefore impossible for the user to sell her "particular" phonorecord on ReDigi, the first sale statute cannot provide a defense. Put another way, the first sale defense is limited to material items, like records, that the copyright owner put into the stream of commerce. Here, ReDigi is not distributing such material items; rather, it is distributing reproductions of the copyrighted code embedded in new material objects, namely, the ReDigi server in Arizona and its users' hard drives. The first sale defense does not cover this any more than it covered the sale of cassette recordings of vinyl records in a bygone era.

> Rejecting such a conclusion, ReDigi argues that, because " 'technological change has rendered its literal terms ambiguous, the Copyright Act must be construed in light of [its] basic purpose,' " namely, to incentivize creative work for the "ultimate[ ] . . . cause of promoting broad public availability of literature, music, and the other arts." [Citation omitted.] Thus, ReDigi asserts that refusal to apply the first sale doctrine to its service would grant Capitol "a Court sanctioned extension of rights under the [C]opyright [A]ct . . . which is against policy, and should not be endorsed by this Court."

> The Court disagrees. ReDigi effectively requests that the Court amend the statute to achieve ReDigi's broader policy goals—goals that happen to advance ReDigi's economic interests. However, ReDigi's argument fails for two reasons.

First, while technological change may have rendered Section 109(a) unsatisfactory to many contemporary observers and consumers, it has not rendered it ambiguous. The statute plainly applies to the lawful owner's "particular" phonorecord, a phonorecord that by definition cannot be uploaded and sold on ReDigi's website. Second, amendment of the Copyright Act in line with ReDigi's proposal is a legislative prerogative that courts are unauthorized and ill suited to attempt.

Nor are the policy arguments as straightforward or uncontested as ReDigi suggests. Indeed, when confronting this precise subject in its report on the Digital Millennium Copyright Act, 17 U.S.C. § 512, the United States Copyright Office . . . rejected extension of the first sale doctrine to the distribution of digital works, noting that the justifications for the first sale doctrine in the physical world could not be imported into the digital domain. . . . Thus, while ReDigi mounts attractive policy arguments, they are not as one-sided as it contends.

Finally, ReDigi feebly argues that the Court's reading of Section 109(a) would in effect exclude digital works from the meaning of the statute. That is not the case. Section 109(a) still protects a lawful owner's sale of her "particular" phonorecord, be it a computer hard disk, iPod, or other memory device onto which the file was originally downloaded. While this limitation clearly presents obstacles to resale that are different from, and perhaps even more onerous than, those involved in the resale of CDs and cassettes, the limitation is hardly absurd—the first sale doctrine was enacted in a world where the ease and speed of data transfer could not have been imagined. There are many reasons, some discussed herein, for why such physical limitations may be desirable. It is left to Congress, and not this Court, to deem them outmoded.

Accordingly, the Court concludes that the first sale defense does not permit sales of digital music files on ReDigi's website.

QUESTIONS

1.   Though ReDigi's system purports to delete uploaded files from the seller's computer, does it (can it?) detect whether the seller has made "back up" copies on other devices before sending her files to ReDigi?

2.   Apart from limiting availability of the service to copies obtained from iTunes, how might ReDigi ascertain whether the uploaded file derived from a lawful source?

3.   Assuming that a "used" digital file "resale" system could be designed to ensure that the seller's file was lawfully obtained, and that she does not make or retain additional copies before "reselling" her file, *should* Congress amend the copyright act to create a "digital first sale doctrine"? How would you draft the legislation, taking into account the necessary safeguards?

Page 735. Add before subsection "3. The § 602(a) Importation Right":

DROIT DE SUITE

The *"droit de suite,"* or artists' resale royalty right, qualifies the freedom to resell at the core of the first sale doctrine: the right requires that, for the duration of the copyright term, the creator of a visual artwork (such as a painting or a sculpture) receive a specified percentage of the price of every subsequent resale. Because there may be no market for reproduction or public display by transmission of many works of art, exploitations of incorporeal copyright rights may not benefit many artists; the *droit de suite* therefore seeks to ensure that artists share in the subsequent disposition of lawfully owned copies of their works. Although the *droit de suite* exists in the European Union, *see* Directive 2001/84/EC of the European Parliaments and of the Council of 27 September 2001 on the resale right for the benefit of the Author of an original work of art, California is the only U.S. state that has enacted a resale royalties statute. California Civil Code section 986 provides that:

> Whenever a work of fine art is sold and the seller resides in California or the sale takes place in California, the seller or his agent shall pay to the artist of such work of fine art or to such artist's agent 5 percent of the amount of such sale.

The artist's right is nonwaivable and may be enforced by an action for damages with a three-year period of limitations; moneys payable to the artist will be paid to the state Arts Council if the seller cannot locate the artist within 90 days, and all moneys due the artist are exempt from attachment or execution of judgment by creditors of the seller. Among those sales exempted from the statute are resales for a gross price of less than $1,000, resales made more than 20 years after the death of the artist, and resales for a gross sales price less than the purchase price paid by the seller.

In *Sam Francis Foundation v. Christies*, 784 F.3d 1320 (9th Cir. 2015), the Ninth Circuit sitting en banc concluded that the statute violated the dormant commerce clause "as an impermissible regulation of wholly out-of-state conduct" where it applies to sales outside California by sellers who reside in California. The court gave the example of "a California resident [who] has a parttime apartment in New York, buys a sculpture in New York from a North Dakota artist to furnish her apartment, and later sells the sculpture to a friend in New York." The court read the California law as requiring "the payment of a royalty to the North Dakota artist—even if the sculpture, the artist, and the buyer never traveled to, or had any connection with, California." This, the court concluded, violated the Supreme Court's interpretation that " '. . . the Commerce Clause precludes the application of a state statute to commerce that takes place wholly outside of the State's borders, whether or not the commerce has effects within the State.' " *Id.* at ___ (quoting *Healy v. Beer Institute*, 491 U.S. 324, 336 (1989)). But the court concluded that the invalidated provision was severable, so that the law would continue to apply to sales that take place in California.

Three of the eleven judges concurred in part, but would have limited the invalidation to the regulation of out-of-state sales by out-of-state *agents* of California sellers (such as the defendant auction houses Christies and Sotheby's in this case). As to the validity of requiring the California-resident sellers *themselves* to pay the resale royalty, two of the concurring judges would not have reached that question, and one of them would have upheld that requirement.

On the federal level, the "American Royalties Too Act of 2015" is currently pending in Congress. H.R. 1881, 114th Cong., 1st Sess. (2015);

S. 977, 114th Cong., 1st Sess. (2015). The bills would add to section 106 a new right, "in the case of a work of visual art, to collect a royalty for the work if the work is sold by a person other than the author of the work for a price of not less than $5,000 as the result of an auction." The royalty would be the lesser of 5% of the price paid for the work or $35,000 (and the $35,000 cap would be adjusted annually for inflation); the entity that conducts the auction would have 90 days after the auction to collect the royalty and pay it to a visual artists' copyright collecting society, which would then make distributions (at least four times a year) of collected royalties to "the author or his or her successor as copyright owner." The new royalty right would not be assignable or waivable, and failure to pay the royalty would constitute copyright infringement subjecting the infringer to liability for both statutory damages and the full amount of the royalty due.

The bills would amend the current definition of "work of visual art" by replacing the first two paragraphs with the following text:

A 'work of visual art' is a painting, drawing, print, sculpture, or photograph, existing either in the original embodiment or in a limited edition of 200 copies or fewer that bear the signature or other identifying mark of the author and are consecutively numbered by the author, or, in the case of a sculpture, in multiple cast, carved, or fabricated sculptures of 200 or fewer that are consecutively numbered by the author and bear the signature or other identifying mark of the author.

In December 2013, the Copyright Office issued a report (updating a report it issued in 1992 on the resale royalty) concluding that "under the current legal system, visual artists are uniquely limited in their ability to fully benefit from the success of their works over time" and that "therefore the Office supports congressional consideration of a resale royalty right." REGISTER OF COPYRIGHTS, RESALE ROYALTIES: AN UPDATED ANALYSIS 1–2 (2013), *at* http://www.copyright.gov/docs/resaleroyalty/usco-resaleroyalty.pdf. The report also noted that while "adoption of a resale royalty right is one option to address the disparate treatment of artists under the law, it is not the only option, and more deliberation is necessary to determine if it is the best option." *Id.* at 3.

The Office recommended that if Congress should wish to adopt a resale royalty, the law adopted should:

— apply to sales by auction houses, galleries, private dealers, and others in the business of selling visual art;

— apply at a relatively low threshold value to benefit as many artists as possible;

— establish a royalty rate of 3 to 5 percent of gross resale price for works that have increased in value, and cap the royalty payment due for each sale;

— apply prospectively to the resale of works acquired after the law takes effect;

— provide for collective management by private collecting societies;

— require copyright registration as a prerequisite for receiving royalties;

— limit remedies for failure to pay the royalty to a specified amount (rather than actual or statutory damages); and

— apply only for the life of the artist.

Id. at 3–4.

QUESTIONS

1. Which artists are covered by the proposed federal law? How would the amendment to the definition of a "work of visual art" affect VARA claims?

2. The California statute applies to sales over $1000; the federal bill to sales over $5,000. Is the federal cut-off too high to benefit the kinds of artists for whom the right may be particularly meaningful—that is, artists whose works are not licensed for reproduction in various forms?

3. Does the provision for payment of the proposed federal resale royalty to the original artist *or* to "his or her successor as copyright owner" threaten to undermine the effectiveness of requiring the royalty payment?

3.   THE § 602(a) IMPORTATION RIGHT, AND ITS RELATIONSHIP TO THE DISTRIBUTION RIGHT

Pages 735–746. Replace the *Quality King* and *Pearson v. Liu* decisions, and the QUESTIONS that follow them, with the following:

Kirtsaeng v. John Wiley & Sons, Inc.

__ U.S. __, 133 S.Ct. 1351 (2013).

■ JUSTICE BREYER delivered the opinion of the Court.

Section 106 of the Copyright Act grants "the owner of copyright under this title" certain "exclusive rights," including the right "to distribute copies . . . of the copyrighted work to the public by sale or other transfer of ownership." 17 U.S.C. § 106(3). These rights are qualified, however, by the application of various limitations set forth in the next several sections of the Act, §§ 107 through 122. . . .

Section 109(a) sets forth the "first sale" doctrine as follows:

"Notwithstanding the provisions of section 106(3), the owner of a particular copy or phonorecord *lawfully made under this title* . . . is entitled, without the authority of the copyright owner, to sell or otherwise dispose of the possession of that copy or phonorecord." (Emphasis added.)

Thus, even though § 106(3) forbids distribution of a copy of, say, the copyrighted novel Herzog without the copyright owner's permission, § 109(a) adds that, once a copy of Herzog has been lawfully sold (or its ownership otherwise lawfully transferred), the buyer of *that copy* and subsequent owners are free to dispose of it as they wish. In copyright jargon, the "first sale" has "exhausted" the copyright owner's § 106(3) exclusive distribution right.

What, however, if the copy of Herzog was printed abroad and then initially sold with the copyright owner's permission? Does the "first sale" doctrine still apply? Is the buyer, like the buyer of a domestically manufactured copy, free to bring the copy into the United States and dispose of it as he or she wishes?

To put the matter technically, an "importation" provision, § 602(a)(1), says that

"[i]mportation into the United States, without the authority of the owner of copyright under this title, of copies . . . of a work that have been acquired outside the United States is an infringement of the exclusive right to distribute copies . . . *under section 106*. . . ." 17 U.S.C. § 602(a)(1) (emphasis added).

Thus § 602(a)(1) makes clear that importing a copy without permission violates the owner's exclusive distribution right. But in doing so, § 602(a)(1) refers explicitly to the *§ 106(3)* exclusive distribution right. As we have just said, § 106 is by its terms "[s]ubject to" the various doctrines and principles contained in §§ 107 through 122, including § 109(a)'s "first sale" limitation. Do those same modifications apply—in particular, does the "first sale" modification apply—when considering whether § 602(a)(1) prohibits importing a copy?

In *Quality King Distribs. v. L'anza Research Int'l*, 523 U.S. 135, 145 (1998), we held that § 602(a)(1)'s reference to § 106(3)'s exclusive distribution right incorporates the later subsections' limitations, including, in particular, the "first sale" doctrine of § 109. Thus, it might seem that, § 602(a)(1) notwithstanding, one who buys a copy abroad can freely import that copy into the United States and dispose of it, just as he could had he bought the copy in the United States.

But *Quality King* considered an instance in which the copy, though purchased abroad, was initially manufactured in the United States (and then sent abroad and sold). This case is like *Quality King* but for one important fact. The copies at issue here were manufactured abroad. That fact is important because § 109(a) says that the "first sale" doctrine applies to "a particular copy or phonorecord *lawfully made under this title*." And we must decide here whether the five words, "lawfully made under this title," make a critical legal difference.

Putting section numbers to the side, we ask whether the "first sale" doctrine applies to protect a buyer or other lawful owner of a copy (of a copyrighted work) lawfully manufactured abroad. Can that buyer bring that copy into the United States (and sell it or give it away) without obtaining permission to do so from the copyright owner? Can, for example, someone who purchases, say at a used bookstore, a book printed abroad subsequently resell it without the copyright owner's permission?

In our view, the answers to these questions are, yes. We hold that the "first sale" doctrine applies to copies of a copyrighted work lawfully made abroad.

I

A

Respondent, John Wiley & Sons, Inc., publishes academic textbooks. Wiley obtains from its authors various foreign and domestic copyright assignments, licenses and permissions—to the point that we can, for present purposes, refer to Wiley as the relevant American copyright owner. See 654 F.3d 210, 213, n. 6 (CA2 2011). Wiley often assigns to its wholly owned foreign subsidiary, John Wiley & Sons (Asia) Pte Ltd., rights to publish, print, and sell Wiley's English language textbooks abroad. Each copy of a Wiley Asia foreign edition will likely contain language making clear that the copy is to be sold only in a particular country or geographical region outside the United States.

For example, a copy of Wiley's American edition says, "Copyright © 2008 John Wiley & Sons, Inc. All rights reserved. . . . Printed in the United States of America." J. Walker, Fundamentals of Physics, p. vi (8th ed. 2008). A copy of Wiley Asia's Asian edition of that book says:

> "Copyright © 2008 John Wiley & Sons (Asia) Pte Ltd[.] All rights reserved. This book is authorized for sale in Europe, Asia, Africa, and the Middle East only and may be not exported out of these territories. Exportation from or importation of this book to another region without the Publisher's authorization is illegal and is a violation of the Publisher's rights. The Publisher may take legal action to enforce its rights. . . . Printed in Asia." J. Walker, Fundamentals of Physics, p. vi (8th ed. 2008 Wiley Int'l Student ed.).

Both the foreign and the American copies say:

> "No part of this publication may be reproduced, stored in a retrieval system, or transmitted in any form or by any means . . . except as permitted under Sections 107 or 108 of the 1976 United States Copyright Act." Compare, *e.g., ibid.* (Int'l ed.), with Walker, *supra,* at vi (American ed.).

The upshot is that there are two essentially equivalent versions of a Wiley textbook, each version manufactured and sold with Wiley's permission: (1) an American version printed and sold in the United States, and (2) a foreign version manufactured and sold abroad. And Wiley makes certain that copies of the second version state that they are not to be taken (without permission) into the United States.

Petitioner, Supap Kirtsaeng, a citizen of Thailand, moved to the United States in 1997 to study mathematics at Cornell University. He paid for his education with the help of a Thai Government scholarship which required him to teach in Thailand for 10 years on his return. Kirtsaeng successfully completed his undergraduate courses at Cornell, successfully completed a Ph.D. program in mathematics at the University of Southern California, and then, as promised, returned to Thailand to teach. While he was studying in the United States, Kirtsaeng asked his friends and family in Thailand to buy copies of foreign edition English-language textbooks at Thai book shops, where they sold at low prices, and mail them to him in the United States. Kirtsaeng would then sell them, reimburse his family and friends, and keep the profit.

B

In 2008 Wiley brought this federal lawsuit against Kirtsaeng for copyright infringement. Wiley claimed that Kirtsaeng's unauthorized importation of its books and his later resale of those books amounted to an infringement of Wiley's § 106(3) exclusive right to distribute as well as § 602's related import prohibition. . . . Kirtsaeng replied that the books he had acquired were " 'lawfully made' " and that he had acquired them legitimately. Thus, in his view, § 109(a)'s "first sale" doctrine permitted him to resell or otherwise dispose of the books without the copyright owner's further permission.

The District Court held that Kirtsaeng could not assert the "first sale" defense because, in its view, that doctrine does not apply to "foreign-manufactured goods" (even if made abroad with the copyright owner's permission). The jury then found that Kirtsaeng had willfully infringed Wiley's American copyrights by selling and importing without authorization copies of eight of Wiley's copyrighted titles. And it assessed statutory damages of $600,000 ($75,000 per work).

On appeal, a split panel of the Second Circuit agreed with the District Court. It pointed out that § 109(a)'s "first sale" doctrine applies only to "the owner of a particular copy . . . *lawfully made under this title.*" And, in the majority's view, this language means that the "first sale" doctrine does not apply to copies of American copyrighted works manufactured abroad. A dissenting judge thought that the words "lawfully made under this title" do not refer "to a place of manufacture" but rather "focu[s] on whether a particular copy was manufactured lawfully under" America's copyright statute, and that "the lawfulness of the manufacture of a particular copy should be judged by U.S. copyright law."

We granted Kirtsaeng's petition for certiorari to consider this question in light of different views among the Circuits.

II

We must decide whether the words "lawfully made under this title" restrict the scope of § 109(a)'s "first sale" doctrine geographically. The Second Circuit, the Ninth Circuit, Wiley, and the Solicitor General (as *amicus*) all read those words as imposing a form of *geographical* limitation. The Second Circuit held that they limit the "first sale" doctrine to particular copies "made in territories *in which the Copyright Act is law,*" which (the Circuit says) are copies "manufactured domestically," not "outside of the United States." 654 F.3d, at 221–222 (emphasis added). Wiley agrees that those five words limit the "first sale" doctrine "to copies made in conformance with the [United States] Copyright Act *where the Copyright Act is applicable,*" which (Wiley says) means it does not apply to copies made "outside the United States" and at least not to "foreign production of a copy for distribution exclusively abroad." Similarly, the Solicitor General says that those five words limit the "first sale" doctrine's applicability to copies " '*made subject to* and in compliance with [the Copyright Act],' " which (the Solicitor General says) are copies "made in the United States." Brief for United States as *Amicus Curiae* 5 (hereinafter Brief for United States) (emphasis added). And the Ninth Circuit has held that those words limit the "first sale" doctrine's applicability (1) to copies lawfully made in the United States, and (2) to copies lawfully made outside the United States but initially sold in the United States with the copyright owner's permission. *Denbicare U.S.A. Inc. v. Toys "R" Us, Inc.,* 84 F.3d 1143, 1149–1150 (1996).

Under any of these geographical interpretations, § 109(a)'s "first sale" doctrine would not apply to the Wiley Asia books at issue here. And, despite an American copyright owner's permission to *make* copies abroad, one who *buys* a copy of any such book or other copyrighted work— whether at a retail store, over the Internet, or at a library sale—could not resell (or otherwise dispose of) that particular copy without further permission.

Kirtsaeng, however, reads the words "lawfully made under this title" as imposing a *non*-geographical limitation. He says that they mean made "in accordance with" or "in compliance with" the Copyright Act. In that case, § 109(a)'s "first sale" doctrine would apply to copyrighted works as long as their manufacture met the requirements of American copyright law. In particular, the doctrine would apply where, as here, copies are manufactured abroad with the permission of the copyright owner. See § 106 (referring to the owner's right to authorize).

In our view, § 109(a)'s language, its context, and the common-law history of the "first sale" doctrine, taken together, favor a *non*-geographical interpretation. We also doubt that Congress would have intended to create the practical copyright-related harms with which a geographical interpretation would threaten ordinary scholarly, artistic, commercial, and consumer activities. We consequently conclude that Kirtsaeng's nongeographical reading is the better reading of the Act.

A

The language of § 109(a) read literally favors Kirtsaeng's nongeographical interpretation, namely, that "lawfully made under this title" means made "in accordance with" or "in compliance with" the Copyright Act. The language of § 109(a) says nothing about geography. The word "under" can mean "[i]n accordance with." 18 Oxford English Dictionary 950 (2d ed. 1989). See also Black's Law Dictionary 1525 (6th ed. 1990) ("according to"). And a nongeographical interpretation provides each word of the five-word phrase with a distinct purpose. The first two words of the phrase, "lawfully made," suggest an effort to distinguish those copies that were made lawfully from those that were not, and the last three words, "under this title," set forth the standard of "lawful[ness]." Thus, the nongeographical reading is simple, it promotes a traditional copyright objective (combatting piracy), and it makes word-by-word linguistic sense.

The geographical interpretation, however, bristles with linguistic difficulties. It gives the word "lawfully" little, if any, linguistic work to do. (How could a book be *un*lawfully "made under this title"?) It imports geography into a statutory provision that says nothing explicitly about it. And it is far more complex than may at first appear.

To read the clause geographically, Wiley, like the Second Circuit and the Solicitor General, must first emphasize the word "under." Indeed, Wiley reads "under this title" to mean "in conformance with the Copyright Act *where the Copyright Act is applicable.*" Wiley must then take a second step, arguing that the Act "is applicable" only in the United States. And the Solicitor General must do the same. See Brief for United States 6 ("A copy is '*lawfully* made under this title' if Title 17 governs the copy's creation *and* the copy is made in compliance with Title 17's requirements"). See also [*infra*] (GINSBURG, J., dissenting) ("under" describes something "governed or regulated by another").

One difficulty is that neither "under" nor any other word in the phrase means "where." See, *e.g.*, 18 Oxford English Dictionary, *supra,* at 947–952 (definition of "under"). It might mean "subject to," but as this Court has repeatedly acknowledged, the word evades a uniform, consistent meaning.

A far more serious difficulty arises out of the uncertainty and complexity surrounding the second step's effort to read the necessary geographical limitation into the word "applicable" (or the equivalent). Where, precisely, is the Copyright Act "applicable"? The Act does not instantly *protect* an American copyright holder from unauthorized piracy taking place abroad. But that fact does not mean the Act is *inapplicable* to copies made abroad. As a matter of ordinary English, one can say that a statute imposing, say, a tariff upon "any rhododendron grown in Nepal" applies to *all* Nepalese rhododendrons. And, similarly, one can say that the American Copyright Act is *applicable* to *all* pirated copies, including those printed overseas. Indeed, the Act itself makes clear that (in the Solicitor General's language) foreign-printed pirated copies are "subject to" the Act. § 602(a)(2) (referring to importation of copies "the making of which either constituted an infringement of copyright, or which would have constituted an infringement of copyright if this title had been applicable"); Brief for United States 5.

The appropriateness of this linguistic usage is underscored by the fact that § 104 of the Act itself says that works *"subject to protection under this title"* include unpublished works "without regard to the nationality or domicile of the author," and works "first published" in any one of the nearly 180 nations that have signed a copyright treaty with the United States. §§ 104(a), (b) (emphasis added); § 101 (defining "treaty party"); U.S. Copyright Office, Circular No. 38A, International Copyright Relations of the United States (2010). Thus, ordinary English permits us to say that the Act "applies" to an Irish manuscript lying in its author's Dublin desk drawer as well as to an original recording of a ballet performance first made in Japan and now on display in a Kyoto art gallery. . . .

The Ninth Circuit's geographical interpretation produces still greater linguistic difficulty. As we said, that Circuit interprets the "first sale" doctrine to cover both (1) copies manufactured in the United States and (2) copies manufactured abroad but first sold in the United States with the American copyright owner's permission. *Denbicare U.S.A.*, 84 F.3d, at 1149–1150. . . .

We can understand why the Ninth Circuit may have thought it necessary to add the second part of its definition. As we shall later describe, without some such qualification a copyright holder could prevent a buyer from domestically reselling or even giving away copies of a video game made in Japan, a film made in Germany, or a dress (with a design copyright [sic]) made in China, *even* if the copyright holder has granted permission for the foreign manufacture, importation, and an initial domestic sale of the copy. A publisher such as Wiley would be free to print its books abroad, allow their importation and sale within the United States, but prohibit students from later selling their used texts at a campus bookstore. We see no way, however, to reconcile this half-geographical/half-nongeographical interpretation with the language of the phrase, "lawfully made under this title." As a matter of English, it would seem that those five words either do cover copies lawfully made abroad or they do not.

In sum, we believe that geographical interpretations create more linguistic problems than they resolve. And considerations of simplicity and coherence tip the purely linguistic balance in Kirtsaeng's, nongeographical, favor.

B

Both historical and contemporary statutory context indicate that Congress, when writing the present version of § 109(a), did not have geography in mind. In respect to history, we compare § 109(a)'s present language with the language of its immediate predecessor. That predecessor said:

> "[N]othing in this Act shall be deemed to forbid, prevent, or restrict the transfer of any copy of a copyrighted work *the possession of which has been lawfully obtained*." Copyright Act of 1909, § 41, 35 Stat. 1084 (emphasis added).

The predecessor says nothing about geography (and Wiley does not argue that it does). So we ask whether Congress, in changing its language implicitly *introduced* a geographical limitation that previously was lacking.

A comparison of language indicates that it did not. The predecessor says that the "first sale" doctrine protects "the transfer of any copy *the possession of which has been lawfully obtained*." The present version says that "*the owner* of a particular copy or phonorecord lawfully made under this title is entitled to sell or otherwise dispose of the possession of that copy or phonorecord." What does this change in language accomplish?

The language of the former version referred to those *who are not owners* of a copy, but mere possessors who "lawfully obtained" a copy. The present version covers only those who are *owners* of a "lawfully made" copy. Whom does the change leave out? Who might have lawfully *obtained* a copy of a copyrighted work but not *owned* that copy? One answer is owners of movie theaters, who during the 1970's (and before) often *leased* films from movie distributors or filmmakers. Because the theater owners had "lawfully obtained" their copies, the earlier version could be read as allowing them to sell that copy, *i.e.*, it might have given them "first sale" protection. Because the theater owners were lessees, not owners, of their copies, the change in language makes clear that they (like bailees and other lessees) cannot take advantage of the "first sale" doctrine. . . .

This objective perfectly well explains the new language of the present version, including the five words here at issue. Section 109(a) now makes clear that a lessee of a copy will *not* receive "first sale" protection but one who *owns* a copy *will* receive "first sale" protection, *provided,* of course, that the copy was "*lawfully made*" and not pirated. The new language also takes into account that a copy may be "lawfully made under this title" when the copy, say of a phonorecord, comes into its owner's possession through use of a compulsory license, which "this title" provides for elsewhere, namely, in § 115. . . .

. . .

Finally, we normally presume that the words "lawfully made under this title" carry the same meaning when they appear in different but related sections. But doing so here produces surprising consequences. Consider:

(1) Section 109(c) says that, despite the copyright owner's exclusive right "to display" a copyrighted work (provided in § 106(5)), the owner of a particular copy "lawfully made under this title" may publicly display it without further authorization. To interpret these words geographically would mean that one who buys a copyrighted work of art, a poster, or even a bumper sticker, in Canada, in Europe, in Asia, could not display it in America without the copyright owner's further authorization.

(2) Section 109(e) specifically provides that the owner of a particular copy of a copyrighted video arcade game "lawfully made under this title" may "publicly perform or display that game in coin-operated equipment" without the authorization of the copyright owner. To interpret these words geographically means that an arcade owner could not ("without the authority of the copyright owner") perform or display arcade games (whether new or used) originally made in Japan.

(3) Section 110(1) says that a teacher, without the copyright owner's authorization, is allowed to perform or display a copyrighted work (say, an audiovisual work) "in the course of face-to-face teaching activities"—unless the teacher knowingly used "a copy that was not lawfully made under this title." To interpret these words geographically would mean that the teacher could not (without further authorization) use a copy of a film during class if the copy was lawfully made in Canada, Mexico, Europe, Africa, or Asia.

(4) In its introductory sentence, § 106 provides the Act's basic exclusive rights to an "owner of a copyright under this title." The last three words cannot support a geographic interpretation.

Wiley basically accepts the first three readings, but argues that Congress intended the restrictive consequences. And it argues that context simply requires that the words of the fourth example receive a different interpretation. Leaving the fourth example to the side, we shall explain in Part II-D, *infra,* why we find it unlikely that Congress would have intended these, and other related consequences.

C

A relevant canon of statutory interpretation favors a nongeographical reading. "[W]hen a statute covers an issue previously governed by the common law," we must presume that "Congress intended to retain the substance of the common law."

. . .

The "first sale" doctrine also frees courts from the administrative burden of trying to enforce restrictions upon difficult-to-trace, readily movable goods. And it avoids the selective enforcement inherent in any such effort. Thus, it is not surprising that for at least a century the "first sale" doctrine has played an important role in American copyright law. See *Bobbs-Merrill Co.* v. *Straus*, 210 U.S. 339 (1908); Copyright Act of 1909, § 41, 35 Stat. 1084. See also Copyright Law Revision, Further Discussions and Comments on Preliminary Draft for Revised U.S. Copyright Law, 88th Cong., 2d Sess., pt. 4, p. 212 (Comm. Print 1964) (Irwin Karp of Authors' League of America expressing concern for "the very basic concept of copyright law that, once you've sold a copy legally, you can't restrict its resale").

The common-law doctrine makes no geographical distinctions; nor can we find any in *Bobbs-Merrill* (where this Court first applied the "first sale" doctrine) or in § 109(a)'s predecessor provision, which Congress enacted a year later. Rather, as the Solicitor General acknowledges, "a straightforward application of *Bobbs-Merrill*" would not preclude the "first sale" defense from applying to authorized copies made overseas. And we can find no language, context, purpose, or history that would rebut a "straightforward application" of that doctrine here.

. . .

D

Associations of libraries, used-book dealers, technology companies, consumer-goods retailers, and museums point to various ways in which a geographical interpretation would fail to further basic constitutional copyright objectives, in particular "promot[ing] the Progress of Science and useful Arts."

The American Library Association tells us that library collections contain at least 200 million books published abroad (presumably, many were first published in one of the nearly 180 copyright-treaty nations and enjoy American copyright protection under 17 U.S.C. § 104); that many others were first published in the United States but printed abroad because of lower costs; and that a geographical interpretation will likely require the libraries to obtain permission (or at least create significant uncertainty) before circulating or otherwise distributing these books.

How, the American Library Association asks, are the libraries to obtain permission to distribute these millions of books? How can they find, say, the copyright owner of a foreign book, perhaps written decades ago? They may not know the copyright holder's present address. And, even where addresses can be found, the costs of finding them, contacting owners, and negotiating may be high indeed. Are the libraries to stop circulating or distributing or displaying the millions of books in their collections that were printed abroad?

Used-book dealers tell us that, from the time when Benjamin Franklin and Thomas Jefferson built commercial and personal libraries of foreign books, American readers have bought used books published and printed abroad. The dealers say that they have "operat[ed] . . . for centuries" under the assumption that the "first sale" doctrine applies. But under a geographical interpretation a contemporary tourist who buys, say, at Shakespeare and Co. (in Paris), a dozen copies of a foreign book for American friends might find that she had violated the copyright law. The used-book dealers cannot easily predict what the foreign copyright holder may think about a reader's effort to sell a used copy of a novel. And they believe that a geographical interpretation will injure a large portion of the used-book business.

Technology companies tell us that "automobiles, microwaves, calculators, mobile phones, tablets, and personal computers" contain copyrightable software programs or packaging. Many of these items are made abroad with the American copyright holder's permission and then sold and imported (with that permission) to the United States. A geographical interpretation would prevent the resale of, say, a car, without the permission of the holder of each copyright on each piece of copyrighted automobile software. Yet there is no reason to believe that foreign auto manufacturers regularly obtain this kind of permission from their software component suppliers, and Wiley did not indicate to the contrary when asked. Without that permission a foreign car owner could not sell his or her used car.

Retailers tell us that over $2.3 trillion worth of foreign goods were imported in 2011. American retailers buy many of these goods after a first sale abroad. And, many of these items bear, carry, or contain copyrighted "packaging, logos, labels, and product inserts and instructions for [the use of] everyday packaged goods from floor cleaners and health and beauty products to breakfast cereals." The retailers add that American sales of more traditional copyrighted works, "such as books, recorded music, motion pictures, and magazines" likely amount to over $220 billion. A geographical interpretation would subject many, if not all, of them to the disruptive impact of the threat of infringement suits.

Art museum directors ask us to consider their efforts to display foreign-produced works by, say, Cy Twombly, René Magritte, Henri Matisse, Pablo Picasso, and others. A geographical interpretation, they say, would require the museums to obtain permission from the copyright owners before they could display the work, even if the copyright owner has already sold or donated the work to a foreign museum. What are the museums to do, they ask, if the artist retained the copyright, if the artist cannot be found, or if a group of heirs is arguing about who owns which copyright?

These examples . . . help explain *why* American copyright law has long applied [the first sale] doctrine.

Neither Wiley nor any of its many *amici* deny that a geographical interpretation could bring about these "horribles"—at least in principle. Rather, Wiley essentially says that the list is artificially invented. It points out that a federal court first adopted a geographical interpretation more than 30 years ago. *CBS, Inc.* v. *Scorpio Music Distributors, Inc.*, 569 F. Supp. 47, 49 (ED Pa. 1983), summarily aff'd, 738 F.2d 424 (CA3 1984) (table). Yet, it adds, these problems have not occurred. Why not? Because, says Wiley, the problems and threats are purely theoretical; they are unlikely to reflect reality.

We are less sanguine. For one thing, the law has not been settled for long in Wiley's favor. The Second Circuit, in its decision below, is the first Court of Appeals to adopt a purely geographical interpretation. The Third Circuit has favored a nongeographical interpretation. *Sebastian Int'l*, 847 F.2d 1093. The Ninth Circuit has favored a modified geographical interpretation with a nongeographical (but textually unsustainable) corollary designed to diminish the problem. *Denbicare U.S.A.*, 84 F.3d 1143. And other courts have hesitated to adopt, and have cast doubt upon, the validity of the geographical interpretation.

For another thing, reliance upon the "first sale" doctrine is deeply embedded in the practices of those, such as booksellers, libraries, museums, and retailers, who have long relied upon its protection. Museums, for example, are not in the habit of asking their foreign counterparts to check with the heirs of copyright owners before sending, *e.g.*, a Picasso on tour. That inertia means a dramatic change is likely necessary before these institutions, instructed by their counsel, would begin to engage in the complex permission-verifying process that a geographical interpretation would demand. And this Court's adoption of the geographical interpretation could provide that dramatic change. These intolerable consequences (along with the absurd result that the copyright owner can exercise downstream control even when it authorized the import or first sale) have understandably led the Ninth Circuit, the Solicitor General as *amicus*, and the dissent to adopt textual readings of the statute that attempt to mitigate these harms. But those readings are not defensible, for they require too many unprecedented jumps over linguistic and other hurdles that in our view are insurmountable. . . .

Finally, the fact that harm has proved limited so far may simply reflect the reluctance of copyright holders so far to assert geographically based resale rights. They may decide differently if the law is clarified in their favor. Regardless, a copyright law that can work in practice only if unenforced is not a sound copyright law. It is a law that would create uncertainty, would bring about selective enforcement, and, if widely unenforced, would breed disrespect for copyright law itself.

Thus, we believe that the practical problems that petitioner and his *amici* have described are too serious, too extensive, and too likely to come about for us to dismiss them as insignificant—particularly in light of the ever-growing importance of foreign trade to America. The upshot is that copyright-related consequences along with language, context, and interpretive canons argue strongly against a geographical interpretation of § 109(a).

III

Wiley and the dissent make several additional important arguments in favor of the geographical interpretation. *First*, they say that our *Quality King* decision strongly supports its geographical interpretation. In that case we asked whether the Act's "importation provision," now § 602(a)(1) (then § 602(a)), barred importation (without permission) of a copyrighted item (labels affixed to hair care products) where an American copyright owner authorized the first sale and export of hair care products with copyrighted labels made in the United States, and where a buyer sought to import them back into the United States without the copyright owner's permission.

We held that the importation provision did *not* prohibit sending the products back into the United States (without the copyright owner's permission). . . .

We pointed out that this section makes importation an infringement of the "exclusive right to distribute . . . *under 106.*" We noted that § 109(a)'s "first sale" doctrine limits the scope of the § 106 exclusive distribution right. We took as given the fact that the products at issue had at least once been sold. And we held that consequently, importation of the copyrighted labels does not violate § 602(a)(1).

In reaching this conclusion we endorsed *Bobbs-Merrill* and its statement that the copyright laws were not "intended to create a right which would permit the holder of the copyright to fasten, by notice in a book . . . a restriction upon the subsequent alienation of the subject-matter of copyright after the owner had parted with the title to one who had acquired full dominion over it." 210 U.S., at 349–350.

We also explained why we rejected the claim that our interpretation would make § 602(a)(1) pointless. Those advancing that claim had pointed out that the 1976 Copyright Act amendments retained a prior anti-piracy provision, prohibiting the importation of *pirated* copies. Thus, they said, § 602(a)(1) must prohibit the importation of lawfully made copies, for to allow the importation of those lawfully made copies *after a first sale,* as *Quality King's* holding would do, would leave § 602(a)(1) without much to prohibit. It would become superfluous, without any real work to do.

We do not believe that this argument is a strong one. Under *Quality King's* interpretation, § 602(a)(1) would still forbid importing (without permission, and subject to the exceptions in § 602(a)(3)) copies lawfully made abroad, for example, where (1) a foreign publisher operating as the licensee of an American publisher prints copies of a book overseas but, prior to any authorized sale, seeks to send them to the United States; (2) a foreign printer or other manufacturer (if not the "owner" for purposes of § 109(a), *e.g.,* before an authorized sale) sought to send copyrighted goods to the United States; (3) "a book publisher transports copies to a wholesaler" and the wholesaler (not yet the owner) sends them to the United States, see Copyright Law Revision, pt. 4, at 211 (giving this example); or (4) a foreign film distributor, having leased films for distribution, or any other licensee, consignee, or bailee sought to send them to the United States. . . . These examples show that § 602(a)(1) retains significance. We concede it has less significance than the dissent believes appropriate, but the dissent also adopts a construction of § 106(3) that "significantly curtails" § 109(a)'s effect, and so limits the scope of that provision to a similar, or even greater, degree.

In *Quality King* we rejected the "superfluous" argument for similar reasons. But, when rejecting it, we said that, where an author gives exclusive American distribution rights to an American publisher and exclusive British distribution rights to a British publisher, "presumably *only those [copies] made by the publisher of the United States edition would be 'lawfully made under this title'* within the meaning of § 109(a)." 523 U.S., at 148 (emphasis added). Wiley now argues that this phrase in the *Quality King* opinion means that books published abroad (under license) must fall outside the words "lawfully made under this title" and that we have consequently already given those words the geographical interpretation that it favors.

We cannot, however, give the *Quality King* statement the legal weight for which Wiley argues. The language "lawfully made under this title" was not at issue in *Quality King*; the point before us now was not then fully argued; we did not canvas the considerations we have here set forth; we there said nothing to suggest that the example assumes a "first sale"; and we there hedged our statement with the word "presumably." Most importantly, the statement is pure dictum. It is dictum contained in a rebuttal to a counterargument. And it is *unnecessary* dictum even in that respect. Is the Court having once written dicta calling a tomato a vegetable bound to deny that it is a fruit forever after?

To the contrary, we have written that we are not necessarily bound by dicta should more complete argument demonstrate that the dicta is not correct. And, given the bit part that our *Quality King* statement played in our *Quality King* decision, we believe the view of *stare decisis* set forth in these opinions applies to the matter now before us.

Second, Wiley and the dissent argue (to those who consider legislative history) that the Act's legislative history supports their interpretation. But the historical events to which it points took place more than a decade before the enactment of the Act and, at best, are inconclusive.

. . .

Third, Wiley and the dissent claim that a nongeographical interpretation will make it difficult, perhaps impossible, for publishers (and other copyright holders) to divide foreign and domestic markets. We concede that is so. A publisher may find it more difficult to charge different prices for the same book in different geographic markets. But we do not see how these facts help Wiley, for we can find no basic principle of copyright law that suggests that publishers are especially entitled to such rights.

The Constitution describes the nature of American copyright law by providing Congress with the power to "secur[e]" to "[a]uthors" "for limited [t]imes" the *"exclusive [r]ight to their . . . [w]ritings."* Art. I, § 8, cl. 8. The Founders, too, discussed the need to grant an author a limited right to exclude competition. But the Constitution's language nowhere suggests that its limited exclusive right should include a right to divide markets or a concomitant right to charge different purchasers different prices for the same book, say to increase or to maximize gain. Neither, to our knowledge, did any Founder make any such suggestion. We have found no precedent suggesting a legal preference for interpretations of copyright statutes that would provide for market divisions. Cf. Copyright Law Revision, pt. 2, at 194 (statement of Barbara Ringer, Copyright Office) (division of territorial markets was "primarily a matter of private contract").

To the contrary, Congress enacted a copyright law that (through the "first sale" doctrine) limits copyright holders' ability to divide domestic markets. And that limitation is consistent with antitrust laws that ordinarily forbid market divisions. Whether copyright owners should, or should not, have more than ordinary commercial power to divide international markets is a matter for Congress to decide. We do no more here than try to determine what decision Congress has taken.

Fourth, the dissent and Wiley contend that our decision launches United States copyright law into an unprecedented regime of "international exhaustion." But they point to nothing indicative of congressional intent in 1976. The dissent also claims that it is clear that the United States now opposes adopting such a regime, but the Solicitor General as *amicus* has taken no such position in this case. In fact, when pressed at oral argument, the Solicitor General stated that the consequences of Wiley's reading of the statute (perpetual downstream control) were "worse" than those of Kirtsaeng's reading (restriction of market segmentation). And the dissent's reliance on the Solicitor General's position in *Quality King* is undermined by his agreement in that case with our reading of § 109(a). Brief for United States as *Amicus Curiae* in *Quality King*, O. T. 1996, No. 1470, p. 30 ("When . . . Congress wishes to make the location of manufacture relevant to Copyright Act protection, it does so expressly"); *ibid.* (calling it "distinctly unlikely" that Congress would have provided an incentive for overseas manufacturing).

Moreover, the exhaustion regime the dissent apparently favors would provide that "the sale in one country of a good" does not "exhaus[t] the intellectual-property owner's right to control the distribution of that good elsewhere." But our holding in *Quality King* that § 109(a) is a defense in U.S. courts even when "the first sale occurred abroad," 523 U.S., at 145, n. 14, has already significantly eroded such a principle.

IV

For these reasons we conclude that the considerations supporting Kirtsaeng's nongeographical interpretation of the words "lawfully made under this title" are the more persuasive. The judgment of the Court of Appeals is reversed, and the case is remanded for further proceedings consistent with this opinion.

It is so ordered.

■ JUSTICE KAGAN, with whom JUSTICE ALITO joins, concurring.

I concur fully in the Court's opinion. Neither the text nor the history of 17 U.S.C. § 109(a) supports removing first-sale protection from every copy of a protected work manufactured abroad. I recognize, however, that the combination of today's decision and *Quality King Distribs. v. L'anza Research Int'l*, 523 U.S. 135 (1998), constricts the scope of § 602(a)(1)'s ban on unauthorized importation. I write to suggest that any problems associated with that limitation come not from our reading of § 109(a) here, but from *Quality King*'s holding that § 109(a) limits § 602(a)(1).

As the Court explains, the first-sale doctrine has played an integral part in American copyright law for over a century. See *Bobbs-Merrill Co. v. Straus*, 210 U.S. 339 (1908). No codification of the doctrine prior to 1976 even arguably limited its application to copies made in the United States. And nothing in the text or history of § 109(a)—the Copyright Act of 1976's first-sale provision—suggests that Congress meant to enact the new, geographical restriction John Wiley proposes, which at once would deprive American consumers of important rights and encourage copyright holders to manufacture abroad.

That said, John Wiley is right that the Court's decision, when combined with *Quality King*, substantially narrows § 602(a)(1)'s ban on unauthorized importation. *Quality King* held that the importation ban does not reach any copies receiving first-sale protection under § 109(a). So notwithstanding § 602(a)(1), an "owner of a particular copy . . . lawfully made under this title" can import that copy without the copyright owner's permission. § 109(a). In now holding that copies "lawfully made under this title" include copies manufactured abroad, we unavoidably diminish § 602(a)(1)'s scope—indeed, limit it to a fairly esoteric set of applications.

But if Congress views the shrinking of § 602(a)(1) as a problem, it should recognize *Quality King*—not our decision today—as the culprit. Here, after all, we merely construe § 109(a); *Quality King* is the decision holding that § 109(a) limits § 602(a)(1). Had we come out the opposite way in that case, § 602(a)(1) would allow a copyright owner to restrict the importation of copies irrespective of the first-sale doctrine.[1] That result would enable the copyright owner to divide international markets in the way John Wiley claims Congress intended when enacting § 602(a)(1). But it would do so without imposing downstream liability on those who purchase and resell in the United States copies that happen to have been manufactured abroad. In other words, that outcome would target unauthorized importers alone, and not the "libraries, used-book dealers, technology companies, consumer-goods retailers, and museums" with whom the Court today is rightly concerned. Assuming Congress adopted § 602(a)(1) to permit market segmentation, I suspect that is how Congress thought the provision would work—not by removing first-sale protection from every copy manufactured abroad (as John Wiley urges us to do here), but by enabling the copyright holder to control imports even when the first-sale doctrine applies (as *Quality King* now prevents).[2]

At bottom, John Wiley (together with the dissent) asks us to misconstrue § 109(a) in order to restore § 602(a)(1) to its purportedly rightful function of enabling copyright holders to segment international markets. I think John Wiley may have a point about what § 602(a)(1) was designed to do; that gives me pause about *Quality King*'s holding that the first-sale doctrine limits the importation ban's scope. But the Court today correctly declines the invitation to save § 602(a)(1) from *Quality King* by destroying the first-sale protection that § 109(a) gives to every owner of a copy manufactured abroad. That would swap one (possible) mistake for a much worse one, and make our reading of the statute only less reflective of Congressional intent. If Congress thinks copyright owners need greater power to restrict importation and thus divide markets, a ready solution is at hand—not the one John Wiley offers in this case, but the one the Court rejected in *Quality King*.

■ JUSTICE GINSBURG, with whom JUSTICE KENNEDY joins, and with whom JUSTICE SCALIA joins except as to Parts III and V-B-1, dissenting.

"In the interpretation of statutes, the function of the courts is easily stated. It is to construe the language so as to give effect to the intent of Congress." *United States* v. *American Trucking Assns., Inc.*, 310 U.S. 534, 542 (1940). Instead of adhering to the Legislature's design, the Court today adopts an interpretation of the Copyright Act at odds with

---

[1]   Although *Quality King* concluded that the statute's text foreclosed that outcome, the Solicitor General offered a cogent argument to the contrary. He reasoned that § 109(a) does not limit § 602(a)(1) because the former authorizes owners only to "sell" or "dispose" of copies—not to import them: The Act's first-sale provision and its importation ban thus regulate separate, non-overlapping spheres of conduct. That reading remains the Government's preferred way of construing the statute. See Tr. of Oral Arg. 44 ("[W]e think that we still would adhere to our view that section 109(a) should not be read as a limitation on section 602(a)(1)") . . .

[2]   Indeed, allowing the copyright owner to restrict imports irrespective of the first-sale doctrine—*i.e.,* reversing *Quality King*—would yield a far more sensible scheme of market segmentation than would adopting John Wiley's argument here. That is because only the former approach turns on the *intended market* for copies; the latter rests instead on their *place of manufacture*. To see the difference, imagine that John Wiley prints all its textbooks in New York, but wants to distribute certain versions only in Thailand. Without *Quality King*, John Wiley could do so—*i.e.,* produce books in New York, ship them to Thailand, and prevent anyone from importing them back into the United States. But with *Quality King*, that course is not open to John Wiley even under its reading of § 109(a): To prevent someone like Kirtsaeng from reimporting the books—and so to segment the Thai market—John Wiley would have to move its printing facilities abroad. I can see no reason why Congress would have conditioned a copyright owner's power to divide markets on outsourcing its manufacturing to a foreign country.

Congress' aim to protect copyright owners against the unauthorized importation of low-priced, foreign-made copies of their copyrighted works. The Court's bold departure from Congress' design is all the more stunning, for it places the United States at the vanguard of the movement for "international exhaustion" of copyrights—a movement the United States has steadfastly resisted on the world stage.

To justify a holding that shrinks to insignificance copyright protection against the unauthorized importation of foreign-made copies, the Court identifies several "practical problems." The Court's parade of horribles, however, is largely imaginary. Congress' objective in enacting 17 U.S.C. § 602(a)(1)'s importation prohibition can be honored without generating the absurd consequences hypothesized in the Court's opinion. I dissent from the Court's embrace of "international exhaustion," and would affirm the sound judgment of the Court of Appeals.

I

Because economic conditions and demand for particular goods vary across the globe, copyright owners have a financial incentive to charge different prices for copies of their works in different geographic regions. Their ability to engage in such price discrimination, however, is undermined if arbitrageurs are permitted to import copies from low-price regions and sell them in high-price regions. The question in this case is whether the unauthorized importation of foreign-made copies constitutes copyright infringement under U.S. law.

To answer this question, one must examine three provisions of Title 17 of the U.S. Code: § § 106(3), 109(a), and 602(a)(1). Section 106 sets forth the "exclusive rights" of a copyright owner, including the right "to distribute copies or phonorecords of the copyrighted work to the public by sale or other transfer of ownership, or by rental, lease, or lending." § 106(3). This distribution right is limited by § 109(a), which . . . codifies the "first sale doctrine," a doctrine articulated in *Bobbs-Merrill Co.* v. *Straus*, 210 U.S. 339, 349–351 (1908), which held that a copyright owner could not control the price at which retailers sold lawfully purchased copies of its work. . . .

Section 602(a)(1)—last, but most critical, of the three copyright provisions bearing on this case—is an importation ban. . . .

In *Quality King Distribs.* v. *L'anza Research Int'l*, 523 U.S. 135, 143–154 (1998), the Court held that a copyright owner's right to control importation under § 602(a)(1) is a component of the distribution right set forth in § 106(3) and is therefore subject to § 109(a)'s codification of the first sale doctrine. *Quality King* thus held that the importation of copies *made in the United States* but sold abroad did not rank as copyright infringement under § 602(a)(1). Important to the Court's holding, the copies at issue in *Quality King* had been " 'lawfully made under [Title 17]' "—a prerequisite for application of § 109(a). Section 602(a)(1), the Court noted, would apply to "copies that were 'lawfully made' not under the United States Copyright Act, but instead, under the law of some other country." *Id.*, at 147. Drawing on an example discussed during a 1964 public meeting on proposed revisions to the U.S. copyright laws, the Court stated:

"If the author of [a] work gave the exclusive United States distribution rights—enforceable under the Act—to the publisher of the United States edition and the exclusive British distribution rights to the publisher of the British edition, . . . presumably only those [copies] made by the publisher of the United States edition would be 'lawfully made under this title' within the meaning of § 109(a). The first sale doctrine would not provide the publisher of the British edition who decided to sell in the American market with a defense to an action under § 602(a) (or, for that matter, to an action under § 106(3), if there was a distribution of the copies)." *Id.*, at 148.

As the District Court and the Court of Appeals concluded, application of the *Quality King* analysis to the facts of this case would preclude any invocation of § 109(a). Petitioner Supap Kirtsaeng imported and then sold at a profit over 600 copies of copyrighted textbooks printed outside the United States by the Asian subsidiary of respondent John Wiley & Sons, Inc. (Wiley). In the words the Court used in *Quality King*, these copies "were 'lawfully made' not under the United States Copyright Act, but instead, under the law of some other country." Section 109(a) therefore does not apply, and Kirtsaeng's unauthorized importation constitutes copyright infringement under § 602(a)(1).

The Court does not deny that under the language I have quoted from *Quality King*, Wiley would prevail. Nevertheless, the Court dismisses this language, to which all Members of the *Quality King* Court subscribed, as ill-considered dictum. I agree that the discussion was dictum in the sense that it was not essential to the Court's judgment. But I disagree with the Court's conclusion that this dictum was ill considered. Instead, for the reasons explained below, I would hold, consistently with *Quality King*'s dictum, that § 602(a)(1) authorizes a copyright owner to bar the importation of a copy manufactured abroad for sale abroad.

II

The text of the Copyright Act demonstrates that Congress intended to provide copyright owners with a potent remedy against the importation of foreign-made copies of their copyrighted works. As the Court recognizes, this case turns on the meaning of the phrase "lawfully made under this title" in § 109(a). In my view, that phrase is most sensibly read as referring to instances in which a copy's creation is governed by, and conducted in compliance with, Title 17 of the U.S. Code. This reading is consistent with the Court's interpretation of similar language in other statutes.

Section 109(a), properly read, affords Kirtsaeng no defense against Wiley's claim of copyright infringement. The Copyright Act, it has been observed time and again, does not apply extraterritorially. The printing of Wiley's foreign-manufactured textbooks therefore was not governed by Title 17. The textbooks thus were not "lawfully made under [Title 17]," the crucial precondition for application of § 109(a). And if § 109(a) does not apply, there is no dispute that Kirtsaeng's conduct constituted copyright infringement under § 602(a)(1).

The Court's point of departure is similar to mine. According to the Court, the phrase " 'lawfully made under this title' means made 'in accordance with' or 'in compliance with' the Copyright Act." But the Court overlooks that, according to the very dictionaries it cites, the word "under" commonly signals a relationship of subjection, where one thing is governed or regulated by another. See Black's Law Dictionary 1525 (6th ed. 1990) ("under" "frequently" means "inferior" or "subordinate" (internal quotation marks omitted)); 18 Oxford English Dictionary 950 (2d ed. 1989) ("under" means, among other things, "[i]n accordance with (*some regulative power or principle*)" (emphasis added)). Only by disregarding this established meaning of "under" can the Court arrive at the conclusion that Wiley's foreign-manufactured textbooks were "lawfully made under" U.S. copyright law, even though that law did not govern their creation. It is anomalous, however, to speak of particular conduct as "lawful" under an inapplicable law. For example, one might say that driving on the right side of the road in England is "lawful" under U.S. law, but that would be so only because U.S. law has nothing to say about the subject. The governing law is English law, and English law demands that driving be done on the left side of the road.

The logical implication of the Court's definition of the word "under" is that *any* copy manufactured abroad—even a piratical one made without the copyright owner's authorization and in violation of the law of the country where it was created—would fall within the scope of § 109(a). Any such copy would have been made "in accordance with" or "in compliance with" the U.S. Copyright Act, in the sense that manufacturing the copy did not violate the Act (because the Act does not apply extraterritorially).

The Court rightly refuses to accept such an absurd conclusion. Instead, it interprets § 109(a) as applying only to copies whose making actually complied with Title 17, or would have complied with Title 17 had Title 17 been applicable (*i.e.*, had the copies been made in the United States). ("§ 109(a)'s 'first sale' doctrine would apply to copyrighted works as long as their manufacture met the requirements of American copyright law."). Congress, however, used express language when it called for such a counterfactual inquiry in 17 U.S.C. §§ 602(a)(2) and (b). See § 602(a)(2) ("Importation into the United States or exportation from the United States, without the authority of the owner of copyright under this title, of copies or phonorecords, the making of which either constituted an infringement of copyright, or *which would have constituted an infringement of copyright if this title had been applicable*, is an infringement of the exclusive right to distribute copies or phonorecords under section 106." (emphasis added)); § 602(b) ("In a case where the making of the copies or phonorecords *would have constituted an infringement of copyright if this title had been applicable*, their importation is prohibited." (emphasis added)). Had Congress intended courts to engage in a similarly hypothetical inquiry under § 109(a), Congress would presumably have included similar language in that section.

Not only does the Court adopt an unnatural construction of the § 109(a) phrase "lawfully made under this title." Concomitantly, the Court reduces § 602(a)(1) to insignificance. As the Court appears to acknowledge, the only independent effect § 602(a)(1) has under today's decision is to prohibit unauthorized importations carried out by persons who merely have possession of, but do not own, the imported copies. If this is enough to avoid rendering § 602(a)(1) entirely "superfluous," it hardly suffices to give the owner's importation right the scope Congress intended it to have. Congress used broad language in § 602(a)(1); it did so to achieve a broad objective. Had Congress intended simply to provide a copyright remedy against larcenous lessees, licensees, consignees, and bailees of films and other copyright-protected goods, it likely would have used language tailored to that narrow purpose. . . .

The Court's decision also overwhelms 17 U.S.C. § 602(a)(3)'s exceptions to § 602(a)(1)'s importation prohibition. 2 P. Goldstein, Copyright § 7.6.1.2(a), p. 7:141 (3d ed. 2012) (hereinafter Goldstein). Those exceptions permit the importation of copies without the copyright owner's authorization for certain governmental, personal, scholarly, educational, and religious purposes. Copies imported under these exceptions "will often be lawfully made gray market goods purchased through normal market channels abroad." 2 Goldstein § 7.6.1.2(a), at 7:141. But if, as the Court holds, such copies can in any event be imported by virtue of § 109(a), § 602(a)(3)'s work has already been done. For example, had Congress conceived of § 109(a)'s sweep as the Court does, what earthly reason would there be to provide, as Congress did in § 602(a)(3)(C), that a library may import "no more than five copies" of a non-audiovisual work for its "lending or archival purposes"?

The far more plausible reading of § § 109(a) and 602(a), then, is that Congress intended § 109(a) to apply to copies made in the United States, not to copies manufactured and sold abroad. That reading of the first sale and importation provisions leaves § 602(a)(3)'s exceptions with real, meaningful work to do. . . . In the range of circumstances covered by the exceptions, § 602(a)(3) frees individuals and entities who purchase foreign-made copies abroad from the requirement they would otherwise face under § 602(a)(1) of obtaining the copyright owner's permission to import the copies into the United States.

III

The history of § 602(a)(1) reinforces the conclusion I draw from the text of the relevant provisions: § 109(a) does not apply to copies manufactured abroad. . . .

[T]he legislative history of the Copyright Act of 1976 is hardly "inconclusive." To the contrary, it confirms what the plain text of the Act conveys: Congress intended § 602(a)(1) to provide copyright owners with a remedy against the unauthorized importation of foreign-made copies of their works, even if those copies were made and sold abroad with the copyright owner's authorization.

IV

Unlike the Court's holding, my position is consistent with the stance the United States has taken in international-trade negotiations. This case bears on the highly contentious trade issue of interterritorial exhaustion. The issue arises because intellectual property law is territorial in nature, which means that creators of intellectual property "may hold a set of parallel" intellectual property rights under the laws of different nations. Chiappetta, The Desirability of Agreeing to Disagree: The WTO, TRIPS, International IPR Exhaustion and a Few Other Things, 21 Mich. J. Int'l L. 333, 340–341 (2000) There is no international consensus on whether the sale in one country of a good incorporating protected intellectual property exhausts the intellectual property owner's right to control the distribution of that good elsewhere. Indeed, the members of the World Trade Organization, "agreeing to disagree," provided in Article 6 of the Agreement on Trade-Related Aspects of Intellectual Property Rights (TRIPS), Apr. 15, 1994, 33 I.L.M. 1197, 1200, that "nothing in this Agreement shall be used to address the issue of . . . exhaustion."

In the absence of agreement at the international level, each country has been left to choose for itself the exhaustion framework it will follow. One option is a national-exhaustion regime, under which a copyright owner's right to control distribution of a particular copy is exhausted only within the country in which the copy is sold. Another option is a rule of international exhaustion, under which the authorized distribution of a particular copy anywhere in the world exhausts the copyright owner's distribution right everywhere with respect to that copy. The European Union has adopted the intermediate approach of regional exhaustion, under which the sale of a copy anywhere within the European Economic Area exhausts the copyright owner's distribution right throughout that region. Section 602(a)(1), in my view, ties the United States to a national-exhaustion framework. The Court's decision, in contrast, places the United States solidly in the international-exhaustion camp.

Strong arguments have been made both in favor of, and in opposition to, international exhaustion. International exhaustion subjects copyright-protected goods to competition from lower priced imports and, to that extent, benefits consumers. Correspondingly, copyright owners profit from a national-exhaustion regime, which also enlarges the monetary incentive to create new copyrightable works.

Weighing the competing policy concerns, our Government reached the conclusion that widespread adoption of the international-exhaustion framework would be inconsistent with the long-term economic interests of the United States. See Brief for United States as *Amicus Curiae* in *Quality King*, O. T. 1997, No. 96–1470, pp. 22–26 (hereinafter *Quality King* Brief). Accordingly, the United States has steadfastly "taken the position in international trade negotiations that domestic copyright owners should . . . have the right to prevent the unauthorized importation of copies of their work sold abroad." *Id.* at 22. The United States has "advanced this position in multilateral trade negotiations," including the negotiations on the TRIPS Agreement. *Id.* at 24. It has also taken a dim view of our trading partners' adoption of legislation incorporating elements of international exhaustion.

Even if the text and history of the Copyright Act were ambiguous on the answer to the question this case presents—which they are not—I would resist a holding out of accord with the firm position the United States has taken on exhaustion in international negotiations. *Quality King*, I acknowledge, discounted the Government's concerns about potential inconsistency with United States obligations under certain bilateral trade agreements. That decision, however, dealt only with copyright-protected products made in the United States. *Quality King* left open the question whether owners of U.S. copyrights could retain control over the importation of copies manufactured and sold abroad—a point the Court obscures (arguing that *Quality King* "significantly eroded" the national-exhaustion principle that, in my view, § 602(a)(1) embraces). The Court today answers that question with a resounding "no," and in doing so, it risks undermining the United States' credibility on the world stage. While the Government has urged our trading partners to refrain from adopting international-exhaustion regimes that could benefit consumers within their borders but would impact adversely on intellectual-property producers in the United States, the Court embraces an international-exhaustion rule that could benefit U.S. consumers but would likely disadvantage foreign holders of U.S. copyrights. This dissonance scarcely enhances the United States' " role as a trusted partner in multilateral endeavors." *Vimar Seguros y Reaseguros, S. A. v. M/V Sky Reefer*, 515 U. S. 528, 539 (1995).

V

I turn now to the Court's justifications for a decision difficult to reconcile with the Copyright Act's text and history.

A

The Court asserts that its holding "is consistent with antitrust laws that ordinarily forbid market divisions." Section 602(a)(1), however, read as I do and as the Government does, simply facilitates copyright owners' efforts to impose "vertical restraints" on distributors of copies of their works. We have held that vertical restraints are not *per se* illegal under § 1 of the Sherman Act, 15 U.S.C. § 1, because such "restraints can have procompetitive effects." 551 U.S., at 881–882.

B

The Court sees many "horribles" following from a holding that the § 109(a) phrase "lawfully made under this title" does not encompass foreign-made copies. If § 109(a) excluded foreign-made copies, the Court fears, then copyright owners could exercise perpetual control over the downstream distribution or public display of such copies. A ruling in Wiley's favor, the Court asserts, would shutter libraries, put used-book dealers out of business, cripple art museums, and prevent the resale of a wide range of consumer goods, from cars to calculators. . . . Copyright law and precedent, however, erect barriers to the anticipated horribles.

1

Recognizing that foreign-made copies fall outside the ambit of § 109(a) would not mean they are forever free of the first sale doctrine. As earlier observed, see the Court stated that doctrine initially in its 1908 *Bobbs-Merrill* decision. At that time, no statutory provision expressly codified the first sale doctrine. Instead, copyright law merely provided that copyright owners had "the sole liberty of printing, reprinting, publishing, completing, copying, executing, finishing, and vending" their works. Copyright Act of 1891, § 1, 26 Stat. 1107.

In *Bobbs-Merrill*, the Court addressed the scope of the statutory right to "ven[d]." In granting that right, the Court held, Congress did not intend to permit copyright owners "to fasten . . . a restriction upon the subsequent alienation of the subject-matter of copyright after the owner had parted with the title to one who had acquired full dominion over it and had given a satisfactory price for it." 210 U.S., at 349–350. "[O]ne who has sold a copyrighted article . . . without restriction," the Court explained, "has parted with all right to control the sale of it." *Id.*, at 350. Thus, "[t]he purchaser of a book, once sold by authority of the owner of the copyright, may sell it again, although he could not publish a new edition of it." *Ibid.*

Under the logic of *Bobbs-Merrill*, the sale of a foreign-manufactured copy in the United States carried out with the copyright owner's authorization would exhaust the copyright owner's right to "vend" that copy. The copy could thenceforth be resold, lent out, or otherwise redistributed without further authorization from the copyright owner. Although § 106(3) uses the word "distribute" rather than "vend," there is no reason to think Congress intended the word "distribute" to bear a meaning different from the construction the Court gave to the word "vend" in *Bobbs-Merrill*. Thus, in accord with *Bobbs-Merrill*, the first authorized distribution of a foreign-made copy in the United States exhausts the copyright owner's distribution right under § 106(3). After such an authorized distribution, a library may lend, or a used-book dealer may resell, the foreign-made copy without seeking the copyright owner's permission.

For example, if Wiley, rather than Kirtsaeng, had imported into the United States and then sold the foreign-made textbooks at issue in this case, Wiley's § 106(3) distribution right would have been exhausted under the rationale of *Bobbs-Merrill*. Purchasers of the textbooks would thus be free to dispose of the books as they wished without first gaining a license from Wiley.

This line of reasoning, it must be acknowledged, significantly curtails the independent effect of § 109(a). If, as I maintain, the term "distribute" in § 106(3) incorporates the first sale doctrine by virtue of *Bobbs-Merrill*, then § 109(a)'s codification of that doctrine adds little to the regulatory regime.[20] Section 109(a), however, does serve as a statutory bulwark against courts deviating from *Bobbs-Merrill* in a way that increases copyright owners' control over downstream distribution, and legislative history indicates that is precisely the role Congress intended § 109(a) to play. Congress first codified the first sale doctrine in § 41 of the Copyright Act of 1909, 35 Stat. 1084. It did so, the House Committee Report on the 1909 Act explains, "in order to make . . . clear that [Congress had] no intention [of] enlarg[ing] in any way the construction to be given to the word 'vend.' " H. R. Rep. No. 2222, 60th Cong., 2d Sess., 19 (1909). According to the Committee Report, § 41 was "not intended to change [existing law] in any way." *Ibid.* The position I have stated and explained accords with this expression of congressional intent. In enacting § 41 and its successors, I would hold, Congress did not "change . . . existing law," *ibid.*, by stripping the word "vend" (and thus its substitute "distribute") of the limiting construction imposed in *Bobbs-Merrill*.

In any event, the reading of the Copyright Act to which I subscribe honors Congress' aim in enacting § 109(a) while the Court's reading of the Act severely diminishes § 602(a)(1)'s role. My position in no way tugs against the principle underlying § 109(a)—*i.e.*, that certain conduct by the copyright owner exhausts the owner's § 106(3) distribution right. The

---

[20] My position that *Bobbs-Merrill* lives on as a limiting construction of the § 106(3) distribution right does not leave § 109(a) with no work to do. There can be little doubt that the books at issue in *Bobbs-Merrill* were published and first sold in the United States. . . . Thus, exhaustion occurs under *Bobbs-Merrill* only when a copy is distributed within the United States with the copyright owner's permission, not when it is distributed abroad. But under § 109(a), as interpreted in *Quality King*, any authorized distribution of a U.S.-made copy, even a distribution occurring in a foreign country, exhausts the copyright owner's distribution right under § 106(3). Section 109(a) therefore provides for exhaustion in a circumstance not reached by *Bobbs-Merrill*.

Court, in contrast, fails to give meaningful effect to Congress' manifest intent in § 602(a)(1) to grant copyright owners the right to control the importation of foreign-made copies of their works.

2

Other statutory prescriptions provide further protection against the absurd consequences imagined by the Court. For example, § 602(a)(3)(C) permits "an organization operated for scholarly, educational, or religious purposes" to import, without the copyright owner's authorization, up to five foreign-made copies of a non-audiovisual work—notably, a book—for "library lending or archival purposes." But cf. [majority opinion] (suggesting that affirming the Second Circuit's decision might prevent libraries from lending foreign-made books).

The Court also notes that *amici* representing art museums fear that a ruling in Wiley's favor would prevent museums from displaying works of art created abroad. These *amici* observe that a museum's right to display works of art often depends on 17 U.S.C. § 109(c). That provision addresses exhaustion of a copyright owner's exclusive right under § 106(5) to publicly display the owner's work. Because § 109(c), like § 109(a), applies only to copies "lawfully made under this title," *amici* contend that a ruling in Wiley's favor would prevent museums from invoking § 109(c) with respect to foreign-made works of art.

Limiting § 109(c) to U.S.-made works, however, does not bar art museums from lawfully displaying works made in other countries. Museums can, of course, seek the copyright owner's permission to display a work. Furthermore, the sale of a work of art to a U.S. museum may carry with it an implied license to publicly display the work. Displaying a work of art as part of a museum exhibition might also qualify as a "fair use" under 17 U.S.C. § 107.

The Court worries about the resale of foreign-made consumer goods "contain[ing] copyrightable software programs or packaging." For example, the Court observes that a car might be programmed with diverse forms of software, the copyrights to which might be owned by individuals or entities other than the manufacturer of the car. Must a car owner, the Court asks, obtain permission from all of these various copyright owners before reselling her car? Although this question strays far from the one presented in this case and briefed by the parties, principles of fair use and implied license (to the extent that express licenses do not exist) would likely permit the car to be resold without the copyright owners' authorization.

Most telling in this regard, no court, it appears, has been called upon to answer any of the Court's "horribles" in an actual case. Three decades have passed since a federal court first published an opinion reading § 109(a) as applicable exclusively to copies made in the United States. See *Columbia Broadcasting System, Inc.* v. *Scorpio Music Distributors, Inc.*, 569 F. Supp. 47, 49 (ED Pa. 1983), summarily aff'd, 738 F.2d 424 (CA3 1984) (table). Yet Kirtsaeng and his supporting *amici* cite not a single case in which the owner of a consumer good authorized for sale in the United States has been sued for copyright infringement after reselling the item or giving it away as a gift or to charity. The absence of such lawsuits is unsurprising. Routinely suing one's customers is hardly a best business practice. Manufacturers, moreover, may be hesitant to do business with software programmers taken to suing consumers. Manufacturers may also insist that software programmers agree to contract terms barring such lawsuits.

The Court provides a different explanation for the absence of the untoward consequences predicted in its opinion—namely, that lower court decisions regarding the scope of § 109(a)'s first sale prescription have not been uniform. Uncertainty generated by these conflicting decisions, the Court notes, may have deterred some copyright owners from pressing infringement claims. But if, as the Court suggests, there are a multitude of copyright owners champing at the bit to bring lawsuits against libraries, art museums, and consumers in an effort to exercise perpetual control over the downstream distribution and public display of foreign-made copies, might one not expect that at least a handful of such lawsuits would have been filed over the past 30 years? The absence of such suits indicates that the "practical problems" hypothesized by the Court are greatly exaggerated.[27] They surely do not warrant disregarding Congress' intent, expressed in § 602(a)(1), to grant copyright owners the authority to bar the importation of foreign-made copies of their works.

VI

To recapitulate, the objective of statutory interpretation is "to give effect to the intent of Congress." Here, two congressional aims are evident. First, in enacting § 602(a)(1), Congress intended to grant copyright owners permission to segment international markets by barring the importation of foreign-made copies into the United States. Second, as codification of the first sale doctrine underscores, Congress did not want the exclusive distribution right conferred in § 106(3) to be boundless. Instead of harmonizing these objectives, the Court subordinates the first entirely to the second. It is unsurprising that none of the three major treatises on U.S. copyright law embrace the Court's construction of § 109(a). See 2 Nimmer § 8.12[B][6][c], at 8–184.34 to 8–184.35; 2 Goldstein § 7.6.1.2(a), at 7:141; 4 Patry §§ 13:22, 13:44, 13:44.10.

Rather than adopting the very international-exhaustion rule the United States has consistently resisted in international-trade negotiations, I would adhere to the national-exhaustion framework set by the Copyright Act's text and history. Under that regime, codified in § 602(a)(1), Kirtsaeng's unauthorized importation of the foreign-made textbooks involved in this case infringed Wiley's copyrights. I would therefore affirm the Second Circuit's judgment.

---

[27] It should not be overlooked that the ability to prevent importation of foreign-made copies encourages copyright owners such as Wiley to offer copies of their works at reduced prices to consumers in less developed countries who might otherwise be unable to afford them. The Court's holding, however, prevents copyright owners from barring the importation of such low-priced copies into the United States, where they will compete with the higher priced editions copyright owners make available for sale in this country. To protect their profit margins in the U.S. market, copyright owners may raise prices in less developed countries or may withdraw from such markets altogether. Such an outcome would disserve consumers—and especially students—in developing nations and would hardly advance the "American foreign policy goals" of supporting education and economic development in such countries. *Quality King* Brief 25–26.

QUESTION

Assume that Congress has the following objectives:

(a) give a copyright owner the ability to exclude others from importing into the United States from another country copies of her work, even if those copies were produced by or under the authority of the copyright owner in that other country;

(b) allow a traveler to bring copies into the United States from abroad in her luggage for personal use, and allow any U.S. resident or institution to import from abroad a limited number of copies for personal use or library lending; and

(c) allow any person in the United States who lends, rents, or resells copies of copyrighted works in the United States to do so if the particular copy was legitimately produced either in the United States or overseas.

Can you draft language to revise the statute in order to accomplish those objectives?

D. RIGHTS OF PUBLIC PERFORMANCE AND DISPLAY UNDER § 106(4), (5), (6)

2. "PUBLIC" PERFORMANCES UNDER THE 1976 ACT

Pages 759–65. Replace *Cartoon Network v. Cablevision* and QUESTIONS with the following:

American Broadcasting Cos., Inc. v. Aereo, Inc.

576 U.S. ___, 134 S.Ct. 2498 (2014).

■ JUSTICE BREYER delivered the opinion of the Court.

[In 2012, a New York City company called Aereo began a service that allowed subscribers, for a monthly fee, to access live (or recorded) broadcast television via a Web browser from the subscriber's Internet-connected mobile device. The service worked by allowing a subscriber to connect to a very small antenna, located at Aereo's data center, that receives broadcast television signals; no two subscribers were simultaneously connected to the same antenna. As a result, the same program could be received by multiple subscribers, but each transmission of the program was individualized, via the multiple personal antennae. Aereo claimed that it was not "performing" the television programming, but was merely providing equipment that enabled its subscribers to perform. A majority of the Supreme Court, 6–3, disagreed.]

. . .

Does Aereo "perform"? See § 106(4) ("[T]he owner of [a] copyright . . . has the exclusive righ[t] . . . to *perform* the copyrighted work publicly" (emphasis added)); § 101 ("To *perform* . . . a work 'publicly' means [among other things] to transmit . . . a performance . . . of the work . . . to the public . . . " (emphasis added)). Phrased another way, does Aereo "transmit . . . a performance" when a subscriber watches a show using Aereo's system, or is it only the subscriber who transmits? In Aereo's view, it does not perform. It does no more than supply equipment that "emulate[s] the operation of a home antenna and [digital video recorder (DVR)]." Brief for Respondent 41. Like a home antenna and DVR, Aereo's equipment simply responds to its subscribers' directives. So it is only the subscribers who "perform" when they use Aereo's equipment to stream television programs to themselves.

Considered alone, the language of the Act does not clearly indicate when an entity "perform[s]" (or "transmit[s]") and when it merely supplies equipment that allows others to do so. But when read in light of its purpose, the Act is unmistakable: An entity that engages in activities like Aereo's performs.

[The court reviewed two prior decisions—*Fortnightly Corp. v. United Artists Television, Inc.*, 392 U.S. 390 (1968), and *Teleprompter Corp. v. Columbia Broadcasting System, Inc.*, 415 U.S. 394 (1974)—in which it had held that under the 1909 Copyright Act cable television services were not "performing" the programming they retransmitted, and Congress' amendment of the Copyright Act in 1976 to clarify that the public performance right encompassed cable retransmissions.]

C.

This history makes clear that Aereo is not simply an equipment provider. Rather, Aereo, and not just its subscribers, "perform[s]" (or "transmit[s]"). Aereo's activities are substantially similar to those of the CATV companies that Congress amended the Act to reach. [Citation.] Aereo sells a service that allows subscribers to watch television programs, many of which are copyrighted, almost as they are being broadcast. In providing this service, Aereo uses its own equipment, housed in a centralized warehouse, outside of its users' homes. By means of its technology (antennas, transcoders, and servers), Aereo's system "receive[s] programs that have been released to the public and carr[ies] them by private channels to additional viewers." *Fortnightly*, 392 U. S., at 400. It "carr[ies] . . . whatever programs [it]receive[s]," and it offers "all the programming" of each over-the-air station it carries. *Id.*, at 392, 400.

Aereo's equipment may serve a "viewer function"; it may enhance the viewer's ability to receive a broadcaster's programs. It may even emulate equipment a viewer could use at home. But the same was true of the equipment that was before the Court, and ultimately before Congress, in *Fortnightly* and *Teleprompter*.

We recognize, and Aereo and the dissent emphasize, one particular difference between Aereo's system and the cable systems at issue in *Fortnightly* and *Teleprompter*. The systems in those cases transmitted constantly; they sent continuous programming to each subscriber's television set. In contrast, Aereo's system remains inert until a subscriber indicates that she wants to watch a program. Only at that moment, in automatic response to the subscriber's request, does Aereo's system activate an antenna and begin to transmit the requested program.

This is a critical difference, says the dissent. It means that Aereo's subscribers, not Aereo, "selec[t] the copyrighted content" that is "perform[ed]," (opinion of SCALIA, J.), and for that reason they, not Aereo, "transmit" the performance. Aereo is thus like "a copy shop that provides its patrons with a library card." A copy shop is not directly liable whenever a patron uses the shop's machines to "reproduce" copyrighted materials found in that library. . . . And by the same token, Aereo should not be directly liable whenever its patrons use its equipment to "transmit" copyrighted television programs to their screens.

In our view, however, the dissent's copy shop argument, in whatever form, makes too much out of too little. Given Aereo's overwhelming likeness to the cable companies targeted by the 1976 amendments, this sole technological difference between Aereo and traditional cable companies does not make a critical difference here. The subscribers of the *Fortnightly* and *Teleprompter* cable systems also selected what programs to display on their receiving sets. Indeed, as we explained in *Fortnightly*, such a subscriber "could choose any of the . . . programs he wished to view by simply turning the knob on his own television set." 392 U. S., at 392. The same is true of an Aereo subscriber. Of course, in *Fortnightly* the television signals, in a sense, lurked behind the screen, ready to emerge when the subscriber turned the knob. Here the signals pursue their ordinary course of travel through the universe until today's "turn of the knob"—a click on a website—activates machinery that intercepts and reroutes them to Aereo's subscribers over the Internet. But this difference means nothing to the subscriber. It means nothing to the broadcaster. We do not see how this single difference, invisible to subscriber and broadcaster alike, could transform a system that is for all practical purposes a traditional cable system into "a copy shop that provides its patrons with a library card."

In other cases involving different kinds of service or technology providers, a user's involvement in the operation of the provider's equipment and selection of the content transmitted may well bear on whether the provider performs within the meaning of the Act. But the many similarities between Aereo and cable companies, considered in light of Congress' basic purposes in amending the Copyright Act, convince us that this difference is not critical here. We conclude that Aereo is not just an equipment supplier and that Aereo "perform[s]."

. . .

III

Next, we must consider whether Aereo performs petitioners' works "publicly," within the meaning of the Transmit Clause. Under the Clause, an entity performs a work publicly when it "transmit[s] . . . a performance . . . of the work . . . to the public." § 101. Aereo denies that it satisfies this definition. It reasons as follows: First, the "performance" it "transmit[s]" is the performance created by its act of transmitting. And second, because each of these performances is capable of being received by one and only one subscriber, Aereo transmits privately, not publicly. Even assuming Aereo's first argument is correct, its second does not follow.

We begin with Aereo's first argument. What performance does Aereo transmit? Under the Act, "[t]o 'transmit' a performance . . . is to communicate it by any device or process whereby images or sounds are received beyond the place from which they are sent." *Ibid.* And "[t]o 'perform' " an audiovisual work means "to show its images in any sequence or to make the sounds accompanying it audible." *Ibid.*

Petitioners say Aereo transmits a *prior* performance of their works. Thus when Aereo retransmits a network's prior broadcast, the underlying broadcast (itself a performance) is the performance that Aereo transmits. Aereo, as discussed above, says the performance it transmits is the *new* performance created by its act of transmitting. That performance comes into existence when Aereo streams the sounds and images of a broadcast program to a subscriber's screen.

We assume *arguendo* that Aereo's first argument is correct. . . . But what about the Clause's further requirement that Aereo transmit a performance "to the public"? As we have said, an Aereo subscriber receives broadcast television signals with an antenna dedicated to him alone. Aereo's system makes from those signals a personal copy of the selected program. It streams the content of the copy to the same subscriber and to no one else. One and only one subscriber has the ability to see and hear each Aereo transmission. The fact that each transmission is to only one subscriber, in Aereo's view, means that it does not transmit a performance "to the public."

In terms of the Act's purposes, these differences do not distinguish Aereo's system from cable systems, which do perform "publicly." Viewed in terms of Congress' regulatory objectives, why should any of these technological differences matter? They concern the behind-the-scenes way in which Aereo delivers television programming to its viewers' screens. They do not render Aereo's commercial objective any different from that of cable companies. Nor do they significantly alter the viewing experience of Aereo's subscribers. Why would a subscriber who wishes to watch a television show care much whether images and sounds are delivered to his screen via a large multisubscriber antenna or one small dedicated antenna, whether they arrive instantaneously or after a few seconds' delay, or whether they are transmitted directly or after a personal copy is made? And why, if Aereo is right, could not modern CATV systems simply continue the same commercial and consumer-oriented activities, free of copyright restrictions, provided they substitute such new technologies for old? Congress would as much have intended to protect a copyright holder from the unlicensed activities of Aereo as from those of cable companies.

The text of the Clause effectuates Congress' intent. Aereo's argument to the contrary relies on the premise that "to transmit . . . a performance" means to make a single transmission. But the Clause suggests that an entity may transmit a performance through multiple, discrete transmissions. That is because one can "transmit" or "communicate" something through a *set* of actions. Thus one can transmit a message to one's friends, irrespective of whether one sends separate identical e-mails to each friend or a single e-mail to all at once. So can an elected official communicate an idea, slogan, or speech to her constituents, regardless of whether she communicates that idea, slogan, or speech during individual phone calls to each constituent or in a public square.

. . . [A]n entity may transmit a performance through one or several transmissions, where the performance is of the same work.

The Transmit Clause must permit this interpretation, for it provides that one may transmit a performance to the public "whether the members of the public capable of receiving the performance . . . receive it . . . at the same time or at different times." § 101. Were the words "to transmit . . . a performance" limited to a single act of communication, members of the public could not receive the performance communicated "at different times." Therefore, in light of the purpose and text of the Clause, we conclude that when an entity communicates the same contemporaneously perceptible images and sounds to multiple people, it transmits a performance to them regardless of the number of discrete communications it makes.

We do not see how the fact that Aereo transmits via personal copies of programs could make a difference. The Act applies to transmissions "by means of any device or process." *Ibid.* And retransmitting a television program using user-specific copies is a "process" of transmitting a performance. A "cop[y]" of a work is simply a "material objec[t] . . . in which a work is fixed . . . and from which the work can be perceived, reproduced, or otherwise communicated." *Ibid.* So whether Aereo transmits from the same or separate copies, it performs the same work; it shows the same images and makes audible the same sounds. Therefore, when Aereo streams the same television program to multiple subscribers, it "transmit[s] . . . a performance" to all of them.

Moreover, the subscribers to whom Aereo transmits television programs constitute "the public." Aereo communicates the same contemporaneously perceptible images and sounds to a large number of people who are unrelated and unknown to each other. This matters because, although the Act does not define "the public," it specifies that an entity performs publicly when it performs at "any place where a substantial number of persons outside of a normal circle of a family and its social acquaintances is gathered." *Ibid.* The Act thereby suggests that "the public" consists of a large group of people outside of a family and friends.

Neither the record nor Aereo suggests that Aereo's subscribers receive performances in their capacities as owners or possessors of the underlying works. This is relevant because when an entity performs to a set of people, whether they constitute "the public" often depends upon their relationship to the underlying work. When, for example, a valet parking attendant returns cars to their drivers, we would not say that the parking service provides cars "to the public." We would say that it provides the cars to their owners. We would say that a car dealership, on the other hand, does provide cars to the public, for it sells cars to individuals who lack a pre-existing relationship to the cars. Similarly, an entity that transmits a performance to individuals in their capacities as owners or possessors does not perform to "the public," whereas an entity like Aereo that transmits to large numbers of paying subscribers who lack any prior relationship to the works does so perform.

Finally, we note that Aereo's subscribers may receive the same programs at different times and locations. This fact does not help Aereo, however, for the Transmit Clause expressly provides that an entity may perform publicly "whether the members of the public capable of receiving the performance . . . receive it in the same place or in separate places and at the same time or at different times." *Ibid.* In other words, "the public" need not be situated together, spatially or temporally. For these reasons, we conclude that Aereo transmits a performance of petitioners' copyrighted works to the public, within the meaning of the Transmit Clause.

IV

Aereo and many of its supporting *amici* argue that to apply the Transmit Clause to Aereo's conduct will impose copyright liability on other technologies, including new technologies, that Congress could not possibly have wanted to reach. We agree that Congress, while intending the Transmit Clause to apply broadly to cable companies and their equivalents, did not intend to discourage or to control the emergence or use of different kinds of technologies. But we do not believe that our limited holding today will have that effect.

For one thing, the history of cable broadcast transmissions that led to the enactment of the Transmit Clause informs our conclusion that Aereo "perform[s]," but it does not determine whether different kinds of providers in different contexts also "perform." For another, an entity only transmits a performance when it communicates contemporaneously perceptible images and sounds of a work. See Brief for Respondent 31 ("[I]f a distributor . . . sells [multiple copies of a digital video disc] by mail to consumers, . . . [its] distribution of the DVDs merely makes it possible for the recipients to perform the work themselves—it is not a 'device or process' by which the *distributor* publicly performs the work" (emphasis in original)).

Further, we have interpreted the term "the public" to apply to a group of individuals acting as ordinary members of the public who pay primarily to watch broadcast television programs, many of which are copyrighted. We have said that it does not extend to those who act as owners or possessors of the relevant product. And we have not considered whether the public performance right is infringed when the user of a service pays primarily for something other than the transmission of copyrighted works, such as the remote storage of content. See Brief for United States as *Amicus Curiae* 31 (distinguishing cloud-based storage services because they "offer consumers more numerous and convenient means of playing back copies that the consumers have *already* lawfully acquired" (emphasis in original)). In addition, an entity does not transmit to the public if it does not transmit to a substantial number of people outside of a family and its social circle.

. . .

We cannot now answer more precisely how the Transmit Clause or other provisions of the Copyright Act will apply to technologies not before us. We agree with the Solicitor General that "[q]uestions involving cloud computing, [remote storage] DVRs, and other novel issues not before the Court, as to which 'Congress has not plainly marked [the] course,' should await a case in which they are squarely presented." Brief for United States as *Amicus Curiae* 34. . . . And we note that, to the extent commercial actors or other interested entities may be concerned with the relationship between the development and use of such technologies and the Copyright Act, they are of course free to seek action from Congress. . . .

■ JUSTICE SCALIA, with whom JUSTICE THOMAS and JUSTICE ALITO join, dissenting.

. . .

The Networks claim that Aereo *directly* infringes their public-performance right. Accordingly, the Networks must prove that Aereo "perform[s]" copyrighted works, § 106(4), when its subscribers log in, select a channel, and push the "watch" button. That process undoubtedly results in a performance; the question is *who* does the performing. See *Cartoon Network LP, LLLP* v. *CSC Holdings, Inc.*, 536 F. 3d 121, 130 (CA2 2008). If Aereo's subscribers perform but Aereo does not, the claim necessarily fails.

The Networks' claim is governed by a simple but profoundly important rule: A defendant may be held directly liable only if it has engaged in volitional conduct that violates the Act. This requirement is firmly grounded in the Act's text, which defines "perform" in active, affirmative terms: One "perform[s]" a copyrighted "audiovisual work," such as a movie or news broadcast, by "show[ing] its images in any sequence" or "mak[ing] the sounds accompanying it audible." § 101. And since the Act makes it unlawful to copy or perform copyrighted works, not to copy or perform in general, see § 501(a), the volitional-act requirement demands conduct directed to the plaintiff's copyrighted material. Every Court of Appeals to have considered an automated-service provider's direct liability for copyright infringement has adopted that rule. Although we have not opined on the issue, our cases are fully consistent with a volitional-conduct requirement. . . .

. . .

A comparison between copy shops and video-on-demand services illustrates the point. A copy shop rents out photocopiers on a per-use basis. One customer might copy his 10-year-old's drawings—a perfectly lawful thing to do—while another might duplicate a famous artist's copyrighted photographs—a use clearly prohibited by § 106(1). Either way, *the customer* chooses the content and activates the copying function; the photocopier does nothing except in response to the customer's commands. Because the shop plays no role in selecting the content, it cannot be held directly liable when a customer makes an infringing copy.

Video-on-demand services, like photocopiers, respond automatically to user input, but they differ in one crucial respect: *They choose the content.* When a user signs in to Netflix, for example, "thousands of . . . movies [and] TV episodes" carefully curated by Netflix are "available to watch instantly." That selection and arrangement by the service provider constitutes a volitional act directed to specific copyrighted works and thus serves as a basis for direct liability.

The distinction between direct and secondary liability would collapse if there were not a clear rule for determining whether *the defendant* committed the infringing act. The volitional-conduct requirement supplies that rule; its purpose is not to excuse defendants from accountability, but to channel the claims against them into the correct analytical track. Thus, in the example given above, the fact that the copy shop does not choose the content simply means that its culpability will be assessed using secondary-liability rules rather than direct-liability rules.

II.   Application to Aereo

So which is Aereo: the copy shop or the video-on-demand service? In truth, it is neither. Rather, it is akin to a copy shop that provides its patrons with a library card. Aereo offers access to an automated system consisting of routers, servers, transcoders, and dime-sized antennae.

Like a photocopier or VCR, that system lies dormant until a subscriber activates it. When a subscriber selects a program, Aereo's system picks up the relevant broadcast signal, translates its audio and video components into digital data, stores the data in a user-specific file, and transmits that file's contents to the subscriber via the Internet—at which point the subscriber's laptop, tablet, or other device displays the broadcast just as an ordinary television would. The result of that process fits the statutory definition of a performance to a tee: The subscriber's device "show[s]" the broadcast's "images" and "make[s] the sounds accompanying" the broadcast "audible." § 101. The only question is whether those performances are the product of Aereo's volitional conduct.

They are not. Unlike video-on-demand services, Aereo does not provide a prearranged assortment of movies and television shows. Rather, it assigns each subscriber an antenna that—like a library card— can be used to obtain whatever broadcasts are freely available. Some of those broadcasts are copyrighted; others are in the public domain. The key point is that subscribers call all the shots: Aereo's automated system does not relay any program, copyrighted or not, until a subscriber selects the program and tells Aereo to relay it. Aereo's operation of that system is a volitional act and a but-for cause of the resulting performances, but, as in the case of the copy shop, that degree of involvement is not enough for direct liability. . . .

. . .

[On remand, the trial judge rejected Aereo's argument that it was not infringing because of Section 111 of the Copyright Act, which grants cable television operators a compulsory license for certain cable retransmissions. 112 U.S.P.Q.2d 1582 (S.D.N.Y. 2014). (Congress enacted the Section 111 license in the 1976 Act, at the same time that it revised the understanding of public performance to reject the Supreme Court's interpretation that cable systems were not within the 1909 Act's public performance right.) The court rejected Aereo's argument that "simply because an entity performs copyrighted works in a way similar to cable systems it must then be deemed a cable system for all other purposes of the Copyright Act," noting that while the *Aereo* Court had discussed Aereo's *similarity* to CATV systems, it had not stated that Aereo *was* a cable system. Essentially, the court concluded, "while all cable systems may perform publicly, not all entities that perform publicly are necessarily cable systems." Instead, the court ruled that binding Second Circuit precedent established that the Section 111 license does not extend to Internet transmissions. *WPIX, Inc. v. ivi, Inc.*, 691 F.3d 275 (2d Cir. 2012). The court therefore granted the copyright owners a preliminary injunction against Aereo's service.]

QUESTIONS

1. What are the implications of the majority and dissenting views of "to perform"? Is the dissent's "volition" approach incompatible with basing direct liability on the offering of access to copyrighted works? Is there a textual basis in the Copyright Act for a "volition" requirement?

2. Does the court require that the entity engaging in a public performance have in fact made a transmission, or does offering a transmission suffice?

3. Who is "the public" to which a public performance is transmitted?

4. What does the Court mean by its distinction of "subscribers [who] receive performances in their capacities as owners or possessors of the underlying works."?

5. If Aereo too closely resembled a cable operator to be held not to be publicly performing the broadcast content, what other services may be found, under the Supreme Court's interpretation of the "transmit clause" to be publicly performing? What if the service does not offer streams until some portion of the original broadcast has been transmitted? What if the service's streams commence only after the initial broadcast has been completed? What if the service, in lieu of transmitting streams of the broadcast content, records the content—at the subscriber's request—and then sends her a "mute" file (a download); the "performance" of the work will originate from the subscriber's computer or device?

6. Recall *ReDigi, supra* this Supplement, page 113. After *Aereo*, can you think of a way to redesign ReDigi's service without triggering any of the exclusive rights under section 106?

Fox Broadcasting Co. v. DISH Network LLC, 114 U.S.P.Q.2d 1100 (C.D.Cal. 2015). In this litigation, involving the use of the defendant's "Hopper" digital videorecorder (DVR) with technology that allows a user to "sling" content to a mobile device, the court addressed the scope of the public performance right after *Aereo*.

1. The Hopper and the Hopper with Sling

In January of 2012, DISH announced the Hopper "Whole Home" High Definition DVR to its subscribers. One year later, in January of 2013, DISH debuted the "Hopper with Sling," which is DISH's next-generation Hopper. The new Hopper includes a faster processor, built-in wireless capability, [and] built-in Sling functionality . . .

2. Sling Technology

DISH offers various products, including the "Hopper with Sling," that make use of "Sling" technology. Sling technology allows consumers to view television content from their home [set-top boxes (STBs)] over the Internet by use of a device that communicates using Internet protocols, such as a laptop, tablet, or smartphone.

Sling technology involves the use of both hardware and software. The Sling hardware is a computer chip that rapidly "transcodes" small packets of audiovisual data from either the live satellite signal coming off of the Hopper tuner or from a pre-existing Hopper DVR recording. Using the Sling hardware together with the Sling software loaded on a tablet, smartphone, laptop, or personal computer, the subscriber can send the television content to herself to watch in another location. Sling can only be used by a subscriber to gain access to her own home STB/DVR and the content on that box, either live or recorded. The programming content to which DISH subscribers have access using Sling is that which they have already received via their DISH subscription.

DISH has a "SlingService Services Agreement" with Sling Media, Inc., which is owned by EchoStar.

It is undisputed that the Sling process or architecture that enables DISH subscribers to watch live TV on DISH Anywhere requires the operation of various servers and equipment located outside the home. The parties dispute whether, when a subscriber requests television content using DISH Anywhere, the programming travels entirely "point-to-point" over the Internet or home WiFi from the subscriber's STB to her Internet-connected device without any assistance from DISH's, EchoStar's, or Sling Media's external equipment and technicians, or whether that external equipment and those technicians are necessary for DISH Anywhere to function.

3. DISH Anywhere

DISH Anywhere refers to Sling technology that enables subscribers who have either a Hopper with Sling or a Sling Adapter to access live and recorded programming from their STBs remotely on computers and mobile devices. In its quick-start features guide for the Hopper with Sling, DISH states that "[o]nly Dish Anywhere lets you access all of your live TV channels . . . while on the go via your Internet-connected smartphone, computer, or tablet."

To use DISH Anywhere, a subscriber must either log in to DISHAnywhere.com on a personal computer and download a browser extension called SlingPlayer or download the free DISH Anywhere app for a tablet or smartphone. The subscriber may then send herself live or recorded television on her computer or mobile device. When a DISH subscriber logs into the DISH Anywhere website and clicks "Live TV," she will see a progress bar that shows the process of sending the video to the transcoder, starting to transcode, sending the information to the client, buffering it, and then starting to display it to the end user.

A subscriber need only create an online ID and download the SlingPlayer once. A subscriber who is not in good standing with DISH because she has not paid her bill (or multiple bills) cannot use the Hopper with Sling to activate DISH Anywhere.

DISH subscribers can *stream* certain live programming (as opposed to viewing via a Sling-enabled STB, as described above) of certain cable television networks—but *not* Fox programming—on the DISHAnywhere.com website under the "Shows" tab. The networks available for live streaming include USA, MSNBC and others, but not Fox. This programming stream does originate from centralized servers, but does not involve Sling technology or require a Sling-enabled STB.

. . .

Fox contends that DISH has publicly performed Fox's copyrighted works by streaming them over the Internet to DISH subscribers using DISH Anywhere with Sling. The Copyright Act grants the owner of a copyright the "exclusive right" to "perform the copyrighted work publicly." 17 U.S.C. § 106(4). . . .

For the Transmit Clause to apply, there must be (1) a transmission or other communication; (2) of a performance of a work; (3) to the public. Not all transmissions are performances, and not all performances are transmissions. *See United States v. Am. Soc. of Composers, Authors, Publishers,* 627 F.3d 64, 74 (2d Cir.2010) ("transmittal without a performance does not constitute a 'public performance.' ").

It is undisputed that, under the 2002 [Retransmission Consent] Agreement [between DISH and Fox], DISH has the right to retransmit Fox programming to its subscribers via satellite. This initial transmission clearly constitutes a public performance under the Copyright Act in that DISH (1) shows images and sounds from an audiovisual work; (2) beyond the place from which they are sent; (3) to a large number of people outside of a normal circle of family and friends. DISH has a valid license for this initial public performance. The salient question is whether any of the additional products or features that DISH offers to its subscribers—DISH Anywhere with Sling Technology, in particular—constitute a public performance that infringes on Fox's exclusive copyrights.

a. DISH Anywhere Does Not "Publicly Perform" Fox's Copyrighted Works

Fox contends that the Supreme Court's recent decision in *American Broadcasting Companies, Inc. v. Aereo, Inc.* is a game-changer that governs the outcome of its copyright claims in this case. The Court disagrees.

In *Aereo,* the Supreme Court held that Aereo, a service which streamed broadcast television programming to subscribers over the Internet, "publicly performed" the programming as defined by the Transmit Clause. 573 U.S. ___, 134 S.Ct. 2498, 2503 (2014). Aereo neither owned the copyright to the broadcast works nor held a license from the copyright owners to perform those works publicly. *Id.*

. . . The Supreme Court determined that Aereo "performed" the copyrighted material. . . . The Court noted that "[i]n other cases involving different kinds of service or technology providers, a user's involvement in the operation of the provider's equipment and selection of the content transmitted may well bear on whether the provider performs within the meaning of the Act." In an effort to cabin the potential overreach of its decision, however, the Court specifically cautioned that its "limited holding" should not be construed to "discourage or to control the emergence or use of different kinds of technologies." *Id.* at 2510. The Court specifically reserved "questions involving cloud computing, remote storage DVRs, and other novel issues not before the Court, as to which Congress has not plainly marked the course," as not before the Court. *Id.* at 2510 (internal quotation marks omitted).

The Supreme Court did not expressly address the general volitional conduct requirement for direct liability under the Copyright Act. The volitional conduct doctrine is a significant and long-standing rule, adopted by all Courts of Appeal to have considered it, and it would be folly to presume that *Aereo* categorically jettisoned it by implication. *See Fox Broadcasting Co. v. Dish Network, LLC,* 723 F.3d 1067, 1073–1074 (9th Cir.2013); *Cartoon Network LP, LLP v. CSC Holdings, Inc.* *("Cablevision"),* 536 F.3d 121, 131 (2d Cir.2008); *Parker v. Google,* 242 Fed. App'x 833, 837 (3d Cir.2007); *CoStar Group, Inc. v. LoopNet, Inc.,* 373 F.3d 544, 550 (4th Cir.2004).

The *Aereo* majority's analysis can be reconciled with the volitional-conduct requirement for direct infringement. The *Aereo* Court distinguishes between an entity that "engages in activities like Aereo's" and one that "merely supplies equipment that allows others to do so." *Id.* at 2504. The Court held that a sufficient likeness to a cable company amounts to a presumption of direct performance, but the distinction between active and passive participation remains a central part of the analysis of an alleged infringement.

The *Aereo* Court cited three points of comparison that established Aereo's "overwhelming likeness" to traditional cable providers: (1) Aereo sold a service that allowed subscribers to watch television programs almost as they were being broadcast; (2) Aereo used its own equipment, housed in a centralized warehouse, outside of its users' homes; and (3) by means of its technology (antennas, transcoders, and servers), Aereo's system received programs that had been released to the public and carried them by private channels to the additional viewers. 134 S.Ct. at 2506.

DISH Anywhere also allows subscribers to watch television programs almost as they are being broadcast. DISH Anywhere depends on equipment and technology both inside and outside of the user's home.

DISH does not, however, receive programs that have been released to the public and then carry them by private channels to additional viewers in the same sense that Aereo did. DISH has a *license* for the analogous initial retransmission of the programming to users via satellite. Aereo streamed a subscriber-specific copy of its programing *from Aereo's hard drive* to the subscriber's screen via individual satellite when the subscriber requested it, whereas DISH Anywhere can only be used by a subscriber to gain access to *her own home STB/DVR* and the authorized recorded content on that box. Any subsequent transfer of the programming by DISH Anywhere takes place after the subscriber has validly received it, whereas Aereo transmitted its programming to subscribers directly, without a license to do so.

Once the DISH subscribers receive the authorized programming, DISH Anywhere facilitates the transfer of those recordings in the STB/DVR to other devices owned by the subscriber. While the parties dispute the extent to which external equipment and employees are involved in this transfer process, there is no material dispute that . . . the programming does not *originate* from the external servers. The ultimate function of DISH Anywhere is to transmit programming that is already legitimately on a user's in-home hardware to a user's Internet-connected mobile device. Relying on external servers and equipment to ensure that content travels between those devices properly does not transform that service into a traditional cable company. *Aereo* 's holding that entities bearing an "overwhelming likeness" to cable companies publicly perform within the meaning of the Transmit Clause does not extend to DISH Anywhere.

b. Direct Infringement: DISH Does Not Engage in Volitional Conduct to Infringe

As discussed above, volitional conduct remains the touchstone of direct infringement. If any public performance occurs when subscribers use DISH Anywhere, DISH may be directly liable if it engages in sufficient volitional conduct enabling that performance. As the Ninth Circuit noted at the preliminary injunction stage in this case, direct infringement turns on *who* commits the infringement. *Fox Broadcasting,* 723 F.3d at 1074. "[O]perating a system . . . at the user's command does not mean that the system operator, rather than the user, caused the [infringement]." *Id.*

To use DISH Anywhere, a subscriber must create an online ID and download the SlingPlayer. DISH's system verifies the subscriber's log-in information, and verifies that the subscriber is in good standing and has paid her bills. The subscriber logs in to DISH Anywhere or opens the DISH Anywhere app, selects the television program she would like to watch, and requests that the live or recorded television programming be sent from the STB in her home to her computer or mobile device. The programming either travels "point-to-point" between the STB and the mobile device [Redacted]. This process depends to some extent on external equipment and services provided by DISH, but it is the user who initiates the process, selects the content, and receives the transmission. No DISH employee actively responds to the user's specific request or directly intervenes in the process of sending the programming between the devices. DISH subscribers, not DISH, engage in the volitional conduct necessary for any direct infringement.

c. Secondary Infringement: DISH Subscribers do not "Publicly" Perform by using DISH Anywhere

DISH may still be liable for secondary liability if its users are engaging in direct infringement by using DISH Anywhere. . . .

DISH Anywhere users "transmit" a "performance" within the meaning of Section 101 of the Copyright Act, in that they use a device or process to transmit images and sounds from audiovisual work beyond the place from which they are sent. The remaining question is whether they perform a copyrighted work "publicly."

In rejecting Aereo's argument that it did not transmit a performance "to the public," the *Aereo* Court noted that nothing in the record before it suggested that the subscribers received the performances "in their capacities as owners or possessors of the underlying works," and that this factor could affect whether or not the subscribers constituted "the public." 134 S.Ct. at 2510.

DISH subscribers are not "owners" of the copyrighted programming. DISH has expressly disclaimed any ownership rights in the underlying programming, and agreed to various restrictions on its use of the material as a condition of the license. DISH is a licensee, and therefore cannot transfer title or ownership to its subscribers.

DISH subscribers are, however, valid "possessors" of the copyrighted works that are stored in the STB in their home. *See Sony Corp. of Am. v. Universal City Studios, Inc.,* 464 U.S. 417, 456 (1984). DISH has a valid license and is permitted to transmit Fox programming to subscribers accordingly.

When an individual DISH subscriber transmits programming *rightfully in her possession* to another device, that transmission does not travel to "a large number of people who are unknown to each other." The transmission travels either to the subscriber herself or to someone in her household using an authenticated device. This is simply not a "public" performance within the meaning of the Transmit Clause. Because DISH Anywhere subscribers do not directly infringe the public performance right, DISH cannot be liable for secondary infringement.

The Court **GRANTS** DISH's motion for summary judgment as to the claim for copyright infringement by DISH Anywhere with Sling and **DENIES** Fox's motion for partial summary judgment as to the same.

For a discussion of copyright claims related to other features of DISH's Hopper service, see the excerpt in Chapter 7.C.3, infra this Supplement, page 205. In that regard, think again after reading that excerpt about whether the Hopper user is in "rightful possession" of the programming she records.

3. PERFORMING RIGHTS SOCIETIES

Page 772. Add after the carryover paragraph:

Two court decisions in 2013 addressed attempts by music copyright owners to require digital music services to license performance rights directly from them, rather than from the performing rights societies. *In re Pandora Media, Inc.,* 2013 WL 5211927 (S.D.N.Y. 2013); *Broadcast Music, Inc. v. Pandora Media, Inc.,* 109 U.S.P.Q.2d 1964 (S.D.N.Y. 2013). In 2011, in response to pressure from music publishers, ASCAP modified its rules to allow any ASCAP member to withdraw from ASCAP the right to license that member's musical works to "new media" users— essentially, digital music services. BMI made similar changes to its rules effective January 1, 2013. Both societies retained the right to grant performance licenses in the works of withdrawing members to all other types of uses. Sony/EMI became the first publisher to withdraw "new media" rights from both ASCAP and BMI. In rate dispute proceedings between digital music service Pandora and both societies, the rate court faced the question of whether withdrawals of "new media" rights by

Sony/EMI and other publishers were effective and disabled ASCAP and BMI from granting public performance rights to Pandora.

In September 2013, in the ASCAP rate proceeding, the court concluded that the consent decree governing ASCAP, which requires the society to license to all applicants "all of the works in the ASCAP repertory," meant that any work in which an ASCAP member had granted ASCAP any rights was "in the ASCAP repertory" and must be licensed to "new media" users just as to other users. The court concluded that under the consent decree "ASCAP did not have the right to permit the partial withdrawals of rights at issue and thereby acquiesce to a regime in which some music users could not obtain full public performance rights to works in the ASCAP repertory." 2013 WL 5211927 at *7.

In May 2015, the Second Circuit affirmed the district court's ruling and the invalidity of the attempted partial withdrawals. *Pandora Media, Inc. v. ASCAP*, 785 F.3d 73 (2d Cir. 2015).

In December 2013, a different judge on the same court reached a different conclusion as to BMI. The court concluded that the BMI consent decree "requires that all compositions in the BMI repertory by offered to all applicants" and that "[b]y placing a composition in the BMI repertory, the [BMI member] routinely authorizes its inclusion in blanket licenses of BMI's whole repertory to all applicants." 109 U.S.P.Q.2d at 1967. The court viewed copyright law as giving BMI members the right to withdraw from BMI the power to license their works to "new media" users. But the consequence of that withdrawal—preventing BMI from licensing these works to "new media" users—meant that for the works whose digital rights were withdrawn, "their availability does not meet the standards of the BMI Consent Decree, and they cannot be held in BMI's repertory. Since they are not in BMI's repertory, BMI cannot deal in or license those compositions to anyone." *Id.* The court noted that its decision did not affect the right to perform withdrawn compositions under existing BMI licenses because "the rights they granted are not to be altered retroactively" and therefore "they continue according to their terms until their expiration." *Id.* at 1968.

How will the decision in the BMI case affect users who want authorization to publicly perform copyrighted compositions by non-digital means? How will the decision affect the prices BMI can charge to over-the-air radio and TV broadcasters, and to bars, restaurants, and retail stores that play copyrighted music? How should such users decide which music to play going forward? And how will the decision affect the royalties that BMI members who have withdrawn "new media" rights will receive?

4. THE DIGITAL PERFORMANCE RIGHT IN SOUND RECORDINGS . . . AND ITS LIMITATIONS

Page 778. Add before the last paragraph:

Public performances of pre-1972 sound recordings. Recall that only sound recordings fixed on or after February 15, 1972, are subject to *federal* copyright law. *See supra*, this Supplement, pages 40-41. When Congress granted federal copyright to sound recordings, it did so only prospectively, and expressly left state protection for existing sound recordings unpreempted by federal copyright law until Feb. 15, 2067. 17 U.S.C. § 301(c). At the time that Congress granted federal protection to sound recordings, some states offered creators of sound recordings some protection against those who produced "bootleg" copies of such sound recordings, but not much other protection was available.

In 2014, federal district courts in California and New York confronted the question of whether those states' laws granted an exclusive public performance right in pre-1972 sound recordings. *Flo & Eddie, Inc. v. Sirius XM Radio, Inc.*, 62 F.Supp.3d 325 (S.D.N.Y. 2014); *Flo & Eddie, Inc. v. Sirius XM Radio, Inc.*, 112 U.S.P.Q.2d 1307 (C.D. Cal. 2014). Flo & Eddie owns sound recordings made in the 1960s by the rock group The Turtles, including the hit "Happy Together." The company sued Sirius XM Radio, alleging, *inter alia*, that playing those sound recordings on its satellite radio service violated Flo & Eddie's public performance rights in the sound recordings. Each court ruled that the law of its respective state provided owners of pre-1972 sound recordings with the exclusive right to publicly perform their sound recordings, at least by satellite transmission

The question in each case was one of first impression. The California decision was based on a 1982 state statute granting "[t]he author of an original work of authorship consisting of a sound recording initially fixed prior to February 15, 1972 . . . an exclusive ownership interest therein until February 15, 2047, as against all persons . . ." Cal. Civ. Code § 980(a)(2). The court concluded that this "exclusive ownership interest" includes the exclusive right to publicly perform the sound recording. The New York decision was based on a prediction of how the New York Court of Appeals would interpret that state's common law protection for sound recordings (since such protection is purely common law, rather than statutory, and since no New York court had addressed the issue of public performance rights). Both decisions have been appealed. By contrast, a federal court in Florida, noting the absence of either a pertinent statute or caselaw, declined to "creat[e] a new property right in Florida as opposed to interpreting the law," and therefore ruled against the existence of a common law public performance right in sound recordings in Florida. *Flo & Eddie, Inc. v. Sirius XM Radio, Inc.*, 114 U.S.P.Q.2d 1997 (S.D. Fla. 2015)

Do the California and New York decisions simply put pre-1972 sound recordings on an even footing with later, federally copyrighted sound recordings? The limited federal public performance right for sound recordings in § 106(6), first granted by Congress in 1995, gives copyright owners the right to control public performance of their works by satellite transmission as long as the transmission is digital. But that control is subject to the statutory license under § 114(d) if the satellite transmitting service qualifies for the license. Will such a statutory license be available under California or New York law for compliant satellite radio transmitters?

If the decisions are upheld on appeal, will they be limited to satellite radio transmissions, or will they apply to other types of digital audio transmissions, such as webcasting? If the state performance right applies to webcasting, will online transmitting services be able to secure the right to transmit pre-1972 sound recordings through a statutory licensing procedure similar to § 114? If not, how might that shape which music gets played online?

Is there any reason to think that the decisions are limited to *digital* transmissions (which were, of course, essentially unknown at the time Congress granted copyright to sound recordings in 1972, and when California adopted § 980(a)(2) in 1982)? If not, do the decisions apply to over-the-air transmissions by terrestrial radio stations? (Recall that those radio transmissions incur no public performance liability under federal copyright law, either because they are not digital (and therefore not within the scope of § 106(6)) or because if they are digital they are exempt under § 114(d)(1).) If the New York and California *Flo & Eddie* decisions extend to public performance by radio, has every radio station that played a sound recording from before 1972 over the air violated the sound recording owner's state public performance right in California since 1982, and in New York since whenever common-law copyright in sound recordings was first judicially recognized there? Can you offer any explanation why for more than 30 years sound recording copyright owners in California never asserted that any radio station in the state that played pre-1972 recordings was infringing on their common-law copyright? (Consider the evolving economics of sound recording copyright.)

Finally, while the limited federal public performance right in sound recordings in § 106(6) extends only to *transmissions*, the general public performance right in § 106(4) also covers nontransmitted performances that occur in public or semi-public places. Given the two *Flo & Eddie* decisions recognizing that the owners of state common law rights in sound recordings own a "public performance" right, is there any reason that these decisions do not apply to discotheques, restaurants, bars, and retail establishments that play records on their premises? Again, can you explain the lack of enforcement against such establishments for three decades or more?

---

6. LIMITATIONS ON THE RIGHTS OF PUBLIC PERFORMANCE AND DISPLAY

f.   ARE COMPULSORY LICENSES AND OTHER LIMITATIONS ON THE PERFORMANCE AND DISPLAY RIGHTS CONSISTENT WITH INTERNATIONAL OBLIGATIONS?

Page 802. Add following the final paragraph:

Another WTO dispute demonstrates how even international trade obligations not directly related to copyright can nevertheless affect copyright rights. The WTO has determined, in a complaint against the United States by Antigua and Barbuda, that the U.S. ban on Americans betting at gambling sites based in the Caribbean nation violated U.S. obligations under the General Agreement on Trade in Services, and that the violation caused Antigua and Barbuda $21 million in damage annually. Because the United States has not come into compliance with its obligations, in January 2013 the WTO authorized Antigua and Barbuda to suspend its intellectual property obligations to the United States up to $21 million annually. Reports indicated that the Antigua and Barbuda government was considering setting up a website "where viewers could pay a pittance to watch a film or television show with an American copyright." Annie Lowrey, *Caribbean Nation Gets an International Go-Ahead to Break U.S. Copyright Laws*, N.Y. TIMES, Jan. 29, 2013, at B4. See generally, World Trade Organization, Dispute Settlement: Dispute DS285, United States—Measures Affecting the Cross-Border Supply of Gambling and Betting Services, at http://www. wto.org/english/tratop_e/dispu_e/cases_e/ds285_e.htm.

CHAPTER 7

FAIR USE

B. APPLICATION OF FAIR USE DOCTRINE TO CREATION OF NEW WORKS

Pages 840–841. Replace the discussion of *Cariou v. Prince* with the following:

Cariou v. Prince, 714 F.3d 694 (2d Cir. 2013). In 2000, Patrick Cariou, a professional photographer, published a book of photographs, titled *Yes Rasta*, containing both portraits of Rastafarian individuals (and others) in Jamaica and landscape photos taken by Cariou in Jamaica. Richard Prince is a well-known "appropriation artist" who has shown at numerous museums and other institutions, and whose work sells for very high prices. From about December 2007 through February 2008, Prince showed artwork at the Eden Rock hotel in St. Barts. Among the works shown was a collage entitled *Canal Zone* (2007), which consisted of 35 photographs torn from *Yes Rasta* and attached to a wooden backer board. Prince painted over some portions of the 35 photographs, and used only portions of some of the photos, while others were used in their entirety or nearly so. Prince ultimately completed 29 paintings in his contemplated *Canal Zone* series, 28 of which included images taken, some in their entirety, from *Yes Rasta*, albeit collaged, enlarged, cropped, tinted, and/or over-painted. Prince admitted using at least 41 photos from *Yes Rasta* as elements of *Canal Zone* paintings. (Images of the Prince artworks and the *Yes Rasta* photos incorporated in them appear in the online Appendix to the Second Circuit opinion at http://www.ca2.uscourts.gov/11–1197apx.htm.)

Gagosian Gallery showed 22 of the *Canal Zone* paintings in Manhattan in late 2008, and published and sold an exhibition catalog from that show. Cariou's Rasta photos have never been sold or licensed for use other than in the *Yes Rasta* book. Cariou had been negotiating with another Manhattan art gallery to display photographs from *Yes Rasta*, but the show was cancelled when the gallery owner learned of the Prince show. The testimony was ambiguous regarding the reason for the cancellation, whether the gallery owner believed the Prince show preempted hers or instead believed, mistakenly, that Cariou was cooperating with Prince.

Cariou sued Prince for infringement, and the District Court rejected Prince's fair use defense, declining to find "appropriation art" per se "transformative." Given Prince's assertion "that he doesn't 'really have a message,' " "his purpose in using Cariou's Rastafarian portraits was the same as Cariou's original purpose in taking them: a desire to communicate to the viewer core truths about Rastafarians and their culture." On appeal, the Second Circuit reversed, strongly criticizing the district court's analysis:

> The district court based its conclusion that Prince's work is not transformative in large part on Prince's deposition testimony that he "do[es]n't really have a message," that he was

not "trying to create anything with a new meaning or a new message," and that he "do[es]n't have any . . . interest in [Cariou's] original intent." On appeal, Cariou argues that we must hold Prince to his testimony and that we are not to consider how Prince's works may reasonably be perceived unless Prince claims that they were satire or parody. No such rule exists, and we do not analyze satire or parody differently from any other transformative use.

It is not surprising that, when transformative use is at issue, the alleged infringer would go to great lengths to explain and defend his use as transformative. Prince did not do so here. However, the fact that Prince did not provide those sorts of explanations in his deposition—which might have lent strong support to his defense—is not dispositive. What is critical is how the work in question appears to the reasonable observer, not simply what an artist might say about a particular piece or body of work. Prince's work could be transformative even without commenting on Cariou's work or on culture, and even without Prince's stated intention to do so. Rather than confining our inquiry to Prince's explanations of his artworks, we instead examine how the artworks may "reasonably be perceived" in order to assess their transformative nature. The focus of our infringement analysis is primarily on the Prince artworks themselves, and we see twenty-five of them as transformative as a matter of law.

. . .

Here, looking at the artworks and the photographs side-by-side, we conclude that [most of] Prince's images . . . have a different character, give Cariou's photographs a new expression, and employ new aesthetics with creative and communicative results distinct from Cariou's. Our conclusion should not be taken to suggest, however, that any cosmetic changes to the photographs would necessarily constitute fair use. A secondary work may modify the original without being transformative. For instance, a derivative work that merely presents the same material but in a new form, such as a book of synopses of televisions shows, is not transformative. See *Castle Rock*, 150 F.3d at 143; *Twin Peaks Prods., Inc. v. Publications Int'l, Ltd.*, 996 F.2d 1366, 1378 (2d Cir. 1993). In twenty-five of his artworks, Prince has not presented the same material as Cariou in a different manner, but instead has "add[ed] something new" and presented images with a fundamentally different aesthetic.

With respect to the fourth fair use factor, the Second Circuit determined (in reviewing a motion for summary judgment) that the gallery owner did not cancel Cariou's show "because it had already been done at Gagosian, but rather because she mistakenly believed that Cariou had collaborated with Prince on the Gagosian show." Indeed, evoking Prince's celebrity A-list clientele, the court found that Prince's works had no deleterious impact on the market for Cariou's work because the struggling photojournalist and the star of the New York art scene simply did not compete in the same or similar markets:

Although certain of Prince's artworks contain significant portions of certain of Cariou's photographs, neither Prince nor the *Canal Zone* show usurped the market for those photographs. Prince's audience is very different from Cariou's, and there is no evidence that Prince's work ever touched—much less usurped— either the primary or derivative market for Cariou's work. There is nothing in the record to suggest that Cariou would ever develop or license secondary uses of his work in the vein of Prince's artworks. Nor does anything in the record suggest that Prince's artworks had any impact on the marketing of the photographs. Indeed, Cariou has not aggressively marketed his work, and has earned just over $8,000 in royalties from *Yes Rasta* since its publication. He has sold four prints from the book, and only to personal acquaintances.

Prince's work appeals to an entirely different sort of collector than Cariou's. Certain of the *Canal Zone* artworks have sold for two million or more dollars. The invitation list for a dinner that Gagosian hosted in conjunction with the opening of the *Canal Zone* show included a number of the wealthy and famous such as the musicians Jay-Z and Beyonce Knowles, artists Damien Hirst and Jeff Koons, professional football player Tom Brady, model Gisele Bundchen, Vanity Fair editor Graydon Carter, Vogue editor Anna Wintour, authors Jonathan Franzen and Candace Bushnell, and actors Robert DeNiro, Angelina Jolie, and Brad Pitt. Prince sold eight artworks for a total of $10,480,000, and exchanged seven others for works by painter Larry Rivers and by sculptor Richard Serra. Cariou on the other hand has not actively marketed his work or sold work for significant sums, and nothing in the record suggests that anyone will not now purchase Cariou's work, or derivative non-transformative works (whether Cariou's own or licensed by him) as a result of the market space that Prince's work has taken up. This fair use factor therefore weighs in Prince's favor.

The court remanded for a determination whether Prince's almost unadorned appropriations from five of Cariou's photographs were sufficiently transformative to qualify as fair uses of those images. In lieu of litigating the fair use issues regarding the remaining 5 photographs, the parties subsequently settled the dispute. See Randy Kennedy, *Richard Prince Settles Copyright Suit With Patrick Cariou Over Photographs*, NEW YORK TIMES, March 18, 2013, http://artsbeat.blogs.nytimes.com/2014/03/18/richard-prince-settles-copyright-suit-with-patrick-cariou-over-photographs/?_php=true&_type=blogs&_r=0.

QUESTIONS

1. Recall *Rogers v. Koons, supra* page 839 in the main casebook. The Second Circuit there rejected the fair use defense (colorfully charging Koons with sailing under the flag of piracy rather than parody), finding persuasive neither Koons' claim that the inclusion of the "String of Puppies" sculpture in his "Banality Show" brought out the hidden meaning of the underlying photograph, nor his contention that there was no cognizable harm because Rogers' images appeared on mass-market greeting cards, while Koons' limited edition sculpture sold for over $150,000 each. (Perhaps the guest list for Koons' opening was not of record.) Has the Second Circuit effectively overruled its earlier decision?

2.   In *Blanch v. Koons, supra* page 833 in the main casebook, the court's analysis of "transformativeness" emphasized Koons' elaborate explanation of his use of the Blanch photograph. Richard Prince seems to have been less eloquent (or more truculent) in his exposition of his artistic purposes. Making "transformativeness" turn on the artist's loquacity is problematic, as the Second Circuit now recognizes. ("What is critical is how the work in question appears to the reasonable observer, not simply what an artist might say about a particular piece or body of work.") But how helpful is the "reasonable observer" standard the court now applies? And who, in this context, is a "reasonable observer"? The judge? (But see *Bleistein, supra* p. 34 in the main casebook.) The jury? A cross-section of art critics and/or patrons? How much worse (or better) would be a rule deeming appropriation art (or any kind of art, for that matter) per se "transformative"?

3.   Following his fair use success in *Cariou*, Richard Prince exhibited portraits he created (without authorization) from screen captures of other people's Instagram photos, which he enlarged to 55 x 67 cm and printed on canvas via inkjet. He also added his Instagram handle "richardprince1234" below the image. Prince's portraits were displayed at top galleries and reportedly sold for at least $90,000 each. "Missy Suicide," creator of the "Suicidegirls" website, and author of one of the appropriated Instagram photos, responded in kind, reproducing Prince's reproduction of her image, with the addition of a text line, "true art," and offering canvasses for $90 each, with proceeds going to charity. (As she put it, "Beautiful Art, 99.9% off the original price.") A "comparison ad" from her website appears below. Were the author of the initial Instagram photo to have initiated a copyright infringement action against Prince, would his fair use defense prevail? Were Prince to sue Missy Suicide, would her fair use defense prevail? (Could Prince establish a prima facie infringement case that "Missy Suicide" would need to defend against with a fair use claim?)

Page 846. Add new Question 7:

7. Derek Seltzer is street artist. In 2003, he created *Scream Icon*, a drawing of a screaming, contorted face, which he has reproduced as large posters and smaller prints. Many *Scream Icon* posters have been plastered on walls as street art in Los Angeles and elsewhere. Roger Staub is a photographer and professional set-lighting and video designer. In 2008, Staub photographed a brick wall at the corner of Sunset Boulevard and Gardner Avenue in Los Angeles which was covered in graffiti and posters—including a weathered and torn copy of Scream Icon. Staub subsequently incorporated his photograph of the wall as part of a 4-minute video backdrop to a concert performance by the rock group Green Day. According to the court, "Throughout the video, the center of the frame is dominated by an unchanging, but modified, *Scream Icon*. Staub used the photograph he had taken at Sunset and Gardner, cut out the image of *Scream Icon* and modified it by adding a large red 'spray-painted' cross over the middle of the screaming face. He also changed the contrast and color and added black streaks running down the right side of the face. Staub's image further differs from *Scream Icon* because Staub's original photograph was of a weathered, slightly defaced, and torn poster. *Scream Icon* is nonetheless clearly identifiable in the middle of the screen throughout the video." The original image and its appearance in the concert backdrop are reproduced below. In defense to Seltzer's infringement claim, Green Day asserts that the incorporation of the image of *Scream Icon* as part of Green Day's concert performances was "transformative," did not "substitute for the primary market for Seltzer's art," and therefore was a fair use. How should the court rule? See *Seltzer v. Green Day, Inc.*, 725 F.3d 1170 (9th Cir. 2013).

Kienitz v. Sconnie Nation, 766 F.3d 756 (7th Cir. 2014). Photographer Michael Kienitz brought an infringement action against the reproduction of an altered version of his photo of the mayor of Madison, Wisconsin, on t-shirts sold by supporters of an anti-establishment block party which the mayor, in his younger and more reckless days, had attended. Now middle-aged and part of the Establishment, the mayor sought to ban the block party. The retaliatory t-shirt bore the legend "Sorry for partying" beneath the image of the mayor in his maturity. The district court ruled for defendant, holding that the t-shirts made a "transformative" fair use of the photograph. The Seventh Circuit affirmed, but took the occasion to query the pertinence of a work's transformativeness.

The district court and the parties have debated whether the t-shirts are a "transformative use" of the photo—and, if so, just how "transformative" the use must be. That's not one of the statutory factors, though the Supreme Court mentioned it in *Campbell v. Acuff-Rose Music, Inc.*, 510 U.S. 569, 579 (1994). The Second Circuit has run with the suggestion and concluded that "transformative use" is enough to bring a modified copy within the scope of § 107. See, e.g., *Cariou v. Prince*, 714 F.3d 694, 706 (2d Cir. 2013). *Cariou* applied this to an example of "appropriation art," in which some of the supposed value comes from the very fact that the work was created by someone else.

We're skeptical of *Cariou*'s approach, because asking exclusively whether something is "transformative" not only replaces the list in § 107 but also could override 17 U.S.C. § 106(2), which protects derivative works. To say that a new use transforms the work is precisely to say that it is derivative and thus, one might suppose, protected under § 106(2). *Cariou* and its predecessors in the Second Circuit do not explain how every "transformative use" can be "fair use" without extinguishing the author's rights under § 106(2).

We think it best to stick with the statutory list, of which the most important usually is the fourth (market effect). We have asked whether the contested use is a complement to the protected work (allowed) rather than a substitute for it (prohibited). [Citations.] A t-shirt or tank top is no substitute for the original photograph. Nor does Kienitz say that defendants disrupted a plan to license this work for apparel. Kienitz does not argue that defendants' products have reduced the demand for the original work or any use of it that he is contemplating.

QUESTION

Has the Second Circuit asked "exclusively" whether a use is transformative in evaluating whether that use is fair? Have the Second Circuit cases found that "every" transformative use is a "fair use"? On the issue of whether considering transformativeness in fair use analysis "extinguishes" the derivative work right, see R. Anthony Reese, *Transformativeness and the Derivative Work Right*, 31 COLUMB. J. L. & ARTS 467 (2008).

Page 859. Insert before QUESTIONS:

Swatch Group Management Services Ltd. v. Bloomberg L.P., 756 F.3d 73 (2d Cir. 2014). The Swatch Group Ltd, a foreign public company, convened a conference call with invited investment analysts to discuss the company's recently released earnings report. Bloomberg L.P., a financial news and data reporting service obtained a copy of that sound recording without authorization and disseminated it to paying subscribers. Bloomberg asserts that its purpose in obtaining and disseminating the recording at issue was to make important financial information about Swatch Group available to investors and analysts., The court ruled that Bloomberg was engaged in news reporting, and that the context of its use made the verbatim communication of the sound recording "transformative":

> In the context of news reporting and analogous activities, moreover, the need to convey information to the public accurately may in some instances make it desirable and consonant with copyright law for a defendant to faithfully reproduce an original work without alteration. Courts often find such uses transformative by emphasizing the altered purpose or context of the work, as evidenced by surrounding commentary or criticism. Here, Bloomberg provided no additional commentary or analysis of Swatch Group's earnings call. But by disseminating not just a written transcript or article but an actual sound recording, Bloomberg was able to convey with precision not only the raw data of the Swatch Group executives' words, but also more subtle indications of meaning inferable from their hesitation, emphasis, tone of voice, and other such aspects of their delivery. This latter type of information may be just as valuable to investors and analysts as the former, since a speaker's demeanor, tone, and cadence can often elucidate his or her true beliefs far beyond what a stale transcript or summary can show. . . .

> Furthermore, a secondary work "can be transformative in function or purpose without altering or actually adding to the original work." Here, notwithstanding that the data disseminated by Bloomberg was identical to what Swatch Group had disseminated, the two works had different messages and purposes. To begin with, while Swatch Group purported to convey true answers to the analysts' questions and to justify the propriety and reliability of its published earnings statement, Bloomberg made no representation one way or another as to whether the answers given by Swatch Group executives were true or reliable. Nor did Bloomberg purport to support the propriety or reliability of Swatch Group's earnings statement. Bloomberg was simply revealing the newsworthy information of what Swatch Group executives had said. Bloomberg's message—"This is what they said"—is a very different message from Swatch Group's—"This is what you should believe."

> Moreover, Swatch Group intended to exclude members of the press and to restrict the information supplied by its executives to a relatively small group of analysts who had identified themselves to the company in advance. Bloomberg's

objective in rebroadcasting the call, by contrast, was to make this information public, defeating Swatch Group's effort to restrict access. Bloomberg's purpose, in other words, was to publish this factual information to an audience from which Swatch Group's purpose was to withhold it. These differences give Bloomberg's use at least an arguably transformative character.

In any event, regardless of how transformative the use is, we conclude that the first fair use factor, focusing on the purpose and character of the secondary use, favors fair use. We of course recognize that a news reporting purpose by no means guarantees a finding of fair use. *See Harper & Row, . . .* A news organization thus may not freely copy creative expression solely because the expression itself is newsworthy. Nevertheless, we agree with the district court's conclusion that, under the unusual circumstances of this case, the purpose and character of Bloomberg's unaltered dissemination of Swatch Group's expression weighs in favor of fair use, for two reasons.

First, as noted above, by disseminating a full, unadulterated recording of the earnings call, Bloomberg was able to convey valuable factual information that would have been impaired if Bloomberg had undertaken to alter the speech of the Swatch Group executives by interjecting its own interpretations. As we explained in a fair use case involving verbatim copying of a written work, "[w]here an evaluation or description is being made, copying the exact words may be the only valid way precisely to report the evaluation." So too here, copying the exact spoken performance of Swatch Group's executives was reasonably necessary to convey their full meaning. Bloomberg's faithful reproduction thus served "the interest of accuracy, not piracy."

Second, Bloomberg's use did no harm to the legitimate copyright interests of the original author. Importantly, Swatch has admitted that it "did not seek to profit from the publication of the February 8, 2011 Earnings Call in audio or written format." The copyright-protected aspects of the earnings call— that is, the manner by which the facts were expressed—thus were of no value to Swatch or Swatch Group except insofar as they served to convey important information to the analysts in attendance. But Bloomberg's copying of the Swatch Group executives' words, as needed to communicate factual information about the company's earnings report, in no way diminished Swatch Group's ability to communicate with analysts, and thus caused no harm to Swatch's copyright interests. In this way, the case at bar stands in stark contrast to a case like *Harper & Row*, where a magazine disseminated an unpublished excerpt of President Ford's memoirs. This kind of gun-jumping, which scooped the publication of the copyrighted work and, in doing so, did considerable harm to the value of the original author's copyright, is not present here.

Page 870. Add before the paragraph preceding the *Sega* opinion:

Because fair use is determined on a case-by-case basis by applying a fact-intensive multifactor balancing test, it is often difficult to know for sure whether a use is or is not fair until a court (or sometimes one or more reviewing courts) makes a final decision. Does that give a copyright owner an incentive to sue for every possibly infringing use, even if the owner suspects that it will eventually lose on a fair use claim, in the hope of at least reaching some settlement with the defendant? Does the possibility that the court will require the copyright owner plaintiff to pay a prevailing defendant's attorney's fees change the incentives? See *SOFA Entertainment, Inc. v. Dodger Productions, Inc.*, 709 F.3d 1273 (9th Cir. 2013) (upholding award of $155,000 in attorney's fees to defendant after determining that the use of seven-second clip from plaintiff's copyrighted television program showing Ed Sullivan introducing musical group the Four Seasons in defendants' biographical musical *Jersey Boys* was "undoubtably" fair use).

C. APPLICATION OF FAIR USE DOCTRINE TO NEW TECHNOLOGIES

1. PHOTOCOPYING BY COMMERCIAL AND NONCOMMERCIAL INTERMEDIARIES

Page 897. After the end of Question 4, add the following:

Cambridge Univ. Press v. Patton

769 F.3d 1232 (11th Cir. 2014)

■ Tjoflat, Circuit Judge.

[This case involved claims by three academic publishers (Cambridge and Oxford University Presses and Sage Publications) that copyright infringement occurred when Georgia State University (GSU) faculty members made excerpts from the plaintiffs' works available as electronic course reserves through the university library's website ("ERes") and the university's course management system ("uLearn"). Because the university itself enjoyed sovereign immunity, the plaintiffs sought injunctive and declaratory relief under the *Ex Parte Young* doctrine, and the question before the court was whether the university's 2009 Copyright Policy had "led to continuing abuse of the fair use privilege." That policy "makes professors responsible for determining whether a particular use is a fair use" and requires the professor to complete a "fair use checklist" to do so.

The plaintiffs identified 75 instances of alleged infringement during the three full semesters after the Copyright Policy was adopted, and the opinion centered on whether those 75 instances of the plaintiffs' material being placed on electronic reserve constituted infringement or fair use.

The excerpts at issue were assigned by faculty members as supplemental (but often required) reading in graduate or upper-level undergraduate courses in language or social science. The books from which the excerpts came were generally not textbooks, but rather single-author monographs or edited collections of multiple chapters by a variety of authors. The "great majority" of the excerpts at issue constituted "a chapter or less from a multi-chapter book." The average copied excerpt constituted about 10% of the book from which it was copied "(though some were considerably more and some were considerably less)". Excerpts placed on electronic reserve were available by password only to students enrolled in the course, and only during the semester in which the student was enrolled, but students could download or print the reserve readings for their courses.

The court held a bench trial on the infringement claims and assertions of fair use, finding all the factors to weigh in favor of most of the instances of copying.

On appeal, the Eleventh Circuit reversed, although it sustained much of the District Court's analysis. The Eleventh Circuit differed primarily with respect to the second (nature of the copyrighted work) and third factors (amount and substantiality), and to the overall weighting of the factors. Judge Vinson, concurring specially, would have rejected the fair use defense in its entirety, principally because he viewed the electronic reserves program as substituting for paper coursepacks for which the University had taken licenses from the publishers.]

. . .

C.

Before we turn to the District Court's analysis of each of the four fair use factors, we must first address the District Court's overarching fair use methodology. . . .

Plaintiffs . . . argue that the District Court erred in giving each of the four factors equal weight, essentially taking a mechanical "add up the factors" approach, finding fair use if three factors weighed in favor of fair use and one against and vice versa, and only performing further analysis in case of a "tie." We agree that the District Court's arithmetic approach was improper.

Congress, in the Copyright Act, spoke neither to the relative weight courts should attach to each of the four factors nor to precisely how the factors ought to be balanced. However, the Supreme Court has explained that "the four statutory factors [may not] be treated in isolation, one from another. All are to be explored, and the results weighed together, in light of the purposes of copyright." [*Campbell*] at 578. In keeping with this approach, a given factor may be more or less important in determining whether a particular use should be considered fair under the specific circumstances of the case. . . . Accordingly, we find that the District Court erred in giving each of the four factors equal weight, and in treating the four factors as a simple mathematical formula. As we will explain, because of the circumstances of this case, some of the factors weigh more heavily on the fair use determination than others.

D.

We now turn to the District Court's analysis of each individual fair use factor. Although we have found that the District Court's method for weighing the four factors against one another was erroneous, this does not mean that the District Court's reasoning under each of the four factors is also necessarily flawed. Rather, we must determine the correct analysis under each factor and then ascertain whether the District Court properly applied that analysis.

Plaintiffs argue that the District Court erred in its application of each of the four fair use factors. Plaintiffs' argument centers on a comparison of the circumstances of the instant case to those of the so-called "coursepack cases," in which courts rejected a defense of fair use for commercial copyshops that assembled paper coursepacks containing unlicensed excerpts of copyrighted works for use in university courses.

. . .

In essence, Plaintiffs argue that the coursepack cases should have guided the District Court's analysis in this case, because GSU cannot alter the fair use calculus simply by choosing to distribute course readings in an electronic rather than paper format. In making this argument, Plaintiffs invoke the "media neutrality" principle, which "mandates that the 'transfer of a work between media does not alter the character of that work for copyright purposes.'" [Citations.]

Plaintiffs' reliance on the media neutrality doctrine is misplaced. Congress established that doctrine to ensure that works created with new technologies, perhaps not in existence at the time of the Copyright Act of 1976, would qualify for copyright protection. . . . The media neutrality doctrine concerns copyrightability and does not dictate the result in a fair use inquiry. Congress would not have intended this doctrine to effectively displace the flexible work-by-work fair use analysis in favor of a one dimensional analysis as to whether the case involves a transfer of a work between media.

Likewise, because the fair use analysis is highly fact-specific and must be performed on a work-by-work basis, *see Cariou*, 714 F.3d at 694, the coursepack cases provide guidance but do not dictate the results here, which must be based upon a careful consideration of the circumstances of the individual instances of alleged infringement involved in this case.

1.

. . .

Our initial inquiry under the first factor asks whether Defendants' use is transformative, . . .

Here, Defendants' use of excerpts of Plaintiffs' works is not transformative. The excerpts of Plaintiffs' works posted on GSU's electronic reserve system are verbatim copies of portions of the original books which have merely been converted into a digital format. Although a professor may arrange these excerpts into a particular order or combination for use in a college course, this does not imbue the excerpts themselves with any more than a de minimis amount of new meaning. *See Princeton University Press*, 99 F.3d at 1389 ("[I]f you make verbatim copies of 95 pages of a 316-page book, you have not transformed the 95 pages very much—even if you juxtapose them to excerpts from other works.").

Nor do Defendants use the excerpts for anything other than the same intrinsic purpose—or at least one of the purposes—served by Plaintiffs' works: reading material for students in university courses. Although an electronic reserve system may facilitate easy access to excerpts of Plaintiffs' works, it does nothing to transform those works. *But see Authors Guild, Inc. v. HathiTrust*, 755 F.3d 87, 97 (2d Cir. 2014) (holding that universities' systematic digitization of copyrighted books was transformative because the digital copies were used to create a searchable database which supplied users with lists of page numbers and not with copies of the original works, and so the copies served a different purpose than the original works). Rather, Defendants' use of excerpts of Plaintiffs' works "supersede[s] the objects of the original creation." *See Campbell*, 510 U.S. at 579 (alteration in original) (quotation marks omitted). Were this element by itself dispositive, we would be compelled to find that the first factor weighs against a finding of fair use.

However, we must also consider under the first factor whether Defendants' use is for a nonprofit educational purpose, as opposed to a commercial purpose. "[T]he commercial or non-transformative uses of a work are to be regarded as 'separate factor[s] that tend[ ] to weigh against a finding of fair use,' and 'the force of that tendency will vary with the context.'" *Peter Letterese & Assocs.*, 533 F.3d at 1309 (alteration in original) (quoting *Campbell*, 510 U.S. at 585). Indeed, the Supreme Court has recognized in dicta that nonprofit educational use may weigh in favor of a finding of fair use under the first factor, even when nontransformative. *Campbell*, 510 U.S. at 579 n.11 ("The obvious statutory exception to this focus on transformative uses is the straight reproduction of multiple copies for classroom distribution.").

Because "copyright has always been used to promote learning," *Suntrust Bank*, 268 F.3d at 1261, allowing some leeway for educational fair use furthers the purpose of copyright by providing students and teachers with a means to lawfully access works in order to further their learning in circumstances where it would be unreasonable to require permission. But, as always, care must be taken not to allow too much educational use, lest we undermine the goals of copyright by enervating the incentive for authors to create the works upon which students and teachers depend.

In the coursepack cases, *Princeton University Press*, 99 F.3d at 1389, and *Basic Books*, 758 F.Supp. at 1531–32, the first factor weighed against a finding of fair use when the nontransformative, educational use in question was performed by a for-profit copyshop, and was therefore commercial. In a more recent case, a district court refused to allow a commercial copyshop to sidestep the outcome of the coursepack cases by requiring its student customers to perform the photocopying themselves (for a fee) when assembling paper coursepacks from master copies held by the copyshop. *Blackwell Publ'g, Inc. v. Excel Research Grp., LLC*, 661 F.Supp.2d 786, 794 (E.D. Mich. 2009). In all three instances, the court refused to allow the defendants, who were engaged in commercial operations, to stand in the shoes of students and professors in claiming that their making of multiple copies of scholarly works was for nonprofit educational purposes.

However, in both of the coursepack cases, the court expressly declined to conclude that the copying would fall outside the boundaries of fair use if conducted by professors, students, or academic institutions. . . . In *Blackwell Publishing*, the District Court noted that, conversely, "the fact that students do the copying does not ipso facto mean that a commercial use cannot be found." 661 F. Supp. 2d at 793.

Furthermore, where we previously held that the first factor weighed against a finding of fair use in a case involving use that was nontransformative but educational, the use in question was commercial. *Peter Letterese & Assocs.*, 533 F.3d at 1309–12 (finding that the first factor weighed against a finding of fair use in a case involving the verbatim use of copyrighted material in an instructional coursepack for use by the Church of Scientology, where defendants charged a fee or obtained a promissory note in exchange for the coursepacks and hence the use was for commercial purposes).

Thus, the question becomes whether Defendants' use of Plaintiffs' works is truly a nonprofit educational use under § 107(1), and if so, whether this places sufficient weight on the first factor scales to justify a finding that this factor favors fair use despite the nontransformativeness of Defendants' use.

GSU is a nonprofit educational institution. While this is relevant, our inquiry does not end there: we must consider not only the nature of the user, but the use itself. . . . Defendants' use of Plaintiffs' works in the teaching of university courses is clearly for educational purposes. Nevertheless, it is not entirely clear that use by a nonprofit entity for educational purposes is always a "nonprofit" use as contemplated by § 107(1). The Supreme Court has explained that "[t]he crux of the profit/nonprofit distinction is not whether the sole motive of the use is monetary gain but whether the user stands to profit from exploitation of the copyrighted material without paying the customary price." *Harper & Row*, 471 U.S. at 562. . . .

Under this line of reasoning, Defendants' educational use of Plaintiffs' works is a for-profit use despite GSU's status as a nonprofit educational institution, and despite the fact that GSU does not directly sell access to Plaintiffs' works on Eres and uLearn. Defendants "exploited" Plaintiffs' copyrighted material for use in university courses without "paying the customary price"—a licensing fee. Defendants profited from the use of excerpts of Plaintiffs' works—however indirectly—because GSU collects money from students in the form of tuition and fees (which students pay in part for access to ERes and uLearn) and reduces its costs by avoiding fees it might have otherwise paid for the excerpts.

However, this reasoning is somewhat circular, and hence of limited usefulness to our fair use inquiry. Of course, any unlicensed use of copyrighted material profits the user in the sense that the user does not pay a potential licensing fee, allowing the user to keep his or her money. If this analysis were persuasive, no use could qualify as "nonprofit" under the first factor. Moreover, if the use is a fair use, then the copyright owner is not entitled to charge for the use, and there is no "customary price" to be paid in the first place.

Accordingly, evaluating the indirect profit GSU gained by refusing to pay to license Plaintiffs' works provides little useful guidance under the first factor. Simply put, the greater the amount of a work taken by the secondary user (or the more valuable the portion taken), the more the user "profits" by not paying for the use. Thus, the concern we have identified with profit in this sense is better dealt with under the third factor, which directs us to consider the amount of the original work that the secondary user appropriated, and the substantiality of the portion used. *See* 17 U.S.C. § 107(3).

. . .

Although GSU certainly benefits from its use of Plaintiffs' works by being able to provide the works conveniently to students, and profits in the sense that it avoids paying licensing fees, Defendants' use is not fairly characterized as "commercial exploitation." Even if Defendants' use profits GSU in some sense, we are not convinced that this type of benefit is indicative of "commercial" use. There is no evidence that Defendants capture significant revenues as a direct consequence of copying Plaintiffs' works. At the same time, the use provides a broader public benefit— furthering the education of students at a public university.

Thus, we find that Defendants' use of Plaintiffs' works is of the nonprofit educational nature that Congress intended the fair use defense to allow under certain circumstances. Furthermore, we find this sufficiently weighty that the first factor favors a finding of fair use despite the nontransformative nature of the use.

The text of the fair use statute highlights the importance Congress placed on educational use. The preamble to the statute provides that fair uses may include "teaching (including multiple copies for classroom use), scholarship, or research" and the first factor singles out "nonprofit educational purposes." 17 U.S.C. § 107. The legislative history of § 107 further demonstrates that Congress singled out educational purposes for special consideration. In the years leading up to passage of the Copyright Act of 1976 (which introduced § 107), Congress devoted considerable attention to working out the proper scope of the fair use defense as applied to copying for educational and classroom purposes, going so far as to include in a final report the Classroom Guidelines developed by representatives of educator, author, and publisher groups at the urging of Congress. *See* H.R. Rep. No. 2237, at 59–66 (1966); S. Rep. No. 93–983, at 116–19 (1974); S. Rep. No. 94–473, at 63–65 (1975); H.R. Rep. No. 94–1476, at 66–70 (1976).

Notably, early drafts of § 107 did not include the parenthetical "including multiple copies for classroom use" or the specific direction to consider "whether [the] use is of a commercial nature or is for nonprofit educational purposes." This language was not inserted until one month before the passage of the Copyright Act of 1976.

In sum, Congress devoted extensive effort to ensure that fair use would allow for educational copying under the proper circumstances and was sufficiently determined to achieve this goal that it amended the text of the statute at the eleventh hour in order to expressly state it. Furthermore, as described above, allowing latitude for educational fair use promotes the goals of copyright. Thus, we are persuaded that, despite the recent focus on transformativeness under the first factor, use for teaching purposes by a nonprofit, educational institution such as Defendants' favors a finding of fair use under the first factor, despite the nontransformative nature of the use.

Accordingly, we find that the District Court did not err in holding that the first factor favors a finding of fair use. Nevertheless, because

Defendants' use of Plaintiffs' works is nontransformative, the threat of market substitution is significant. We note that insofar as the first factor is concerned with uses that supplant demand for the original, this factor is "closely related" to "[t]he fourth fair use factor, the effect on the potential market for the work." [Citation.] We will thus revisit this concern when we analyze the fourth factor.

2.

. . .

Here, the District Court held that "[b]ecause all of the excerpts are informational and educational in nature and none are fictional, fair use factor two weighs in favor of Defendants." 863 F.Supp.2d at 1242. We disagree.

. . .

Defendants argue that GSU professors chose the excerpts of Plaintiffs' works for their factual content, not for any expressive content the works may contain, noting that several professors testified that if the use of a particular excerpt was not a fair use, they would have found another source. Of course, other professors testified that they chose particular excerpts because of the author's interpretative originality and significance. Regardless of whether GSU faculty chose the excerpts for their expressive or factual content, the excerpts were copied wholesale—facts, ideas, and original expression alike. Which aspect the secondary user was interested in is irrelevant to the disposition of the second factor.

Accordingly, we find that the District Court erred in holding that the second factor favored fair use in every instance. Where the excerpts of Plaintiffs' works contained evaluative, analytical, or subjectively descriptive material that surpasses the bare facts necessary to communicate information, or derives from the author's experiences or opinions, the District Court should have held that the second factor was neutral, or even weighed against fair use in cases of excerpts that were dominated by such material. That being said, the second fair use factor is of relatively little importance in this case.

3.

. . . Here, the District Court found that the third factor favored fair use in instances where Defendants copied no more than 10 percent of a work, or one chapter in case of a book with ten or more chapters. 863 F. Supp. 2d at 1243. The District Court's blanket 10 percent-or-one-chapter benchmark was improper. The fair use analysis must be performed on a case-by-case/work-by-work basis. *Campbell*, 510 U.S. at 577. We must avoid "hard evidentiary presumption[s] . . . and 'eschew[ ] a rigid, bright-line approach to fair use.'" *Campbell*, 510 U.S. at 584–85 (quoting Sony, 464 U.S. at 449 n. 31). By holding that the third factor favored fair use whenever the amount of copying fell within a 10 percent-or-one-chapter baseline, the District Court abdicated its duty to analyze the third factor for each instance of alleged infringement individually.

Defendants argue that the District Court's 10 percent-or-one-chapter baseline served as a starting point only. However, this "starting point" in fact served as a substantive safe harbor in the third factor analysis, an approach which is incompatible with the prescribed work-by-work analysis. Even if we consider the baseline as a starting point only, application of the same non-statutory starting point to each instance of infringement is not a feature of a proper work-by-work analysis under the third fair use factor.

Defendants also argue that the District Court's 10 percent-or-one-chapter approach is supported by the record. Defendants' explain that a CCC white paper, Using Electronic Reserves: Guidelines and Best Practices for Copyright Compliance (2011), identifies "best practices" for electronic reserves, stating that electronic reserve materials should be limited to "small excerpts" and that "[m]ost experts advise using a single article or . . . chapter of a copyrighted work. . . ." However, even if we accept that the 10 percent-or-one-chapter approach represents a general industry "best practice" for electronic reserves, this is not relevant to an individualized fair use analysis.

. . . Plaintiffs argue that the District Court erred in measuring the amount taken based on the length of the entire book even where the copied material was an independently authored chapter in an edited volume. Rather, Plaintiffs contend, the relevant "work" in the case of an edited volume is the chapter copied, not the entire book; to conclude otherwise would create the anomalous result that a work bound with other works in an edited volume would enjoy less copyright protection than if the same work were published in a journal. *See Texaco*, 60 F.3d at 926 (treating individual articles in a journal as discrete works of authorship for purposes of third factor analysis).

As noted earlier, the District Court declined to consider this argument because Plaintiffs raised it late in the proceedings. The decision whether to hear an argument raised late in litigation is squarely within the discretion of the District Court. . . .

. . . Plaintiffs [also] argue that the copying permitted by the District Court exceeds the amounts outlined in the Classroom Guidelines. We note that the Classroom Guidelines, although part of the legislative history of the Copyright Act, do not carry force of law. In any case, to treat the Classroom Guidelines as indicative of what is allowable would be to create the type of "hard evidentiary presumption" that the Supreme Court has cautioned against, because fair use must operate as a "'sensitive balancing of interests.'" *Campbell*, 510 U.S. at 584 (quoting *Sony*, 464 U.S. at 455, n. 40). As discussed, the fair use analysis must be performed on a work-by-work basis, and so we must not give undue weight to the amounts of copying set forth in the Classroom Guidelines.

Furthermore, although Plaintiffs characterize the amounts set forth in the Classroom Guidelines as "limits," the Classroom Guidelines were intended to suggest a minimum, not maximum, amount of allowable educational copying that might be fair use, and were not intended to limit fair use in any way: . . . Thus, while the Classroom Guidelines may be seen to represent Congress' tentative view of the permissible amount of educational copying in 1976, we are not persuaded by the Plaintiffs' argument that the Classroom Guidelines should control the analysis under factor three in this case.

. . .

Accordingly, we find that the District Court properly considered whether the individual instances of alleged infringement were excessive in relation to Defendants' pedagogical purpose, properly measured the amounts taken in all cases based on the length of the entire book, and properly declined to tie its analysis under the third factor to the Classroom Guidelines or to the coursepack cases. However, we find that the District Court erred in applying a 10 percent-or-one-chapter safe harbor in it analysis of the individual instances of alleged infringement. The District Court should have analyzed each instance of alleged copying individually, considering the quantity and the quality of the material taken—including whether the material taken constituted the heart of the work—and whether that taking was excessive in light of the educational purpose of the use and the threat of market substitution.

4.

. . .

The central question under the fourth factor is not whether Defendants' use of Plaintiffs' works caused Plaintiffs to lose some potential revenue. Rather, it is whether Defendants' use—taking into account the damage that might occur if "everybody did it"—would cause substantial economic harm such that allowing it would frustrate the purposes of copyright by materially impairing Defendants' incentive to publish the work. . . .

We agree with the District Court that the small excerpts Defendants used do not substitute for the full books from which they were drawn. "Plaintiffs offered no trial testimony or evidence showing that they lost any book sales in or after 2009 on account of any actions by anyone at Georgia State." 863 F. Supp. 2d at 1217. Thus, the District Court did not err in finding that "Defendants' use of small excerpts did not affect Plaintiffs' actual or potential sales of books." Id. at 1236.

However, CCC's various programs for academic permissions—and Plaintiffs' own permissions programs—constitute a workable market through which universities like GSU may purchase licenses to use excerpts of Plaintiffs' works. Plaintiffs contend that, by failing to purchase digital permissions to use excerpts of Plaintiffs' works on ERes and uLearn, Defendants caused substantial harm to the market for licenses, and that widespread adoption of this practice would cause substantial harm to the potential market. Plaintiffs also argue that, even if a license for a digital excerpt of a work was unavailable, this should not weigh in favor of fair use because the copyright owner is not obliged to accommodate prospective users.

Defendants argue that, because permissions income for academic books represents a miniscule percentage of Plaintiffs' overall revenue, Defendants' practices have not caused substantial harm to the market for Plaintiffs works, and would not do so even if widely adopted. Defendants further argue that unavailability of licensing opportunities for particular works should weigh in favor of fair use.

We note that it is not determinative that programs exist through which universities may license excerpts of Plaintiffs' works. In other words, the fact that Plaintiffs have made paying easier does not automatically dictate a right to payment. "[A] copyright holder can always assert some degree of adverse [effect] on its potential licensing revenues as a consequence of the secondary use at issue simply because the copyright holder has not been paid a fee to permit that particular use." *Texaco*, 60 F.3d at 929 n.17 (citations omitted). The goal of copyright is to stimulate the creation of new works, not to furnish copyright holders with control over all markets. Accordingly, the ability to license does not demand a finding against fair use.

Nevertheless, "it is sensible that a particular unauthorized use should be considered 'more fair' when there is no ready market or means to pay for the use, while such an unauthorized use should be considered 'less fair' when there is a ready market or means to pay for the use. The vice of circular reasoning arises only if the availability of payment is conclusive against fair use." *Id.* at 931. Put simply, absent evidence to the contrary, if a copyright holder has not made a license available to use a particular work in a particular manner, the inference is that the author or publisher did not think that there would be enough such use to bother making a license available. In such a case, there is little damage to the publisher's market when someone makes use of the work in that way without obtaining a license, and hence the fourth factor should generally weigh in favor of fair use. This is true of Plaintiffs' works for which no license for a digital excerpt was available.[32]

Plaintiffs argue that even though a use is less fair when licensing is readily available, it does not follow that a use becomes more fair if, for a legitimate reason, the copyright holder has not offered to license the work. Plaintiffs cite several cases which have found that the fourth factor weighs against fair use even though the copyright holder was not actively marketing the work in question because the secondary use negatively impacted the potential market for the work. *See . . . Castle Rock Entm't, Inc. v. Carol Publ'g Grp., Inc.,* 150 F.3d 132, 145–46 (2d Cir. 1998) (finding that the fourth factor weighed against a defendant who published a book containing trivia questions about the plaintiff's copyrighted television program where the plaintiff "ha[d] evidenced little if any interest in exploiting [the] market for derivative works based on" the program, noting that "copyright law must respect that creative and economic choice"). We note that our own precedent also supports this theory in some circumstances. *See Pac. & S. Co.,* 744 F.2d at 1496 (finding harm to the potential market for plaintiff's news broadcasts where a defendant videotaped the broadcasts and sold tapes to the subjects of the news reports because "[c]opyrights protect owners who immediately market a work no more stringently than owners who delay before entering the market" and so "[t]he fact that [the plaintiff] does not actively market copies of the news programs does not matter, for Section 107 looks to the 'potential market' in analyzing the effects of an alleged infringement").

However, this reasoning need not dictate the result in this case, which concerns not the market for Plaintiffs' original works themselves or for derivative works based upon those works, but rather a market for licenses to use Plaintiffs' works in a particular way. As previously explained, licensing poses a particular threat that the fair use analysis will become circular, and Plaintiffs may not head off a defense of fair use

---

[32] Of course, it need not *always* be true that a publisher's decision not to make a work available for digital permissions conclusively establishes that the publisher envisioned little or no demand, and that the value of the permissions market is zero. After all, a number of other factors might influence a publisher's distribution decision: the publisher may not yet have figured out how to sell work in a different medium, or it might want to restrict circulation in one medium to promote another.

by complaining that every potential licensing opportunity represents a potential market for purposes of the fourth fair use factor.

An analogy is helpful. A publisher acts like a securities underwriter. A publisher determines the value of a work, which is set by the anticipated demand for the work. Thus, the greater the demand for the work—the greater the market—the more the publisher will pay the author of the work up front, and the more the publisher will endeavor to make the work widely available. If a publisher makes licenses available for some uses but not for others, this indicates that the publisher has likely made a reasoned decision not to enter the licensing market for those uses, which implies that the value of that market is minimal.

With regard to the works for which digital permissions were unavailable, Plaintiffs choose to enter those works into some markets—print copies of the whole work, or perhaps licenses for paper copies of excerpts—but not the digital permission market. This tells us that Plaintiffs likely anticipated that there would be little to no demand for digital excerpts of the excluded works and thus saw the value of that market as de minimis or zero. If the market for digital excerpts were in fact de minimis or zero, then neither Defendants' particular use nor a widespread use of similar kind would be likely to cause significant market harm. Of course, if publishers choose to participate in the market the calculation will change.

In its individual analysis under the fourth factor of each of the forty-eight works for which it found Plaintiffs had made a prima facie case of infringement, the District Court performed a sufficiently nuanced review of the evidence regarding license availability. Where the evidence showed that there was a ready market for digital excerpts of a work in 2009, the time of the purported infringements, the District Court found that there was small—due to the amount of money involved—but actual damage to the value of Plaintiffs' copyright.[33] The District Court also properly took into account that widespread use of similar unlicensed excerpts could cause substantial harm to the potential market. Thus, where there was a license for digital excerpts available, the District Court generally held that the fourth factor weighed against a finding of fair use. In close cases, the District Court went further and examined the amount of permissions income a work had generated in order to determine how much this particular revenue source contributed to the value of the copyright in the work, noting that where there is no significant demand for excerpts, the likelihood of repetitive unpaid use is diminished. Where there was no evidence in the record to show that a license for digital excerpts was available—as was the case for seventeen works published by Oxford and

---

[33] Plaintiffs argue that the District Court improperly focused on the availability of digital licenses in 2009. Such availability, Plaintiffs point out, is irrelevant because Plaintiffs seek only prospective injunctive relief, and the status of licensing in 2009 has no bearing on the question of whether GSU's copyright policy going forward should require an investigation of whether a license is available.

However, the fair use analysis must be performed on a work-by-work basis. Campbell, 510 U.S. at 577. As such, the District Court had to examine specific instances of infringement in order to determine whether prospective relief was warranted, and what shape that relief should take. In deciding those individual cases, the availability of licensing at the time of an alleged infringement—not at some undefined time in the future—is the relevant evidence.

. . .

Cambridge—the District Court held that the fourth factor weighted in favor of fair use. We find that the District Court's analysis under the fourth factor was correct, and that the District Court properly took license availability into account in determining whether the fourth factor weighted for or against fair use.

Plaintiffs argue that the District Court erred by placing the burden on Plaintiffs to show that digital licenses for the particular works in question were reasonably available through CCC in 2009. Cognizant that fair use is an affirmative defense, the District Court kept the overall burden on Defendants to show that "no substantial damage was caused to the potential market for or the value of Plaintiffs' works" in order to prevail on the question of whether the fourth factor should favor fair use. 863 F.Supp.2d at 1237. However, the District Court found that because Plaintiffs were "advocates of the theory that the availability of licenses shifts the factor four fair use analysis in their favor . . . it is appropriate for them to be called upon to show that CCC provided in 2009 reasonably efficient, reasonably priced, convenient access to the particular excerpts which are in question in this case." Id. Plaintiffs argue that this amounted to relieving the Defendants of their burden of proof on the fourth factor

We disagree. Fair use is an affirmative defense, and the evidentiary burden on all four of its factors rests on the alleged infringer. However, Plaintiffs—as publishers—can reasonably be expected to have the evidence as to availability of licenses for their own works. It is therefore reasonable to place on Plaintiffs the burden of going forward with the evidence on this question.

In effect, this creates a presumption that no market for digital permissions exists for a particular work.[34] . . . This is reasonable, because if a license was available during the relevant time period, Plaintiffs can rebut the presumption of no market by going forward with evidence of license availability. If there is evidence of a potential, future market, Plaintiffs can rebut the presumption by going forward with that. Then, Defendants—retaining the overall burden of persuasion on the fourth factor—must demonstrate that their use does not materially impair the existing or potential market in order to prevail.

Although the District Court did not articulate its approach to the evidentiary burden on license availability in exactly this manner, the District Court did essentially what we have described. The District Court required Plaintiffs to put on evidence as to the availability of digital permissions in 2009, and Plaintiffs provided such evidence for some of the works in question but not for others. For those seventeen works for which Plaintiffs presented no evidence that digital permissions were available, the District Court—noting that, because access was limited to particular classes, it was unlikely that Defendants' use would result in exposure of the works to the general public and so there was little risk of widespread market substitution for excerpts of the works—held that

---

[34] We note that placing the burden of going forward with the evidence regarding license availability on Plaintiffs does not create a proscribed "hard evidentiary presumption" regarding categories of use that are fair use against. *See Campbell*, 510 U.S. at 584. Placing this burden on Plaintiffs creates no presumption about whether a given instance of copying will be fair use. This approach merely recognizes that this is a case wherein one party has all the evidence on a particular issue, and so it is equitable to require that party to go forward with the evidence.

there was no harm to the actual or potential market. For those works for which Plaintiffs demonstrated that digital permissions were available, the District Court considered the evidence demonstrating that the actual harm to the value of Plaintiffs' copyright was minor (because the fees Defendants would have paid for a small number of licenses for the works in question amounted to a relatively small amount), but reasonably concluded that widespread conduct of the sort engaged in by Defendants would cause substantial harm. Thus, although the District Court required Plaintiffs to go forward with evidence of license availability, the District Court properly kept the ultimate burden of persuasion on Defendants on the question of market harm under the fourth factor. Accordingly, the District Court did not engage in improper burden shifting.

. . .

The District Court engaged in a careful investigation of the evidence in the record, properly considered the availability of digital permissions in 2009, and appropriately placed the burden of going forward with the evidence on this issue on Plaintiffs. Accordingly, we find that the District Court did not err in its application of the fourth factor. However, because Defendants' copying was nontransformative and the threat of market substitution was therefore serious, the District Court erred by not affording the fourth factor additional weight in its overall fair use calculus.

. . .

E.

In sum, we hold that the District Court did not err in performing a work-by-work analysis of individual instances of alleged infringement in order to determine the need for injunctive relief. However, the District Court did err by giving each of the four fair use factors equal weight, and by treating the four factors mechanistically. The District Court should have undertaken a holistic analysis which carefully balanced the four factors in the manner we have explained.

The District Court did not err in holding that the first factor—the purpose and character of the use—favors fair use. Although Defendants' use was nontransformative, it was also for nonprofit educational purposes, which are favored under the fair use statute. However, the District Court did err in holding that the second fair use factor—the nature of the copyrighted work—favors fair use in every case. Though this factor is of comparatively little weight in this case particularly because the works at issue are neither fictional nor unpublished, where the excerpts in question contained evaluative, analytical, or subjectively descriptive material that surpasses the bare facts, or derives from the author's own experiences or opinions, the District Court should have held that the second factor was neutral or even weighed against fair use where such material dominated.

With regard to the third factor—the amount used in relation to the copyrighted work as a whole—the District Court erred in setting a 10 percent-or-one-chapter benchmark. The District Court should have performed this analysis on a work-by-work basis, taking into account whether the amount taken—qualitatively and quantitatively—was reasonable in light of the pedagogical purpose of the use and the threat of market substitution. However, the District Court appropriately measured the amount copied based on the length of the entire book in all cases, declined to give much weight to the Classroom Guidelines, and found that the Defendants' educational purpose may increase the amount of permissible copying.

With regard to the fourth factor—the effect of Defendants' use on the market for the original—the District Court did not err. However, because Defendants' unpaid copying was nontransformative and they used Plaintiffs' works for one of the purposes for which they are marketed, the threat of market substitution is severe. Therefore, the District Court should have afforded the fourth fair use factor more significant weight in its overall fair use analysis. . . .

Because the District Court's grant of injunctive relief to Plaintiffs was predicated on its finding of infringement, which was in turn based on the District Court's legally flawed methodology in balancing the four fair use factors and erroneous application of factors two and three, we find that the District Court abused its discretion in granting the injunction and the related declaratory relief. Similarly, because the District Court's designation of Defendants as the prevailing party and consequent award of fees and costs were predicated on its erroneous fair use analysis, we find that the District Court erred in designating Defendants as the prevailing party and awarding fees and costs to Defendants.

QUESTIONS

1. For books for which CCC licenses for digital access are available, does it matter in the fair use analysis how large an excerpt the defendant uses?

2. What difference would (or should) it have made if the publishers had from the outset argued that the relevant unit of the copyrighted work was not the book as a whole, but each separate chapter? Would it matter if the book were a collection of chapters by different authors, rather than a multi-chapter book by a single author?

3. Since the plaintiffs were seeking only injunctive relief, why is it relevant whether a digital license for a particular book was available in 2009, so long as a license for e-reserves was and remained available at the time of the court's decision?

2. DIGITAL COPYING BY COMMERCIAL INTERMEDIARIES

Pages 902–906: Replace the excerpt from the *Perfect 10, Inc. v. Amazon.com, Inc.*, decision with the following excerpt:

Perfect 10, Inc. v. Amazon.com, Inc.

508 F.3d 1146 (9th Cir. 2007).

■ IKUTA, CIRCUIT JUDGE.

[For the facts of this case, see the excerpt starting at page 785 in the main casebook.]

. . .

C.   *Fair Use Defense*

Because Perfect 10 has succeeded in showing it would prevail in its prima facie case that Google's thumbnail images infringe Perfect 10's display rights, the burden shifts to Google to show that it will likely succeed in establishing an affirmative defense. Google contends that its use of thumbnails is a fair use of the images and therefore does not constitute an infringement of Perfect 10's copyright. . . .

In applying the fair use analysis in this case, we are guided by *Kelly v. Arriba Soft Corp.,* [336 F.3d 811 (9th Cir. 2003)] which considered substantially the same use of copyrighted photographic images as is at issue here. In *Kelly,* a photographer brought a direct infringement claim against Arriba, the operator of an Internet search engine. The search engine provided thumbnail versions of the photographer's images in response to search queries. We held that Arriba's use of thumbnail images was a fair use primarily based on the transformative nature of a search engine and its benefit to the public. We also concluded that Arriba's use of the thumbnail images did not harm the photographer's market for his image.

In this case, the district court determined that Google's use of thumbnails was not a fair use and distinguished *Kelly.* We consider these distinctions in the context of the four-factor fair use analysis. . . .[8] . . .

Google's use of thumbnails is highly transformative. In *Kelly,* we concluded that Arriba's use of thumbnails was transformative because "Arriba's use of the images serve[d] a different function than Kelly's use—improving access to information on the [I]nternet versus artistic expression." *Kelly,* 336 F.3d at 819. Although an image may have been created originally to serve an entertainment, aesthetic, or informative function, a search engine transforms the image into a pointer directing a user to a source of information. Just as a "parody has an obvious claim to transformative value" because "it can provide social benefit, by shedding light on an earlier work, and, in the process, creating a new one," *Campbell,* 510 U.S. at 579, a search engine provides social benefit by incorporating an original work into a new work, namely, an electronic reference tool. Indeed, a search engine may be more transformative than a parody because a search engine provides an entirely new use for the

---

[8]   We reject at the outset Perfect 10's argument that providing access to infringing websites cannot be deemed transformative and is inherently not fair use. Perfect 10 relies on *Video Pipeline, Inc. v. Buena Vista Home Entm't, Inc.,* 342 F.3d 191 (3d Cir. 2003), and *Atari Games Corp. v. Nintendo of Am. Inc.,* 975 F.2d 832, 843 (Fed.Cir. 1992). But these cases, in essence, simply apply the general rule that a party claiming fair use must act in a manner generally compatible with principles of good faith and fair dealing. *See Harper & Row,* 471 U.S. at 562–63. For this reason, a company whose business is based on providing scenes from copyrighted movies without authorization could not claim that it provided the same public benefit as the search engine in *Kelly. See Video Pipeline,* 342 F.3d at 198–200. Similarly, a company whose overriding desire to replicate a competitor's computer game led it to obtain a copy of the competitor's source code from the Copyright Office under false pretenses could not claim fair use with respect to its purloined copy. *Atari Games,* 975 F.2d at 843.

Unlike the alleged infringers in *Video Pipeline* and *Atari Games,* who intentionally misappropriated the copyright owners' works for the purpose of commercial exploitation, Google is operating a comprehensive search engine that only incidentally indexes infringing websites. This incidental impact does not amount to an abuse of the good faith and fair dealing underpinnings of the fair use doctrine. Accordingly, we conclude that Google's inclusion of thumbnail images derived from infringing websites in its Internet-wide search engine activities does not preclude Google from raising a fair use defense.

original work, while a parody typically has the same entertainment purpose as the original work. . . .

The fact that Google incorporates the entire Perfect 10 image into the search engine results does not diminish the transformative nature of Google's use. As the district court correctly noted, *Perfect 10*, 416 F.Supp.2d at 848–49, we determined in *Kelly* that even making an exact copy of a work may be transformative so long as the copy serves a different function than the original work. For example, the First Circuit has held that the republication of photos taken for a modeling portfolio in a newspaper was transformative because the photos served to inform, as well as entertain. *See Nunez v. Caribbean Int'l News Corp.*, 235 F.3d 18, 22–23 (1st Cir. 2000). In contrast, duplicating a church's religious book for use by a different church was not transformative. *See Worldwide Church of God v. Phila. Church of God, Inc.*, 227 F.3d 1110, 1117 (9th Cir. 2000). Nor was a broadcaster's simple retransmission of a radio broadcast over telephone lines transformative, where the original radio shows were given no "new expression, meaning, or message." *Infinity Broad. Corp. v. Kirkwood*, 150 F.3d 104, 108 (2d Cir. 1998). Here, Google uses Perfect 10's images in a new context to serve a different purpose.

The district court nevertheless determined that Google's use of thumbnail images was less transformative than Arriba's use of thumbnails in *Kelly* because Google's use of thumbnails superseded Perfect 10's right to sell its reduced-size images for use on cell phones. The district court stated that "mobile users can download and save the thumbnails displayed by Google Image Search onto their phones," and concluded "to the extent that users may choose to download free images to their phone rather than purchase [Perfect 10's] reduced-size images, Google's use supersedes [Perfect 10's]."

Additionally, the district court determined that the commercial nature of Google's use weighed against its transformative nature. *Id.* Although *Kelly* held that the commercial use of the photographer's images by Arriba's search engine was less exploitative than typical commercial use, and thus weighed only slightly against a finding of fair use, the district court here distinguished *Kelly* on the ground that some website owners in the AdSense program had infringing Perfect 10 images on their websites. The district court held that because Google's thumbnails "lead users to sites that directly benefit Google's bottom line," the AdSense program increased the commercial nature of Google's use of Perfect 10's images.

In conducting our case-specific analysis of fair use in light of the purposes of copyright, we must weigh Google's superseding and commercial uses of thumbnail images against Google's significant transformative use, as well as the extent to which Google's search engine promotes the purposes of copyright and serves the interests of the public. Although the district court acknowledged the "truism that search engines such as Google Image Search provide great value to the public," the district court did not expressly consider whether this value outweighed the significance of Google's superseding use or the commercial nature of Google's use. The Supreme Court, however, has directed us to be mindful of the extent to which a use promotes the purposes of copyright and serves the interests of the public.

We note that the superseding use in this case is not significant at present: the district court did not find that any downloads for mobile phone use had taken place. Moreover, while Google's use of thumbnails to direct users to AdSense partners containing infringing content adds a commercial dimension that did not exist in *Kelly*, the district court did not determine that this commercial element was significant. The district court stated that Google's AdSense programs as a whole contributed "$630 million, or 46% of total revenues" to Google's bottom line, but noted that this figure did not "break down the much smaller amount attributable to websites that contain infringing content."

We conclude that the significantly transformative nature of Google's search engine, particularly in light of its public benefit, outweighs Google's superseding and commercial uses of the thumbnails in this case. In reaching this conclusion, we note the importance of analyzing fair use flexibly in light of new circumstances. . . . We are also mindful of the Supreme Court's direction that "the more transformative the new work, the less will be the significance of other factors, like commercialism, that may weigh against a finding of fair use." *Campbell*, 510 U.S. at 579.

Accordingly, we disagree with the district court's conclusion that because Google's use of the thumbnails could supersede Perfect 10's cell phone download use and because the use was more commercial than Arriba's, this fair use factor weighed "slightly" in favor of Perfect 10. Instead, we conclude that the transformative nature of Google's use is more significant than any incidental superseding use or the minor commercial aspects of Google's search engine and website. Therefore, this factor weighs heavily in favor of Google.

The nature of the copyrighted work. With respect to the second factor, "the nature of the copyrighted work," 17 U.S.C. § 107(2), our decision in *Kelly* is directly on point. There we held that the photographer's images were "creative in nature" and thus "closer to the core of intended copyright protection than are more fact-based works." *Kelly*, 336 F.3d at 820 (internal quotation omitted). However, because the photos appeared on the Internet before Arriba used thumbnail versions in its search engine results, this factor weighed only slightly in favor of the photographer. *Id.*

Here, the district court found that Perfect 10's images were creative but also previously published. The right of first publication is "the author's right to control the first public appearance of his expression." *Harper & Row*, 471 U.S. at 564. Because this right encompasses "the choices of when, where, and in what form first to publish a work," *id.*, an author exercises and exhausts this one-time right by publishing the work in any medium. *See, e.g., Batjac Prods. Inc. v. GoodTimes Home Video Corp.*, 160 F.3d 1223, 1235 (9th Cir. 1998) (noting, in the context of the common law right of first publication, that such a right "does not entail multiple first publication rights in every available medium"). Once Perfect 10 has exploited this commercially valuable right of first publication by putting its images on the Internet for paid subscribers, Perfect 10 is no longer entitled to the enhanced protection available for an unpublished work. Accordingly the district court did not err in holding that this factor weighed only slightly in favor of Perfect 10.

The amount and substantiality of the portion used. . . . In *Kelly*, we held Arriba's use of the entire photographic image was reasonable in light of the purpose of a search engine. Specifically, we noted, "[i]t was necessary for Arriba to copy the entire image to allow users to recognize the image and decide whether to pursue more information about the image or the originating [website]. If Arriba only copied part of the image, it would be more difficult to identify it, thereby reducing the usefulness of the visual search engine." Accordingly, we concluded that this factor did not weigh in favor of either party. Because the same analysis applies to Google's use of Perfect 10's image, the district court did not err in finding that this factor favored neither party.

Effect of use on the market. . . . In *Kelly*, we concluded that Arriba's use of the thumbnail images did not harm the market for the photographer's full-size images. *See Kelly*, 336 F.3d at 821–22. We reasoned that because thumbnails were not a substitute for the full-sized images, they did not harm the photographer's ability to sell or license his full-sized images. *Id.* The district court here followed *Kelly's* reasoning, holding that Google's use of thumbnails did not hurt Perfect 10's market for full-size images. *See Perfect 10*, 416 F.Supp.2d at 850–51. We agree.

Perfect 10 argues that the district court erred because the likelihood of market harm may be presumed if the intended use of an image is for commercial gain. However, this presumption does not arise when a work is transformative because "market substitution is at least less certain, and market harm may not be so readily inferred." *Campbell*, 510 U.S. at 591. As previously discussed, Google's use of thumbnails for search engine purposes is highly transformative, and so market harm cannot be presumed.

Perfect 10 also has a market for reduced-size images, an issue not considered in *Kelly*. The district court held that "Google's use of thumbnails likely does harm the potential market for the downloading of [Perfect 10's] reduced-size images onto cell phones." The district court reasoned that persons who can obtain Perfect 10 images free of charge from Google are less likely to pay for a download, and the availability of Google's thumbnail images would harm Perfect 10's market for cell phone downloads. *Id.* As we discussed above, the district court did not make a finding that Google users have downloaded thumbnail images for cell phone use. This potential harm to Perfect 10's market remains hypothetical. We conclude that this factor favors neither party.

Having undertaken a case-specific analysis of all four factors, we now weigh these factors together "in light of the purposes of copyright." In this case, Google has put Perfect 10's thumbnail images (along with millions of other thumbnail images) to a use fundamentally different than the use intended by Perfect 10. In doing so, Google has provided a significant benefit to the public. Weighing this significant transformative use against the unproven use of Google's thumbnails for cell phone downloads, and considering the other fair use factors, all in light of the purpose of copyright, we conclude that Google's use of Perfect 10's thumbnails is a fair use. . . .

[For a subsequent decision applying the Ninth Circuit's analysis to infringement claims brought by the same copyright owner against a different search engine, *see Perfect 10, Inc. v. Yandex N.V.*, 2013 WL 4777189 (N.D.Cal. 2013).]

Page 907. Add new Question 4:

4. With the development of search engines, particularly Google, the practice of "crawling" and "scraping" websites for reproduction of extracts in search results, or on a site aggregating links to the indexed content, has refocused the fair use defense as an adjunct to the defense of implied license. Arguably, anyone who posts a website wants that website to be found on the internet; to be found, one's site has to be "indexed," that is, copied and stored in the search engine's database, as well as partly reproduced in search results. Copyright owners who do not wish to have their sites copied can "opt out" of being crawled by including an instruction to the search engine's "robot" not to copy the site. *See Field v. Google*, 412 F.Supp.2d 1106 (D.Nev. 2006), discussed in Question 7 on page 352 in the main casebook. Otherwise, in this fully automated process (whose defaults the search engine nonetheless sets), the website will be included. Failure to withdraw completely from the indexing process (there currently appears to be no halfway setting, allowing the "bot" to reproduce some but not all of the content of an openly accessible webpage) may be construed as acceptance of the search engine's conduct. The more widespread the practice of implied licensing, the more "fair" it becomes. While the outcome seems reasonable in the context of search results, is it more problematic in other contexts? Is it appropriate to intertwine fair use with implied license arguments which themselves presume copyright owner acceptance of search engines' unilaterally-imposed design choices?

Pages 911–912. Delete Question 1 and renumber Question 2 as Question 1. After the newly renumbered Question 1, insert the following:

MASS DIGITIZATION

Authors Guild, Inc. v. HathiTrust

755 F.3d 87 (2d Cir. 2014)

■ PARKER, CIRCUIT JUDGE.

Beginning in 2004, several research universities including the University of Michigan, the University of California at Berkeley, Cornell University, and the University of Indiana agreed to allow Google to electronically scan the books in their collections. In October 2008, thirteen universities announced plans to create a repository for the digital copies and founded an organization called HathiTrust to set up and operate the HathiTrust Digital Library (or "HDL"). Colleges, universities, and other nonprofit institutions became members of HathiTrust and made the books in their collections available for inclusion in the HDL. HathiTrust currently has 80 member institutions and the HDL contains digital copies of more than ten million works, published over many centuries, written in a multitude of languages, covering almost every subject imaginable. This appeal requires us to decide whether the HDL's use of copyrighted material is protected against a claim of copyright infringement under the doctrine of fair use.

BACKGROUND
A. The HathiTrust Digital Library

Below is an example of the results a user might see after running an HDL full-text search:

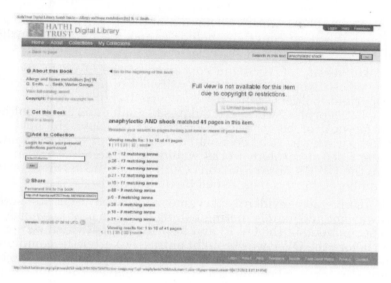

Second, the HDL allows member libraries to provide patrons with certified print disabilities access to the full text of copyrighted works. A "print disability" is any disability that prevents a person from effectively reading printed material. Blindness is one example, but print disabilities also include those that prevent a person from physically holding a book or turning pages. To use this service, a patron must obtain certification of his disability from a qualified expert. Through the HDL, a print-disabled user can obtain access to the contents of works in the digital library using adaptive technologies such as software that converts the text into spoken words, or that magnifies the text. Currently, the University of Michigan's library is the only HDL member that permits such access, although other member libraries intend to provide it in the future.

Third, by preserving the copyrighted books in digital form, the HDL permits members to create a replacement copy of the work, if the member already owned an original copy, the member's original copy is lost, destroyed, or stolen, and a replacement copy is unobtainable at a "fair" price elsewhere.

The HDL stores digital copies of the works in four different locations. One copy is stored on its primary server in Michigan, one on its secondary server in Indiana, and two on separate backup tapes at the University of Michigan.[3] Each copy contains the full text of the work, in a machine

---

[3]   Separate from the HDL, one copy is also kept by Google. Google's use of its copy is the subject of a separate lawsuit currently pending in this Court. *See Authors Guild, Inc. v. Google, Inc.*, 721 F.3d 132 (2d Cir. 2013), *on remand*, 954 F.Supp.2d 282 (S.D.N.Y. 2013), *appeal docketed*, No. 13–4829 (2d Cir. Dec. 23, 2013).

readable format, as well as the images of each page in the work as they appear in the print version.

B.   The Orphan Works Project

Separate and apart from the HDL, in May 2011, the University of Michigan developed a project known as the Orphan Works Project (or "OWP"). An "orphan work" is an out-of-print work that is still in copyright, but whose copyright holder cannot be readily identified or located.

The University of Michigan conceived of the OWP in two stages: First, the project would attempt to identify out-of-print works, try to find their copyright holders, and, if no copyright holder could be found, publish a list of orphan works candidates to enable the copyright holders to come forward or be otherwise located. If no copyright holder came forward, the work was to be designated as an orphan work. Second, those works identified as orphan works would be made accessible in digital format to the OWP's library patrons (with simultaneous viewers limited to the number of hard copies owned by the library).

The University evidently became concerned that its screening process was not adequately distinguishing between orphan works (which were to be included in the OWP) and in-print works (which were not). As a result, before the OWP was brought online, but after the complaint was filed in this case, the University indefinitely suspended the project. No copyrighted work has been distributed or displayed through the project and it remains suspended as of this writing.

C.   Proceedings in the District Court

This case began when twenty authors and authors' associations (collectively, the "Authors") sued HathiTrust, one of its member universities, and the presidents of four other member universities (collectively, the "Libraries") for copyright infringement seeking declaratory and injunctive relief. The National Federation of the Blind and three print-disabled students (the "Intervenors") were permitted to intervene to defend their ability to continue using the HDL.

. . .

The district court granted the Libraries' and Intervenors' motions for summary judgment on the infringement claims on the basis that the three uses permitted by the HDL were fair uses. In this assessment, the district court gave considerable weight to what it found to be the "transformative" nature of the three uses and to what it described as the HDL's "invaluable" contribution to the advancement of knowledge, *Authors Guild, Inc. v. HathiTrust,* 902 F.Supp.2d 445, 460–64 (S.D.N.Y. 2012). The district court explained:

> Although I recognize that the facts here may on some levels be without precedent, I am convinced that they fall safely within the protection of fair use such that there is no genuine issue of material fact. I cannot imagine a definition of fair use that would not encompass the transformative uses made by [the HDL] and would require that I terminate this invaluable contribution to the progress of science and cultivation of the arts that at the same time effectuates the ideals espoused by the

[Americans With Disabilities Act of 1990 (codified as amended at 42 U.S.C. §§ 12101, *et seq.*)].

Id. at 464.

. . . [T]his appeal followed.

DISCUSSION

We review *de novo* under well-established standards the district court's decisions granting summary judgment and judgment on the pleadings.

As a threshold matter, we consider whether the authors' associations have standing to assert infringement claims on behalf of their members. [The court affirmed the district court's ruling that three authors' associations asserting claims did not have standing based on U.S. law, but that four associations claiming standing based on foreign law authorization to sue on behalf of their members did have standing.]

I.   Fair Use[4]

A.

As the Supreme Court has explained, the overriding purpose of copyright is " '[t]o promote the Progress of Science and useful Arts . . . .' " *Campbell v. Acuff-Rose Music, Inc.,* 510 U.S. 569, 574 (1994); *see also Twentieth Century Music Corp. v. Aiken,* 422 U.S. 151, 156 (1975). This goal has animated copyright law in Anglo-American history, beginning with the first copyright statute, the Statute of Anne of 1709, which declared itself to be "[a]n Act for the Encouragement of Learning, by Vesting the Copies of Printed Books in the Authors . . . during the Times therein mentioned." In short, our law recognizes that copyright is "not an inevitable, divine, or natural right that confers on authors the absolute ownership of their creations. It is designed rather to stimulate activity and progress in the arts for the intellectual enrichment of the public." Pierre N. Leval, *Toward a Fair Use Standard,* 103 HARV. L. REV. 1105,1107 (1990).

The Copyright Act furthers this core purpose by granting authors a limited monopoly over (and thus the opportunity to profit from) the dissemination of their original works of authorship. The Copyright Act confers upon authors certain enumerated exclusive rights over their works during the term of the copyright, including the rights to reproduce the copyrighted work and to distribute those copies to the public. The Act also gives authors the exclusive right to prepare certain new works— called "derivative works"—that are based upon the copyrighted work. Paradigmatic examples of derivative works include the translation of a novel into another language, the adaptation of a novel into a movie or a play, or the recasting of a novel as an e-book or an audiobook. As a

---

[4]   Plaintiffs argue that the fair use defense is inapplicable to the activities at issue here, because the Copyright Act includes another section, 108, which governs "Reproduction [of copyrighted works] by Libraries . . ." 17 U.S.C. § 108. However, section 108 also includes a "savings clause," which states, "Nothing in this section in any way affects the right of fair use as provided by section 107. . . ." § 108(f)(4). Thus, we do not construe § 108 as foreclosing our analysis of the Libraries' activities under fair use, and we proceed with that analysis.

general rule, for works created after January 1, 1978, copyright protection lasts for the life of the author plus an additional 70 years.

At the same time, there are important limits to an author's rights to control original and derivative works. One such limit is the doctrine of "fair use," which allows the public to draw upon copyrighted materials without the permission of the copyright holder in certain circumstances. *See id.* § 107 ("[T]he fair use of a copyrighted work . . . is not an infringement of copyright."). "From the infancy of copyright protection, some opportunity for fair use of copyrighted materials has been thought necessary to fulfill copyright's very purpose, '[t]o promote the Progress of Science and useful Arts. . . .'" *Campbell,* 510 U.S. at 574.

Under the fair-use doctrine, a book reviewer may, for example, quote from an original work in order to illustrate a point and substantiate criticisms, *see Folsom v. Marsh,* 9 F.Cas. 342, 344 (C.C.D.Mass. 1841) (No. 4901), and a biographer may quote from unpublished journals and letters for similar purposes, *see Wright v. Warner Books, Inc.,* 953 F.2d 731 (2d Cir. 1991). An artist may employ copyrighted photographs in a new work that uses a fundamentally different artistic approach, aesthetic, and character from the original. *See Cariou v. Prince,* 714 F.3d 694, 706 (2d Cir. 2013). An internet search engine can display low-resolution versions of copyrighted images in order to direct the user to the website where the original could be found. *See Perfect 10, Inc. v. Amazon.com, Inc.,* 508 F.3d 1146, 1165 (9th Cir. 2007); *Kelly v. Arriba Soft Corp.,* 336 F.3d 811, 818–22 (9th Cir. 2002). A newspaper can publish a copyrighted photograph 18 (taken for a modeling portfolio) in order to inform and entertain the newspaper's readership about a news story. *See Nunez v. Caribbean Int'l News Corp.,* 235 F.3d 18, 25 (1st Cir. 2000). A viewer can create a recording of a broadcast television show in order to view it at a later time. *See Sony Corp. of Am. v. Universal City Studios, Inc.,* 464 U.S. 417, 447–450 (1984). And a competitor may create copies of copyrighted software for the purpose of analyzing that software and discovering how it functions (a process called "reverse engineering"). *See Sony Comp. Entertainment, Inc. v. Connectix Corp.,* 203 F.3d 596, 599–601 (9th Cir. 2000).

The doctrine is generally subject to an important proviso: A fair use must not excessively damage the market for the original by providing the public with a substitute for that original work. Thus, a book review may fairly quote a copyrighted book "for the purposes of fair and reasonable criticism," *Folsom,* 9 F.Cas. at 344, but the review may not quote extensively from the "heart" of a forthcoming memoir in a manner that usurps the right of first publication and serves as a substitute for purchasing the memoir, *Harper & Row, Publishers, Inc. v. Nation Enters.,* 471 U.S. 539 (1985).

In 1976, as part of a wholesale revision of the Copyright Act, Congress codified the judicially created fair-use doctrine at 17 U.S.C. § 107. Section 107 requires a court to consider four nonexclusive factors which are to be weighed together to assess whether a particular use is fair . . .

An important focus of the first factor is whether the use is "transformative." A use is transformative if it does something more than repackage or republish the original copyrighted work. The inquiry is whether the work "adds something new, with a further purpose or different character, altering the first with new expression, meaning or message. . . ." *Campbell,* 510 U.S. at 579 (citing Leval, 103 HARV. L. REV. at 1111). "[T]he more transformative the new work, the less will be the significance of other factors . . . that may weigh against a finding of fair use." *Id.* Contrary to what the district court implied, a use does not become transformative by making an "invaluable contribution to the progress of science and cultivation of the arts." *HathiTrust,* 902 F.Supp.2d at 464. Added value or utility is not the test: a transformative work is one that serves a new and different function from the original work and is not a substitute for it.

The second factor considers whether the copyrighted work is "of the creative or instructive type that the copyright laws value and seek to foster." Leval, 103 HARV. L. REV. at 1117; *see also Folsom,* 9 F.Cas. at 348 ("[W]e must often . . . look to the nature and objects of the selections made. . . ."). For example, the law of fair use "recognizes a greater need to disseminate factual works than works of fiction or fantasy." *Harper & Row,* 471 U.S. at 563.

The third factor asks whether the secondary use employs more of the copyrighted work than is necessary, and whether the copying was excessive in relation to any valid purposes asserted under the first factor. *Campbell,* 510 U.S. at 586–87. In weighing this factor, we assess the quantity and value of the materials used and whether the amount copied is reasonable in relation to the purported justifications for the use under the first factor. Leval, 103 HARV. L. REV. at 1123.

Finally, the fourth factor requires us to assess the impact of the use on the traditional market for the copyrighted work. This is the "single most important element of fair use." *Harper & Row,* U.S. at 566. To defeat a claim of fair use, the copyright holder must point to market harm that results because the secondary use serves as a substitute for the original work. *See Campbell,* 510 U.S. at 591 ("cognizable market harm" is limited to "market substitution"); *see also NXIVM Corp. v. Ross Inst.,* 364 F.3d 471, 481–82 (2d Cir. 2004).

B.

As discussed above, the Libraries permit three uses of the digital copies deposited in the HDL. We now consider whether these uses are "fair" within the meaning of our copyright law.

1.   Full-Text Search

It is not disputed that, in order to perform a full-text search of books, the Libraries must first create digital copies of the entire books. Importantly, as we have seen, the HDL does not allow users to view any portion of the books they are searching. Consequently, in providing this service, the HDL does not add into circulation any new, human-readable copies of any books. Instead, the HDL simply permits users to "word search"—that is, to locate where specific words or phrases appear in the digitized books. Applying the relevant factors, we conclude that this use is a fair use.

i.

Turning to the first factor, we conclude that the creation of a full-text searchable database is a quintessentially transformative use. As the example, *supra,* demonstrates, the result of a word search is different in purpose, character, expression, meaning, and message from the page (and the book) from which it is drawn. Indeed, we can discern little or no resemblance between the original text and the results of the HDL full-text search.

There is no evidence that the Authors write with the purpose of enabling text searches of their books. Consequently, the full-text search function does not "supersede[ ] the objects [or purposes] of the original creation," *Campbell*, 510 U.S. at 579 (internal quotation marks omitted). The HDL does not "merely repackage[ ] or republish[ ] the original[s]," Leval, 103 HARV. L. REV. at 1111, or merely recast "an original work into a new mode of presentation," *Castle Rock Entm't, Inc. v. Carol Publ'g Grp., Inc. .*, 150 F.3d 132, 143 (2d Cir. 1998). Instead, by enabling full-text search, the HDL adds to the original something new with a different purpose and a different character.

Full-text search adds a great deal more to the copyrighted works at issue than did the transformative uses we approved in several other cases. For example, in *Cariou v. Prince,* we found that certain photograph collages were transformative, even though the collages were cast in the same medium as the copyrighted photographs. 714 F.3d at 706. Similarly, in *Bill Graham Archives v. Dorling Kindersley Ltd.,* we held that it was a transformative use to include in a biography copyrighted concert photos, even though the photos were unaltered (except for being reduced in size). 448 F.3d 605, 609–11 (2d Cir. 2006); *see also Blanch v. Koons,* 467 F.3d 244, 252–53 (2d Cir. 2006) (transformative use of copyrighted photographs in collage painting); *Leibovitz v. Paramount Pictures Corp.,* 137 F.3d 109, 114 (2d Cir. 1998) (transformative use of copyrighted photograph in advertisement).

Cases from other Circuits reinforce this conclusion. In *Perfect 10, Inc.,* the Ninth Circuit held that the use of copyrighted thumbnail images in internet search results was transformative because the thumbnail copies served a different function from the original copyrighted images. 508 F.3d at 1165. And in *A.V. ex rel. Vanderhye v. iParadigms, LLC,* a company created electronic copies of unaltered student papers for use in connection with a computer program that detects plagiarism. Even though the electronic copies made no "substantive alteration to" the copyrighted student essays, the Fourth Circuit held that plagiarism detection constituted a transformative use of the copyrighted works. 562 F.3d 630, 639–40.

ii.

The second fair-use factor—the nature of the copyrighted work—is not dispositive. The HDL permits the full-text search of every type of work imaginable. Consequently, there is no dispute that the works at issue are of the type that the copyright laws value and seek to protect. However, "this factor 'may be of limited usefulness where,' as here, 'the creative work . . . is being used for a transformative purpose'." *Cariou,* 714 F.3d at 710 (quoting *Bill Graham Archives,* 448 F.3d at 612). Accordingly, our fair-use analysis hinges on the other three factors.

iii.

The third factor asks whether the copying used more of the copyrighted work than necessary and whether the copying was excessive. As we have noted, "[t]here are no absolute rules as to how much of a copyrighted work may be copied and still be considered a fair use." *Maxtone-Graham v. Burtchaell*, 803 F.2d 1253, 1263 (2d Cir. 1986). "[T]he extent of permissible copying varies with the purpose and character of the use." *Campbell*, 510 U.S. at 586–87. The crux of the inquiry is whether "no more was taken than necessary." *Id.* at 589. For some purposes, it may be necessary to copy the entire copyrighted work, in which case Factor Three does not weigh against a finding of fair use.

In order to enable the full-text search function, the Libraries, as we have seen, created digital copies of all the books in their collections.[5] Because it was reasonably necessary for the HDL to make use of the entirety of the works in order to enable the full-text search function, we do not believe the copying was excessive.

The Authors also contend that the copying is excessive because the HDL creates and maintains copies of the works at four different locations. But the record demonstrates that these copies are also reasonably necessary in order to facilitate the HDL's legitimate uses. In particular, the HDL's services are offered to patrons through two servers, one at the University of Michigan (the primary server) and an identical one at the University of Indiana (the "mirror" server). Both servers contain copies of the digital works at issue. According to the HDL executive director, the "existence of a[n] [identical] mirror site allows for balancing the load of user web traffic to avoid overburdening a single site, and each site acts as a back-up of the HDL collection in the event that one site were to cease operation (for example, due to failure caused by a disaster, or even as a result of routine maintenance)." To further guard against the risk of data loss, the HDL stores copies of the works on two encrypted backup tapes, which are disconnected from the internet and are placed in separate secure locations on the University of Michigan campus. The HDL creates these backup tapes so that the data could be restored in "the event of a disaster causing large-scale data loss" to the primary and mirror servers.

We have no reason to think that these copies are excessive or unreasonable in relation to the purposes identified by the Libraries and permitted by the law of copyright. In sum, even viewing the evidence in the light most favorable to the Authors, the record demonstrates that these copies are reasonably necessary to facilitate the services HDL provides to the public and to mitigate the risk of disaster or data loss. Accordingly, we conclude that this factor favors the Libraries.

iv.

The fourth factor requires us to consider "the effect of the use upon the potential market for or value of the copyrighted work," 17 U.S.C. § 107(4), and, in particular, whether the secondary use "usurps the market of the original work," *NXIVM Corp.*, 364 F.3d at 482.

The Libraries contend that the full-text-search use poses no harm to any existing or potential traditional market and point to the fact that, in discovery, the Authors admitted that they were unable to identify "any specific, quantifiable past harm, or any documents relating to any such

---

[5] The HDL also creates digital copies of the images of each page of the books. As the Libraries acknowledge, the HDL does not need to retain these copies to enable the full-text search use. We discuss the fair-use justification for these copies in the context of the disability-access use.

past harm," resulting from any of the Libraries' uses of their works (including full-text search). The district court agreed with this contention, as do we.

At the outset, it is important to recall that the Factor Four analysis is concerned with only one type of economic injury to a copyright holder: the harm that results because the secondary use serves as a substitute for the original work. *See Campbell,* 510 U.S. at 591 ("cognizable market harm" is limited to "market substitution"). In other words, under Factor Four, any economic "harm" caused by transformative uses does not count because such uses, by definition, do not serve as substitutes for the original work.

To illustrate why this is so, consider how copyright law treats book reviews. Book reviews often contain quotations of copyrighted material to illustrate the reviewer's points and substantiate his criticisms; this is a paradigmatic fair use. And a negative book review can cause a degree of economic injury to the author by dissuading readers from purchasing copies of her book, even when the review does not serve as a substitute for the original. But, obviously, in that case, the author has no cause for complaint under Factor Four: The only market harms that count are the ones that are caused because the secondary use serves as a substitute for the original, not when the secondary use is transformative (as in quotations in a book review). *See Campbell,* 510 U.S. at 591–92 ("[W]hen a lethal parody, like a scathing theater review, kills demand for the original, it does not produce a harm cognizable under the Copyright Act.").

The Authors assert two reasons why the full-text-search function harms their traditional markets. The first is a "lost sale" theory which posits that a market for licensing books for digital search could possibly develop in the future, and the HDL impairs the emergence of such a market because it allows patrons to search books without any need for a license. Thus, according to the Authors, every copy employed by the HDL in generating full-text searches represents a lost opportunity to license the book for search.

This theory of market harm does not work under Factor Four, because the full-text search function does not serve as a substitute for the books that are being searched. Thus, it is irrelevant that the Libraries might be willing to purchase licenses in order to engage in this transformative use (if the use were deemed unfair). Lost licensing revenue counts under Factor Four only when the use serves as a substitute for the original and the full-text-search use does not.

Next, the Authors assert that the HDL creates the risk of a security breach which might impose irreparable damage on the Authors and their works. In particular, the Authors speculate that, if hackers were able to obtain unauthorized access to the books stored at the HDL, the full text of these tens of millions of books might be distributed worldwide without restriction, "decimat[ing]" the traditional market for those works.

The record before us documents the extensive security measures the Libraries have undertaken to safeguard against the risk of a data breach. Some of those measures were described by the HDL executive director as follows:

First, [HDL] maintains . . . rigorous physical security controls. HDL servers, storage, and networking equipment at Michigan and Indiana University are mounted in locked racks, and only six individuals at Michigan and three at Indiana University have keys. The data centers housing HDL servers, storage, and networking equipment at each site location are monitored by video surveillance, and entry requires use of both a keycard and a biometric sensor.

Second, network access to the HDL corpus is highly restricted, even for the staff of the data centers housing HDL equipment at Michigan and Indiana University. For example, two levels of network firewalls are in place at each site, and Indiana University data center staff do not have network access to the HDL corpus, only access to the physical equipment. For the backup tapes, network access is limited to the administrators of the backup system, and these individuals are not provided the encryption key that would be required to access the encrypted files on the backup tapes.

Web access to the HDL corpus is also highly restricted. Access by users of the HDL service is governed by primarily by [*sic*] the HDL rights database, which classifies each work by presumed copyright status, and also by a user's authentication to the system (e.g., as an individual certified to have a print disability by Michigan's Office of Services for Students with Disabilities).

. . .

Even where we do permit a work to be read online, such as a work in the public domain, we make efforts to ensure that inappropriate levels of access do not take place. For example, a mass download prevention system called "choke" is used to measure the rate of activity (such as the rate a user is reading pages) by each individual user. If a user's rate of activity exceeds certain thresholds, the system assumes that the user is mechanized (e.g., a web robot) and blocks that user's access for a set period of time.

This showing of the security measures taken by the Libraries is essentially unrebutted. Consequently, we see no basis in the record on which to conclude that a security breach is likely to occur, much less one that would result in the public release of the specific copyrighted works belonging to any of the plaintiffs in this case. Factor Four thus favors a finding of fair use.

Without foreclosing a future claim based on circumstances not now predictable, and based on a different record, we hold that the balance of relevant factors in this case favors the Libraries. In sum, we conclude that the doctrine of fair use allows the Libraries to digitize copyrighted works for the purpose of permitting full-text searches.

2.   Access to the Print-Disabled

The HDL also provides print-disabled patrons with versions of all of the works contained in its digital archive in formats accessible to them. In order to obtain access to the works, a patron must submit documentation from a qualified expert verifying that the disability prevents him or her from reading printed materials, and the patron must be affiliated with an HDL member that has opted-into the program. Currently, the University of Michigan is the only HDL member institution that has opted-in. We conclude that this use is also protected by the doctrine of fair use.

i

In applying the Factor One analysis, the district court concluded that "[t]he use of digital copies to facilitate access for print-disabled persons is [a] transformative" use. *HathiTrust*, 902 F.Supp.2d at 461. This is a misapprehension; providing expanded access to the print disabled is not "transformative."

As discussed above, a transformative use adds something new to the copyrighted work and does not merely supersede the purposes of the original creation. The Authors state that they "write books to be read (or listened to)." By making copyrighted works available in formats accessible to the disabled, the HDL enables a larger audience to read those works, but the underlying purpose of the HDL's use is the same as the author's original purpose.

Indeed, when the HDL recasts copyrighted works into new formats to be read by the disabled, it appears, at first glance, to be creating derivative works over which the author ordinarily maintains control. *See* 17 U.S.C. § 106(2). As previously noted, paradigmatic examples of derivative works include translations of the original into a different language, or adaptations of the original into different forms or media. *See id.* § 101 (defining "derivative work"). The Authors contend that by converting their works into a different, accessible format, the HDL is simply creating a derivative work.

It is true that, oftentimes, the print-disabled audience has no means of obtaining access to the copyrighted works included in the HDL. But, similarly, the non-English-speaking audience cannot gain access to untranslated books written in English and an unauthorized translation is not transformative simply because it enables a new audience to read a work.

This observation does not end the analysis. "While a transformative use generally is more likely to qualify as fair use, 'transformative use is not absolutely necessary for a finding of fair use.' " *Swatch Grp. Mgmt. Servs. Ltd. v. Bloomberg L.P.,* ___ F.3d ___, ___, 2014 WL 2219162, at *7 (2d Cir. 2014) (quoting *Campbell,* 510 U.S. at 579). We conclude that providing access to the print-disabled is still a valid purpose under Factor One even though it is not transformative. We reach that conclusion for several reasons.

First, the Supreme Court has already said so. As Justice Stevens wrote for the Court: "Making a copy of a copyrighted work for the convenience of a blind person is expressly identified by the House Committee Report as an example of fair use, with no suggestion that anything more than a purpose to entertain or to inform need motivate the copying." *Sony Corp. of Am.,* 464 U.S. at 455 n. 40.

Our conclusion is reinforced by the legislative history on which he relied. The House Committee Report that accompanied codification of the fair use doctrine in the Copyright Act of 1976 expressly stated that making copies accessible "for the use of blind persons" posed a "special instance illustrating the application of the fair use doctrine. . . ." H.R. REP. NO. 94–1476, at 73 (1976). The Committee noted that "special [blind-accessible formats] . . . are not usually made by the publishers for commercial distribution." *Id.* In light of its understanding of the market (or lack thereof) for books accessible to the blind, the Committee explained that "the making of a single copy or phonorecord by an individual as a free service for a blind persons [*sic*] would properly be considered a fair use under section 107." *Id.* We believe this guidance supports a finding of fair use in the unique circumstances presented by print-disabled readers.

Since the passage of the 1976 Copyright Act, Congress has reaffirmed its commitment to ameliorating the hardships faced by the blind and the print disabled. In the Americans with Disabilities Act, Congress declared that our "Nation's proper goals regarding individuals with disabilities are to assure equality of opportunity, full participation, independent living, and economic self-sufficiency for such individuals." 42 U.S.C. § 12101(7). Similarly, the Chafee Amendment illustrates Congress's intent that copyright law make appropriate accommodations for the blind and print disabled. *See* 17 U.S.C. § 121.

ii.

Through the HDL, the disabled can obtain access to copyrighted works of all kinds, and there is no dispute that those works are of the sort that merit protection under the Copyright Act. As a result, Factor Two weighs against fair use. This does not preclude a finding of fair use, however, given our analysis of the other factors.

iii.

Regarding Factor Three, as previously noted, the HDL retains copies as digital image files and as text-only files, which are then stored in four separate locations. The Authors contend that this amount of copying is excessive because the Libraries have not demonstrated their need to retain the digital *image* files in addition to the text files.

We are unconvinced. The text files are required for text searching and to create text-to-speech capabilities for the blind and disabled. But the image files will provide an additional and often more useful method by which many disabled patrons, especially students and scholars, can obtain access to these works. These image files contain information, such as pictures, charts, diagrams, and the layout of the text on the printed page that cannot be converted to text or speech. None of this is captured by the HDL's text-only copies. Many legally blind patrons are capable of viewing these images if they are sufficiently magnified or if the color contrasts are increased. And other disabled patrons, whose physical impairments prevent them from turning pages or from holding books, may also be able to use assistive devices to view all of the content contained in the image files for a book. For those individuals, gaining access to the HDL's image files—in addition to the text-only files—is necessary to perceive the books fully. Consequently, it is reasonable for the Libraries to retain both the text and image copies.[6]

---

[6] The Authors also complain that the HDL creates and maintains four separate copies of the copyrighted works at issue. For reasons discussed in the full-text search section, this does not preclude a finding of fair use.

iv.

The fourth factor also weighs in favor of a finding of fair use. It is undisputed that the present-day market for books accessible to the handicapped is so insignificant that "it is common practice in the publishing industry for authors to forgo royalties that are generated through the sale of books manufactured in specialized formats for the blind. . . ." Appellants' Br. 34. "[T]he number of accessible books currently available to the blind for borrowing is a mere few hundred thousand titles, a minute percentage of the world's books. In contrast, the HDL contains more than ten million accessible volumes." J.A. 173 ¶ 10 (Maurer Decl.). When considering the 1976 Act, Congress was well aware of this problem. The House Committee Report observed that publishers did not "usually ma[ke]" their books available in specialized formats for the blind. H.R. REP. NO. 94–1476, at 73. That observation remains true today.

Weighing the factors together, we conclude that the doctrine of fair use allows the Libraries to provide full digital access to copyrighted works to their print-disabled patrons.[7]

3.   Preservation

By storing digital copies of the books, the HDL preserves them for generations to come, and ensures that they will still exist when their copyright terms lapse. Under certain circumstances, the HDL also proposes to make one additional use of the digitized works while they remain under copyright: The HDL will permit member libraries to create a replacement copy of a book, to be read and consumed by patrons, if (1) the member already owned an original copy, (2) the member's original copy is lost, destroyed, or stolen, and (3) a replacement copy is unobtainable at a fair price. The Authors claim that this use infringes their copyrights.

Even though the parties assume that this issue is appropriate for our determination, we are not convinced that this is so. The record before the district court does not reflect whether the plaintiffs own copyrights in any works that would be effectively irreplaceable at a fair price by the Libraries and, thus, would be potentially subject to being copied by the Libraries in case of the loss or destruction of an original. The Authors are not entitled to make this argument on behalf of others, because § 501 of "the Copyright Act does not permit copyright holders to choose third parties to bring suits on their behalf." *ABKCO Music,* 944 F.2d at 980.

Because the record before us does not reflect the existence of a non-speculative risk that the HDL might create replacement copies of the *plaintiffs'* copyrighted work, we do not believe plaintiffs have standing to bring this claim, and this concern does not present a live controversy for adjudication. Accordingly, we vacate the district court's judgment insofar as it adjudicated this issue without first considering whether plaintiffs have standing to challenge the preservation use of the HDL, and we remand for the district court to so determine.

---

[7]   In light of our holding, we need not consider whether the disability-access use is protected under the Chafee Amendment, 17 U.S.C. § 121.

[The court also affirmed the district court's ruling that the infringement claims asserted in connection with the OWP were not ripe for adjudication.]

CONCLUSION

The judgment of the district court is AFFIRMED, in part, insofar as the district court concluded that certain plaintiffs-appellants lack associational standing; that the doctrine of "fair use" allows defendants-appellees to create a full-text searchable database of copyrighted works and to provide those works in formats accessible to those with disabilities; and that claims predicated upon the Orphan Works Project are not ripe for adjudication. We VACATE the judgment, in part, insofar as it rests on the district court's holding related to the claim of infringement predicated upon defendants-appellees' preservation of copyrighted works, and we REMAND for further proceedings consistent with this opinion.

Authors Guild, Inc. v. Google Inc., 954 F.Supp.2d 282 (S.D.N.Y. 2013). Google, a major online search engine, scanned the contents of millions of physical books, both in and out of copyright. The contents were indexed, and both the full text of the digitized books and the index reside in a database owned and controlled by Google. To obtain the books for scanning, Google worked with several university libraries who, in return, received a digital copy of each library's scanned holdings. Google did not seek authorization for the scanning, but placed the burden on copyright holders to notify Google that they did not wish their books included in the program.

Users who search for particular words or phrases receive search results identifying the books in which the queried text appears. If the book has been scanned without the copyright holder's permission, the user receives only a short "snippet" of text showing the queried words, and a couple of lines of text above and below. The user cannot reconstruct whole pages through repeated searches. While advertising accompanies the general book search program, pages reporting returns from books included without permission will not carry advertising. Although Google does not publicly display more than "snippets" from in-copyright books it was not authorized to scan, Google retains the full text of these books in its database, which it exploits for a variety of "non-display" uses, such as enhancement of search results and of its translation program. Google thus derives economic value from the books it scans, but its internal exploitations arguably are "transformative" (or even *prima facie* non-infringing) because it is using the books' content as data rather than for its expressive value.

Prior to the Second Circuit's decision in the *HathiTrust* case, the district court in a suit by the Authors Guild against Google held that Google's book search activities constituted fair use. The court, following the district court decision (by a different S.D.N.Y. judge) in the *HathiTrust* case, emphasized the public benefit conferred by the search service. The court accorded little weight to the commercial character of Google's use:

> Google does not sell the scans it has made of books for Google Books; it does not sell the snippets that it displays; and it does not run ads on the About the Book pages that contain snippets.

> It does not engage in the direct commercialization of copyrighted works. Google does, of course, benefit commercially in the sense that users are drawn to the Google websites by the ability to search Google Books. While this is a consideration to be acknowledged in weighing all the factors, even assuming Google's principal motivation is profit, the fact is that Google Books serves several important educational purposes.

With respect to the fourth factor, the court ruled that

> a reasonable factfinder could only find that Google Books enhances the sales of books to the benefit of copyright holders. An important factor in the success of an individual title is whether it is discovered—whether potential readers learn of its existence. Google Books provides a way for authors' works to become noticed, much like traditional in-store book displays. Indeed, both librarians and their patrons use Google Books to identify books to purchase. Many authors have noted that online browsing in general and Google Books in particular helps readers find their work, thus increasing their audiences. Further, Google provides convenient links to booksellers to make it easy for a reader to order a book. In this day and age of on-line shopping, there can be no doubt but that Google Books improves books sales.

> In light of the Second Circuit's reasoning in *HathiTrust*, how would you predict the circuit court will rule on the Authors Guild's appeal of the trial court decision? Are there any salient differences between the Google book search service and the uses made in *HathiTrust*?

Fox News Network, LLC v. TVEyes, Inc., 43 F.Supp.3d 379 (S.D.N.Y. 2014).

> TVEyes is a media-monitoring service that enables its subscribers to track when keywords or phrases of interest are uttered on the television or radio. To do this, TVEyes records the content of more than 1,400 television and radio stations, twenty-four hours a day, seven days a week. Using closed captions and speech-to-text technology, TVEyes records the entire content of television and radio broadcasts and creates a searchable database of that content. The database, with services running from it, is the cornerstone of the service TVEyes provides to its subscribers.

> The database allows its subscribers, who include the United States Army, the White House, numerous members of the United States Congress, and local and state police departments, to track the news coverage of particular events. For example, police departments use TVEyes to track television coverage of public safety messages across different stations and locations, and to adjust outreach efforts accordingly. Without a service like TVEyes, the only way for the police department to know how every station is constantly reporting the situation would be to have an individual watch every station that broadcast news for twenty-four hours a day taking notes on each station's simultaneous coverage.

> . . .

Upon logging into its TVEyes account, the subscriber is taken to the Watch List Page. This page monitors all of the subscriber's desired keywords and terms, and organizes search results by day, tabulating the total number of times the keyword was mentioned by all 1,400 television and radio stations each day over a 32 day period. While on the Watch List Page, a user can also run a "Google News" search, comparing the mentions of the keyword or term on the internet with the mentions of the keyword or term on the TVEyes database. A subscriber can also create a custom time range to tabulate the number of times a term has been used in a certain time period, and the relative frequency of such use compared to other terms. Subscribers can set up email alerts for specific keywords or terms, and receive responses one to five minutes after the keyword or term is mentioned on any of the 1,400 television and radio stations TVEyes monitors. TVEyes' responses to subscribers provides a thumbnail image of the show, a snippet of transcript, and a short video clip beginning 14 seconds before the word was used.

When a subscriber on the Watch List Page clicks on the hyperlink showing the number of times the term was mentioned on a particular day, the subscriber is brought to the Results List Page. The Results List Page displays each mention of the keyword or term in reverse chronological order. Each individual result includes a portion of transcript highlighting the keyword and a thumbnail image of the particular show that used the term. When the user clicks the thumbnail image of the show, the video clip begins to play automatically alongside the transcript on the Transcript Page, beginning 14 seconds before the keyword is mentioned.

. . .

TVEyes is available only to businesses [subscribers pay a monthly fee of $500] and not to the general public. As of October 2013, TVEyes had over 2,200 subscribers including the White House, 100 current members of Congress, the Department of Defense, the United States House Committee on the Budget, the Associated Press, MSNBC, Reuters, the United States Army and Marines, the American Red Cross, AARP, Bloomberg, Cantor Fitzgerald, Goldman Sachs, ABC Television Group, CBS Television Network, the Association of Trial Lawyers, and many others.

. . .

[Applying the first fair use factor, the court found TVEyes' use to be "transformative"] I find that TVEyes' search engine together with its display of result clips is transformative, and "serves a new and different function from the original work and is not a substitute for it." *HathiTrust*, 755 F.3d 87, 2014 WL 2576342, at *6. In making this finding, I am guided by the Second Circuit's determination that databases that convert copyrighted works into a research tool to further learning are transformative. TVEyes' message, " 'this is what they said'—is a very different message from [Fox News']—'this is what you should [know or] believe.' " *Swatch*, 756 F.3d 73, 2014 WL

2219162, at *8. TVEyes' evidence, that its subscribers use the service for research, criticism, and comment, is undisputed and shows fair use as explicitly identified in the preamble of the statute. 17 U.S.C. § 107.

The issue of fair use is affected by the issue of profits. Clearly, TVEyes is a for profit company, and enjoys revenue and income from the service it provides. However, the consideration of profits is just one factor, among many others. "[T]he more transformative the new work, the less will be the significance of other factors, like commercialism, that may weigh against a finding of fair use." [Citations.] If "commerciality carried presumptive force against a finding of fairness, the presumption would swallow nearly all of the illustrative uses listed in the preamble paragraph of § 107, including news reporting, comment, criticism, teaching, scholarship, and research, since these activities are generally conducted for profit in this country." *Campbell*, 510 U.S. at 584. Thus I find that the first factor weighs in favor of TVEyes' fair use defense.

          . . .

[As to the third factor, h]ere, there is no question that TVEyes copies all of Fox News' content—that is the essence of TVEyes' business model. The third factor does not, however, counsel a simple, crude quantitative comparison. It asks rather "whether the secondary use employs more of the copyrighted work than is necessary, and whether the copying was excessive in relation to any valid purpose asserted under the first factor." *Authors Guild, Inc. v. HathiTrust*, 755 F.3d 87 (2d Cir. 2014). Thus, where copying the entire work is necessary to accomplish the transformative function or purpose, as is the case, here, this factor, like the second factor, bows to the importance and priority of the first factor's finding of transformative use. . . .

Here TVEyes copies all of Fox News' television content (and other stations' contents) in its entirety, a service no one, including Fox News itself provides. The value of TVEyes' database depends on its all-inclusive nature, copying everything that television and radio stations broadcast. One cannot say that TVEyes copies more than is necessary to its transformative purpose for, if TVEyes were to copy less, the reliability of its all-inclusive service would be compromised. I find that the third factor, the extent of the copying, weighs neither in favor or against a fair use finding . . .

          . . .

[Applying the fourth factor, the court found no economic harm to Fox.] No reasonable juror could find that people are using TVEyes as a substitute for watching Fox News broadcasts on television. There is no history of any such use, and there is no realistic danger of any potential harm to the overall market of television watching from an "unrestricted and widespread conduct of the sort engaged in by defendant." *Campbell*, 510 U.S. at 590 (internal citations and quotations omitted). Fox News has not shown that TVEyes poses a risk to it of reduced returns on advertising rates or revenues because of alleged diversions of television viewers.

. . .

TVEyes argues that its service provides an immense benefit to the public interest because it assembles from scratch a library of television broadcast content that otherwise would not exist and renders it easily and efficiently text-searchable. Without TVEyes, there is no other way to sift through more than 27,000 hours of programming broadcast on television daily, most of which is not available online or anywhere else, to track and discover information.

TVEyes subscribers use this service to comment on and criticize broadcast news channels. Government bodies use it to monitor the accuracy of facts reported by the media so they can make timely corrections when necessary. Political campaigns use it to monitor political advertising and appearances of candidates in election years. Financial firms use it to track and archive public statements made by their employees for regulatory compliance. The White House uses TVEyes to evaluate news stories and give feedback to the press corps. The United States Army uses TVEyes to track media coverage of military operations in remote locations, to ensure national security and the safety of American troops. Journalists use TVEyes to research, report on, compare, and criticize broadcast news coverage. Elected officials use TVEyes to confirm the accuracy of information reported on the news and seek timely corrections of misinformation. Clearly, TVEyes provides substantial benefit to the public.

. . .

I therefore find that TVEyes' copying of Fox News' broadcast content for indexing and clipping services to its subscribers constitutes fair use. . . .

QUESTIONS

1. How significant to the court's analysis do you think was the use by the White House, the U.S. Army and various police departments of TVEyes' video clipping service? Do we know whether TVEyes' subscribers are predominantly for-profit businesses? Should that matter?

2. What is "transformative" about reproducing a work in whole or in part in order to communicate what the work says?

3. In *TVEyes*, *HathiTrust*, and *Google Books*, the courts emphasized the transformative uses to which the defendants' users might put the copied works. Why is that relevant to whether the defendants' uses are transformative?

3. COPYING BY END USERS

Page 920. Add after Question 6:

Fox Broadcasting Company Inc. v. Dish Network, L.C.C., 723 F.3d 1067 (9th Cir. 2013). Dish Network, a satellite TV transmission service, which retransmits television programming under license, began providing its customers with a new offering called the Hopper, which the court described:

In March 2012, Dish released to its customers the Hopper, a set-top box with digital video recorder (DVR) and video on demand capabilities. The Hopper provides service to up to four televisions in a home using companion boxes (known as Joeys) wired to each television. Dish customers can also watch Hopper content on their computers and mobile devices using a product called the Sling Adapter.

At the same time it released the Hopper, Dish introduced a feature called PrimeTime Anytime that works only on the Hopper. PrimeTime Anytime allows a subscriber to set a single timer to record any and all primetime programming on the four major broadcast networks (including Fox) every night of the week. To enable PrimeTime Anytime, a Hopper user presses the " * " button on the remote control to reach the PrimeTime Anytime setup screen. The user selects "Enable,' and a new menu appears where the viewer can disable recordings of certain networks on certain days of the week and change the length of time that the shows are saved (between two and eight days). By default, PrimeTime Anytime records primetime shows on all four networks each night of the week and saves all recordings for eight days.

Dish determines the start and end time of the PrimeTime Anytime recordings each night and sometimes alters these times to record programming outside the traditional primetime window of 8 p.m. to 11 p.m. Eastern and Pacific time Monday through Saturday and 7 p.m. to 11 p.m. on Sunday (Primetime starts and ends one hour earlier in the Mountain and Central time zones.). For instance, Dish altered the times to accommodate Olympic programming on NBC in summer 2012. If at least half of a program falls within the primetime window, Dish includes the entire show in the PrimeTime Anytime recording.

A user may start watching recorded programs immediately after PrimeTime Anytime starts recording. The user must enable PrimeTime Anytime at least 15 minutes before the primetime recording begins and can cancel a PrimeTime Anytime recording up to 15 minutes before the recording begins; after that, a user can no longer cancel that day's PrimeTime Anytime recording.

All PrimeTime Anytime recordings are stored locally on a customer's Hopper for the preselected number of days (typically eight), at which time they are automatically deleted. Before that time, a customer cannot actually delete or save a PrimeTime Anytime recording. Rather, if the customer selects "Save" or "Save Series" from the PrimeTime Anytime menu, an icon is created in the customer's "My Recordings" folder, but the icon is simply linked to the PrimeTime Anytime recording until the time of automatic deletion, at which time a duplicate copy is created. Similarly, if a customer "deletes" a show recorded through PrimeTime Anytime, the icon for that show disappears from the user's graphical user interface, but the recording remains on the customer's hard drive until it is automatically deleted.

. . .

In May 2012, Dish started offering a new feature, AutoHop, that allows users to automatically skip commercials. AutoHop is only available on shows recorded using PrimeTime Anytime, typically on the morning after the live broadcast. It is not available for all primetime programs. When a user plays back a PrimeTime Anytime recording, if AutoHop is available, a pop-up screen appears that allows the user to select the option to "automatically skip over" commercial breaks. By default, AutoHop is not selected.

If a customer enables AutoHop, the viewer sees only the first and last few seconds of each commercial break. A red kangaroo icon appears in the corner of the screen to demonstrate that AutoHop is skipping commercials. Unlike the 30-second skip feature available on many DVRs, once a user has enabled AutoHop, the user does not press anything to skip through commercials. AutoHop does not delete commercials from the recording. Customers can see the commercials if they manually rewind or fast-forward into a commercial break.

To create the AutoHop functionality, Dish technicians in Cheyenne, Wyoming manually view Fox's primetime programing each night and technologically mark the beginning and end of each commercial. The program content is not altered in any way. The electronically marked files are then uplinked in Wyoming and eventually transmitted to subscribers in an "announcement" file that Dish makes available to subscribers after the show has aired. Simultaneously with the uplink, three "beta Hoppers" record the Fox primetime block for transmissions in Kentucky, Pennsylvania, and Florida to test the marking announcement. These copies remain at the uplink facility and are used to make sure the commercials have been accurately marked and that no portion of the program has been cut off.

Fox sued, alleging that DISH was infringing on Fox's copyrights in television programming. In ruling on Fox's motion for a preliminary injunction, the district court ruled that Fox was not likely to succeed on the merits of its claim from infringement of its reproduction rights, and focused on the quality assurance copies made in Wyoming, which no one disputed were made by Dish (in contrast to the PrimeTime Anytime copies stored on a user's set top box, as the court concluded that Fox had not established a likelihood of success in showing that Dish, rather that Dish's customer, made the PrimeTime Anytime copies). Assessing the fair use factors, the district court concluded that "Fox has demonstrated a likelihood of success on the merits of its claims that AutoHop's [quality assurance] copies infringe its exclusive reproduction right," but it also stated that "neither the marking announcements nor the ad-skipping effect of AutoHop implicates any copyright interest . . . on the current record." And because the court concluded that Fox had not shown it would likely suffer irreparable harm from the infringement, as opposed to harm compensable with money damages, it denied the preliminary injunction.

The Ninth Circuit affirmed. Applying a "deferential standard of review" of a denial of a preliminary injunction ("We do not reverse 'simply because the appellate court would have arrived at a different result if it had applied the law to the facts of the case' "), "and without determining the ultimate merits of the case," the court held the district court did not abuse its discretion in holding that Fox was unlikely to succeed on its claim of direct or contributory copyright infringement regarding PrimeTime Anytime, and that Fox "did not demonstrate a likelihood of irreparable harm from Dish's creation of the 'quality assurance' copies used to perfect the functioning of AutoHop." With respect to direct copyright infringement, the Ninth Circuit ruled that the district court did not abuse its discretion in determining, on the current record, that Dish had not itself made the allegedly infringing copies: "operating a system used to make copies at the user's command does not mean that the system operator, rather than the user, caused copies to be made. Here, Dish's program creates the copy only in response to the user's command. Therefore, the district court did not err in concluding that the user, not Dish, makes the copy."

Regarding secondary infringement, the Ninth Circuit upheld the district court's determination that Dish's customers' use of PrimeTime Anywhere to make time-shifting copies was a fair use; accordingly, in the absence of a primary infringement, there could be no contributory infringement.

> Fox and its amici argue that Dish customers use PrimeTime Anytime and AutoHop for purposes other than time-shifting—namely, commercial-skipping and library-building. These uses were briefly discussed in *Sony*, in which the Court recognized that some Betamax customers used the device to avoid viewing advertisements and accumulate libraries of tapes. In *Sony*, about 25 percent of Betamax users fast-forwarded through commercials. Additionally, a "substantial number of interviewees had accumulated libraries of tapes." One user owned about 100 tapes and bought his Betamax intending to "build a library of cassettes," but this "proved too expensive." Because the Betamax was primarily used for time-shifting, the Court in *Sony* never expressly decided whether commercial-skipping and library-building were fair uses. Cf. *Metro-Goldwyn-Mayer Studios Inc. v. Grokster, Ltd.*, 545 U.S. 913, 931 (2005) (explaining that "[a]lthough *Sony*'s advertisements urged consumers to buy the VCR to 'record favorite shows' or 'build a library' of recorded programs, neither of these uses was necessarily infringing" (citations omitted)).

> Yet, as the district court held, commercial-skipping does not implicate Fox's copyright interest because Fox owns the copyrights to the television programs, not to the ads aired in the commercial breaks. If recording an entire copyrighted program is a fair use, the fact that viewers do not watch the ads not copyrighted by Fox cannot transform the recording into a copyright violation.

Indeed, a recording made with PrimeTime Anytime still includes commercials; AutoHop simply skips those recorded commercials unless a viewer manually rewinds or fast-forwards into a commercial break. Thus, any analysis of the market harm should exclude consideration of AutoHop because ad-skipping does not implicate Fox's copyright interests.

Analyzing PrimeTime Anytime under the fair use factors, Dish has demonstrated a likelihood of success on its customers' fair use defense. As for the first factor, . . . Dish customers' home viewing is noncommercial under *Sony*, which held that "time-shifting for private home use" was a "noncommercial, nonprofit activity." Here, the district court found that PrimeTime Anytime is used for time-shifting, and that the Hopper is available only to private consumers.

Sony also governs the analysis of the second and third factors. . . . *Sony* held that "when one considers the nature of a televised copyrighted audiovisual work, and that time-shifting merely enables a viewer to see such a work which he had been invited to witness in its entirety free of charge, the fact that the entire work is reproduced, does not have its ordinary effect of militating against a finding of fair use." The same analysis applies here, and thus the fact that Dish users copy Fox's entire copyrighted broadcasts does not have its ordinary effect of militating against a finding of fair use.

Finally, we consider the "effect of the use upon the potential market for or value of the copyrighted work." . . . Because Fox licenses its programs to distributors such as Hulu and Apple, the market harm analysis is somewhat different than in *Sony*, where no such secondary market existed for the copyright-holders' programs. However, the record before the district court establishes that the market harm that Fox and its amici allege results from the automatic commercial-skipping, not the recording of programs through PrimeTime Anytime. Indeed, Fox often charges no additional license fees for providers to offer Fox's licensed video on demand, so long as providers disable fast-forwarding. This indicates that the ease of skipping commercials, rather than the on-demand availability of Fox programs, causes any market harm. And as we have discussed, the commercial-skipping does not implicate any copyright interest.

[After the Ninth Circuit's affirmance, the district court ruled on cross-motions for summary judgment. 114 U.S.P.Q.2d 1100 (C.D.Cal. 2015). The ruling on the copyright claims closely followed the determinations at the preliminary injunction stage: the court granted Fox summary judgment on its claim that DISH's quality assurance copies infringed Fox's reproduction right (and did not constitute fair use), and granted DISH's motion for summary judgment that DISH's Prime Time Anytime and AutoHop services did not infringe.]

QUESTIONS

1. Are you persuaded that furnishing a device that both records entire programs and enables commercial-skipping inflicts no cognizable market impact? Recall that *Sony* emphasized that the public was invited to view the over-the-air television programming for free. What economic model enabled the producers of the programming to offer free viewing?

2. If commercial skipping does not implicate any copyright interests of the copyright owner of broadcast television programming, why did the courts in the *Sony* case pay any attention to the commercial-skipping habits of Betamax users in evaluating whether or not time-shifting by those users was fair use (see *Sony, supra* page 914 n.36 in the main casebook), given that the plaintiffs in *Sony* were the copyright owners of broadcast television shows and movies, and not the owners of copyright in the commercials shown during those programs?

3. The court states, "If recording an entire copyrighted program is a fair use, the fact that viewers do not watch the ads not copyrighted by Fox cannot transform the recording into a copyright violation." Why not? Recall that the *Sony* court defined time-shifting as "the practice of recording a program to view it once at a later time, and thereafter erasing it." 464 U.S. at 423. If a VCR user records a program, views it once at a later time, and then decides not to erase the recording but instead to add it to her library of VCR tapes for future viewing (or to sell it to a third-party), is it also the case that her actions "cannot transform" her act of recording into a copyright violation?

4. To what extent do changes in technology and markets suggest that *Sony*'s determination that timeshifting is fair use may not be directly applicable to new technological means of timeshifting?

> [W]e should not treat *Sony* as imprimatur for any and all timeshifting whatsoever. *Sony* was far from a blanket authorization of any and all consumer time-deferred copying of television broadcasts. While the *Sony* Court assumed that consumers should be entitled to watch at their convenience programming that they had been invited to view for free, the Court reached the conclusion that the copies made there were noninfringing only after considering market harm, cost and difficulty of copying, and the nonexistence of copyright owner-supplied alternatives to broadcast times.
>
> Technologies such as Aereo are readily distinguishable from Sony's Betamax. Most importantly, they have much more potential to compete with remunerated markets for making the same content conveniently available on demand (which have developed significantly since the 1980s, now offering multiple alternative viewing opportunities to the original broadcast time). Moreover, the technologies have eliminated a great deal of "friction" from the copying process (notably, as in the case of Dish's AutoHop service, by automatically deleting the advertisements). In an environment where there is less and less difference between commercially-aided timeshifting and video on demand . . . , the reflexive assumption that timeshifting equals fair use should be questioned.

Rebecca Giblin & Jane C. Ginsburg, *We Still Need to Talk About* Aereo: *New Controversies and Unresolved Questions After the Supreme Court's Decision*, 38 COLUM. J. L. & THE ARTS 109, 131–32 (2015). Does this view offer reasons to think that even the timeshifting approved in *Sony* would no longer be fair use?

GENERAL REVIEW QUESTIONS

Page 934. Replace the first paragraph with the following updated paragraph:

(Fairey subsequently admitted that he used the photo the AP identified, and that he fabricated evidence to make it appear that he had used the photo he originally claimed to have used. In February 2012, he pleaded guilty to criminal contempt for his misconduct, and in September 2012 he was sentenced to two years of probation and a $25,000 fine. Dave Itzkoff, *Arts, Briefly: Probation and a Fine for Shephard Fairey*, N.Y. TIMES, Sep. 8, 2012.)

Page 934. Add new Questions 3 and 4:

3.   When an inventor applies to the U.S. Patent and Trademark Office for a patent on an invention, the PTO must determine whether the invention is novel and nonobvious by comparing it to the "prior art"—the previously existing state of knowledge and invention in the field. In many instances, prior art includes articles that are published in scientific or technical journals and protected by copyright. In the course of patent prosecution, and in post-grant proceedings reconsidering the validity of an issued patent, copies of scientific articles are sometimes made—by the PTO in notifying an applicant of a reason for not granting a patent on the application as submitted, by the patent applicant as part of the application or a response to a PTO action on the application, and by third-parties or members of the public who believe the article is relevant to the patentability of a claimed invention. Indeed, the PTO's regulations impose on patent applicants a duty to disclose to the PTO all material that the applicant knows to be material to the patentability of the claimed application, and an applicant who files an Information Disclosure Statement with his application is required to include a copy of each publication listed in the statement. 37 C.F.R. §§ 1.56, 1.98.

Academic publishers have brought suit against law firms that prosecute patent applications on behalf of paying clients. The publishers argue that those law firms committed copyright infringement when they copied a number of the publishers' academic articles and submitted them to the PTO in the course of patent prosecution. The publishers also allege, and seek discovery to confirm, that the law firms made additional copies (beyond those submitted to the PTO) of the articles identified in the complaint, and made copies of other of the publishers' copyrighted articles that were considered in connection with patent applications but not ultimately submitted to the PTO.

The law firms have responded that the alleged activities constitute noninfringing fair use under Section 107. The PTO has intervened in the suits and in at least one instance has filed a counterclaim, seeking a declaration that

> the copying of copyrighted [scientific and technical articles] and distribution thereof, which copying and/or distribution is necessary and incidental to the filing and prosecution of a U.S. patent application and/or the conduct of other USPTO proceedings concerning or relating to the scope or validity of any issued U.S. Patent, including copies of [such articles] actually submitted to the

USPTO and copies . . . initially considered but ultimately rejected for inclusion in submissions to the USPTO, by or at the direction of patent applicants, patentees, patent challengers, and/or their representatives, . . . constitutes a fair use of such copyrighted works under 17 U.S.C. § 107, and therefore is not an infringement of copyright.

See also *USPTO Position on Fair Use of Copies of [Non-Patent Literature] Made in Patent Examination*, available at http://www.uspto.gov/about/offices/ogc/USPTOPositiononFairUse_of_CopiesofNPLMadeinPatent Examination.pdf.

How should the courts rule on the fair use claims? See *American Institute of Physics v. Schwegman, Lundberg & Woessner, P.A.*, 2013 WL 4666330 (D.Minn. 2013); *American Institute of Physics v. Winstead PC*, 2013 WL 6242843 (N.D.Tex. 2013); John Wiley & Sons, Ltd. v. McDonnell Boehnen Hulbert & Berghoff LLP, No. 12–cv–01446, 2012 WL 870238 (N.D.Ill. filed 2/29/12).

4. Consider the following facts (drawn, with some emendations, from *National Football Scouting, Inc. v. Rang*, 912 F.Supp.2d 985, 2012 WL 6444226 (W.D.Wash. 2012)):

> National Football Scouting (National) is a scouting organization whose sole purpose is to provide yearly Scouting Reports to its shareholders—twenty one different National Football League Clubs. (Many of the remaining eleven NFL teams are clients of a competing scouting organization known as BLESTO, and a few teams are customers of neither.) National's scouts travel the country to evaluate college talent and to discover player information for the Scouting Reports. National then organizes the information into Reports and copyrights them as unpublished works. Each Report includes six pages of information on each prospective draftee, including injuries, the player's morals and family background, and the player's college statistics. Based on the player's information, National assigns each player an over-all Player Grade, which is a numerical score. National prepares hundreds of Scouting Reports each year. Member Clubs each pay $75,000 per year for the Reports, which they receive under strict confidentiality provisions.

> Defendant Sports Xchange is a for-profit Internet media company. Defendant Robert Rang is a full-time high school teacher who moonlights as a sports writer for Sports Xchange. He is currently a senior NFL Draft analyst for one of Sports Xchange's website, NFLDraftScout.com. During 2010–2011, Rang published eight articles on NFLDraftScout.com about players eligible for the upcoming draft. Six of the articles disclose National's Player Grade, while two of the articles merely allude to the prospective draftees rank among other players. The articles, in addition to stating Player Grades, reported other publicly available information about the players and provided Rang's commentary on the players and their draft prospects in his view. In total, Rang disclosed eighteen Player Grades.

National wrote a series of letters to Rang, demanding that he stop infringing on their copyright and disclosing their trade secrets. A telephone call from National's attorneys followed every letter. In National's view, Rang published the Player Grades in his stories in order to look like an "insider." Despite this series of warnings, Rang continued posting the Player Grades, believing that his use of the Player Grades was fair.

National has now sued Rang and Sports Xchange for, among other claims, copyright infringement. Assuming that National's Player Grades are copyrightable (are they?), how should the court rule on the defendant's claim that its copying of those Player Grades is fair use?

CHAPTER 8

SECONDARY LIABILITY

A. GENERAL PRINCIPLES

Page 954. Add a new note before the QUESTIONS:

[Victoria Espinel, the White House Intellectual Property Enforcement Coordinator, testified before the Senate Judiciary Committee in May 2012 that "[i]n June 2011, American Express, Discover, MasterCard, PayPal and Visa—major credit card companies and payment processors—reached an agreement to develop voluntary best practices to withdraw payment services for sites selling counterfeit and pirated goods." *Oversight of the Office of the Intellectual Property Enforcement Coordinator: Hearing Before the S. Comm. on the Judiciary*, 112th Cong. (2012) (statement of Victoria Espinel, Intellectual Property Enforcement Coordinator, Office of Management and Budget).]

Page 954. Add new Question 4:

4. Pharmatext.org is a website offering "Free Pharma E-Books." Images of available books appear on the screen along with invitations to click on "Download" to obtain the entire text of the books at no cost. For many of the books, Pharmatext does not have permission from the copyright owners to make the texts available. Chitika places advertising on various websites, including Pharmatext. Chitika receives payments from advertisers and pays Pharmatext a share of those payments in exchange for the right to display ads on the Pharmatext website.

Elsevier is a leading publisher of medical textbooks. It alleges that Chitika is liable for contributory infringement, because it "holds itself out to the public as 'a proven channel for targeting on-line consumers and qualified buyers,' " it "directly profited from the infringement carried out through Pharmatext," and it "enabled Pharmatext to stay in the infringement business by supplying it with income."

Chitika rejoins that it lacks the requisite knowledge and that it did not materially contribute to any infringement. With respect to knowledge, Chitika asserts that it

> simply offers technology that presents a display ad on a publisher's website. Chitika's technology selects the ad to display automatically, without human intervention, by means of a complex proprietary algorithm to present advertisements on a publisher's website, based upon many factors, including, among many others, information about the visitor to the website, terms entered into a search engine, and the words that appear on the publisher's website. Chitika did not and does not have any knowledge or notice of whether a site contains allegedly infringing materials, and it does not have any mechanism by which it can determine whether a publisher's site contains allegedly infringing materials. When publishers join Chitika's network, they expressly acknowledge that they have full responsibility for the content and operation of their

sites, and they expressly represent that they do not contain any infringing or illegal content.

Respecting materiality, Chitika, citing *Perfect10 v Visa Int'l.*, urges that while its advertising payments might make it easier for Pharmatext to be profitable, Chitika did not create, operate, advertise, or promote the infringing websites, and its advertisements were not the "site" of the infringement. Does it suffice to avoid liability to fully automate one's ad-placement program and warn the ad-carrying websites that they should not infringe? Is an advertisement ever "the 'site' of the infringement"? *See Elsevier v. Chitika, Inc.*, 826 F.Supp.2d 398 (D.Mass. 2011).

B. FACILITATION OF INFRINGEMENT BY END-USERS

Page 960. Add to end of Question:

See *In re AutoHop Litigation (Dish Network v. American Broadcasting Cos., Inc.)*, 2013 WL 5477495 (S.D.N.Y. 2013).

Page 988. In the first paragraph, replace the *Lime Group* citation with "784 F.Supp.2d 398 (S.D.N.Y. 2011)".

C. SECONDARY LIABILITY OF INTERNET SERVICE PROVIDERS

2. SERVICE PROVIDER LIABILITY UNDER THE STATUTORY SAFE HARBORS

Pages 995–1013. Replace the material beginning after the QUESTIONS on page 995 up to the note on ERRONEOUS TAKE-DOWN NOTICES with the following:

Viacom International, Inc. v. YouTube, Inc.
676 F.3d 19 (2d Cir. 2012).

■ CABRANES, CIRCUIT JUDGE.

This appeal requires us to clarify the contours of the "safe harbor" provision of the Digital Millennium Copyright Act (DMCA) that limits the liability of online service providers for copyright infringement that occurs "by reason of the storage at the direction of a user of material that resides on a system or network controlled or operated by or for the service provider." 17 U.S.C. § 512(c).

The plaintiffs-appellants in these related actions—Viacom International, Inc. ("Viacom"), The Football Association Premier League Ltd. ("Premier League"), and various film studios, television networks, music publishers, and sports leagues (jointly, the "plaintiffs")—appeal from an August 10, 2010 judgment of the United States District Court for the Southern District of New York, which granted summary judgment to defendants-appellees YouTube, Inc., YouTube, LLC, and Google Inc. (jointly, "YouTube" or the "defendants"). The plaintiffs alleged direct and secondary copyright infringement based on the public performance, display, and reproduction of approximately 79,000 audiovisual "clips" that appeared on the YouTube website between 2005 and 2008. They demanded, *inter alia,* statutory damages pursuant to 17 U.S.C. § 504(c) or, in the alternative, actual damages from the alleged infringement, as well as declaratory and injunctive relief.

In a June 23, 2010 Opinion and Order (the "June 23 Opinion"), the District Court held that the defendants were entitled to DMCA safe harbor protection primarily because they had insufficient notice of the particular infringements in suit. *Viacom Int'l, Inc. v. YouTube, Inc.,* 718 F.Supp.2d 514, 529 (S.D.N.Y. 2010). In construing the statutory safe harbor, the District Court concluded that the "actual knowledge" or "aware[ness] of facts or circumstances" that would disqualify an online service provider from safe harbor protection under § 512(c)(1)(A) refer to "knowledge of specific and identifiable infringements." The District Court further held that item-specific knowledge of infringing activity is required for a service provider to have the "right and ability to control" infringing activity under § 512(c)(1)(B). Finally, the District Court held that the replication, transmittal, and display of videos on YouTube constituted activity "by reason of the storage at the direction of a user" within the meaning of § 512(c)(1).

These related cases present a series of significant questions of statutory construction. We conclude that the District Court correctly held that the § 512(c) safe harbor requires knowledge or awareness of specific infringing activity, but we vacate the order granting summary judgment because a reasonable jury could find that YouTube had actual knowledge or awareness of specific infringing activity on its website. We further hold that the District Court erred by interpreting the "right and ability to control" provision to require "item-specific" knowledge. Finally, we affirm the District Court's holding that three of the challenged YouTube software functions fall within the safe harbor for infringement that occurs "by reason of" user storage; we remand for further fact-finding with respect to a fourth software function.

BACKGROUND

A. The DMCA Safe Harbors

"The DMCA was enacted in 1998 to implement the World Intellectual Property Organization Copyright Treaty," *Universal City Studios, Inc. v. Corley,* 273 F.3d 429, 440 (2d Cir. 2001), and to update domestic copyright law for the digital age, *see Ellison v. Robertson,* 357 F.3d 1072, 1076 (9th Cir. 2004). Title II of the DMCA, separately titled the "Online Copyright Infringement Liability Limitation Act" (OCILLA), was designed to "clarif[y] the liability faced by service providers who transmit potentially infringing material over their networks." S.Rep. No. 105–190 at 2 (1998). But "[r]ather than embarking upon a wholesale clarification" of various copyright doctrines, Congress elected "to leave current law in its evolving state and, instead, to create a series of 'safe harbors[ ]' for certain common activities of service providers." *Id.* at 19. To that end, OCILLA established a series of four "safe harbors" that allow qualifying service providers to limit their liability for claims of copyright infringement based on (a) "transitory digital network communications," (b) "system caching," (c) "information residing on systems or networks at [the] direction of users," and (d) "information location tools." 17 U.S.C. § 512(a)–(d).

To qualify for protection under any of the safe harbors, a party must meet a set of threshold criteria. First, the party must in fact be a "service provider," defined, in pertinent part, as "a provider of online services or network access, or the operator of facilities therefor." 17 U.S.C. § 512(k)(1)(B). A party that qualifies as a service provider must also satisfy certain "conditions of eligibility," including the adoption and reasonable implementation of a "repeat infringer" policy that "provides for the termination in appropriate circumstances of subscribers and account holders of the service provider's system or network." *Id.* § 512(i)(1)(A). In addition, a qualifying service provider must accommodate "standard technical measures" that are "used by copyright owners to identify or protect copyrighted works." *Id.* § 512(i)(1)(B), (i)(2).

Beyond the threshold criteria, a service provider must satisfy the requirements of a particular safe harbor. In this case, the safe harbor at issue is § 512(c), which covers infringement claims that arise "by reason of the storage at the direction of a user of material that resides on a system or network controlled or operated by or for the service provider." *Id.* § 512(c)(1). The § 512(c) safe harbor will apply only if the service provider:

> (A)(i) does not have actual knowledge that the material or an activity using the material on the system or network is infringing;

> (ii) in the absence of such actual knowledge, is not aware of facts or circumstances from which infringing activity is apparent; or

> (iii) upon obtaining such knowledge or awareness, acts expeditiously to remove, or disable access to, the material;

> (B) does not receive a financial benefit directly attributable to the infringing activity, in a case in which the service provider has the right and ability to control such activity; and

> (C) upon notification of claimed infringement as described in paragraph (3), responds expeditiously to remove, or disable access to, the material that is claimed to be infringing or to be the subject of infringing activity.

Id. § 512(c)(1)(A)–(C). Section 512(c) also sets forth a detailed notification scheme that requires service providers to "designate[ ] an agent to receive notifications of claimed infringement," id. § 512(c)(2), and specifies the components of a proper notification, commonly known as a "takedown notice," to that agent, see id. § 512(c)(3). Thus, actual knowledge of infringing material, awareness of facts or circumstances that make infringing activity apparent, or receipt of a takedown notice will each trigger an obligation to expeditiously remove the infringing material.

With the statutory context in mind, we now turn to the facts of this case.

B.   Factual Background

YouTube was founded in February 2005 by Chad Hurley ("Hurley"), Steve Chen ("Chen"), and Jawed Karim ("Karim"), three former employees of the internet company Paypal. When YouTube announced the "official launch" of the website in December 2005, a press release described YouTube as a "consumer media company" that "allows people to watch, upload, and share personal video clips at www.YouTube.com." Under the slogan "Broadcast yourself," YouTube achieved rapid prominence and profitability, eclipsing competitors such as Google Video and Yahoo Video by wide margins. In November 2006, Google acquired YouTube in a stock-for-stock transaction valued at $1.65 billion. By March 2010, at the time of summary judgment briefing in this litigation, site traffic on YouTube had soared to more than 1 billion daily video views, with more than 24 hours of new video uploaded to the site every minute.

The basic function of the YouTube website permits users to "upload" and view video clips free of charge. Before uploading a video to YouTube, a user must register and create an account with the website. The registration process requires the user to accept YouTube's Terms of Use agreement, which provides, *inter alia,* that the user "will not submit material that is copyrighted . . . unless [he is] the owner of such rights or ha[s] permission from their rightful owner to post the material and to grant YouTube all of the license rights granted herein." When the registration process is complete, the user can sign in to his account, select a video to upload from the user's personal computer, mobile phone, or other device, and instruct the YouTube system to upload the video by clicking on a virtual upload "button."

Uploading a video to the YouTube website triggers a series of automated software functions. During the upload process, YouTube makes one or more exact copies of the video in its original file format. YouTube also makes one or more additional copies of the video in "Flash" format,[4] a process known as "transcoding." The transcoding process ensures that YouTube videos are available for viewing by most users at their request. The YouTube system allows users to gain access to video content by "streaming" the video to the user's computer in response to a playback request. YouTube uses a computer algorithm to identify clips that are "related" to a video the user watches and display links to the "related" clips.

C. Procedural History

Plaintiff Viacom, an American media conglomerate, and various Viacom affiliates filed suit against YouTube on March 13, 2007, alleging direct and secondary copyright infringement based on the public performance, display, and reproduction of their audiovisual works on the YouTube website. Plaintiff Premier League, an English soccer league, and Plaintiff Bourne Co. filed a putative class action against YouTube on May 4, 2007, alleging direct and secondary copyright infringement on behalf of all copyright owners whose material was copied, stored, displayed, or performed on YouTube without authorization. Specifically at issue were some 63,497 video clips identified by Viacom, as well as 13,500 additional clips (jointly, the "clips-in-suit") identified by the putative class plaintiffs.

The plaintiffs in both actions principally demanded statutory damages pursuant to 17 U.S.C. § 504(c) or, in the alternative, actual damages plus the defendants' profits from the alleged infringement, as

---

[4] The "Flash" format "is a highly compressed streaming format that begins to play instantly. Unlike other delivery methods, it does not require the viewer to download the entire video file before viewing."

well as declaratory and injunctive relief . . . At the close of discovery, the parties in both actions cross-moved for partial summary judgment with respect to the applicability of the DMCA safe harbor defense.[7]

In the dual-captioned June 23 Opinion, the District Court denied the plaintiffs' motions and granted summary judgment to the defendants, finding that YouTube qualified for DMCA safe harbor protection with respect to all claims of direct and secondary copyright infringement. The District Court prefaced its analysis of the DMCA safe harbor by holding that, based on the plaintiffs' summary judgment submissions, "a jury could find that the defendants not only were generally aware of, but welcomed, copyright-infringing material being placed on their website." However, the District Court also noted that the defendants had properly designated an agent pursuant to § 512(c)(2), and "when they received specific notice that a particular item infringed a copyright, they swiftly removed it." Accordingly, the District Court identified the crux of the inquiry with respect to YouTube's copyright liability as follows:

> [T]he critical question is whether the statutory phrases "actual knowledge that the material or an activity using the material on the system or network is infringing," and "facts or circumstances from which infringing activity is apparent" in § 512(c)(1)(A)(i) and (ii) mean a general awareness that there are infringements (here, claimed to be widespread and common), or rather mean actual or constructive knowledge of specific and identifiable infringements of individual items.

After quoting at length from the legislative history of the DMCA, the District Court held that "the phrases 'actual knowledge that the material or an activity' is infringing, and 'facts or circumstances' indicating infringing activity, describe knowledge of specific and identifiable infringements of particular individual items." "Mere knowledge of [the] prevalence of such activity in general," the District Court concluded, "is not enough."

In a final section labeled "Other Points," the District Court rejected two additional claims. First, it rejected the plaintiffs' argument that the replication, transmittal and display of YouTube videos are functions that fall outside the protection § 512(c)(1) affords for "infringement of copyright by reason of . . . storage at the direction of the user." Second, it rejected the plaintiffs' argument that YouTube was ineligible for safe harbor protection under the control provision, holding that the "right and ability to control" infringing activity under § 512(c)(1)(B) requires "item-specific" knowledge thereof, because "the provider must know of the particular case before he can control it."

Following the June 23 Opinion, final judgment in favor of YouTube was entered on August 10, 2010. These appeals followed.

DISCUSSION

. . .

A.   Actual and "Red Flag" Knowledge: § 512(c)(1)(A)

The first and most important question on appeal is whether the DMCA safe harbor at issue requires "actual knowledge" or "aware[ness]"

---

[7]   It is undisputed that all clips-in-suit had been removed from the YouTube website by the time of summary judgment, mostly in response to DMCA takedown notices.

of facts or circumstances indicating "specific and identifiable infringements." *Viacom*, 718 F.Supp.2d at 523. We consider first the scope of the statutory provision and then its application to the record in this case.

1.   The Specificity Requirement

"As in all statutory construction cases, we begin with the language of the statute," *Barnhart v. Sigmon Coal Co.*, 534 U.S. 438, 450 (2002). Under § 512(c)(1)(A), safe harbor protection is available only if the service provider:

> (i) does not have actual knowledge that the material or an activity using the material on the system or network is infringing;

> (ii) in the absence of such actual knowledge, is not aware of facts or circumstances from which infringing activity is apparent; or

> (iii) upon obtaining such knowledge or awareness, acts expeditiously to remove, or disable access to, the material. . . .

17 U.S.C. § 512(c)(1)(A). As previously noted, the District Court held that the statutory phrases "actual knowledge that the material . . . is infringing" and "facts or circumstances from which infringing activity is apparent" refer to "knowledge of specific and identifiable infringements." *Viacom*, 718 F.Supp.2d at 523. For the reasons that follow, we substantially affirm that holding.

Although the parties marshal a battery of other arguments on appeal, it is the text of the statute that compels our conclusion. In particular, we are persuaded that the basic operation of § 512(c) requires knowledge or awareness of specific infringing activity. Under § 512(c)(1)(A), knowledge or awareness alone does not disqualify the service provider; rather, the provider that gains knowledge or awareness of infringing activity retains safe-harbor protection if it "acts expeditiously to remove, or disable access to, the material." 17 U.S.C. § 512(c)(1)(A)(iii). Thus, the nature of the removal obligation itself contemplates knowledge or awareness of specific infringing material, because expeditious removal is possible only if the service provider knows with particularity which items to remove. Indeed, to require expeditious removal in the absence of specific knowledge or awareness would be to mandate an amorphous obligation to "take commercially reasonable steps" in response to a generalized awareness of infringement. Viacom Br. 33. Such a view cannot be reconciled with the language of the statute, which requires "expeditious[ ]" action to remove or disable *the material* "at issue. 17 U.S.C. § 512(c)(1)(A)(iii) (emphasis added).

On appeal, the plaintiffs dispute this conclusion by drawing our attention to § 512(c)(1)(A)(ii), the so-called "red flag" knowledge provision. In their view, the use of the phrase "facts or circumstances" demonstrates that Congress did not intend to limit the red flag provision to a particular type of knowledge. The plaintiffs contend that requiring awareness of specific infringements in order to establish "aware[ness] of facts or circumstances from which infringing activity is apparent," 17 U.S.C. § 512(c)(1)(A)(ii), renders the red flag provision superfluous, because that provision would be satisfied only when the "actual knowledge" provision is also satisfied. For that reason, the plaintiffs urge the Court to hold that the red flag provision "requires less specificity" than the actual knowledge provision.

This argument misconstrues the relationship between "actual" knowledge and "red flag" knowledge. It is true that "we are required to 'disfavor interpretations of statutes that render language superfluous.'" *Conn. ex rel. Blumenthal v. U.S. Dep't of the Interior,* 228 F.3d 82, 88 (2d Cir. 2000) (quoting *Conn. Nat'l Bank v. Germain,* 503 U.S. 249, 253 (1992)). But contrary to the plaintiffs' assertions, construing § 512(c)(1)(A) to require actual knowledge or awareness of specific instances of infringement does not render the red flag provision superfluous. The phrase "actual knowledge," which appears in § 512(c)(1)(A)(i), is frequently used to denote subjective belief. By contrast, courts often invoke the language of "facts or circumstances," which appears in § 512(c)(1)(A)(ii), in discussing an objective reasonableness standard.

The difference between actual and red flag knowledge is thus not between specific and generalized knowledge, but instead between a subjective and an objective standard. In other words, the actual knowledge provision turns on whether the provider actually or "subjectively" knew of specific infringement, while the red flag provision turns on whether the provider was subjectively aware of facts that would have made the specific infringement "objectively" obvious to a reasonable person. The red flag provision, because it incorporates an objective standard, is not swallowed up by the actual knowledge provision under our construction of the § 512(c) safe harbor. Both provisions do independent work, and both apply only to specific instances of infringement.

The limited body of case law interpreting the knowledge provisions of the § 512(c) safe harbor comports with our view of the specificity requirement. Most recently, a panel of the Ninth Circuit addressed the scope of § 512(c) in *UMG Recordings, Inc. v. Shelter Capital Partners LLC,* 667 F.3d 1022 (9th Cir. 2011), a copyright infringement case against Veoh Networks, a video-hosting service similar to YouTube. As in this case, various music publishers brought suit against the service provider, claiming direct and secondary copyright infringement based on the presence of unauthorized content on the website, and the website operator sought refuge in the § 512(c) safe harbor. The Court of Appeals affirmed the district court's determination on summary judgment that the website operator was entitled to safe harbor protection. With respect to the actual knowledge provision, the panel declined to "adopt[ ] a broad conception of the knowledge requirement," holding instead that the safe harbor "[r]equir[es] specific knowledge of particular infringing activity." The Court of Appeals "reach[ed] the same conclusion" with respect to the red flag provision, noting that "[w]e do not place the burden of determining whether [materials] are actually illegal on a service provider." *Id.* at 1038 (alterations in original) (quoting *Perfect 10, Inc. v. CCBill LLC,* 488 F.3d 1102, 1114 (9th Cir. 2007)).

Although *Shelter Capital* contains the most explicit discussion of the § 512(c) knowledge provisions, other cases are generally in accord.

Based on the text of § 512(c)(1)(A), as well as the limited case law on point, we affirm the District Court's holding that actual knowledge or awareness of facts or circumstances that indicate specific and identifiable instances of infringement will disqualify a service provider from the safe harbor.

2. The Grant of Summary Judgment

The corollary question on appeal is whether, under the foregoing construction of § 512(c)(1)(A), the District Court erred in granting summary judgment to YouTube on the record presented. For the reasons that follow, we hold that although the District Court correctly interpreted § 512(c)(1)(A), summary judgment for the defendants was premature.

i. Specific Knowledge or Awareness

The plaintiffs argue that, even under the District Court's construction of the safe harbor, the record raises material issues of fact regarding YouTube's actual knowledge or "red flag" awareness of specific instances of infringement. To that end, the plaintiffs draw our attention to various estimates regarding the percentage of infringing content on the YouTube website. For example, Viacom cites evidence that YouTube employees conducted website surveys and estimated that 75–80% of all YouTube streams contained copyrighted material. The class plaintiffs similarly claim that Credit Suisse, acting as financial advisor to Google, estimated that more than 60% of YouTube's content was "premium" copyrighted content—and that only 10% of the premium content was authorized. These approximations suggest that the defendants were conscious that significant quantities of material on the YouTube website were infringing. *See Viacom Int'l,* 718 F.Supp.2d at 518 ("[A] jury could find that the defendants not only were generally aware of, but welcomed, copyright-infringing material being placed on their website."). But such estimates are insufficient, standing alone, to create a triable issue of fact as to whether YouTube actually knew, or was aware of facts or circumstances that would indicate, the existence of particular instances of infringement.

Beyond the survey results, the plaintiffs rely upon internal YouTube communications that do refer to particular clips or groups of clips. The class plaintiffs argue that YouTube was aware of specific infringing material because, *inter alia,* YouTube attempted to search for specific Premier League videos on the site in order to gauge their "value based on video usage." In particular, the class plaintiffs cite a February 7, 2007 e-mail from Patrick Walker, director of video partnerships for Google and YouTube, requesting that his colleagues calculate the number of daily searches for the terms "soccer," "football," and "Premier League" in preparation for a bid on the global rights to Premier League content. On another occasion, Walker requested that any "clearly infringing, official broadcast footage" from a list of top Premier League clubs—including Liverpool Football Club, Chelsea Football Club, Manchester United Football Club, and Arsenal Football Club—be taken down in advance of a meeting with the heads of "several major sports teams and leagues." YouTube ultimately decided not to make a bid for the Premier League rights—but the infringing content allegedly remained on the website.

The record in the *Viacom* action includes additional examples. For instance, YouTube founder Jawed Karim prepared a report in March 2006 which stated that, "[a]s of today[,] episodes and clips of the following well-known shows can still be found [on YouTube]: Family Guy, South Park, MTV Cribs, Daily Show, Reno 911, [and] Dave Chapelle [sic]."

Karim further opined that, "although YouTube is not legally required to monitor content . . . and complies with DMCA takedown requests, we would benefit from *preemptively* removing content that is blatantly illegal and likely to attract criticism." He also noted that "a more thorough analysis" of the issue would be required. At least some of the TV shows to which Karim referred are owned by Viacom. A reasonable juror could conclude from the March 2006 report that Karim knew of the presence of Viacom-owned material on YouTube, since he presumably located specific clips of the shows in question before he could announce that YouTube hosted the content "[a]s of today." A reasonable juror could also conclude that Karim believed the clips he located to be infringing (since he refers to them as "blatantly illegal"), and that YouTube did not remove the content from the website until conducting "a more thorough analysis," thus exposing the company to liability in the interim.

Furthermore, in a July 4, 2005 e-mail exchange, YouTube founder Chad Hurley sent an e-mail to his co-founders with the subject line "budlight commercials," and stated, "we need to reject these too." Steve Chen responded, "can we please leave these in a bit longer? another week or two can't hurt." Karim also replied, indicating that he "added back in all 28 bud videos." Similarly, in an August 9, 2005 e-mail exchange, Hurley urged his colleagues "to start being *diligent* about rejecting copyrighted/inappropriate content," noting that "there is a cnn clip of the shuttle clip on the site today, if the boys from Turner would come to the site, they might be pissed?" Again, Chen resisted:

> but we should just keep that stuff on the site. i really don't see what will happen. what? someone from cnn sees it? he happens to be someone with power? he happens to want to take it down right away. he gets in touch with cnn legal. 2 weeks later, we get a cease & desist letter. we take the video down.

And again, Karim agreed, indicating that "the CNN space shuttle clip, I like. we can remove it once we're bigger and better known, but for now that clip is fine."

Upon a review of the record, we are persuaded that the plaintiffs may have raised a material issue of fact regarding YouTube's knowledge or awareness of specific instances of infringement. The foregoing Premier League e-mails request the identification and removal of "clearly infringing, official broadcast footage." The March 2006 report indicates Karim's awareness of specific clips that he perceived to be "blatantly illegal." Similarly, the Bud Light and space shuttle e-mails refer to particular clips in the context of correspondence about whether to remove infringing material from the website. On these facts, a reasonable juror could conclude that YouTube had actual knowledge of specific infringing activity, or was at least aware of facts or circumstances from which specific infringing activity was apparent. *See* § 512(c)(1)(A)(i)–(ii). Accordingly, we hold that summary judgment to YouTube on all clips-in-suit, especially in the absence of any detailed examination of the extensive record on summary judgment, was premature.[9]

---

[9]   We express no opinion as to whether the evidence discussed above will prove sufficient to withstand a renewed motion for summary judgment by YouTube on remand. In particular, we note that there is at least some evidence that the search requested by Walker in his February 7, 2007 e-mail was never carried out. We also note that the class plaintiffs have failed to identify evidence indicating that any infringing content discovered as a result of Walker's request in fact

We hasten to note, however, that although the foregoing e-mails were annexed as exhibits to the summary judgment papers, it is unclear whether the clips referenced therein are among the current clips-in-suit. By definition, only the current clips-in-suit are at issue in this litigation. Accordingly, we vacate the order granting summary judgment and instruct the District Court to determine on remand whether any specific infringements of which YouTube had knowledge or awareness correspond to the clips-in-suit in these actions.

ii. "Willful Blindness"

The plaintiffs further argue that the District Court erred in granting summary judgment to the defendants despite evidence that YouTube was "willfully blind" to specific infringing activity. On this issue of first impression, we consider the application of the common law willful blindness doctrine in the DMCA context.

"The principle that willful blindness is tantamount to knowledge is hardly novel." *Tiffany (NJ) Inc. v. eBay, Inc.,* 600 F.3d 93, 110 n. 16 (2d Cir. 2010) (collecting cases); *see In re Aimster Copyright Litig.,* 334 F.3d 643, 650 (7th Cir. 2003) ("Willful blindness is knowledge, in copyright law . . . as it is in the law generally."). A person is "willfully blind" or engages in "conscious avoidance" amounting to knowledge where the person " 'was aware of a high probability of the fact in dispute and consciously avoided confirming that fact.' " *United States v. Aina-Marshall,* 336 F.3d 167, 170 (2d Cir. 2003) (quoting *United States v. Rodriguez,* 983 F.2d 455, 458 (2d Cir. 1993)). Writing in the trademark infringement context, we have held that "[a] service provider is not . . . permitted willful blindness. When it has reason to suspect that users of its service are infringing a protected mark, it may not shield itself from learning of the particular infringing transactions by looking the other way." *Tiffany,* 600 F.3d at 109.

The DMCA does not mention willful blindness. As a general matter, we interpret a statute to abrogate a common law principle only if the statute "speak[s] directly to the question addressed by the common law." *Matar v. Dichter,* 563 F.3d 9, 14 (2d Cir. 2009) (internal quotation marks omitted). The relevant question, therefore, is whether the DMCA "speak[s] directly" to the principle of willful blindness. The DMCA provision most relevant to the abrogation inquiry is § 512(m), which provides that safe harbor protection shall not be conditioned on "a service provider monitoring its service or affirmatively seeking facts indicating infringing activity, except to the extent consistent with a standard technical measure complying with the provisions of subsection (i)." 17 U.S.C. § 512(m)(1). Section 512(m) is explicit: DMCA safe harbor protection cannot be conditioned on affirmative monitoring by a service provider. For that reason, § 512(m) is incompatible with a broad common law duty to monitor or otherwise seek out infringing activity based on general awareness that infringement may be occurring. That fact does not, however, dispose of the abrogation inquiry; as previously noted, willful blindness cannot be defined as an affirmative duty to monitor. Because the statute does not "speak[ ] directly" to the willful blindness

---

remained on the YouTube website. The class plaintiffs, drawing on the voluminous record in this case, may be able to remedy these deficiencies in their briefing to the District Court on remand.

doctrine, § 512(m) limits—but does not abrogate—the doctrine. Accordingly, we hold that the willful blindness doctrine may be applied, in appropriate circumstances, to demonstrate knowledge or awareness of specific instances of infringement under the DMCA.

The District Court cited § 512(m) for the proposition that safe harbor protection does not require affirmative monitoring, but did not expressly address the principle of willful blindness or its relationship to the DMCA safe harbors. As a result, whether the defendants made a "deliberate effort to avoid guilty knowledge," *In re Aimster,* 334 F.3d at 650, remains a fact question for the District Court to consider in the first instance on remand.[10]

B.   Control and Benefit: § 512(c)(1)(B)

Apart from the foregoing knowledge provisions, the § 512(c) safe harbor provides that an eligible service provider must "not receive a financial benefit directly attributable to the infringing activity, in a case in which the service provider has the right and ability to control such activity." 17 U.S.C. § 512(c)(1)(B). The District Court addressed this issue in a single paragraph, quoting from § 512(c)(1)(B), the so-called "control and benefit" provision, and concluding that "[t]he 'right and ability to control' the activity requires knowledge of it, which must be item-specific." For the reasons that follow, we hold that the District Court erred by importing a specific knowledge requirement into the control and benefit provision, and we therefore remand for further fact-finding on the issue of control.

1.   "Right and Ability to Control" Infringing Activity

On appeal, the parties advocate two competing constructions of the "right and ability to control" infringing activity. Because each is fatally flawed, we reject both proposed constructions in favor of a fact-based inquiry to be conducted in the first instance by the District Court.

The first construction, pressed by the defendants, is the one adopted by the District Court, which held that "the provider must know of the particular case before he can control it." *Viacom,* 718 F.Supp.2d at 527. The Ninth Circuit recently agreed, holding that "until [the service provider] becomes aware of specific unauthorized material, it cannot exercise its 'power or authority' over the specific infringing item. In practical terms, it does not have the kind of ability to control infringing activity the statute contemplates." *Shelter Capital,* 667 F.3d at 1041. The trouble with this construction is that importing a specific knowledge requirement into § 512(c)(1)(B) renders the control provision duplicative of § 512(c)(1)(A). Any service provider that has item-specific knowledge of infringing activity and thereby obtains financial benefit would already be excluded from the safe harbor under § 512(c)(1)(A) for having specific knowledge of infringing material and failing to effect expeditious removal. No additional service provider would be excluded by § 512(c)(1)(B) that was not already excluded by § 512(c)(1)(A). Because

---

[10]   Our recent decision in *Tiffany (NJ) Inc. v. eBay Inc.,* 600 F.3d 93 (2d Cir. 2010), lends support to this result. In *Tiffany,* we rejected a willful blindness challenge, holding that although eBay "knew as a general matter that counterfeit Tiffany products were listed and sold through its website," such knowledge "is insufficient to trigger liability." In so holding, however, we rested on the extensive findings of the district court with respect to willful blindness. Thus, the *Tiffany* holding counsels in favor of explicit fact-finding on the issue of willful blindness.

statutory interpretations that render language superfluous are disfavored, we reject the District Court's interpretation of the control provision.

The second construction, urged by the plaintiffs, is that the control provision codifies the common law doctrine of vicarious copyright liability. The common law imposes liability for vicarious copyright infringement "[w]hen the right and ability to supervise coalesce with an obvious and direct financial interest in the exploitation of copyrighted materials—even in the absence of actual knowledge that the copyright mono[poly] is being impaired." *Shapiro, Bernstein & Co. v. H.L. Green Co.*, 316 F.2d 304, 307 (2d Cir. 1963). . . .

. . . The general rule with respect to common law codification is that when "Congress uses terms that have accumulated settled meaning under the common law, a court must infer, unless the statute otherwise dictates, that Congress means to incorporate the established meaning of those terms." *Neder v. United States,* 527 U.S. 1, 21 (1999) (ellipsis and internal quotation marks omitted). Under the common law vicarious liability standard, " '[t]he ability to block infringers' access to a particular environment for any reason whatsoever is evidence of the right and ability to supervise.' " *Arista Records LLC v. Usenet.com, Inc.,* 633 F.Supp.2d 124, 157 (S.D.N.Y. 2009) (alteration in original) (quoting *A & M Records, Inc. v. Napster, Inc.,* 239 F.3d 1004, 1023 (9th Cir. 2001)). To adopt that principle in the DMCA context, however, would render the statute internally inconsistent. Section 512(c) actually presumes that service providers have the ability to "block . . . access" to infringing material. *Id.* at 157; *see Shelter Capital,* 667 F.3d at 1042–43. Indeed, a service provider who has knowledge or awareness of infringing material or who receives a takedown notice from a copyright holder is *required* to "remove, or disable access to, the material" in order to claim the benefit of the safe harbor. 17 U.S.C. § 512(c)(1)(A)(iii) & (C). But in taking such action, the service provider would—in the plaintiffs' analysis—be admitting the "right and ability to control" the infringing material. Thus, the prerequisite to safe harbor protection under § 512(c)(1)(A)(iii) & (C) would at the same time be a disqualifier under § 512(c)(1)(B).

Moreover, if Congress had intended § 512(c)(1)(B) to be coextensive with vicarious liability, "the statute could have accomplished that result in a more direct manner." *Shelter Capital,* 667 F.3d at 1045.

It is conceivable that Congress . . . intended that [service providers] which receive a financial benefit directly attributable to the infringing activity would not, under any circumstances, be able to qualify for the subsection (c) safe harbor. But if that was indeed their intention, it would have been far simpler and much more straightforward to simply say as much.

Id. (alteration in original).

In any event, the foregoing tension—elsewhere described as a "predicament" and a "catch 22"—is sufficient to establish that the control provision "dictates" a departure from the common law vicarious liability standard. Accordingly, we conclude that the "right and ability to control" infringing activity under § 512(c)(1)(B) "requires something more than the ability to remove or block access to materials posted on a service provider's website." *MP3tunes, LLC,* 821 F.Supp.2d at 645; *accord Wolk* *v. Kodak Imaging Network, Inc.,* ___ F.Supp.2d ___, ___, 2012 WL 11270, at *21 (S.D.N.Y. Jan. 3, 2012); *UMG II,* 665 F.Supp.2d at 1114–15; *Io Grp., Inc. v. Veoh Networks, Inc.,* 586 F.Supp.2d 1132, 1151 (N.D.Cal. 2008); *Corbis Corp. v. Amazon.com, Inc.,* 351 F.Supp.2d 1090, 1110 (W.D.Wash. 2004). The remaining—and more difficult—question is how to define the "something more" that is required.

To date, only one court has found that a service provider had the right and ability to control infringing activity under § 512(c)(1)(B).[13] In *Perfect 10, Inc. v. Cybernet Ventures, Inc.,* 213 F.Supp.2d 1146 (C.D.Cal. 2002), the court found control where the service provider instituted a monitoring program by which user websites received "detailed instructions regard[ing] issues of layout, appearance, and content." *Id.* at 1173. The service provider also forbade certain types of content and refused access to users who failed to comply with its instructions. Similarly, inducement of copyright infringement under *Metro-Goldwyn-Mayer Studios Inc. v. Grokster, Ltd.,* 545 U.S. 913 (2005), which "premises liability on purposeful, culpable expression and conduct," *id.* at 937, might also rise to the level of control under § 512(c)(1)(B). Both of these examples involve a service provider exerting substantial influence on the activities of users, without necessarily—or even frequently—acquiring knowledge of specific infringing activity.

In light of our holding that § 512(c)(1)(B) does not include a specific knowledge requirement, we think it prudent to remand to the District Court to consider in the first instance whether the plaintiffs have adduced sufficient evidence to allow a reasonable jury to conclude that YouTube had the right and ability to control the infringing activity and received a financial benefit directly attributable to that activity.

C.   "By Reason of" Storage: § 512(c)(1)

The § 512(c) safe harbor is only available when the infringement occurs "by reason of the storage at the direction of a user of material that resides on a system or network controlled or operated by or for the service provider." 17 U.S.C. § 512(c)(1). In this case, the District Court held that YouTube's software functions fell within the safe harbor for infringements that occur "by reason of" user storage. *Viacom,* 718 F.Supp.2d at 526 (noting that a contrary holding would "confine[ ] the word 'storage' too narrowly to meet the statute's purpose"). For the reasons that follow, we affirm that holding with respect to three of the challenged software functions—the conversion (or "transcoding") of videos into a standard display format, the playback of videos on "watch" pages, and the "related videos" function. We remand for further fact-finding with respect to a fourth software function, involving the third-party syndication of videos uploaded to YouTube.

As a preliminary matter, we note that "the structure and language of OCILLA indicate that service providers seeking safe harbor under [§] 512(c) are not limited to merely storing material." *Io Grp.,* 586 F.Supp.2d

---

[13]   Other courts have suggested that control may exist where the service provider is "actively involved in the listing, bidding, sale and delivery" of items offered for sale, *Hendrickson v. eBay, Inc.,* 165 F.Supp.2d 1082, 1094 (C.D.Cal. 2001), or otherwise controls vendor sales by previewing products prior to their listing, editing product descriptions, or suggesting prices, *Corbis Corp.,* 351 F.Supp.2d at 1110. Because these cases held that control did *not* exist, however, it is not clear that the practices cited therein are individually sufficient to support a finding of control.

at 1147. The structure of the statute distinguishes between so-called "conduit only" functions under § 512(a) and the functions addressed by § 512(c) and the other subsections. *See* 17 U.S.C. § 512(n) ("Subsections (a), (b), (c), and (d) describe separate and distinct functions for purposes of applying this section."). Most notably, OCILLA contains two definitions of "service provider." 17 U.S.C. § 512(k)(1)(A)–(B). The narrower definition, which applies only to service providers falling under § 512(a), is limited to entities that "offer[ ] the transmission, routing or providing of connections for digital online communications, between or among points specified by a user, of material of the user's choosing, *without modification to the content of the material* as sent or received." *Id.* § 512(k)(1)(A) (emphasis added). No such limitation appears in the broader definition, which applies to service providers—including YouTube—falling under § 512(c). Under the broader definition, "the term 'service provider' means a provider of online services or network access, or the operator of facilities therefor, and includes an entity described in subparagraph (A)." *Id.* § 512(k)(1)(B). In the absence of a parallel limitation on the ability of a service provider to modify user-submitted material, we conclude that § 512(c) "is clearly meant to cover more than mere electronic storage lockers." *UMG Recordings, Inc. v. Veoh Networks, Inc.,* 620 F.Supp.2d 1081, 1088 (C.D.Cal. 2008) ("*UMG I* ").

The relevant case law makes clear that the § 512(c) safe harbor extends to software functions performed "for the purpose of facilitating access to user-stored material." *Id.; see Shelter Capital,* 667 F.3d at 1031–35. Two of the software functions challenged here—transcoding and playback—were expressly considered by our sister Circuit in *Shelter Capital,* which held that liability arising from these functions occurred "by reason of the storage at the direction of a user." Transcoding involves "[m]aking copies of a video in a different encoding scheme" in order to render the video "viewable over the Internet to most users." The playback process involves "deliver[ing] copies of YouTube videos to a user's browser cache" in response to a user request. The District Court correctly found that to exclude these automated functions from the safe harbor would eviscerate the protection afforded to service providers by § 512(c).

A similar analysis applies to the "related videos" function, by which a YouTube computer algorithm identifies and displays "thumbnails" of clips that are "related" to the video selected by the user. The plaintiffs claim that this practice constitutes content promotion, not "access" to stored content, and therefore falls beyond the scope of the safe harbor. Citing similar language in the Racketeer Influenced and Corrupt Organizations Act ("RICO"), 18 U.S.C. §§ 1961–68, and the Clayton Act, 15 U.S.C. §§ 12 *et seq.,* the plaintiffs argue that the statutory phrase "by reason of" requires a finding of proximate causation between the act of storage and the infringing activity. But even if the plaintiffs are correct that § 512(c) incorporates a principle of proximate causation—a question we need not resolve here—the indexing and display of related videos retain a sufficient causal link to the prior storage of those videos. The record makes clear that the related videos algorithm "is fully automated and operates solely in response to user input without the active involvement of YouTube employees." Furthermore, the related videos function serves to help YouTube users locate and gain access to material stored at the direction of other users. Because the algorithm "is closely related to, and follows from, the storage itself," and is "narrowly directed

toward providing access to material stored at the direction of users,"
UMG I, 620 F.Supp.2d at 1092, we conclude that the related videos
function is also protected by the § 512(c) safe harbor.

The final software function at issue here—third-party syndication—
is the closest case. In or around March 2007, YouTube transcoded a select
number of videos into a format compatible with mobile devices and
"syndicated" or licensed the videos to Verizon Wireless and other
companies. The plaintiffs argue—with some force—that business
transactions do not occur at the "direction of a user" within the meaning
of § 512(c)(1) when they involve the manual selection of copyrighted
material for licensing to a third party. The parties do not dispute,
however, that none of the clips-in-suit were among the approximately
2,000 videos provided to Verizon Wireless. In order to avoid rendering an
advisory opinion on the outer boundaries of the storage provision, we
remand for fact-finding on the question of whether any of the clips-in-
suit were in fact syndicated to any other third party.

D.   Other Arguments

1.   Repeat Infringer Policy

The class plaintiffs briefly argue that YouTube failed to comply with
the requirements of § 512(i), which conditions safe harbor eligibility on
the service provider having "adopted and reasonably implemented . . . a
policy that provides for the termination in appropriate circumstances of
subscribers and account holders of the service provider's system or
network who are repeat infringers." 17 U.S.C. § 512(i)(1)(A). Specifically,
the class plaintiffs allege that YouTube "deliberately set up its
identification tools to try to avoid identifying infringements of class
plaintiffs' works." This allegation rests primarily on the assertion that
YouTube permitted only designated "partners" to gain access to content
identification tools by which YouTube would conduct network searches
and identify infringing material.

Because the class plaintiffs challenge YouTube's deployment of
search technology, we must consider their § 512(i) argument in
conjunction with § 512(m). As previously noted, § 512(m) provides that
safe harbor protection cannot be conditioned on "a service provider
monitoring its service or affirmatively seeking facts indicating infringing
activity, *except to the extent consistent with a standard technical measure
complying with the provisions of subsection (i).*" 17 U.S.C. § 512(m)(1)
(emphasis added). In other words, the safe harbor expressly disclaims
any affirmative monitoring requirement—except to the extent that such
monitoring comprises a "standard technical measure" within the
meaning of § 512(i). Refusing to accommodate or implement a "standard
technical measure" exposes a service provider to liability; refusing to
provide access to mechanisms by which a service provider affirmatively
monitors its own network has no such result. In this case, the class
plaintiffs make no argument that the content identification tools
implemented by YouTube constitute "standard technical measures," such
that YouTube would be exposed to liability under § 512(i). For that
reason, YouTube cannot be excluded from the safe harbor by dint of a
decision to restrict access to its proprietary search mechanisms.

2. Affirmative Claims

Finally, the plaintiffs argue that the District Court erred in denying summary judgment to the plaintiffs on their claims of direct infringement, vicarious liability, and contributory liability under *Metro-Goldwyn-Mayer Studios Inc. v. Grokster, Ltd.,* 545 U.S. 913 (2005). In granting summary judgment to the defendants, the District Court held that YouTube "qualif[ied] for the protection of . . . § 512(c)," and therefore denied the plaintiffs' cross-motion for summary judgment without comment.

The District Court correctly determined that a finding of safe harbor application necessarily protects a defendant from all affirmative claims for monetary relief. 17 U.S.C. § 512(c)(1); *cf.* 17 U.S.C. § 512(j) (setting forth the scope of injunctive relief available under § 512). For the reasons previously stated, further fact-finding is required to determine whether YouTube is ultimately entitled to safe harbor protection in this case. Accordingly, we vacate the order denying summary judgment to the plaintiffs and remand the cause without expressing a view on the merits of the plaintiffs' affirmative claims.

CONCLUSION

To summarize, we hold that:

(1) The District Court correctly held that 17 U.S.C. § 512(c)(1)(A) requires knowledge or awareness of facts or circumstances that indicate specific and identifiable instances of infringement;

(2) However, the June 23, 2010 order granting summary judgment to YouTube is **VACATED** because a reasonable jury could conclude that YouTube had knowledge or awareness under § 512(c)(1)(A) at least with respect to a handful of specific clips; the cause is **REMANDED** for the District Court to determine whether YouTube had knowledge or awareness of any specific instances of infringement corresponding to the clips-in-suit;

(3) The willful blindness doctrine may be applied, in appropriate circumstances, to demonstrate knowledge or awareness of specific instances of infringement under § 512(c)(1)(A); the cause is **REMANDED** for the District Court to consider the application of the willful blindness doctrine in the first instance;

(4) The District Court erred by requiring "item-specific" knowledge of infringement in its interpretation of the "right and ability to control" infringing activity under 17 U.S.C. § 512(c)(1)(B), and the judgment is **REVERSED** insofar as it rests on that erroneous construction of the statute; the cause is **REMANDED** for further fact-finding by the District Court on the issues of control and financial benefit;

(5) The District Court correctly held that three of the challenged YouTube software functions—replication, playback, and the related videos feature—occur "by reason of the storage at the direction of a user" within the meaning of 17 U.S.C. § 512(c)(1), and the judgment is **AFFIRMED** insofar as it so held; the cause is **REMANDED** for further fact-finding regarding a fourth software function, involving the syndication of YouTube videos to third parties.

. . .

Viacom International, Inc. v. YouTube, Inc., 940 F.Supp.2d 110 (S.D.N.Y. 2013). On remand, the district court, applying a standard of "blindness to 'specific and identifiable instances of infringement,' " did not find facts sufficient to support the claim of willful blindness.

In general, the law has long included the doctrine of "willful blindness." Nevertheless, willful blindness is not the same as an affirmative duty to monitor . . .

Applying the doctrine, however, requires attention to its scope. In imputing knowledge of the willfully disregarded fact, one must not impute more knowledge than the fact conveyed. Under appropriate circumstances the imputed knowledge of the willfully-avoided fact may impose a duty to make further inquiries that a reasonable person would make—but that depends on the law governing the factual situation. As shown by the Court of Appeals' discussion of "red flags," under the DMCA, what disqualifies the service provider from the DMCA's protection is blindness to "specific and identifiable instances of infringement." 676 F.3d at 32.

. . .

Here, the examples proffered by plaintiffs (to which they claim YouTube was willfully blind) give at most information that infringements were occurring with particular works, and occasional indications of promising areas to locate and remove them. The specific locations of infringements are not supplied: at most, an area of search is identified, and YouTube is left to find the infringing clip. . . .

The Karim memorandum states that infringing clips of some well-known shows "can still be found," but does not identify the specific clips he saw or where he found them. The Wilkens declaration submitted by plaintiffs asserts that there were over 450 such clips on YouTube at the time, and presumably some of them contained the infringing matter seen by Mr. Karim. To find them would require YouTube to locate and review over 450 clips. The DMCA excuses YouTube from doing that search. Under § 512 (m), nothing in the applicable section of the DMCA shall be construed to require YouTube's "affirmatively seeking facts indicating infringing activity."

Mr. Karim's memorandum does not tie his observations to any specific clips. Application of the principle of willful blindness to his memorandum thus does not produce knowledge or awareness of infringement of specific clips-in-suit, out of the 450 available candidates. Nor does any other example tendered by plaintiffs.

. . .

There is no showing of willful blindness to specific infringements of clips-in-suit.

[In March 2014 the parties announced that they had settled the case, though the terms of the settlement were not disclosed. Leslie Kaufman, *Viacom and YouTube Settle Suit Over Copyright Violations*, N.Y. TIMES, Mar. 19, 2014, at B4.]

Capitol Records, Inc. v. MP3tunes, LLC

821 F.Supp.2d. 627 (S.D.N.Y. 2011).

■ PAULEY, DISTRICT JUDGE.

Plaintiffs, EMI, Inc. and fourteen record companies and music publishers (collectively, "EMI"), bring this copyright infringement action against Defendants MP3tunes, LLC ("MP3tunes") and Michael Robertson ("Robertson"). All parties move for summary judgment. For the following reasons, EMI's motion is granted in part and denied in part and MP3tunes and Robertson's motion is granted in part and denied in part.

BACKGROUND

I. *MP3tunes' Websites and Services*

Robertson is an online music entrepreneur familiar with high-stakes copyright litigation. Years ago, he founded MP3.com, an entity which was the subject of a copyright infringement action . . . *See UMG Recordings, Inc. v. MP3.com, Inc.,* 92 F.Supp.2d 349 (S.D.N.Y. 2000). MP3.com offered users online access to music if they could demonstrate they already owned the same music on CD. Various record labels brought suit and a multi-million dollar judgment was entered against MP3.com for copying thousands of music files. In the wake of that judgment, MP3.com was sold and its locker service abandoned. MP3tunes—the subject of this litigation—is Robertson's current foray into online music services.

Robertson founded MP3 tunes in February 2005 and launched the website MP3tunes.com to sell independent artists' songs in the mp3 file format. In the fall of 2005, MP3tunes added a storage service allowing users to store music files in personal online storage "lockers." Songs uploaded to a user's locker could be played and downloaded through any internet-enabled device. MP3tunes offers free lockers with limited storage space and premium lockers with expanded storage for a subscription fee. Over 300,000 users have signed up for a locker. LockerSync, a free software program provided on the website, enables users to automatically upload to their lockers mp3 files stored on their personal hard drives. Another feature of the website called Webload allows a user to enter the web address of a music file stored on a third-party server connected to the internet, and transfer the file to the user's locker.

MP3tunes uses a standard algorithm known as a Content-Addressable Storage system to store music files on its servers. Based on the sequence of data bits in a particular music file, the algorithm creates an identification number called a hash tag. If different users upload the same song containing identical blocks of data to MP3tunes' servers, those blocks will be assigned the same hash tag and typically saved only once. If a user plays or downloads a song from a locker, the storage system uses the hash tags associated with the uploaded song to reconstruct the exact file the user originally uploaded to his locker.

MP3tunes owns and operates a second website located at www. sideload.com. That website allows users to search for free song files on the internet. Like other search engines, a user can enter keywords (e.g., "Sinatra" or "Watchtower") and Sideload.com returns a list of potential matches. That list is generated by searching an index or list of websites with free song files and cross-referencing the keywords with information associated with each song file. The index is maintained on MP3tunes' servers. By clicking on a search return, the user is taken to a page where he can play the song, follow a link to the third-party website hosting the song, or download the song to another computer. If the user has a locker on MP3tunes.com, Sideload.com displays a link that if clicked, will "sideload" (i.e., download) the song from the third-party website and save it to his locker. Sideload.com is free as is storage of sideloaded-songs in MP3tunes.com lockers. MP3tunes keeps track of the sources of songs in its users' lockers. Thus, MP3tunes can identify the third-party websites from which users copied songs to their lockers. . . .

Sideload.com also offers users free Sideload Plug-in software. When a user with the Sideload Plug-in surfs the internet and comes across a website with a free song file, a button appears on the third-party website that will copy the song directly to the user's MP3tunes locker, without visiting Sideload.com. When a user sideloads a song from a third-party site, either through the Sideload Plug-in or Webload software, that third-party website is added to Sideload.com's index of searchable songs. Information associated with the song, such as artist, album, title, and track is automatically stored on a "Track Details" page, and the information becomes part of the searchable index. From then on, Sideload.com returns a potential match whenever any other user searches for that song on Sideload.com by entering keywords that match the song file. Thus, as users discover free songs on the internet, the number of songs available through Sideload.com increases. When a downloadable song is removed from a third-party source, the sideload feature becomes inoperable and users can no longer add the song to their lockers. But, users who sideloaded the song before it was removed from the third-party source may continue to access the song through their MP3tunes lockers.

MP3tunes' executives, including Robertson, have personal accounts with MP3tunes and sideload songs from various third-party websites. . . .

II. *MP3tunes' Anti-Infringement Policies and Reaction to EMI's Takedown Notices*

Before users activate an MP3tunes locker, they must agree to abide by MP3tunes' policy prohibiting the storage of content that infringes copyrights. Users must also acknowledge MP3tunes' right to sever its relationship with repeat infringers. Sideload.com does not impose similar conditions for use, but MP3tunes places links to its anti-infringement policy on both Sideload.com and MP3tunes.com. . . .

On September 4, 2007, MP3tunes received a takedown notice from non-party EMI Music Group North America ("EMGNA") identifying 350 song titles and web addresses that allegedly infringed EMI's copyrights. EMGNA also provided a list of EMI artists and demanded that MP3tunes "remove all of EMI's copyrighted works, even those not specifically identified." MP3tunes responded by removing links to the specific web addresses listed in EMGNA's letter, but did not remove infringing songs from its users' lockers. In addition, by letter dated September 13, 2007, MP3tunes asked EMGNA to identify any other infringing links. EMGNA declined to identify other links and asserted that its representative list was sufficient to obligate MP3tunes to takedown all other infringing material.

On October 25, 2007, MP3tunes received two additional takedown notices: another from EMGNA and one from non-party EMI Entertainment World ("EEW"). Each notice identified specific infringing songs and URLs and demanded that MP3tunes takedown all other EMI copyrighted works. Once again, MP3tunes removed the specific links on Sideload.com but did not remove any content from users' lockers. MP3tunes reiterated its earlier request that EMGNA and now EEW specifically identify any other infringing links. Neither EMGNA nor EEW responded. Rather, on November 9, 2007, EMI filed this lawsuit.

DISCUSSION

. . .

II. *DMCA Safe Harbors*

This case turns in large part on whether MP3tunes is eligible for protection under the safe harbors created by the Digital Millennium Copyright Act ("DMCA"), 17 U.S.C. § 512. . . .

A.   *Subsection 512(i)—Repeat Infringer Policy*

EMI argues that MP3tunes failed to reasonably implement a repeat infringer policy and is therefore ineligible for protection under subsection 512(i) . . . This requirement is a prerequisite for every DMCA safe harbor and is a fundamental safeguard for copyright owners. . . .

The key terms "reasonably implemented" and "repeat infringer" are not defined in the DMCA. Courts have held that implementation is reasonable if the service provider (1) has a system for responding to takedown notices, (2) does not interfere with the copyright owners' ability to issue notices, and (3) under "appropriate circumstances" terminates users who repeatedly or blatantly infringe copyrights. *See Perfect 10 v. CCBill,* 488 F.3d 1102, 1109–1110 (9th Cir. 2007). The purpose of subsection 512(i) is to deny protection to websites that tolerate users who flagrantly disrespect copyrights. Thus, service providers that purposefully fail to keep adequate records of the identity and activities of their users and fail to terminate users despite their persistent and flagrant infringement are not eligible for protection under the safe harbor. On the other hand, service providers have no affirmative duty to police their users. In cases of video and file sharing sites, courts have found reasonable implementation where service providers terminated the accounts of users who had been warned yet continued to upload material that had been the subject of a takedown notice. *See, e.g., UMG Recordings, Inc. v. Veoh Networks Inc.,* 665 F.Supp.2d 1099, 1117–18 (C.D.Cal. 2009).

EMI argues that MP3tunes purposefully blinded itself to its users' infringement and failed to take any action against hundreds of users who sideloaded copies of songs identified in EMGNA's and EEW's takedown notices. EMI also maintains that MP3tunes ignored blatant infringement by its executives. MP3tunes counters that they have implemented a procedure for responding to takedown notices and have complied with EMGNA's and EEW's notices by removing the identified infringing links on Sideload.com. In addition, MP3tunes notes that it terminated the accounts of 153 repeat infringers who violated copyrights by sharing the contents of their lockers with other users.

Blatant infringers typically are those who upload or post unauthorized content, allowing others to experience or copy the work. *See Viacom v. YouTube,* 718 F.Supp.2d 514, 528–29 (S.D.N.Y. 2010) (finding reasonable a policy that terminated users who uploaded content after warning); *see also Io Grp., Inc. v. Veoh Networks, Inc.,* 586 F.Supp.2d 1132, 1143 (N.D.Cal. 2008). The record reveals that MP3tunes' users do not upload content to the internet, but copy songs from third-party sites for their personal entertainment. There is a difference between (1) users who know they lack authorization and nevertheless upload content to the internet for the world to experience or copy, and (2) users who download content for their personal use and are otherwise oblivious to the copyrights of others. The former are blatant infringers that internet service providers are obligated to ban from their websites. The latter, like MP3tunes users who sideload content to their lockers for personal use, do not know for certain whether the material they download violates the copyrights of others.

It is not surprising that the cases cited by EMI require the termination of users who repeatedly upload copyrighted material to service providers' websites, but absolve service providers from policing users who merely consume that content. *See Viacom,* 718 F.Supp.2d at 529; *see also Io Grp.,* 586 F.Supp.2d at 1143; *UMG Recordings,* 665 F.Supp.2d at 1116; [*Corbis Corp. v. Amazon.com,* 351 F.Supp.2d 1090, 1100–01 (W.D.Wash. 2004)]. This applies to MP3tunes executives. Like their users, they do not post content to the internet and cannot be certain whether content on third-party sites actually infringes. For example, MP3tunes employee e-mails reveal discussions about the legitimacy of some third-party sites and, on at least one occasion, a recommendation that a site be removed from Sideload.com. But ultimately there is no evidence that MP3tunes executives or employees had firsthand knowledge that websites linked on Sideload.com were unauthorized. While knowledge is not an element of copyright infringement, it is relevant to a services provider's decision whether appropriate circumstances exist to terminate a user's account. *See CCBill,* 488 F.3d at 1109; *see also Corbis Corp.,* 351 F.Supp.2d at 1104 ("Because it does not have an affirmative duty to police its users, failure to properly implement an infringement policy requires a showing of instances where a service provider fails to terminate a user even though it has sufficient evidence to create *actual knowledge* of that user's blatant, repeat infringement of a willful and commercial nature.") (emphasis added).

Moreover, MP3tunes does not purposefully blind itself to its users' identities and activities. . . . In contrast [to Aimster], MP3tunes tracks the source and web address of every sideloaded song in its users' lockers and can terminate the accounts of repeat infringers. And Robertson asserted that MP3tunes employed those resources and terminated the accounts of 153 users who allowed others to access their lockers and copy music files without authorization. . . .

Finally, MP3tunes demonstrated that it has a procedure for responding to DMCA takedown notifications and does not interfere with copyright owners' ability to issue such notices. MP3tunes reacted to EMGNA's and EEW's notices and removed the links listed on Sideload.com. EMI argues that MP3tunes had an obligation to terminate any user who added multiple links to Sideload.com that appeared on one or more takedown notices. EMI argues that such users are automatic repeat infringers. But, takedown notices themselves are not evidence of blatant infringement and users could not be certain that they had downloaded infringing content. Thus, MP3tunes' decision to refrain from terminating those user accounts was appropriate. Accordingly, there is no genuine dispute that MP3tunes satisfies the threshold requirements to qualify for safe harbor protection under the DMCA.

B. *Subsections 512(c)(3) and (d)(3)—Compliance with EMI's Takedown Notices*

EMI argues that MP3tunes failed to comply with the DMCA takedown notices sent by EMGNA and EEW as required by subsections 512(c)(3) and (d)(3). Specifically, EMI asserts that MP3tunes failed to remove songs from users' lockers that were sideloaded from specific websites identified in the notices.

Subsection 512(c) governs material stored on the service provider's servers at the direction of a user. This safe harbor potentially applies to MP3tunes' locker service. Subsection 512(d) governs information location tools, e.g., search engines. This safe harbor potentially applies to Sideload.com. The parties agree that, in relevant part, the eligibility requirements for subsections 512(c) and (d) protection are the same and that each service must independently qualify. . . .

1. *Pre-1972 Recordings*

[As an initial matter, the court rejected EMI's argument that because sound recordings first fixed before February 15, 1972 are not protected by federal copyright, 17 U.S.C. § 301(c), the DMCA does not apply to claims of infringement in those works. The court concluded that the DMCA's text limits immunity for the "infringement of copyrights" without drawing any distinction between federal and state law, and that the common law meaning of the term "copyright infringement" encompasses violations of both federal and state protections. The court also noted that excluding pre-1972 sound recordings from the scope of § 512 "would spawn legal uncertainty and subject otherwise innocent internet service providers to liability for the acts of third parties." As a result, the court ruled that the DMCA's safe harbors cover both state and federal copyright claims, and therefore apply to sound recordings fixed prior to February 15, 1972.]

2. *Sufficiency of the Takedown Notices*

The notification requirements of subsections 512(c)(3) and (d) (3) are identical . . . A proper DMCA notice must, *inter alia,* identify the copyrighted work or provide a representative list, if multiple works on a single site are subject to the same notice, *and* identify the infringing material with enough information to locate it. . . .

The EMGNA and EEW letters list hundreds of copyrighted works and provide web addresses for the infringing links on Sideload.com. EMI argues that such notice required MP3tunes to remove all of the songs sideloaded from those links to users' lockers. Defendants counter that [§ 512] only requires removal of the identified link from Sideload.com because that was the only infringing material listed in the notices. In addition, MP3tunes argues that it would be subject to lawsuits by users if it removed personal property from user lockers.

While [§ 512] does not require service providers to locate additional infringing copyrighted work other than the specific work noticed, MP3tunes was obligated to remove specific works traceable to users' lockers. Because MP3tunes keeps track of the source and web address for each sideloaded song in each user's locker, EMI's notices gave sufficient information for MP3tunes to locate copies of infringing songs in user lockers. All MP3tunes had to do was search for the offending web address in its database of information regarding user lockers.

MP3tunes interprets the reach of a notice too narrowly. Under its reading, EMI would be required to identify each and every user who copied a song from an unauthorized web site to a locker. Of course, EMI could not meet that burden because it has no way of identifying such users without conducting burdensome discovery. Thus, this case is distinguishable from *Viacom*. There, the copyright owner could freely search YouTube for its copyrighted work and identify infringing material. Where service providers such as MP3tunes allow users to search for copyrighted works posted to the internet and to store those works in private accounts, to qualify for DMCA protection, those service providers must (1) keep track of the source and web address of stored copyrighted material, and (2) take content down when copyright owners identify the infringing sources in otherwise compliant notices.

MP3tunes exaggerates the potential liability of removing content from users' lockers. MP3tunes' Terms of Use clearly authorize it to block a user's access to material in lockers. And the DMCA provides MP3tunes with immunity and a procedure for dealing with claims from its users. 17 U.S.C. § 512(g). Accordingly, there is no genuine dispute that MP3tunes does not qualify for safe harbor protection for songs stored in users lockers that were sideloaded from the unauthorized websites identified in the EMGNA and EEW takedown notices.

EMI also contends that MP3tunes should have taken down all EMI content because the notices provided a representative list. However, EMI's argument misconstrues the DMCA and applicable case law. Even assuming the representative lists properly identified EMI's copyrighted works, EMI had to provide sufficient information—namely, additional web addresses—for MP3tunes to locate other infringing material. EMI's notifications provided only enough information for MP3tunes to remove the noticed websites from Sideload.com and to find and remove copies of songs sideloaded from those websites. They did not identify the location of additional infringing material, let alone all of EMI's copyrighted works. Absent adequate notice, MP3tunes would need to conduct a burdensome investigation in order to determine whether songs in its users' accounts were unauthorized copies. As discussed, the DMCA does not place this burden on service providers. Thus, there is no genuine dispute that MP3tunes complies with the requirements of the DMCA with respect to songs sideloaded from websites not listed in the takedown notices.

. . .

Capitol Records, Inc. v. MP3Tunes, LLC, 48 F.Supp.3d 703 (S.D.N.Y. 2014). At a jury trial in this case, "found MP3tunes directly liable for infringement of Plaintiffs' reproduction and public display rights in cover art and for unfair competition with respect to pre-1972 sound recordings. Concluding that MP3tunes acted with both red flag knowledge and willful blindness, the jurors found MP3tunes secondarily liable for infringements by MP3tunes' users, third-party websites, and MP3tunes' Executives," but did not find MP3tunes secondarily liable for violating the plaintiffs' distribution rights. The jury imposed secondary liability on Robertson himself for every claim on which it found MP3tunes liable, except for MP3tunes' failure to remove certain works from lockers in response to takedown notices. The jury awarded $48,061,073 in damages.

In response to defendants' motion for judgment as a matter of law, the court reviewed, among other issues, the application of the § 512(c) safe harbor in the case.

The crux of this case is whether MP3tunes and Robertson are insulated from liability under the DMCA. Congress enacted the DMCA to comply with treaty obligations "and to update domestic copyright law for the digital age." *Viacom Int'l, Inc. v. YouTube, Inc.,* 676 F.3d 19, 26 (2d Cir.2012). To that end, Congress established four safe harbors that protect service providers from liability for certain types of copyright infringement. 17 U.S.C. § 512.

The safe harbor at issue in this case protects qualifying service providers from liability for "information residing on systems or networks at [the] direction of users." 17 U.S.C. § 512(c). The DMCA's protection must be earned. A service provider qualifies for § 512(c) immunity only if the service provider:

(i) does not have actual knowledge that the material or an activity using the material on the system or network is infringing;

(ii) in the absence of such actual knowledge, is not aware of facts or circumstances from which infringing activity is apparent; or

(iii) upon obtaining such knowledge or awareness, acts expeditiously to remove, or disable access to, the material;

17 U.S.C. § 512(c)(1)(A). The second provision has come to be known as the "'red flag' knowledge" provision. In *Viacom,* the Second Circuit "establish[ed] an exquisite 'subjective/objective' standard for distinguishing between 'actual' and 'red flag' knowledge." *MP3tunes II,* 2013 WL 1987225, at *3 (citation omitted). Actual knowledge refers to subjective awareness of infringement, and "red flag" knowledge arises where a provider is aware of facts that would have made specific infringement objectively obvious to a reasonable person. *Viacom,* 676 F.3d at 31.

In addition to red flag knowledge, knowledge may be imputed to a service provider through the common law doctrine of willful blindness. *Viacom,* 676 F.3d at 35. A provider acts with willful blindness if it is aware of a high probability that specific material is infringing but consciously avoids confirming that fact. *Viacom,* 676 F.3d at 35. Section 512(m)'s command that "DMCA safe harbor protection cannot be conditioned on affirmative monitoring by a service provider" limits the reach of the common law doctrine. *Viacom,* 676 F.3d at 35 (citing 17 U.S.C. § 512(m)). "*Viacom* offers little guidance on how to reconcile the tension between the doctrine of willful blindness and the DMCA's explicit repudiation of any affirmative duty on the part of service providers to monitor user content." *Capitol Records, LLC v. Vimeo, LLC,* 972 F.Supp.2d 500, 523, *amended on reconsideration in part,* 972 F.Supp.2d 537 (S.D.N.Y.2013) (quoting *MP3tunes II,* 2013 WL 1987225, at *2).

Only knowledge of specific instances of infringement bars a service provider from the safe harbor, regardless of whether the knowledge is actual, or supplied though red flag knowledge or willful blindness. *Viacom,* 676 F.3d at 32, 35. The requirement is a practical one—only specific knowledge enables the service provider to expeditiously remove infringing material. *Viacom,* 676 F.3d at 30. The statute does not impose "an amorphous obligation to 'take commercially reasonable steps' in response to a generalized awareness of infringement." *Viacom,* 676 F.3d at 31 (citing 17 U.S.C. § 512(c)(1)(A)); *see also* 17 U.S.C. § 512(m). Thus, when a provider knows that material at a specific location is infringing, it must act expeditiously to remove it or risk losing the safe harbor for infringements of that material. And that knowledge can be actual or as a result of red flag knowledge or willful blindness. *See Viacom,* 676 F.3d at 32.[6]

The jury held Defendants liable for MP3tunes' users' copyright infringement by finding red flag knowledge and willful blindness as to four categories of works: (1) takedown notices identifying ten or more infringing files on a domain; (2) Sideloads of MP3s before January 2007; (3) Sideloads by MP3tunes Executives; and (4) works by The Beatles. Those categories were not court imposed; they were constructed by Plaintiffs, presumably to streamline their trial presentation. The decision to cabin thousands of works into one or more of these categories foreshadowed a strategy that aggregated claims instead of focusing on specific instances of infringement. Robertson argues that the evidence was insufficient to conclude the Defendants possessed knowledge of specific instances of infringement.

1. *Takedown Notices Identifying 10 or More Infringing Files on a Domain*

Plaintiffs sent MP3tunes takedown notices listing thousands of songs and the source URLs from which they were sideloaded. Thirteen domains were listed at least ten times.[7] At trial, Plaintiffs argued Defendants knew those domains likely hosted other infringing content sideloaded by users but failed to remove that content. The jury agreed and found Defendants

---

[6] The Section 512(c) safe harbor also requires that providers "not receive a financial benefit directly attributable to the infringing activity, in a case in which the service provider has the right and ability to control such activity." 17 U.S.C. § 512(c)(1)(B). This provision does not include a specific knowledge requirement. *Viacom,* 676 F.3d at 38. This Court found MP3tunes met this requirement, *MP3tunes I,* 821 F.Supp.2d at 645–46, and this issue was not submitted to the jury.

[7] The number of files per domain ranged from 10 to 56.

acted with red flag knowledge and willful blindness in permitting users to continue to sideload content from those domains.

Red flag knowledge requires awareness of facts that would have made specific instances of infringement objectively obvious to a reasonable person. *Viacom,* 676 F.3d at 31–32. General knowledge is insufficient. For example, knowledge that a high percentage of content on a domain is infringing does not establish actual or red flag knowledge of particular instances of infringement. *Viacom,* 676 F.3d at 33. In this case, MP3tunes lacked even general knowledge. Even if MP3tunes tracked domains posting infringing files, a fact not in evidence, MP3tunes would still need to investigate how much content the domain hosted before it could calculate what percentage was infringing.

To ascribe red flag knowledge to MP3tunes because it was possible for MP3tunes to research and identify other instances of infringing content hosted by these domains and sideloaded by users would "mandate an amorphous obligation to 'take commercially reasonable steps' in response to generalized awareness of infringement." *Viacom,* 676 F.3d at 31. But the DMCA imposes a duty on providers to track repeat infringement by users, not third parties. *See* 17 U.S.C. § 512(i)(1)(A).

The same reasoning disposes of the willful blindness argument. Imputing knowledge to MP3tunes would impose an obligation to affirmatively monitor content, which would contravene Section 512(m)'s clear instruction that no such obligation exists. *See Viacom,* 676 F.3d at 35. Therefore, Robertson's motion for judgment as a matter of law is granted as to his liability for secondary infringement of tracks sideloaded by users from these domains.

2. *Sideloads of MP3s before January 2007*

The major record labels offered no MP3s for sale until 2007, and Robertson knew this. Although Amazon.com and some industry websites, such as South by Southwest (sxsw.com), offered promotional MP3's before 2007, the vast majority of promotional works were offered in other formats. Plaintiffs argued that because industry insiders knew MP3s of major-label works available before 2007 were illicit, MP3 tunes knew that all pre-2007 sideloads of major-label MP3s were infringing. The jury agreed and found that MP3tunes acted with red flag knowledge and willful blindness in enabling sideloads of MP3s before January 2007.

Knowledge that a high percentage of a type of content is infringing is insufficient to create red flag knowledge. *Viacom,* 676 F.3d at 33. A party is willfully blind, however, when it is aware of a high probability that a specific type of content is infringing, available on a service, and consciously avoids confirming that fact. *Viacom,* 676 F.3d at 33. Here, the jury heard evidence from which it could conclude Defendants were aware that major record labels had not offered MP3s until 2007.

But in the context of the DMCA, willful blindness is limited by the express statutory disavowal of a duty to affirmatively monitor. *Viacom,* 676 F.3d at 35. The common law doctrine would require Defendants to actively conduct routine searches and eliminate material likely to be infringing.[8] But under *Viacom's* interpretation of the DMCA, even when service providers possess sophisticated monitoring technology, they are under no obligation to use it to seek out infringement. *See Vimeo, LLC,* 972 F.Supp.2d at 525. Thus, MP3tunes cannot be held liable for failing to routinely search its servers for major-label MP3s released before January 2007. And therefore, Robertson's motion for judgment as a matter of law is granted as to sideloads of MP3s before January 2007.

3. *Sideloads by MP3tunes Executives and Related Claims*

MP3tunes' Executives sideloaded songs. As MP3tunes' Executives sideloaded tracks, they viewed the source domain's URL along with the artist and track title. The MP3tunes' Executives knew personal sites on storage service domains and student pages on college websites had a high probability of hosting infringing material. Because MP3Tunes' Executives observed those clearly infringing source domains, the jury could conclude that it would be objectively obvious to a reasonable person (here, MP3Tunes) that any tracks sideloaded from those domains were infringing. Accordingly, Robertson's motion for judgment as a matter of law is denied as to tracks sideloaded by MP3tunes' Executives and users from those domains.

4. *The Beatles*

MP3tunes' users sideloaded numerous tracks by The Beatles. In 2009, Robertson sent an email acknowledging that "the Beatles have never authorized their songs to be available digitally." Although Robertson testified that he did not learn the Labels' position that no songs by the Beatles were available legitimately over the Internet until that year, the jury was free to disregard that testimony, especially since it heard evidence that it was widely known in the music industry that authorized digital tracks by The Beatles were not available during that time period. Thus, Plaintiffs adduced evidence at trial that MP3 tunes was aware of facts that would indicate to a reasonable person that sideloading any Beatles song before 2010 was an act of infringement.

However, MP3tunes loses the protection of the safe harbor only if it also knew of specific instances of infringement. MP3tunes' Executives personally sideloaded songs by The Beatles. Therefore, the Executives possessed actual knowledge of those specific instances of infringement, and MP3tunes acted with red flag knowledge that those specific songs sideloaded by the Executives were infringing.

---

[8] Although MP3tunes had software that could identify the copyright holder of each work individually, there was no evidence MP3tunes could search for major-label content or by file format.

In addition, a user sent MP3tunes an email indicating the song "Strawberry Fields Forever" by The Beatles was available on Sideload.com. Therefore, MP3tunes possessed red flag knowledge that its users had sideloaded infringing copies of "Strawberry Fields Forever." *See UMG Recordings, Inc. v. Shelter Capital Partners LLC,* 718 F.3d 1006, 1024–25 (9th Cir.2013) (holding that a user's email to a service provider identifying infringing content on its service may be sufficient to establish red flag knowledge).

Plaintiffs also contend that Robertson had actual knowledge that he was infringing copyrights of works by The Beatles because he was "unable to deny that he personally demonstrated how to sideload works by using The Beatles as an example." But that is a bridge too far. When asked if he had searched for works by The Beatles, Robertson testified that he could not recall. Robertson's ambiguous response was not probed to any depth. His "I don't recall that" answer was not distilled to a "no, it did not happen," a "yes, it happened" or an "It could have happened but I just don't remember" answer. And there was no other evidence that answered counsel's question.

"[I]t is black letter law that questions asked by counsel are not evidence." *Washington v. Schriver,* 255 F.3d 45, 61 (2d Cir.2001) (citation omitted). While the jury could have disregarded Robertson's answer as a feigned lack of recollection, it could not, in the absence of other evidence, use it to conclude that Robertson sideloaded works by The Beatles.[9] And the record is bereft of any other evidence supporting the jury's finding of red flag knowledge and willful blindness as to specific works by The Beatles.

Despite proffering only evidence of the specific knowledge of Executive-sideloaded Beatles tracks and "Strawberry Fields Forever," Plaintiffs argue that MP3tunes possessed knowledge of all songs by The Beatles sideloaded by its users. The MP3tunes' Executives' personal sideloads and the user's email may have put MP3tunes on notice that its service probably linked to other songs by The Beatles. But MP3tunes cannot be required to search for links to Beatles songs to retain the protection of a DMCA safe harbor. *See Viacom,* 676 F.3d at 35 & n. 10. Therefore, the jury heard insufficient evidence to support a finding of red flag knowledge and willful blindness as to songs by The Beatles other than "Strawberry Fields Forever" and those sideloaded by MP3tunes' Executives.

In sum, the jury's determination that MP3tunes possessed red flag knowledge as to instances of "Strawberry Fields Forever" and songs by The Beatles sideloaded by MP3tunes' Executives is supported by the evidence. But Robertson's motion

---

[9] Another witness testified that Robertson advised her generally "just to say 'I don't recall,' " in response to questions posed at deposition. While her testimony undermines Robertson's credibility, Robertson's response to counsel's question at trial is not affirmative evidence that Robertson searched for tracks by The Beatles.

for judgment as a matter of law is granted as to the other Beatles tracks.

The court also largely upheld the jury's damage award, though it ordered remittitur of the punitive damages award on the plaintiff's state-law claims involving pre-1972 sound recordings from $7.5 million to $750,00.

QUESTIONS

1. The *Viacom* court read section 512(c)(1)(A)(i) and (ii) as differentiating, respectively, a service provider's subjective and objective knowledge, and not differentiating between specific and generalized knowledge. Is this result consistent with section 512(c)(1)(A)(ii)'s reference to whether "infringing activity" is apparent, or does that language suggest that this subsection requires a lower level of specificity of knowledge?

2. The court in *MP3tunes* described "the DMCA's purpose" as "innovation and growth of internet services," and rejected readings of the statute that would in its view undermine that purpose. Was the court sufficiently protective of another Congressional purpose for the DMCA—dividing responsibility for reducing online infringement between copyright owners and internet service providers?

3. While the *MP3Tunes* court concluded that § 512 covered pre-1972 sound recordings, New York State courts have since determined differently. In *UMG Recordings, Inc. v. Escape Media Group, Inc.,* 964 N.Y.S.2d 106 (N.Y.App.Div. 2013) the appellate court ruled that § 512 does not reach claims for infringement of common law copyright in pre-1972 recordings. Unless the U.S. Supreme Court issues an authoritative interpretation of § 512 (whose literal text in fact accords with the Appellate Division's reading), the liability of internet service providers for direct or derivative copyright infringement of pre-1972 sound recordings may depend on whether the sound recording producer brings the claim in federal or state court (and on whether the defendant, if alien to New York, removes the case to federal court). Does this make sense?

At least one federal court has disagreed with the *MP3Tunes* decision and held that § 512 does not apply to pre-1972 sound recordings. *Capitol Records, LLC v. Vimeo, LLC,* 972 F.Supp.2d 500 (S.D.N.Y. 2013). In addition, the Copyright Office, in its December 2011 report on pre-1972 sound recordings, see *supra* this Supplement at pages 40–41, also took the position that such recordings are not covered by § 512.

4. What should constitute the "something more" (beyond the right and ability to remove infringing material) that would give a service provider the "right and ability to control" infringing activity under section 512(c)(1)(B)? In reading the following decision, consider whether the Ninth Circuit has identified an aspect of right and ability to control that is not redundant with some aspect of what a service provider must do to comply with section 512.

5. How do the notice and takedown provisions of section 512 interact with section 411's requirement that a claim of copyright be registered before a suit for infringement is brought? If a copyright owner sends a takedown notice regarding an unregistered work and the ISP receives a counter notice from the alleged infringer, will the copyright owner be able to prevent the ISP from putting the material back online by filing an infringement suit? *See Schenck v. Orosz,* 109 U.S.P.Q.2d 1099 (M.D.Tenn. 2013).

———

Disney Enterprises, Inc. v. Hotfile Corp., 2013 WL 6336286 (S.D.Fla. 2013). Hotfile provides an online storage service that allows users to upload files; it the provides the user with a URL where the file can be retrieved. Files uploaded to Hotfile can be downloaded an unlimited number of times and by anyone who has the URL for the file. Five major film studios sued Hotfile for copyright infringement, and eligibility for the safe harbors—in particular, compliance with the repeat infringer policy requirement—was in dispute. Hotfile had received 10 million takedown notices, identifying 8 million unique files alleged to infringe. While it removed the content, it did not keep track of the notices or the users who had posted the allegedly infringing material. Evidence showed that nearly 25,000 users had been the subject of at least three complaints, about half of those had received more than 10 complaints, half again had received 25 or more complaints, over 1200 had been the subject of 100 or more complaints, and 61 had received 300 or more complaints. Although these were less than one percent of Hotfile's total users, they had uploaded 44% of all files uploaded to the service, and over 15 million of those 50 million uploaded files were eventually the subject of takedown notices. These 50 million files accounted for 1.5 billion downloads, roughly half of all downloads ever made from Hotfile. As far as Hotfile's implementation of a repeat infringer policy was concerned, the court determined that it was Hotfile's practice to ignore the identity of users whose uploaded files led to takedown notices, rather than to terminate the users' accounts with which they were associated. The court concluded that the scale of activity indicated to Hotfile "that a substantial number of blatant repeat infringers made the system a conduit for infringing activity" but that Hotfile "failed to devise any actual policy of dealing with those offenders." As a result, the court concluded that the implementation of Hotfile's repeat infringer policy was legally insufficient under 512(i) and therefore Hotfile was not eligible for the safe harbors.

Columbia Pictures Industries, Inc. v. Fung

710 F.3d 1020 (9th Cir. 2013).

■ BERZON, CIRCUIT JUDGE.

This case is yet another concerning the application of established intellectual property concepts to new technologies. Various film studios alleged that the services offered and websites maintained by Appellants Gary Fung and his company, isoHunt Web Technologies, Inc. (isohunt.com, torrentbox.com, podtropolis.com, and ed2k-it.com, collectively referred to in this opinion as "Fung" or the "Fung sites") induced third parties to download infringing copies of the studios' copyrighted works. The district court agreed, holding that the undisputed facts establish that Fung is liable for contributory copyright infringement. The district court also held as a matter of law that Fung is not entitled to protection from damages liability under any of the "safe harbor" provisions of the Digital Millennium Copyright Act ("DMCA"), 17 U.S.C. § 512, Congress's foray into mediating the competing interests in protecting intellectual property interests and in encouraging creative development of devices for using the Internet to make information available. By separate order, the district court permanently enjoined Fung from engaging in a number of activities that ostensibly facilitate the infringement of Plaintiffs' works.

Fung contests the copyright violation determination as well as the determination of his ineligibility for safe harbor protection under the DMCA. . . .

TECHNOLOGICAL BACKGROUND

This case concerns a peer-to-peer file sharing protocol known as BitTorrent. We begin by providing basic background information useful to understanding the role the Fung sites play in copyright infringement.

I.   Client-server vs. peer-to-peer networks

The traditional method of sharing content over a network is the relatively straightforward client-server model. In a client-server network, one or more central computers (called "servers") store the information; upon request from a user (or "client"), the server sends the requested information to the client. In other words, the server supplies information resources to clients, but the clients do not share any of their resources with the server. Client-server networks tend to be relatively secure, but they have a few drawbacks: if the server goes down, the entire network fails; and if many clients make requests at the same time, the server can become overwhelmed, increasing the time it takes the server to fulfill requests from clients. Client-server systems, moreover, tend to be more expensive to set up and operate than other systems. Websites work on a client-server model, with the server storing the website's content and delivering it to users upon demand.

"Peer-to-peer" (P2P) networking is a generic term used to refer to several different types of technology that have one thing in common: a decentralized infrastructure whereby each participant in the network (typically called a "peer," but sometimes called a "node") acts as both a supplier and consumer of information resources. Although less secure, P2P networks are generally more reliable than client-server networks and do not suffer from the same bottleneck problems. These strengths make P2P networks ideally suited for sharing large files, a feature that has led to their adoption by, among others, those wanting access to pirated media, including music, movies, and television shows. But there also are a great number of non-infringing uses for peer-to-peer networks; copyright infringement is in no sense intrinsic to the technology, any more than making unauthorized copies of television shows was to the video tape recorder.

II.   Architecture of P2P networks

In a client-server network, clients can easily learn what files the server has available for download, because the files are all in one central place. In a P2P network, in contrast, there is no centralized file repository, so figuring out what information other peers have available is more challenging. The various P2P protocols permit indexing in different ways.

A.   "Pure" P2P networks

In "pure" P2P networks, a user wanting to find out which peers have particular content available for download will send out a search query to several of his neighbor peers. As those neighbor peers receive the query, they send a response back to the requesting user reporting whether they have any content matching the search terms, and then pass the query on to some of their neighbors, who repeat the same two steps; this process is known as "flooding." In large P2P networks, the query does not get to every peer on the network, because permitting that amount of signaling traffic would either overwhelm the resources of the peers or use up all of the network's bandwidth (or both). Therefore, the P2P protocol will usually specify that queries should no longer be passed on after a certain amount of time (the so-called "time to live") or after they have already been passed on a certain number of times (the "hop count"). Once the querying user has the search results, he can go directly to a peer that has the content desired to download it.

This search method is an inefficient one for finding content (especially rare content that only a few peers have), and it causes a lot of signaling traffic on the network. The most popular pure P2P protocol was Gnutella. Streamcast, a *Grokster* defendant, used Gnutella to power its software application, Morpheus.

B. "Centralized" P2P networks

"Centralized" P2P networks, by contrast, use a centralized server to index the content available on all the peers: the user sends the query to the indexing server, which tells the user which peers have the content available for download. At the same time the user tells the indexing server what files he has available for others to download. Once the user makes contact with the indexing server, he knows which specific peers to contact for the content sought, which reduces search time and signaling traffic as compared to a "pure" P2P protocol.

Although a centralized P2P network has similarities with a client-server network, the key difference is that the indexing server does not store or transfer the content. It just tells users which other peers have the content they seek. In other words, searching is centralized, but file transfers are peer-to-peer. One consequent disadvantage of a centralized P2P network is that it has a single point of potential failure: the indexing server. If it fails, the entire system fails. Napster was a centralized P2P network, as, in part, is eDonkey, the technology upon which one of the Fung sites, ed2k-it.com, is based.

C. Hybrid P2P networks

Finally, there are a number of hybrid protocols. The most common type of hybrid systems use what are called "supernodes." In these systems, each peer is called a "node," and each node is assigned to one "supernode." A supernode is a regular node that has been "promoted," usually because it has more bandwidth available, to perform certain tasks. Each supernode indexes the content available on each of the nodes attached to it, called its "descendants." When a node sends out a search query, it goes just to the supernode to which it is attached. The supernode responds to the query by telling the node which of its descendant nodes has the desired content. The supernode may also forward the query on to other supernodes, which may or may not forward the query on further, depending on the protocol.

The use of supernodes is meant to broaden the search pool as much as possible while limiting redundancy in the search. As with centralized

P2P systems, supernodes only handle search queries, telling the nodes the addresses of the other nodes that have the content sought; they are not ordinarily involved in the actual file transfers themselves. Grokster's software application was based on a P2P protocol, FastTrack, that uses supernodes.

III. BitTorrent protocol

The BitTorrent protocol, first released in 2001, is a further variant on the P2P theme. BitTorrent is a hybrid protocol with some key differences from "supernode" systems. We discuss those differences after first describing BitTorrent's distinguishing feature: how it facilitates file transfers.

A.   BitTorrent file transfers.

Traditionally, if a user wanted to download a file on a P2P network, he would locate another peer with the desired file and download the entire file from that peer. Alternatively, if the download was interrupted—if, for example, the peer sending the file signed off—the user would find another peer that had the file and resume the download from that peer. The reliability and duration of the download depended on the strength of the connection between those two peers. Additionally, the number of peers sharing a particular file was limited by the fact that a user could only begin sharing his copy of the file with other peers once he had completed the download.

With the BitTorrent protocol, however, the file is broken up into lots of smaller "pieces," each of which is usually around 256 kilobytes (one-fourth of one megabyte) in size. Whereas under the older protocols the user would download the entire file in one large chunk from a single peer at a time, BitTorrent permits users to download lots of different pieces at the same time from different peers. Once a user has downloaded all the pieces, the file is automatically reassembled into its original form.

BitTorrent has several advantages over the traditional downloading method. Because a user can download different pieces of the file from many different peers at the same time, downloading is much faster. Additionally, even before the entire download is complete, a user can begin sharing the pieces he has already downloaded with other peers, making the process faster for others. Generally, at any given time, each user is both downloading and uploading several different pieces of a file from and to multiple other users; the collection of peers swapping pieces with each other is known as a "swarm."

B.   BitTorrent architecture

To describe the structure of BitTorrent further, an example is helpful. Let us suppose that an individual (the "publisher") decides to share via BitTorrent her copy of a particular movie. The movie file, we shall assume, is quite large, and is already on the publisher's computer; the publisher has also already downloaded and installed a BitTorrent "client" program on her computer.

To share her copy of the movie file, the publisher first creates a very small file called a "torrent" or "dot-torrent" file, which has the file extension ".torrent." The torrent file is quite small, as it contains none of the actual content that may be copyrighted but, instead, a minimal amount of vital information: the size of the (separate) movie file being shared; the number of "pieces" the movie file is broken into; a cryptographic "hash" that peers will use to authenticate the downloaded file as a true and complete copy of the original; and the address of one or more "trackers." Trackers, discussed more below, serve many of the functions of an indexing server; there are many different trackers, and they typically are not connected or related to each other.

Second, the publisher makes the torrent file available by uploading it to one or more websites ("torrent sites") that collect, organize, index, and host torrent files. Whereas Napster and Grokster had search functionality built into their client programs, the standard BitTorrent client program has no such capability. BitTorrent users thus rely on torrent sites to find and share torrent files. There is no central repository of torrent files, but torrent sites strive to have the most comprehensive torrent collection possible.

The Fung sites have two primary methods of acquiring torrent files: soliciting them from users, who then upload the files; and using several automated processes (called "bots," "crawlers," or "spiders") that collect torrent files from *other* torrent sites. Because of this latter route, which other torrent sites also routinely use, torrent sites tend to have largely overlapping collections of torrents. According to a declaration Fung signed in April 2008, there were then over 400 torrent sites. Because the torrent sites typically contain only torrent files, no copyrighted material resides on these sites.

Lastly, the publisher leaves her computer on and connected to the Internet, with her BitTorrent program running. The publisher's job is essentially done; her computer will continue to communicate with the tracker assigned to the torrent file she uploaded, standing ready to distribute the movie file (or, more accurately, parts thereof) to others upon request.

A user seeking the uploaded movie now goes to the torrent site to which the torrent file was uploaded and runs a search for the movie. The search results then provide the torrent file for the user to download. Once the user downloads the torrent file and opens it with his BitTorrent program, the program reads the torrent file, learns the address of the tracker, and contacts it. The program then informs the tracker that it is looking for the movie associated with the downloaded torrent file and asks if there are any peers online that have the movie available for download. Assuming that publishers of that movie are online, the tracker will communicate their address to the user's BitTorrent program. The user's BitTorrent program will then contact the publishers' computers directly and begin downloading the pieces of the movie. At this point, the various publishers are known as "seeders," and the downloading user a "leecher." Once the leecher has downloaded one or more pieces of the movie, he, too, can be a seeder by sending other leechers the pieces that he has downloaded.

A final few words on trackers. Although no content is stored on or passes through trackers, they serve as a central hub of sorts, managing traffic for their associated torrents. The tracker's primary purpose is to provide a list of peers that have files available for download. Fung avers that this function is the only one provided by his two trackers, discussed below.

Because trackers are periodically unavailable—they can go offline for routine maintenance, reach capacity, be shuttered by law enforcement, and so on—torrent files will often list addresses for more than one tracker. That way, if the first (or "primary") tracker is down, the user's client program can proceed to contact the backup tracker(s).

IV. Fung's role

Three of Fung's websites—isohunt.com ("isoHunt"); torrentbox.com ("Torrentbox"), and podtropolis.com ("Podtropolis")—are torrent sites. As described above, they collect and organize torrent files and permit users to browse in and search their collections. Searching is done via keyword; users can also browse by category (movies, television shows, music, etc.).

IsoHunt, however, which appears to be Fung's "flagship" site, goes a step beyond merely collecting and organizing torrent files. Each time a torrent file is added to isoHunt, the website automatically modifies the torrent file by adding additional backup trackers to it. That way, if the primary tracker is down, the users' BitTorrent client program will contact the backup trackers, making it more likely that the user will be successful in downloading the content sought. In other words, isoHunt alters the torrent files it hosts, making them more reliable than when they are uploaded to the site.

Torrentbox and Podtropolis, in addition to being torrent sites, run associated trackers. Their collections of torrent files appear to be fairly small. Every torrent file available on Torrentbox and Podtropolis is tracked by the Torrentbox and Podtropolis trackers, respectively, but the Torrentbox and Podtropolis trackers are *much* busier than the Torrentbox and Podtropolis websites. For example, a torrent file for the movie "Casino Royale" was downloaded from Torrentbox.com 50,000 times, but the Torrentbox tracker registered approximately 1.5 million downloads of the movie. This disparity indicates that users obtain the torrent files tracked by Torrentbox and Podtropolis from torrent sites other than Torrentbox.com and Podtropolis.com. The Torrentbox and Podtropolis websites both have continually-updated lists of, *inter alia*, the "Top 20 TV Shows," the "Top 20 Movies," and the "Top 20 Most Active Torrents." These rankings are based on the number of seeders and leechers for each particular torrent file, as measured by the Torrentbox and Podtropolis trackers. IsoHunt does not run a tracker, so it cannot measure how frequently the content associated with each torrent file is downloaded; instead, it keeps a continually updated list of the "Top Searches."

IsoHunt also hosts an electronic message board, or "forum," where users can post comments, queries, and the like. In addition to posting to the forum himself, Fung also had some role in moderating posts to the forum.

PROCEDURAL HISTORY

[Columbia sued Fung, alleging he] was liable for vicarious and contributory copyright infringement, in violation of 17 U.S.C. § 106.

On Columbia's motion for summary judgment on liability, the district court held Fung liable for contributory infringement, for inducing others to infringe Plaintiffs' copyrighted material. Although Fung sought protection in the DMCA safe harbors for "[t]ransitory digital network communications," 17 U.S.C. § 512(a), "[i]nformation residing on systems or networks at direction of users," *id.* § 512(c), and "[i]nformation location tools," *id.* § 512(d), the district court concluded that none of the safe harbors were applicable.

The district court later entered a permanent injunction that prohibits, generally speaking, "knowingly engaging in any activities having the object or effect of fostering infringement of Plaintiffs' Copyrighted Works, including without limitation by engaging in" certain specified activities. . . .

Fung timely appealed . . .

DISCUSSION

. . .

I.   Liability

A.   Inducement liability under Grokster III

The "inducement" theory, on which the district court's liability holding was grounded, was spelled out in the Internet technology context by the Supreme Court in *Grokster III.* Considering how to apply copyright law to file sharing over P2P networks, *Grokster III* addressed the circumstances in which individuals and companies are secondarily liable for the copyright infringement of others using the Internet to download protected material.

. . .

. . . Th[e] inducement principle, as enunciated in *Grokster III*, has four elements: (1) the distribution of a device or product, (2) acts of infringement, (3) an object of promoting its use to infringe copyright, and (4) causation.

i. Distribution of a "device" or "product"

In describing the inducement liability standard, *Grokster III* phrased it as applying to one who distributes a "device," although it also used the word "product," seemingly interchangeably. The "device" or "product" was the software developed and distributed by the defendants—for Grokster, its eponymous software, based on FastTrack technology; and for StreamCast, also a defendant in *Grokster*, its software application, Morpheus, based on Gnutella.

The analogy between *Grokster III* and this case is not perfect. Here, Fung did not develop and does not provide the client programs used to download media products, nor did he develop the BitTorrent protocol (which is maintained by non-party BitTorrent, Inc., a privately-held company founded by the creators of the protocol). Fung argues that because he did not develop or distribute any "device"—that is, the software or technology used for downloading—he is not liable under the inducement rule enunciated in *Grokster III.*

We cannot agree. Unlike patents, copyrights protect expression, not products or devices. Inducement liability is not limited, either logically or as articulated in *Grokster III*, to those who distribute a "device." As a result, one can infringe a copyright through culpable actions resulting in the impermissible reproduction of copyrighted expression, whether those actions involve making available a device or product or providing some service used in accomplishing the infringement. For example, a retail copying service that accepts and copies copyrighted material for customers after broadly promoting its willingness to do so may be liable for the resulting infringement although it does not produce any copying machines or sell them; all it provides is the "service" of copying. Whether the service makes copies using machines of its own manufacture, machines it owns, or machines in someone else's shop would not matter, as copyright liability depends on one's purposeful involvement in the process of reproducing copyrighted material, not the precise nature of that involvement.

Grokster III did phrase the rule it applied principally in terms of a "device." But that was because it was responding to the main argument made by the defendants in that case—that they were entitled to protection for commercial products capable of significant non-infringing uses, just as Sony was insulated from liability for infringing use of the Betamax. When explaining the *rationale* for permitting secondary infringement liability, *Grokster III* used more general language:

> When a widely shared *service or product* is used to commit infringement, it may be impossible to enforce rights in the protected work effectively against all direct infringers, the only practical alternative being to go against the distributor of *the copying device* for secondary liability on a theory of contributory or vicarious infringement.

[545 U.S.] at 929–30 (emphases added); *see also id.* at 924 (describing Napster as a "notorious file-sharing service"); *id.* at 925 (describing one defendant's efforts "to market its service as the best Napster alternative"); *id.* at 937–38; *id.* at 939 (describing the import of defendants' "efforts to supply services to former Napster users").

Since *Grokster III*, we have not considered a claim of inducement liability on facts closely comparable to those here. But we have, in two cases, considered claims of inducement liability against parties providing services as opposed to products, without suggesting that the difference matters. *Perfect 10, Inc. v. Visa Int'l Serv. Ass'n*, 494 F.3d 788, 800–02 (9th Cir. 2007); *Perfect 10, Inc. v. Amazon.com, Inc.*, 508 F.3d 1146, 1170 n.11 (9th Cir. 2007). The two *Perfect* 10 cases confirm that, as one would expect, the inducement copyright doctrine explicated in *Grokster III* applies to services available on the Internet as well as to devices or products.

We hold that Columbia has carried its burden on summary judgment as to the first element of the *Grokster III* test for inducement liability.

ii. Acts of infringement

To prove copyright infringement on an inducement theory, Columbia also had to adduce "evidence of actual infringement by" users of Fung's services. *Grokster III*, 545 U.S. at 940. This they have done.

Both uploading and downloading copyrighted material are infringing acts. The former violates the copyright holder's right to distribution, the latter the right to reproduction. Based on statistical sampling, Columbia's expert averred that between 90 and 96% of the content associated with the torrent files available on Fung's websites are for "confirmed or highly likely copyright infringing" material. Although Fung takes issue with certain aspects of the expert's methodology, he does not attempt to rebut the factual assertion that his services were widely used to infringe copyrights. Indeed, even giving Fung the benefit of all doubts by tripling the margins of error in the expert's reports,

Columbia would still have such overwhelming evidence that any reasonable jury would have to conclude that the vastly predominant use of Fung's services has been to infringe copyrights.

In sum, as in *Grokster III*, "[a]lthough an exact calculation of infringing use, as a basis for a claim of damages, is subject to dispute, there is no question" that Plaintiffs have met their burden on summary judgment to warrant equitable relief. *Grokster III*, 545 U.S. at 940–41.

iii. With the object of promoting its use to infringe copyright

The third, usually dispositive, requirement for inducement liability is that the "device" or service be distributed "with the object of promoting its use to infringe copyright, as shown by clear expression or other affirmative steps taken to foster infringement." *Id.* at 936–37.

As an initial matter, Fung argues that this factor includes two separate elements—the improper object *and* "clear expression or other affirmative steps taken to foster infringement." Not so. "[C]lear expression or other affirmative steps" is not a separate requirement, but, rather, an explanation of how the improper object must be proven. In other words, *Grokster III* requires a high degree of proof of the improper object. . . .

. . .

Using [the] *Grokster III* evidentiary categories and cautions as templates, we conclude that there is more than enough unrebutted evidence in the summary judgment record to prove that Fung offered his services with the object of promoting their use to infringe copyrighted material. No reasonable jury could find otherwise.

As for the necessary "clear expression or other affirmative steps" evidence indicative of unlawful intent, the most important is Fung's active encouragement of the uploading of torrent files concerning copyrighted content. For a time, for example, isoHunt prominently featured a list of "Box Office Movies," containing the 20 highest-grossing movies then playing in U.S. theaters. When a user clicked on a listed title, she would be invited to "upload [a] torrent" file for that movie. In other words, she would be asked to upload a file that, once downloaded by other users, would lead directly to their obtaining infringing content. Fung also posted numerous messages to the isoHunt forum requesting that users upload torrents for specific copyrighted films; in other posts, he provided links to torrent files for copyrighted movies, urging users to download them. Though not the exclusive means of proving inducement, we have characterized a distributor's communication of an inducing message to its users as "crucial" to establishing inducement liability. That crucial requirement was met here. Like Grokster's advertisements—indeed, even more so—Fung's posts were explicitly "designed to stimulate others to commit [copyright] violations," and so are highly probative of an unlawful intent. *Grokster III*, 545 U.S. at 937.

As in *Grokster*, moreover, Fung "communicated a clear message by responding affirmatively to requests for help in locating and playing copyrighted materials." *Id.* at 938. The record is replete with instances of Fung responding personally to queries for assistance in: uploading torrent files corresponding to obviously copyrighted material, finding particular copyrighted movies and television shows, getting pirated material to play properly, and burning the infringing content onto DVDs for playback on televisions.

Two types of supporting evidence, insufficient in themselves—like the similar evidence in *Grokster III*—corroborate the conclusion that Fung "acted with a purpose to cause copyright violations by use of" their services. *Id.* at 938. First, Fung took no steps "to develop filtering tools or other mechanisms to diminish the infringing activity" by those using his services. *Id.* at 939. Second, Fung generates revenue almost exclusively by selling advertising space on his websites. The more users who visit Fung's websites and view the advertisements supplied by Fung's business partners, the greater the revenues to Fung. Because "the extent of the [services'] use determines the gain to [Fung], the commercial sense of [his] enterprise turns on high-volume use, which the record shows is infringing." *Id.* at 940. Given both the clear expression and other affirmative steps and the supporting evidence, Fung's "unlawful objective is unmistakable." *Id.*

iv. Causation

Grokster III mentions causation only indirectly, by speaking of "*resulting* acts of infringement by third parties." *Id.* at 937 (emphasis added). The parties here advance competing interpretations of the causation requirement adopted through that locution: Fung and amicus curiae Google argue that the acts of infringement must be caused by the manifestations of the distributor's improper object—that is, by the inducing messages themselves. Columbia, on the other hand, maintains that it need only prove that the "acts of infringement by third parties" were caused by the product distributed or services provided.

We think Columbia's interpretation of *Grokster III* is the better one. On that view, if one provides a service that could be used to infringe copyrights, with the manifested intent that the service actually be used in that manner, that person is liable for the infringement that occurs through the use of the service. As *Grokster III* explained:

> It is not only that encouraging a particular consumer to infringe a copyright can give rise to secondary liability for the infringement that results. Inducement liability goes beyond that, and the distribution of a product can itself give rise to liability where evidence shows that the distributor intended and encouraged the product to be used to infringe. In such a case, the culpable act is not merely the encouragement of infringement but also the distribution of the tool intended for infringing use.

Id. at 940 n.13.

We are mindful, however, of the potential severity of a loose causation theory for inducement liability. Under this theory of liability, the only causation requirement is that the product or service at issue was used to infringe the plaintiff's copyrights. The possible reach of liability is enormous, particularly in the digital age.

Copyright law attempts to strike a balance amongst three competing interests: those of the copyright holders in benefitting from their labor; those of entrepreneurs in having the latitude to invent new technologies without fear of being held liable if their innovations are used by others in unintended infringing ways; and those of the public in having access both to entertainment options protected by copyright and to new technologies that enhance productivity and quality of life. Because copyright law's "ultimate aim is . . . to stimulate artistic creativity for the general public good," *Sony*, 464 U.S. at 432 (quoting *Twentieth Century Music Corp. v. Aiken*, 422 U.S. 151, 156 (1975)), it is important that we not permit inducement liability's relatively lax causation requirement to "enlarge the scope of [copyright's] statutory monopolies to encompass control over an article of commerce"—such as technology capable of substantial non-infringing uses—"that is not the subject of copyright protection." *Sony*, 464 U.S. at 421.

We emphasize a few points in this regard. First, as previously discussed, proper proof of the defendant's intent that its product or service be used to infringe copyrights is paramount. "[M]ere knowledge of infringing potential or of actual infringing uses" does not subject a product distributor or service provider to liability. *Grokster III*, 545 U.S. at 937. When dealing with corporate or entity defendants, moreover, the relevant intent must be that of the entity itself, as defined by traditional agency law principles; liability cannot be premised on stray or unauthorized statements that cannot fairly be imputed to the entity.

Moreover, proving that an entity had an unlawful purpose at a particular time in providing a product or service does not infinitely expand its liability in either temporal direction. If an entity begins providing a service with infringing potential at time *A*, but does not appreciate that potential until later and so does not develop and exhibit the requisite intent to support inducement liability until time *B*, it would not be held liable for the infringement that occurred between time *A* and *B*. Relatedly, an individual or entity's unlawful objective at time *B* is not a virus that infects all future actions. People, companies, and technologies must be allowed to rehabilitate, so to speak, through actions actively discouraging the infringing use of their product, lest the public be deprived of the useful good or service they are still capable of producing.

We also note, as Fung points out, that *Grokster III* seemingly presupposes a condition that is absent in this case: that there is but a single producer of the "device" in question. Only Sony sold the Betamax, and only Grokster and Streamcast distributed their respective software applications. Assessing causation was thus a straightforward task. In *Sony*, for example, there was no question that some customers would purchase and use the Betamax in ways that infringed copyright. Thus, in a "but-for" sense, there was no question that Sony *caused* whatever infringement resulted from the use of Betamax sets; the Court nonetheless held Sony not liable on the ground that even if Sony caused the infringement, it was not at *fault*, with fault measured by Sony's intent. But as *Grokster III* explained, "nothing in *Sony* requires courts to ignore evidence of intent if there is such evidence, and the case was never meant to foreclose rules of fault-based liability." 545 U.S. at 934. *Grokster III* thus held that where there is sufficient evidence of fault—that is, an unlawful objective—distributors are liable for causing the infringement that resulted from use of their products. In other words, *Grokster III* and *Sony* were able to assume causation and assess liability (or not) based on fault. In the present case, however, where other individuals and entities provide services identical to those offered by Fung, causation, even in the relatively loose sense we have delineated, cannot be assumed, even though fault is unquestionably present.

Fung argues, on this basis, that some of the acts of infringement by third parties relied upon by the district court may not have involved his websites at all. He points out, for example, that by far the largest number of torrents tracked by the Torrentbox tracker are obtained from somewhere *other* than Torrentbox.com. If a user obtained a torrent from a source other than his websites, Fung maintains, he cannot be held liable for the infringement that resulted.

On the other hand, Fung's services encompass more than the provision of torrent files. Fung's trackers manage traffic for torrent files, obtained from Torrentbox and Podtropolis as well as other torrent sites, which enables users to download copyrighted content. If Plaintiffs can show a sufficient casual connection between users' infringing activity and the use of Fung's trackers, the fact that torrent files were obtained from elsewhere may not relieve Fung of liability.

We do not decide the degree to which Fung can be held liable for having caused infringements by users of his sites or trackers. The only issue presently before us is the permanent injunction, which, as in *Grokster III*, does not in this case depend on the "exact calculation of infringing use[ ] as a basis for a claim of damages." 545 U.S. at 941. We therefore need not further entertain Fung's causation arguments at this time, but leave it to the district court to consider them, in light of the observations we have made, when it calculates damages.

In sum, we affirm the district court's holding that Columbia has carried its burden of proving, on the basis of undisputed facts, Fung's liability for inducing others to infringe Columbia's copyrights.

B.   DMCA Safe Harbors

Fung asserts affirmative defenses under three of the DMCA's safe harbor provisions, 17 U.S.C. § 512(a), (c), and (d). Because the DMCA safe harbors are affirmative defenses, Fung has the burden of establishing that he meets the statutory requirements.

Columbia argues, and the district court agreed, that inducement liability is inherently incompatible with protection under the DMCA safe harbors. This court has already rejected the notion that there can *never* be a DMCA safe harbor defense to contributory copyright liability . . . We note, in this connection, that the DMCA does not in terms exempt from protection any mode of copyright liability, including liability under the doctrine of inducement. Moreover, the DMCA's legislative history confirms that Congress intended to provide protection for at least some vicarious and contributory infringement.

Nor is there any inherent incompatibility between inducement liability and the requirements that apply to all of the DMCA safe harbors. For example, a prerequisite for the safe harbors is that the service provider implement a policy of removing repeat infringers. *See* 17 U.S.C. § 512(i)(1)(A). Although at first glance that requirement that might seem impossible to establish where the requisites for inducing infringement are met, *see In re Aimster Copyright Litig.*, 334 F.3d 643, 655 (7th Cir. 2003), on closer examination the appearance of *inherent* incompatibility dissipates. In some instances, for example, the *Grokster* standard for inducement might be met even where a service provider has a policy of removing proven repeat infringers. It is therefore *conceivable* that a service provider liable for inducement could be entitled to protection under the safe harbors.

In light of these considerations, we are not clairvoyant enough to be sure that there are no instances in which a defendant otherwise liable for contributory copyright infringement could meet the prerequisites for one or more of the DMCA safe harbors. We therefore think it best to conduct the two inquiries independently—although, as will appear, aspects of the inducing behavior that give rise to liability are relevant to the operation of some of the DMCA safe harbors and can, in some circumstances, preclude their application.

i. "Transitory digital network communications" (17 U.S.C. § 512(a))

The first safe harbor at issue, which Fung asserts only as to his trackers, [is set out at] 17 U.S.C. § 512(a). For purposes of this safe harbor only, "the term 'service provider' means an entity offering the transmission, routing, or providing of connections for digital online communications, between or among points specified by a user, of material of the user's choosing, without modification to the content of the material as sent or received." 17 U.S.C. § 512(k)(1)(A). The district court dismissed the application of this safe harbor in a footnote, stating that it did not apply to Fung "[b]ecause infringing materials do not pass through or reside on [Fung's] system."

The district court should not have rejected this safe harbor on the ground it did. *Perfect 10, Inc. v. CCBill LLC*, 488 F.3d 1102 (9th Cir. 2007), held that the § 512(a) safe harbor does not require that the service provider transmit or route infringing material, explaining that "[t]here is no requirement in the statute that the communications must themselves be infringing, and we see no reason to import such a requirement." *Id*. at 1116; *see also id*. ("Service providers are immune for transmitting all digital online communications, not just those that directly infringe.").

We could, perhaps, end our analysis of the § 512(a) safe harbor there. The district court seemingly held Fung liable for inducement based not on Fung's trackers' routing services, but, instead, on the dot-torrent files Fung collects and indexes. And it is not clear that Columbia is seeking to establish liability based directly on the tracking functions of Fung's trackers.

It appears, however, that Fung's trackers generate information concerning the torrent files transmitted that Fung then compiles and uses to induce further infringing use of his websites and trackers. In that sense, the tracking function is connected to the basis on which liability was sought and found. Without determining whether that information-generating use would itself affect the availability of the § 512(a) safe harbor, we hold that safe harbor not available for Fung's trackers on other grounds.

Unlike a P2P network like Napster, in which users select particular files to download from particular users, Fung's trackers manage a "swarm" of connections that source tiny pieces of each file from numerous users; the user seeking to download a file chooses only the file, not the particular users who will provide it, and the tracker identifies the source computers to the user seeking to download a work.

Given these characteristics, Fung's trackers do not fit the definition of "service provider" that applies to this safe harbor. The definition provides that a "service provider" provides "connections . . . between or among points *specified by a user*." 17 U.S.C. § 512(k)(1)(A) (emphasis added). Here, it is Fung's tracker that selects the *"points"* to which a user's client will connect in order to download a file. The tracker, not the requesting user, selects the publishers from which chunks of data will be transmitted.

We have held that § 512(a) applies to service provides who act only as "conduits" for the transmission of information. Because they select which users will communicate with each other, Fung's trackers serve as more than "conduits" between computer users. Fung's trackers therefore are not "service providers" for purposes of § 512(a), and are not eligible for the § 512(a) safe harbor.

> . . .

ii. "Information residing on systems or networks at direction of users" (17 U.S.C. § 512(c))

> . . .

The district court held that Fung is ineligible for this safe harbor for the same reason it rejected the § 512(a) safe harbor—that is, because the infringing material does not actually reside on Fung's servers. As with § 512(a), this holding was in error. As *CCBill* emphasized, we will not read requirements into the safe harbors that are not contained in the text of the statute. Moreover, § 512(c) explicitly covers not just the storage of infringing material, but also infringing "activit[ies]" that "us[e] the material [stored] on the system or network." 17 U.S.C. § 512(c)(1)(A)(i). Here, as we have explained, the infringing activity associated with Fung—the peer-to-peer transfer of pirated content—relies upon torrents stored on Fung's websites. According to the record, sometimes those torrents are uploaded by users of the sites, while other torrents are collected for storage by Fung's websites themselves. The former situation would be at least facially eligible for the safe harbor, assuming the other criteria are met.

a.   Actual and "Red Flag" Knowledge (512(c)(1)(A)(i)—(ii))

We nonetheless hold that Fung is not eligible for the § 512(c) safe harbor, on different grounds. The § 512(c) safe harbor is available only if the service provider "does not have actual knowledge that the material or an activity using the material on the system or network is infringing," 17 U.S.C. § 512(c)(1)(A)(i), or "is not aware of facts or circumstances from which infringing activity is apparent," *id.* § 512(c)(1)(A)(ii). In *UMG Recordings*, ___ F.3d at ___, this court endorsed the Second Circuit's interpretation of § 512(c)(1)(A), that "the actual knowledge provision turns on whether the provider actually or 'subjectively' knew of specific infringement, while the red flag provision turns on whether the provider was subjectively aware of facts that would have made the specific infringement 'objectively' obvious to a reasonable person." *Viacom Int'l, Inc.*, 676 F.3d at 31.

Fung maintains that he lacked either type of knowledge, because Columbia failed to provide statutorily compliant notification of infringement. Under § 512(c)(3)(B), notification of infringement that fails to comply with the requirements set forth in § 512(c)(3)(A) "shall not be considered . . . in determining whether a service provider has actual knowledge or is aware of facts or circumstances from which infringing activity is apparent." 17 U.S.C. § 512(c)(3)(B)(i). And, as Fung points out, the district court noted that there was at least a "triable issue of fact as to the adequacy of the statutory notice that Plaintiffs provided to [Fung]."

We need not determine the adequacy of Columbia's notification of claimed infringement—indeed, as the district court held, it would not be appropriate to do so at this stage. Fung had "red flag" knowledge of a broad range of infringing activity for reasons independent of any notifications from Columbia, and therefore is ineligible for the § 512(c) safe harbor.

As noted, the record is replete with instances of Fung actively encouraging infringement, by urging his users to both upload and download particular copyrighted works, providing assistance to those seeking to watch copyrighted films, and helping his users burn copyrighted material onto DVDs. The material in question was sufficiently current and well-known that it would have been objectively obvious to a reasonable person that the material solicited and assisted was both copyrighted and not licensed to random members of the public, and that the induced use was therefore infringing. Moreover, Fung does not dispute that he personally used the isoHunt website to download infringing material. Thus, while Fung's inducing actions do not necessarily render him per se ineligible for protection under § 512(c), they are relevant to our determination that Fung had "red flag" knowledge of infringement.

Fung introduced no contrary facts with regard to identified torrents involved in these documented activities, responding only with the generalized assertion that he "ha[s] a robust copyright compliance system." But "conclusory allegations, standing alone, are insufficient to prevent summary judgment." [Citation omitted.]

As Fung has not carried his burden as the non-moving party of demonstrating a genuine dispute as to the material facts regarding his eligibility for the § 512(c) safe harbor, Columbia is entitled to summary judgment as to this issue.

b. "Financial benefit" & "the right and ability to control" (§ 512(c)(1)(B))

Under § 512(c)(1)(B), a service provider loses protection under the safe harbor if two conditions are met: (1) the provider "receive[s] a financial benefit directly attributable to the infringing activity"; and (2) the "service provider has the right and ability to control such activity." 17 U.S.C. § 512(c)(1)(B). Fung meets both requirements and is therefore ineligible for protection under the § 512(c) safe harbor.

As to the first prong of § 512(c)(1)(B), we have held, in the context of service providers who charge for their services, that a service provider receives a direct financial benefit from infringing activity where "there is a causal relationship between the infringing activity and any financial benefit a defendant reaps, regardless of *how substantial* the benefit is in proportion to a defendant's overall profits." *Ellison*, 357 F.3d at 1079. Thus, where a service provider obtains revenue from "subscribers," the relevant inquiry is " 'whether the infringing activity constitutes a draw for subscribers, not just an added benefit.' " *CCBill*, 488 F.3d at 1117 (quoting *Ellison*, 357 F.3d at 1079).

At the same time, our opinions have not suggested that the "financial benefit" prong of § 512(c)(1)(B) is peripheral or lacks teeth. *Ellison* ultimately concluded that the financial benefit standard was not met, because there was inadequate proof that "customers either subscribed because of the available infringing material or cancelled subscriptions because it was no longer available." *Ellison*, 357 F.3d at 1079. And *CCBill* similarly found that evidence that the service provider hosted, for a fee, websites that contain infringing material inadequate to establish the requisite financial benefit. In so holding, *CCBill* cited to DMCA legislative history stating that a direct financial benefit cannot be established showing that a service provider "receive[d] a one-time set-up fee and flat, periodic payments for service from a person engaging in infringing activities." 488 F.3d at 1118 (quoting H.R. Rep. 105–551(II), 54 (1998)).

Moreover, the structure of § 512(c)(1)(B) indicates that the lack of direct financial benefit prong of the safe harbor requirement is central, rather than peripheral. The statute sets out as the requirement that the service provider "not receive a financial benefit directly attributable to the infringing activity." It then states the "right and ability to control" in a dependent clause, describing a limitation on the financial benefit requirement to certain circumstances. The grammatical emphasis, then, is on the lack of direct financial benefit requirement, with the right to control prong secondary.

Against this background, we note that we have never specified what constitutes a "financial benefit *directly* attributable to the infringing activity," 17 U.S.C. § 512(c)(1)(B) (emphasis added), where, as here, the service provider's revenue is derived from advertising, and not from users. We do so now.

Here, the record shows that Fung generated revenue by selling advertising space on his websites. The advertising revenue depended on the number of users who viewed and then clicked on the advertisements. Fung marketed advertising to one advertiser by pointing to the "TV and movies . . . at the top of the most frequently searched by our viewers," and provided another with a list of typical user search queries, including popular movies and television shows. In addition, there was a vast amount of infringing material on his websites—whether 90–96% or somewhat less—supporting an inference that Fung's revenue stream is predicated on the broad availability of infringing materials for his users, thereby attracting advertisers. And, as we have seen, Fung actively induced infringing activity on his sites.

Under these circumstances, we hold the connection between the infringing activity and Fung's income stream derived from advertising is sufficiently direct to meet the direct "financial benefit" prong of § 512(c)(1)(B). Fung promoted advertising by pointing to infringing activity; obtained advertising revenue that depended on the number of visitors to his sites; attracted primarily visitors who were seeking to engage in infringing activity, as that is mostly what occurred on his sites;

and encouraged that infringing activity. Given this confluence of circumstances, Fung's revenue stream was tied directly to the infringing activity involving his websites, both as to his ability to attract advertisers and as to the amount of revenue he received.

With respect to the second prong of § 512(c)(1)(B), we recently explained in *UMG* that the "right and ability to control" infringing activity involves "something more" than "merely having the general ability to locate infringing material and terminate users' access." *UMG*, ___ F.3d ___. Adopting the Second Circuit's interpretation of § 512(c)(1)(B), we held that "in order to have the 'right and ability to control,' the service provider must [also] 'exert[ ] substantial influence on the activities of users.'" *Id.* (quoting *Viacom Int'l, Inc.*, 676 F.3d at 38) (second alteration in original). In doing so, we noted that " '[s]ubstantial influence' may include . . . purposeful conduct, as in *Grokster*." *Id.* In the absence of any evidence of inducement or any other reason to suggest the defendant exerted substantial influence over its users' activities, we concluded the defendant was not ineligible for protection under this provision.

Here, we are confronted with the opposite situation. Fung unquestionably had the ability to locate infringing material and terminate users' access. In addition to being able to locate material identified in valid DMCA notices, Fung organized torrent files on his sites using a program that matches file names and content with specific search terms describing material likely to be infringing, such as "screener" or "PPV." And when users could not find certain material likely to be infringing on his sites, Fung personally assisted them in locating the files. Fung also personally removed "fake[ ], infected, or otherwise bad or abusive torrents" in order to "protect[ ] the integrity of [his websites'] search index[es]."

Crucially, Fung's ability to control infringing activity on his websites went well beyond merely locating and terminating users' access to infringing material. As noted, there is overwhelming evidence that Fung engaged in culpable, inducing activity like that in *Grokster III*. Although Fung's inducement actions do not *categorically* remove him from protection under § 512(c), they demonstrate the substantial influence Fung exerted over his users' infringing activities, and thereby supply one essential component of the financial benefit/right to control exception to the § 512(c) safe harbor.

Because he meets both prongs of § 512(c)(1)(B), Fung is not eligible for protection under the § 512(c) safe harbor.

We have no difficulty concluding that where the § 512(c)(1)(B) safe harbor requirements are not met, the service provider loses protection with regard to any infringing activity using the service. As we held in *UMG*, the § 512(c)(1)(B) "right and ability to control" requirement does not depend only upon the ability to remove known or apparent infringing material. Instead, there must also be substantial influence on the infringing activities of users, indicating that it is the overall relationship between the service provider and infringing users that matters. Also, to the degree this DMCA provision had its origin in vicarious liability concepts, those concepts rest on the overall relationship between the defendant and the infringers, rather than on specific instances of infringement. The term "right and ability to control such activity" so reflects, as it emphasizes a general, structural relationship and speaks of "such activity," not any particular activity.

We therefore hold that because Fung does not meet the requirements of § 512(c)(1)(B), he is outside of the § 512(c) safe harbor with respect to all infringement activity on the sites that are the subject of this suit.

iii. "Information location tools" (17 U.S.C. § 512(d))

. . .

We affirm the grant of summary judgment to Columbia on Fung's claim to the § 512(d) safe harbor for the reasons just discussed with regard to § 512(c): Fung was broadly "aware of facts or circumstances from which infringing activity [wa]s apparent." 17 U.S.C. § 512(d)(1)(B). Moreover, he received a direct financial benefit from that infringing activity, and had the "right and ability to control such activity." *Id*. § 512(d)(2).

. . .

Page 1017. Add before the Question:

At a later stage of the litigation, in denying cross-motions for summary judgment on Lenz's claim, the court considered the effect of Universal's failure to consider whether Lenz's video constituted fair use in light of *Rossi*'s standards for a § 512 misrepresentation claim:

> In *Rossi,* the court held that "the 'good faith belief' requirement in § 512(c)(3)(A)(v) encompasses a subjective, rather than objective, standard." [391 F.3d] at 1004. The plaintiff in that case asserted that had the defendant conducted a reasonable investigation into the plaintiff's allegedly offending website, the defendant necessarily would have realized that there was no copyright infringement. The Court of Appeals concluded that "[a] copyright owner cannot be liable simply because an unknowing mistake is made, even if the copyright owner acted unreasonably in making the mistake." *Id*. at 1005. "Rather, there must be a demonstration of some actual knowledge of misrepresentation on the part of the copyright owner." *Id*. In light of *Rossi,* it appears that Universal's mere failure to consider fair use would be insufficient to give rise to liability under § 512(f). Lenz thus must demonstrate that Universal had some actual knowledge that its Takedown Notice contained a material misrepresentation.

Lenz v. Universal Music Corp., 2013 WL 271673 (N.D.Cal. 2013). The court ruled that neither party was entitled to summary judgment on that issue.

Page 1018. Add at the top of the page at the end of the Question:

See also Disney Enterprises, Inc. v. Hotfile Corp., 2013 WL 6336286 (S.D.Fla. 2013), less redacted version at https://www.eff.org/document/order-denying-summary-judgment-hotfile-counterclaim-ecf-534 (discussing issue of human review but ultimately denying summary judgment on § 512(f) claim because evidence in the record suggested copyright owner intentionally targeted files it knew it had no right to remove).

In July 2011, a number of major movie and music copyright owners (and their trade associations MPAA and RIAA) entered into a Memorandum of Understanding with major ISPs (a variety of AT & T and Verizon companies, Comcast, Cablevision, and Time Warner Cable) to create the Center for Copyright Information (CCI) in order to "help educate the public and deter copyright infringement and offer information about legal content options and protecting personal computers from unintentional file sharing through P2P networks." (The original MOU, and later amendments, are available at http://www.copyrightinformation.org/resources-faq/.)

A primary activity of CCI, which launched in February 2013, is the Copyright Alert System. At the time, CCI described the system as follows:

> Under this system content owners (represented by MPAA and RIAA) will notify a participating ISP when they believe their copyrights are being misused online by a specific computer (identified by its Internet Protocol ("IP") address which indicates the connection to the Internet). The ISP will determine which of its subscriber accounts was allocated the specified IP address at the applicable date and time and then send an alert to the subscriber whose account has been identified. The alert will notify the subscriber that his/her account may have been misused for potentially illegal file sharing, explain . . . why the action is illegal and a violation of the ISP's policies and provide advice about how to avoid receiving further alerts as well as how to locate film, television and music content legally.

> Alerts will be non-punitive and progressive in nature. Successive alerts will reinforce the seriousness of the copyright infringement and inform the recipient how to address the activity that is precipitating the alerts. For users who repeatedly fail to respond to alerts, the alerts will inform them of steps that will be taken to mitigate the ongoing distribution of copyrighted content through their accounts.

An example of the alert system is below:

- **First Alert**: In response to a notice from a copyright owner, an ISP will send an online alert to a subscriber, such as an email, notifying the subscriber that his/her account may have been misused or involved in copyright infringement. This first alert will also direct the subscriber to educational resources which will (i) help him/her to check the security of his/her computer and network, (ii) provide explanatory steps which will help to avoid copyright infringement in the future and (iii) provide information about the abundant legal sources of music, film and TV content.

- **Second Alert**: If the alleged activity persists despite the receipt of the first alert, the subscriber will get a second similar alert that will underscore the educational messages.

- **Third Alert**: If the subscriber's account again appears to have been used for copyright infringement, he/she will receive another alert, much like the initial alerts. However, this alert will provide a conspicuous mechanism (a click-through pop-up notice, landing page, or similar mechanism) requiring the subscriber to acknowledge receipt of this alert. This is designed to ensure that the subscriber is aware of the third copyright alert as well as the previous educational alerts.

- **Fourth Alert**: If the subscriber's account again appears to have been used for copyright infringement, the subscriber will receive yet another alert that again requires the subscriber to acknowledge receipt.

- **Fifth Alert**: At this time, the ISP may take one of several steps, specified in its published policies and the alert itself, reasonably calculated to stop future copyright infringement. These steps, referred to as "Mitigation Measures," may include, for example: temporary reductions of Internet speeds, redirection to a landing page until the subscriber contacts the ISP to discuss the matter or reviews and responds to some educational information about copyright, or other measures that the ISP may deem necessary to help resolve the matter. The ISP may decide to waive the Mitigation Measure at this point—but it would be applied if a further notice of copyright infringement associated with the same subscriber's account is received.

- **Sixth Alert**: If the subscriber's account again appears to have been used for copyright infringement, the ISP will send another alert and will implement a Mitigation Measure as described above. As described above, it's likely that very few subscribers who after having received multiple alerts, will persist (or allow others to persist) in the copyright infringement.

CCI, "How CAS Works," available at https://web.archive.org/ web/20120614112258/http://www.copyrightinformation.org/alerts.

The system also provides that before any "mitigation measure" is imposed, the subscriber may seek an independent review "to invalidate the alert and avoid any Mitigation if s/he believes that the alert is not justified." The subscriber will have to pay a $35 filing fee (unless the review body waives it). The American Arbitration Association administers the Independent Review Program.

Grounds on which an alert may be challenged include misidentification or unauthorized use of the subscriber's account, misidentification of the allegedly infringing material, and authorization for the subscriber's use (either by the copyright owner, under fair use, or because the material was published before 1923 and has entered the public domain).

What advantages or disadvantages does the Copyright Alert System have, compared to the statutory safe harbors, for copyright owners, for ISPs, and for internet users? How will this system interact with the provisions of Section 512?

CHAPTER 9

ENFORCEMENT OF COPYRIGHT

A. REMEDIES

1. INJUNCTIONS

Page 1022. Add at the end of the paragraph ending with the citation to *Silverstein*:

See also *Bouchat v. Baltimore Ravens LP*, 105 U.S.P.Q.2d 1403 (D.Md. 2012) (adopting the circuit court's approach in *Abend v. MCA* and denying plaintiff an injunction against the defendant's use of film footage from the 1996–1998 football seasons showing defendant's players wearing uniforms bearing a logo that infringes on plaintiff's copyrighted logo, but instead awarding a one-time royalty of $721.65 for future use of such footage in the sale of highlight films and an ongoing royalty of $100 for each instance in which the defendants show such footage on the scoreboard during games).

Page 1028. Insert before QUESTIONS:

The Ninth Circuit has followed the Second Circuit in interpreting *eBay* to preclude presumptions of irreparable harm arising from a ruling of likelihood of success on the merits of a copyright infringement claim. In *Perfect 10 v. Google*, 653 F.3d 976 (9th Cir. 2011), the court acknowledged that its prior caselaw upheld presumptions of irreparable harm, but that the Supreme Court's *eBay* decision now barred such categorical rules, and required plaintiffs to satisfy the four *Winter* factors.

> We agree with the Second Circuit. . . . Nothing in the [copyright] statute indicates congressional intent to authorize a "major departure" from "the traditional four-factor framework that governs the award of injunctive relief," or to undermine the equitable principle that such relief is an "extraordinary and drastic remedy" that "is never awarded as of right." We therefore conclude that the propriety of injunctive relief in cases arising under the Copyright Act must be evaluated on a case-by-case basis in accord with traditional equitable principles and without the aid of presumptions or a "thumb on the scale" in favor of issuing such relief.

> Although *eBay* dealt with a permanent injunction, the rule enunciated in that case is equally applicable to preliminary injunctive relief. This conclusion is compelled by Supreme Court precedent, cited in *eBay*, holding that "[t]he standard for a preliminary injunction is essentially the same as for a permanent injunction with the exception that the plaintiff must show a likelihood of success on the merits rather than actual success."

> In sum, we conclude that our longstanding rule that "[a] showing of a reasonable likelihood of success on the merits in a

copyright infringement claim raises a presumption of irreparable harm," "is clearly irreconcilable with the reasoning" of the Court's decision in eBay and has therefore been "effectively overruled."

The Seventh Circuit has also agreed with the view of the Second and the Ninth Circuits. *Flava Works, Inc. v. Gunter*, 689 F.3d 754, 755 (7th Cir. 2012).

Although courts after *eBay* have declined to presume irreparable harm upon a showing of likely success on the merits, a review of post *eBay* copyright cases indicates that denial of preliminary or permanent injunctive relief in copyright cases falls far short of general or systematic. With respect to permanent injunctions, only five of 23 cases studied through 2013 withheld injunctive relief despite plaintiff's success on the merits, and with one exception, none involved a finding of likely future infringement. Regarding preliminary injunctions, only three of ten decisions found a likelihood of success on the merits but then declined to find sufficient irreparable harm to warrant injunctive relief. See Jane C. Ginsburg, *Fair Use For Free, or Permitted-But-Paid?*, 29 BERKELEY TECH. L. J. 1383, 1435 and nn. 197–199 (2014).

On the importance of a showing of likelihood of future infringement, see, e.g., *Harper Collins v. Open Road,* 112 U.S.P.Q.2d 1809 (S.D.N.Y. 2014): "[T]he critical question for a district court in deciding whether to issue a permanent injunction is whether there is a reasonable likelihood that the wrong will be repeated. Thus, in copyright cases, the prevailing plaintiff must show some probability that the defendant would resume its infringement in the future. Although courts may not presume irreparable harm, courts have consistently found that harm can be irreparable, and adequate remedies at law lacking, where . . . , absent an injunction, the defendant is likely to continue infringing the copyright." (Citations and internal quotation marks omitted). The court granted the permanent injunction after finding that the defendant, "rather than taking immediate steps to conform to [the court's liability] decision, . . . apparently viewed that decision as merely a prelude to negotiations."

Beastie Boys v. Monster Energy Co., 114 U.S.P.Q.2d 1063 (S.D.N.Y. 2015). In this infringement action against the unauthorized incorporation of the Beastie Boys' recorded compositions into a promotional video for Monster energy drinks, the plaintiffs emphasized that they had never licensed their music for product advertisements. In evaluating irreparable harm, the court—which had earlier held that the evidence supported plaintiff's claims that Monster, a sophisticated economic actor, had used plaintiff's recorded music in reckless disregard of plaintiff's copyrights—gave particular weight to plaintiff's refusal to license advertisements:

> [T]he two surviving members of the Beastie Boys testified, emphatically, that, "since the beginning," they have refused to license their music for product advertisements because they view such licenses as "a form of selling out." The evidence at trial corroborated that claim. The Beastie Boys' manager testified that, with one arguable exception, the Beastie Boys had never authorized use of their music or names in connection with a product. The Beastie Boys' extensive licensing history, which was received into evidence at trial, similarly demonstrated that,

although the Beastie Boys have licensed their music for use in television programs, motion pictures, movie trailers, and video games, they have never done so for product commercials. Beyond the group's general policy against licensing their music for product advertisements, the surviving band members testified, credibly, that, had they been asked, they would not have granted permission for Monster to use their music in the Ruckus video because they did not want to associate with Monster's products and disliked the portrayal of women in Monster's video.

Under these circumstances, Monster's exploitation of the Beastie Boys' works and persona for its own benefit inflicted an intangible, yet very real, injury on plaintiffs. Against their will, the Beastie Boys were forced to associate publicly with, and advance the cause of, a corporation and marketing campaign for which they had evident disdain. As the Second Circuit has held, the " 'loss of First Amendment freedoms,' " namely, "infringement of the right not to speak, 'for even minimal periods of time, unquestionably constitutes irreparable injury.' " *Salinger*, 607 F.3d at 81 (quoting *Elrod v. Burns*, 427 U.S. 347, 373 (1976)); *see also Silverstein v. Penguin Putnam, Inc.*, 368 F.3d 77, 84 (2d Cir. 2004) ("[A]n injunction should be granted if denial would amount to a forced license to use the creative work of another.").

It is, further, apparent that the monetary damages awarded by the jury did not capture—or attempt to capture—this injury. The parties agreed here, and the Court charged the jury, that the value of actual copyright damages was set by the market: the price that a willing buyer and a willing seller would have agreed upon for a license to use the Beastie Boys' music and names in Monster's video, for the duration of time that video was available. . . . And the award of statutory damages under the Copyright Act was keyed to the willfulness of Monster's conduct, including "Monster's state of mind"; "the expenses saved, and profits earned, if any, by Monster in connection with the infringement"; and "the deterrent effect of such an award on Monster and third parties." None of these awards, as charged, took into account or sought to compensate the Beastie Boys for the injury caused by the forced association with Monster and its products. Nor could this injury be easily measured, "given the difficulty of protecting a right to exclude through monetary remedies." *eBay*, 547 U.S. at 395 (Roberts, C.J., concurring) . . .

While the court therefore granted the Beastie Boys' request for a permanent injunction against the dissemination of the promotional video, it declined to enter plaintiff's requested broader injunction "from using their music, videos, voices, names and trademarks in any advertisement or other trade-related context":

The Beastie Boys have not pointed to any other act of infringement, or evidence outside of the episode involving the [infringing] video, that indicates a propensity by Monster to infringe on others' intellectual property rights generally or the rights of the Beastie Boys specifically. On the basis of the trial evidence, the Court finds that the infringement and false endorsement here, egregious though they were, were transgressions that are unlikely to recur. [Citation.] Any contrary conclusion would be based on impermissible speculation. To the extent the Beastie Boys seek a permanent injunction that sweeps beyond the use of the infringing Ruckus video on which this case focused, the Court therefore denies the Beastie Boys' request for a permanent injunction.

Page 1029. Add new Questions 4 and 5:

4. A copyright owner sues the operator of a website, alleging that the operator has infringed the copyright in the plaintiff's works by posting those works on the website. The plaintiff requests that, if it prevails on its claim, the court order that the website's domain name be transferred to the plaintiff. Does the Copyright Act give the court authority to order such a transfer? Consider section 503, which supplements section 502's injunctive provisions with authority regarding the impoundment and disposition of infringing articles. See *Righthaven, LLC v. DiBiase*, 98 U.S.P.Q.2d 1598 (D.Nev. 2011).

5. What kind of harm is "irreparable" for purposes of issuing an injunction? See *Garcia v. Google*, 786 F.3d 733 (9th Cir. 2015, en banc), *supra* this Supplement, page 5, holding that death threats Garcia received as a result of her performance in the film *Innocence of Muslims* are not cognizable harm: "[T]here is a mismatch between her substantive copyright claim and the dangers she hopes to remedy through an injunction. Garcia seeks a preliminary injunction under copyright law, not privacy, fraud, false light or any other tort-based cause of action. Hence, Garcia's harm must stem from copyright—namely, harm to her legal interests *as an author*." *Id.* at 744 (emphasis in original).

2. DAMAGES

a. ACTUAL DAMAGES & INFRINGER'S PROFITS

Page 1036. Add the following after *Davis v. The Gap*:

Dash v. Mayweather, 731 F.3d 303 (4th Cir. 2013). Dash claimed that Floyd Mayweather, Jr. and World Wrestling Entertainment, Inc. ("WWE") performed Dash's musical composition without authorization during Mayweather's entrance at two WWE events. Although the district court held Dash's copyright to have been infringed, the court declined to award damages. The Fourth Circuit affirmed.

> . . . The statute does not define the term "actual damages," nor does it prescribe a method for calculating such damages. Generally, the term "actual damages" is "broadly construed to favor victims of infringement." *On Davis v. The Gap, Inc.,* 246 F.3d 152, 164 (2d Cir. 2001) (collecting cases and commentaries).

> Consistent with this approach, courts have recognized several methods for calculating the compensable loss suffered by a copyright owner as a result of infringement. It is generally accepted that "the primary measure of recovery is the extent to which the market value of the copyrighted work at the time of

the infringement has been injured or destroyed by the infringement." [Citations.] The fair market value of a copyrighted work is derived from an objective, not a subjective, inquiry. . . .

Injury to a copyrighted work's market value can be measured in a variety of ways. The first possible measure is the amount of revenue that the copyright holder lost as a result of infringement, such as his own lost sales of the work. Another cognizable measure is the fair market value of the licensing "fee the owner was entitled to charge for [the infringer's] use" of his copyrighted work. *On Davis* . . .

Regardless of the measure or combination of measures used to establish actual damages, a copyright holder asserting such damages "must prove the existence of a causal connection between the alleged infringement and some loss of anticipated revenue." *Thoroughbred Software Int'l, Inc. v. Dice Corp.*, 488 F.3d 352, 358 (6th Cir. 2007). Although the nature of actual damages will often require a court to "engage in some degree of speculation," *Stevens Linen Assocs., Inc. v. Mastercraft Corp.*, 656 F.2d 11, 14 (2d Cir. 1981), the amount of damages sought cannot be based on "undue speculation," *On Davis*, 246 F.3d at 166. In the summary judgment context, once a defendant has properly supported his claim that there are no actual damages resulting from infringement, the plaintiff must respond with nonspeculative evidence that such damages do, in fact, exist.

The district court concluded that Dash was not entitled to actual damages under § 504(b) because he had not offered "sufficient, concrete evidence to indicate an actual value of his beat." . . . Dash . . . relies on his lost licensing fee as the only measure of his actual damages claim.

Under the lost licensing fee theory, actual damages are generally calculated based on "what a willing buyer would have been reasonably required to pay to a willing seller for [the] plaintiffs' work." *Jarvis v. K2 Inc.*, 486 F.3d 526, 533 (9th Cir. 2007) (quoting *Frank Music Corp.*, 772 F.2d at 512) (internal quotation marks omitted). "The question is not what the owner would have charged," nor what the infringer might have been willing to pay. *On Davis*, 246 F.3d at 166. Rather, the objective inquiry focuses on the fair market value of the work as "negotiat[ed] between a willing buyer and a willing seller" contemplating the use the infringer made.

. . . [O]n the question of actual damages, Appellees were required to show that there was no genuine dispute among the parties as to the existence of any actual damages and, accordingly, that Appellees were entitled to judgment on Dash's actual damages claim because the record did not reveal that "a willing buyer would have been reasonably required to pay a willing seller" for the use of TGB at the WWE events. Appellees satisfied this initial burden by providing the district court with Dash's admission that he had never commercially exploited TGB, with copies of Dash's income tax returns from 2003 to present (none of which reflect income related to the sale or licensing of any musical composition), and with Dash's failure to offer any other proof that he had previously sold one of his beats. Once Appellees properly made and supported their motions for summary judgment on Dash's actual damages claim, the burden shifted to Dash to provide nonspeculative evidence establishing a genuine dispute as to the existence of such damages. Dash has failed to meet that burden.

Crunchyroll, Inc. v. Pledge, 2014 U.S. Dist. LEXIS 47025 (N.D. Cal.2015). Plaintiff is the U.S. licensee of the leading Japanese producer of anime. U.S. viewers may subscribe to the plaintiff's website, or watch the episodes for free, but with advertising. Defendant posted to YouTube thousands of anime episodes in which plaintiff held licenses, and then defaulted in plaintiff's infringement action. Plaintiff obtained the requested injunctive relief, but the court declined to award actual damages. Plaintiff alleged that users viewed the 3,265 unlawfully posted "Anime Episodes" a total of 470,829,627 times, and requested $4,087,950.65 in damages, based on its assumption that all of the Anime Episodes uploaded by Defendant on YouTube would have been watched in Crunchyroll's ad-supported environment had they not been available for free on YouTube.

The Court finds . . . that this claim is unsupported. Plaintiffs offer no evidence that all of Pledge's YouTube viewers necessarily would have watched the Anime Episodes on Crunchyroll's ad supported site. As Plaintiffs themselves note, viewers may prefer to watch an episode on YouTube in order to avoid having to be subjected to advertising. . . . As such, it is entirely speculative to assume that all YouTube viewers would automatically watch the Anime Episodes using Crunchyroll's ad-supported site in lieu of their availability on YouTube. Moreover, Plaintiffs offer no evidence that the viewership on Crunchyroll's ad-supported site declined during the time-period that the Anime Episodes were available on YouTube. . . .

The law of this Circuit requires that Plaintiff demonstrate a nexus between the claimed damages and the infringing conduct. See *Polar Bear Prods., Inc.*, 384 F.3d at 708 ("Under § 504(b), actual damages *must* be suffered '*as a result of* the infringement,' and recoverable profits must be '*attributable* to the infringement.' ") (emphasis added). Evidence that Crunchyroll's viewership declined during the period of infringement arguably would have supported the inference that Pledge's YouTube viewers would have watched the programs on Crunchyroll's site if those programs were not posted on YouTube. Consequently, the fact that Plaintiffs made no such showing undermines any claim that Pledge's infringing conduct proximately caused any injury to Plaintiffs. . . .

Plaintiffs have made no showing that Crunchyroll's viewership was adversely affected during the time period that the YouTube videos were available. [By contrast] [t]he plaintiff in *Millennium* [*TGA, Inc. v. Leon*, No. 12-CV-01360, 2013 WL 5719079 (E.D.N.Y. Oct. 18, 2013)] presented evidence that after defendant's blog was removed, plaintiff's revenues increased by 11%. A logical inference from such evidence is that defendant's infringing conduct did, in fact, negatively affect plaintiff's sales. Notably, Plaintiffs, who were notified of the evidentiary deficiencies by the Magistrate, offer no analogous evidence in this case.

———

Gaylord v. United States, 678 F.3d 1339 (Fed. Cir. 2012). In 1995, Frank Gaylord created "The Column," a group of nineteen stainless steel sculptures representing a platoon of soldiers. The Column is the centerpiece of the Korean War Veterans' Memorial on the National Mall in Washington, D.C. In 2002, the United States Postal Service issued a 37-cent stamp commemorating the 50th anniversary of the armistice of the Korean War. The stamp featured a photograph of The Column, which the Postal Service licensed from photographer John Alli. Alli did not obtain a license from Gaylord to photograph The Column. The Postal Service issued roughly 86.8 million of the stamps, sold retail goods carrying the stamp image, and licensed the stamp image to retailers. The Postal Service did not seek or obtain Mr. Gaylord's permission to depict The Column on the stamp or the related merchandise. Having prevailed on his infringement claim, Gaylord sought actual damages corresponding to a 10% royalty on about $30.2 million in revenue allegedly generated by the Postal Service's infringing use, arguing that he typically receives a 10% license fee for various collectibles (such as t-shirts and miniature statues) based on The Column, and that the 10% royalty accurately represents the fair market value of a license to his work. The Postal Service objected that a $5,000 one-time lump-sum royalty was the highest amount he would have received in negotiations with the Postal Service, and therefore constituted just compensation for the infringement. The Federal Circuit declined to adopt the Postal Service's basis for calculating actual damages:

> It is incorrect in a hypothetical negotiation inquiry for a court to limit its analysis to only one side of the negotiating table because the court's task is to determine the "reasonable license fee on which a willing buyer and a willing seller would have agreed for the use taken by the infringer." See *On Davis*, 246 F.3d at 167. The trial court erred in this case by restricting its focus to the Postal Service's past payments: $1,500–$5,000. Defendants cannot insulate themselves from paying for the damages they caused by resting on their past agreements and by creating internal "policies" that shield them from paying fair market value for what they took. See *Rite-Hite Corp. v. Kelley Co.*, 56 F.3d 1538, 1555 (Fed. Cir. 1995) ("[W]hat an infringer would prefer to pay is not the test for damages."). Instead, the trial court must look at the evidence presented by both sides to determine the fair market value of a license to which the parties would have agreed. Hence, while the evidence may indicate that the Postal Service has not paid more than $5,000, it is equally clear that Mr. Gaylord has consistently licensed images of The Column for retail and commemorative items at approximately 10%.

> The trial court legally erred in this case by failing to calculate the fair market value of a license based on a

hypothetical negotiation between Mr. Gaylord and the Postal Service. In applying the so-called "zone of reasonableness" test, the court improperly limited its inquiry to the Postal Service's past licenses and, as a result, erroneously capped Mr. Gaylord's maximum damages without considering other evidence supporting a higher award. . . . We thus vacate and remand for the court to determine the fair market value of a license for the full scope of the Postal Service's infringing use based on a hypothetical negotiation with Mr. Gaylord.

On remand, 112 Fed. Cl. 539 (Fed. Cl. 2013), the U.S. Court of Federal Claims held Gaylord entitled to just compensation of $684,844.94. The court based its conclusion on a finding that a 10% running royalty corresponded to the royalty rate Gaylord consistently charged licensees of "The Column" for various collectibles, such as t-shirts and miniature statues, and therefore accurately captured the fair market value of a license to Gaylord's copyright. The court did not award any damages for the sale of stamps used by purchasers to send mail, but did add prejudgment interest.

On appeal, the Federal Circuit rejected a challenge to the trial court's award of a 10% royalty for sales of unused stamps purchased by collectors. 777 F.3d 1363 (Fed. Cir. 2015). The appellate judges saw no clear error in the trial court's factual finding that the hypothetical negotiation would have resulted in a per-unit royalty rather than a lump-sum payment (even though the postal service had never before agreed to a per-unit royalty for stamp sales) or in the conclusion that the parties would have agreed on 10% as the royalty rate.

b.   STATUTORY DAMAGES

Page 1052. In Question 8, replace the *Lime Group* citation with "784 F.Supp.2d 313 (S.D.N.Y. 2011)".

Pages 1053–1065. Replace the *Tenenbaum* opinion and QUESTIONS with the following:

Capitol Records, Inc. v. Thomas-Rasset, 692 F.3d 899 (8th Cir. 2012). Record company copyright owners sued Jammie Thomas-Rasset, asserting that she infringed their copyrights on 24 sound recordings by exchanging them over peer-to-peer networks. A jury awarded the plaintiffs statutory damages of $9,250 for each of 24 works, for a total award of $222,000. The defendant moved for a new trial or remittitur, and challenged the award as unconstitutionally excessive. The district court granted a new trial because it concluded that it had given an erroneous jury instruction. 579 F.Supp.2d 1210 (D.Minn. 2008). After the second trial, a second jury awarded statutory damages of $80,000 per sound recording infringed, for a total award of $1,920,000. The court granted the defendant's motion for remittitur and reduced the award to $2,250, three times the statutory minimum per work infringed, for a total award of $54,000. 680 F.Supp.2d 1045 (D.Minn. 2010).) (The court declined to reach Thomas-Rasset's claim that the award violated the Due Process Clause.) The common law considerations that the court addressed in assessing whether the jury's award was outrageously excessive included the relationship of the statutory damages award to actual damages, the damages plaintiffs in fact suffered, the reprehensibility of defendant's conduct, and the need for deterrence. The court's award represented in its view the maximum amount that the jury could properly have awarded.

The plaintiffs did not accept the remitted award and a new trial on damages was held. In November 2010, the third jury returned a verdict awarding $62,500 per song, or a total of $1,500,000 in damages. The defendant moved to have that damages award reduced, again raising the claim that the award was unconstitutionally excessive. The court noted that "[a]lthough, in the past, the Court endeavored to avoid unnecessary adjudication of a constitutional issue by relying upon remittitur, based on Plaintiffs' demonstrated refusal to accept remittitur, the Court must now address the constitutionality of the damages award, because, after yet another trial on damages, the Court would face the same constitutional question." 799 F.Supp.2d 999 (D.Minn.2011). Relying in part on the factors it had used in deciding to grant remittitur after the second trial, the court concluded that the jury award violated due process. The court reduced the award again to $2,250 per work infringed, for a total award of $54,000. The parties cross-appealed, and the Eighth Circuit evaluated the damages award:

> On the question of damages, we conclude that a statutory damages award of $9,250 for each of the twenty-four infringed songs, for a total of $222,000, does not contravene the Due Process Clause. The district court erred in reducing the third jury's verdict to $2,250 per work, for a total of $54,000, on the ground that this amount was the maximum permitted by the Constitution.

> The Supreme Court long ago declared that damages awarded pursuant to a statute violate due process only if they are "so severe and oppressive as to be wholly disproportioned to the offense and obviously unreasonable." *St. Louis, I. M. & S. Ry. Co. v. Williams,* 251 U.S. 63, 67 (1919). Under this standard, Congress possesses a "wide latitude of discretion" in setting statutory damages. *Id.* at 66. *Williams* is still good law, and the district court was correct to apply it.

> Thomas-Rasset urges us to consider instead the "guideposts" announced by the Supreme Court for the review of punitive damages awards under the Due Process Clause. When a party challenges an award of punitive damages, a reviewing court is directed to consider three factors in determining whether the award is excessive and unconstitutional: "(1) the degree of reprehensibility of the defendant's misconduct; (2) the disparity between the actual or potential harm suffered by the plaintiff and the punitive damages award; and (3) the difference between the punitive damages awarded by the jury and the civil penalties authorized or imposed in comparable cases." *State Farm Mut. Auto. Ins. Co. v. Campbell,* 538 U.S. 408, 418 (2003); *see also BMW of N. Am., Inc. v. Gore,* 517 U.S. 559, 574–75 (1996).

> The Supreme Court never has held that the punitive damages guideposts are applicable in the context of statutory damages. Due process prohibits excessive punitive damages because " '[e]lementary notions of fairness enshrined in our

constitutional jurisprudence dictate that a person receive fair notice not only of the conduct that will subject him to punishment, but also of the severity of the penalty that a State may impose.' " *Campbell,* 538 U.S. at 417 (quoting *Gore,* 517 U.S. at 574). This concern about fair notice does not apply to statutory damages, because those damages are identified and constrained by the authorizing statute. The guideposts themselves, moreover, would be nonsensical if applied to statutory damages. It makes no sense to consider the disparity between "actual harm" and an award of statutory damages when statutory damages are designed precisely for instances where actual harm is difficult or impossible to calculate. Nor could a reviewing court consider the difference between an award of statutory damages and the "civil penalties authorized," because statutory damages *are* the civil penalties authorized.

Applying the *Williams* standard, we conclude that an award of $9,250 per each of twenty-four works is not "so severe and oppressive as to be wholly disproportioned to the offense and obviously unreasonable." 251 U.S. at 67. Congress, exercising its "wide latitude of discretion," *id.* at 66, set a statutory damages range for willful copyright infringement of $750 to $150,000 per infringed work. 17 U.S.C. § 504(c). The award here is toward the lower end of this broad range. As in *Williams,* "the interests of the public, the numberless opportunities for committing the offense, and the need for securing uniform adherence to [federal law]" support the constitutionality of the award. *Id.* at 67.

Congress's protection of copyrights is not a "special private benefit," but is meant to achieve an important public interest: "to motivate the creative activity of authors and inventors by the provision of a special reward, and to allow the public access to the products of their genius after the limited period of exclusive control has expired." *Sony Corp. of Am. v. Universal City Studios, Inc.,* 464 U.S. 417, 429 (1984). With the rapid advancement of technology, copyright infringement through online file-sharing has become a serious problem in the recording industry. Evidence at trial showed that revenues across the industry decreased by fifty percent between 1999 and 2006, a decline that the record companies attributed to piracy. This decline in revenue caused a corresponding drop in industry jobs and a reduction in the number of artists represented and albums released. *See Sony BMG Music Entm't v. Tenenbaum,* 660 F.3d 487, 492 (1st Cir. 2011).

Congress no doubt was aware of the serious problem posed by online copyright infringement, and the "numberless opportunities for committing the offense," when it last revisited the Copyright Act in 1999. To provide a deterrent against such infringement, Congress amended § 504(c) to increase the minimum per-work award from $500 to $750, the maximum per-work award from $20,000 to $30,000, and the maximum per-work award for willful infringement from $100,000 to $150,000.

Thomas-Rasset contends that the range of statutory damages established by § 504(c) reflects only a congressional judgment "at a very general level," but that courts have authority to declare it "severe and oppressive" and "wholly disproportioned" in particular cases. The district court similarly emphasized that Thomas-Rasset was "not a business acting for profit, but rather an individual consumer illegally seeking free access to music for her own use." By its terms, however, the statute plainly encompasses infringers who act without a profit motive, and the statute already provides for a broad range of damages that allows courts and juries to calibrate the award based on the nature of the violation. For those who favor resort to legislative history, the record also suggests that Congress was well aware of the threat of noncommercial copyright infringement when it established the lower end of the range. *See* H.R. Rep. 106–216, at 3 (1999).[1] . . .

In holding that any award over $2,250 per work would violate the Constitution, the district court effectively imposed a treble damages limit on the $750 minimum statutory damages award. The district court based this holding on a "broad legal practice of establishing a treble award as the upper limit permitted to address willful or particularly damaging behavior." Any "broad legal practice" of treble damages for statutory violations, however, does not control whether an award of statutory damages is within the limits prescribed by the Constitution. The limits of treble damages to which the district court referred, such as in the antitrust laws or other intellectual property laws, represent congressional judgments about the appropriate maximum in a given context. They do not establish a *constitutional* rule that can be substituted for a different congressional judgment in the area of copyright infringement. Although the United States seems to think that the district court's ruling did not question the constitutionality of the statutory damages statute, the district court's approach in our view would make the statute unconstitutional as applied to a significant category of copyright infringers. The evidence against Thomas-Rasset demonstrated an aggravated case of willful infringement by an individual consumer who acted to download and distribute copyrighted recordings without profit motive. If an award near the bottom of the statutory range is unconstitutional as applied to her infringement of twenty-four

---

[1] According to the House report in 1999:

By the turn of the century the Internet is projected to have more than 200 million users, and the development of new technology will create additional incentive for copyright thieves to steal protected works. The advent of digital video discs, for example, will enable individuals to store far more material than on conventional discs, and at the same time, produce perfect secondhand copies. . . . Many computer users are either ignorant that copyright laws apply to Internet activity, or they simply believe that they will not be caught or prosecuted for their conduct. Also, many infringers do not consider the current copyright infringement penalties a real threat and continue infringing, even after a copyright owner puts them on notice that their actions constitute infringement and that they should stop the activity or face legal action. In light of this disturbing trend, it is manifest that Congress respond appropriately with updated penalties to dissuade such conduct.

works, then it would be the rare case of noncommercial infringement to which the statute could be applied.

Thomas-Rasset's cross-appeal goes so far as to argue that *any* award of statutory damages would be unconstitutional, because even the minimum damages award of $750 per violation would be "wholly disproportioned to the offense" and thus unconstitutional. This is so, Thomas-Rasset argues, because the damages award is not based on any evidence of harm caused by her specific infringement, but rather reflects the harm caused by file-sharing in general. The district court similarly concluded that "statutory damages must still bear *some* relation to actual damages." The Supreme Court in *Williams,* however, disagreed that the constitutional inquiry calls for a comparison of an award of statutory damages to actual damages caused by the violation. 251 U.S. at 66. Because the damages award "is imposed as a punishment for the violation of a public law, the Legislature may adjust its amount to the public wrong rather than the private injury, just as if it were going to the state." *Id.* The protection of copyrights is a vindication of the public interest, and statutory damages are "by definition a substitute for unproven or unprovable actual damages." *Cass Cnty. Music Co.,* 88 F.3d at 643. For copyright infringement, moreover, statutory damages are "designed to discourage wrongful conduct," in addition to providing "restitution of profit and reparation for injury." *F.W. Woolworth Co. v. Contemporary Arts,* 344 U.S. 228, 233 (1952).

Thomas-Rasset highlights that if the recording companies had sued her based on infringement of 1,000 copyrighted recordings instead of the twenty-four recordings that they selected, then an award of $9,250 per song would have resulted in a total award of $9,250,000. Because that hypothetical award would be obviously excessive and unreasonable, she reasons, an award of $222,000 based on the same amount per song must likewise be invalid. Whatever the constitutionality of the hypothetical award, we disagree that the validity of the lesser amount sought here depends on whether the Due Process Clause would permit the extrapolated award that she posits. The absolute amount of the award, not just the amount per violation, is relevant to whether the award is "so severe and oppressive as to be wholly disproportioned to the offense and obviously unreasonable." *Williams,* 251 U.S. at 67. The recording companies here opted to sue over twenty-four recordings. If they had sued over 1,000 recordings, then a finder of fact may well have considered the number of recordings and the proportionality of the total award as factors in determining where within the range to assess the statutory damages. If and when a jury returns a multi-million dollar award for noncommercial online copyright infringement, then there will be time enough to consider it.

In June 2013, the First Circuit reached a similar conclusion based on similar analysis. *Sony BMG Music Entertainment v. Tenenbaum*, 719 F.3d 67.

QUESTION

Canada's copyright act has a statutory damages provision very similar to that in Title 17, with a range for awards between $500 to $20,000. Recent amendments to Canadian law limit awards to a range between $100 and $5000 "for all infringements involved in the proceedings for all works . . . if the infringements are for non-commercial purposes." Would you support a similar change to U.S. law? Why or why not? If such a change were adopted, how should "non-commercial purposes" be defined?

For a thoughtful examination of issues presented by large statutory damage awards and the Supreme Court's punitive damages jurisprudence, see Pamela Samuelson & Tara Wheatland, *Statutory Damages in Copyright Law: A Remedy in Need of Reform*, 51 William & Mary L. Rev. 439 (2009).

3. COSTS AND ATTORNEY'S FEES

Page 1069. Add after the second full paragraph:

Klinger v. Conan Doyle Estate, Ltd., 761 F.3d 789 (7th Cir. 2014). The court's decision on the merits of this case, rejecting the defendant's claim of copyright in characters appearing in Sherlock Holmes stories in which the copyright had already expired, appears in Chapter 2.H on page 25, *supra* this Supplement. In this opinion, the court ruled on Klinger's request for an award of the $30,679.93 in attorneys' fees incurred in the appeal. (Klinger separately petitioned for an award of $39,123.44 for costs and fees incurred in the trial court.)

> . . . The estate opposes Klinger's request on the same hopeless grounds that it had urged in its appeal, but does not question the amount of fees as distinct from Klinger's entitlement to an award of *any* amount of fees in this case.

> The Copyright Act authorizes the "award [of] a reasonable attorney's fee to the prevailing party as part of the costs." 17 U.S.C. § 505. We said in *Assessment Technologies of Wisconsin, LLC v. WIREdata, Inc.,* 361 F.3d 434, 436–37 (7th Cir.2004) (and reaffirmed in *DeliverMed Holdings, LLC v. Schaltenbrand,* 734 F.3d 616, 625–26 (7th Cir.2013)) that the two most important considerations in deciding whether to award fees "are the strength of the prevailing party's case and the amount of damages or other relief the party obtained. If the case was a toss-up and the prevailing party obtained generous damages, or injunctive relief of substantial monetary value, there is no urgent need to add an award of attorneys' fees. But if at the other extreme the claim or defense was frivolous and the prevailing party obtained no relief at all, the case for awarding attorneys' fees is compelling" (citations omitted). We said that as a consequence of the successful defense of an infringement suit the defendant is entitled to a "very strong" presumption in favor of receiving attorneys' fees, in order to ensure that an infringement defendant does not abandon a meritorious defense in situations in which "the cost of vindication exceeds the private benefit to the party." 361 F.3d at 437. "For without the prospect of such an award, [an infringement defendant] might

be forced into a nuisance settlement or deterred altogether from exercising [its] rights." *Id.*

We're not alone in expressing these concerns. See Michael J. Meurer, "Controlling Opportunistic and Anti-Competitive Intellectual Property Litigation," 44 *Boston College L.Rev.* 509, 521 (2003). See also Ben Depoorter & Robert Kirk Walker, "Copyright False Positives," 89 *Notre Dame L.Rev.* 319, 343–45 (2013), where we read that many persons or firms accused of copyright infringement find that "it is more cost-effective to simply capitulate" than to fight, even when the alleged claim is of dubious merit. Copyright holders, the authors explain, have larger potential upsides and smaller downside risks to filing suit, since if they win they obtain damages but if they lose they don't have to pay damages (although a loss, especially if recorded in a published opinion as in this case, may make it more difficult for them to play their extortionate game in future cases). So copiers or alleged copiers may be "induced into licensing [that is, paying a fee for a license to reproduce] the underlying work, even if this license is unnecessary or conveys non-existent rights." *Id.* at 345. Depoorter and Walker (*id.* at 345 n. 172) give the example of the Summy-Brichard Company, a subsidiary of Warner Music Group, which "receives approximately $2 million per year in royalty payments for licenses to the song 'Happy Birthday to You,' despite the fact that the song is most likely in the public domain," as argued in Robert Brauneis, "Copyright and the World's Most Popular Song," 56 *J. Copyright Society U.S.A.* 335, 338–40 (2009).

This case illustrates the concerns expressed both in the articles we've just cited and in our opinions in *Assessment Technologies* and *DeliverMed Holdings.* Unless Klinger is awarded his attorneys' fees, he will have lost money—to be precise, $25,679.93 ($30,679.93–$5,000 [the amount the Doyle estate demanded for a license])—in winning an appeal in which the defendant's only defense bordered on the frivolous: a Pyrrhic victory if ever there was one. It's irrelevant that in *Assessment Technologies* and *DeliverMed Holdings,* the alleged infringer was the defendant, and in this case it's the plaintiff; a declaratory judgment plaintiff in a copyright case is in effect a defendant permitted to precipitate the infringement suit.

The Doyle estate's business strategy is plain: charge a modest license fee for which there is no legal basis, in the hope that the "rational" writer or publisher asked for the fee will pay it rather than incur a greater cost, in legal expenses, in challenging the legality of the demand. The strategy had worked with Random House [which published Klinger's first anthology]; Pegasus[, the publisher of his second anthology,] was ready to knuckle under; only Klinger (so far as we know) resisted. In effect he was a private attorney general, combating a disreputable business practice—a form of extortion—and he is seeking by the present motion not to obtain a reward but merely to avoid a loss. He has performed a public service—and with substantial risk to himself, for had he lost he would have been out of pocket for the $69,803.37 in fees and costs incurred at the trial and appellate levels ($30,679.93 + $39,123.44). The willingness of someone in Klinger's position to sue rather than pay Doyle's estate a modest license fee is important because it injects risk into the estate's business model. As a result of losing the suit, the estate has lost its claim to own copyrights in characters in the Sherlock Holmes stories published by Arthur Conan Doyle before 1923. For exposing the estate's unlawful business strategy, Klinger deserves a reward but asks only to break even.

We note finally that the estate was playing with fire in asking Amazon and other booksellers to cooperate with it in enforcing its nonexistent copyright claims against Klinger. For it was enlisting those sellers in a boycott of a competitor of the estate, and boycotts of competitors violate the antitrust laws. The usual boycott is of a purchaser by his suppliers, induced by a competitor of the purchaser in order to eliminate competition from that purchaser . . . This case is different, in its facts but not in economic substance or legal relevance, because the boycotters enlisted by the Doyle estate were buyers from the victim, rather than sellers to it. But functionally they *were* suppliers—suppliers of essential distribution services to Klinger.

It's time the estate, in its own self-interest, changed its business model.

Klinger's motion is granted and the Doyle estate ordered to pay him $30,679.93 for the legal fees that he incurred in his successful defense of the district court's judgment in his favor.

4.   PROCEDURAL ISSUES

a.   JURISDICTION

Page 1071. Before the last paragraph ("On the issue of personal jurisdiction over a defendant in a copyright infringement suit, see *Penguin Group (USA) Inc. v. American Buddha*, page 1246, infra."), add:

The Copyright Office, recognizing that many authors and small claimants cannot afford to vindicate their exclusive rights under copyright because of the prohibitive cost of bringing an infringement action in federal court, has recommended creation of small claims tribunals to adjudicate infringement actions by authors and copyright owners seeking relief for "modest-sized copyright claims." The Copyright Office's report addresses potential constitutional impediments to vesting non-Article III tribunals with jurisdiction over small copyright claims: "Concerns of pragmatism and efficiency are core considerations, but they are not the only ones, and they must be viewed in the larger context of federal powers. Our Constitution protects both the role of the federal judiciary and the rights of those who participate in adjudicatory proceedings. These principles are enshrined in Article III and the Fifth and Seventh Amendments, and in judicial interpretations of these and other constitutional provisions. Any alternative process must fit comfortably within the constitutional parameters."

The Copyright Office's recommendations include the following measures:

- Congress should create a centralized tribunal within the Copyright Office, which would administer proceedings through online and teleconferencing facilities without the requirement of personal appearances. The tribunal would be staffed by three adjudicators, two of whom would have significant experience in copyright law—together having represented or presided over the interests of both owners and users of copyrighted works—with the third to have a background in alternative dispute resolution.

- The tribunal would be a voluntary alternative to federal court. Its focus would be on small infringement cases valued at no more than $30,000 in damages. Copyright owners would be required to have registered their works or filed an application before bringing an action. They would be eligible to recover either actual or statutory damages up to the $30,000 cap, but statutory damages would be limited to $15,000 per work (or $7,500 for a work not registered by the normally applicable deadline for statutory damages).

- Claimants who initiated a proceeding would provide notice of the claim to responding parties, who would need to agree to the process, either through an opt-out mechanism or by affirmative written consent. Respondents would be permitted to assert all relevant defenses, including fair use, as well as limited counterclaims arising from the infringing conduct at issue. Certain DMCA-related matters relating to takedown notices, including claims of misrepresentation, could also be considered, and parties threatened with an infringement action could seek a declaration of noninfringement.

- Parties would provide written submissions and hearings would be conducted through telecommunications facilities. Proceedings would be streamlined, with limited discovery and no formal motion practice. A responding party's agreement to cease infringing activity could be considered by the tribunal and reflected in its determination. The tribunal would retain the discretion to dismiss without prejudice any claim that it did not believe could fairly be adjudicated through the small claims process.

- Determinations of the small claims tribunal would be binding only with respect to the parties and claims at issue and would have no precedential effect. They would be subject to limited administrative review for error and could be challenged in federal district court for fraud, misconduct, or other improprieties. Final determinations could be filed in federal court, if necessary, to ensure their enforceability.

See Copyright Small Claims: A Report of the Register of Copyrights, U.S. COPYRIGHT OFFICE (September 2013), *available at* http://www.copyright. gov/docs/smallclaims

Page 1071. Following the last paragraph ("On the issue of personal jurisdiction over a defendant in a copyright infringement suit, see *Penguin Group (USA) Inc. v. American Buddha*, page 1246, infra."), add:

See also Mavrix Photo v. Brand Technologies, 647 F.3d 1218 (9th Cir. 2011), *infra*, Chapter 11.D.2, page 301, this Supplement.

b.   STANDING

Page 1072. Add at the end of the carryover paragraph:

In *Broadcast Music, Inc. v. McDade & Sons, Inc.*, 928 F.Supp.2d 1120 (D.Ariz. 2013), in response to the defendants' challenge to BMI's standing as a nonexclusive licensee to sue for infringement of the public performance right, the court wrote, "The non-exclusive nature of BMI's licensing agreements, however, does not deprive BMI of the right to enforce the copyrights at issue. See Broadcast Music, Inc. v. TTJ's Inc., 2010 WL 2867814, *1 (D.Idaho Jul. 20, 2010) (noting BMI rights are "nonexclusive" and granting summary judgment for BMI on its copyright infringement claims). The assignments BMI receives from its "affiliates" (songwriters and music publishers who assign their copyrights to BMI) for the millions of songs in the BMI repertoire are non-exclusive because each BMI affiliate retains the right to separately grant permission to a particular user for the public performance of its songs. Absent such direct permission, however, a user must purchase a BMI license to obtain the right to publicly perform a song in the BMI repertoire." Is the court correct, in light of the provisions of § 501(b) and the definition of "transfer of copyright ownership"? (Is the court's description of the transactions between BMI and its affiliates as "assignments" correct)?

Page 1072. Insert before *Righthaven LLC v. Democratic Underground LLC*:

What is the relationship between a beneficial owner's standing to sue, and compliance with the pre-suit registration requirement? Although section 501(b) confers standing on a beneficial owner (who often will be the work's author), does section 411(a) require the author or other beneficial owner also to have registered the work with the copyright office in order to pursue the infringement claim? In **Smith v. Casey**, 741 F.3d 1236 (11th Cir. 2014), the court ruled that the transferee's registration of the work sufficed for purposes of section 411(a).

> Section 501(b), however, contains a caveat. Even the beneficial owner of an exclusive right in a copyrighted work must still demonstrate compliance with the Act's formalities, which require "preregistration or registration of the copyright claim . . . in accordance with this title." 17 U.S.C. § 411(a). Harrick Music registered the copyright in the [plaintiff composer's] "Spank" composition, but [plaintiff] Smith did not file a separate registration. Because Smith had not registered the work, the district court concluded, he lacked statutory standing. In reaching that conclusion, the district court rejected the Smith estate's contention that it could rely on the registration Harrick Music had filed to satisfy § 411(a).

The district court's construction of § 411(a) was too narrow. Harrick Music registered a claim to copyright in the "Spank" composition, specifically identifying Smith as the composer and informing the Copyright Office the work was not made for hire. Nothing in § 411(a) indicates that a composer who has agreed to assign his legal interest in a composition, along with the right to register it, in exchange for royalties, may not rely on the registration his assignee files. Where a publisher has registered a claim to copyright in a work not made for hire, we conclude the beneficial owner has statutory standing to sue for infringement.

In reaching this conclusion, we are in good company. As best we can tell, the only other court of appeals to have addressed the issue held, under nearly identical circumstances, that composers who retained a beneficial interest could rely upon the registration their music publisher filed. See *Batiste*, 179 F.3d at 220–21 & n. 2. In that case, three brothers wrote a song entitled "Funky Soul" and then signed an agreement transferring all rights in the composition, including "the exclusive right to secure copyright," to a publisher in exchange for royalties. *Id.* at 219. The Fifth Circuit affirmed the denial of a motion to dismiss the brothers' infringement claims for lack of standing, finding "no merit" in the contention that they "could not demonstrate that they had obtained or applied to obtain a valid copyright registration for 'Funky Soul.' " *Id.* at 220–21 & n.2. Composers who agree to assign their legal rights to a work in exchange for royalties, the court concluded, "may properly assert their copyright infringement claims as beneficial owners of [the publisher's] registered copyright." [Citations.]

. . . Were we to ignore the weight of this authority and hold otherwise, redundant registrations would be necessary for statutory standing purposes every time legal and beneficial ownership of the same exclusive right rested with two distinct parties, even if they joined together in filing suit against an alleged infringer. Absent clear statutory language requiring it, we do not believe Congress would have intended such a result. We hold the Smith estate has adequately alleged facts to support its statutory standing to sue for infringement of the "Spank" copyright.

. . .

QUESTION

What public policy underlies the sec. 411 pre-suit registration requirement? What is to be gained by obliging the author, beneficial owner of copyright, to register the copyright if the transferee has already done so?

Page 1074. Replace the citation to *Righthaven, LLC v. Hoehn* in the second paragraph with the following:

In *Righthaven, LLC v. Hoehn*, 716 F.3d 1166, 2013 WL 1908876 (9th Cir. 2013), another case involving claims by Righthaven of infringement of *Las Vegas Journal-Review* articles, the Ninth Circuit took the same approach to the agreements between the newspaper and Righthaven.

The court noted that the fact that "some language in the contract described Righthaven as the owner . . . does not itself prove that Righthaven owned any exclusive rights" as required for standing to sue. Noting that "we look not just at the labels parties use but also at the substance and effect of the contract," the court concluded that the SAA's limits on what Righthaven could do with any copyright assigned to it "left Righthaven without any ability to . . . exploit any . . . exclusive right under the Copyright Act." As a result, Righthaven was not a legal or beneficial owner of an exclusive copyright right and therefore did not have standing to sue under § 501(b).

c.   STATUTE OF LIMITATIONS

Page 1075: Insert into paragraph beginning "First, is the running of the statute "tolled" . . . after case cites to *Taylor v. Meirick* and *Polar Bear Prods.*:

Accord, Psihoyos v. John Wiley & Sons, 748 F.3d 120 (2d Cir. 2014); *Diversey v. Schmidly*, 738 F.3d 1196 (10th Cir. 2013).

Page 1076. Insert at end of first full paragraph, following citations:

Accord, Diversey v. Schmidly, 738 F.3d 1196 (10th Cir. 2013) ("discovery" rule for running of the statute of limitations makes "continuing wrong" exception "unnecessary.")

Page 1076. Replace the last full paragraph with the following:

Is the statute of limitations the only possible time bar on bringing a copyright infringement claim? Might some claims be barred, even though brought during the statutory limitations period, by laches, which generally denies equitable relief when a plaintiff's failure to diligently assert its rights unduly prejudices the defendant? The Supreme Court addressed this question in **Petrella v. Metro-Goldwyn-Mayer, Inc.,** ___ U.S. ___, 134 S.Ct. 1962 (2014). In 1963, Frank Petrella registered the copyright in a screenplay, and in 1976 licensed MGM's predecessor to make a film based on that screenplay. (The license also included the right to use a later screenplay and book, but by the time of the litigation those works had entered the public domain.) In 1980, MGM released Martin Scorsese's film *Raging Bull*, allegedly derivative of the 1963 screenplay. Petrella died in 1981, and in 1991 his daughter Paula Petrella renewed the copyright. In 1998, Petrella notified MGM of her ownership of the renewal copyright, and for two years MGM denied any infringement and Petrella threatened to sue, but she did not file suit until January 6, 2009 (eighteen years after she had acquired the renewal copyright), seeking relief for infringements occurring since January 6, 2006 (and thus within the statute of limitations under § 507). In the meantime, MGM had released the film on DVD and Blu-ray. During the litigation, Petrella stated that she had waited to sue because she believed, based in part on representations from MGM, that the film was still in debt and would probably never make a profit. The district court and the Ninth Circuit held that laches barred Petrella's suit, though Circuit Judge William Fletcher, concurring, called for a reexamination of the role of laches in copyright suits.

The Supreme Court granted certiorari and reversed 6–3 (with Justice Breyer, joined by Chief Justice Roberts and Justice Kennedy, dissenting), ruling that a defendant cannot invoke laches to bar a claim for damages within the three-year statute of limitations. Writing for the Court, Justice Ginsburg explained that Congress had already taken a copyright owner's delay in bringing suit into account in adopting the three-year statute of limitations, which bars all recovery for infringements committed more than 3 years before a suit is brought. (In this connection, the Court noted approvingly the "widely recognized" separate-accrual rule, under which the statute of limitations "runs separately from each violation," so that "each infringing act starts a new limitations period," *id.* at ___ (slip op. at 5), and a recent act of infringement will not allow a copyright owner to bring a suit and reach back to recover for infringements older than three years.) And even for infringements occurring within the limitations period, the Court observed that the statutory provisions for apportioning profits mean that a defendant "may retain the return on investment shown to be attributable to its own enterprise, as distinct from the value created by the infringed work." *Id.* at ___ (slip op. at 12).

The Court also observed that a copyright owner might legitimately delay bringing an infringement suit:

> It is hardly incumbent on copyright owners . . . to challenge each and every actionable infringement. And there is nothing untoward about waiting to see whether an infringer's exploitation undercuts the value of the copyrighted work, has no effect on the original work, or even complements it. Fan sites prompted by a book or film, for example, may benefit the copyright owner. See Wu, Tolerated Use, 31 Colum. J. L. & Arts 617, 619–620 (2008). Even if an infringement is harmful, the harm may be too small to justify the cost of litigation.

> If the rule were, as MGM urges, "sue soon, or forever hold your peace," copyright owners would have to mount a federal case fast to stop seemingly innocuous infringements, lest those infringements eventually grow in magnitude. Section 507(b)'s three-year limitations period, however, coupled to the separate-accrual rule, avoids such litigation profusion. It allows a copyright owner to defer suit until she can estimate whether litigation is worth the candle. She will miss out on damages for periods prior to the three-year look-back, but her right to prospective injunctive relief should, in most cases, remain unaltered.

Id. at ___ (slip op. at 16–17).

Regarding concerns that delay could prejudice a defendant by making relevant evidence unavailable, the majority noted that some evidentiary unavailability was an inevitable part of a Congressional scheme that grants very long copyright terms and a renewal opportunity after 28 years to a deceased author's descendants. The Court also asserted that copyright's registration mechanism would help reduce the need for extrinsic evidence in copyright litigation.

The majority observed that delay by a copyright owner could still be taken into account in determining the remedies to be awarded should the owner prevail in an infringement suit. Delay could be relevant, the Court noted, in assessing the recovery of the defendant's profits (which the

Court viewed as an equitable remedy), and in fashioning appropriate injunctive relief (which, the Court noted, might involve allowing a defendant like MGM to continue to exploit its work upon payment of a reasonable royalty to the copyright owner).

While the Court ruled that laches could not, as the lower courts had held in this case, bar a copyright owner's infringement claims entirely at the very threshold of litigation, in "extraordinary circumstances" courts could conclude at the very outset of the litigation that the copyright owner's delay in bringing suit would bar the owner, if successful, from certain equitable relief, especially the destruction of infringing copies or in some situations a complete injunction against a work containing infringing material.

Finally, the Court noted that the equitable defense of estoppel—based not on delay but on a copyright owner's "intentionally misleading representations concerning his abstention from suit" and the accused infringer's detrimental reliance on "the copyright owner's deception"—remained available to bar the copyright owner's claims completely in appropriate cases.

The *Petrella* Court's reasoning relies heavily on the "separate accrual" rule for applying the statute of limitations to infringement claims. Does the opinion therefore doom the "continuing wrong" approach to the limitations period taken by some lower courts?

d.   STATE SOVEREIGN IMMUNITY

Page 1079. Add at the end of the section before "Criminal Liability":

Note that the *federal* government has enacted a limited waiver of its sovereign immunity, allowing copyright owners to bring infringement claims against it under certain conditions:

> [W]henever the copyright in any work protected under the copyright laws of the United States shall be infringed by the United States, the exclusive action which may be brought for such infringement shall be an action by the copyright owner against the United States in the Court of Federal Claims for the recovery of his reasonable and entire compensation as damages for such infringement, including the minimum statutory damages as set forth in section 504(c) of title 17, United States Code.

28 U.S.C. § 1498(b). Can a copyright owner suing the U.S. government and electing statutory damages recover enhanced statutory damages if she shows that the government infringed willfully? Can she recover a statutory damage award anywhere in the range set by statute, or is she limited to an award of the minimum amount of $750? See *Cohen v. U.S.*, 105 Fed.Cl. 733 (2012).

5.   CRIMINAL LIABILITY

Page 1079. Insert at line 9 of first paragraph, following "(rather than merely to make or distribute copies)":

See, e.g., U.S. v. Liu, 731 F.3d 982 (9th Cir. 2013) (citing decisions).

Page 1082. Add after the second full paragraph:

Can an employer legally fire an at-will employee if the employee refuses to perform acts ordered by the employer that would constitute criminal copyright infringement? What if the employee only reasonably believes that the act would constitute criminal copyright infringement? What if the acts would constitute only civil copyright infringement? See *Young v. Nortex Foundation Designs, Inc.*, 105 U.S.P.Q.2d 1793 (Tex.Ct.App. 2013) (exception to employment-at-will doctrine for discharge of employee for refusing to perform an illegal act applied to a drafter at an architectural firm who was ordered to create a foundation design plan from a copy of architectural plans labeled as an "illegal" copy).

B. TECHNOLOGICAL PROTECTION MEASURES

1. PROTECTION AGAINST CIRCUMVENTION

a. WHAT § 1201 PROTECTS

Page 1106. Add a new subsection:

iv. What Constitutes a Criminally Actionable Violation of § 1201?

Section 1204 provides that "Any person who violates section 1201 or 1202 willfully and for purposes of commercial advantage or private financial gain" is subject to fines and imprisonment. As in cases involving infringement of section 106 rights, the willfulness standard is met when the government shows beyond a reasonable doubt that the defendant intentionally engaged in acts he knew to be unlawful. In **U.S. v. Reichert**, 747 F.3d 445 (6th Cir. 2014), the defendant was prosecuted for selling "mod chips" that circumvent a videogame console's security settings, thus allowing users to play infringing copies of videogames. The judge instructed the jury that it could convict on the basis of "deliberate ignorance," which the court explained as meaning:

> No one can avoid responsibility for a crime by deliberately ignoring the obvious. If you are convinced that the Defendant deliberately ignored a high probability that he was trafficking in technology primarily designed to circumvent technological measures designed to effectively control access to a work copyrighted under federal law, then you may find that he knew he was violating the Digital Millennium Copyright Act.

> But to find this, you must be convinced beyond a reasonable doubt that the Defendant was aware of a high probability that he was violating the Digital Millennium Copyright Act, and that the Defendant deliberately closed his eyes to what was obvious.

Reichert appealed his conviction on the ground that "the deliberate ignorance instruction incorrectly implemented the pattern jury instruction and consequently eviscerated the DMCA's willfulness requirement by allowing the jury to convict him upon finding only that he knew that he was trafficking in circumvention technology, rather than after finding that he knew that he was violating the law by trafficking in such technology." The Sixth Circuit affirmed:

. . . [D]evoid of context, this part of the instruction lends some support to Reichert's position, as it seems to inform the jury that if Reichert deliberately ignored a high probability that he merely engaged in the conduct at issue, then the jury could find that Reichert knew that his conduct violated the DMCA.

But Reichert's focus is too myopic. Even to the extent that the challenged portion of the instruction could have been more precise, it was not given in a vacuum. Instead, it was sandwiched between two instructions that stated the stricter requirement and clarified the challenged language. Immediately before giving the challenged instruction, the district court gave an instruction on "willfulness," explaining that an act is willful if done "with the intent either to disobey or disregard the law," that the defendant "must have acted with the intent to do something the law forbids," and that the government must prove "that the law imposed a duty on the Defendant, that the Defendant knew of this duty, and that he voluntarily and intentionally violated that duty." And immediately after giving the portion of the deliberate ignorance instruction to which Reichert objects, the district court cautioned the jury that, to find that Reichert knew that he was violating the DMCA, "you must be convinced beyond a reasonable doubt that the Defendant was aware of a high probability that he was violating the Digital Millennium Copyright Act, and that the Defendant deliberately closed his eyes to what was obvious."

In context, therefore, the language relied upon by Reichert did not detract from the jury instructions' overall import: when viewed "as a whole," the jury instructions given in this case properly instructed the jury on the issue of willfulness. [Citation] Reichert has never objected to the district court's willfulness instruction, and it informed the jury that, for a defendant's conduct to be willful, he "need not be aware of the specific law or the rule his conduct is violating." Even in Reichert's formulation, then, the jury was not required to find that Reichert knew that his conduct violated any specific statute; all that was required to convict Reichert was a finding that he knew that his conduct was illegal. This is exactly what the district court's "willfulness" instruction told the jury, and the mildly imprecise deliberate ignorance instruction did not fatally undermine it.

b. EXCEPTIONS AND LIMITATIONS

i. *Statutory Scheme*

Pages 1106–1111. Replace the text on the Statutory Scheme with the following:

Although the exceptions to § 1201(a) are multiple, they are also very narrowly defined, and do not admit of expansive judicial construction. As a result, Congress instructed the Librarian of Congress, in consultation with the Register of Copyrights, to conduct a rulemaking every three years to identify particular classes of works whose users would be "adversely affected by the prohibition . . . in their ability to make noninfringing uses under this title" and to suspend the application of the prohibition on the act of access control circumvention as to those works until the next rulemaking period. Each rulemaking is de novo: a class identified in a prior rulemaking is not automatically reinstated; the Copyright Office must determine whether a need for an exemption still exists. It is important to recognize, however, that the prohibitions against trafficking in access circumvention devices continue to apply.

The Copyright Office has now conducted five Rulemakings, the most recent of which resulted in a final rule issued by the Librarian of Congress on October 26, 2012.

That rulemaking provided two pairs of exemptions relating to circumventing measures protecting motion pictures in order to use short excerpts for criticism and commentary. 37 C.F.R. § 201.40(b)(4)–(7). Each pair contains two separate exemptions that are virtually identical, except that one applies to motion pictures "on DVDs that are lawfully made and acquired and that are protected by the Content Scrambling System," 37 C.F.R. § 201.40(b)(4), (6), and the other applies to motion pictures "that are lawfully made and acquired via online distribution services and that are protected by various technological protection measures," 37 C.F.R. § 201.40(b)(5), (7). (The Register concluded that the record did not support extending the exemption to motion pictures distributed on Blu-ray discs. 77 Fed.Reg. at 65,269.)

Both pairs of exemptions apply "where [the] circumvention is undertaken solely in order to make use of short portions of the motion pictures for the purpose of criticism or comment." 37 C.F.R. § 201.40(b)(4)–(7). And both pairs apply where the criticism or comment is in (i) "noncommercial videos;" (ii) "documentary films;" and (iii) "nonfiction multimedia ebooks offering film analysis." *Id.* The Register determined that the use of short excerpts for such criticism or commentary was likely to be fair use (though she concluded that the record did not establish that uses in fictional films were likely to be noninfringing). 77 Fed.Reg. at 65,268–69.

The first pair of exemptions only applies, though, "where the person engaging in circumvention believes and has reasonable grounds for believing that circumvention is necessary because reasonably available alternatives . . . are not able to produce the level of high-quality content required to achieve the desired criticism or comment on such motion pictures." 37 C.F.R. § 201.40(b)(4),(5). In those instances, the Register concluded that alternatives such screen-capture technology did not necessarily provide an adequate alternative to circumvention, because the lower-quality images that such alternatives produced would likely impair in many instances the criticism or comment being made. That conclusion explains the limitation of these exemptions to situations in which alternatives are reasonably believed "not able to produce the level of high-quality content required to achieve the desired criticism or comment." And in addition to the three instances identified above, these exemptions also apply to uses "[f]or educational purposes in film studies or other courses requiring close analysis of film and media excerpts, by college and university faculty, college and university students, and kindergarten through twelfth grade educators." *Id.*

The second pair of exemptions applies

> where the circumvention, if any, is undertaken using screen capture technology that is reasonably represented and offered to the public as enabling the reproduction of motion picture content after such content has been lawfully decrypted, when such representations have been reasonably relied upon by the user of such technology, when the person engaging in the circumvention believes and has reasonable grounds for believing that the circumvention is necessary to achieve the desired criticism or comment . . .

37 C.F.R. § 201.40(b)(6),(7). The Register acknowledged an "unsettled legal landscape" as to whether use of screen capture technology was noncircumventing, and therefore determined that limited exemptions were needed "to address the *possible* circumvention" when using such technology. 77 Fed.Reg. at 65,269 (emphasis added). These exemptions contain a broader educational category, allowing circumvention when the use is "[f]or educational purposes by college and university faculty, college and university students, and kindergarten through twelfth grade educators." 37 C.F.R. § 201.40(b)(6),(7).

This exemption continues an approach begun in the 2006 rulemaking, *see* 71 Fed.Reg. 68,472 (Nov. 27, 2006), which marked the first time that an exempt "class of works" was defined in part by the type of user or the type of use at issue. In earlier rulemakings, the Register had concluded that the statute limited her authority to declaring classes of works without reference to classes of users. *See* 65 Fed.Reg. 64,556 (Oct. 27, 2000); 68 Fed.Reg. 62,011 (Oct. 31, 2003). In 2006, however, she reassessed the scope of her authority and reached a different conclusion:

> The Register reached this conclusion in reviewing a request to exempt a class of works consisting of "audiovisual works included in the educational library of a college or university's film or media studies department and that are protected by technological measures that prevent their educational use." Concluding that a "class" must be properly tailored not only to address the harm demonstrated, but also to limit the adverse consequences that may result from the creation of an exempted class, the Register has concluded that given the facts demonstrated by the film professor proponents of the exemption and the legitimate concerns expressed by the opponents of the proposed exemption, it makes sense that a class may, in appropriate cases, be additionally refined by reference to the particular type of use and/or user.

71 Fed.Reg. at 68,473. In the case of technologically protected films, the "works only" approach would have produced results that would have been overbroad had the exemption been granted, or underinclusive had it been denied. Defining the class as films in protected digital format would have opened all DVDs and access-protected videostreams or downloads to circumvention. But refusing any exemption would have frustrated specific noninfringing educational uses of the films, according to the record the Register found persuasive.

While defining exempted classes narrowly helps avoid the danger that an overbroad exemption could possibly vitiate the protection of access controls in the first place, the need to limit user-defined classes to well-circumscribed (and thus controllable) sets of users may have the effect of confining the practice of certain fair uses to traditional fair use communities, such as library or university research and instructional staff, while excluding the population at large. As may be inferred from the specificity of the exceptions resulting from the triennial rulemakings, assisting the latter group's fair uses may be beyond the Register's statutory power to recommend; whether these broader goals may be achieved by other means remains to be seen.

The most recent rulemaking seemed to acknowledge that defining an exempted class in part by the type of use or user means that the more specific the exemption, the greater the onus on someone wishing to rely on the exemption:

> The Register stressed that prospective users of the recommended [motion picture] exemptions . . . should take care to ensure that they satisfy each requirement of the narrowly tailored exemptions before seeking to operate under their benefits, and consider whether there is an adequate alternative before engaging in circumvention under [an] exemption. The Register noted that screen capture technology should only be employed when it is reasonably represented, and offered to the public, as enabling the reproduction of motion picture content after such content has been lawfully decrypted—that is, when it is offered as a noncircumventing technology. And, finally, users of the limited exemptions should be prepared to defend their activities in light of the alternatives as they exist at the time of their use of the exemption, including any further innovations in screen capture or other technologies that may produce higher-quality results than were obtainable as of the Register's Recommendation.

77 Fed.Reg. at 65,269–70.

> The most recent rulemaking also exempted

> > Literary works, distributed electronically, that are protected by technological measures which either prevent the enabling of read-aloud functionality or interfere with screen readers or other applications or assistive technologies in the following instances:

> > > (i) When a copy of such a work is lawfully obtained by a blind or other person with a disability, as such a person is defined in 17 U.S.C. 121; provided, however, the rights owner is remunerated, as appropriate, for the price of the mainstream copy of the work as made available to the general public through customary channels . . .

37 C.F.R. § 201.40(b)(1)(i). This exemption is similar to one granted in the 2006 and 2010 rulemakings, which had concluded "that making an ebook accessible to blind and visually impaired persons is a noninfringing use," 75 Fed.Reg. at 43,837. But while the previous rulemakings had focused on whether "*all* existing ebook editions of the work" contained access controls, in the current proceeding the Register noted that the development of multiple ebook platforms created a different problem:

> Proponents cited . . . *The Mill River Recluse* by Darcie Chan, ebook editions of which are available in each of the three major ebook stores. Only the iBookstore edition is accessible, however. An individual with a print disability would thus be required to have an iPhone, iPad, or other Apple device in order to access the book. . . . [T]here are often substantial costs associated with owning dedicated reading devices, and there are inefficiencies associated with having to own more than one such device.

77 Fed.Reg. at 65,262–63. The Register emphasized that the "lawfully obtained copy" condition ensures that those with a print disability "have access through the open market, while also ensuring that rights owners receive appropriate remuneration." 77 Fed.Reg. at 65,263.

A third category of exemption allows circumvention of motion pictures and audiovisual works, either on CSS-protected DVDs or in protected online formats, in order to obtain embedded information embedded necessary to develop players capable of providing captions or descriptive audio to accompany the work for those with visual or auditory impairments. 37 C.F.R. § 201.40(b)(8). The Register concluded that the evidence demonstrated that a substantial amount of content was distributed without captioning or descriptive audio, and that circumvention to obtain timing information embedded in copies of the works "did not implicate the copyrighted content itself, but only certain non-protectable information *about* the work." 77 Fed.Reg. at 65,271.

The two final exemptions deal with cellular telephones and carry forward to some extent exemptions adopted in prior proceedings. The first addresses the ability of a "smartphone" user to run software on her phone, and deals with circumvention where needed to enable lawfully obtained software applications to interoperate with the phone's operating system. The exemption is directed at, for example, the practice colloquially known as "jailbreaking," which allows an iPhone user to run an application on her iPhone even if Apple has not approved the application. In 2010, the Register concluded that "when one jailbreaks a smartphone in order to make the operating system on that phone interoperable with an independently created application that has not been approved by the maker of the smartphone or the maker of its operating system, the modifications that are made purely for the purpose of such interoperability are fair uses," and noted case decisions and Congressional enactments that "reflect a judgment that interoperability is favored." 75 Fed.Reg. at 43,830. In the current rulemaking, the Register concluded that the factual record and legal landscape was substantially the same as it had been two years earlier, and supported renewing the exemption for

> [c]omputer programs that enable wireless telephone handsets to execute lawfully obtained software applications, where circumvention is accomplished for the sole purpose of enabling interoperability of such applications with computer programs on the telephone handset.

37 C.F.R. § 201.40(b)(2); 77 Fed.Reg. at 65,264. The Register concluded, however, that the record did not support extending the exemption to include "tablets," as had been proposed, in large part because those proposing the extension had not sufficiently defined the term "tablet."

The final, cellular phone-related exemption is designed to allow cell phone owners to "unlock" their phones in order to switch networks, and addresses a different kind of anticircumvention problem. The other exemptions and their predecessors arose in the context of a statutory scheme that was working as designed to protect works of authorship, where the design acknowledges the potential for encroachment on noninfringing uses, and accordingly, through the triennial rulemaking process, builds in its own safeguards against inflexibility. The need for the cell phone exception arose because of arguable misuse of the anticircumvention protections to achieve a goal the statute was not designed to achieve.

Like the producers of garage doors and printer cartridges in the *Chamberlain* and *Lexmark* cases, discussed *supra*, proprietors of wireless networks appear to be bootstrapping access to their network service to protection of the technological measure that controls access to the software which causes the cell phone to function in connection with the service. The courts in the garage door and printer cartridge cases pierced through the veil of the access-controlled computer programs, correctly perceiving the plaintiffs' commercial objective to be control over use of a utilitarian device, not control over enjoyment of copyrightable expression. However, a cell phone operating system is complex software, which surely contains some minimally original expression that has not merged with its function (conditions perhaps not met in the printer and garage door cases). Therefore, it is a "work protected under this title," whose associated access control may not be circumvented under § 1201(a)(1). In general, the more elaborate the computer program, the more a prohibition on circumventing a technological measure that controls access to that program seems consonant at least with the statutory text, albeit not at all with its purpose. As a result, Copyright Office intervention through declaration of an anticircumvention exception may have been needed to parry such attempts to leverage control over access to computer programs into control over use of utilitarian articles or services.

The 2006 and 2010 Rulemakings therefore each granted a similar exemption covering computer programs that enable used wireless phones to connect to a wireless network, when the owner of the computer program initiates the circumvention solely to connect to a wireless network. In the 2010 Rulemaking, the Register concluded that "unlocking a mobile phone to be used on another wireless network does not ordinarily constitute copyright infringement," but that "mobile phone locks prevent consumers from legally accessing alternative wireless networks with the phone of their choice." 75 Fed.Reg. at 43,830–31. In reviewing the statutory factors to be considered in granting an exemption (§ 1201(a)(1)(C)(i)–(iv)), the Register concluded that the first four weighed neither in favor or against.

> Moreover, because it appears that the opposition to designating the proposed class is based primarily on the desires of wireless carriers to preserve an existing business model that has little if anything to do with protecting works of authorship, it is appropriate to address the additional factor ("such other factors as the Librarian considers appropriate") set forth in Section 1201(a)(1)(C)(v). It seems clear that the primary purpose of the

locks is to keep consumers bound to their existing networks, rather than to protect the rights of copyright owners in their capacity as copyright owners. This observation is not a criticism of the mobile phone industry's business plans and practices, which may well be justified for reasons having nothing to do with copyright law and policy, but simply a recognition of existing circumstances. [But] there appear to be no copyright-based reasons why circumvention under these circumstances should not be permitted . . .

Id. at 43,831.

The 2012 Rulemaking, however, resulted in a narrower exemption. The Register concluded that for new cell phones, circumvention was not needed because there is "a wide array of unlocked phone options available to consumers" and "there is a wide range of alternatives from which consumers may choose in order to obtain an unlocked wireless phone." 77 Fed.Reg. at 65,265. The Register therefore concluded that the exemption was only warranted for "legacy" phones—those acquired prior to the exemption's effective date (October 26, 2012) or within 90 days thereafter—and only if the operator of the network to which the phone is locked "has failed to unlock it within a reasonable period of time following a request by the owner" of the phone. 37 C.F.R. § 201.40(b)(3).

Some in Congress were dissatisfied with the more limited exemption, and several bills were introduced to expand it. In December 2013, the Federal Communications Commission announced that it had reached an agreement with the leading cell phone industry group, CTIA—The Wireless Association, to add provisions on cell phone unlocking to the group's Consumer Code for Wireless Service, the signatories to which cover nearly 97% of wireless subscribers in the United States. The principles agreed to provide that:

- each carrier will clearly post on their websites their policies regarding mobile phone unlocking;

- carriers will unlock postpaid wireless devices on consumer request or provide consumers with information on how to do it themselves;

- carriers will unlock prepaid wireless devices, on consumer request, no later than one year after initial activation;

- carriers will clearly notify consumers when their devices are eligible for unlocking or automatically unlock them with no additional fees;

- carriers will respond to consumer requests to unlock eligible phones within two days of the request; and

- carriers will unlock mobile devices for deployed military personnel.

Bryce Baschuk, *FCC Pens Voluntary Agreement for Wireless Industry to Permit Mobile Phone Unlocking*, 87 PATENT, TRADEMARK & COPYRIGHT JOURNAL (BNA) 371 (2013). The signatories agreed to implement three of the six standards by May 2014, and the remaining three by February 2015. *See generally* CTIA, *Consumer Code for Wireless Service*, at http://www.ctia.org/policy-initiatives/voluntary-guidelines/consumer-code-for-wireless-service; Federal Communications Commission, *Mobile*

Phone and Device Unlocking FAQs, at http://www.fcc.gov/device-unlocking-faq.

Congressional dissatisfaction remained, and in August 2014, the Unlocking Consumer Choice and Wireless Competition Act became law. Pub. L. 113–144. Among other provisions, the act repealed the exemption adopted in the 2012 Rulemaking and replaced it with the broader 2010 exemption, and required the Register and the Librarian to determine, in the next triennial rulemaking, "whether to extend the exemption . . . to include any other category of wireless devices in addition to wireless telephone handsets." In addition, the Act provided that circumvention permitted under a Section 1201 rulemaking to allow wireless devices to connect to a wireless network may be initiated not only by the device's owner, but also by someone authorized by the owner.

The Copyright Office began conducting the sixth 1201 Rulemaking with a notice of inquiry published in September 2014, and a final rule is expected in October 2015. See http://copyright.gov/1201/ for more details.

2.   COPYRIGHT MANAGEMENT INFORMATION

a.   WHAT CONSTITUTES PROTECTED COPYRIGHT MANAGEMENT INFORMATION?

Page 1124. Replace the citation for *Murphy* with "650 F.3d 295 (3d Cir. 2011)".

b.   WHERE MUST COPYRIGHT MANAGEMENT INFORMATION APPEAR IN ORDER TO BE PROTECTED?

Page 1132. Add after *BanxCorp v. Costco Wholesale Corp.*:

Personal Keepsakes, Inc. v. Personalizationmall.com, 101 U.S.P.Q.2d 1855 (N.D.Ill. 2012). Personal Keepsakes, a website for personalized gifts and knickknacks, alleged that its competitor Personalizationmall.com copied poems from its website and displayed them on the competitor's own site. The plaintiff argued that the defendant had, by placing copyright notices on the parts of its own site that contained the allegedly infringing poems (thereby attributing to itself the authorship of plaintiff's poems), supplied false CMI in violation of § 1202. While the court held that plaintiff's assertion that defendant's placement of a copyright notice directly within the title of one of the allegedly copied poems stated a claim for relief under the DMCA, it also ruled that the more remote location of a copyright notice relative to the other allegedly copied poems did not "convey" the CMI "with" the other alleged infringements: "If a general copyright notice appears on an entirely different webpage than the work at issue, then that CMI is not 'conveyed' with the work and no claim will lie under the DMCA." In requiring that the false CMI be "conveyed with" the infringing works, is the court reading "conveyed *in connection with*" out of the statute? If, contrary to the court's ruling, the statute does leave room for more distant placement, how many more clicks can the website require to access the CMI, before a court should decline to find a connection between the work and the "conveyance" of its CMI to the end user?

C. OVERENFORCEMENT: MISUSE

Page 1141. Add new Questions 4 and 5:

4.   Apple Computer licenses its Mac OS X software subject to the condition that the licensee not install, use, or run it on a non-Apple computer. Psystar made and installed copies of the operating system on its "Open Computers," which it sold to the public. In Apple's ensuing infringement action, Psystar defends on grounds of copyright misuse, contending that Apple's attempt through its licensing agreements to bar use of the Apple software on non-Apple computers impermissibly extends the reach of Apple's copyright. Recall that, in the Ninth Circuit, software distributed subject to a license may not be considered "sold," so that the first sale doctrine does not apply. *See Vernor v. Autodesk, supra* Chapter 6.C.2, in the main casebook. Does the licensing agreement nonetheless restrict competition in a manner triggering the misuse doctrine? *See Apple Inc. v. Psystar*, 658 F.3d 1150 (9th Cir. 2011).

CHAPTER 10

FEDERAL PREEMPTION OF STATE LAW

A. STATE LAWS RESTRICTING COPYING

Page 1147. In the second paragraph, replace the *Montz* citation with "649 F.3d 975 (9th Cir. 2011) (en banc)".

C. COPYRIGHT PREEMPTION UNDER SECTION 301 OF THE 1976 ACT

2. RIGHTS EQUIVALENT TO COPYRIGHT

a. MISAPPROPRIATION

Page 1185. Replace the *Barclays Capital* citation with "650 F.3d 876 (2d Cir. 2011)".

b. CONTRACT

Page 1198. Replace the *Montz* citation with "649 F.3d 975 (9th Cir. 2011) (en banc)".

Page 1207. Renumber Questions 3 and 4 as 4 and 5. Add new Questions 3 and 6:

3. *Montz* holds that claims of breach of promise to pay based on implied-in-fact contracts to compensate the idea-submitter for the use of her idea are not preempted under section 301. What about a *quantum meruit* claim arising out of an alleged implied-in-law contract to compensate the creator of a work of authorship for the use of her work? Compare *Design Data Corp. v. Unigate Enterprise, Inc.*, 105 U.S.P.Q.2d 1718 (N.D.Cal. 2013) (software program) with *Forest Park Pictures v. Universal Television Network, Inc.*, 683 F.3d 424 (2d Cir. 2012) (television series treatment).

6. Alice Author's publishing contract provides that "In the event that litigation is instituted with regard to this Agreement, the prevailing party shall be entitled to its costs of the suit, including reasonable attorney's fees." Alice subsequently prevailed in a copyright infringement suit against her publisher in which she alleged that the publisher had exceeded the scope of the contract by licensing the production of unauthorized derivative works. Because the copyright in Alice's work was not registered prior to the infringement, she did not qualify for a statutory award of attorneys' fees. Instead she claimed entitlement to attorneys' fees on the basis of the contract. Her publisher asserts that the Copyright Act preempts the application of the asserted contractual entitlement to attorneys' fees. How should the court rule? See *Ryan v. Editions Limited West, Inc.*, 786 F.3d 754 (9th Cir. 2015). Cf. *Rano v. Sipa Press, Inc.*, 987 F.2d 580 (9th Cir. 1993) (discussed and criticized *infra* main casebook at 1222).

3.   A SUGGESTED PREEMPTION ANALYSIS

Page 1224. Add new Question 8:

5.   Aereo, an Internet start-up company, takes broadcast television signals for New York-area television stations and retransmits them over the Internet to Aereo subscribers as described *supra*, Chapter 6.D.2., page 142, this Supplement. Plaintiff television stations allege, in addition to federal copyright infringement, unfair competition under New York law, claiming that "by commercially exploiting Plaintiffs' programming and broadcasting infrastructure without authorization," Aereo is "unfairly exploiting Plaintiffs' property interests in their audiovisual works for Aereo's own commercial benefit and in bad faith." Aereo has moved to dismiss the state law claim as preempted under section 301, on the ground that a state law unfair competition claim founded on the *private* performance of copyrighted works seeks to vindicate rights that fall into the general scope of the exclusive rights created by the Copyright Act. Is a claim arising out of unauthorized private performances "equivalent to" a right under section 106(4)? *See WNET v. Aereo, Inc.*, 871 F.Supp.2d 281 (S.D.N.Y. 2012).

CHAPTER 11

INTERNATIONAL DIMENSIONS OF COPYRIGHT

D. U.S.-BASED COPYRIGHT ACTIONS WITH AN INTERNATIONAL DIMENSION

1. PROTECTION OF ALIEN AUTHORS

Page 1239. In Question 4, replace the *Kernal Records* citation with "794 F.Supp.2d 1355 (S.D.Fla. 2011)".

Page 1241. In the last paragraph, replace the *Kernal Records* citation with "794 F.Supp.2d 1355 (S.D.Fla. 2011)".

Page 1243. Insert after carryover paragraph:

The Eleventh Circuit affirmed, 694 F.3d 1294 (11th Cir. 2012), holding that "Kernel cannot demonstrate that *Acidjazzed Evening* is a foreign work exempt from registration." The court nonetheless determined that the district court erred in characterizing the dissemination of plaintiff's work as "Internet publication."

> [T]o proceed with a copyright infringement action, a plaintiff that claims his published work is exempt from the registration requirement must prove that the first publication occurred abroad. See 17 U.S.C. §§ 101, 411(a). This requires the plaintiff to first prove a publication: that the method, extent, and purpose of the distribution meets the Copyright Act's requirements for publication. Once the plaintiff has proven publication, he must then prove that the publication was, in fact, the first publication, and that the geographic extent of this first publication diverges from the statutory definition of a "United States work."

V. TECHNOLOGY REVIEW

. . .

> To determine the countries to which these other online methods distribute material would require additional evidence, such as the country of residence of the users of a certain restricted website or peer-to-peer network, or the recipient of a certain e-mail. For example, if a restricted website has subscribers only in the United States, Germany, and Japan, placing a file on that website would not make the file simultaneously available to a worldwide audience. Similarly, if the software for a peer-to-peer network was downloaded only in Canada, Egypt, and the Netherlands, offering a file for download on the peer-to-peer network would not make the file simultaneously available to a worldwide audience. Finally, if the recipients of an e-mail are all located in Mexico, sending a

file by e-mail attachment would not make the file simultaneously available to a worldwide audience. Each of these "online" distribution methods utilizes the Internet, but none of them can be presumed to result in simultaneous, worldwide distribution.

Throughout this case, the district court (as well as the parties) confounded "the Internet" and "online" with "World Wide Web" and "website." Because of the strict temporal and geographic requirements contained in the statutory definition of "United States work," conflating these terms had a profound impact on the district court's evidentiary analysis. By confounding "Internet" with "website," the district court erroneously assumed that all "Internet publication" must occur on the "World Wide Web" or a "website." The district court then erroneously assumed all "Internet publication" results in simultaneous, worldwide distribution.

2. PERSONAL JURISDICTION OVER OFFSHORE ACTORS ALLEGEDLY INFRINGING U.S. COPYRIGHTS

Pages 1246–1249. At the direction of the instructor, either (a) replace the *Penguin Group (USA) Inc. v. American Buddha* opinion and the QUESTION that follows it with the *Mavrix Photo* opinion that follows or (b) at page 1249 after the QUESTION, add the following casenote and the *Mavrix Photo* opinion:

On remand, *Penguin Group (USA) Inc. v. American Buddha*, 106 U.S.P.Q.2d 1306 (S.D.N.Y. 2013), however, the Southern District of New York held that defendant did not derive substantial revenue from interstate commerce "because it 'operates on a strictly eleemosynary model' and has no revenue whatsoever." The court acknowledged that:

> It is true that Internet companies can operate without any costs or even revenue. It is also true that an online library such as American Buddha's is indeed far from an industry with a "local character;" and that its reach, like that of other Internet sites, is inherently global in nature. Nonetheless, the statutory language remains the same, requiring proof of "substantial" revenue to apply New York's long-arm statute.

Thus, while the New York Court of Appeals interpreted the statutory criterion of "injury within the state" flexibly in light of the characteristics of the Internet, the Southern District of New York did not find the New York long-arm statute permitted a lower threshold of revenue substantiality, even though the Internet enables a non-profit (or unprofitable) defendant to wreak substantial injury on New York businesses. Unless the S.D.N.Y.'s reading of the long-arm statute is reversed, the Court of Appeals' expansive interpretation will apply only to commercial actors on the Internet, and perhaps only to commercial actors whose for-profit endeavors prove successful.

Mavrix Photo v. Brand Technologies

647 F.3d 1218 (9th Cir. 2011).

■ W. FLETCHER, CIRCUIT JUDGE.

Mavrix Photo, Inc. ("Mavrix") sued Brand Technologies, Inc. and its CEO, Brad Mandell (collectively, "Brand"), in federal district court for the Central District of California, alleging that Brand infringed Mavrix's copyright by posting its copyrighted photos on its web-site. Brand moved to dismiss for lack of personal jurisdiction. *See* Fed. R. Civ. P. 12(b)(2). The district court denied Mavrix's motion for jurisdictional discovery and granted Brand's motion to dismiss. We reverse. We hold that Brand is not subject to general personal jurisdiction in California, but that its contacts with California are sufficiently related to the dispute in this case that it is subject to specific personal jurisdiction.

I. Background

Mavrix, a Florida corporation with its principal place of business in Miami, is a celebrity photo agency. Mavrix pays photographers for candid photos of celebrities. Its primary business is licensing and selling those photos to purveyors of celebrity news such as *People* and *Us Weekly* magazines. Many of the celebrities whom Mavrix photographs live and work in Southern California. Mavrix keeps a Los Angeles office, employs Los Angeles-based photographers, has a registered agent for service of process in California, and pays fees to the California Franchise Tax Board.

Brand, an Ohio corporation with its principal place of business in Toledo, operates a website called celebrity-gossip.net. As its name suggests, the website covers popular personalities in the entertainment industry and features photo galleries, videos, and short articles (for example, . . . "Shiloh Jolie-Pitt Named Most Influential Infant"). The website has several interactive features. . . . The website is very popular. When this litigation began, Alexa.com, an Internet tracking service, ranked celebrity-gossip.net as number 3,622 out of approximately 180 million websites world-wide based on traffic. By comparison, the national news website MSNBC.com was then ranked number 2,521. In its marketing materials, Brand claims that celebrity-gossip.net currently receives more than 12 million unique U.S. visitors and 70 million U.S. page views per month. . . . The record does not reflect how many of the website's visitors are California residents.

Like any large media entity, celebrity-gossip.net courts a national audience, not restricted to California. However, the website has some specific ties to California. Brand makes money from third-party advertisements for jobs, hotels, and vacations in California. The website also features a "Ticket Center," which is a link to the website of a third-party vendor that sells tickets to nationwide events. Some of these events are in California. Brand has agreements with several California businesses. A California Internet advertising agency solicits buyers and places advertisements on celebrity-gossip.net. A California wireless provider designed and hosts on its servers a version of celebrity-gossip.net accessible to mobile phone users. A California firm designed the website and performs site maintenance. Finally, Brand has entered a "link-sharing" agreement with a California-based national news site, according to which each site agrees to promote the other's top stories.

However, Brand has no offices, real property, or staff in California, is not licensed to do business in California, and pays no California taxes.

In 2008, a photographer working for Mavrix shot thirty-five pictures of Stacy Ferguson and Josh Duhamel while the couple was bathing, sunning, and jet skiing in the Bahamas. Ferguson, better known by her stage name Fergie, is a singer in the hip-hop group the Black Eyed Peas. The group has sold some 56 million records in the last decade . . . Ferguson's husband Duhamel is an actor who has appeared, most notably, in the trilogy of Transformers movies. . . . Mavrix registered its copyright in the photos and posted them on its website. Mavrix alleges that shortly thereafter Brand reposted the photos on celebrity-gossip.net in violation of Mavrix's copyright. Mavrix alleges that in doing so Brand destroyed the market value of the photos. . . .

III. Discussion

A. General Jurisdiction

[The court ruled that Brand lacked the "substantial, continuous and systematic" contacts with California sufficient to justify an assertion of general jurisdiction. Although Mavrix contended that Brand's website made it a continuous presence in California, the court determined that maintenance of a "highly interactive website," while pertinent to specific jurisdiction, was inadequate for general jurisdiction.]

. . . Brand's operation of an interactive website—even a "highly interactive" website—does not confer general jurisdiction. Mavrix relies on *Zippo Mfg. Co. v. Zippo Dot Com, Inc.*, 952 F. Supp. 1119 (W.D. Pa. 1997), but that reliance, in the context of general jurisdiction, is misplaced. The court in *Zippo* developed a "sliding scale" test to characterize the "nature and quality of commercial activity that an entity conducts over the Internet." At one end of the scale were active sites "where a defendant clearly does business over the Internet" and "enters into contracts with residents of a foreign jurisdiction that involve the knowing and repeated transmission of computer files over the Internet," which support jurisdiction. At the other end were passive sites "where a defendant has simply posted information on an Internet Website which is accessible to users in foreign jurisdictions," and which do not support jurisdiction. Id. Under the *Zippo* analysis, the availability of jurisdiction is determined by examining the "level of interactivity and commercial nature of the exchange . . . that occurs on the Web site."

We have followed *Zippo. See, e.g., Cybersell, Inc. v. Cybersell, Inc.*, 130 F.3d 414, 418–19 (9th Cir. 1997). But *Zippo*'s sliding scale test was formulated in the context of a specific jurisdiction inquiry. The level of interactivity of a nonresident defendant's website provides limited help in answering the distinct question whether the defendant's forum contacts are sufficiently substantial, continuous, and systematic to justify general jurisdiction. *See, e.g., Lakin v. Prudential Sec., Inc.*, 348 F.3d 704, 712 (8th Cir. 2003) ("Under the *Zippo* test, it is possible for a Web site to be very interactive, but to have no quantity of contacts. In other words, the contacts would be continuous, but not substantial. This is untenable in a general jurisdiction analysis."); *Revell v. Lidov*, 317 F.3d 467, 471 (5th Cir. 2002) (*Zippo* test "is not well adapted to the general jurisdiction inquiry, because even repeated contacts with forum residents by a foreign defendant may not constitute the requisite substantial, continuous and systematic contacts required for a finding of general jurisdiction"); *accord* 4A Charles Alan Wright & Arthur R. Miller, Federal Practice & Procedure § 1073.1, at 331 (3d ed. 2002) ("[T]he *Zippo* case's sliding scale approach should be of little value in a general jurisdiction analysis.").

Many of the features on which Mavrix relies to show *Zippo* interactivity—commenting, receiving email newsletters, voting in polls, uploading user-generated content—are standard attributes of many websites. Such features require a minimal amount of engineering expense and effort on the part of a site's owner and do not signal a non-resident defendant's intent to "sit down and make itself at home" in the forum by cultivating deep, persistent ties with forum residents. To permit the exercise of general jurisdiction based on the accessibility in the forum of a non-resident interactive website would expose most large media entities to nationwide general jurisdiction. That result would be inconsistent with the constitutional requirement that "the continuous corporate operations within a state" be "so substantial and of such a nature as to justify suit against [the nonresident defendant] on causes of action arising from dealings entirely distinct from those activities." *International Shoe*, 326 U.S. at 318.

In sum, Brand's contacts with California, even considered collectively, do not justify the exercise of general jurisdiction.

B. Specific Jurisdiction

In the alternative, Mavrix argues that Brand has sufficient "minimum contacts" with California arising out of, or related to, its actions in reposting the photos of Ferguson and Duhamel to justify the exercise of specific jurisdiction. We analyze specific jurisdiction under a three-prong test:

> (1) The non-resident defendant must *purposefully direct his activities* or consummate some transaction with the forum or resident thereof; *or* perform some act by which he *purposefully avails himself* of the privilege of conducting activities in the forum, thereby invoking the benefits and protections of its laws; (2) the claim must be one which arises out of or relates to the defendant's forum-related activities; and (3) the exercise of jurisdiction must comport with fair play and substantial justice, i.e. it must be reasonable.

Schwarzenegger, 374 F.3d at 802. . . .

Only the first prong is at issue here. As to the second prong, Mavrix's claim of copyright infringement arises out of Brand's publication of the photos on a website accessible to users in the forum state. As to the third prong, Brand does not argue that the exercise of jurisdiction would be unreasonable. . . .

The first prong of the specific jurisdiction test refers to both purposeful direction and purposeful availment. We have explained that in cases involving tortious conduct, we most often employ a purposeful direction analysis. The "effects" test, which is based on the Supreme Court's decision in *Calder v. Jones*, 465 U.S. 783 (1984), requires that "the defendant allegedly must have (1) committed an intentional act, (2) expressly aimed at the forum state, (3) causing harm that the defendant knows is likely to be suffered in the forum state." *Brayton Purcell,* 606

F.3d at 1128 (quoting *Yahoo!*, 433 F.3d at 1206). Because Mavrix has alleged copyright infringement, a tort-like cause of action, purposeful direction "is the proper analytical framework."

. . .

First, we conclude that Brand "committed an intentional act." There is no question that it acted intentionally reposting the allegedly infringing photos of Ferguson and Duhamel.

Second, we conclude that Brand "expressly aimed at the forum state." In prior cases, we have struggled with the question whether tortious conduct on a nationally accessible website is expressly aimed at any, or all, of the forums in which the website can be viewed. On the one hand, we have made clear that "maintenance of a passive website alone cannot satisfy the express aiming prong." *Brayton Purcell,* 606 F.3d at 1129. On the other, we have held that "operating even a passive website in conjunction with 'something more'—conduct directly targeting the forum—is sufficient." *Rio Props.,* 284 F.3d at 1020. In determining whether a nonresident defendant has done "something more," we have considered several factors, including the interactivity of the defendant's website; the geographic scope of the defendant's commercial ambitions; and whether the defendant "individually targeted" a plaintiff known to be a forum resident.

In this case, we find most salient the fact that Brand used Mavrix's copyrighted photos as part of its exploitation of the California market for its own commercial gain. The Court's decision in *Keeton* is directly relevant. The plaintiff in *Keeton* was a New York resident. She sued Hustler magazine, an Ohio corporation, for libel in New Hampshire based on the circulation in New Hampshire of copies of the magazine that contained the allegedly libelous material. The plaintiff sued in New Hampshire in order to take advantage of the state's unusually long statute of limitations, even though she had virtually no connection with the forum. Hustler had a circulation of 10,000–15,000 copies per month in New Hampshire, but no other contacts with the forum. The Court concluded that Hustler's

> regular circulation of magazines in the forum State is sufficient to support an exercise of jurisdiction in a libel action based on the contents of the magazine. . . . Such regular monthly sales of thousands of magazines cannot by any stretch of the imagination be characterized as random, isolated, or fortuitous. It is, therefore, unquestionable that New Hampshire jurisdiction over a complaint based on those contacts would ordinarily satisfy the requirement of the Due Process Clause that a State's assertion of personal jurisdiction over a nonresident defendant be predicated on 'minimum contacts' between the defendant and the State.

[465 U.S. at 773–774.] The Court acknowledged that New Hampshire accounted for a share of Hustler's overall business that was too small to support the exercise of general jurisdiction, but noted that Hustler was "carrying on a 'part of its general business' in New Hampshire, and that is sufficient to support jurisdiction when the cause of action arises out of the very activity being conducted, in part, in New Hampshire." Finally, the Court specified that because Hustler has continuously and deliberately exploited the New Hampshire market, it must reasonably anticipate being haled into court there in a libel action based on the contents of its magazine. . . . [Hustler] produces a national publication aimed at a nationwide audience. There is no unfairness in calling it to answer for the contents of that publication wherever a substantial number of copies are regularly sold and distributed.

Id. at 781.

As did Hustler in distributing its magazine in New Hampshire, Brand "continuously and deliberately exploited" the California market for its website. Brand makes money by selling advertising space on its website to third-party advertisers: the more visitors there are to the site, the more hits that are made on the advertisements; the more hits that are made on the advertisements, the more money that is paid by the advertisers to Brand. A substantial number of hits to Brand's website came from California residents. One of the ways we know this is that some of the third-party advertisers on Brand's website had advertisements directed to Californians. In this context, it is immaterial whether the third-party advertisers or Brand targeted California residents. The fact that the advertisements targeted California residents indicates that Brand knows—either actually or constructively—about its California user base, and that it exploits that base for commercial gain by selling space on its website for advertisements. . . .

The record does not show that Brand marketed its website in California local media. But it is clear from the record that Brand operated a very popular website with a specific focus on the California-centered celebrity and entertainment industries. Based on the website's subject matter, as well as the size and commercial value of the California market, we conclude that Brand anticipated, desired, and achieved a substantial California viewer base. This audience is an integral component of Brand's business model and its profitability. As in *Keeton*, it does not violate due process to hold Brand answerable in a California court for the contents of a website whose economic value turns, in significant measure, on its appeal to Californians.

The applicability of *Keeton* to this case depends on two similarities between celebrity-gossip.net and Hustler magazine. First, both were large publications that sought and attracted nationwide audiences. Both publications could count on reaching consumers in all fifty states. Second, both publications cultivated their nationwide audiences for commercial gain. Accordingly, neither could characterize the consumption of its products in any state as "random," "fortuitous," or "attenuated." Rather, consumption was a predictable consequence of their business models. The same would not necessarily be true, for example, of a local newspaper, an individual, or an unpaid blogger who posted an allegedly actionable comment or photo to a website accessible in all fifty states, but who could not be as certain as Brand or Hustler that his actions would be so widely observed and who did not seek commercial gain from users outside his locality. Not all material placed on the Internet is, solely by virtue of its universal accessibility, expressly aimed at every state in which it is accessed. But where, as here, a website with national viewership and scope appeals to, and profits from, an audience in a particular state, the site's operators can be said to have "expressly aimed" at that state.

We acknowledge the burden that our conclusion may impose on some popular commercial websites. But we note that the alternative proposed by Brand's counsel at oral argument—that Mavrix can sue Brand only in Ohio or Florida—would substantially undermine the "interests . . . of the plaintiff in proceeding with the cause in the plaintiff's forum of choice." *Kulko v. Superior Court of Cal.*, 436 U.S. 84, 92 (1978). Brand's theory of jurisdiction would allow corporations whose websites exploit a national market to defeat jurisdiction in states where those websites generate substantial profits from local consumers. We also note that the "expressly aimed" requirement is a necessary but not sufficient condition for jurisdiction. In order to establish specific jurisdiction, a plaintiff must also show that jurisdictionally significant harm was suffered in the forum state.

We therefore turn to the question of harm, the third element of the *Calder* effects test. We conclude that Brand has "caus[ed] harm that [it] knows is likely to be suffered in the forum state." In determining the situs of a corporation's injury, "[o]ur precedents recognize that in appropriate circumstances a corporation can suffer economic harm both where the bad acts occurred and where the corporation has its principal place of business." *Dole Food Co., Inc. v. Watts,* 303 F.3d 1104, 1113 (9th Cir. 2002). "[J]urisdictionally sufficient harm may be suffered in multiple forums." *Id.* Mavrix alleges that, by republishing the photos of Ferguson and Duhamel, Brand interfered with Mavrix's exclusive ownership of the photos and destroyed their market value. The economic loss caused by the intentional infringement of a plaintiff's copyright is foreseeable. It was foreseeable that this economic loss would be inflicted not only in Florida, Mavrix's principal place of business, but also in California. A substantial part of the photos' value was based on the fact that a significant number of Californians would have bought publications such as *People* and *Us Weekly* in order to see the photos. Because Brand's actions destroyed this California-based value, a jurisdictionally significant amount of Mavrix's economic harm took place in California.

In sum, we conclude that Mavrix has presented a prima facie case of purposeful direction by Brand sufficient to survive a motion to dismiss for lack of personal jurisdiction.

QUESTIONS

1.   So long as the website is "directed" to users in every State (that is, seeks to attract users from all States), may the copyright infringement plaintiff assert jurisdiction in every State, or only in the State of the plaintiff's headquarters (where the economic impact of the infringement will be greatest)? If "foreseeability" of economic harm in that State is required, must the defendant know where the plaintiff's headquarters are?

2.   Defendant is an Indian software company that makes and distributes software in India that allegedly infringes the copyrights in plaintiff's software. Plaintiff, a U.S. software developer, claims that the defendant accessed an unauthorized copy of the software from its U.S. co-defendant's U.S.-based website and, through frequent visits to the co-defendant's site, developed a derivative work for use in India. Do the Indian defendant's U.S.-

related activities meet the minimum contacts standard sufficient to found personal jurisdiction where the U.S. co-defendant is located? See *Rhapsody Solutions LLC v. Cryogenic Vessel Alternatives, Inc.*, 106 U.S.P.Q.2d 1219 (S.D.Tex. 2013).

3. Defendant, who resides in the U.K., sent a take-down notice to a California-based server hosting a blog which defendant asserted contained infringing content. Plaintiffs allege that the defendant's notices constituted willful misrepresentation under section 512(f), because defendant had no copyright interest in the blog's contents, but rather objected to the blog's message. Does the sending of take-down notices to a California host service provider suffice to establish specific personal jurisdiction over the foreign national defendant? See *Automattic, Inc. v. Steiner*, 2015 WL 1022655 (N.D. Cal., March 2, 2015).

4. [For instructors choosing to include both *American Buddha* and *Mavrix*:] The New York Court of Appeals in *American Buddha* applied the New York Civil Practice Law and Rules; the 9th Circuit in *Mavrix* applied constitutional due process principles. Do the different sources produce different analyses? Differences in the scope of outcome?

4. WHEN U.S. COURTS EXERCISE JURISDICTION OVER CLAIMS PRESENTING EXTRATERRITORIAL ELEMENTS, WHAT LAW APPLIES—

a. —TO DETERMINE COPYRIGHT OWNERSHIP OF A FOREIGN WORK

Page 1264. Add new Question 5 following the carryover paragraph:

5. For an extensive inquiry into the copyright law of the source country in order to determine whether the copyright in the work would have belonged to the employer in the work's country of origin, see *Games Workshop v. Chapterhouse Studios*, 105 U.S.P.Q.2d 1524 (N.D.Ill. 2012) (assessing copyright ownership under U.K. copyright law of science fiction war game with figurines).

b. —TO INFRINGEMENTS OCCURRING, AT LEAST IN PART, BEYOND U.S. BORDERS

Pages 1271–1275. Delete *Update Art v. Modiin Publishing, Curb v. MCA*, and *Peter Rosenbaum Photography v. Otto Doosan Mail Order, Ltd.*, and replace with the following:

Shropshire v. Canning, 809 F.Supp.2d 1139 (C.D.Cal. 2011). Elmo Shropshire is a co-owner of the musical composition copyright in the immortal seasonal anthem "Grandma Got Run Over By A Reindeer." Aubrey Canning, a resident of Canada, uploaded to You Tube and refused to remove an allegedly infringing video incorporating the composition. Canning moved to dismiss Shropshire's U.S. infringement action on the ground that the alleged infringing act—uploading the Grandma video to YouTube—took place in Canada and thus fell outside the reach of the Copyright Act. Because U.S. law does not apply to Canadian infringements, Canning argued the U.S. federal district court lacked subject matter jurisdiction over the claim. The court first ruled that extraterritoriality (or more precisely, the presence of a territorial point of attachment) should be treated as an element of the claim, rather than as a "jurisdictional" issue.

Turning to the extraterritorial applicability of the Copyright Act, courts are split on whether the infringing act must occur wholly within the United States or if the infringing act only must not occur wholly outside of the United States. Put differently, the dispute is whether all parts of the infringing act must take place in the United States, or if it is sufficient that some part of the infringing acts take place in the United States. . . .

The Court finds that in this case, the alleged act of direct copyright infringement—uploading a video from Canada to YouTube's servers in California for display within the United States—constitutes an act of infringement that is not "wholly extraterritorial" to the United States. Those cases holding that the Copyright Act requires at least one infringing act to occur entirely within the United States dealt with situations in which the infringing transmission was authorized or sent from within the U.S. but received and accessed abroad. In this case, however, we face the opposite scenario. The allegedly infringing act in this case began in Canada, where Defendant created his Grandma song video. Had Defendant stopped there, there is no doubt that the strict presumption against extraterritoriality would apply and Plaintiff would not have a claim. As noted in the Court's January 11, 2011 Order: "The creation of the video, however, occurred entirely in Canada, and thus cannot constitute copyright infringement under well-settled law."

The problem is that Defendant did not stop at the mere creation of the Grandma song video in Canada, but instead allegedly uploaded it to YouTube's California servers for display in the United States after agreeing to YouTube's Terms of Service agreement. Thus, according to the allegations in the [complaint], Defendant's direct action led to the creation of a copy of the Grandma video on YouTube's servers in California, and to the subsequent viewing of the video by potentially thousands in the United States.

Tire Engineering and Distribution, LLC v. Shandong Linglong Rubber Company, Ltd.

682 F.3d. 292 (4th Cir. 2012).

■ PER CURIAM:

Alpha, a domestic producer of mining tires, sued Al Dobowi and Linglong, foreign corporations. Alpha alleged that the defendants conspired to steal its tire blueprints, produce infringing tires, and sell them to entities that had formerly purchased products from Alpha. . . . We affirm the district court's judgment that Al Dobowi and Linglong are liable to Alpha under the Copyright Act . . .

[Al Dobowi obtained the blueprints from a former Alpha employee; copies were sent to Linglong in China to manufacture tires from the blueprints. Linglong was aware that the blueprints had been stolen.]

III.

. . .

A.

Appellants first argue that the Copyright Act has no extraterritorial reach. Because the only claims raised by Alpha involve conduct abroad, Appellants maintain that the Copyright Act affords Alpha no remedy. Alternatively, even if the Copyright Act sometimes reaches foreign conduct that flows from a domestic violation, Appellants urge us to consider that foreign conduct only where, unlike here, the domestic violation is not barred by the Copyright Act's three-year statute of limitations.

We hold that Alpha has presented a cognizable claim under the Copyright Act and therefore uphold the jury's finding of liability on that count. We adopt the predicate-act doctrine, which posits that a plaintiff may collect damages from foreign violations of the Copyright Act so long as the foreign conduct stems from a domestic infringement. . . .

1.

As a general matter, the Copyright Act is considered to have no extraterritorial reach. *E.g., Nintendo of Am., Inc. v. Aeropower Co.*, 34 F.3d 246, 249 n.5 (4th Cir. 1994). But courts have recognized a fundamental exception: "when the type of infringement permits further reproduction abroad," a plaintiff may collect damages flowing from the foreign conduct. *Update Art, Inc. v. Modiin Pub., Ltd.*, 843 F.2d 67, 73 (2d Cir. 1988).

This predicate-act doctrine traces its roots to a famous Second Circuit opinion penned by Learned Hand. *See Sheldon v. Metro-Goldwyn Pictures Corp.*, 106 F.2d 45, 52 (2d Cir. 1939). The Second Circuit in *Sheldon* was confronted with an undisputed domestic Copyright Act violation. The defendant had converted the plaintiff's motion picture while in the United States and then exhibited the picture abroad. The court was required to decide whether the damages award could include profits made from foreign exhibition of the film. Answering the question in the affirmative, Judge Hand articulated the framework of the predicate-act doctrine:

> The Culver Company made the negatives in this country, or had them made here, and shipped them abroad, where the positives were produced and exhibited. The negatives were 'records' from which the work could be 'reproduced,' and it was a tort to make them in this country. The plaintiffs acquired an equitable interest in them as soon as they were made, which attached to any profits from their exploitation, whether in the form of money remitted to the United States, or of increase in the value of shares of foreign companies held by the defendants. . . . [A]s soon as any of the profits so realized took the form of property whose situs was in the United States, our law seized upon them and impressed them with a constructive trust, whatever their form.

Id. Once a plaintiff demonstrates a domestic violation of the Copyright Act, then, it may collect damages from foreign violations that are directly linked to the U.S. infringement.

The Second Circuit has reaffirmed the continuing vitality of the predicate-act doctrine. *Update Art*, 843 F.2d at 73. In *Update Art*, the plaintiff owned the rights to distribute and publish a certain graphic art design. Without authorization from the plaintiff, the defendant published the image in an Israeli newspaper. The court reasoned that "the applicability of American copyright laws over the Israeli newspapers depends on the occurrence of a predicate act in the United States." "If the illegal reproduction of the poster occurred in the United States and then was exported to Israel," the court continued, "the magistrate properly could include damages accruing from the Israeli newspapers." But if the predicate act of reproduction occurred outside of the United States, the district court could award no damages from newspaper circulation in Israel.

More recently, the Ninth Circuit embraced the predicate-act doctrine. *Los Angeles News Serv. v. Reuters TV Int'l.*, 149 F.3d 987, 990–92 (9th Cir. 1998). The court endorsed Second Circuit precedent, which it construed as holding that "[r]ecovery of damages arising from overseas infringing uses was allowed because the predicate act of infringement occurring within the United States enabled further reproduction abroad." To invoke the predicate-act doctrine, according to the Ninth Circuit, damages must flow from "extraterritorial exploitation of an infringing act that occurred in the United States." The court distinguished a previous decision, *Subafilms, Ltd. v. MGM-Pathe Commc'ns Co.*, 24 F.3d 1088 (9th Cir. 1994), as controlling only a narrow class of cases dealing with the Copyright Act's "authorization" provision, in which a plaintiff alleges merely a domestic authorization of infringing conduct that otherwise takes place wholly abroad. Such a case presents concerns not relevant to disputes in which a predicate act of infringement—going beyond mere authorization—occurred in the United States. The Ninth Circuit further noted that the predicate-act doctrine does not abrogate a defendant's right to be free from stale claims.

At least two other circuits have recognized the validity of the predicate-act doctrine, even if they have not had occasion to squarely apply it to the facts before them. *Litecubes, LLC v. N. Light Prods., Inc.*, 523 F.3d 1353, 1371 (Fed. Cir. 2008) (endorsing principle that "courts have generally held that the Copyright Act only does not reach activities 'that take place entirely abroad' " (quoting *Subafilms*, 24 F.3d at 1098)); *Liberty Toy Co. v. Fred Silber Co.*, 149 F.3d 1183 (6th Cir. 1998) (unpublished table decision) ("[I]f all the copying or infringement occurred outside the United States, the Copyright Act would not apply. However, as long as some act of infringement occurred in the United States, the Copyright Act applies."

We join our sister circuits that have adopted the predicate-act doctrine. The doctrine strikes an appropriate balance between competing concerns, protecting aggrieved plaintiffs from savvy defendants while also safeguarding a defendant's freedom from stale claims. Absent the predicate-act doctrine, a defendant could convert a plaintiff's intellectual property in the United States, wait for the Copyright Act's three-year statute of limitations to expire, and then reproduce the property abroad with impunity. Such a result would jeopardize intellectual property rights and subvert Congress's goals as engrafted on to the Copyright Act. But lest the doctrine lead to a windfall for plaintiffs and force a defendant to face liability for stale claims, plaintiffs may collect only those damages "suffered during the statutory period for bringing claims, regardless of where they may have been incurred," *Los Angeles News*, 149 F.3d at 992.

2.

Applying the predicate-act doctrine to this case, we conclude that Alpha has presented a valid claim under the Copyright Act. Accordingly, we sustain the jury's finding of liability on that count.

Distilling applicable case law, we find that a plaintiff is required to show a domestic violation of the Copyright Act and damages flowing from foreign exploitation of that infringing act to successfully invoke the predicate-act doctrine. Alpha has shown both. Appellants concede on appeal that Alpha has established a domestic violation of the Copyright Act. While in the United States, Vance [Alpha's former employee] and Al Dobowi unlawfully converted Alpha's blueprints and reproduced them absent authorization. These acts constitute infringing conduct under the Copyright Act. *See Update Art*, 843 F.2d at 73 (concluding there would be an actionable violation if defendant illegally reproduced image while in the United States). And Alpha has demonstrated damages flowing from extraterritorial exploitation of this infringing conduct. Al Dobowi and Linglong used the converted blueprints to produce mining tires almost identical to those of Alpha. They then sold these tires to former customers of Alpha, causing Alpha substantial damage. *See Sheldon*, 106 F.2d at 52 (finding damages flowing from foreign exploitation of infringing act where defendant converted negatives of motion picture in United States and exhibited the film abroad).

Pages 1275–1276. Delete Questions 3 and 5. Renumber Question 4 as Question 3 and add a new Question 4:

4. Should it matter whether the further communications for which a U.S.-made copy is the source include U.S. recipients? What if the Canadian uploaded the "Grandma" song to a California server that allowed access only by Canadians (or by non-U.S. users)? Is the "predicate act" doctrine more or less persuasive when applied to Internet communications?

Page 1279. Insert following PROBLEM:

Notwithstanding the "predicate act" cases and other caselaw applying U.S. copyright law to a multiterritorial alleged infringement, territoriality remains a fundamental principle of international copyright law, even in the U.S., as the following decision illustrates.

Perfect 10, Inc. v. Yandex, NV, 962 F. Supp. 2d 1146 (N.D. Cal. 2013). Perfect10, publisher of "adult" images, alleged that Yandex, a Russian search engine, had violated U.S. copyright law by hosting full-sized copies of user-uploaded infringing Perfect 10 images; and hosting infringing thumbnail-sized copies of Perfect 10 images and linked them to Yandex-created pages that display similar full-sized versions of the images often adjacent to Yandex ads, and that all Yandex pages or hosted sites are accessible in the US. Yandex replied that most of the content was hosted on servers located in Russia, to which the U.S. copyright law did not apply.

A. Servers Outside the United States.

Yandex moves for summary judgment on Perfect 10's direct infringement claims "premised on the 1,474 acts of alleged infringement concerning user-generated content" [i.e. user-uploaded Perfect 10 images] hosted on Yandex's narod.ru, fotki.ru, ya.ru, and moikrug.ru services. Yandex argues that the evidence is undisputed that these Yandex services are, and have always been, hosted on servers in Russia. The "server test" applied by our court of appeals makes the hosting website's computer, rather than the search engine's computer, the situs of direct copyright infringement liability. [Citation.] Therefore, Yandex argues, these foreign-hosted images are extraterritorial and not actionable under the Act. This order agrees.

Perfect 10 does not contest that the servers for these Yandex services are located in Russia. Rather, Perfect 10 objects that fotki.ru and narod.ru (and presumably Yandex's other, similar sites) commit "direct infringement by display." According to Perfect 10, when its images are hosted on servers located in Russia, Yandex violates Perfect 10's "exclusive display right" because users in the United States could download them. Perfect 10 supplies declarations establishing that a United States user *could* download Perfect 10 images from a Yandex server in Russia, but no evidence of *actual* downloads in the United States.

This theory of liability is rejected. Although Perfect 10 cites *Amazon* in support of its argument, nowhere in that decision did our court of appeals endorse the idea that display of a copyrighted image anywhere in the world creates direct copyright liability in the United States merely because the image could be downloaded from a server abroad by someone in the United States. Such a principle would destroy the concept of territoriality inherent in the Copyright Act for works on the internet.

In a more plausible variation of this argument, Perfect 10 points out that when Yandex's servers were located in the United States for a nine-month period, a Yandex.com image search performed by a server in the United States *could have linked* to a Perfect 10 image hosted on a Yandex server in Russia. Perfect 10 argues that Yandex should not escape direct copyright liability by international distribution of its hosting and searching servers.

It is not necessary to address the validity of this theory's merits. It fails for lack of proof. Perfect 10 does not demonstrate that Yandex in fact stored or displayed full-sized copies of the Perfect 10 images on Yandex's United States servers. . . . Perfect 10 only submits that "Yandex suggests it keeps duplicate copies of images on all of its servers . . . so full-size Perfect 10 images *may very well have been* stored on yandex.com's U.S. servers" Perfect 10's speculation that full-size image storage may have occurred in the United States is insufficient at the summary judgment stage, which is the point in litigation to stand and deliver on admissible evidence. Nor is there any evidence of an effort by Yandex to intentionally circumvent copyright liability through clever placement of its servers or through manipulation of the corporate form.

This order accordingly holds that Yandex's hosting of full-sized Perfect 10 images on servers in Russia does not constitute direct copyright infringement in the United States. To this extent, Yandex's motion for partial summary judgment is **Granted**.

APPENDIX A

THE COPYRIGHT ACT OF 1976

Public Law 94–553, 90 Stat. 2541, as amended
through July 1, 2009

TITLE 17—COPYRIGHTS

CHAPTER 1.—SUBJECT MATTER AND SCOPE OF COPYRIGHT

Sec. 101.   Definitions

Except as otherwise provided in this title, as used in this title, the following terms and their variant forms mean the following:

An "anonymous work" is a work on the copies or phonorecords of which no natural person is identified as author.

An "architectural work" is the design of a building as embodied in any tangible medium of expression, including a building, architectural plans, or drawings. The work includes the overall form as well as the arrangement and composition of spaces and elements in the design, but does not include individual standard features.

"Audiovisual works" are works that consist of a series of related images which are intrinsically intended to be shown by the use of machines or devices such as projectors, viewers, or electronic equipment, together with accompanying sounds, if any, regardless of the nature of the material objects, such as films or tapes, in which the works are embodied.

The "Berne Convention" is the Convention for the Protection of Literary and Artistic Works, signed at Berne, Switzerland, on September 9, 1886, and all acts, protocols, and revisions thereto.

The "best edition" of a work is the edition, published in the United States at any time before the date of deposit, that the Library of Congress determines to be most suitable for its purposes.

A person's "children" are that person's immediate offspring, whether legitimate or not, and any children legally adopted by that person.

A "collective work" is a work, such as a periodical issue, anthology, or encyclopedia, in which a number of contributions, constituting separate and independent works in themselves, are assembled into a collective whole.

A "compilation" is a work formed by the collection and assembling of preexisting materials or of data that are selected, coordinated, or arranged in such a way that the resulting work as a whole constitutes an original work of authorship. The term "compilation" includes collective works.

A "computer program" is a set of statements or instructions to be used directly or indirectly in a computer in order to bring about a certain result.

"Copies" are material objects, other than phonorecords, in which a work is fixed by any method now known or later developed, and from which the work can be perceived, reproduced, or otherwise communicated, either directly or with the aid of a machine or device. The term "copies" includes the material object, other than a phonorecord, in which the work is first fixed.

"Copyright owner", with respect to any one of the exclusive rights comprised in a copyright, refers to the owner of that particular right.

A "Copyright Royalty Judge" is a Copyright Royalty Judge appointed under section 802 of this title, and includes any individual serving as an interim Copyright Royalty Judge under such section.

A work is "created" when it is fixed in a copy or phonorecord for the first time; where a work is prepared over a period of time, the portion of it that has been fixed at any particular time constitutes the work as of that time, and where the work has been prepared in different versions, each version constitutes a separate work.

A "derivative work" is a work based upon one or more preexisting works, such as a translation, musical arrangement, dramatization, fictionalization, motion picture version, sound recording, art reproduction, abridgment, condensation, or any other form in which a work may be recast, transformed, or adapted. A work consisting of editorial revisions, annotations, elaborations, or other modifications which, as a whole, represent an original work of authorship, is a "derivative work".

A "device", "machine", or "process" is one now known or later developed.

A "digital transmission" is a transmission in whole or in part in a digital or other non-analog format.

To "display" a work means to show a copy of it, either directly or by means of a film, slide, television image, or any other device or process or, in the case of a motion picture or other audiovisual work, to show individual images nonsequentially.

An "establishment" is a store, shop, or any similar place of business open to the general public for the primary purpose of selling goods or services in which the majority of the gross square feet of space that is nonresidential is used for that purpose, and in which nondramatic musical works are performed publicly.

The term "financial gain" includes receipt, or expectation of receipt, of anything of value, including the receipt of other copyrighted works.

A work is "fixed" in a tangible medium of expression when its embodiment in a copy or phonorecord, by or under the authority of the author, is sufficiently permanent or stable to permit it to be perceived, reproduced, or otherwise communicated for a period of more than transitory duration. A work consisting of sounds, images, or both, that are being transmitted, is "fixed" for purposes of this title if a fixation of the work is being made simultaneously with its transmission.

A "food service or drinking establishment" is a restaurant, inn, bar, tavern, or any other similar place of business in which the public or patrons assemble for the primary purpose of being served food or drink, in which the majority of the gross square feet of space that is nonresidential is used for that purpose, and in which nondramatic musical works are performed publicly.

The "Geneva Phonograms Convention" is the Convention for the Protection of Producers of Phonograms Against Unauthorized Duplication of Their Phonograms, concluded at Geneva, Switzerland, on October 29, 1971.

The "gross square feet of space" of an establishment means the entire interior space of that establishment, and any adjoining outdoor space used to serve patrons, whether on a seasonal basis or otherwise.

The terms "including" and "such as" are illustrative and not limitative.

An "international agreement" is—

(1) the Universal Copyright Convention;

(2) the Geneva Phonograms Convention;

(3) the Berne Convention;

(4) the WTO Agreement;

(5) the WIPO Copyright Treaty;

(6) the WIPO Performances and Phonograms Treaty; and

(7) any other copyright treaty to which the United States is a party.

A "joint work" is a work prepared by two or more authors with the intention that their contributions be merged into inseparable or interdependent parts of a unitary whole.

"Literary works" are works, other than audiovisual works, expressed in words, numbers, or other verbal or numerical symbols or indicia, regardless of the nature of the material objects, such as books, periodicals, manuscripts, phonorecords, film, tapes, disks, or cards, in which they are embodied.

The term "motion picture exhibition facility" means a movie theater, screening room, or other venue that is being used primarily for the exhibition of a copyrighted motion picture, if such exhibition is open to the public or is made to an assembled group of viewers outside of a normal circle of a family and its social acquaintances.

"Motion pictures" are audiovisual works consisting of a series of related images which, when shown in succession, impart an impression of motion, together with accompanying sounds, if any.

To "perform" a work means to recite, render, play, dance, or act it, either directly or by means of any device or process or, in the case of a motion picture or other audiovisual work, to show its images in any sequence or to make the sounds accompanying it audible.

A "performing rights society" is an association, corporation, or other entity that licenses the public performance of nondramatic musical works on behalf of copyright owners of such works, such as the American Society of Composers, Authors and Publishers (ASCAP), Broadcast Music, Inc. (BMI), and SESAC, Inc.

"Phonorecords" are material objects in which sounds, other than those accompanying a motion picture or other audiovisual work, are fixed by any method now known or later developed, and from which the sounds can be perceived, reproduced, or otherwise communicated, either directly or with the aid of a machine or device. The term "phonorecords" includes the material object in which the sounds are first fixed.

"Pictorial, graphic, and sculptural works" include two-dimensional and three-dimensional works of fine, graphic, and applied art, photographs, prints and art reproductions, maps, globes, charts, diagrams, models, and technical drawings, including architectural plans. Such works shall include works of artistic craftsmanship insofar as their form but not their mechanical or utilitarian aspects are concerned; the design of a useful article, as defined in this section, shall be considered a pictorial, graphic, or sculptural work only if, and only to the extent that, such design incorporates pictorial, graphic, or sculptural features that can be identified separately from, and are capable of existing independently of, the utilitarian aspects of the article.

For purposes of section 513, a "proprietor" is an individual, corporation, partnership, or other entity, as the case may be, that owns an establishment or a food service or drinking establishment, except that no owner or operator of a radio or television station licensed by the Federal Communications Commission, cable system or satellite carrier, cable or satellite carrier service or programmer, provider of online services or network access or the operator of facilities therefor, telecommunications company, or any other such audio or audiovisual service or programmer now known or as may be developed in the future, commercial subscription music service, or owner or operator of any other transmission service, shall under any circumstances be deemed to be a proprietor.

A "pseudonymous work" is a work on the copies or phonorecords of which the author is identified under a fictitious name.

"Publication" is the distribution of copies or phonorecords of a work to the public by sale or other transfer of ownership, or by rental, lease, or lending. The offering to distribute copies or phonorecords to a group of persons for purposes of further distribution, public performance, or public display, constitutes publication. A public performance or display of a work does not of itself constitute publication.

To perform or display a work "publicly" means—

(1) to perform or display it at a place open to the public or at any place where a substantial number of persons outside of a normal circle of a family and its social acquaintances is gathered; or

(2) to transmit or otherwise communicate a performance or display of the work to a place specified by clause (1) or to the public, by means of any device or process, whether the members of the public capable of receiving the performance or display receive it in the same place or in separate places and at the same time or at different times.

"Registration," for purposes of sections 205(c)(2), 405, 406, 410(d), 411, 412, and 506(e), means a registration of a claim in the original or the renewed and extended term of copyright.

"Sound recordings" are works that result from the fixation of a series of musical, spoken, or other sounds, but not including the sounds accompanying a motion picture or other audiovisual work, regardless of the nature of the material objects, such as disks, tapes, or other phonorecords, in which they are embodied.

"State" includes the District of Columbia and the Commonwealth of Puerto Rico, and any territories to which this title is made applicable by an Act of Congress.

A "transfer of copyright ownership" is an assignment, mortgage, exclusive license, or any other conveyance, alienation, or hypothecation of a copyright or of any of the exclusive rights comprised in a copyright, whether or not it is limited in time or place of effect, but not including a nonexclusive license.

A "transmission program" is a body of material that, as an aggregate, has been produced for the sole purpose of transmission to the public in sequence and as a unit.

To "transmit" a performance or display is to communicate it by any device or process whereby images or sounds are received beyond the place from which they are sent.

A "treaty party" is a country or intergovernmental organization other than the United States that is a party to an international agreement.

The "United States", when used in a geographical sense, comprises the several States, the District of Columbia and the Commonwealth of Puerto Rico, and the organized territories under the jurisdiction of the United States Government.

For purposes of section 411, a work is a "United States work" only if—

(1) in the case of a published work, the work is first published—

(A) in the United States;

(B) simultaneously in the United States and another treaty party or parties, whose law grants a term of copyright protection that is the same as or longer than the term provided in the United States;

(C) simultaneously in the United States and a foreign nation that is not a treaty party; or

(D) in a foreign nation that is not a treaty party, and all of the authors of the work are nationals, domiciliaries, or habitual residents of, or in the case of an audiovisual work legal entities with headquarters in, the United States;

(2) in the case of an unpublished work, all the authors of the work are nationals, domiciliaries, or habitual residents of the United States, or, in the case of an unpublished audiovisual work, all the authors are legal entities with headquarters in the United States; or

(3) in the case of a pictorial, graphic, or sculptural work incorporated in a building or structure, the building or structure is located in the United States.

A "useful article" is an article having an intrinsic utilitarian function that is not merely to portray the appearance of the article or to convey information. An article that is normally a part of a useful article is considered a "useful article".

The author's "widow" or "widower" is the author's surviving spouse under the law of the author's domicile at the time of his or her death, whether or not the spouse has later remarried.

The "WIPO Copyright Treaty" is the WIPO Copyright Treaty concluded at Geneva, Switzerland, on December 20, 1996.

The "WIPO Performance and Phonograms Treaty" is the WIPO Performances and Phonograms Treaty concluded at Geneva, Switzerland, on December 20, 1996.

A "work of visual art" is—

(1) a painting, drawing, print, or sculpture, existing in a single copy, in a limited edition of 200 copies or fewer that are signed and consecutively numbered by the author, or, in the case of a sculpture, in multiple cast, carved, or fabricated sculptures of 200 or fewer that are consecutively numbered by the author and bear the signature or other identifying mark of the author; or

(2) a still photographic image produced for exhibition purposes only, existing in a single copy that is signed by the author, or in a limited edition of 200 copies or fewer that are signed and consecutively numbered by the author.

A work of visual art does not include—

(A)(i) any poster, map, globe, chart, technical drawing, diagram, model, applied art, motion picture or other audiovisual work, book, magazine, newspaper, periodical, data base, electronic information service, electronic publication, or similar publication;

(ii) any merchandising item or advertising, promotional, descriptive, covering, or packaging material or container;

(iii) any portion or part of any item described in clause (i) or (ii);

(B) any work made for hire; or

(C) any work not subject to copyright protection under this title.

A "work of the United States Government" is a work prepared by an officer or employee of the United States Government as part of that person's official duties.

A "work made for hire" is—

(1) a work prepared by an employee within the scope of his or her employment; or

(2) a work specially ordered or commissioned for use as a contribution to a collective work, as a part of a motion picture or other audiovisual work, as a translation, as a supplementary work, as a compilation, as an instructional text, as a test, as answer material for a test, or as an atlas, if the parties expressly agree in a written instrument signed by them that the work shall be considered a work made for hire. For the purpose of the foregoing sentence, a "supplementary work" is a work prepared for publication as a secondary adjunct to a work by another author for the purpose of introducing, concluding, illustrating, explaining, revising, commenting upon, or assisting in the use of the other work, such as forewords, afterwords, pictorial illustrations, maps, charts, tables, editorial notes, musical arrangements, answer material for tests, bibliographies, appendixes, and indexes, and an "instructional text" is a literary, pictorial, or graphic work prepared for publication and with the purpose of use in systematic instructional activities.

In determining whether any work is eligible to be considered a work made for hire under paragraph (2), neither the amendment contained in section 1011(d) of the Intellectual Property and Communications Omnibus Reform Act of 1999, as enacted by section 1000(a)(9) of Public Law 106–113, nor the deletion of the words added by that amendment—

    (A) shall be considered or otherwise given any legal significance, or

    (B) shall be interpreted to indicate congressional approval or disapproval of, or acquiescence in, any judicial determination,

by the courts or the Copyright Office. Paragraph (2) shall be interpreted as if both section 2(a)(1) of the Work Made For Hire and Copyright Corrections Act of 2000 and section 1011(d) of the Intellectual Property and Communications Omnibus Reform Act of 1999, as enacted by section 1000(a)(9) of Public Law 106–113, were never enacted, and without regard to any inaction or awareness by the Congress at any time of any judicial determinations.

    The terms "WTO Agreement" and "WTO member country" have the meanings given those terms in paragraphs (9) and (10), respectively, of section 2 of the Uruguay Round Agreements Act.

Sec. 102.   Subject Matter of Copyright: In General

    (a) Copyright protection subsists, in accordance with this title, in original works of authorship fixed in any tangible medium of expression, now known or later developed, from which they can be perceived, reproduced, or otherwise communicated, either directly or with the aid of a machine or device. Works of authorship include the following categories:

    (1) literary works;

    (2) musical works, including any accompanying words;

    (3) dramatic works, including any accompanying music;

    (4) pantomimes and choreographic works;

    (5) pictorial, graphic, and sculptural works;

    (6) motion pictures and other audiovisual works;

    (7) sound recordings; and

    (8) architectural works.[a]

    (b) In no case does copyright protection for an original work of authorship extend to any idea, procedure, process, system, method of operation, concept, principle, or discovery, regardless of the form in which it is described, explained, illustrated, or embodied in such work.

---

    [a] The Architectural Works Copyright Protection Act, Title VII of Pub.L. 101–650, 104 Stat. 5089 (1990), enacted Dec. 1, 1990, further provides:

Sec. 706.   **Effective Date.**

    The amendments made by this title apply to—

    (1) any architectural work created on or after the date of the enactment of this Act; and

    (2) any architectural work that, on the date of the enactment of this Act, is unconstructed and embodied in unpublished plans or drawings, except that protection for such architectural work under title 17, United States Code, by virtue of the amendments made by this title, shall terminate on December 31, 2002, unless the work is constructed by that date.

Sec. 103.   Subject Matter of Copyright: Compilations and Derivative Works

(a) The subject matter of copyright as specified by section 102 includes compilations and derivative works, but protection for a work employing preexisting material in which copyright subsists does not extend to any part of the work in which such material has been used unlawfully.

(b) The copyright in a compilation or derivative work extends only to the material contributed by the author of such work, as distinguished from the preexisting material employed in the work, and does not imply any exclusive right in the preexisting material. The copyright in such work is independent of, and does not affect or enlarge the scope, duration, ownership, or subsistence of, any copyright protection in the preexisting material.

Sec. 104.   Subject Matter of Copyright: National Origin

(a) Unpublished Works.—The works specified by sections 102 and 103, while unpublished, are subject to protection under this title without regard to the nationality or domicile of the author.

(b) Published Works.—The works specified by sections 102 and 103, when published, are subject to protection under this title if—

(1) on the date of first publication, one or more of the authors is a national or domiciliary of the United States, or is a national, domiciliary, or sovereign authority of a treaty party, or is a stateless person, wherever that person may be domiciled; or

(2) the work is first published in the United States or in a foreign nation that, on the date of first publication, is a treaty party; or

(3) the work is a sound recording that was first fixed in a treaty party; or

(4) the work is a pictorial, graphic, or sculptural work that is incorporated in a building or other structure, or an architectural work that is embodied in a building and the building or structure is located in the United States or a treaty party; or

(5) the work is first published by the United Nations or any of its specialized agencies, or by the Organization of American States; or

(6) the work comes within the scope of a Presidential proclamation. Whenever the President finds that a particular foreign nation extends, to works by authors who are nationals or domiciliaries of the United States or to works that are first published in the United States, copyright protection on substantially the same basis as that on which the foreign nation extends protection to works of its own nationals and domiciliaries and works first published in that nation, the President may by proclamation extend protection under this title to works of which one or more of the authors is, on the date of first publication, a national, domiciliary, or sovereign authority of that nation, or which was first published in that nation. The President may revise, suspend, or revoke any such proclamation or impose any conditions or limitations on protection under a proclamation.

For purposes of paragraph (2), a work that is published in the United States or a treaty party within 30 days after publication in a foreign nation that is not a treaty party shall be considered to be first published in the United States or such treaty party, as the case may be.

(c) Effect of Berne Convention.—No right or interest in a work eligible for protection under this title may be claimed by virtue of, or in reliance upon, the provisions of the Berne Convention, or the adherence of the United States thereto. Any rights in a work eligible for protection under this title that derive from this title, other Federal or State statutes, or the common law, shall not be expanded or reduced by virtue of, or in reliance upon, the provisions of the Berne Convention, or the adherence of the United States thereto.

(d) Effect of Phonograms Treatises.—Notwithstanding the provisions of subsection (b), no works other than sound recordings shall be eligible for protection under this title solely by virtue of the adherence of the United States to the Geneva Phonograms Convention or the WIPO Performances and Phonograms Treaty.

Sec. 104A. Copyright in Restored Works

(a) Automatic Protection and Term.—

(1) Term.—

(A) Copyright subsists, in accordance with this section, in restored works, and vests automatically on the date of restoration.

(B) Any work in which copyright is restored under this section shall subsist for the remainder of the term of copyright that the work would have otherwise been granted in the United States if the work never entered the public domain in the United States.

(2) Exception.—Any work in which the copyright was ever owned or administered by the Alien Property Custodian and in which the restored copyright would be owned by a government or instrumentality thereof, is not a restored work.

(b) Ownership of Restored Copyright.—A restored work vests initially in the author or initial rightholder of the work as determined by the law of the source country of the work.

(c) Filing of Notice of Intent to Enforce Restored Copyright Against Reliance Parties.—On or after the date of restoration, any person who owns a copyright in a restored work or an exclusive right therein may file with the Copyright Office a notice of intent to enforce that person's copyright or exclusive right or may serve such a notice directly on a reliance party. Acceptance of a notice by the Copyright Office is effective as to any reliance parties but shall not create a presumption of the validity of any of the facts stated therein. Service on a reliance party is effective as to that reliance party and any other reliance parties with actual knowledge of such service and of the contents of that notice.

(d) Remedies for Infringement of Restored Copyrights.—

(1) Enforcement of copyright in restored works in the absence of a reliance party.—As against any party who is not a reliance party, the remedies provided in chapter 5 of this title shall be available on or after the date of restoration of a restored copyright with respect to an act of infringement of the restored copyright that is commenced on or after the date of restoration.

(2) **Enforcement of copyright in restored works as against reliance parties.**—As against a reliance party, except to the extent provided in paragraphs (3) and (4), the remedies provided in chapter 5 of this title shall be available, with respect to an act of infringement of a restored copyright, on or after the date of restoration of the restored copyright if the requirements of either of the following subparagraphs are met:

(A)(i) The owner of the restored copyright (or such owner's agent) or the owner of an exclusive right therein (or such owner's agent) files with the Copyright Office, during the 24–month period beginning on the date of restoration, a notice of intent to enforce the restored copyright; and

(ii)(I) the act of infringement commenced after the end of the 12–month period beginning on the date of publication of the notice in the Federal Register;

(II) the act of infringement commenced before the end of the 12–month period described in subclause (I) and continued after the end of that 12–month period, in which case remedies shall be available only for infringement occurring after the end of that 12–month period; or

(III) copies or phonorecords of a work in which copyright has been restored under this section are made after publication of the notice of intent in the Federal Register.

(B)(i) The owner of the restored copyright (or such owner's agent) or the owner of an exclusive right therein (or such owner's agent) serves upon a reliance party a notice of intent to enforce a restored copyright; and

(ii)(I) the act of infringement commenced after the end of the 12–month period beginning on the date the notice of intent is received;

(II) the act of infringement commenced before the end of the 12–month period described in subclause (I) and continued after the end of that 12–month period, in which case remedies shall be available only for the infringement occurring after the end of that 12–month period; or

(III) copies or phonorecords of a work in which copyright has been restored under this section are made after receipt of the notice of intent.

In the event that notice is provided under both subparagraphs (A) and (B), the 12–month period referred to in such subparagraphs shall run from the earlier of publication or service of notice.

(3) **Existing derivative works.**—(A) In the case of a derivative work that is based upon a restored work and is created—

(i) before the date of the enactment of the Uruguay Round Agreements Act, if the source country of the restored work is an eligible country on such date, or

(ii) before the date on which the source country of the restored work becomes an eligible country, if that country is not an eligible country on such date of enactment,

a reliance party may continue to exploit that derivative work for the duration of the restored copyright if the reliance party pays to the owner of the restored copyright reasonable compensation for conduct which would be subject to a remedy for infringement but for the provisions of this paragraph.

(B) In the absence of an agreement between the parties, the amount of such compensation shall be determined by an action in United States district court, and shall reflect any harm to the actual or potential market for or value of the restored work from the reliance party's continued exploitation of the work, as well as compensation for the relative contributions of expression of the author of the restored work and the reliance party to the derivative work.

(4) Commencement of infringement for reliance parties.—For purposes of section 412, in the case of reliance parties, infringement shall be deemed to have commenced before registration when acts which would have constituted infringement had the restored work been subject to copyright were commenced before the date of restoration.

(e) Notices of Intent to Enforce a Restored Copyright.—

(1) Notices of intent filed with the Copyright Office.—

(A)(i) A notice of intent filed with the Copyright Office to enforce a restored copyright shall be signed by the owner of the restored copyright or the owner of an exclusive right therein, who files the notice under subsection (d)(2)(A)(i) (hereafter in this paragraph referred to as the "owner"), or by the owner's agent, shall identify the title of the restored work, and shall include an English translation of the title and any other alternative titles known to the owner by which the restored work may be identified, and an address and telephone number at which the owner may be contacted. If the notice is signed by an agent, the agency relationship must have been constituted in a writing signed by the owner before the filing of the notice. The Copyright Office may specifically require in regulations other information to be included in the notice, but failure to provide such other information shall not invalidate the notice or be a basis for refusal to list the restored work in the Federal Register.

(ii) If a work in which copyright is restored has no formal title, it shall be described in the notice of intent in detail sufficient to identify it.

(iii) Minor errors or omissions may be corrected by further notice at any time after the notice of intent is filed. Notices of corrections for such minor errors or omissions shall be accepted after the period established in subsection (d)(2)(A)(i). Notices shall be published in the Federal Register pursuant to subparagraph (B).

(B)(i) The Register of Copyrights shall publish in the Federal Register, commencing not later than 4 months after the date of restoration for a particular nation and every 4 months thereafter for a period of 2 years, lists identifying restored works and the ownership thereof if a notice of intent to enforce a restored copyright has been filed.

(ii) Not less than 1 list containing all notices of intent to enforce shall be maintained in the Public Information Office of the Copyright Office and shall be available for public inspection and copying during regular business hours pursuant to sections 705 and 708.

(C) The Register of Copyrights is authorized to fix reasonable fees based on the costs of receipt, processing, recording, and publication of notices of intent to enforce a restored copyright and corrections thereto.

(D)(i) Not later than 90 days before the date the Agreement on Trade-Related Aspects of Intellectual Property referred to in section 101(d)(15) of the Uruguay Round Agreements Act enters into force with respect to the United States, the Copyright Office shall issue and publish in the Federal Register regulations governing the filing under this subsection of notices of intent to enforce a restored copyright.

(ii) Such regulations shall permit owners of restored copyrights to file simultaneously for registration of the restored copyright.

(2) Notices of intent served on a reliance party.—

(A) Notices of intent to enforce a restored copyright may be served on a reliance party at any time after the date of restoration of the restored copyright.

(B) Notices of intent to enforce a restored copyright served on a reliance party shall be signed by the owner or the owner's agent, shall identify the restored work and the work in which the restored work is used, if any, in detail sufficient to identify them, and shall include an English translation of the title, any other alternative titles known to the owner by which the work may be identified, the use or uses to which the owner objects, and an address and telephone number at which the reliance party may contact the owner. If the notice is signed by an agent, the agency relationship must have been constituted in writing and signed by the owner before service of the notice.

(3) Effect of material false statements.—Any material false statement knowingly made with respect to any restored copyright identified in any notice of intent shall make void all claims and assertions made with respect to such restored copyright.

(f) Immunity From Warranty and Related Liability.—

(1) In general.—Any person who warrants, promises, or guarantees that a work does not violate an exclusive right granted in section 106 shall not be liable for legal, equitable, arbitral, or administrative relief if the warranty, promise, or guarantee is breached by virtue of the restoration of copyright under this section, if such warranty, promise, or guarantee is made before January 1, 1995.

(2) Performances.—No person shall be required to perform any act if such performance is made infringing by virtue of the restoration of copyright under the provisions of this section, if the obligation to perform was undertaken before January 1, 1995.

(g) Proclamation of Copyright Restoration.—Whenever the President finds that a particular foreign nation extends, to works by authors who are nationals or domiciliaries of the United States, restored copyright protection on substantially the same basis as provided under this section, the President may by proclamation extend restored protection provided under this section to any work—

(1) of which one or more of the authors is, on the date of first publication, a national, domiciliary, or sovereign authority of that nation; or

(2) which was first published in that nation. The President may revise, suspend, or revoke any such proclamation or impose any conditions or limitations on protection under such a proclamation.

(h) Definitions.—For purposes of this section and section 109(a):

(1) The term "date of adherence or proclamation" means the earlier of the date on which a foreign nation which, as of the date the WTO Agreement enters into force with respect to the United States, is not a nation adhering to the Berne Convention or a WTO member country, becomes—

(A) a nation adhering to the Berne Convention;

(B) a WTO member country;

(C) a nation adhering to the WIPO Copyright Treaty;

(D) a nation adhering to the WIPO Performance and Phonograms Treaty; or

(E) subject to a Presidential proclamation under subsection (g).

(2) The "date of restoration" of a restored copyright is—

(A) January 1, 1996, if the source country of the restored work is a nation adhering to the Berne Convention or a WTO member country on such date, or

(B) the date of adherence or proclamation, in the case of any other source country of the restored work.

(3) The term "eligible country" means a nation, other than the United States, that—

(A) becomes a WTO member country after the date of the enactment of the Uruguay Round Agreements Act;

(B) on such date of enactment is, or after such date of enactment becomes, a nation adhering to the Berne Convention;

(C) adheres to the WIPO Copyright Treaty;

(D) adheres to the WIPO Performance and Phonograms Treaty; or

(E) after such date of enactment becomes subject to a proclamation under subsection (g).

(4) The term "reliance party" means any person who—

(A) with respect to a particular work, engages in acts, before the source country of that work becomes an eligible country, which would have violated section 106 if the restored work had been subject to copyright protection, and who, after the source country becomes an eligible country, continues to engage in such acts;

(B) before the source country of a particular work becomes an eligible country, makes or acquires 1 or more copies or phonorecords of that work; or

(C) as the result of the sale or other disposition of a derivative work covered under subsection (d)(3), or significant assets of a person described in subparagraph (A) or (B), is a successor, assignee, or licensee of that person.

(5) The term "restored copyright" means copyright in a restored work under this section.

(6) The term "restored work" means an original work of authorship that—

(A) is protected under subsection (a);

(B) is not in the public domain in its source country through expiration of term of protection;

(C) is in the public domain in the United States due to—

(i) noncompliance with formalities imposed at any time by United States copyright law, including failure of renewal, lack of proper notice, or failure to comply with any manufacturing requirements;

(ii) lack of subject matter protection in the case of sound recordings fixed before February 15, 1972; or

(iii) lack of national eligibility;

(D) has at least one author or rightholder who was, at the time the work was created, a national or domiciliary of an eligible country, and if published, was first published in an eligible country and not published in the United States during the 30–day period following publication in such eligible country; and

(E) if the source country for the work is an eligible country solely by virtue of its adherence to the WIPO Performance and Phonograms Treaty, is a sound recording.

(7) The term "rightholder" means the person—

(A) who, with respect to a sound recording, first fixes a sound recording with authorization, or

(B) who has acquired rights from the person described in subparagraph (A) by means of any conveyance or by operation of law.

(8) The "source country" of a restored work is—

(A) a nation other than the United States;

(B) in the case of an unpublished work—

(i) the eligible country in which the author or rightholder is a national or domiciliary, or, if a restored work has more than 1 author or rightholder, of which the majority of foreign authors or rightholders are nationals or domiciliaries; or

(ii) if the majority of authors or rightholders are not foreign, the nation other than the United States which has the most significant contacts with the work; and

(C) in the case of a published work—

(i) the eligible country in which the work is first published, or

(ii) if the restored work is published on the same day in 2 or more eligible countries, the eligible country which has the most significant contacts with the work.

Sec. 105.   Subject   Matter   of   Copyright: United   States Government Works

Copyright protection under this title is not available for any work of the United States Government, but the United States Government is not precluded from receiving and holding copyrights transferred to it by assignment, bequest, or otherwise.

Sec. 106.   Exclusive Rights in Copyrighted Works

Subject to sections 107 through 122, the owner of copyright under this title has the exclusive rights to do and to authorize any of the following:

(1) to reproduce the copyrighted work in copies or phonorecords;

(2) to prepare derivative works based upon the copyrighted work;

(3) to distribute copies or phonorecords of the copyrighted work to the public by sale or other transfer of ownership, or by rental, lease, or lending;

(4) in the case of literary, musical, dramatic, and choreographic works, pantomimes, and motion pictures and other audiovisual works, to perform the copyrighted work publicly;

(5) in the case of literary, musical, dramatic, and choreographic works, pantomimes, and pictorial, graphic, or sculptural works, including the individual images of a motion picture or other audiovisual work, to display the copyrighted work publicly; and

(6) in the case of sound recordings, to perform the copyrighted work publicly by means of a digital audio transmission.

Sec. 106A. Rights of Certain Authors to Attribution and Integrity

(a) Rights of Attribution and Integrity.—Subject to section 107 and independent of the exclusive rights provided in section 106, the author of a work of visual art—

(1) shall have the right—

(A) to claim authorship of that work, and

(B) to prevent the use of his or her name as the author of any work of visual art which he or she did not create;

(2) shall have the right to prevent the use of his or her name as the author of the work of visual art in the event of a distortion, mutilation, or other modification of the work which would be prejudicial to his or her honor or reputation; and

(3) subject to the limitations set forth in section 113(d), shall have the right—

(A) to prevent any intentional distortion, mutilation, or other modification of that work which would be prejudicial to his or her honor or reputation, and any intentional distortion, mutilation, or modification of that work is a violation of that right, and

(B) to prevent any destruction of a work of recognized stature, and any intentional or grossly negligent destruction of that work is a violation of that right.

(b) Scope and Exercise of Rights.—Only the author of a work of visual art has the rights conferred by subsection (a) in that work, whether or not the author is the copyright owner. The authors of a joint work of visual art are coowners of the rights conferred by subsection (a) in that work.

(c) Exceptions.—

(1) The modification of a work of visual art which is a result of the passage of time or the inherent nature of the materials is not distortion, mutilation, or other modification described in subsection (a)(3)(A).

(2) The modification of a work of visual art which is the result of conservation, or of the public presentation, including lighting and placement, of the work is not a destruction, distortion, mutilation, or other modification described in subsection (a)(3) unless the modification is caused by gross negligence.

(3) The rights described in paragraphs (1) and (2) of subsection (a) shall not apply to any reproduction, depiction, portrayal, or other use of a work in, upon, or in any connection with any item described in subparagraph (A) or (B) of the definition of "work of visual art" in section 101, and any such reproduction, depiction, portrayal, or other use of a work is not a destruction, distortion, mutilation, or other modification described in paragraph (3) of subsection (a).

(d) Duration of Rights.—

(1) With respect to works of visual art created on or after the effective date set forth in section 9(a) of the Visual Artists Rights Act

of 1990, the rights conferred by subsection (a) shall endure for a term consisting of the life of the author.

(2) With respect to works of visual art created before the effective date set forth in section 9(a) of the Visual Artists Rights Act of 1990, but title to which has not, as of such effective date, been transferred from the author, the rights conferred by subsection (a) shall be coextensive with, and shall expire at the same time as, the rights conferred by section 106.

(3) In the case of a joint work prepared by two or more authors, the rights conferred by subsection (a) shall endure for a term consisting of the life of the last surviving author.

(4) All terms of the right conferred by subsection (a) run to the end of the calendar year in which they would otherwise expire.

(e) Transfer and Waiver.—

(1) The rights conferred by subsection (a) may not be transferred, but those rights may be waived if the author expressly agrees to such waiver in a written instrument signed by the author. Such instrument shall specifically identify the work, and uses of that work, to which the waiver applies, and the waiver shall apply only to the work and uses so identified. In the case of a joint work prepared by two or more authors, a waiver of rights under this paragraph made by one such author waives such rights for all such authors.

(2) Ownership of the rights conferred by subsection (a) with respect to a work of visual art is distinct from ownership of any copy of that work, or of a copyright or any exclusive right under a copyright in that work. Transfer of ownership of any copy of a work of visual art, or of a copyright or any exclusive right under a copyright, shall not constitute a waiver of the rights conferred by subsection (a). Except as may otherwise be agreed by the author in a written instrument signed by the author, a waiver of the rights conferred by subsection (a) with respect to a work of visual art shall not constitute a transfer of ownership of any copy of that work, or of ownership of a copyright or of any exclusive right under a copyright in that work.[b]

Sec. 107.   Limitations on Exclusive Rights: Fair Use

Notwithstanding the provisions of sections 106 and 106A, the fair use of a copyrighted work, including such use by reproduction in copies

---

[b]   The Visual Artists Rights Act of 1990, Title VI of Pub.L. 101–650, 104 Stat. 5089 (1990), enacted Dec. 1, 1990, further provides:

SEC. 610.   EFFECTIVE DATE.

(a) In General.—Subject to subsection (b) and except as provided in subsection (c), this title and the amendments made by this title take effect 6 months after the date of the enactment of this Act.

(b) Applicability.—The rights created by section 106A of title 17, United States Code, shall apply to—

(1) works created before the effective date set forth in subsection (a) but title to which has not, as of such effective date, been transferred from the author, and

(2) works created on or after such effective date, but shall not apply to any destruction, distortion, mutilation, or other modification (as described in section 106A(a)(3) of such title) of any work which occurred before such effective date.

or phonorecords or by any other means specified by that section, for purposes such as criticism, comment, news reporting, teaching (including multiple copies for classroom use), scholarship, or research, is not an infringement of copyright. In determining whether the use made of a work in any particular case is a fair use the factors to be considered shall include—

> (1) the purpose and character of the use, including whether such use is of a commercial nature or is for nonprofit educational purposes;

> (2) the nature of the copyrighted work;

> (3) the amount and substantiality of the portion used in relation to the copyrighted work as a whole; and

> (4) the effect of the use upon the potential market for or value of the copyrighted work.

The fact that a work is unpublished shall not itself bar a finding of fair use if such finding is made upon consideration of all the above factors.

Sec. 108.   Limitations on Exclusive Rights: Reproduction by Libraries and Archives

(a) Except as otherwise provided in this title and notwithstanding the provisions of section 106, it is not an infringement of copyright for a library or archives, or any of its employees acting within the scope of their employment, to reproduce no more than one copy or phonorecord of a work, except as provided in subsections (b) and (c), or to distribute such copy or phonorecord, under the conditions specified by this section, if—

> (1) the reproduction or distribution is made without any purpose of direct or indirect commercial advantage;

> (2) the collections of the library or archives are (i) open to the public, or (ii) available not only to researchers affiliated with the library or archives or with the institution of which it is a part, but also to other persons doing research in a specialized field; and

> (3) the reproduction or distribution of the work includes a notice of copyright that appears on the copy or phonorecord that is reproduced under the provisions of this section, or includes a legend stating that the work may be protected by copyright if no such notice can be found on the copy or phonorecord that is reproduced under the provisions of this section.

(b) The rights of reproduction and distribution under this section apply to three copies or phonorecords of an unpublished work duplicated solely for purposes of preservation and security or for deposit for research use in another library or archives of the type described by clause (2) of subsection (a), if—

> (1) the copy or phonorecord reproduced is currently in the collections of the library or archives; and

> (2) any such copy or phonorecord that is reproduced in digital format is not otherwise distributed in that format and is not made available to the public in that format outside the premises of the library or archives.

(c) The right of reproduction under this section applies to three copies or phonorecords of a published work duplicated solely for the purpose of replacement of a copy or phonorecord that is damaged, deteriorating, lost, or stolen, or of the existing format in which the work is stored has become obsolete, if—

    (1) the library or archives has, after a reasonable effort, determined that an unused replacement cannot be obtained at a fair price; and

    (2) any such copy or phonorecord that is reproduced in digital format is not made available to the public in that format outside the premises of the library or archives in lawful possession of such copy.

For purposes of this subsection, a format shall be considered obsolete if the machine or device necessary to render perceptible a work stored in that format is no longer manufactured or is no longer reasonably available in the commercial marketplace.

(d) The rights of reproduction and distribution under this section apply to a copy, made from the collection of a library or archives where the user makes his or her request or from that of another library or archives, of no more than one article or other contribution to a copyrighted collection or periodical issue, or to a copy or phonorecord of a small part of any other copyrighted work, if—

    (1) the copy or phonorecord becomes the property of the user, and the library or archives has had no notice that the copy or phonorecord would be used for any purpose other than private study, scholarship, or research; and

    (2) the library or archives displays prominently, at the place where orders are accepted, and includes on its order form, a warning of copyright in accordance with requirements that the Register of Copyrights shall prescribe by regulation.

(e) The rights of reproduction and distribution under this section apply to the entire work, or to a substantial part of it, made from the collection of a library or archives where the user makes his or her request or from that of another library or archives, if the library or archives has first determined, on the basis of a reasonable investigation, that a copy, or phonorecord of the copyrighted work cannot be obtained at a fair price, if—

    (1) the copy or phonorecord becomes the property of the user, and the library or archives has had no notice that the copy or phonorecord would be used for any purpose other than private study, scholarship, or research; and

    (2) the library or archives displays prominently, at the place where orders are accepted, and includes on its order form, a warning of copyright in accordance with requirements that the Register of Copyrights shall prescribe by regulation.

(f) Nothing in this section—

    (1) shall be construed to impose liability for copyright infringement upon a library or archives or its employees for the unsupervised use of reproducing equipment located on its premises: *Provided,* That such equipment displays a notice that the making of a copy may be subject to the copyright law;

(2) excuses a person who uses such reproducing equipment or who requests a copy or phonorecord under subsection (d) from liability for copyright infringement for any such act, or for any later use of such copy or phonorecord, if it exceeds fair use as provided by section 107;

(3) shall be construed to limit the reproduction and distribution by lending of a limited number of copies and excerpts by a library or archives of an audiovisual news program, subject to clauses (1), (2), and (3) of subsection (a); or

(4) in any way affects the right of fair use as provided by section 107, or any contractual obligations assumed at any time by the library or archives when it obtained a copy or phonorecord of a work in its collections.

(g) The rights of reproduction and distribution under this section extend to the isolated and unrelated reproduction or distribution of a single copy or phonorecord of the same material on separate occasions, but do not extend to cases where the library or archives, or its employee—

(1) is aware or has substantial reason to believe that it is engaging in the related or concerted reproduction or distribution of multiple copies or phonorecords of the same material, whether made on one occasion or over a period of time, and whether intended for aggregate use by one or more individuals or for separate use by the individual members of a group; or

(2) engages in the systematic reproduction or distribution of single or multiple copies or phonorecords of material described in subsection (d): *Provided,* That nothing in this clause prevents a library or archives from participating in interlibrary arrangements that do not have, as their purpose or effect, that the library or archives receiving such copies or phonorecords for distribution does so in such aggregate quantities as to substitute for a subscription to or purchase of such work.

(h)(1) For purposes of this section, during the last 20 years of any term of copyright of a published work, a library or archives, including a nonprofit educational institution that functions as such, may reproduce, distribute, display, or perform in facsimile or digital form a copy or phonorecord of such work, or portions thereof, for purposes of preservation, scholarship, or research, if such library or archives has first determined, on the basis of a reasonable investigation, that none of the conditions set forth in subparagraphs (A), (B), and (C) of paragraph (2) apply.

(2) No reproduction, distribution, display, or performance is authorized under this subsection if—

(A) the work is subject to normal commercial exploitation;

(B) a copy or phonorecord of the work can be obtained at a reasonable price; or

(C) the copyright owner or its agent provides notice pursuant to regulations promulgated by the Register of Copyrights that either of the conditions set forth in subparagraphs (A) and (B) applies.

(3) The exemption provided in this subsection does not apply to any subsequent uses by users other than such library or archives.

(i) The rights of reproduction and distribution under this section do not apply to a musical work, a pictorial, graphic or sculptural work, or a motion picture or other audiovisual work other than an audiovisual work dealing with news, except that no such limitation shall apply with respect to rights granted by subsections (b), (c), and (h), or with respect to pictorial or graphic works published as illustrations, diagrams, or similar adjuncts to works of which copies are reproduced or distributed in accordance with subsections (d) and (e).

Sec. 109.   Limitations on Exclusive Rights: Effect of Transfer of Particular Copy or Phonorecord

(a) Notwithstanding the provisions of section 106(3), the owner of a particular copy or phonorecord lawfully made under this title, or any person authorized by such owner, is entitled, without the authority of the copyright owner, to sell or otherwise dispose of the possession of that copy or phonorecord. Notwithstanding the preceding sentence, copies or phonorecords of works subject to restored copyright under section 104A that are manufactured before the date of restoration of copyright or, with respect to reliance parties, before publication or service of notice under section 104A(e), may be sold or otherwise disposed of without the authorization of the owner of the restored copyright for purposes of direct or indirect commercial advantage only during the 12–month period beginning on—

(1) the date of the publication in the Federal Register of the notice of intent filed with the Copyright Office under section 104A(d)(2)(A), or

(2) the date of the receipt of actual notice served under section 104A(d)(2)(B),

whichever occurs first.

(b)(1)(A) Notwithstanding the provisions of subsection (a), unless authorized by the owners of copyright in the sound recording or the owner of copyright in a computer program (including any tape, disk, or other medium embodying such program), and in the case of a sound recording in the musical works embodied therein, neither the owner of a particular phonorecord nor any person in possession of a particular copy of a computer program (including any tape, disk, or other medium embodying such program), may, for the purposes of direct or indirect commercial advantage, dispose of, or authorize the disposal of, the possession of that phonorecord or computer program (including any tape, disk, or other medium embodying such program) by rental, lease, or lending, or by any other act or practice in the nature of rental, lease, or lending. Nothing in the preceding sentence shall apply to the rental, lease, or lending of a phonorecord for nonprofit purposes by a nonprofit library or nonprofit educational institution. The transfer of possession of a lawfully made copy of a computer program by a nonprofit educational institution to another nonprofit educational institution or to faculty, staff, and students does not constitute rental, lease, or lending for direct or indirect commercial purposes under this subsection.

(B) This subsection does not apply to—

(i) a computer program which is embodied in a machine or product and which cannot be copied during the ordinary operation or use of the machine or product; or

(ii) a computer program embodied in or used in conjunction with a limited purpose computer that is designed for playing video games and may be designed for other purposes.

(C) Nothing in this subsection affects any provision of chapter 9 of this title.

(2)(A) Nothing in this subsection shall apply to the lending of a computer program for nonprofit purposes by a nonprofit library, if each copy of a computer program which is lent by such library has affixed to the packaging containing the program a warning of copyright in accordance with requirements that the Register of Copyrights shall prescribe by regulation.

(B) Not later than three years after the date of the enactment of the Computer Software Rental Amendments Act of 1990, and at such times thereafter as the Register of Copyrights considers appropriate, the Register of Copyrights, after consultation with representatives of copyright owners and librarians, shall submit to the Congress a report stating whether this paragraph has achieved its intended purpose of maintaining the integrity of the copyright system while providing nonprofit libraries the capability to fulfill their function. Such report shall advise the Congress as to any information or recommendations that the Register of Copyrights considers necessary to carry out the purposes of this subsection.

(3) Nothing in this subsection shall affect any provision of the antitrust laws. For purposes of the preceding sentence, "antitrust laws" has the meaning given that term in the first section of the Clayton Act and includes section 5 of the Federal Trade Commission Act to the extent that section relates to unfair methods of competition.

(4) Any person who distributes a phonorecord[c] or a copy of a computer program[d] (including any tape, disk, or other medium

---

[c]   The Record Rental Amendment, Pub.L. 98–450, 98 Stat. 1727 (1984), enacted Oct. 4, 1984, concludes as follows:

Sec. 4. (a) The amendments made by this Act shall take effect on the date of the enactment of this Act.

(b) The provisions of section 109(b) of title 17, United States Code, as added by section 2 of this Act, shall not affect the right of an owner of a particular phonorecord of a sound recording, who acquired such ownership before the date of the enactment of this Act, to dispose of the possession of that particular phonorecord on or after such date of enactment in any manner permitted by section 109 of title 17, United States Code, as in effect on the day before the date of the enactment of this Act.

[d]   The Computer Software Rental Amendments Act of 1990, Title VIII of Pub.L. 101–650, 104 Stat. 5089 (1990), enacted Dec. 1, 1990, further provides:

(a) In General.—Subject to subsection (b), this title and the amendments made in section 802 shall take effect on the date of the enactment of this Act. The amendment made by section 803 [adding § 109(e)] shall take effect one year after such date of enactment.

(b) Prospective Application.—Section 109(b) of title 17, United States Code, as amended by section 802 of this Act, shall not affect the right of a person in possession of a particular copy of a computer program, who acquired such copy before the date of the enactment of this Act, to dispose of the possession of that copy on or after such date embodying such program) in violation of paragraph (1) is an infringer of copyright under section 501 of this title and is subject to the remedies set forth in sections 502, 503, 504 and 505. Such violation shall not be a criminal offense under section 506 or cause such person to be subject to the criminal penalties set forth in section 2319 of title 18.

(c) Notwithstanding the provisions of section 106(5), the owner of a particular copy lawfully made under this title, or any person authorized by such owner, is entitled, without the authority of the copyright owner, to display that copy publicly, either directly or by the projection of no more than one image at a time, to viewers present at the place where the copy is located.

(d) The privileges prescribed by subsections (a) and (c) do not, unless authorized by the copyright owner, extend to any person who has acquired possession of the copy or phonorecord from the copyright owner, by rental, lease, loan, or otherwise, without acquiring ownership of it.

(e) Notwithstanding the provisions of sections 106(4) and 106(5), in the case of an electronic audiovisual game intended for use in coin-operated equipment, the owner of a particular copy of such a game lawfully made under this title, is entitled, without the authority of the copyright owner of the game, to publicly perform or display that game in coin-operated equipment, except that this subsection shall not apply to any work of authorship embodied in the audiovisual game if the copyright owner of the electronic audiovisual game is not also the copyright owner of the work of authorship.

Sec. 110.   Limitations on Exclusive Rights: Exemption of Certain Performances and Displays

Notwithstanding the provisions of section 106, the following are not infringements of copyright:

(1) performance or display of a work by instructors or pupils in the course of face-to-face teaching activities of a nonprofit educational institution, in a classroom or similar place devoted to instruction, unless, in the case of a motion picture or other audiovisual work, the performance, or the display of individual images, is given by means of a copy that was not lawfully made under this title, and that the person responsible for the performance knew or had reason to believe was not lawfully made;

(2) except with respect to a work produced or marketed primarily for performance or display as part of mediated instructional activities transmitted via digital networks, or a performance or display that is given by means of a copy or phonorecord that is not lawfully made and acquired under this title, and the transmitting government body or accredited nonprofit educational institution knew or had reason to believe was not lawfully made and acquired, the performance of a nondramatic literary or musical work or reasonable and limited portions of any other work, or display of a work in an amount comparable to that

---

of enactment in any manner permitted by section 109 of title 17, United States Code, as in effect on the day before such date of enactment.

(c) Termination.—The amendments made by section 803 [adding § 109(e)] shall not apply to public performances or displays that occur on or after October 1, 1995.

which is typically displayed in the course of a live classroom session, by or in the course of a transmission, if—

    (A) the performance or display is made by, at the direction of, or under the actual supervision of an instructor as an integral part of a class session offered as a regular part of the systematic mediated instructional activities of a governmental body or an accredited nonprofit educational institution;

    (B) the performance or display is directly related and of material assistance to the teaching content of the transmission;

    (C) the transmission is made solely for, and, to the extent technologically feasible, the reception of such transmission is limited to—

        (i) students officially enrolled in the course for which the transmission is made; or

        (ii) officers or employees of governmental bodies as a part of their official duties or employment; and

    (D) the transmitting body or institution—

        (i) institutes policies regarding copyright, provides informational materials to faculty, students, and relevant staff members that accurately describe, and promote compliance with, the laws of the United States relating to copyright, and provides notice to students that materials used in connection with the course may be subject to copyright protection; and

        (ii) in the case of digital transmissions—

            (I) applies technological measures that reasonably prevent—

            (aa) retention of the work in accessible form by recipients of the transmission from the transmitting body or institution for longer than the class session; and

            (bb) unauthorized further dissemination of the work in accessible form by such recipients to others; and

            (II) does not engage in conduct that could reasonably be expected to interfere with technological measures used by copyright owners to prevent such retention or unauthorized further dissemination;

    (3) performance of a nondramatic literary or musical work or of a dramatico-musical work of a religious nature, or display of a work, in the course of services at a place of worship or other religious assembly;

    (4) performance of a nondramatic literary or musical work otherwise than in a transmission to the public, without any purpose of direct or indirect commercial advantage and without payment of any fee or other compensation for the performance to any of its performers, promoters, or organizers, if—

    (A) there is no direct or indirect admission charge; or

(B) the proceeds, after deducting the reasonable costs of producing the performance, are used exclusively for educational, religious, or charitable purposes and not for private financial gain, except where the copyright owner has served notice of objection to the performance under the following conditions:

(i) the notice shall be in writing and signed by the copyright owner or such owner's duly authorized agent; and

(ii) the notice shall be served on the person responsible for the performance at least seven days before the date of the performance, and shall state the reasons for the objection; and

(iii) the notice shall comply, in form, content, and manner of service, with requirements that the Register of Copyrights shall prescribe by regulation;

(5)(A) except as provided in subparagraph (B), communication of a transmission embodying a performance or display of a work by the public reception of the transmission on a single receiving apparatus of a kind commonly used in private homes, unless—

(i) a direct charge is made to see or hear the transmission; or

(ii) the transmission thus received is further transmitted to the public;

(B) communication by an establishment of a transmission or retransmission embodying a performance or display of a nondramatic musical work intended to be received by the general public, originated by a radio or television broadcast station licensed as such by the Federal Communications Commission, or, if an audiovisual transmission, by a cable system or satellite carrier, if—

(i) in the case of an establishment other than a food service or drinking establishment, either the establishment in which the communication occurs has less than 2,000 gross square feet of space (excluding space used for customer parking and for no other purpose), or the establishment in which the communication occurs has 2,000 or more gross square feet of space (excluding space used for customer parking and for no other purpose) and—

(I) if the performance is by audio means only, the performance is communicated by means of a total of not more than 6 loudspeakers, of which not more than 4 loudspeakers are located in any 1 room or adjoining outdoor space; or

(II) if the performance or display is by audiovisual means, any visual portion of the performance or display is communicated by means of a total of not more than 4 audiovisual devices, of which not more than 1 audiovisual device is located in any 1 room, and no such audiovisual device has a diagonal screen size greater than 55 inches, and any audio portion of the performance or display is communicated by means of a total of not more than 6 loudspeakers, of which not more than 4 loudspeakers are located in any 1 room or adjoining outdoor space;

(ii) in the case of a food service or drinking establishment, either the establishment in which the communication occurs has less than 3,750 gross square feet of space (excluding space used for customer parking and for no other purpose), or the establishment in which the communication occurs has 3,750 gross square feet of space or more (excluding space used for customer parking and for no other purpose) and—

(I) if the performance is by audio means only, the performance is communicated by means of a total of not more than 6 loudspeakers, of which not more than 4 loudspeakers are located in any 1 room or adjoining outdoor space; or

(II) if the performance or display is by audiovisual means, any visual portion of the performance or display is communicated by means of a total of not more than 4 audiovisual devices, of which not more than one audiovisual device is located in any 1 room, and no such audiovisual device has a diagonal screen size greater than 55 inches, and any audio portion of the performance or display is communicated by means of a total of not more than 6 loudspeakers, of which not more than 4 loudspeakers are located in any 1 room or adjoining outdoor space;

(iii) no direct charge is made to see or hear the transmission or retransmission;

(iv) the transmission or retransmission is not further transmitted beyond the establishment where it is received; and

(v) the transmission or retransmission is licensed by the copyright owner of the work so publicly performed or displayed;

(6) performance of a nondramatic musical work by a governmental body or a nonprofit agricultural or horticultural organization, in the course of an annual agricultural or horticultural fair or exhibition conducted by such body or organization; the exemption provided by this clause shall extend to any liability for copyright infringement that would otherwise be imposed on such body or organization, under doctrines of vicarious liability or related infringement, for a performance by a concessionnaire, business establishment, or other person at such fair or exhibition, but shall not excuse any such person from liability for the performance;

(7) performance of a nondramatic musical work by a vending establishment open to the public at large without any direct or indirect admission charge, where the sole purpose of the performance is to promote the retail sale of copies or phonorecords of the work, or of the audiovisual or other devices utilized in such performance, and the performance is not transmitted beyond the place where the establishment is located and is within the immediate area where the sale is occurring;

(8) performance of a nondramatic literary work, by or in the course of a transmission specifically designed for and primarily

directed to blind or other handicapped persons who are unable to read normal printed material as a result of their handicap, or deaf or other handicapped persons who are unable to hear the aural signals accompanying a transmission of visual signals, if the performance is made without any purpose of direct or indirect commercial advantage and its transmission is made through the facilities of: (i) a governmental body; or (ii) a noncommercial educational broadcast station (as defined in section 397 of title 47); or (iii) a radio subcarrier authorization (as defined in 47 CFR 73.293–73.295 and 73.593–73.595); or (iv) a cable system (as defined in section 111(f));

(9) performance on a single occasion of a dramatic literary work published at least ten years before the date of the performance, by or in the course of a transmission specifically designed for and primarily directed to blind or other handicapped persons who are unable to read normal printed material as a result of their handicap, if the performance is made without any purpose of direct or indirect commercial advantage and its transmission is made through the facilities of a radio subcarrier authorization referred to in clause (8)(iii), *Provided,* That the provisions of this clause shall not be applicable to more than one performance of the same work by the same performers or under the auspices of the same organization;

(10) notwithstanding paragraph (4), the following is not an infringement of copyright: performance of a nondramatic literary or musical work in the course of a social function which is organized and promoted by a nonprofit veterans' organization or a nonprofit fraternal organization to which the general public is not invited, but not including the invitees of the organizations, if the proceeds from the performance, after deducting the reasonable costs of producing the performance, are used exclusively for charitable purposes and not for financial gain. For purposes of this section the social functions of any college or university fraternity or sorority shall not be included unless the social function is held solely to raise funds for a specific charitable purpose; and

(11) the making imperceptible, by or at the direction of a member of a private household, of limited portions of audio or video content of a motion picture, during a performance in or transmitted to that household for private home viewing, from an authorized copy of the motion picture, or the creation or provision of a computer program or other technology that enables such making imperceptible and that is designed and marketed to be used, at the direction of a member of a private household, for such making imperceptible, if no fixed copy of the altered version of the motion picture is created by such computer program or other technology.

The exemptions provided under paragraph (5) shall not be taken into account in any administrative, judicial, or other governmental proceeding to set or adjust the royalties payable to copyright owners for the public performance or display of their works. Royalties payable to copyright owners for any public performance or display of their works other than such performances or displays as are exempted under paragraph (5) shall not be diminished in any respect as a result of such exemption

In paragraph (2), the term "mediated instructional activities" with respect to the performance or display of a work by digital transmission under this section refers to activities that use such work as an integral part of the class experience, controlled by or under the actual supervision of the instructor and analogous to the type of performance or display that would take place in a live classroom setting. The term does not refer to activities that use, in one or more class sessions of a single course, such works as textbooks, course packs, or other material in any media, copies or phonorecords of which are typically purchased or acquired by the students in higher education for their independent use and retention or are typically purchased or acquired for elementary and secondary students for their possession and independent use.

For purposes of paragraph (2), accreditation—

(A) with respect to an institution providing post-secondary education, shall be as determined by a regional or national accrediting agency recognized by the Council on Higher Education Accreditation or the United States Department of Education; and

(B) with respect to an institution providing elementary or secondary education, shall be as recognized by the applicable state certification or licensing procedures.

For purposes of paragraph (2), no governmental body or accredited nonprofit educational institution shall be liable for infringement by reason of the transient or temporary storage of material carried out through the automatic technical process of a digital transmission of the performance or display of that material as authorized under paragraph (2). No such material stored on the system or network controlled or operated by the transmitting body or institution under this paragraph shall be maintained on such system or network in a manner ordinarily accessible to anyone other than anticipated recipients. No such copy shall be maintained on the system or network in a manner ordinarily accessible to such anticipated recipients for a longer period than is reasonably necessary to facilitate the transmissions for which it was made.

For purposes of paragraph (11), the term "making imperceptible" does not include the addition of audio or video content that is performed or displayed over or in place of existing content in a motion picture.

Nothing in paragraph (11) shall be construed to imply further rights under section 106 of this title, or to have any effect on defenses or limitations on rights granted under any other section of this title or under any other paragraph of this section.

Sec. 111. Limitations on Exclusive Rights: Secondary Transmissions of Broadcast Programming by Cable

(a) **Certain secondary transmissions exempted.**—The secondary transmission of a performance or display of a work embodied in a primary transmission is not an infringement of copyright if—

(1) the secondary transmission is not made by a cable system, and consists entirely of the relaying, by the management of a hotel, apartment house, or similar establishment, of signals transmitted by a broadcast station licensed by the Federal Communications Commission, within the local service area of such station, to the

private lodgings of guests or residents of such establishment, and no direct charge is made to see or hear the secondary transmission; or

(2) the secondary transmission is made solely for the purpose and under the conditions specified by paragraph (2) of section 110; or

(3) the secondary transmission is made by any carrier who has no direct or indirect control over the content or selection of the primary transmission or over the particular recipients of the secondary transmission, and whose activities with respect to the secondary transmission consist solely of providing wires, cables, or other communications channels for the use of others: *Provided,* That the provisions of this paragraph extend only to the activities of said carrier with respect to secondary transmissions and do not exempt from liability the activities of others with respect to their own primary or secondary transmissions;

(4) the secondary transmission is made by a satellite carrier pursuant to a statutory license under section 119 or section 122;

(5) the secondary transmission is not made by a cable system but is made by a governmental body, or other nonprofit organization, without any purpose of direct or indirect commercial advantage, and without charge to the recipients of the secondary transmission other than assessments necessary to defray the actual and reasonable costs of maintaining and operating the secondary transmission service.

(b) Secondary transmission of primary transmission to controlled group.—Notwithstanding the provisions of subsections (a) and (c), the secondary transmission to the public of a performance or display of a work embodied in a primary transmission is actionable as an act of infringement under section 501, and is fully subject to the remedies provided by sections 502 through 506, if the primary transmission is not made for reception by the public at large but is controlled and limited to reception by particular members of the public: *Provided,* however, That such secondary transmission is not actionable as an act of infringement if—

(1) the primary transmission is made by a broadcast station licensed by the Federal Communications Commission; and

(2) the carriage of the signals comprising the secondary transmission is required under the rules, regulations, or authorizations of the Federal Communications Commission; and

(3) the signal of the primary transmitter is not altered or changed in any way by the secondary transmitter.

(c) Secondary transmissions by cable systems.—

(1) Subject to the provisions of paragraphs (2), (3), and (4) of this subsection and section 114(d), secondary transmissions to the public by a cable system of a performance or display of a work embodied in a primary transmission made by a broadcast station licensed by the Federal Communications Commission or by an appropriate governmental authority of Canada or Mexico shall be subject to statutory licensing upon compliance with the requirements of subsection (d) where the carriage of the signals comprising the

secondary transmission is permissible under the rules, regulations, or authorizations of the Federal Communications Commission.

(2) Notwithstanding the provisions of paragraph (1) of this subsection, the willful or repeated secondary transmission to the public by a cable system of a primary transmission made by a broadcast station licensed by the Federal Communications Commission or by an appropriate governmental authority of Canada or Mexico and embodying a performance or display of a work is actionable as an act of infringement under section 501, and is fully subject to the remedies provided by sections 502 through 506, in the following cases:

(A) where the carriage of the signals comprising the secondary transmission is not permissible under the rules, regulations, or authorizations of the Federal Communications Commission; or

(B) where the cable system has not deposited the statement of account and royalty fee required by subsection (d).

(3) Notwithstanding the provisions of paragraph (1) of this subsection and subject to the provisions of subsection (e) of this section, the secondary transmission to the public by a cable system of a performance or display of a work embodied in a primary transmission made by a broadcast station licensed by the Federal Communications Commission or by an appropriate governmental authority of Canada or Mexico is actionable as an act of infringement under section 501, and is fully subject to the remedies provided by sections 502 through 506 and section 510, if the content of the particular program in which the performance or display is embodied, or any commercial advertising or station announcements transmitted by the primary transmitter during, or immediately before or after, the transmission of such program, is in any way willfully altered by the cable system through changes, deletions, or additions, except for the alteration, deletion, or substitution of commercial advertisements performed by those engaged in television commercial advertising market research: *Provided*, That the research company has obtained the prior consent of the advertiser who has purchased the original commercial advertisement, the television station broadcasting that commercial advertisement, and the cable system performing the secondary transmission: *And provided further*, That such commercial alteration, deletion, or substitution is not performed for the purpose of deriving income from the sale of that commercial time.

(4) Notwithstanding the provisions of paragraph (1) of this subsection, the secondary transmission to the public by a cable system of a performance or display of a work embodied in a primary transmission made by a broadcast station licensed by an appropriate governmental authority of Canada or Mexico is actionable as an act of infringement under section 501, and is fully subject to the remedies provided by sections 502 through 506, if (A) with respect to Canadian signals, the community of the cable system is located more than 150 miles from the United States—Canadian border and is also located south of the forty-second parallel of latitude, or (B) with respect to Mexican signals, the secondary transmission is made by a

cable system which received the primary transmission by means other than direct interception of a free space radio wave emitted by such broadcast television station, unless prior to April 15, 1976, such cable system was actually carrying, or was specifically authorized to carry, the signal of such foreign station on the system pursuant to the rules, regulations, or authorizations of the Federal Communications Commission.

(d) Statutory license for secondary transmissions by cable systems.—

(1) **Statement of account and royalty fees.**—Subject to paragraph (5), a cable system whose secondary transmissions have been subject to statutory licensing under subsection (c) shall, on a semiannual basis, deposit with the Register of Copyrights, in accordance with requirements that the Register shall prescribe by regulation the following:

(A) A statement of account, covering the six months next preceding, specifying the number of channels on which the cable system made secondary transmissions to its subscribers, the names and locations of all primary transmitters whose transmissions were further transmitted by the cable system, the total number of subscribers, the gross amounts paid to the cable system for the basic service of providing secondary transmissions of primary broadcast transmitters, and such other data as the Register of Copyrights may from time to time prescribe by regulation. In determining the total number of subscribers and the gross amounts paid to the cable system for the basic service of providing secondary transmissions of primary broadcast transmitters, the system shall not include subscribers and amounts collected from subscribers receiving secondary transmissions pursuant to section 119. Such statement shall also include a special statement of account covering any non-network television programming that was carried by the cable system in whole or in part beyond the local service area of the primary transmitter, under rules, regulations, or authorizations of the Federal Communications Commission permitting the substitution or addition of signals under certain circumstances, together with logs showing the times, dates, stations, and programs involved in such substituted or added carriage.

(B) Except in the case of a cable system whose royalty fee is specified in subparagraph (E) or (F), a total royalty fee payable to copyright owners pursuant to paragraph (3) for the period covered by the statement, computed on the basis of specified percentages of the gross receipts from subscribers to the cable service during such period for the basic service of providing secondary transmissions of primary broadcast transmitters, as follows:

(i) 1.064 percent of such gross receipts for the privilege of further transmitting, beyond the local service area of such primary transmitter, any non-network programming of a primary transmitter in whole or in part, such amount to be applied against the fee, if any, payable pursuant to clauses (ii) through (iv);

(ii) 1.064 percent of such gross receipts for the first distant signal equivalent;

(iii) 0.701 percent of such gross receipts for each of the second, third, and fourth distant signal equivalents; and

(iv) 0.330 percent of such gross receipts for the fifth distant signal equivalent and each distant signal equivalent thereafter.

(C) In computing amounts under clauses (ii) through (iv) of subparagraph (B)—

(i) any fraction of a distant signal equivalent shall be computed at its fractional value;

(ii) in the case of any cable system located partly within and partly outside of the local service area of a primary transmitter, gross receipts shall be limited to those gross receipts derived from subscribers located outside of the local service area of such primary transmitter; and

(iii) if a cable system provides a secondary transmission of a primary transmitter to some but not all communities served by that cable system—

(I) the gross receipts and the distant signal equivalent values for such secondary transmission shall be derived solely on the basis of the subscribers in those communities where the cable system provides such secondary transmission; and

(II) the total royalty fee for the period paid by such system shall not be less than the royalty fee calculated under subparagraph (B)(i) multiplied by the gross receipts from all subscribers to the system.

(D) A cable system that, on a statement submitted before the date of the enactment of the Satellite Television Extension and Localism Act of 2010, computed its royalty fee consistent with the methodology under subparagraph (C)(iii), or that amends a statement filed before such date of enactment to compute the royalty fee due using such methodology, shall not be subject to an action for infringement, or eligible for any royalty refund or offset, arising out of its use of such methodology on such statement.

(E) If the actual gross receipts paid by subscribers to a cable system for the period covered by the statement for the basic service of providing secondary transmissions of primary broadcast transmitters are $263,800 or less—

(i) gross receipts of the cable system for the purpose of this paragraph shall be computed by subtracting from such actual gross receipts the amount by which $263,800 exceeds such actual gross receipts, except that in no case shall a cable system's gross receipts be reduced to less than $10,400; and

(ii) the royalty fee payable under this paragraph to copyright owners pursuant to paragraph (3) shall be 0.5 percent, regardless of the number of distant signal equivalents, if any.

(F) If the actual gross receipts paid by subscribers to a cable system for the period covered by the statement for the basic service of providing secondary transmissions of primary broadcast transmitters are more than $263,800 but less than $527,600, the royalty fee payable under this paragraph to copyright owners pursuant to paragraph (3) shall be—

(i) 0.5 percent of any gross receipts up to $263,800, regardless of the number of distant signal equivalents, if any; and

(ii) 1 percent of any gross receipts in excess of $263,800, but less than $527,600, regardless of the number of distant signal equivalents, if any.

(G) A filing fee, as determined by the Register of Copyrights pursuant to section 708(a).

(2) **Handling of fees.**—The Register of Copyrights shall receive all fees (including the filing fee specified in paragraph (1)(G)) deposited under this section and, after deducting the reasonable costs incurred by the Copyright Office under this section, shall deposit the balance in the Treasury of the United States, in such manner as the Secretary of the Treasury directs. All funds held by the Secretary of the Treasury shall be invested in interest-bearing United States securities for later distribution with interest by the Librarian of Congress upon authorization by the Copyright Royalty Judges.

(3) **Distribution of royalty fees to copyright owners.**—The royalty fees thus deposited shall, in accordance with the procedures provided by paragraph (4), be distributed to those among the following copyright owners who claim that their works were the subject of secondary transmissions by cable systems during the relevant semiannual period:

(A) Any such owner whose work was included in a secondary transmission made by a cable system of a non-network television program in whole or in part beyond the local service area of the primary transmitter.

(B) Any such owner whose work was included in a secondary transmission identified in a special statement of account deposited under paragraph (1)(A).

(C) Any such owner whose work was included in non-network programming consisting exclusively of aural signals carried by a cable system in whole or in part beyond the local service area of the primary transmitter of such programs.

(4) **Procedures for royalty fee distribution.**—The royalty fees thus deposited shall be distributed in accordance with the following procedures:

(A) During the month of July in each year, every person claiming to be entitled to statutory license fees for secondary transmissions shall file a claim with the Copyright Royalty Judges, in accordance with requirements that the Copyright Royalty Judges shall prescribe by regulation. Notwithstanding any provisions of the antitrust laws, for purposes of this clause any claimants may agree among themselves as to the proportionate division of statutory licensing fees among them, may lump their claims together and file them jointly or as a single claim, or may designate a common agent to receive payment on their behalf.

(B) After the first day of August of each year, the Copyright Royalty Judges shall determine whether there exists a controversy concerning the distribution of royalty fees. If the Copyright Royalty Judges determine that no such controversy exists, the Copyright Royalty Judges shall authorize the Librarian of Congress to proceed to distribute such fees to the copyright owners entitled to receive them, or to their designated agents, subject to the deduction of reasonable administrative costs under this section. If the Copyright Royalty Judges find the existence of a controversy, the Copyright Royalty Judges shall, pursuant to chapter 8 of this title, conduct a proceeding to determine the distribution of royalty fees.

(C) During the pendency of any proceeding under this subsection, the Copyright Royalty Judges shall have the discretion to authorize the Librarian of Congress to proceed to distribute any amounts that are not in controversy.

(5) **3.75 percent rate and syndicated exclusivity surcharge not applicable to multicast streams.**—The royalty rates specified in sections 256. 2(c) and 256.2(d) of title 37, Code of Federal Regulations (commonly referred to as the "3.75 percent rate" and the "syndicated exclusivity surcharge", respectively), as in effect on the date of the enactment of the Satellite Television Extension and Localism Act of 2010, as such rates may be adjusted, or such sections redesignated, thereafter by the Copyright Royalty Judges, shall not apply to the secondary transmission of a multicast stream.

(6) **Verification of accounts and fee payments.**—The Register of Copyrights shall issue regulations to provide for the confidential verification by copyright owners whose works were embodied in the secondary transmissions of primary transmissions pursuant to this section of the information reported on the semiannual statements of account filed under this subsection for accounting periods beginning on or after January 1, 2010, in order that the auditor designated under subparagraph (A) is able to confirm the correctness of the calculations and royalty payments reported therein. The regulations shall—

(A) establish procedures for the designation of a qualified independent auditor—

(i) with exclusive authority to request verification of such a statement of account on behalf of all copyright owners whose works were the subject of secondary transmissions of primary transmissions by the cable system (that deposited the statement) during the accounting period covered by the statement; and

(ii) who is not an officer, employee, or agent of any such copyright owner for any purpose other than such audit;

(B) establish procedures for safeguarding all non-public financial and business information provided under this paragraph;

(C)(i) require a consultation period for the independent auditor to review its conclusions with a designee of the cable system;

(ii) establish a mechanism for the cable system to remedy any errors identified in the auditor's report and to cure any underpayment identified; and

(iii) provide an opportunity to remedy any disputed facts or conclusions;

(D) limit the frequency of requests for verification for a particular cable system and the number of audits that a multiple system operator can be required to undergo in a single year; and

(E) permit requests for verification of a statement of account to be made only within 3 years after the last day of the year in which the statement of account is filed.

(7) **Acceptance of additional deposits.**—Any royalty fee payments received by the Copyright Office from cable systems for the secondary transmission of primary transmissions that are in addition to the payments calculated and deposited in accordance with this subsection shall be deemed to have been deposited for the particular accounting period for which they are received and shall be distributed as specified under this subsection.

(e) **Nonsimultaneous secondary transmissions by cable systems.**—

(1) Notwithstanding those provisions of the subsection (f)(2) relating to nonsimultaneous secondary transmissions by a cable system, any such transmissions are actionable as an act of infringement under section 501, and are fully subject to the remedies provided by sections 502 through 506 and section 510, unless—

(A) the program on the videotape is transmitted no more than one time to the cable system's subscribers;

(B) the copyrighted program, episode, or motion picture videotape, including the commercials contained within such program, episode, or picture, is transmitted without deletion or editing;

(C) an owner or officer of the cable system (i) prevents the duplication of the videotape while in the possession of the system, (ii) prevents unauthorized duplication while in the possession of the facility making the videotape for the system if the system owns or controls the facility, or takes reasonable precautions to prevent such duplication if it does not own or control the facility, (iii) takes adequate precautions to prevent duplication while the tape is being transported, and (iv) subject to paragraph (2), erases or destroys, or causes the erasure or destruction of, the videotape;

(D) within forty-five days after the end of each calendar quarter, an owner or officer of the cable system executes an affidavit attesting (i) to the steps and precautions taken to prevent duplication of the videotape, and (ii) subject to paragraph (2), to the erasure or destruction of all videotapes made or used during such quarter;

(E) such owner or officer places or causes each such affidavit, and affidavits received pursuant to paragraph (2)(C), to be placed in a file, open to public inspection, at such system's main office in the community where the transmission is made or in the nearest community where such system maintains an office; and

(F) the nonsimultaneous transmission is one that the cable system would be authorized to transmit under the rules, regulations, and authorizations of the Federal Communications Commission in effect at the time of the nonsimultaneous transmission if the transmission had been made simultaneously, except that this subparagraph shall not apply to inadvertent or accidental transmissions.

(2) If a cable system transfers to any person a videotape of a program nonsimultaneously transmitted by it, such transfer is actionable as an act of infringement under section 501, and is fully subject to the remedies provided by sections 502 through 506, except that, pursuant to a written, nonprofit contract providing for the equitable sharing of the costs of such videotape and its transfer, a videotape nonsimultaneously transmitted by it, in accordance with paragraph (1), may be transferred by one cable system in Alaska to another system in Alaska, by one cable system in Hawaii permitted to make such nonsimultaneous transmissions to another such cable system in Hawaii, or by one cable system in Guam, the Northern Mariana Islands, the Federated States of Micronesia, the Republic of Palau, or the Republic of the Marshall Islands, to another cable system in any of those five entities, if—

(A) each such contract is available for public inspection in the offices of the cable systems involved, and a copy of such contract is filed, within thirty days after such contract is entered into, with the Copyright Office (which Office shall make each such contract available for public inspection);

(B) the cable system to which the videotape is transferred complies with paragraph (1)(A), (B), (C)(i), (iii), and (iv), and (D) through (F); and

(C) such system provides a copy of the affidavit required to be made in accordance with paragraph (1)(D) to each cable system making a previous nonsimultaneous transmission of the same videotape.

(3) This subsection shall not be construed to supersede the exclusivity protection provisions of any existing agreement, or any such agreement hereafter entered into, between a cable system and

a television broadcast station in the area in which the cable system is located, or a network with which such station is affiliated.

(4) As used in this subsection, the term "videotape" means the reproduction of the images and sounds of a program or programs broadcast by a television broadcast station licensed by the Federal Communications Commission, regardless of the nature of the material objects, such as tapes or films, in which the reproduction is embodied.

(f) Definitions.—As used in this section, the following terms mean the following:

(1) **Primary transmission.**—A "primary transmission" is a transmission made to the public by a transmitting facility whose signals are being received and further transmitted by a secondary transmission service, regardless of where or when the performance or display was first transmitted. In the case of a television broadcast station, the primary stream and any multicast streams transmitted by the station constitute primary transmissions.

(2) **Secondary transmission.**—A "secondary transmission" is the further transmitting of a primary transmission simultaneously with the primary transmission, or nonsimultaneously with the primary transmission if by a cable system not located in whole or in part within the boundary of the forty-eight contiguous States, Hawaii, or Puerto Rico: *Provided, however*, That a nonsimultaneous further transmission by a cable system located in Hawaii of a primary transmission shall be deemed to be a secondary transmission if the carriage of the television broadcast signal comprising such further transmission is permissible under the rules, regulations, or authorizations of the Federal Communications Commission.

(3) **Cable system.**—A "cable system" is a facility, located in any State, territory, trust territory, or possession of the United States, that in whole or in part receives signals transmitted or programs broadcast by one or more television broadcast stations licensed by the Federal Communications Commission, and makes secondary transmissions of such signals or programs by wires, cables, microwave, or other communications channels to subscribing members of the public who pay for such service. For purposes of determining the royalty fee under subsection (d)(1), two or more cable systems in contiguous communities under common ownership or control or operating from one headend shall be considered as one system.

(4) **Local service area of a primary transmitter.**—The "local service area of a primary transmitter", in the case of both the primary stream and any multicast streams transmitted by a primary transmitter that is a television broadcast station, comprises the area where such primary transmitter could have insisted upon its signal being retransmitted by a cable system pursuant to the rules, regulations, and authorizations of the Federal Communications Commission in effect on April 15, 1976, or such station's television market as defined in section 76.55(e) of title 47, Code of Federal Regulations (as in effect on September 18, 1993), or any

modifications to such television market made, on or after September 18, 1993, pursuant to section 76.55(e) or 76.59 of title 47, Code of Federal Regulations, or within the noise-limited contour as defined in 73.622(e)(1) of title 47, Code of Federal Regulations, or in the case of a television broadcast station licensed by an appropriate governmental authority of Canada or Mexico, the area in which it would be entitled to insist upon its signal being retransmitted if it were a television broadcast station subject to such rules, regulations, and authorizations. In the case of a low power television station as defined by the rules and regulations of the Federal Communications Commission, the "local service area of a primary transmitter" comprises the designated market area, as defined in section 122(j)(2)(C), that encompasses the community of license of such station and any community that is located outside such designated market area that is either wholly or partially within 35 miles of the transmitter site or, in the case of such a station located in a standard metropolitan statistical area which has one of the 50 largest populations of all standard metropolitan statistical areas (based on the 1980 decennial census of population taken by the Secretary of Commerce), wholly or partially within 20 miles of such transmitter site. The "local service area of a primary transmitter", in the case of a radio broadcast station, comprises the primary service area of such station, pursuant to the rules and regulations of the Federal Communications Commission.

(5) **Distant signal equivalent.**—

(A) **In general.**—Except as provided under subparagraph (B), a "distant signal equivalent"—

(i) is the value assigned to the secondary transmission of any non-network television programming carried by a cable system in whole or in part beyond the local service area of the primary transmitter of such programming; and

(ii) is computed by assigning a value of one to each primary stream and to each multicast stream (other than a simulcast) that is an independent station, and by assigning a value of one-quarter to each primary stream and to each multicast stream (other than a simulcast) that is a network station or a noncommercial educational station.

(B) **Exceptions.**—The values for independent, network, and noncommercial educational stations specified in subparagraph (A) are subject to the following:

(i) Where the rules and regulations of the Federal Communications Commission require a cable system to omit the further transmission of a particular program and such rules and regulations also permit the substitution of another program embodying a performance or display of a work in place of the omitted transmission, or where such rules and regulations in effect on the date of the enactment of the Copyright Act of 1976 permit a cable system, at its election, to effect such omission and substitution of a nonlive program or to carry additional programs not transmitted by primary transmitters within whose local service area the cable system is located, no value shall be assigned for the substituted or additional program.

(ii) Where the rules, regulations, or authorizations of the Federal Communications Commission in effect on the date of the enactment of the Copyright Act of 1976 permit a cable system, at its election, to omit the further transmission of a particular program and such rules, regulations, or authorizations also permit the substitution of another program embodying a performance or display of a work in place of the omitted transmission, the value assigned for the substituted or additional program shall be, in the case of a live program, the value of one full distant signal equivalent multiplied by a fraction that has as its numerator the number of days in the year in which such substitution occurs and as its denominator the number of days in the year.

(iii) In the case of the secondary transmission of a primary transmitter that is a television broadcast station pursuant to the late-night or specialty programming rules of the Federal Communications Commission, or the secondary transmission of a primary transmitter that is a television broadcast station on a part-time basis where full-time carriage is not possible because the cable system lacks the activated channel capacity to retransmit on a full-time basis all signals that it is authorized to carry, the values for independent, network, and noncommercial educational stations set forth in subparagraph (A), as the case may be, shall be multiplied by a fraction that is equal to the ratio of the broadcast hours of such primary transmitter retransmitted by the cable system to the total broadcast hours of the primary transmitter.

(iv) No value shall be assigned for the secondary transmission of the primary stream or any multicast streams of a primary transmitter that is a television broadcast station in any community that is within the local service area of the primary transmitter.

(6) **Network station.—**

(A) **Treatment of primary stream.—**The term "network station" shall be applied to a primary stream of a television broadcast station that is owned or operated by, or affiliated with, one or more of the television networks in the United States providing nationwide transmissions, and that transmits a substantial part of the programming supplied by such networks for a substantial part of the primary stream's typical broadcast day.

(B) **Treatment of multicast streams.—**The term "network station" shall be applied to a multicast stream on which a television broadcast station transmits all or substantially all of the programming of an interconnected program service that—

(i) is owned or operated by, or affiliated with, one or more of the television networks described in subparagraph (A); and

(ii) offers programming on a regular basis for 15 or more hours per week to at least 25 of the affiliated television licensees of the interconnected program service in 10 or more States.

(7) **Independent station.**—The term "independent station" shall be applied to the primary stream or a multicast stream of a television broadcast station that is not a network station or a noncommercial educational station.

(8) **Noncommercial educational station.**—The term "noncommercial educational station" shall be applied to the primary stream or a multicast stream of a television broadcast station that is a noncommercial educational broadcast station as defined in section 397 of the Communications Act of 1934, as in effect on the date of the enactment of the Satellite Television Extension and Localism Act of 2010.

(9) **Primary stream.**—A "primary stream" is—

(A) the single digital stream of programming that, before June 12, 2009, was substantially duplicating the programming transmitted by the television broadcast station as an analog signal; or

(B) if there is no stream described in subparagraph (A), then the single digital stream of programming transmitted by the television broadcast station for the longest period of time.

(10) **Primary transmitter.**—A "primary transmitter" is a television or radio broadcast station licensed by the Federal Communications Commission, or by an appropriate governmental authority of Canada or Mexico, that makes primary transmissions to the public.

(11) **Multicast stream.**—A "multicast stream" is a digital stream of programming that is transmitted by a television broadcast station and is not the station's primary stream.

(12) **Simulcast.**—A "simulcast" is a multicast stream of a television broadcast station that duplicates the programming transmitted by the primary stream or another multicast stream of such station.

(13) **Subscriber; subscribe.**—

(A) **Subscriber.**—The term "subscriber" means a person or entity that receives a secondary transmission service from a cable system and pays a fee for the service, directly or indirectly, to the cable system.

(B) **Subscribe.**—The term "subscribe" means to elect to become a subscriber.

Sec. 112.   Limitations   on   Exclusive   Rights: Ephemeral Recordings

(a)(1) Notwithstanding the provisions of section 106, and except in the case of a motion picture or other audiovisual work, it is not an infringement of copyright for a transmitting organization entitled to transmit to the public a performance or display of a work, under a license, including a statutory license under section 114(f), or transfer of the copyright or under the limitations on exclusive rights in sound recordings specified by section 114(a), or for a transmitting organization that is a broadcast radio or television station licensed as such by the Federal Communications Commission and that makes a broadcast transmission of a performance of a sound recording in a digital format on a nonsubscription basis, to make no more than one copy or phonorecord of a particular transmission program embodying the performance or display, if—

(A) the copy or phonorecord is retained and used solely by the transmitting organization that made it, and no further copies or phonorecords are reproduced from it; and

(B) the copy or phonorecord is used solely for the transmitting organization's own transmissions within its local service area, or for purposes of archival preservation or security; and

(C) unless preserved exclusively for archival purposes, the copy or phonorecord is destroyed within six months from the date the transmission program was first transmitted to the public.

(2) In a case in which a transmitting organization entitled to make a copy or phonorecord under paragraph (1) in connection with the transmission to the public of a performance or display of a work is prevented from making such copy or phonorecord by reason of the application by the copyright owner of technical measures that prevent the reproduction of the work, the copyright owner shall make available to the transmitting organization the necessary means for permitting the making of such copy or phonorecord as permitted under that paragraph, if it is technologically feasible and economically reasonable for the copyright owner to do so. If the copyright owner fails to do so in a timely manner in light of the transmitting organization's reasonable business requirements, the transmitting organization shall not be liable for a violation of section 1201(a)(1) of this title for engaging in such activities as are necessary to make such copies or phonorecords as permitted under paragraph (1) of this subsection.

(b) Notwithstanding the provisions of section 106, it is not an infringement of copyright for a governmental body or other nonprofit organization entitled to transmit a performance or display of a work, under section 110(2) or under the limitations on exclusive rights in sound recordings specified by section 114(a), to make no more than thirty copies or phonorecords of a particular transmission program embodying the performance or display, if—

(1) no further copies or phonorecords are reproduced from the copies or phonorecords made under this clause; and

(2) except for one copy or phonorecord that may be preserved exclusively for archival purposes, the copies or phonorecords are

destroyed within seven years from the date the transmission program was first transmitted to the public.

(c) Notwithstanding the provisions of section 106, it is not an infringement of copyright for a governmental body or other nonprofit organization to make for distribution no more than one copy or phonorecord, for each transmitting organization specified in clause (2) of this subsection, of a particular transmission program embodying a performance of a nondramatic musical work of a religious nature, or of a sound recording of such a musical work, if—

(1) there is no direct or indirect charge for making or distributing any such copies or phonorecords; and

(2) none of such copies or phonorecords is used for any performance other than a single transmission to the public by a transmitting organization entitled to transmit to the public a performance of the work under a license or transfer of the copyright; and

(3) except for one copy or phonorecord that may be preserved exclusively for archival purposes, the copies or phonorecords are all destroyed within one year from the date the transmission program was first transmitted to the public.

(d) Notwithstanding the provisions of section 106, it is not an infringement of copyright for a governmental body or other nonprofit organization entitled to transmit a performance of a work under section 110(8) to make no more than ten copies or phonorecords embodying the performance, or to permit the use of any such copy or phonorecord by any governmental body or nonprofit organization entitled to transmit a performance of a work under section 110(8), if—

(1) any such copy or phonorecord is retained and used solely by the organization that made it, or by a governmental body or nonprofit organization entitled to transmit a performance of a work under section 110(8), and no further copies or phonorecords are reproduced from it; and

(2) any such copy or phonorecord is used solely for transmissions authorized under section 110(8), or for purposes of archival preservation or security; and

(3) the governmental body or nonprofit organization permitting any use of any such copy or phonorecord by any governmental body or nonprofit organization under this subsection does not make any charge for such use.

(e) Statutory license.—

(1) A transmitting organization entitled to transmit to the public a performance of a sound recording under the limitation on exclusive rights specified by section 114(d)(1)(C)(iv) or under a statutory license in accordance with section 114(f) is entitled to a statutory license, under the conditions specified by this subsection, to make no more than 1 phonorecord of the sound recording (unless the terms and conditions of the statutory license allow for more), if the following conditions are satisfied:

(A) The phonorecord is retained and used solely by the transmitting organization that made it, and no further phonorecords are reproduced from it.

(B) The phonorecord is used solely for the transmitting organization's own transmissions originating in the United States under a statutory license in accordance with section 114(f) or the limitation on exclusive rights specified by section 114(d)(1)(C)(iv).

(C) Unless preserved exclusively for purposes of archival preservation, the phonorecord is destroyed within 6 months from the date the sound recording was first transmitted to the public using the phonorecord.

(D) Phonorecords of the sound recording have been distributed to the public under the authority of the copyright owner or the copyright owner authorizes the transmitting entity to transmit the sound recording, and the transmitting entity makes the phonorecord under this subsection from a phonorecord lawfully made and acquired under the authority of the copyright owner.

(2) Notwithstanding any provision of the antitrust laws, any copyright owners of sound recordings and any transmitting organizations entitled to a statutory license under this subsection may negotiate and agree upon royalty rates and license terms and conditions for making phonorecords of such sound recordings under this section and the proportionate division of fees paid among copyright owners, and may designate common agents to negotiate, agree to, pay, or receive such royalty payments.

(3) Proceedings under chapter 8 shall determine reasonable rates and terms of royalty payments for the activities specified by paragraph (1) during the 5–year period beginning on January 1 of the second year following the year in which the proceedings are to be commenced, or such other period as the parties may agree. Such rates shall include a minimum fee for each type of service offered by transmitting organizations. Any copyright owners of sound recordings or any transmitting organizations entitled to a statutory license under this subsection may submit to the Copyright Royalty Judges licenses covering such activities with respect to such sound recordings. The parties to each proceeding shall bear their own costs.

(4) The schedule of reasonable rates and terms determined by the Copyright Royalty Judges shall, subject to paragraph (5), be binding on all copyright owners of sound recordings and transmitting organizations entitled to a statutory license under this subsection during the 5–year period specified in paragraph (3), or such other period as the parties may agree. Such rates shall include a minimum fee for each type of service offered by transmitting organizations. The Copyright Royalty Judges shall establish rates that most clearly represent the fees that would have been negotiated in the marketplace between a willing buyer and a willing seller. In determining such rates and terms, the Copyright Royalty Judges shall base their decision on economic, competitive, and programming information presented by the parties, including—

(A) whether use of the service may substitute for or may promote the sales of phonorecords or otherwise interferes with or enhances the copyright owner's traditional streams of revenue; and

(B) the relative roles of the copyright owner and the transmitting organization in the copyrighted work and the service made available to the public with respect to relative creative contribution, technological contribution, capital investment, cost, and risk.

In establishing such rates and terms, the Copyright Royalty Judges may consider the rates and terms under voluntary license agreements described in paragraphs (2) and (3). The Copyright Royalty Judges shall also establish requirements by which copyright owners may receive reasonable notice of the use of their sound recordings under this section, and under which records of such use shall be kept and made available by transmitting organizations entitled to obtain a statutory license under this subsection.

(5) License agreements voluntarily negotiated at any time between 1 or more copyright owners of sound recordings and 1 or more transmitting organizations entitled to obtain a statutory license under this subsection shall be given effect in lieu of any decision by the Librarian of Congress or determination by the Copyright Royalty Judges.

(6)(A) Any person who wishes to make a phonorecord of a sound recording under a statutory license in accordance with this subsection may do so without infringing the exclusive right of the copyright owner of the sound recording under section 106(1)—

(i) by complying with such notice requirements as the Copyright Royalty Judges shall prescribe by regulation and by paying royalty fees in accordance with this subsection; or

(ii) if such royalty fees have not been set, by agreeing to pay such royalty fees as shall be determined in accordance with this subsection.

(B) Any royalty payments in arrears shall be made on or before the 20th day of the month next succeeding the month in which the royalty fees are set.

(7) If a transmitting organization entitled to make a phonorecord under this subsection is prevented from making such phonorecord by reason of the application by the copyright owner of technical measures that prevent the reproduction of the sound recording, the copyright owner shall make available to the transmitting organization the necessary means for permitting the making of such phonorecord as permitted under this subsection, if it is technologically feasible and economically reasonable for the copyright owner to do so. If the copyright owner fails to do so in a timely manner in light of the transmitting organization's reasonable business requirements, the transmitting organization shall not be liable for a violation of section 1201(a)(1) of this title for engaging in such activities as are necessary to make such phonorecords as permitted under this subsection.

(8) Nothing in this subsection annuls, limits, impairs, or otherwise affects in any way the existence or value of any of the exclusive rights of the copyright owners in a sound recording, except as otherwise provided

in this subsection, or in a musical work, including the exclusive rights to reproduce and distribute a sound recording or musical work, including by means of a digital phonorecord delivery, under sections 106(1), 106(3), and 115, and the right to perform publicly a sound recording or musical work, including by means of a digital audio transmission, under sections 106(4) and 106(6).

(f)(1) Notwithstanding the provisions of section 106, and without limiting the application of subsection (b), it is not an infringement of copyright for a governmental body or other nonprofit educational institution entitled under section 110(2) to transmit a performance or display to make copies or phonorecords of a work that is in digital form and, solely to the extent permitted in paragraph (2), of a work that is in analog form, embodying the performance or display to be used for making transmissions authorized under section 110(2), if—

    (A) such copies or phonorecords are retained and used solely by the body or institution that made them, and no further copies or phonorecords are reproduced from them, except as authorized under section 110(2); and

    (B) such copies or phonorecords are used solely for transmissions authorized under section 110(2).

(2) This subsection does not authorize the conversion of print or other analog versions of works into digital formats, except that such conversion is permitted hereunder, only with respect to the amount of such works authorized to be performed or displayed under section 110(2), if—

    (A) no digital version of the work is available to the institution; or

    (B) the digital version of the work that is available to the institution is subject to technological protection measures that prevent its use for section 110(2).

(g) The transmission program embodied in a copy or phonorecord made under this section is not subject to protection as a derivative work under this title except with the express consent of the owners of copyright in the preexisting works employed in the program.

Sec. 113.   Scope of Exclusive Rights in Pictorial, Graphic, and Sculptural Works

(a) Subject to the provisions of subsections (b) and (c) of this section, the exclusive right to reproduce a copyrighted pictorial, graphic, or sculptural work in copies under section 106 includes the right to reproduce the work in or on any kind of article, whether useful or otherwise.

(b) This title does not afford, to the owner of copyright in a work that portrays a useful article as such, any greater or lesser rights with respect to the making, distribution, or display of the useful article so portrayed than those afforded to such works under the law, whether title 17 or the common law or statutes of a State, in effect on December 31, 1977, as held applicable and construed by a court in an action brought under this title.

(c) In the case of a work lawfully reproduced in useful articles that have been offered for sale or other distribution to the public, copyright does not include any right to prevent the making, distribution, or display of pictures or photographs of such articles in connection with advertisements or commentaries related to the distribution or display of such articles, or in connection with news reports.

(d)(1) In a case in which—

(A) a work of visual art has been incorporated in or made part of a building in such a way that removing the work from the building will cause the destruction, distortion, mutilation, or other modification of the work as described in section 106A(a)(3), and

(B) the author consented to the installation of the work in the building either before the effective date set forth in section 9(a) of the Visual Artists Rights Act of 1990, or in a written instrument executed on or after such effective date that is signed by the owner of the building and the author and that specifies that installation of the work may subject the work to destruction, distortion, mutilation, or other modification, by reason of its removal,

then the rights conferred by paragraphs (2) and (3) of section 106A(a) shall not apply.

(2) If the owner of a building wishes to remove a work of visual art which is a part of such building and which can be removed from the building without the destruction, distortion, mutilation, or other modification of the work as described in section 106A(a)(3), the author's rights under paragraphs (2) and (3) of section 106A(a) shall apply unless—

(A) the owner has made a diligent, good faith attempt without success to notify the author of the owner's intended action affecting the work of visual art, or

(B) the owner did provide such notice in writing and the person so notified failed, within 90 days after receiving such notice, either to remove the work or to pay for its removal.

For purposes of subparagraph (A), an owner shall be presumed to have made a diligent, good faith attempt to send notice if the owner sent such notice by registered mail to the author at the most recent address of the author that was recorded with the Register of Copyrights pursuant to paragraph (3). If the work is removed at the expense of the author, title to that copy of the work shall be deemed to be in the author.

(3) The Register of Copyrights shall establish a system of records whereby any author of a work of visual art that has been incorporated in or made part of a building, may record his identity and address with the Copyright Office. The Register shall also establish procedures under which any such author may update the information so recorded, and procedures under which owners of buildings may record with the Copyright Office evidence of their efforts to comply with this subsection.

Sec. 114.   Scope of Exclusive Rights in Sound Recordings

(a) The exclusive rights of the owner of copyright in a sound recording are limited to the rights specified by clauses (1), (2), (3) and (6) of section 106, and do not include any right of performance under section 106(4).

(b) The exclusive right of the owner of copyright in a sound recording under clause (1) of section 106 is limited to the right to duplicate the sound recording in the form of phonorecords or copies that directly or indirectly recapture the actual sounds fixed in the recording. The exclusive right of the owner of copyright in a sound recording under clause (2) of section 106 is limited to the right to prepare a derivative work in which the actual sounds fixed in the sound recording are rearranged, remixed, or otherwise altered in sequence or quality. The exclusive rights of the owner of copyright in a sound recording under clauses (1) and (2) of section 106 do not extend to the making or duplication of another sound recording that consists entirely of an independent fixation of other sounds, even though such sounds imitate or simulate those in the copyrighted sound recording. The exclusive rights of the owner of copyright in a sound recording under clauses (1), (2), and (3) of section 106 do not apply to sound recordings included in educational television and radio programs (as defined in section 397 of title 47) distributed or transmitted by or through public broadcasting entities (as defined by section 118(f)): Provided, That copies or phonorecords of said programs are not commercially distributed by or through public broadcasting entities to the general public.

(c) This section does not limit or impair the exclusive right to perform publicly, by means of a phonorecord, any of the works specified by section 106(4).

(d) Limitations on Exclusive Right.—Notwithstanding the provisions of section 106(6)—

(1) Exempt transmissions and retransmissions.—The performance of a sound recording publicly by means of a digital audio transmission, other than as a part of an interactive service, is not an infringement of section 106(6) if the performance is part of—

(A) a nonsubscription broadcast transmission;

(B) a retransmission of a nonsubscription broadcast transmission: *Provided,* That, in the case of a retransmission of a radio station's broadcast transmission—

(i) the radio station's broadcast transmission is not willfully or repeatedly retransmitted more than a radius of 150 miles from the site of the radio broadcast transmitter, however—

(I) the 150 mile limitation under this clause shall not apply when a nonsubscription broadcast transmission by a radio station licensed by the Federal Communications Commission is retransmitted on a nonsubscription basis by a terrestrial broadcast station, terrestrial translator, or terrestrial repeater licensed by the Federal Communications Commission; and

(II) in the case of a subscription retransmission of a nonsubscription broadcast retransmission covered by subclause (I), the 150 mile radius shall be measured from the transmitter site of such broadcast retransmitter;

(ii) the retransmission is of radio station broadcast transmissions that are—

(I) obtained by the retransmitter over the air;

(II) not electronically processed by the retransmitter to deliver separate and discrete signals; and

(III) retransmitted only within the local communities served by the retransmitter;

(iii) the radio station's broadcast transmission was being retransmitted to cable systems (as defined in section 111(f)) by a satellite carrier on January 1, 1995, and that retransmission was being retransmitted by cable systems as a separate and discrete signal, and the satellite carrier obtains the radio station's broadcast transmission in an analog format: *Provided,* That the broadcast transmission being retransmitted may embody the programming of no more than one radio station; or

(iv) the radio station's broadcast transmission is made by a noncommercial educational broadcast station funded on or after January 1, 1995, under section 396(k) of the Communications Act of 1934 (47 U.S.C. 396(k)), consists solely of noncommercial educational and cultural radio programs, and the retransmission, whether or not simultaneous, is a nonsubscription terrestrial broadcast retransmission; or

(C) a transmission that comes within any of the following categories—

(i) a prior or simultaneous transmission incidental to an exempt transmission, such as a feed received by and then retransmitted by an exempt transmitter: *Provided,* That such incidental transmissions do not include any subscription transmission directly for reception by members of the public;

(ii) a transmission within a business establishment, confined to its premises or the immediately surrounding vicinity;

(iii) a retransmission by any retransmitter, including a multichannel video programming distributor as defined in section 602(12) of the Communications Act of 1934 (47 U.S.C. 522(12)), of a transmission by a transmitter licensed to publicly perform the sound recording as a part of that transmission, if the retransmission is simultaneous with the licensed transmission and authorized by the transmitter; or

(iv) a transmission to a business establishment for use in the ordinary course of its business: *Provided,* That the business recipient does not retransmit the transmission outside of its premises or the immediately surrounding vicinity, and that the transmission does not exceed the sound recording performance complement. Nothing in this clause shall limit the scope of the exemption in clause (ii).

(2) Statutory licensing of certain transmissions.—The performance of a sound recording publicly by means of a subscription digital audio transmission not exempt under paragraph (1), an eligible nonsubscription transmission, or a transmission not exempt under paragraph (1) that is made by a preexisting satellite digital audio radio service shall be subject to statutory licensing, in accordance with subsection (f) if—

(A)(i) the transmission is not part of an interactive service;

(ii) except in the case of a transmission to a business establishment, the transmitting entity does not automatically and intentionally cause any device receiving the transmission to switch from one program channel to another; and

(iii) except as provided in section 1002(e), the transmission of the sound recording is accompanied, if technically feasible, by the information encoded in that sound recording, if any, by or under the authority of the copyright owner of that sound recording, that identifies the title of the sound recording, the featured recording artist who performs on the sound recording, and related information, including information concerning the underlying musical work and its writer;

(B) in the case of a subscription transmission not exempt under paragraph (1) that is made by a preexisting subscription service in the same transmission medium used by such service on July 31, 1998, or in the case of a transmission not exempt under paragraph (1) that is made by a preexisting satellite digital audio radio service—

(i) the transmission does not exceed the sound recording performance complement; and

(ii) the transmitting entity does not cause to be published by means of an advance program schedule or prior announcement the titles of the specific sound recordings or phonorecords embodying such sound recordings to be transmitted; and

(C) in the case of an eligible nonsubscription transmission or a subscription transmission not exempt under paragraph (1) that is made by a new subscription service or by a preexisting subscription service other than in the same transmission medium used by such service on July 31, 1998—

(i) the transmission does not exceed the sound recording performance complement, except that this requirement shall not apply in the case of a retransmission of a broadcast transmission if the retransmission is made by a transmitting entity that does not have the right or ability to control the programming of the broadcast station making the broadcast transmission, unless—

(I) the broadcast station makes broadcast transmissions—

(aa) in digital format that regularly exceed the sound recording performance complement; or

(bb) in analog format, a substantial portion of which, on a weekly basis, exceed the sound recording performance complement; and

(II) the sound recording copyright owner or its representative has notified the transmitting entity in writing that broadcast transmissions of the copyright owner's sound recordings exceed the sound recording performance complement as provided in this clause;

(ii) the transmitting entity does not cause to be published, or induce or facilitate the publication, by means of an advance program schedule or prior announcement, the titles

of the specific sound recordings to be transmitted, the phonorecords embodying such sound recordings, or, other than for illustrative purposes, the names of the featured recording artists, except that this clause does not disqualify a transmitting entity that makes a prior announcement that a particular artist will be featured within an unspecified future time period, and in the case of a retransmission of a broadcast transmission by a transmitting entity that does not have the right or ability to control the programming of the broadcast transmission, the requirement of this clause shall not apply to a prior oral announcement by the broadcast station, or to an advance program schedule published, induced, or facilitated by the broadcast station, if the transmitting entity does not have actual knowledge and has not received written notice from the copyright owner or its representative that the broadcast station publishes or induces or facilitates the publication of such advance program schedule, or if such advance program schedule is a schedule of classical music programming published by the broadcast station in the same manner as published by that broadcast station on or before September 30, 1998;

(iii) the transmission—

(I) is not part of an archived program of less than 5 hours duration;

(II) is not part of an archived program of 5 hours or greater in duration that is made available for a period exceeding 2 weeks;

(III) is not part of a continuous program which is of less than 3 hours duration; or

(IV) is not part of an identifiable program in which performances of sound recordings are rendered in a predetermined order, other than an archived or continuous program, that is transmitted at—

(aa) more than 3 times in any 2–week period that have been publicly announced in advance, in the case of a program of less than 1 hour in duration, or

(bb) more than 4 times in any 2–week period that have been publicly announced in advance, in the case of a program of 1 hour or more in duration,

except that the requirement of this subclause shall not apply in the case of a retransmission of a broadcast transmission by a transmitting entity that does not have the right or ability to control the programming of the broadcast transmission, unless the transmitting entity is given notice in writing by the copyright owner of the sound recording that the broadcast station makes broadcast transmissions that regularly violate such requirement;

(iv) the transmitting entity does not knowingly perform the sound recording, as part of a service that offers transmissions of visual images contemporaneously with transmissions of sound recordings, in a manner that is likely to cause confusion, to cause mistake, or to deceive, as to the affiliation, connection, or association of the copyright owner or featured recording artist with the transmitting entity or a particular product or service advertised by the transmitting entity, or as to the origin, sponsorship, or approval by the copyright owner or featured recording artist of the activities of the transmitting entity other than the performance of the sound recording itself;

(v) the transmitting entity cooperates to prevent, to the extent feasible without imposing substantial costs or burdens, a transmission recipient or any other person or entity from automatically scanning the transmitting entity's transmissions alone or together with transmissions by other transmitting entities in order to select a particular sound recording to be transmitted to the transmission recipient, except that the requirement of this clause shall not apply to a satellite digital audio service that is in operation, or that is licensed by the Federal Communications Commission, on or before July 31, 1998;

(vi) the transmitting entity takes no affirmative steps to cause or induce the making of a phonorecord by the transmission recipient, and if the technology used by the transmitting entity enables the transmitting entity to limit the making by the transmission recipient of phonorecords of the transmission directly in a digital format, the transmitting entity sets such technology to limit such making of phonorecords to the extent permitted by such technology;

(vii) phonorecords of the sound recording have been distributed to the public under the authority of the copyright owner or the copyright owner authorizes the transmitting entity to transmit the sound recording, and the transmitting entity makes the transmission from a phonorecord lawfully made under the authority of the copyright owner, except that the requirement of this clause shall not apply to a retransmission of a broadcast transmission by a transmitting entity that does not have the right or ability to control the programming of the broadcast transmission, unless the transmitting entity is given notice in writing by the copyright owner of the sound recording that the broadcast station makes broadcast transmissions that regularly violate such requirement;

(viii) the transmitting entity accommodates and does not interfere with the transmission of technical measures that are widely used by sound recording copyright owners to identify or protect copyrighted works, and that are technically feasible of being transmitted by the transmitting entity without imposing substantial costs on the transmitting entity or resulting in perceptible aural or visual degradation of the digital signal, except that the requirement of this clause shall not apply to a satellite digital audio service that is in operation, or that is licensed under the authority of the Federal Communications Commission, on or before July 31, 1998, to the extent that such service has designed, developed, or made commitments to procure equipment or technology that is not compatible with such technical measures before such technical measures are widely adopted by sound recording copyright owners; and

(ix) the transmitting entity identifies in textual data the sound recording during, but not before, the time it is performed, including the title of the sound recording, the title of the phonorecord embodying such sound recording, if any, and the featured recording artist, in a manner to permit it to be displayed to the transmission recipient by the device or technology intended for receiving the service provided by the transmitting entity, except that the obligation in this clause shall not take effect until 1 year after the date of the enactment of the Digital Millennium Copyright Act and shall not apply in the case of a retransmission of a broadcast transmission by a transmitting entity that does not have the right or ability to control the programming of the broadcast transmission, or in the case in which devices or technology intended for receiving the service provided by the transmitting entity that have the capability to display such textual data are not common in the marketplace.

(3) Licenses for transmissions by interactive services.—

(A) No interactive service shall be granted an exclusive license under section 106(6) for the performance of a sound recording publicly by means of digital audio transmission for a period in excess of 12 months, except that with respect to an exclusive license granted to an interactive service by a licensor that holds the copyright to 1,000 or fewer sound recordings, the period of such license shall not exceed 24 months: *Provided, however,* That the grantee of such exclusive license shall be ineligible to receive another exclusive license for the performance of that sound recording for a period of 13 months from the expiration of the prior exclusive license.

(B) The limitation set forth in subparagraph (A) of this paragraph shall not apply if—

(i) the licensor has granted and there remain in effect licenses under section 106(6) for the public performance of sound recordings by means of digital audio transmission by at least 5 different interactive services: *Provided, however,* That each such license must be for a minimum of 10 percent of the copyrighted sound recordings owned by the licensor that have been licensed to interactive services, but in no event less than 50 sound recordings; or

(ii) the exclusive license is granted to perform publicly up to 45 seconds of a sound recording and the sole purpose of the performance is to promote the distribution or performance of that sound recording.

(C) Notwithstanding the grant of an exclusive or nonexclusive license of the right of public performance under section 106(6), an interactive service may not publicly perform a sound recording unless a license has been granted for the public performance of any copyrighted musical work contained in the sound recording: *Provided,* That such license to publicly perform the copyrighted musical work may be granted either by a performing rights society representing the copyright owner or by the copyright owner.

(D) The performance of a sound recording by means of a retransmission of a digital audio transmission is not an infringement of section 106(6) if—

(i) the retransmission is of a transmission by an interactive service licensed to publicly perform the sound recording to a particular member of the public as part of that transmission; and

(ii) the retransmission is simultaneous with the licensed transmission, authorized by the transmitter, and limited to that particular member of the public intended by the interactive service to be the recipient of the transmission.

(E) For the purposes of this paragraph—

(i) a "licensor" shall include the licensing entity and any other entity under any material degree of common ownership, management, or control that owns copyrights in sound recordings; and

(ii) a "performing rights society" is an association or corporation that licenses the public performance of nondramatic musical works on behalf of the copyright owner, such as the American Society of Composers, Authors and Publishers, Broadcast Music, Inc., and SESAC, Inc.

(4) Rights not otherwise limited.—

(A) Except as expressly provided in this section, this section does not limit or impair the exclusive right to perform a sound recording publicly by means of a digital audio transmission under section 106(6).

(B) Nothing in this section annuls or limits in any way—

(i) the exclusive right to publicly perform a musical work, including by means of a digital audio transmission, under section 106(4);

(ii) the exclusive rights in a sound recording or the musical work embodied therein under sections 106(1), 106(2) and 106(3); or

(iii) any other rights under any other clause of section 106, or remedies available under this title, as such rights or remedies exist either before or after the date of enactment of the Digital Performance Right in Sound Recordings Act of 1995.

(C) Any limitations in this section on the exclusive right under section 106(6) apply only to the exclusive right under section 106(6) and not to any other exclusive rights under section 106. Nothing in this section shall be construed to annul, limit, impair or otherwise affect in any way the ability of the owner of a copyright in a sound recording to exercise the rights under sections 106(1), 106(2) and 106(3), or to obtain the remedies available under this title pursuant to such rights, as such rights and remedies exist either before or after the date of enactment of the Digital Performance Right in Sound Recordings Act of 1995.

(e) Authority for Negotiations.—

(1) Notwithstanding any provision of the antitrust laws, in negotiating statutory licenses in accordance with subsection (f), any copyright owners of sound recordings and any entities performing sound recordings affected by this section may negotiate and agree upon the royalty rates and license terms and conditions for the performance of such sound recordings and the proportionate division of fees paid among copyright owners, and may designate common agents on a nonexclusive basis to negotiate, agree to, pay, or receive payments.

(2) For licenses granted under section 106(6), other than statutory licenses, such as for performances by interactive services or performances that exceed the sound recording performance complement—

(A) copyright owners of sound recordings affected by this section may designate common agents to act on their behalf to grant licenses and receive and remit royalty payments: *Provided,* That each copyright owner shall establish the royalty rates and material license terms and conditions unilaterally, that is, not in agreement, combination, or concert with other copyright owners of sound recordings; and

(B) entities performing sound recordings affected by this section may designate common agents to act on their behalf to obtain licenses and collect and pay royalty fees: *Provided,* That each entity performing sound recordings shall determine the royalty rates and material license terms and conditions unilaterally, that is, not in agreement, combination, or concert with other entities performing sound recordings.

(f) Licenses for Certain Nonexempt Transmissions.—

(1)(A) Proceedings under chapter 8 shall determine reasonable rates and terms of royalty payments for subscription transmissions by preexisting subscription services and transmissions by preexisting satellite digital audio radio services specified by subsection (d)(2) during the 5–year period beginning on January 1 of the second year following the year in which the proceedings are to be commenced, except in the case of a different transitional period provided under section 6(b)(3) of the Copyright Royalty and Distribution Reform Act of 2004, or such other period as the parties may agree. Such terms and rates shall distinguish among the different types of digital audio transmission services then in operation. Any copyright owners of sound recordings, preexisting subscription services, or preexisting satellite digital audio radio services may submit to the Copyright Royalty Judges licenses covering such subscription transmissions with respect to such sound recordings. The parties to each proceeding shall bear their own costs.

(B) The schedule of reasonable rates and terms determined by the Copyright Royalty Judges shall, subject to paragraph (3), be binding on all copyright owners of sound recordings and entities performing sound recordings affected by this paragraph during the 5–year period specified in subparagraph (A), a transitional period provided under section 6(b)(3) of the Copyright Royalty and Distribution Reform Act of 2004, or such other period as the parties may agree. In establishing rates and terms for preexisting subscription services and preexisting satellite digital audio radio services, in addition to the objectives set forth in section 801(b)(1), the Copyright Royalty Judges may consider the rates and terms for comparable types of subscription digital audio transmission services and comparable circumstances under voluntary license agreements described in subparagraph (A).

(C) The procedures under subparagraphs (A) and (B) also shall be initiated pursuant to a petition filed by any copyright owners of sound recordings, any preexisting subscription services, or any preexisting satellite digital audio radio services indicating that a new type of subscription digital audio transmission service on which sound recordings are performed is or is about to become operational, for the purpose of determining reasonable terms and rates of royalty payments with respect to such new type of transmission service for the period beginning with the inception of such new type of service and ending on the date on which the royalty rates and terms for subscription digital audio transmission services most recently determined under subparagraph (A) or (B) and chapter 8 expire, or such other period as the parties may agree.

(2)(A) Proceedings under chapter 8 shall determine reasonable rates and terms of royalty payments for public performances of sound recordings by means of eligible nonsubscription transmission services and new subscription services specified by subsection (d)(2) during the 5–year period beginning on January 1 of the second year following the year in which the proceedings are to be commenced, except in the case of a different transitional period provided under section 6(b)(3) of the Copyright Royalty and Distribution Reform Act of 2004, or such other period as the parties may agree. Such rates and terms shall distinguish among the different types of eligible nonsubscription transmission services and new subscription services then in operation and shall include a minimum fee for each such type of service. Any copyright owners of sound recordings or any entities performing sound recordings affected by this paragraph may submit to the Copyright Royalty Judges licenses covering such eligible nonsubscription transmissions and new subscription services with respect to such sound recordings. The parties to each proceeding shall bear their own costs.

(B) The schedule of reasonable rates and terms determined by the Copyright Royalty Judges shall, subject to paragraph (3), be binding on all copyright owners of sound recordings and entities performing sound recordings affected by this paragraph during the 5–year period specified in subparagraph (A), a transitional period provided under section 6(b)(3) of the Copyright Royalty and Distribution Reform Act of 2004, or such other period as the parties may agree. Such rates and terms shall distinguish among the different types of eligible nonsubscription transmission services then in operation and shall include a minimum fee for each such type of service, such differences to be based on criteria including, but not limited to, the quantity and nature of the use of sound recordings and the degree to which use of the service may substitute for or may promote the purchase of phonorecords by consumers. In establishing rates and terms for transmissions by eligible nonsubscription services and new subscription services, the Copyright Royalty Judges shall establish rates and terms that most clearly represent the rates and terms that would have been negotiated in the marketplace between a willing buyer and a willing seller. In determining such rates and terms, the Copyright Royalty Judges shall base their decision on economic, competitive and programming information presented by the parties, including—

(i) whether use of the service may substitute for or may promote the sales of phonorecords or otherwise may interfere with or may enhance the sound recording copyright owner's other streams of revenue from its sound recordings; and

(ii) the relative roles of the copyright owner and the transmitting entity in the copyrighted work and the service made available to the public with respect to relative creative contribution, technological contribution, capital investment, cost, and risk.

In establishing such rates and terms, the Copyright Royalty Judges may consider the rates and terms for comparable types of digital audio transmission services and comparable circumstances under voluntary license agreements described in subparagraph (A).

(C) The procedures under subparagraphs (A) and (B) shall also be initiated pursuant to a petition filed by any copyright owners of sound recordings or any eligible nonsubscription service or new subscription service indicating that a new type of eligible nonsubscription service or new subscription service on which sound recordings are performed is or is about to become operational, for the purpose of determining reasonable terms and rates of royalty payments with respect to such new type of service for the period beginning with the inception of such new type of service and ending on the date on which the royalty rates and terms for eligible nonsubscription services and new subscription services, as the case may be, most recently determined under subparagraph (A) or (B) and chapter 8 expire, or such other period as the parties may agree.

(3) License agreements voluntarily negotiated at any time between 1 or more copyright owners of sound recordings and 1 or more entities performing sound recordings shall be given effect in lieu of any decision by the Librarian of Congress or determination by the Copyright Royalty Judges.

(4)(A) The Copyright Royalty Judges shall also establish requirements by which copyright owners may receive reasonable notice of the use of their sound recordings under this section, and under which records of such use shall be kept and made available by entities performing sound recordings. The notice and recordkeeping rules in effect on the day before the effective date of the Copyright Royalty and Distribution Reform Act of 2004 shall remain in effect unless and until new regulations are promulgated by the Copyright Royalty Judges. If new regulations are promulgated under this subparagraph, the Copyright Royalty Judges shall take into account the substance and effect of the rules in effect on the day before the effective date of the Copyright Royalty and Distribution Reform Act of 2004 and shall, to the extent practicable, avoid significant disruption of the functions of any designated agent authorized to collect and distribute royalty fees.

(B) Any person who wishes to perform a sound recording publicly by means of a transmission eligible for statutory licensing under this subsection may do so without infringing the exclusive right of the copyright owner of the sound recording—

(i) by complying with such notice requirements as the Copyright Royalty Judges shall prescribe by regulation and by paying royalty fees in accordance with this subsection; or

(ii) if such royalty fees have not been set, by agreeing to pay such royalty fees as shall be determined in accordance with this subsection.

(C) Any royalty payments in arrears shall be made on or before the twentieth day of the month next succeeding the month in which the royalty fees are set.

(5)(A) Notwithstanding section 112(e) and the other provisions of this subsection, the receiving agent may enter into agreements for the reproduction and performance of sound recordings under section

112(e) and this section by any one or more commercial webcasters or noncommercial webcasters for a period of not more than 11 years beginning on January 1, 2005, that, once published in the Federal Register pursuant to subparagraph (B), shall be binding on all copyright owners of sound recordings and other persons entitled to payment under this section, in lieu of any determination by the Copyright Royalty Judges. Any such agreement for commercial webcasters may include provisions for payment of royalties on the basis of a percentage of revenue or expenses, or both, and include a minimum fee. Any such agreement may include other terms and conditions, including requirements by which copyright owners may receive notice of the use of their sound recordings and under which records of such use shall be kept and made available by commercial webcasters or noncommercial webcasters. The receiving agent shall be under no obligation to negotiate any such agreement. The receiving agent shall have no obligation to any copyright owner of sound recordings or any other person entitled to payment under this section in negotiating any such agreement, and no liability to any copyright owner of sound recordings or any other person entitled to payment under this section for having entered into such agreement.

(B) The Copyright Office shall cause to be published in the Federal Register any agreement entered into pursuant to subparagraph (A). Such publication shall include a statement containing the substance of subparagraph (C). Such agreements shall not be included in the Code of Federal Regulations. Thereafter, the terms of such agreement shall be available, as an option, to any commercial webcaster or noncommercial webcaster meeting the eligibility conditions of such agreement.

(C) Neither subparagraph (A) nor any provisions of any agreement entered into pursuant to subparagraph (A), including any rate structure, fees, terms, conditions, or notice and recordkeeping requirements set forth therein, shall be admissible as evidence or otherwise taken into account in any administrative, judicial, or other government proceeding involving the setting or adjustment of the royalties payable for the public performance or reproduction in ephemeral phonorecords or copies of sound recordings, the determination of terms or conditions related thereto, or the establishment of notice or recordkeeping requirements by the Copyright Royalty Judges under paragraph (4) or section 112(e)(4). It is the intent of Congress that any royalty rates, rate structure, definitions, terms, conditions, or notice and recordkeeping requirements, included in such agreements shall be considered as a compromise motivated by the unique business, economic and political circumstances of webcasters, copyright owners, and performers rather than as matters that would have been negotiated in the marketplace between a willing buyer and a willing seller, or otherwise meet the objectives set forth in section 801(b). This subparagraph shall not apply to the extent that the receiving agent and a webcaster that is party to an agreement entered into pursuant to subparagraph (A) expressly authorize the submission of the agreement in a proceeding under this subsection.

(D) Nothing in the Webcaster Settlement Act of 2008, the Webcaster Settlement Act of 2009, or any agreement entered into pursuant to subparagraph (A) shall be taken into account by the United States Court of Appeals for the District of Columbia Circuit in its review of the determination by the Copyright Royalty Judges of May 1, 2007, of rates and terms for the digital performance of sound recordings and ephemeral recordings, pursuant to sections 112 and 114.

(E) As used in this paragraph—

(i) the term "noncommercial webcaster" means a webcaster that—

(I) is exempt from taxation under section 501 of the Internal Revenue Code of 1986 (26 U.S.C. 501);

(II) has applied in good faith to the Internal Revenue Service for exemption from taxation under section 501 of the Internal Revenue Code and has a commercially reasonable expectation that such exemption shall be granted; or

(III) is operated by a State or possession or any governmental entity or subordinate thereof, or by the United States or District of Columbia, for exclusively public purposes;

(ii) the term "receiving agent" shall have the meaning given that term in section 261.2 of title 37, Code of Federal Regulations, as published in the Federal Register on July 8, 2002; and

(iii) the term "webcaster" means a person or entity that has obtained a compulsory license under section 112 or 114 and the implementing regulations therefor

(F) The authority to make settlements pursuant to subparagraph (A) shall expire at 11:59 p.m. Eastern time on the 30th day after the date of the enactment of the Webcaster Settlement Act of 2009.

(g) Proceeds From Licensing of Transmissions.—

(1) Except in the case of a transmission licensed under a statutory license in accordance with subsection (f) of this section—

(A) a featured recording artist who performs on a sound recording that has been licensed for a transmission shall be entitled to receive payments from the copyright owner of the sound recording in accordance with the terms of the artist's contract; and

(B) a nonfeatured recording artist who performs on a sound recording that has been licensed for a transmission shall be entitled to receive payments from the copyright owner of the sound recording in accordance with the terms of the nonfeatured recording artist's applicable contract or other applicable agreement.

(2) An agent designated to distribute receipts from the licensing of transmissions in accordance with subsection (f) shall distribute such receipts as follows:

(A) 50 percent of the receipts shall be paid to the copyright owner of the exclusive right under section 106(6) of this title to publicly perform a sound recording by means of a digital audio transmission.

(B) 2 1/2 percent of the receipts shall be deposited in an escrow account managed by an independent administrator jointly appointed by copyright owners of sound recordings and the American Federation of Musicians (or any successor entity) to be distributed to nonfeatured musicians (whether or not members of the American Federation of Musicians) who have performed on sound recordings.

(C) 2 1/2 percent of the receipts shall be deposited in an escrow account managed by an independent administrator jointly appointed by copyright owners of sound recordings and the American Federation of Television and Radio Artists (or any successor entity) to be distributed to nonfeatured vocalists (whether or not members of the American Federation of Television and Radio Artists) who have performed on sound recordings.

(D) 45 percent of the receipts shall be paid, on a per sound recording basis, to the recording artist or artists featured on such sound recording (or the persons conveying rights in the artists' performance in the sound recordings).

(3) A nonprofit agent designated to distribute receipts from the licensing of transmissions in accordance with subsection (f) may deduct from any of its receipts, prior to the distribution of such receipts to any person or entity entitled thereto other than copyright owners and performers who have elected to receive royalties from another designated agent and have notified such nonprofit agent in writing of such election, the reasonable costs of such agent incurred after November 1, 1995, in—

(A) the administration of the collection, distribution, and calculation of the royalties;

(B) the settlement of disputes relating to the collection and calculation of the royalties; and

(C) the licensing and enforcement of rights with respect to the making of ephemeral recordings and performances subject to licensing under section 112 and this section, including those incurred in participating in negotiations or arbitration proceedings under section 112 and this section, except that all costs incurred relating to the section 112 ephemeral recordings right may only be deducted from the royalties received pursuant to section 112.

(4) Notwithstanding paragraph (3), any designated agent designated to distribute receipts from the licensing of transmissions in accordance with subsection (f) may deduct from any of its receipts, prior to the distribution of such receipts, the reasonable costs

identified in paragraph (3) of such agent incurred after November 1, 1995, with respect to such copyright owners and performers who have entered with such agent a contractual relationship that specifies that such costs may be deducted from such royalty receipts.

(h) Licensing to Affiliates.—

(1) If the copyright owner of a sound recording licenses an affiliated entity the right to publicly perform a sound recording by means of a digital audio transmission under section 106(6), the copyright owner shall make the licensed sound recording available under section 106(6) on no less favorable terms and conditions to all bona fide entities that offer similar services, except that, if there are material differences in the scope of the requested license with respect to the type of service, the particular sound recordings licensed, the frequency of use, the number of subscribers served, or the duration, then the copyright owner may establish different terms and conditions for such other services.

(2) The limitation set forth in paragraph (1) of this subsection shall not apply in the case where the copyright owner of a sound recording licenses—

(A) an interactive service; or

(B) an entity to perform publicly up to 45 seconds of the sound recording and the sole purpose of the performance is to promote the distribution or performance of that sound recording.

(i) No Effect on Royalties for Underlying Works.—License fees payable for the public performance of sound recordings under section 106(6) shall not be taken into account in any administrative, judicial, or other governmental proceeding to set or adjust the royalties payable to copyright owners of musical works for the public performance of their works. It is the intent of Congress that royalties payable to copyright owners of musical works for the public performance of their works shall not be diminished in any respect as a result of the rights granted by section 106(6).

(j) Definitions.—As used in this section, the following terms have the following meanings:

(1) An "affiliated entity" is an entity engaging in digital audio transmissions covered by section 106(6), other than an interactive service, in which the licensor has any direct or indirect partnership or any ownership interest amounting to 5 percent or more of the outstanding voting or non-voting stock.

(2) An "archived program" is a predetermined program that is available repeatedly on the demand of the transmission recipient and that is performed in the same order from the beginning, except that an archived program shall not include a recorded event or broadcast transmission that makes no more than an incidental use of sound recordings, as long as such recorded event or broadcast transmission does not contain an entire sound recording or feature a particular sound recording.

(3) A "broadcast" transmission is a transmission made by a terrestrial broadcast station licensed as such by the Federal Communications Commission.

(4) A "continuous program" is a predetermined program that is continuously performed in the same order and that is accessed at a point in the program that is beyond the control of the transmission recipient.

(5) A "digital audio transmission" is a digital transmission as defined in section 101, that embodies the transmission of a sound recording. This term does not include the transmission of any audiovisual work.

(6) An "eligible nonsubscription transmission" is a noninteractive nonsubscription digital audio transmission not exempt under subsection (d)(1) that is made as part of a service that provides audio programming consisting, in whole or in part, of performances of sound recordings, including retransmissions of broadcast transmissions, if the primary purpose of the service is to provide to the public such audio or other entertainment programming, and the primary purpose of the service is not to sell, advertise, or promote particular products or services other than sound recordings, live concerts, or other music-related events.

(7) An "interactive service" is one that enables a member of the public to receive a transmission of a program specially created for the recipient, or on request, a transmission of a particular sound recording, whether or not as part of a program, which is selected by or on behalf of the recipient. The ability of individuals to request that particular sound recordings be performed for reception by the public at large, or in the case of a subscription service, by all subscribers of the service, does not make a service interactive, if the programming on each channel of the service does not substantially consist of sound recordings that are performed within 1 hour of the request or at a time designated by either the transmitting entity or the individual making such request. If an entity offers both interactive and noninteractive services (either concurrently or at different times), the noninteractive component shall not be treated as part of an interactive service.

(8) A "new subscription service" is a service that performs sound recordings by means of noninteractive subscription digital audio transmissions and that is not a preexisting subscription service or a preexisting satellite digital audio radio service.

(9) A "nonsubscription" transmission is any transmission that is not a subscription transmission.

(10) A "preexisting satellite digital audio radio service" is a subscription satellite digital audio radio service provided pursuant to a satellite digital audio radio service license issued by the Federal Communications Commission on or before July 31, 1998, and any renewal of such license to the extent of the scope of the original license, and may include a limited number of sample channels representative of the subscription service that are made available on a nonsubscription basis in order to promote the subscription service.

(11) A "preexisting subscription service" is a service that performs sound recordings by means of noninteractive audio-only subscription digital audio transmissions, which was in existence and was making such transmissions to the public for a fee on or before July 31, 1998, and may include a limited number of sample channels representative of the subscription service that are made available on a nonsubscription basis in order to promote the subscription service.

(12) A "retransmission" is a further transmission of an initial transmission, and includes any further retransmission of the same transmission. Except as provided in this section, a transmission qualifies as a "retransmission" only if it is simultaneous with the initial transmission. Nothing in this definition shall be construed to exempt a transmission that fails to satisfy a separate element required to qualify for an exemption under section 114(d)(1).

(13) The "sound recording performance complement" is the transmission during any 3–hour period, on a particular channel used by a transmitting entity, of no more than—

(A) 3 different selections of sound recordings from any one phonorecord lawfully distributed for public performance or sale in the United States, if no more than 2 such selections are transmitted consecutively; or

(B) 4 different selections of sound recordings—

(i) by the same featured recording artist; or

(ii) from any set or compilation of phonorecords lawfully distributed together as a unit for public performance or sale in the United States,

if no more than three such selections are transmitted consecutively:

Provided, That the transmission of selections in excess of the numerical limits provided for in clauses (A) and (B) from multiple phonorecords shall nonetheless qualify as a sound recording performance complement if the programming of the multiple phonorecords was not willfully intended to avoid the numerical limitations prescribed in such clauses.

(14) A "subscription" transmission is a transmission that is controlled and limited to particular recipients, and for which consideration is required to be paid or otherwise given by or on behalf of the recipient to receive the transmission or a package of transmissions including the transmission.

(15) A "transmission" is either an initial transmission or a retransmission.

Sec. 115. Scope of Exclusive Rights in Nondramatic Musical Works: Compulsory License for Making and Distributing Phonorecords

In the case of nondramatic musical works, the exclusive rights provided by clauses (1) and (3) of section 106, to make and to distribute phonorecords of such works, are subject to compulsory licensing under the conditions specified by this section.

(a) Availability and Scope of Compulsory License.—

(1) When phonorecords of a nondramatic musical work have been distributed to the public in the United States under the authority of the copyright owner, any other person, including those who make phonorecords or digital phonorecord deliveries may, by complying with the provisions of this section, obtain a compulsory license to make and distribute phonorecords of the work. A person may obtain a compulsory license only if his or her primary purpose in making phonorecords is to distribute them to the public for private use, including by means of a digital phonorecord delivery. A person may not obtain a compulsory license for use of the work in the making of phonorecords duplicating a sound recording fixed by another, unless: (i) such sound recording was fixed lawfully; and (ii) the making of the phonorecords was authorized by the owner of copyright in the sound recording or, if the sound recording was fixed before February 15, 1972, by any person who fixed the sound recording pursuant to an express license from the owner of the copyright in the musical work or pursuant to a valid compulsory license for use of such work in a sound recording.

(2) A compulsory license includes the privilege of making a musical arrangement of the work to the extent necessary to conform it to the style or manner of interpretation of the performance involved, but the arrangement shall not change the basic melody or fundamental character of the work, and shall not be subject to protection as a derivative work under this title, except with the express consent of the copyright owner.

(b) Notice of Intention to Obtain Compulsory License.—

(1) Any person who wishes to obtain a compulsory license under this section shall, before or within thirty days after making, and before distributing any phonorecords of the work, serve notice of intention to do so on the copyright owner. If the registration or other public records of the Copyright Office do not identify the copyright owner and include an address at which notice can be served, it shall be sufficient to file the notice of intention in the Copyright Office. The notice shall comply, in form, content, and manner of service, with requirements that the Register of Copyrights shall prescribe by regulation.

(2) Failure to serve or file the notice required by clause (1) forecloses the possibility of a compulsory license and, in the absence of a negotiated license, renders the making and distribution of phonorecords actionable as acts of infringement under section 501 and fully subject to the remedies provided by sections 502 through 506 and 509.

(c) Royalty Payable Under Compulsory License.—

(1) To be entitled to receive royalties under a compulsory license, the copyright owner must be identified in the registration or other public records of the Copyright Office. The owner is entitled to royalties for phonorecords made and distributed after being so identified, but is not entitled to recover for any phonorecords previously made and distributed.

(2) Except as provided by clause (1), the royalty under a compulsory license shall be payable for every phonorecord made and distributed in accordance with the license. For this purpose, and other than as provided in paragraph (3), a phonorecord is considered "distributed" if the person exercising the compulsory license has voluntarily and permanently parted with its possession. With respect to each work embodied in the

phonorecord, the royalty shall be either two and three-fourths cents, or one-half of one cent per minute of playing time or fraction thereof, whichever amount is larger.[e]

(3)(A) A compulsory license under this section includes the right of the compulsory licensee to distribute or authorize the distribution of a phonorecord of a nondramatic musical work by means of a digital transmission which constitutes a digital phonorecord delivery, regardless of whether the digital transmission is also a public performance of the sound recording under section 106(6) of this title or of any nondramatic musical work embodied therein under section 106(4) of this title. For every digital phonorecord delivery by or under the authority of the compulsory licensee—

     (i) on or before December 31, 1997, the royalty payable by the compulsory licensee shall be the royalty prescribed under paragraph (2) and chapter 8 of this title; and

     (ii) on or after January 1, 1998, the royalty payable by the compulsory licensee shall be the royalty prescribed under subparagraphs (B) through (E) and chapter 8 of this title.

(B) Notwithstanding any provision of the antitrust laws, any copyright owners of nondramatic musical works and any persons entitled to obtain a compulsory license under subsection (a)(1) may negotiate and agree upon the terms and rates of royalty payments under this section and the proportionate division of fees paid among copyright owners, and may designate common agents on a nonexclusive basis to negotiate, agree to, pay or receive such royalty payments. Such authority to negotiate the terms and rates of royalty payments includes, but is not limited to, the authority to negotiate the year during which the royalty rates prescribed under this subparagraph and subparagraphs (C) through (E) and chapter 8 of this title shall next be determined.

(C) Proceedings under chapter 8 shall determine reasonable rates and terms of royalty payments for the activities specified by this section during the period beginning with the effective date of such rates and terms, but not earlier than January 1 of the second year following the year in which the petition requesting the proceeding is filed, and ending on the effective date of successor rates and terms, or such other period as the parties may agree. Such terms and rates shall distinguish between (i) digital phonorecord deliveries where the reproduction or distribution of a phonorecord is incidental to the transmission which constitutes the digital phonorecord delivery, and (ii) digital phonorecord deliveries in general. Any copyright owners of nondramatic musical works and any persons entitled to obtain a compulsory license under subsection (a)(1) may submit to the Copyright Royalty Judges licenses covering such activities. The parties to each proceeding shall bear their own costs.

(D) The schedule of reasonable rates and terms determined by the Copyright Royalty Judges shall, subject to subparagraph (E), be binding on all copyright owners of nondramatic musical works and persons entitled to obtain a compulsory license under subsection (a)(1) during the period specified in subparagraph (C), such other period as may be determined pursuant to subparagraphs (B) and (C), or such other period

---

[e]   The current royalty rate is set as provided in 37 C.F.R. § 385.3, at http://www.loc.gov/crb/laws/title37/index.htm

as the parties may agree. Such terms and rates shall distinguish between (i) digital phonorecord deliveries where the reproduction or distribution of a phonorecord is incidental to the transmission which constitutes the digital phonorecord delivery, and (ii) digital phonorecord deliveries in general. In addition to the objectives set forth in section 801(b)(1), in establishing such rates and terms, the Copyright Royalty Judges may consider rates and terms under voluntary license agreements described in subparagraphs (B) and (C). The royalty rates payable for a compulsory license for a digital phonorecord delivery under this section shall be established de novo and no precedential effect shall be given to the amount of the royalty payable by a compulsory licensee for digital phonorecord deliveries on or before December 31, 1997. The Copyright Royalty Judges shall also establish requirements by which copyright owners may receive reasonable notice of the use of their works under this section, and under which records of such use shall be kept and made available by persons making digital phonorecord deliveries.

(E)(i) License agreements voluntarily negotiated at any time between one or more copyright owners of nondramatic musical works and one or more persons entitled to obtain a compulsory license under subsection (a)(1) shall be given effect in lieu of any determination by the Librarian of Congress and Copyright Royalty Judges. Subject to clause (ii), the royalty rates determined pursuant to subparagraph (C) and (D) shall be given effect as to digital phonorecord deliveries in lieu of any contrary royalty rates specified in a contract pursuant to which a recording artist who is the author of a nondramatic musical work grants a license under that person's exclusive rights in the musical work under paragraphs (1) and (3) of section 106 or commits another person to grant a license in that musical work under paragraphs (1) and (3) of section 106, to a person desiring to fix in a tangible medium of expression a sound recording embodying the musical work.

(ii) The second sentence of clause (i) shall not apply to—

(I) a contract entered into on or before June 22, 1995, and not modified thereafter for the purpose of reducing the royalty rates determined pursuant to subparagraph (C) and (D) or of increasing the number of musical works within the scope of the contract covered by the reduced rates, except if a contract entered into on or before June 22, 1995, is modified thereafter for the purpose of increasing the number of musical works within the scope of the contract, any contrary royalty rates specified in the contract shall be given effect in lieu of royalty rates determined pursuant to subparagraph (C) and (D) for the number of musical works within the scope of the contract as of June 22, 1995; and

(II) a contract entered into after the date that the sound recording is fixed in a tangible medium of expression substantially in a form intended for commercial release, if at the time the contract is entered into, the recording artist retains the right to grant licenses as to the musical work under paragraphs (1) and (3) of section 106.

(F) Except as provided in section 1002(e) of this title, a digital phonorecord delivery licensed under this paragraph shall be accompanied by the information encoded in the sound recording, if any, by or under the authority of the copyright owner of that sound recording, that identifies the title of the sound recording, the featured recording artist who performs on the sound recording, and related information, including information concerning the underlying musical work and its writer.

(G)(i) A digital phonorecord delivery of a sound recording is actionable as an act of infringement under section 501, and is fully subject to the remedies provided by sections 502 through 506, unless—

(I) the digital phonorecord delivery has been authorized by the copyright owner of the sound recording; and

(II) the owner of the copyright in the sound recording or the entity making the digital phonorecord delivery has obtained a compulsory license under this section or has otherwise been authorized by the copyright owner of the musical work to distribute or authorize the distribution, by means of a digital phonorecord delivery, of each musical work embodied in the sound recording.

(ii) Any cause of action under this subparagraph shall be in addition to those available to the owner of the copyright in the nondramatic musical work under subsection (c)(6) and section 106(4) and the owner of the copyright in the sound recording under section 106(6).

(H) The liability of the copyright owner of a sound recording for infringement of the copyright in a nondramatic musical work embodied in the sound recording shall be determined in accordance with applicable law, except that the owner of a copyright in a sound recording shall not be liable for a digital phonorecord delivery by a third party if the owner of the copyright in the sound recording does not license the distribution of a phonorecord of the nondramatic musical work.

(I) Nothing in section 1008 shall be construed to prevent the exercise of the rights and remedies allowed by this paragraph, paragraph (6), and chapter 5 in the event of a digital phonorecord delivery, except that no action alleging infringement of copyright may be brought under this title against a manufacturer, importer or distributor of a digital audio recording device, a digital audio recording medium, an analog recording device, or an analog recording medium, or against a consumer, based on the actions described in such section.

(J) Nothing in this section annuls or limits (i) the exclusive right to publicly perform a sound recording or the musical work embodied therein, including by means of a digital transmission, under sections 106(4) and 106(6), (ii) except for compulsory licensing under the conditions specified by this section, the exclusive rights to reproduce and distribute the sound recording and the musical work embodied therein under sections 106(1) and 106(3), including by means of a digital phonorecord delivery, or (iii) any other rights under any other provision of section 106, or remedies available under this title, as such rights or remedies exist either before or after the date of enactment of the Digital Performance Right in Sound Recordings Act of 1995.

(K) The provisions of this section concerning digital phonorecord deliveries shall not apply to any exempt transmissions or retransmissions under section 114(d)(1). The exemptions created in section 114(d)(1) do not expand or reduce the rights of copyright owners under section 106(1) through (5) with respect to such transmissions and retransmissions.

(4) A compulsory license under this section includes the right of the maker of a phonorecord of a nondramatic musical work under subsection (a)(1) to distribute or authorize distribution of such phonorecord by rental, lease, or lending (or by acts or practices in the nature of rental, lease, or lending). In addition to any royalty payable under clause (2) and chapter 8 of this title, a royalty shall be payable by the compulsory licensee for every act of distribution of a phonorecord by or in the nature of rental, lease, or lending, by or under the authority of the compulsory licensee. With respect to each nondramatic, musical work embodied in the phonorecord, the royalty shall be a proportion of the revenue received by the compulsory licensee from every such act of distribution of the phonorecord under this clause equal to the proportion of the revenue received by the compulsory licensee from distribution of the phonorecord under clause (2) that is payable by a compulsory licensee under that clause and under chapter 8. The Register of Copyrights shall issue regulations to carry out the purpose of this clause.

(5) Royalty payments shall be made on or before the twentieth day of each month and shall include all royalties for the month next preceding. Each monthly payment shall be made under oath and shall comply with requirements that the Register of Copyrights shall prescribe by regulation. The Register shall also prescribe regulations under which detailed cumulative annual statements of account, certified by a certified public accountant, shall be filed for every compulsory license under this section. The regulations covering both the monthly and the annual statements of account shall prescribe the form, content, and manner of certification with respect to the number of records made and the number of records distributed.

(6) If the copyright owner does not receive the monthly payment and the monthly and annual statements of account when due, the owner may give written notice to the licensee that, unless the default is remedied within thirty days from the date of the notice, the compulsory license will be automatically terminated. Such termination renders either the making or the distribution, or both, of all phonorecords for which the royalty has not been paid, actionable as acts of infringement under section 501 and fully subject to the remedies provided by sections 502 through 506.

(d) Definition.—As used in this section, the following term has the following meaning: A "digital phonorecord delivery" is each individual delivery of a phonorecord by digital transmission of a sound recording which results in a specifically identifiable reproduction by or for any transmission recipient of a phonorecord of that sound recording, regardless of whether the digital transmission is also a public performance of the sound recording or any nondramatic musical work embodied therein. A digital phonorecord delivery does not result from a real-time, non-interactive subscription transmission of a sound recording where no reproduction of the sound recording or the musical work embodied therein is made from the inception of the transmission through to its receipt by the transmission recipient in order to make the sound recording audible.

Sec. 116.   Negotiated Licenses for Public Performances by Means of Coin-Operated Phonorecord Players

(a) Applicability of Section.—This section applies to any nondramatic musical work embodied in a phonorecord.

(b) Negotiated Licenses.—

(1) Authority for Negotiations.—Any owners of copyright in works to which this section applies and any operators of coin-operated phonorecord players may negotiate and agree upon the terms and rates of royalty payments for the performance of such works and the proportionate division of fees paid among copyright owners, and may designate common agents to negotiate, agree to, pay, or receive such royalty payments.

(2) Chapter 8 Proceeding.—Parties not subject to such a negotiation may have the terms and rates and the division of fees described in paragraph (1) determined in a proceeding in accordance with the provisions of chapter 8.

(c) License Agreements Superior to Determinations by Copyright Royalty Judges.—License agreements between one or more copyright owners and one or more operators of coin-operated phonorecord players, which are negotiated in accordance with subsection (b), shall be given effect in lieu of any otherwise applicable determination by the Copyright Royalty Judges.

(d) Definitions.—As used in this section, the following terms mean the following:

(1) A "coin-operated phonorecord player" is a machine or device that—

(A) is employed solely for the performance of nondramatic musical works by means of phonorecords upon being activated by the insertion of coins, currency, tokens, or other monetary units or their equivalent;

(B) is located in an establishment making no direct or indirect charge for admission;

(C) is accompanied by a list which is comprised of the titles of all the musical works available for performance on it, and is affixed to the phonorecord player or posted in the establishment in a prominent position where it can be readily examined by the public; and

(D) affords a choice of works available for performance and permits the choice to be made by the patrons of the establishment in which it is located.

(2) An "operator" is any person who, alone or jointly with others—

(A) owns a coin-operated phonorecord player;

(B) has the power to make a coin-operated phonorecord player available for placement in an establishment for purposes of public performance; or

(C) has the power to exercise primary control over the selection of the musical works made available for public performance on a coin-operated phonorecord player.

Sec. 117. Limitations on Exclusive Rights: Computer Programs

(a) Making of Additional Copy or Adaptation by Owner of Copy.—Notwithstanding the provisions of section 106, it is not an infringement for the owner of a copy of a computer program to make or authorize the making of another copy or adaptation of that computer program provided:

(1) that such a new copy or adaptation is created as an essential step in the utilization of the computer program in conjunction with a machine and that it is used in no other manner, or

(2) that such new copy or adaptation is for archival purposes only and that all archival copies are destroyed in the event that continued possession of the computer program should cease to be rightful.

(b) Leases, Sale, or Other Transfer of Additional Copy or Adaptation.—Any exact copies prepared in accordance with the provisions of this section may be leased, sold, or otherwise transferred, along with the copy from which such copies were prepared, only as part of the lease, sale, or other transfer of all rights in the program. Adaptations so prepared may be transferred only with the authorization of the copyright owner.

(c) Machine Maintenance or Repair.—Notwithstanding the provisions of section 106, it is not an infringement for the owner or lessee of a machine to make or authorize the making of a copy of a computer program if such copy is made solely by virtue of the activation of a machine that lawfully contains an authorized copy of the computer program, for purposes only of maintenance or repair of that machine, if—

(1) such new copy is used in no other manner and is destroyed immediately after the maintenance or repair is completed; and

(2) with respect to any computer program or part thereof that is not necessary for that machine to be activated, such program or part thereof is not accessed or used other than to make such new copy by virtue of the activation of the machine.

(d) Definitions.—For purposes of this section—

(1) the "maintenance" of a machine is the servicing of the machine in order to make it work in accordance with its original specifications and any changes to those specifications authorized for that machine; and

(2) the "repair" of a machine is the restoring of the machine to the state of working in accordance with its original specifications and any changes to those specifications authorized for that machine.

Sec. 118. Scope of Exclusive Rights: Use of Certain Works in Connection With Noncommercial Broadcasting

(a) The exclusive rights provided by section 106 shall, with respect to the works specified by subsection (b) and the activities specified by subsection (d), be subject to the conditions and limitations prescribed by this section.

(b) Notwithstanding any provision of the antitrust laws, any owners of copyright in published nondramatic musical works and published pictorial, graphic, and sculptural works and any public broadcasting entities, respectively, may negotiate and agree upon the terms and rates of royalty payments and the proportionate division of fees paid among various copyright owners, and may designate common agents to negotiate, agree to, pay, or receive payments.

(1) Any owner of copyright in a work specified in this subsection or any public broadcasting entity may submit to the Copyright Royalty Judges proposed licenses covering such activities with respect to such works.

(2) License agreements voluntarily negotiated at any time between one or more copyright owners and one or more public broadcasting entities shall be given effect in lieu of any determination by the Librarian of Congress or the Copyright Royalty Judges, if copies of such agreements are filed with the Copyright Royalty Judges within 30 days of execution in accordance with regulations that the Copyright Royalty Judges shall issue.

(3) Voluntary negotiation proceedings initiated pursuant to a petition filed under section 804(a) for the purpose of determining a schedule of terms and rates of royalty payments by public broadcasting entities to owners of copyright in works specified by this subsection and the proportionate division of fees paid among various copyright owners shall cover the 5–year period beginning on January 1 of the second year following the year in which the petition is filed. The parties to each negotiation proceeding shall bear their own costs. In establishing such rates and terms the Copyright Royalty Judges may consider the rates for comparable circumstances under voluntary license agreements negotiated as provided in paragraph (2) or (3). The Copyright Royalty Judges shall also establish requirements by which copyright owners may receive reasonable notice of the use of their works under this section, and under which records of such use shall be kept by public broadcasting entities.

(4) In the absence of license agreements negotiated under paragraph (2) or (3), the Copyright Royalty Judges shall, pursuant to chapter 8, conduct a proceeding to determine and publish in the Federal Register a schedule of rates and terms which, subject to paragraph (2), shall be binding on all owners of copyright in works specified by this subsection and public broadcasting entities, regardless of whether such copyright owners have submitted proposals to the Copyright Royalty Judges.

(c) Subject to the terms of any voluntary license agreements that have been negotiated as provided by subsection (b)(2) or (3), a public broadcasting entity may, upon compliance with the provisions of this section, including the rates and terms established by the Copyright Royalty Judges under subsection (b)(4), engage in the following activities with respect to published nondramatic musical works and published pictorial, graphic, and sculptural works:

(1) performance or display of a work by or in the course of a transmission made by a noncommercial educational broadcast station referred to in subsection (f); and

(2) production of a transmission program, reproduction of copies or phonorecords of such a transmission program, and distribution of such copies or phonorecords, where such production, reproduction, or distribution is made by a nonprofit institution or organization solely for the purpose of transmissions specified in paragraph (1); and

(3) the making of reproductions by a governmental body or a nonprofit institution of a transmission program simultaneously with its transmission as specified in paragraph (1), and the performance or display of the contents of such program under the conditions specified by paragraph (1) of section 110, but only if the reproductions are used for performances or displays for a period of no more than seven days from the date of the transmission specified in paragraph (1), and are destroyed before or at the end of such period. No person supplying, in accordance with paragraph (2), a reproduction of a transmission program to governmental bodies or nonprofit institutions under this paragraph shall have any liability as a result of failure of such body or institution to destroy such reproduction: *Provided,* That it shall have notified such body or institution of the requirement for such destruction pursuant to this paragraph: *And provided further,* That if such body or institution itself fails to destroy such reproduction it shall be deemed to have infringed.

(d) Except as expressly provided in this subsection, this section shall have no applicability to works other than those specified in subsection (b). Owners of copyright in nondramatic literary works and public broadcasting entities may, during the course of voluntary negotiations, agree among themselves, respectively, as to the terms and rates of royalty payments without liability under the antitrust laws. Any such terms and rates of royalty payments shall be effective upon filing with the Copyright Royalty Judges, in accordance with regulations that the Copyright Royalty Judges shall prescribe as provided in section 803(b)(6).

(e) Nothing in this section shall be construed to permit, beyond the limits of fair use as provided by section 107, the unauthorized dramatization of a nondramatic musical work, the production of a transmission program drawn to any substantial extent from a published compilation of pictorial, graphic, or sculptural works, or the unauthorized use of any portion of an audiovisual work.

(f) As used in this section, the term "public broadcasting entity" means a noncommercial educational broadcast station as defined in section 397 of title 47 and any nonprofit institution or organization engaged in the activities described in paragraph (2) of subsection (c).

Sec. 119.　Limitations on Exclusive Rights: Secondary Transmissions of Distant Television Programming by Satellite

(a) Secondary transmissions by satellite carriers.—

(1) Non-network stations.—Subject to the provisions of paragraphs (4), (5), and (7) of this subsection and section 114(d), secondary transmissions of a performance or display of a work embodied in a primary transmission made by a non-network station shall be subject to statutory licensing under this section if the secondary transmission is made by a satellite carrier to the public for private home viewing or for viewing in a commercial establishment, with regard to secondary transmissions the satellite carrier is in compliance with the rules, regulations, or authorizations of the Federal Communications Commission governing the carriage of television broadcast station signals, and the carrier makes a direct or indirect charge for each retransmission service to each subscriber receiving the secondary transmission or to a distributor that has contracted with the carrier for direct or indirect delivery of the secondary transmission to the public for private home viewing or for viewing in a commercial establishment.

(2) Network stations.—

(A) In general.—Subject to the provisions of subparagraph (B) of this paragraph and paragraphs (4), (5), (6), and (7) of this subsection and section 114(d), secondary transmissions of a performance or display of a work embodied in a primary transmission made by a network station shall be subject to statutory licensing under this section if the secondary transmission is made by a satellite carrier to the public for private home viewing, with regard to secondary transmissions the satellite carrier is in compliance with the rules, regulations, or authorizations of the Federal Communications Commission governing the carriage of television broadcast station signals, and the carrier makes a direct or indirect charge for such retransmission service to each subscriber receiving the secondary transmission.

(B) Secondary transmissions to unserved households.—

(i) In general.—The statutory license provided for in subparagraph (A) shall be limited to secondary transmissions of the signals of no more than two network stations in a single day for each television network to persons who reside in unserved households.

(ii) Accurate determinations of eligibility.—

(I) Accurate predictive model.—In determining presumptively whether a person resides in an unserved household under subsection (d)(10)(A), a court shall rely on the Individual Location Longley-Rice model set forth by the Federal Communications Commission in Docket No. 98–201, as that model may be amended by the Commission over time under section 339(c)(3) of the Communications Act of 1934 to increase the accuracy of that model.

(II) Accurate measurements.—For purposes of site measurements to determine whether a person resides in an unserved household under subsection (d)(10)(A), a court shall rely on section 339(c)(4) of the Communications Act of 1934.

(III) Accurate predictive model with respect to digital signals.—Notwithstanding subclause (I), in determining presumptively whether a person resides in an unserved household under subsection (d)(10)(A) with respect to digital signals, a court shall rely on a predictive model set forth by the Federal Communications Commission pursuant to a rulemaking as provided in section 339(c)(3) of the Communications Act of 1934 (47 U.S.C. 339(c)(3)), as that model may be amended by the Commission over time under such section to increase the accuracy of that model. Until such time as the Commission sets forth such model, a court shall rely on the predictive model as recommended by the Commission with respect to digital signals in its Report to Congress in ET Docket No. 05–182, FCC 05–199 (released December 9, 2005).

(iii) C-band exemption to unserved households.—

(I) In general.—The limitations of clause (i) shall not apply to any secondary transmissions by C-band services of network stations that a subscriber to C-band service received before any termination of such secondary transmissions before October 31, 1999.

(II) Definition.—In this clause, the term "C-band service" means a service that is licensed by the Federal Communications Commission and operates in the Fixed Satellite Service under part 25 of title 47, Code of Federal Regulations.

(C) Submission of subscriber lists to networks.—

(i) Initial lists.—A satellite carrier that makes secondary transmissions of a primary transmission made by a network station pursuant to subparagraph (A) shall, not later than 90 days after commencing such secondary transmissions, submit to the network that owns or is affiliated with the network station a list identifying (by name and address, including street or rural route number, city, State, and 9–digit zip code) all subscribers to which the satellite carrier makes secondary transmissions of that primary transmission to subscribers in unserved households.

(ii) Monthly lists.—After the submission of the initial lists under clause (i), the satellite carrier shall, not later than the 15th of each month, submit to the network a list, aggregated by designated market area, identifying (by name and address, including street or rural route number, city, State, and 9–digit zip code) any persons who have been added or dropped as subscribers under clause (i) since the last submission under this subparagraph.

(iii) Use of subscriber information.—Subscriber information submitted by a satellite carrier under this subparagraph may be used only for purposes of monitoring compliance by the satellite carrier with this subsection.

(iv) Applicability.—The submission requirements of this subparagraph shall apply to a satellite carrier only if the network to which the submissions are to be made places on file with the Register of Copyrights a document identifying the name and address of the person to whom such submissions are to be made. The Register shall maintain for public inspection a file of all such documents.

(3) Statutory license where retransmissions into local market available.—

(A) Rules for subscribers to signals under subsection (e)—

(i) For those receiving distant signals.—In the case of a subscriber of a satellite carrier who is eligible to receive the secondary transmission of the primary transmission of a network station solely by reason of subsection (e) (in this subparagraph referred to as a "distant signal"), and who, as of October 1, 2004, is receiving the distant signal of that network station, the following shall apply:

(I) In a case in which the satellite carrier makes available to the subscriber the secondary transmission of the primary transmission of a local network station affiliated with the same television network pursuant to the statutory license under section 122, the statutory license under paragraph (2) shall apply only to secondary transmissions by that satellite carrier to that subscriber of the distant signal of a station affiliated with the same television network—

(aa) if, within 60 days after receiving the notice of the satellite carrier under section 338(h)(1) of the Communications Act of 1934, the subscriber elects to retain the distant signal; but

(bb) only until such time as the subscriber elects to receive such local signal.

(II) Notwithstanding subclause (I), the statutory license under paragraph (2) shall not apply with respect to any subscriber who is eligible to receive the distant signal of a television network station solely by reason of subsection (e), unless the satellite carrier, within 60 days after the date of the enactment of the Satellite Home Viewer Extension and Reauthorization Act of 2004, submits to that television network a list, aggregated by designated market area (as defined in section 122(j)(2)(C)), that—

(aa) identifies that subscriber by name and address (street or rural route number, city, state, and zip code) and specifies the distant signals received by the subscriber; and

(bb) states, to the best of the satellite carrier's knowledge and belief, after having made diligent and good faith inquiries, that the subscriber is eligible under subsection (e) to receive the distant signals.

(ii) For those not receiving distant signals.—In the case of any subscriber of a satellite carrier who is eligible to receive the distant signal of a network station solely by reason of subsection (e) and who did not receive a distant signal of a station affiliated with the same network on October 1, 2004, the statutory license under paragraph (2) shall not apply to secondary transmissions by that satellite carrier to that subscriber of the distant signal of a station affiliated with the same network.

(B) Rules for lawful subscribers as of date of enactment of 2010 Act.—In the case of a subscriber of a satellite carrier who, on the day before the date of the enactment of the Satellite Television Extension and Localism Act of 2010, was lawfully receiving the secondary transmission of the primary transmission of a network station under the statutory license under paragraph (2) (in this subparagraph referred to as the "distant signal"), other than subscribers to whom subparagraph (A) applies, the statutory license under paragraph (2) shall apply to secondary transmissions by that satellite carrier to that subscriber of the distant signal of a station affiliated with the same television network, and the subscriber's household shall continue to be considered to be an unserved household with respect to such network, until such time as the subscriber elects to terminate such secondary transmissions, whether or not the subscriber elects to subscribe to receive the secondary transmission of the primary transmission of a local network station affiliated with the same network pursuant to the statutory license under section 122.

(C) Future applicability.—

(i) When local signal available at time of subscription.—The statutory license under paragraph (2) shall not apply to the secondary transmission by a satellite carrier of the primary transmission of a network station to a person who is not a subscriber lawfully receiving such secondary transmission as of the date of the enactment of the Satellite Television Extension and Localism Act of 2010 and, at the time such person seeks to subscribe to receive such secondary transmission, resides in a local market where the satellite carrier makes available to that person the secondary transmission of the primary transmission of a local network station affiliated with the same network pursuant to the statutory license under section 122.

(ii) When local signal available after subscription.— In the case of a subscriber who lawfully subscribes to and receives the secondary transmission by a satellite carrier of the primary transmission of a network station under the statutory license under paragraph (2) (in this clause referred to as the "distant signal") on or after the date of the enactment of the Satellite Television Extension and Localism Act of 2010, the statutory license under paragraph (2) shall apply to secondary transmissions by that satellite carrier to that subscriber of the distant signal of a station affiliated with the same television network, and the subscriber's household shall continue to be considered to be an unserved household with respect to such network, until such time as the subscriber elects to terminate such secondary transmissions, but only if such subscriber subscribes to the secondary transmission of the primary transmission of a local network station affiliated with the same network within 60 days after the satellite carrier makes available to the subscriber such secondary transmission of the primary transmission of such local network station.

(D) Other provisions not affected.—This paragraph shall not affect the applicability of the statutory license to secondary transmissions to unserved households included under paragraph (11).

(E) Waiver.—A subscriber who is denied the secondary transmission of a network station under subparagraph (B) or (C) may request a waiver from such denial by submitting a request, through the subscriber's satellite carrier, to the network station in the local market affiliated with the same network where the subscriber is located. The network station shall accept or reject the subscriber's request for a waiver within 30 days after receipt of the request. If the network station fails to accept or reject the subscriber's request for a waiver within that 30–day period, that network station shall be deemed to agree to the waiver request. Unless specifically stated by the network station, a waiver that was granted before the date of the enactment of the Satellite Home Viewer Extension and Reauthorization Act of 2004 under section 339(c)(2) of the Communications Act of 1934 shall not constitute a waiver for purposes of this subparagraph.

(F) Available defined.—For purposes of this paragraph, a satellite carrier makes available a secondary transmission of the primary transmission of a local station to a subscriber or person if the satellite carrier offers that secondary transmission to other subscribers who reside in the same 9–digit zip code as that subscriber or person.

(4) Noncompliance with reporting and payment requirements.—Notwithstanding the provisions of paragraphs (1) and (2), the willful or repeated secondary transmission to the public by a satellite carrier of a primary transmission made by a non-network station or a network station and embodying a performance or display of a work is actionable as an act of infringement under section 501, and is fully subject to the remedies provided by sections 502 through 506, where the satellite carrier has not deposited the statement of account and royalty fee required by subsection (b), or has failed to make the submissions to networks required by paragraph (2)(C).

(5) Willful alterations.—Notwithstanding the provisions of paragraphs (1) and (2), the secondary transmission to the public by a satellite carrier of a performance or display of a work embodied in a primary transmission made by a non-network station or a network station is actionable as an act of infringement under section 501, and is fully subject to the remedies provided by sections 502 through 506 and section 510, if the content of the particular program in which the performance or display is embodied, or any commercial advertising or station announcement transmitted by the primary transmitter during, or immediately before or after, the transmission of such program, is in any way willfully altered by the satellite carrier through changes, deletions, or additions, or is combined with programming from any other broadcast signal.

(6) Violation of territorial restrictions on statutory license for network stations.—

(A) Individual violations.—The willful or repeated secondary transmission by a satellite carrier of a primary transmission made by a network station and embodying a performance or display of a work to a subscriber who is not eligible to receive the transmission under this section is actionable as an act of infringement under section 501 and is fully subject to the remedies provided by sections 502 through 506, except that—

(i) no damages shall be awarded for such act of infringement if the satellite carrier took corrective action by promptly withdrawing service from the ineligible subscriber, and

(ii) any statutory damages shall not exceed $250 for such subscriber for each month during which the violation occurred.

(B) Pattern of violations.—If a satellite carrier engages in a willful or repeated pattern or practice of delivering a primary transmission made by a network station and embodying a performance or display of a work to subscribers who are not eligible to receive the transmission under this section, then in addition to the remedies set forth in subparagraph (A)—

(i) if the pattern or practice has been carried out on a substantially nationwide basis, the court shall order a permanent injunction barring the secondary transmission by the satellite carrier, for private home viewing, of the primary transmissions of any primary network station affiliated with the same network, and the court may order statutory damages of not to exceed $2,500,000 for each 3–month period during which the pattern or practice was carried out; and

(ii) if the pattern or practice has been carried out on a local or regional basis, the court shall order a permanent injunction barring the secondary transmission, for private home viewing in that locality or region, by the satellite carrier of the primary transmissions of any primary network station affiliated with the same network, and the court may order statutory damages of not to exceed $2,500,000 for each 6–month period during which the pattern or practice was carried out.

(C) Previous subscribers excluded.—Subparagraphs (A) and (B) do not apply to secondary transmissions by a satellite carrier to persons who subscribed to receive such secondary transmissions from the satellite carrier or a distributor before November 16, 1988.

(D) Burden of proof.—In any action brought under this paragraph, the satellite carrier shall have the burden of proving that its secondary transmission of a primary transmission by a network station is to a subscriber who is eligible to receive the secondary transmission under this section.

(E) Exception.—The secondary transmission by a satellite carrier of a performance or display of a work embodied in a primary transmission made by a network station to subscribers who do not reside in unserved households shall not be an act of infringement if—

> **(i)** the station on May 1, 1991, was retransmitted by a satellite carrier and was not on that date owned or operated by or affiliated with a television network that offered interconnected program service on a regular basis for 15 or more hours per week to at least 25 affiliated television licensees in 10 or more States;

> **(ii)** as of July 1, 1998, such station was retransmitted by a satellite carrier under the statutory license of this section; and

> **(iii)** the station is not owned or operated by or affiliated with a television network that, as of January 1, 1995, offered interconnected program service on a regular basis for 15 or more hours per week to at least 25 affiliated television licensees in 10 or more States.

The court shall direct one half of any statutory damages ordered under clause (i) to be deposited with the Register of Copyrights for distribution to copyright owners pursuant to subsection (b). The Copyright Royalty Judges shall issue regulations establishing procedures for distributing such funds, on a proportional basis, to copyright owners whose works were included in the secondary transmissions that were the subject of the statutory damages.

(7) Discrimination by a satellite carrier.—Notwithstanding the provisions of paragraph (1), the willful or repeated secondary transmission to the public by a satellite carrier of a performance or display of a work embodied in a primary transmission made by a non-network station or a network station is actionable as an act of infringement under section 501, and is fully subject to the remedies provided by sections 502 through 506, if the satellite carrier unlawfully discriminates against a distributor.

(8) Geographic limitation on secondary transmissions.—The statutory license created by this section shall apply only to secondary transmissions to households located in the United States.

(9) Loser pays for signal intensity measurement; recovery of measurement costs in a civil action.—In any civil action filed relating to the eligibility of subscribing households as unserved households—

> **(A)** a network station challenging such eligibility shall, within 60 days after receipt of the measurement results and a statement of such costs, reimburse the satellite carrier for any signal intensity measurement that is conducted by that carrier in response to a challenge by the network station and that establishes the household is an unserved household; and

> **(B)** a satellite carrier shall, within 60 days after receipt of the measurement results and a statement of such costs, reimburse the network station challenging such eligibility for any signal intensity measurement that is conducted by that station and that establishes the household is not an unserved household.

(10) Inability to conduct measurement.—If a network station makes a reasonable attempt to conduct a site measurement of its signal at a subscriber's household and is denied access for the purpose of conducting the measurement, and is otherwise unable to conduct a measurement, the satellite carrier shall within 60 days notice thereof, terminate service of the station's network to that household.

(11) Service to recreational vehicles and commercial trucks.—

    (A) Exemption.—

        (i) In general.—For purposes of this subsection, and subject to clauses (ii) and (iii), the term "unserved household" shall include—

            (I) recreational vehicles as defined in regulations of the Secretary of Housing and Urban Development under section 3282.8 of title 24, Code of Federal Regulations; and

            (II) commercial trucks that qualify as commercial motor vehicles under regulations of the Secretary of Transportation under section 383.5 of title 49, Code of Federal Regulations.

        (ii) Limitation.—Clause (i) shall apply only to a recreational vehicle or commercial truck if any satellite carrier that proposes to make a secondary transmission of a network station to the operator of such a recreational vehicle or commercial truck complies with the documentation requirements under subparagraphs (B) and (C).

        (iii) Exclusion.—For purposes of this subparagraph, the terms "recreational vehicle" and "commercial truck" shall not include any fixed dwelling, whether a mobile home or otherwise.

    (B) Documentation requirements.—A recreational vehicle or commercial truck shall be deemed to be an unserved household beginning 10 days after the relevant satellite carrier provides to the network that owns or is affiliated with the network station that will be secondarily transmitted to the recreational vehicle or commercial truck the following documents:

        (i) Declaration.—A signed declaration by the operator of the recreational vehicle or commercial truck that the satellite dish is permanently attached to the recreational vehicle or commercial truck, and will not be used to receive satellite programming at any fixed dwelling.

        (ii) Registration.—In the case of a recreational vehicle, a copy of the current State vehicle registration for the recreational vehicle.

        (iii) Registration and license.—In the case of a commercial truck, a copy of—

            (I) the current State vehicle registration for the truck; and

            (II) a copy of a valid, current commercial driver's license, as defined in regulations of the Secretary of Transportation under section 383 of title 49, Code of Federal Regulations, issued to the operator.

(C) Updated documentation requirements.—If a satellite carrier wishes to continue to make secondary transmissions to a recreational vehicle or commercial truck for more than a 2–year period, that carrier shall provide each network, upon request, with updated documentation in the form described under subparagraph (B) during the 90 days before expiration of that 2–year period.

(12) Statutory license contingent on compliance with FCC rules and remedial steps.—Notwithstanding any other provision of this section, the willful or repeated secondary transmission to the public by a satellite carrier of a primary transmission embodying a performance or display of a work made by a broadcast station licensed by the Federal Communications Commission is actionable as an act of infringement under section 501, and is fully subject to the remedies provided by sections 502 through 506, if, at the time of such transmission, the satellite carrier is not in compliance with the rules, regulations, and authorizations of the Federal Communications Commission concerning the carriage of television broadcast station signals.

(13) Waivers.—A subscriber who is denied the secondary transmission of a signal of a network station under subsection (a)(2)(B) may request a waiver from such denial by submitting a request, through the subscriber's satellite carrier, to the network station asserting that the secondary transmission is prohibited. The network station shall accept or reject a subscriber's request for a waiver within 30 days after receipt of the request. If a television network station fails to accept or reject a subscriber's request for a waiver within the 30–day period after receipt of the request, that station shall be deemed to agree to the waiver request and have filed such written waiver. Unless specifically stated by the network station, a waiver that was granted before the date of the enactment of the Satellite Home Viewer Extension and Reauthorization Act of 2004 under section 339(c)(2) of the Communications Act of 1934, and that was in effect on such date of enactment, shall constitute a waiver for purposes of this paragraph.

(14) Restricted transmission of out-of-state distant network signals into certain markets.—

(A) Out-of-state network affiliates.—Notwithstanding any other provision of this title, the statutory license in this subsection and subsection (b) shall not apply to any secondary transmission of the primary transmission of a network station located outside of the State of Alaska to any subscriber in that State to whom the secondary transmission of the primary transmission of a television station located in that State is made available by the satellite carrier pursuant to section 122.

(B) Exception.—The limitation in subparagraph (A) shall not apply to the secondary transmission of the primary transmission of a digital signal of a network station located outside of the State of Alaska if at the time that the secondary transmission is made, no television station licensed to a community in the State and affiliated with the same network makes primary transmissions of a digital signal.

(b) Deposit of statements and fees; verification procedures.—

(1) Deposits with the Register of Copyrights.—A satellite carrier whose secondary transmissions are subject to statutory licensing under subsection (a) shall, on a semiannual basis, deposit with the Register of Copyrights, in accordance with requirements that the Register shall prescribe by regulation—

(A) a statement of account, covering the preceding 6–month period, specifying the names and locations of all non-network stations and network stations whose signals were retransmitted, at any time during that period, to subscribers as described in subsections (a)(1) and (a)(2), the total number of subscribers that received such retransmissions, and such other data as the Register of Copyrights may from time to time prescribe by regulation;

(B) a royalty fee payable to copyright owners pursuant to paragraph (4) for that 6–month period, computed by multiplying the total number of subscribers receiving each secondary transmission of a primary stream or multicast stream of each non-network station or network station during each calendar year month by the appropriate rate in effect under this subsection; and

(C) a filing fee, as determined by the Register of Copyrights pursuant to section 708(a).

(2) Verification of accounts and fee payments.—The Register of Copyrights shall issue regulations to permit interested parties to verify and audit the statements of account and royalty fees submitted by satellite carriers under this subsection.

(3) Investment of fees.—The Register of Copyrights shall receive all fees (including the filing fee specified in paragraph (1)(C)) deposited under this section and, after deducting the reasonable costs incurred by the Copyright Office under this section (other than the costs deducted under paragraph (5)), shall deposit the balance in the Treasury of the United States, in such manner as the Secretary of the Treasury directs. All funds held by the Secretary of the Treasury shall be invested in interest-bearing securities of the United States for later distribution with interest by the Librarian of Congress as provided by this title.

(4) Persons to whom fees are distributed.—The royalty fees deposited under paragraph (3) shall, in accordance with the procedures provided by paragraph (5), be distributed to those copyright owners whose works were included in a secondary transmission made by a satellite carrier during the applicable 6–month accounting period and who file a claim with the Copyright Royalty Judges under paragraph (5).

(5) Procedures for distribution.—The royalty fees deposited under paragraph (3) shall be distributed in accordance with the following procedures:

(A) Filing of claims for fees.—During the month of July in each year, each person claiming to be entitled to statutory license fees for secondary transmissions shall file a claim with the Copyright Royalty Judges, in accordance with requirements that the Copyright Royalty Judges shall prescribe by regulation. For purposes of this paragraph, any claimants may agree among themselves as to the proportionate division of statutory license fees among them, may lump their claims together and file them jointly or as a single claim, or may designate a common agent to receive payment on their behalf.

(B) Determination of controversy; distributions.—After the first day of August of each year, the Copyright Royalty Judges shall determine whether there exists a controversy concerning the distribution of royalty fees. If the Copyright Royalty Judges determine that no such controversy exists, the Copyright Royalty Judges shall authorize the Librarian of Congress to proceed to distribute such fees to the copyright owners entitled to receive them, or to their designated agents, subject to the deduction of reasonable administrative costs under this section. If the Copyright Royalty Judges find the existence of a controversy, the Copyright Royalty Judges shall, pursuant to chapter 8 of this title, conduct a proceeding to determine the distribution of royalty fees.

(C) Withholding of fees during controversy.—During the pendency of any proceeding under this subsection, the Copyright Royalty Judges shall have the discretion to authorize the Librarian of Congress to proceed to distribute any amounts that are not in controversy.

(c) Adjustment of royalty fees.—

(1) Applicability and determination of royalty fees for signals.—

(A) Initial fee.—The appropriate fee for purposes of determining the royalty fee under subsection (b)(1)(B) for the secondary transmission of the primary transmissions of network stations and non-network stations shall be the appropriate fee set forth in part 258 of title 37, Code of Federal Regulations, as in effect on July 1, 2009, as modified under this paragraph.

(B) Fee set by voluntary negotiation.—On or before June 1, 2010, the Copyright Royalty Judges shall cause to be published in the Federal Register of the initiation of voluntary negotiation proceedings for the purpose of determining the royalty fee to be paid by satellite carriers for the secondary transmission of the primary transmissions of network stations and non-network stations under subsection (b)(1)(B).

(C) Negotiations.—Satellite carriers, distributors, and copyright owners entitled to royalty fees under this section shall negotiate in good faith in an effort to reach a voluntary agreement or agreements for the payment of royalty fees. Any such satellite carriers, distributors and copyright owners may at any time negotiate and agree to the royalty fee, and may designate common agents to negotiate, agree to, or pay such fees. If the parties fail to identify common agents, the Copyright Royalty Judges shall do so, after requesting recommendations from the parties to the negotiation proceeding. The parties to each negotiation proceeding shall bear the cost thereof.

(D) Agreements binding on parties; filing of agreements; public notice.—

(i) Voluntary agreements; filing.—Voluntary agreements negotiated at any time in accordance with this paragraph shall be binding upon all satellite carriers, distributors, and copyright owners that are parties thereto. Copies of such agreements shall be filed with the Copyright Office within 30 days after execution in accordance with regulations that the Register of Copyrights shall prescribe.

(ii) Procedure for adoption of fees.—

(I) Publication of notice.—Within 10 days after publication in the Federal Register of a notice of the initiation of voluntary negotiation proceedings, parties who have reached a voluntary agreement may request that the royalty fees in that agreement be applied to all satellite carriers, distributors, and copyright owners without convening a proceeding under subparagraph (F).

(II) Public notice of fees.—Upon receiving a request under subclause (I), the Copyright Royalty Judges shall immediately provide public notice of the royalty fees from the voluntary agreement and afford parties an opportunity to state that they object to those fees.

(III) Adoption of fees.—The Copyright Royalty Judges shall adopt the royalty fees from the voluntary agreement for all satellite carriers, distributors, and copyright owners without convening the proceeding under subparagraph (F) unless a party with an intent to participate in that proceeding and a significant interest in the outcome of that proceeding objects under subclause (II).

(E) Period agreement is in effect.—The obligation to pay the royalty fees established under a voluntary agreement which has been filed with the Copyright Royalty Judges in accordance with this paragraph shall become effective on the date specified in the agreement, and shall remain in effect until December 31, 2019, or in accordance with the terms of the agreement, whichever is later.

(F) Fee set by Copyright Royalty Judges proceeding.—

(i) Notice of initiation of the proceeding.—On or before September 1, 2010, the Copyright Royalty Judges shall cause notice to be published in the Federal Register of the initiation of a proceeding for the purpose of determining the royalty fees to be paid for the secondary transmission of the primary transmissions of network stations and non-network stations under subsection (b)(1)(B) by satellite carriers and distributors—

(I) in the absence of a voluntary agreement filed in accordance with subparagraph (D) that establishes royalty fees to be paid by all satellite carriers and distributors; or

(II) if an objection to the fees from a voluntary agreement submitted for adoption by the Copyright Royalty Judges to apply to all satellite carriers, distributors, and copyright owners is received under subparagraph (D) from a party with an intent to participate in the proceeding and a significant interest in the outcome of that proceeding.

Such proceeding shall be conducted under chapter 8.

(ii) Establishment of royalty fees.—In determining royalty fees under this subparagraph, the Copyright Royalty Judges shall establish fees for the secondary transmissions of the primary transmissions of network stations and non-network stations that most clearly represent the fair market value of secondary transmissions, except that the Copyright Royalty Judges shall adjust royalty fees to account for the obligations of the parties under any applicable voluntary agreement filed with the Copyright Royalty Judges in accordance with subparagraph (D). In determining the fair market value, the Judges shall base their decision on economic, competitive, and programming information presented by the parties, including—

(I) the competitive environment in which such programming is distributed, the cost of similar signals in similar private and compulsory license marketplaces, and any special features and conditions of the retransmission marketplace;

(II) the economic impact of such fees on copyright owners and satellite carriers; and

(III) the impact on the continued availability of secondary transmissions to the public.

(iii) Effective date for decision of Copyright Royalty Judges.—The obligation to pay the royalty fees established under a determination that is made by the Copyright Royalty Judges in a proceeding under this paragraph shall be effective as of January 1, 2010.

(iv) Persons subject to royalty fees.—The royalty fees referred to in clause (iii) shall be binding on all satellite carriers, distributors and copyright owners, who are not party to a voluntary agreement filed with the Copyright Office under subparagraph (D).

(2) Annual royalty fee adjustment.—Effective January 1 of each year, the royalty fee payable under subsection (b)(1)(B) for the secondary transmission of the primary transmissions of network stations and non-network stations shall be adjusted by the Copyright Royalty Judges to reflect any changes occurring in the cost of living as determined by the most recent Consumer Price Index (for all consumers and for all items) published by the Secretary of Labor before December 1 of the preceding year. Notification of the adjusted fees shall be published in the Federal Register at least 25 days before January 1.

(d) Definitions.—As used in this section—

(1) Distributor.—The term "distributor" means an entity that contracts to distribute secondary transmissions from a satellite carrier and, either as a single channel or in a package with other programming, provides the secondary transmission either directly to individual subscribers or indirectly through other program distribution entities in accordance with the provisions of this section.

(2) Network station.—The term "network station" means—

(A) a television station licensed by the Federal Communications Commission, including any translator station or terrestrial satellite station that rebroadcasts all or substantially all of the programming broadcast by a network station, that is owned or operated by, or affiliated with, one or more of the television networks in the United States that offer an interconnected program service on a regular basis for 15 or more hours per week to at least 25 of its affiliated television licensees in 10 or more States; or

    (B) a noncommercial educational broadcast station (as defined in section 397 of the Communications Act of 1934);

except that the term does not include the signal of the Alaska Rural Communications Service, or any successor entity to that service.

    (3) Primary network station.—The term "primary network station" means a network station that broadcasts or rebroadcasts the basic programming service of a particular national network.

    (4) Primary transmission.—The term "primary transmission" has the meaning given that term in section 111(f) of this title.

    (5) Private home viewing.—The term "private home viewing" means the viewing, for private use in a household by means of satellite reception equipment that is operated by an individual in that household and that serves only such household, of a secondary transmission delivered by a satellite carrier of a primary transmission of a television station licensed by the Federal Communications Commission.

    (6) Satellite carrier.—The term "satellite carrier" means an entity that uses the facilities of a satellite or satellite service licensed by the Federal Communications Commission and operates in the Fixed-Satellite Service under part 25 of title 47, Code of Federal Regulations, or the Direct Broadcast Satellite Service under part 100 of title 47, Code of Federal Regulations, to establish and operate a channel of communications for point-to-multipoint distribution of television station signals, and that owns or leases a capacity or service on a satellite in order to provide such point-to-multipoint distribution, except to the extent that such entity provides such distribution pursuant to tariff under the Communications Act of 1934, other than for private home viewing pursuant to this section.

    (7) Secondary transmission.—The term "secondary transmission" has the meaning given that term in section 111(f) of this title.

    (8) Subscriber; subscribe.—

    (A) Subscriber.—The term "subscriber" means a person or entity that receives a secondary transmission service from a satellite carrier and pays a fee for the service, directly or indirectly, to the satellite carrier or to a distributor.

    (B) Subscribe.—The term "subscribe" means to elect to become a subscriber.

    (9) Non-network station.—The term "non-network station" means a television station, other than a network station, licensed by the Federal Communications Commission, that is secondarily transmitted by a satellite carrier.

    (10) Unserved household.—The term "unserved household", with respect to a particular television network, means a household that—

(A) cannot receive, through the use of an antenna, an over-the-air signal containing the primary stream, or, on or after the qualifying date, the multicast stream, originating in that household's local market and affiliated with that network of—

(i) if the signal originates as an analog signal, Grade B intensity as defined by the Federal Communications Commission in section 73.683(a) of title 47, Code of Federal Regulations, as in effect on January 1, 1999; or

(ii) if the signal originates as a digital signal, intensity defined in the values for the digital television noise-limited service contour, as defined in regulations issued by the Federal Communications Commission (section 73.622(e) of title 47, Code of Federal Regulations), as such regulations may be amended from time to time;

(B) is subject to a waiver that meets the standards of subsection (a) (13), whether or not the waiver was granted before the date of the enactment of the Satellite Television Extension and Localism Act of 2010;

(C) is a subscriber to whom subsection (e) applies;

(D) is a subscriber to whom subsection (a)(11) applies; or

(E) is a subscriber to whom the exemption under subsection (a)(2)(B)(iii) applies.

(11) **Local market.**—The term "local market" has the meaning given such term under section 122(j).

(12) **Commercial establishment.**—The term "commercial establishment"—

(A) means an establishment used for commercial purposes, such as a bar, restaurant, private office, fitness club, oil rig, retail store, bank or other financial institution, supermarket, automobile or boat dealership, or any other establishment with a common business area; and

(B) does not include a multi-unit permanent or temporary dwelling where private home viewing occurs, such as a hotel, dormitory, hospital, apartment, condominium, or prison.

(13) **Qualifying date.**—The term "qualifying date", for purposes of paragraph (10)(A), means—

(A) October 1, 2010, for multicast streams that exist on March 31, 2010; and

(B) January 1, 2011, for all other multicast streams.

(14) **Multicast stream.**—The term "multicast stream" means a digital stream containing programming and program-related material affiliated with a television network, other than the primary stream.

(15) **Primary stream.**—The term "primary stream" means—

(A) the single digital stream of programming as to which a television broadcast station has the right to mandatory carriage with a satellite carrier under the rules of the Federal Communications Commission in effect on July 1, 2009; or

(B) if there is no stream described in subparagraph (A), then either—

    (i) the single digital stream of programming associated with the network last transmitted by the station as an analog signal; or

    (ii) if there is no stream described in clause (i), then the single digital stream of programming affiliated with the network that, as of July 1, 2009, had been offered by the television broadcast station for the longest period of time.

(e) Moratorium on copyright liability.—Until December 31, 2019, a subscriber who does not receive a signal of Grade A intensity (as defined in the regulations of the Federal Communications Commission under section 73.683(a) of title 47, Code of Federal Regulations, as in effect on January 1, 1999, or predicted by the Federal Communications Commission using the Individual Location Longley-Rice methodology described by the Federal Communications Commission in Docket No. 98–201) of a local network television broadcast station shall remain eligible to receive signals of network stations affiliated with the same network, if that subscriber had satellite service of such network signal terminated after July 11, 1998, and before October 31, 1999, as required by this section, or received such service on October 31, 1999.

(f) Expedited consideration by Justice Department of voluntary agreements to provide satellite secondary transmissions to local markets.—

(1) In general.—In a case in which no satellite carrier makes available, to subscribers located in a local market, as defined in section 122(j)(2), the secondary transmission into that market of a primary transmission of one or more television broadcast stations licensed by the Federal Communications Commission, and two or more satellite carriers request a business review letter in accordance with section 50.6 of title 28, Code of Federal Regulations (as in effect on July 7, 2004), in order to assess the legality under the antitrust laws of proposed business conduct to make or carry out an agreement to provide such secondary transmission into such local market, the appropriate official of the Department of Justice shall respond to the request no later than 90 days after the date on which the request is received.

(2) Definition.—For purposes of this subsection, the term "antitrust laws"—

(A) has the meaning given that term in subsection (a) of the first section of the Clayton Act (15 U.S.C. 12(a)), except that such term includes section 5 of the Federal Trade Commission Act (15 U.S.C. 45) to the extent such section 5 applies to unfair methods of competition; and

(B) includes any State law similar to the laws referred to in paragraph (1).

(g) Certain waivers granted to providers of local-into-local service to all DMAs.—

(1) Injunction waiver.—A court that issued an injunction pursuant to subsection (a)(7)(B) before the date of the enactment of this subsection shall waive such injunction if the court recognizes the entity against which the injunction was issued as a qualified carrier.

(2) Limited temporary waiver.—

(A) In general.—Upon a request made by a satellite carrier, a court that issued an injunction against such carrier under subsection (a)(7)(B) before the date of the enactment of this subsection shall waive such injunction with respect to the statutory license provided under subsection (a)(2) to the extent necessary to allow such carrier to make secondary transmissions of primary transmissions made by a network station to unserved households located in short markets in which such carrier was not providing local service pursuant to the license under section 122 as of December 31, 2009.

(B) Expiration of temporary waiver.—A temporary waiver of an injunction under subparagraph (A) shall expire after the end of the 120–day period beginning on the date such temporary waiver is issued unless extended for good cause by the court making the temporary waiver.

(C) Failure to provide local-into-local service to all DMAs.—

(i) Failure to act reasonably and in good faith.—If the court issuing a temporary waiver under subparagraph (A) determines that the satellite carrier that made the request for such waiver has failed to act reasonably or has failed to make a good faith effort to provide local-into-local service to all DMAs, such failure—

(I) is actionable as an act of infringement under section 501 and the court may in its discretion impose the remedies provided for in sections 502 through 506 and subsection (a)(6)(B) of this section; and

(II) shall result in the termination of the waiver issued under subparagraph (A).

(ii) Failure to provide local-into-local service.—If the court issuing a temporary waiver under subparagraph (A) determines that the satellite carrier that made the request for such waiver has failed to provide local-into-local service to all DMAs, but determines that the carrier acted reasonably and in good faith, the court may in its discretion impose financial penalties that reflect—

(I) the degree of control the carrier had over the circumstances that resulted in the failure;

(II) the quality of the carrier's efforts to remedy the failure; and

(III) the severity and duration of any service interruption.

(D) Single temporary waiver available.—An entity may only receive one temporary waiver under this paragraph.

(E) Short market defined.—For purposes of this paragraph, the term "short market" means a local market in which programming of one or more of the four most widely viewed television networks nationwide as measured on the date of the enactment of this subsection is not offered on the primary stream transmitted by any local television broadcast station.

(3) Establishment of qualified carrier recognition.—

(A) Statement of eligibility.—An entity seeking to be recognized as a qualified carrier under this subsection shall file a statement of eligibility with the court that imposed the injunction. A statement of eligibility must include—

(i) an affidavit that the entity is providing local-into-local service to all DMAs;

(ii) a motion for a waiver of the injunction;

(iii) a motion that the court appoint a special master under Rule 53 of the Federal Rules of Civil Procedure;

(iv) an agreement by the carrier to pay all expenses incurred by the special master under paragraph (4)(B)(ii); and

(v) a certification issued pursuant to section 342(a) of Communications Act of 1934.

(B) Grant of recognition as a qualified carrier.—Upon receipt of a statement of eligibility, the court shall recognize the entity as a qualified carrier and issue the waiver under paragraph (1). Upon motion pursuant to subparagraph (A)(iii), the court shall appoint a special master to conduct the examination and provide a report to the court as provided in paragraph (4)(B).

(C) Voluntary termination.—At any time, an entity recognized as a qualified carrier may file a statement of voluntary termination with the court certifying that it no longer wishes to be recognized as a qualified carrier. Upon receipt of such statement, the court shall reinstate the injunction waived under paragraph (1).

(D) Loss of recognition prevents future recognition.—No entity may be recognized as a qualified carrier if such entity had previously been recognized as a qualified carrier and subsequently lost such recognition or voluntarily terminated such recognition under subparagraph (C).

(4) Qualified carrier obligations and compliance.—

(A) Continuing obligations.—

(i) In general.—An entity recognized as a qualified carrier shall continue to provide local-into-local service to all DMAs.

(ii) Cooperation with compliance examination.—An entity recognized as a qualified carrier shall fully cooperate with the special master appointed by the court under paragraph (3)(B) in an examination set forth in subparagraph (B).

(B) Qualified carrier compliance examination.—

(i) Examination and report.—A special master appointed by the court under paragraph (3)(B) shall conduct an examination of, and file a report on, the qualified carrier's compliance with the royalty payment and household eligibility requirements of the license under this section. The report shall address the qualified carrier's conduct during the period beginning on the date on which the qualified carrier is recognized as such under paragraph (3)(B) and ending on April 30, 2012.

(ii) Records of qualified carrier.—Beginning on the date that is one year after the date on which the qualified carrier is recognized as such under paragraph (3)(B), but not later than December 1, 2011, the qualified carrier shall provide the special master with all records that the special master considers to be directly pertinent to the following requirements under this section:

    (I) Proper calculation and payment of royalties under the statutory license under this section.

    (II) Provision of service under this license to eligible subscribers only.

(iii) Submission of report.—The special master shall file the report required by clause (i) not later than July 24, 2012, with the court referred to in paragraph (1) that issued the injunction, and the court shall transmit a copy of the report to the Register of Copyrights, the Committees on the Judiciary and on Energy and Commerce of the House of Representatives, and the Committees on the Judiciary and on Commerce, Science, and Transportation of the Senate.

(iv) Evidence of infringement.—The special master shall include in the report a statement of whether the examination by the special master indicated that there is substantial evidence that a copyright holder could bring a successful action under this section against the qualified carrier for infringement.

(v) Subsequent examination.—If the special master's report includes a statement that its examination indicated the existence of substantial evidence that a copyright holder could bring a successful action under this section against the qualified carrier for infringement, the special master shall, not later than 6 months after the report under clause (i) is filed, initiate another examination of the qualified carrier's compliance with the royalty payment and household eligibility requirements of the license under this section since the last report was filed under clause (iii). The special master shall file a report on the results of the examination conducted under this clause with the court referred to in paragraph (1) that issued the injunction, and the court shall transmit a copy to the Register of Copyrights, the Committees on the Judiciary and on Energy and Commerce of the House of Representatives, and the Committees on the Judiciary and on Commerce, Science, and Transportation of the Senate. The report shall include a statement described in clause (iv).

(vi) Compliance.—Upon motion filed by an aggrieved copyright owner, the court recognizing an entity as a qualified carrier shall terminate such designation upon finding that the entity has failed to cooperate with an examination required by this subparagraph.

(vii) Oversight.—During the period of time that the special master is conducting an examination under this subparagraph, the Comptroller General shall monitor the degree to which the entity seeking to be recognized or recognized as a qualified carrier under paragraph (3) is complying with the special master's examination. The qualified carrier shall make available to the Comptroller General all records and individuals that the Comptroller General considers necessary to meet the Comptroller General's obligations under this clause. The Comptroller General shall report the results of the monitoring required by this clause to the Committees on the Judiciary and on Energy and Commerce of the House of Representatives and the Committees on the Judiciary and on Commerce, Science, and Transportation of the Senate at intervals of not less than six months during such period.

(C) Affirmation.—A qualified carrier shall file an affidavit with the district court and the Register of Copyrights 30 months after such status was granted stating that, to the best of the affiant's knowledge, it is in compliance with the requirements for a qualified carrier. The qualified carrier shall attach to its affidavit copies of all reports or orders issued by the court, the special master, and the Comptroller General.

(D) Compliance determination.—Upon the motion of an aggrieved television broadcast station, the court recognizing an entity as a qualified carrier may make a determination of whether the entity is providing local-into-local service to all DMAs.

(E) Pleading requirement.—In any motion brought under subparagraph (D), the party making such motion shall specify one or more designated market areas (as such term is defined in section 122(j)(2)(C)) for which the failure to provide service is being alleged, and, for each such designated market area, shall plead with particularity the circumstances of the alleged failure.

(F) Burden of proof.—In any proceeding to make a determination under subparagraph (D), and with respect to a designated market area for which failure to provide service is alleged, the entity recognized as a qualified carrier shall have the burden of proving that the entity provided local-into-local service with a good quality satellite signal to at least 90 percent of the households in such designated market area (based on the most recent census data released by the United States Census Bureau) at the time and place alleged.

(5) Failure to provide service.—

(A) Penalties.—If the court recognizing an entity as a qualified carrier finds that such entity has willfully failed to provide local-into-local service to all DMAs, such finding shall result in the loss of recognition of the entity as a qualified carrier and the termination of the waiver provided under paragraph (1), and the court may, in its discretion—

(i) treat such failure as an act of infringement under section 501, and subject such infringement to the remedies provided for in sections 502 through 506 and subsection (a)(6)(B) of this section; and

(ii) impose a fine of not less than $250,000 and not more than $5,000,000.

(B) Exception for nonwillful violation.—If the court determines that the failure to provide local-into-local service to all DMAs is nonwillful, the court may in its discretion impose financial penalties for noncompliance that reflect—

(i) the degree of control the entity had over the circumstances that resulted in the failure;

(ii) the quality of the entity's efforts to remedy the failure and restore service; and

(iii) the severity and duration of any service interruption.

(6) Penalties for violations of license.—A court that finds, under subsection (a)(6)(A), that an entity recognized as a qualified carrier has willfully made a secondary transmission of a primary transmission made by a network station and embodying a performance or display of a work to a subscriber who is not eligible to receive the transmission under this section shall reinstate the injunction waived under paragraph (1), and the court may order statutory damages of not more than $2,500,000.

(7) Local-into-local service to all DMAs defined.—For purposes of this subsection:

(A) In general.—An entity provides "local-into-local service to all DMAs" if the entity provides local service in all designated market areas (as such term is defined in section 122(j)(2)(C)) pursuant to the license under section 122.

(B) Household coverage.—For purposes of subparagraph (A), an entity that makes available local-into-local service with a good quality satellite signal to at least 90 percent of the households in a designated market area based on the most recent census data released by the United States Census Bureau shall be considered to be providing local service to such designated market area.

(C) Good quality satellite signal defined.—The term "good quality satellite signal" has the meaning given such term under section 342(e)(2) of Communications Act of 1934.

(h) Termination of License.—This section shall cease to be effective on December 31, 2019.

Sec. 120.   Scope of Exclusive Rights in Architectural Works

(a) Pictorial Representations Permitted.—The copyright in an architectural work that has been constructed does not include the right to prevent the making, distributing, or public display of pictures, paintings, photographs, or other pictorial representations of the work, if the building in which the work is embodied is located in or ordinarily visible from a public place.

(b) Alterations to and Destruction of Buildings.—Notwithstanding the provisions of section 106(2), the owners of a building embodying an architectural work may, without the consent of the author or copyright owner of the architectural work, make or authorize the making of alterations to such building, and destroy or authorize the destruction of such building.

Sec. 121.   Limitations on Exclusive Rights: Reproduction for Blind or Other People with Disabilities

(a) Notwithstanding the provisions of section 106, it is not an infringement of copyright for an authorized entity to reproduce or to distribute copies or phonorecords of a previously published, nondramatic literary work if such copies or phonorecords are reproduced or distributed in specialized formats exclusively for use by blind or other persons with disabilities.

(b)(1) Copies or phonorecords to which this section applies shall—

(A) not be reproduced or distributed in a format other than a specialized format exclusively for use by blind or other persons with disabilities;

(B) bear a notice that any further reproduction or distribution in a format other than a specialized format is an infringement; and

(C) include a copyright notice identifying the copyright owner and the date of the original publication.

(2) The provisions of this subsection shall not apply to standardized, secure, or norm-referenced tests and related testing material, or to computer programs, except the portions thereof that are in conventional human language (including descriptions of pictorial works) and displayed to users in the ordinary course of using the computer programs.

(c) Notwithstanding the provisions of section 106, it is not an infringement of copyright for a publisher of print instructional materials for use in elementary or secondary schools to create and distribute to the National Instructional Materials Access Center copies of the electronic files described in sections 612(a)(23)(C), 613(a)(6), and section 674(e) of the Individuals with Disabilities Education Act that contain the contents of print instructional materials using the National Instructional Material Accessibility Standard (as defined in section 674(e)(3) of that Act), if—

(1) the inclusion of the contents of such print instructional materials is required by any State educational agency or local educational agency;

(2) the publisher had the right to publish such print instructional materials in print formats; and

(3) such copies are used solely for reproduction or distribution of the contents of such print instructional materials in specialized formats.

(d) For purposes of this section, the term—

(1) "authorized entity" means a nonprofit organization or a governmental agency that has a primary mission to provide specialized services relating to training, education, or adaptive reading or information access needs of blind or other persons with disabilities;

(2) "blind or other persons with disabilities" means individuals who are eligible or who may qualify in accordance with the Act entitled "An Act to provide books for the adult blind", approved

March 3, 1931 (2 U.S.C. 135a; 46 Stat. 1487) to receive books and other publications produced in specialized formats;

(3) "print instructional materials" has the meaning given under section 674(e)(3)(C) of the Individuals with Disabilities Education Act; and

(4) "specialized formats" means—

(A) braille, audio, or digital text which is exclusively for use by blind or other persons with disabilities; and

(B) with respect to print instructional materials, includes large print formats when such materials are distributed exclusively for use by blind or other persons with disabilities.

Sec. 122. Limitations on Exclusive Rights: Secondary Transmissions of Local Television Programming by Satellite

(a) Secondary transmissions into local markets.—

(1) Secondary transmissions of television broadcast stations within a local market.—A secondary transmission of a performance or display of a work embodied in a primary transmission of a television broadcast station into the station's local market shall be subject to statutory licensing under this section if—

(A) the secondary transmission is made by a satellite carrier to the public;

(B) with regard to secondary transmissions, the satellite carrier is in compliance with the rules, regulations, or authorizations of the Federal Communications Commission governing the carriage of television broadcast station signals; and

(C) the satellite carrier makes a direct or indirect charge for the secondary transmission to—

(i) each subscriber receiving the secondary transmission; or

(ii) a distributor that has contracted with the satellite carrier for direct or indirect delivery of the secondary transmission to the public.

(2) Significantly viewed stations.—

(A) In general.—A secondary transmission of a performance or display of a work embodied in a primary transmission of a television broadcast station to subscribers who receive secondary transmissions of primary transmissions under paragraph (1) shall be subject to statutory licensing under this paragraph if the secondary transmission is of the primary transmission of a network station or a non-network station to a subscriber who resides outside the station's local market but within a community in which the signal has been determined by the Federal Communications Commission to be significantly viewed in such community, pursuant to the rules, regulations, and authorizations of the Federal Communications Commission in effect on April 15, 1976, applicable to determining with respect to a cable system whether signals are significantly viewed in a community.

(B) Waiver.—A subscriber who is denied the secondary transmission of the primary transmission of a network station or a non-network station under subparagraph (A) may request a waiver from such denial by submitting a request, through the subscriber's satellite carrier, to the network station or non-network station in the local market affiliated with the same network or non-network where the subscriber is located. The network station or non-network station shall accept or reject the subscriber's request for a waiver within 30 days after receipt of the request. If the network station or non-network station fails to accept or reject the subscriber's request for a waiver within that 30–day period, that network station or non-network station shall be deemed to agree to the waiver request.

(3) Secondary transmission of low power programming.—

(A) In general.—Subject to subparagraphs (B) and (C), a secondary transmission of a performance or display of a work embodied in a primary transmission of a television broadcast station to subscribers who receive secondary transmissions of primary transmissions under paragraph (1) shall be subject to statutory licensing under this paragraph if the secondary transmission is of the primary transmission of a television broadcast station that is licensed as a low power television station, to a subscriber who resides within the same designated market area as the station that originates the transmission.

(B) No applicability to repeaters and translators.— Secondary transmissions provided for in subparagraph (A) shall not apply to any low power television station that retransmits the programs and signals of another television station for more than 2 hours each day.

(C) No impact on other secondary transmissions obligations.—A satellite carrier that makes secondary transmissions of a primary transmission of a low power television station under a statutory license provided under this section is not required, by reason of such secondary transmissions, to make any other secondary transmissions.

(4) Special exceptions.—A secondary transmission of a performance or display of a work embodied in a primary transmission of a television broadcast station to subscribers who receive secondary transmissions of primary transmissions under paragraph (1) shall, if the secondary transmission is made by a satellite carrier that complies with the requirements of paragraph (1), be subject to statutory licensing under this paragraph as follows:

(A) States with single full-power network station.—In a State in which there is licensed by the Federal Communications Commission a single full-power station that was a network station on January 1, 1995, the statutory license provided for in this paragraph shall apply to the secondary transmission by a satellite carrier of the primary transmission of that station to any subscriber in a community that is located within that State and that is not within the first 50 television markets as listed in the regulations of the Commission as in effect on such date (47 C.F.R. 76.51).

(B) States with all network stations and non-network stations in same local market.—In a State in which all network stations and non-network stations licensed by the Federal

Communications Commission within that State as of January 1, 1995, are assigned to the same local market and that local market does not encompass all counties of that State, the statutory license provided under this paragraph shall apply to the secondary transmission by a satellite carrier of the primary transmissions of such station to all subscribers in the State who reside in a local market that is within the first 50 major television markets as listed in the regulations of the Commission as in effect on such date (section 76.51 of title 47, Code of Federal Regulations).

(C) Additional stations.—In the case of that State in which are located 4 counties that—

(i) on January 1, 2004, were in local markets principally comprised of counties in another State, and

(ii) had a combined total of 41,340 television households, according to the U.S. Television Household Estimates by Nielsen Media Research for 2004,

the statutory license provided under this paragraph shall apply to secondary transmissions by a satellite carrier to subscribers in any such county of the primary transmissions of any network station located in that State, if the satellite carrier was making such secondary transmissions to any subscribers in that county on January 1, 2004.

(D) Certain additional stations.—If 2 adjacent counties in a single State are in a local market comprised principally of counties located in another State, the statutory license provided for in this paragraph shall apply to the secondary transmission by a satellite carrier to subscribers in those 2 counties of the primary transmissions of any network station located in the capital of the State in which such 2 counties are located, if—

(i) the 2 counties are located in a local market that is in the top 100 markets for the year 2003 according to Nielsen Media Research; and

(ii) the total number of television households in the 2 counties combined did not exceed 10,000 for the year 2003 according to Nielsen Media Research.

(E) Networks of noncommercial educational broadcast stations.—In the case of a system of three or more noncommercial educational broadcast stations licensed to a single State, public agency, or political, educational, or special purpose subdivision of a State, the statutory license provided for in this paragraph shall apply to the secondary transmission of the primary transmission of such system to any subscriber in any county or county equivalent within such State, if such subscriber is located in a designated market area that is not otherwise eligible to receive the secondary transmission of the primary transmission of a noncommercial educational broadcast station located within the State pursuant to paragraph (1).

(5) Applicability of royalty rates and procedures.—The royalty rates and procedures under section 119(b) shall apply to the secondary transmissions to which the statutory license under paragraph (4) applies.

(b) Reporting requirements.—

(1) Initial lists.—A satellite carrier that makes secondary transmissions of a primary transmission made by a network station under subsection (a) shall, within 90 days after commencing such secondary transmissions, submit to the network that owns or is affiliated with the network station—

    (A) a list identifying (by name in alphabetical order and street address, including county and 9–digit zip code) all subscribers to which the satellite carrier makes secondary transmissions of that primary transmission under subsection (a); and

    (B) a separate list, aggregated by designated market area (by name and address, including street or rural route number, city, State, and 9–digit zip code), which shall indicate those subscribers being served pursuant to paragraph (2) of subsection (a).

(2) Subsequent lists.—After the list is submitted under paragraph (1), the satellite carrier shall, on the 15th of each month, submit to the network—

    (A) a list identifying (by name in alphabetical order and street address, including county and 9–digit zip code) any subscribers who have been added or dropped as subscribers since the last submission under this subsection; and

    (B) a separate list, aggregated by designated market area (by name and street address, including street or rural route number, city, State, and 9–digit zip code), identifying those subscribers whose service pursuant to paragraph (2) of subsection (a) has been added or dropped since the last submission under this subsection.

(3) Use of subscriber information.—Subscriber information submitted by a satellite carrier under this subsection may be used only for the purposes of monitoring compliance by the satellite carrier with this section.

(4) Requirements of networks.—The submission requirements of this subsection shall apply to a satellite carrier only if the network to which the submissions are to be made places on file with the Register of Copyrights a document identifying the name and address of the person to whom such submissions are to be made. The Register of Copyrights shall maintain for public inspection a file of all such documents.

(c) No royalty fee required for certain secondary transmissions.—A satellite carrier whose secondary transmissions are subject to statutory licensing under paragraphs (1), (2), and (3) of subsection (a) shall have no royalty obligation for such secondary transmissions.

(d) Noncompliance with reporting and regulatory requirements.—Notwithstanding subsection (a), the willful or repeated secondary transmission to the public by a satellite carrier into the local market of a television broadcast station of a primary transmission embodying a performance or display of a work made by that television broadcast station is actionable as an act of infringement under section 501, and is fully subject to the remedies provided under sections 502 through 506, if the satellite carrier has not complied with the reporting requirements of subsection (b) or with the rules, regulations, and authorizations of the Federal Communications Commission concerning the carriage of television broadcast signals.

(e) Willful alterations.—Notwithstanding subsection (a), the secondary transmission to the public by a satellite carrier into the local market of a television broadcast station of a performance or display of a work embodied in a primary transmission made by that television broadcast station is actionable as an act of infringement under section 501, and is fully subject to the remedies provided by sections 502 through 506 and section 510, if the content of the particular program in which the performance or display is embodied, or any commercial advertising or station announcement transmitted by the primary transmitter during, or immediately before or after, the transmission of such program, is in any way willfully altered by the satellite carrier through changes, deletions, or additions, or is combined with programming from any other broadcast signal.

(f) Violation of territorial restrictions on statutory license for television broadcast stations.—

(1) Individual violations.—The willful or repeated secondary transmission to the public by a satellite carrier of a primary transmission embodying a performance or display of a work made by a television broadcast station to a subscriber who does not reside in that station's local market, and is not subject to statutory licensing under section 119, subject to statutory licensing by reason of paragraph (2)(A), (3), or (4) of subsection (a), or subject to a private licensing agreement, is actionable as an act of infringement under section 501 and is fully subject to the remedies provided by sections 502 through 506, except that—

(A) no damages shall be awarded for such act of infringement if the satellite carrier took corrective action by promptly withdrawing service from the ineligible subscriber; and

(B) any statutory damages shall not exceed $250 for such subscriber for each month during which the violation occurred.

(2) Pattern of violations.—If a satellite carrier engages in a willful or repeated pattern or practice of secondarily transmitting to the public a primary transmission embodying a performance or display of a work made by a television broadcast station to subscribers who do not reside in that station's local market, and are not subject to statutory licensing under section 119, subject to statutory licensing by reason of paragraph (2)(A), (3), or (4) of subsection (a), or subject to a private licensing agreement, then in addition to the remedies under paragraph (1)—

(A) if the pattern or practice has been carried out on a substantially nationwide basis, the court—

(i) shall order a permanent injunction barring the secondary transmission by the satellite carrier of the primary transmissions of that television broadcast station (and if such television broadcast station is a network station, all other television broadcast stations affiliated with such network); and

(ii) may order statutory damages not exceeding $2,500,000 for each 6–month period during which the pattern or practice was carried out; and

(B) if the pattern or practice has been carried out on a local or regional basis with respect to more than one television broadcast station, the court—

>   **(i)** shall order a permanent injunction barring the secondary transmission in that locality or region by the satellite carrier of the primary transmissions of any television broadcast station; and

>   **(ii)** may order statutory damages not exceeding $2,500,000 for each 6–month period during which the pattern or practice was carried out.

(g) Burden of proof.—In any action brought under subsection (f), the satellite carrier shall have the burden of proving that its secondary transmission of a primary transmission by a television broadcast station is made only to subscribers located within that station's local market or subscribers being served in compliance with section 119, paragraph (2)(A), (3), or (4) of subsection (a), or a private licensing agreement.

(h) Geographic limitations on secondary transmissions.—The statutory license created by this section shall apply to secondary transmissions to locations in the United States.

(i) Exclusivity with respect to secondary transmissions of broadcast stations by satellite to members of the public.—No provision of section 111 or any other law (other than this section and section 119) shall be construed to contain any authorization, exemption, or license through which secondary transmissions by satellite carriers of programming contained in a primary transmission made by a television broadcast station may be made without obtaining the consent of the copyright owner.

(j) Definitions.—In this section—

(1) Distributor.—The term "distributor" means an entity that contracts to distribute secondary transmissions from a satellite carrier and, either as a single channel or in a package with other programming, provides the secondary transmission either directly to individual subscribers or indirectly through other program distribution entities.

(2) Local market.—

(A) In general.—The term "local market", in the case of both commercial and noncommercial television broadcast stations, means the designated market area in which a station is located, and—

>   **(i)** in the case of a commercial television broadcast station, all commercial television broadcast stations licensed to a community within the same designated market area are within the same local market; and

>   **(ii)** in the case of a noncommercial educational television broadcast station, the market includes any station that is licensed to a community within the same designated market area as the noncommercial educational television broadcast station.

(B) County of license.—In addition to the area described in subparagraph (A), a station's local market includes the county in which the station's community of license is located.

(C) Designated market area.—For purposes of subparagraph (A), the term "designated market area" means a designated market area, as determined by Nielsen Media Research and published in the 1999–2000 Nielsen Station Index Directory and Nielsen Station Index United States Television Household Estimates or any successor publication.

(D) Certain areas outside of any designated market area.—Any census area, borough, or other area in the State of Alaska that is outside of a designated market area, as determined by Nielsen Media Research, shall be deemed to be part of one of the local markets in the State of Alaska. A satellite carrier may determine which local market in the State of Alaska will be deemed to be the relevant local market in connection with each subscriber in such census area, borough, or other area.

(E) Market Determinations.—The local market of a commercial television broadcast station may be modified by the Federal Communications Commission in accordance with section 338(l) of the Communications Act of 1937 (47 U.S.C. 388).

(3) Low power television station.—The term "low power television station" means a low power TV station as defined in section 74.701(f) of title 47, Code of Federal Regulations, as in effect on June 1, 2004. For purposes of this paragraph, the term 'low power television station' includes a low power television station that has been accorded primary status as a Class A television licensee under section 73.6001(a) of title 47, Code of Federal Regulations.

(4) Network station; non-network station; satellite carrier; secondary transmission.—The terms "network station", "non-network station", "satellite carrier", and "secondary transmission" have the meanings given such terms under section 119(d).

(5) Noncommercial educational broadcast station.—The term "noncommercial educational broadcast station" means a television broadcast station that is a noncommercial educational broadcast station as defined in section 397 of the Communications Act of 1934, as in effect on the date of the enactment of the Satellite Television Extension and Localism Act of 2010.

(6) Subscriber.—The term "subscriber" means a person or entity that receives a secondary transmission service from a satellite carrier and pays a fee for the service, directly or indirectly, to the satellite carrier or to a distributor.

(7) Television broadcast station.—The term "television broadcast station"—

(A) means an over-the-air, commercial or noncommercial television broadcast station licensed by the Federal Communications Commission under subpart E of part 73 of title 47, Code of Federal Regulations, except that such term does not include a low-power or translator television station; and

(B) includes a television broadcast station licensed by an appropriate governmental authority of Canada or Mexico if the station broadcasts primarily in the English language and is a network station as defined in section 119(d)(2)(A).

CHAPTER 2.—COPYRIGHT OWNERSHIP AND TRANSFER

Sec. 201.   Ownership of Copyright

(a) Initial Ownership.—Copyright in a work protected under this title vests initially in the author or authors of the work. The authors of a joint work are coowners of copyright in the work.

(b) Works Made for Hire.—In the case of a work made for hire, the employer or other person for whom the work was prepared is considered the author for purposes of this title, and, unless the parties have expressly agreed otherwise in a written instrument signed by them, owns all of the rights comprised in the copyright.

(c) Contributions to Collective Works.—Copyright in each separate contribution to a collective work is distinct from copyright in the collective work as a whole, and vests initially in the author of the contribution. In the absence of an express transfer of the copyright or of any rights under it, the owner of copyright in the collective work is presumed to have acquired only the privilege of reproducing and distributing the contribution as part of that particular collective work, any revision of that collective work, and any later collective work in the same series.

(d) Transfer of Ownership.—

(1) The ownership of a copyright may be transferred in whole or in part by any means of conveyance or by operation of law, and may be bequeathed by will or pass as personal property by the applicable laws of intestate succession.

(2) Any of the exclusive rights comprised in a copyright, including any subdivision of any of the rights specified by section 106, may be transferred as provided by clause (1) and owned separately. The owner of any particular exclusive right is entitled, to the extent of that right, to all of the protection and remedies accorded to the copyright owner by this title.

(e) Involuntary Transfer.—When an individual author's ownership of a copyright, or of any of the exclusive rights under a copyright, has not previously been transferred voluntarily by that individual author, no action by any governmental body or other official or organization purporting to seize, expropriate, transfer, or exercise rights of ownership with respect to the copyright, or any of the exclusive rights under a copyright, shall be given effect under this title, except as provided under Title 11.

Sec. 202.   Ownership of Copyright as Distinct From Ownership of Material Object

Ownership of a copyright, or of any of the exclusive rights under a copyright, is distinct from ownership of any material object in which the work is embodied. Transfer of ownership of any material object, including the copy or phonorecord in which the work is first fixed, does not of itself convey any rights in the copyrighted work embodied in the object; nor, in the absence of an agreement, does transfer of ownership of a copyright or of any exclusive rights under a copyright convey property rights in any material object.

Sec. 203.   Termination of Transfers and Licenses Granted by the Author

(a) Conditions for Termination.—In the case of any work other than a work made for hire, the exclusive or nonexclusive grant of a transfer or license of copyright or of any right under a copyright, executed by the author on or after January 1, 1978, otherwise than by will, is subject to termination under the following conditions:

(1) In the case of a grant executed by one author, termination of the grant may be effected by that author or, if the author is dead, by the person or persons who, under clause (2) of this subsection, own and are entitled to exercise a total of more than one-half of that author's termination interest. In the case of a grant executed by two or more authors of a joint work, termination of the grant may be effected by a majority of the authors who executed it; if any of such authors is dead, the termination interest of any such author may be exercised as a unit by the person or persons who, under clause (2) of this subsection, own and are entitled to exercise a total of more than one-half of that author's interest.

(2) Where an author is dead, his or her termination interest is owned, and may be exercised, as follows:

(A) The widow or widower owns the author's entire termination interest unless there are any surviving children or grandchildren of the author, in which case the widow or widower owns one-half of the author's interest.

(B) The author's surviving children, and the surviving children of any dead child of the author, own the author's entire termination interest unless there is a widow or widower, in which case the ownership of one-half of the author's interest is divided among them.

(C) The rights of the author's children and grandchildren are in all cases divided among them and exercised on a per stirpes basis according to the number of such author's children represented; the share of the children of a dead child in a termination interest can be exercised only by the action of a majority of them.

(D) In the event that the author's widow or widower, children, and grandchildren are not living, the author's executor, administrator, personal representative, or trustee shall own the author's entire termination interest.

(3) Termination of the grant may be effected at any time during a period of five years beginning at the end of thirty-five years from the date of execution of the grant; or, if the grant covers the right of publication of the work, the period begins at the end of thirty-five years from the date of publication of the work under the grant or at the end of forty years from the date of execution of the grant, whichever term ends earlier.

(4) The termination shall be effected by serving an advance notice in writing, signed by the number and proportion of owners of termination interests required under clauses (1) and (2) of this subsection, or by their duly authorized agents, upon the grantee or the grantee's successor in title.

(A) The notice shall state the effective date of the termination, which shall fall within the five-year period specified by clause (3) of this subsection, and the notice shall be served not less than two or more than ten years before that date. A copy of the notice shall be recorded in the Copyright Office before the effective date of termination, as a condition to its taking effect.

(B) The notice shall comply, in form, content, and manner of service, with requirements that the Register of Copyrights shall prescribe by regulation.

(5) Termination of the grant may be effected notwithstanding any agreement to the contrary, including an agreement to make a will or to make any future grant.

(b) Effect of Termination.—Upon the effective date of termination, all rights under this title that were covered by the terminated grants revert to the author, authors, and other persons owning termination interests under clauses (1) and (2) of subsection (a), including those owners who did not join in signing the notice of termination under clause (4) of subsection (a), but with the following limitations:

(1) A derivative work prepared under authority of the grant before its termination may continue to be utilized under the terms of the grant after its termination, but this privilege does not extend to the preparation after the termination of other derivative works based upon the copyrighted work covered by the terminated grant.

(2) The future rights that will revert upon termination of the grant become vested on the date the notice of termination has been served as provided by clause (4) of subsection (a). The rights vest in the author, authors, and other persons named in, and in the proportionate shares provided by, clauses (1) and (2) of subsection (a).

(3) Subject to the provisions of clause (4) of this subsection, a further grant, or agreement to make a further grant, of any right covered by a terminated grant is valid only if it is signed by the same number and proportion of the owners, in whom the right has vested under clause (2) of this subsection, as are required to terminate the grant under clauses (1) and (2) of subsection (a). Such further grant or agreement is effective with respect to all of the persons in whom the right it covers has vested under clause (2) of this subsection,

including those who did not join in signing it. If any person dies after rights under a terminated grant have vested in him or her, that person's legal representatives, legatees, or heirs at law represent him or her for purposes of this clause.

(4) A further grant, or agreement to make a further grant, of any right covered by a terminated grant is valid only if it is made after the effective date of the termination. As an exception, however, an agreement for such a further grant may be made between the persons provided by clause (3) of this subsection and the original grantee or such grantee's successor in title, after the notice of termination has been served as provided by clause (4) of subsection (a).

(5) Termination of a grant under this section affects only those rights covered by the grants that arise under this title, and in no way affects rights arising under any other Federal, State, or foreign laws.

(6) Unless and until termination is effected under this section, the grant, if it does not provide otherwise, continues in effect for the term of copyright provided by this title.

Sec. 204.   Execution of Transfers of Copyright Ownership

(a) A transfer of copyright ownership, other than by operation of law, is not valid unless an instrument of conveyance, or a note or memorandum of the transfer, is in writing and signed by the owner of the rights conveyed or such owner's duly authorized agent.

(b) A certificate of acknowledgement is not required for the validity of a transfer, but is prima facie evidence of the execution of the transfer if—

(1) in the case of a transfer executed in the United States, the certificate is issued by a person authorized to administer oaths within the United States; or

(2) in the case of a transfer executed in a foreign country, the certificate is issued by a diplomatic or consular officer of the United States, or by a person authorized to administer oaths whose authority is proved by a certificate of such an officer.

Sec. 205.   Recordation of Transfers and Other Documents

(a) Conditions for Recordation.—Any transfer of copyright ownership or other document pertaining to a copyright may be recorded in the Copyright Office if the document filed for recordation bears the actual signature of the person who executed it, or if it is accompanied by a sworn or official certification that it is a true copy of the original, signed document. A sworn official certification may be submitted to the Copyright Office electronically, pursuant to regulations established by the Register of Copyrights.

(b) Certificate of Recordation.—The Register of Copyrights shall, upon receipt of a document as provided by subsection (a) and of the fee provided by section 708, record the document and return it with a certificate of recordation.

(c) Recordation as Constructive Notice.—Recordation of a document in the Copyright Office gives all persons constructive notice of the facts stated in the recorded document, but only if—

(1) the document, or material attached to it, specifically identifies the work to which it pertains so that, after the document is indexed by the Register of Copyrights, it would be revealed by a reasonable search under the title or registration number of the work; and

(2) registration has been made for the work.

(d) Priority Between Conflicting Transfers.—As between two conflicting transfers, the one executed first prevails if it is recorded, in the manner required to give constructive notice under subsection (c), within one month after its execution in the United States or within two months after its execution outside the United States, or at any time before recordation in such manner of the later transfer. Otherwise the later transfer prevails if recorded first in such manner, and if taken in good faith, for valuable consideration or on the basis of a binding promise to pay royalties, and without notice of the earlier transfer.

(e) Priority Between Conflicting Transfer of Ownership and Nonexclusive License.—A nonexclusive license, whether recorded or not, prevails over a conflicting transfer of copyright ownership if the license is evidenced by a written instrument signed by the owner of the rights licensed or such owner's duly authorized agent; and if—

(1) the license was taken before execution of the transfer; or

(2) the license was taken in good faith before recordation of the transfer and without notice of it.

CHAPTER 3.—DURATION OF COPYRIGHT

Sec. 301.   Preemption With Respect to Other Laws

(a) On and after January 1, 1978, all legal or equitable rights that are equivalent to any of the exclusive rights within the general scope of copyright as specified by section 106 in works of authorship that are fixed in a tangible medium of expression and come within the subject matter of copyright as specified by sections 102 and 103, whether created before or after that date and whether published or unpublished, are governed exclusively by this title. Thereafter, no person is entitled to any such right or equivalent right in any such work under the common law or statutes of any State.

(b) Nothing in this title annuls or limits any rights or remedies under the common law or statutes of any State with respect to—

(1) subject matter that does not come within the subject matter of copyright as specified by sections 102 and 103, including works of authorship not fixed in any tangible medium of expression; or

(2) any cause of action arising from undertakings commenced before January 1, 1978;

(3) activities violating legal or equitable rights that are not equivalent to any of the exclusive rights within the general scope of copyright as specified by section 106; or

(4) State and local landmarks, historic preservation, zoning, or building codes, relating to architectural works protected under section 102(a)(8).

(c) With respect to sound recordings fixed before February 15, 1972, any rights or remedies under the common law or statutes of any State shall not be annulled or limited by this title until February 15, 2067. The preemptive provisions of subsection (a) shall apply to any such rights and remedies pertaining to any cause of action arising from undertakings commenced on and after February 15, 2067. Notwithstanding the provisions of section 303, no sound recording fixed before February 15, 1972, shall be subject to copyright under this title before, on, or after February 15, 2067.

(d) Nothing in this title annuls or limits any rights or remedies under any other Federal statute.

(e) The scope of Federal preemption under this section is not affected by the adherence of the United States to the Berne Convention or the satisfaction of obligations of the United States thereunder.

(f)(1) On or after the effective date set forth in section 9(a) of the Visual Artists Rights Act of 1990, all legal or equitable rights that are equivalent to any of the rights conferred by section 106A with respect to works of visual art to which the rights conferred by section 106A apply are governed exclusively by section 106A and section 113(d) and the provisions of this title relating to such sections. Thereafter, no person is entitled to any such right or equivalent right in any work of visual art under the common law or statutes of any State.

(2) Nothing in paragraph (1) annuls or limits any rights or remedies under the common law or statutes of any State with respect to—

(A) any cause of action from undertakings commenced before the effective date set forth in section 9(a) of the Visual Artists Rights Act of 1990;

(B) activities violating legal or equitable rights that are not equivalent to any of the rights conferred by section 106A with respect to works of visual art; or

(C) activities violating legal or equitable rights which extend beyond the life of the author.

Sec. 302.   Duration of Copyright: Works Created on or After January 1, 1978

(a) In General.—Copyright in a work created on or after January 1, 1978, subsists from its creation and, except as provided by the following subsections, endures for a term consisting of the life of the author and 70 years after the author's death.

(b) Joint Works.—In the case of a joint work prepared by two or more authors who did not work for hire, the copyright endures for a term consisting of the life of the last surviving author and 70 years after such last surviving author's death.

(c) Anonymous Works, Pseudonymous Works, and Works Made for Hire.—In the case of an anonymous work, a pseudonymous work, or a work made for hire, the copyright endures for a term of 95 years from the year of its first publication, or a term of 120 years from the year of its creation, whichever expires first. If, before the end of such term, the identity of one or more of the authors of an anonymous or pseudonymous work is revealed in the records of a registration made for that work under subsections (a) or (d) of section 408, or in the records provided by this subsection, the copyright in the work endures for the term specified by subsection (a) or (b), based on the life of the author or authors whose identity has been revealed. Any person having an interest in the copyright in an anonymous or pseudonymous work may at any time record, in records to be maintained by the Copyright Office for that purpose, a statement identifying one or more authors of the work; the statement shall also identify the person filing it, the nature of that person's interest, the source of the information recorded, and the particular work affected, and shall comply in form and content with requirements that the Register of Copyrights shall prescribe by regulation.

(d) Records Relating to Death of Authors.—Any person having an interest in a copyright may at any time record in the Copyright Office a statement of the date of death of the author of the copyrighted work, or a statement that the author is still living on a particular date. The statement shall identify the person filing it, the nature of that person's interest, and the source of the information recorded, and shall comply in form and content with requirements that the Register of Copyrights shall prescribe by regulation. The Register shall maintain current records of information relating to the death of authors of copyrighted works, based on such recorded statements and, to the extent the Register considers practicable, on data contained in any of the records of the Copyright Office or in other reference sources.

(e) Presumption as to Author's Death.—After a period of 95 years from the year of first publication of a work, or a period of 120 years from the year of its creation, whichever expires first, any person who obtains from the Copyright Office a certified report that the records provided by subsection (d) disclose nothing to indicate that the author of the work is living, or died less than 70 years before, is entitled to the benefit of a presumption that the author has been dead for at least 70 years. Reliance in good faith upon this presumption shall be a complete defense to any action for infringement under this title.

Sec. 303.   Duration of Copyright: Works Created but not Published or Copyrighted Before January 1, 1978

(a) Copyright in a work created before January 1, 1978, but not theretofore in the public domain or copyrighted, subsists from January 1, 1978, and endures for the term provided by section 302. In no case, however, shall the term of copyright in such a work expire before December 31, 2002; and, if the work is published on or before December 31, 2002, the term of copyright shall not expire before December 31, 2047.

(b) The distribution before January 1, 1978, of a phonorecord shall not for any purpose constitute a publication of any musical work, dramatic work, or literary work embodied therein.

Sec. 304.   Duration of Copyright: Subsisting Copyrights

(a) Copyrights in Their First Term on January 1, 1978.—

(1)(A) Any copyright, the first term of which is subsisting on January 1, 1978, shall endure for 28 years from the date it was originally secured.

(B) In the case of—

(i) any posthumous work or of any periodical, cyclopedic, or other composite work upon which the copyright was originally secured by the proprietor thereof, or

(ii) any work copyrighted by a corporate body (otherwise than as assignee or licensee of the individual author) or by an employer for whom such work is made for hire,

the proprietor of such copyright shall be entitled to a renewal and extension of the copyright in such work for the further term of 67 years.

(C) In the case of any other copyrighted work, including a contribution by an individual author to a periodical or to a cyclopedic or other composite work—

(i) the author of such work, if the author is still living,

(ii) the widow, widower, or children of the author, if the author is not living,

(iii) the author's executors, if such author, widow, widower, or children are not living, or

(iv) the author's next of kin, in the absence of a will of the author,

shall be entitled to a renewal and extension of the copyright in such work for a further term of 67 years.

(2)(A) At the expiration of the original term of copyright in a work specified in paragraph (1)(B) of this subsection, the copyright shall endure for a renewed and extended further term of 67 years, which—

(i) if an application to register a claim to such further term has been made to the Copyright Office within 1 year before the expiration of the original term of copyright, and the claim is registered, shall vest, upon the beginning of such further term, in the proprietor of the copyright who is entitled to claim the renewal of copyright at the time the application is made; or

(ii) if no such application is made or the claim pursuant to such application is not registered, shall vest, upon the beginning of such further term, in the person or entity that was the proprietor of the copyright as of the last day of the original term of copyright.

(B) At the expiration of the original term of copyright in a work specified in paragraph (1)(C) of this subsection, the copyright shall endure for a renewed and extended further term of 67 years, which—

(i) if an application to register a claim to such further term has been made to the Copyright Office within 1 year before the expiration of the original term of copyright, and the claim is registered, shall vest, upon the beginning of such further term, in any person who is entitled under paragraph (1)(C) to the renewal and extension of the copyright at the time the application is made; or

(ii) if no such application is made or the claim pursuant to such application is not registered, shall vest, upon the beginning of such further term, in any person entitled under paragraph (1)(C), as of the last day of the original term of copyright, to the renewal and extension of the copyright.

(3)(A) An application to register a claim to the renewed and extended term of copyright in a work may be made to the Copyright Office—

(i) within 1 year before the expiration of the original term of copyright by any person entitled under paragraph (1)(B) or (C) to such further term of 67 years; and

(ii) at any time during the renewed and extended term by any person in whom such further term vested, under paragraph (2)(A) or (B), or by any successor or assign of such person, if the application is made in the name of such person.

(B) Such an application is not a condition of the renewal and extension of the copyright in a work for a further term of 67 years.

(4)(A) If an application to register a claim to the renewed and extended term of copyright in a work is not made within 1 year before the expiration of the original term of copyright in a work, or if the claim pursuant to such application is not registered, then a derivative work prepared under authority of a grant of a transfer or license of the copyright that is made before the expiration of the original term of copyright may continue to be used under the terms of the grant during the renewed and extended term of copyright without infringing the copyright, except that such use does not extend to the preparation during such renewed and extended term of other derivative works based upon the copyrighted work covered by such grant.

(B) If an application to register a claim to the renewed and extended term of copyright in a work is made within 1 year before its expiration, and the claim is registered, the certificate of such registration shall constitute prima facie evidence as to the validity of the copyright during its renewed and extended term and of the facts stated in the certificate. The evidentiary weight to be accorded the certificates of a registration of a renewed and extended term of copyright made after the end of that 1–year period shall be within the discretion of the court.*

---

*   Congress, in revising section 304(a) effective June 26, 1992, stated the following with respect to the effective date of this new renewal provision: "The amendments made by this section shall apply only to those copyrights secured between January 1, 1964, and December 31, 1977. Copyrights secured before January 1, 1964, shall be governed by the provisions of section 304(a) of title 17, United States Code, as in effect on the day before the effective date of this section." Pub. L. 102–307, § 102(g)(2). The text of section 304(a) as enacted in 1976, which thus governs works that were in their first term of copyright prior to January 1, 1964,and which thus would have to be renewed before the end of 1991, was as follows:

(a) Copyrights in their first term on January 1, 1978. Any copyright, the first term of which is subsisting on January 1, 1978, shall endure for twenty-eight years from the date it was originally secured: *Provided*, That in the case of any posthumous work or of any periodical, cyclopedic, or other composite work upon which the copyright was originally secured by the proprietor thereof, or of any work copyrighted by a corporate body (otherwise than as assignee or licensee of the individual author) or by an employer for whom such work is made for hire, the proprietor of such copyright shall be entitled to a renewal and extension of the copyright in such work for the further term of forty-seven years when application for such renewal and extension shall have been made to the Copyright Office and duly registered therein within one year prior to the expiration of the original term of copyright: *And provided further*, That in the case of any

(b) Copyrights in their Renewal Term at the Time of the Effective Date of the Sonny Bono Copyright Term Extension Act.—Any copyright still in its renewal term at the time that the Sonny Bono Copyright Term Extension Act becomes effective shall have a copyright term of 95 years from the date copyright was originally secured.

(c) Termination of Transfers and Licenses Covering Extended Renewal Term.—In the case of any copyright subsisting in either its first or renewal term on January 1, 1978, other than a copyright in a work made for hire, the exclusive or nonexclusive grant of a transfer or license of the renewal copyright or any right under it, executed before January 1, 1978, by any of the persons designated by subsection (a)(1)(C) of this section, otherwise than by will, is subject to termination under the following conditions:

(1) In the case of a grant executed by a person or persons other than the author, termination of the grant may be effected by the surviving person or persons who executed it. In the case of a grant executed by one or more of the authors of the work, termination of the grant may be effected, to the extent of a particular author's share in the ownership of the renewal copyright, by the author who executed it or, if such author is dead, by the person or persons who, under clause (2) of this subsection, own and are entitled to exercise a total of more than one-half of that author's termination interest.

(2) Where an author is dead, his or her termination interest is owned, and may be exercised, as follows:

(A) The widow or widower owns the author's entire termination interest unless there are any surviving children or grandchildren of the author, in which case the widow or widower owns one-half of the author's interest.

(B) The author's surviving children, and the surviving children of any dead child of the author, own the author's entire termination interest unless there is a widow or widower, in which case the ownership of one-half of the author's interest is divided among them.

(C) The rights of the author's children and grandchildren are in all cases divided among them and exercised on a per stirpes basis according to the number of such author's children represented; the share of the children of a dead child in a termination interest can be exercised only by the action of a majority of them.

(D) In the event that the author's widow or widower, children, and grandchildren are not living, the author's

---

other copyrighted work, including a contribution by an individual author to a periodical or to a cyclopedic or other composite work, the author of such work, if still living, or the widow, widower, or children of the author, if the author be not living, or if such author, widow, widower, or children be not living, then the author's executors, or in the absence of a will, his or her next of kin shall be entitled to a renewal and extension of the copyright in such work for a further term of forty-seven years when application for such renewal and extension shall have been made to the Copyright Office and duly registered therein within one year prior to the expiration of the original term of copyright: *And provided further*, That in default of the registration of such application for renewal and extension, the copyright in any work shall terminate at the expiration of twenty-eight years from the date copyright was originally secured.

executor, administrator, personal representative, or trustee shall own the author's entire termination interest.

(3) Termination of the grant may be effected at any time during a period of five years beginning at the end of fifty-six years from the date copyright was originally secured, or beginning on January 1, 1978, whichever is later.

(4) The termination shall be effected by serving an advance notice in writing upon the grantee or the grantee's successor in title. In the case of a grant executed by a person or persons other than the author, the notice shall be signed by all of those entitled to terminate the grant under clause (1) of this subsection, or by their duly authorized agents. In the case of a grant executed by one or more of the authors of the work, the notice as to any one author's share shall be signed by that author or his or her duly authorized agent or, if that author is dead, by the number and proportion of the owners of his or her termination interest required under clauses (1) and (2) of this subsection, or by their duly authorized agents.

(A) The notice shall state the effective date of the termination, which shall fall within the five-year period specified by clause (3) of this subsection, or, in the case of a termination under subsection (d), within the five-year period specified by subsection (d)(2), and the notice shall be served not less than two or more than ten years before that date. A copy of the notice shall be recorded in the Copyright Office before the effective date of termination, as a condition to its taking effect.

(B) The notice shall comply, in form, content, and manner of service, with requirements that the Register of Copyrights shall prescribe by regulation.

(5) Termination of the grant may be effected notwithstanding any agreement to the contrary, including an agreement to make a will or to make any future grant.

(6) In the case of a grant executed by a person or persons other than the author, all rights under this title that were covered by the terminated grant revert, upon the effective date of termination, to all of those entitled to terminate the grant under clause (1) of this subsection. In the case of a grant executed by one or more of the authors of the work, all of a particular author's rights under this title that were covered by the terminated grant revert, upon the effective date of termination, to that author or, if that author is dead, to the persons owning his or her termination interest under clause (2) of this subsection, including those owners who did not join in signing the notice of termination under clause (4) of this subsection. In all cases the reversion of rights is subject to the following limitations:

(A) A derivative work prepared under authority of the grant before its termination may continue to be utilized under the terms of the grant after its termination, but this privilege does not extend to the preparation after the termination of other derivative works based upon the copyrighted work covered by the terminated grant.

(B) The future rights that will revert upon termination of the grant become vested on the date the notice of termination has been served as provided by clause (4) of this subsection.

(C) Where the author's rights revert to two or more persons under clause (2) of this subsection, they shall vest in those persons in the proportionate shares provided by that clause. In such a case, and subject to the provisions of subclause (D) of this clause, a further grant, or agreement to make a further grant, of a particular author's share with respect to any right covered by a terminated grant is valid only if it is signed by the same number and proportion of the owners, in whom the right has vested under this clause, as are required to terminate the grant under clause (2) of this subsection. Such further grant or agreement is effective with respect to all of the persons in whom the right it covers has vested under this subclause, including those who did not join in signing it. If any person dies after rights under a terminated grant have vested in him or her, that person's legal representatives, legatees, or heirs at law represent him or her for purposes of this subclause.

(D) A further grant, or agreement to make a further grant, of any right covered by a terminated grant is valid only if it is made after the effective date of the termination. As an exception, however, an agreement for such a further grant may be made between the author or any of the persons provided by the first sentence of clause (6) of this subsection, or between the persons provided by subclause (C) of this clause, and the original grantee or such grantee's successor in title, after the notice of termination has been served as provided by clause (4) of this subsection.

(E) Termination of a grant under this subsection affects only those rights covered by the grant that arise under this title, and in no way affects rights arising under any other Federal, State, or foreign laws.

(F) Unless and until termination is effected under this subsection, the grant, if it does not provide otherwise, continues in effect for the remainder of the extended renewal term.

(d) Termination Rights Provided in Subsection (c) which have Expired On or Before the Effective Date of the Sonny Bono Copyright Term Extension Act.—In the case of any copyright other than a work made for hire, subsisting in its renewal term on the effective date of the Sonny Bono Copyright Term Extension Act for which the termination right provided in subsection (c) has expired by such date, where the author or owner of the termination right has not previously exercised such termination right, the exclusive or nonexclusive grant of a transfer or license of the renewal copyright or any right under it, executed before January 1, 1978, by any of the persons designated in subsection (a)(1)(C) of this section, other than by will, is subject to termination under the following conditions:

(1) The conditions specified in subsections (c)(1), (2), (4), (5), and (6) of this section apply to terminations of the last 20 years of

copyright term as provided by the amendments made by the Sonny Bono Copyright Term Extension Act.

(2) Termination of the grant may be effected at any time during a period of 5 years beginning at the end of 75 years from the date copyright was originally secured.

Sec. 305.   Duration of Copyright: Terminal Date

All terms of copyright provided by sections 302 through 304 run to the end of the calendar year in which they would otherwise expire.

CHAPTER 4.—COPYRIGHT NOTICE, DEPOSIT, AND REGISTRATION

Sec. 401.   Notice of Copyright: Visually Perceptible Copies

(a) General Provisions.—Whenever a work protected under this title is published in the United States or elsewhere by authority of the copyright owner, a notice of copyright as provided by this section may be placed on publicly distributed copies from which the work can be visually perceived, either directly or with the aid of a machine or device.

(b) Form of Notice.—If a notice appears on the copies, it shall consist of the following three elements:

(1) the symbol © (the letter C in a circle), or the word "Copyright", or the abbreviation "Copr."; and

(2) the year of first publication of the work; in the case of compilations or derivative works incorporating previously published material, the year date of first publication of the compilation or derivative work is sufficient. The year date may be omitted where a pictorial, graphic, or sculptural work, with accompanying text matter, if any, is reproduced in or on greeting cards, postcards, stationery, jewelry, dolls, toys, or any useful articles; and

(3) the name of the owner of copyright in the work, or an abbreviation by which the name can be recognized, or a generally known alternative designation of the owner.

(c) Position of Notice.—The notice shall be affixed to the copies in such manner and location as to give reasonable notice of the claim of copyright. The Register of Copyrights shall prescribe by regulation, as examples, specific methods of affixation and positions of the notice on various types of works that will satisfy this requirement, but these specifications shall not be considered exhaustive.

(d) Evidentiary Weight of Notice.—If a notice of copyright in the form and position specified by this section appears on the published copy or copies to which a defendant in a copyright infringement suit had access, then no weight shall be given to such a defendant's interposition of a defense based on innocent infringement in mitigation of actual or statutory damages, except as provided in the last sentence of section 504(c)(2).

Sec. 402.   Notice   of   Copyright: Phonorecords   of   Sound Recordings

(a) General Provisions.—Whenever a sound recording protected under this title is published in the United States or elsewhere by authority of the copyright owner, a notice of copyright as provided by this section may be placed on publicly distributed phonorecords of the sound recording.

(b) Form of Notice.—If a notice appears on the phonorecords, it shall consist of the following three elements:

(1) the symbol Ⓟ (the letter P in a circle); and

(2) the year of first publication of the sound recording; and

(3) the name of the owner of copyright in the sound recording, or an abbreviation by which the name can be recognized, or a generally known alternative designation of the owner; if the producer of the sound recording is named on the phonorecord labels or containers, and if no other name appears in conjunction with the notice, the producer's name shall be considered a part of the notice.

(c) Position of Notice.—The notice shall be placed on the surface of the phonorecord, or on the phonorecord label or container, in such manner and location as to give reasonable notice of the claim of copyright.

(d) Evidentiary Weight of Notice.—If a notice of copyright in the form and position specified by this section appears on the published phonorecord or phonorecords to which a defendant in a copyright infringement suit had access, then no weight shall be given to such a defendant's interposition of a defense based on innocent infringement in mitigation of actual or statutory damages, except as provided in the last sentence of section 504(c)(2).

Sec. 403.   Notice of Copyright: Publications Incorporating United States Government Works

Sections 401(d) and 402(d) shall not apply to a work published in copies or phonorecords consisting predominantly of one or more works of the United States Government unless the notice of copyright appearing on the published copies or phonorecords to which a defendant in the copyright

infringement suit had access includes a statement identifying, either affirmatively or negatively, those portions of the copies or phonorecords embodying any work or works protected under this title.

Sec. 404.   Notice of Copyright: Contributions to Collective Works

(a) A separate contribution to a collective work may bear its own notice of copyright, as provided by sections 401 through 403. However, a single notice applicable to the collective work as a whole is sufficient to invoke the provisions of section 401(d) or 402(d), as applicable with respect to the separate contributions it contains (not including advertisements inserted on behalf of persons other than the owner of copyright in the collective work), regardless of the ownership of copyright in the contributions and whether or not they have been previously published.

(b) With respect to copies and phonorecords publicly distributed by authority of the copyright owner before the effective date of the Berne Convention Implementation Act of 1988, where the person named in a single notice applicable to a collective work as a whole is not the owner of copyright in a separate contribution that does not bear its own notice, the case is governed by the provisions of section 406(a).

Sec. 405. Notice of Copyright: Omission of Notice on Certain Copies and Phonorecords

(a) **Effect of Omission on Copyright.**—With respect to copies and phonorecords publicly distributed by authority of the copyright owner before the effective date of the Berne Convention Implementation Act of 1988, the omission of the copyright notice described in sections 401 through 403 from copies or phonorecords publicly distributed by authority of the copyright owner does not invalidate the copyright in a work if—

(1) the notice has been omitted from no more than a relatively small number of copies or phonorecords distributed to the public; or

(2) registration for the work has been made before or is made within five years after the publication without notice, and a reasonable effort is made to add notice to all copies or phonorecords that are distributed to the public in the United States after the omission has been discovered; or

(3) the notice has been omitted in violation of an express requirement in writing that, as a condition of the copyright owner's authorization of the public distribution of copies or phonorecords, they bear the prescribed notice.

(b) **Effect of Omission on Innocent Infringers.**—Any person who innocently infringes a copyright, in reliance upon an authorized copy or phonorecord from which the copyright notice has been omitted and which was publicly distributed by authority of the copyright owner before the effective date of the Berne Convention Implementation Act of 1988, incurs no liability for actual or statutory damages under section 504 for any infringing acts committed before receiving actual notice that registration for the work has been made under section 408, if such person proves that he or she was misled by the omission of notice. In a suit for infringement in such a case the court may allow or disallow recovery of any of the infringer's profits attributable to the infringement, and may enjoin the continuation of the infringing undertaking or may require, as a condition for permitting the continuation of the infringing undertaking, that the infringer pay the copyright owner a reasonable license fee in an amount and on terms fixed by the court.

(c) **Removal of Notice.**—Protection under this title is not affected by the removal, destruction, or obliteration of the notice, without the authorization of the copyright owner, from any publicly distributed copies or phonorecords.

Sec. 406.   Notice of Copyright: Error in Name or Date on Certain Copies and Phonorecords

(a) **Error in Name.**—With respect to copies and phonorecords publicly distributed by authority of the copyright owner before the effective date of the Berne Convention Implementation Act of 1988, where the person named in the copyright notice on copies or phonorecords publicly distributed by authority of the copyright owner is not the owner of copyright, the validity and ownership of the copyright are not affected. In such a case, however, any person who innocently begins an undertaking that infringes the copyright has a complete defense to any action for such infringement if such person proves that he or she was misled by the notice and began the undertaking in good faith under a purported transfer or license from the person named therein, unless before the undertaking was begun—

(1) registration for the work had been made in the name of the owner of copyright; or

(2) a document executed by the person named in the notice and showing the ownership of the copyright had been recorded.

The person named in the notice is liable to account to the copyright owner for all receipts from transfers or licenses purportedly made under the copyright by the person named in the notice.

(b) **Error in Date.**—When the year date in the notice on copies or phonorecords distributed before the effective date of the Berne Convention Implementation Act of 1988 by authority of the copyright owner is earlier than the year in which publication first occurred, any period computed from the year of first publication under section 302 is to be computed from the year in the notice. Where the year date is more than one year later than the year in which publication first occurred, the work is considered to have been published without any notice and is governed by the provisions of section 405.

(c) **Omission of Name or Date.**—Where copies or phonorecords publicly distributed before the effective date of the Berne Convention Implementation Act of 1988 by authority of the copyright owner contain no name or no date that could reasonably be considered a part of the notice, the work is considered to have been published without any notice and is governed by the provisions of section 405 as in effect on the day before the effective date of the Berne Convention Implementation Act of 1988.

Sec. 407.   Deposit of Copies or Phonorecords for Library of Congress

(a) Except as provided by subsection (c), and subject to the provisions of subsection (e), the owner of copyright or of the exclusive right of publication in a work published in the United States shall deposit, within three months after the date of such publication—

(1) two complete copies of the best edition; or

(2) if the work is a sound recording, two complete phonorecords of the best edition, together with any printed or other visually perceptible material published with such phonorecords.

Neither the deposit requirements of this subsection nor the acquisition provisions of subsection (e) are conditions of copyright protection.

(b) The required copies or phonorecords shall be deposited in the Copyright Office for the use or disposition of the Library of Congress. The Register of Copyrights shall, when requested by the depositor and upon payment of the fee prescribed by section 708, issue a receipt for the deposit.

(c) The Register of Copyrights may by regulation exempt any categories of material from the deposit requirements of this section, or require deposit of only one copy or phonorecord with respect to any categories. Such regulations shall provide either for complete exemption from the deposit requirements of this section, or for alternative forms of deposit aimed at providing a satisfactory archival record of a work without imposing practical or financial hardships on the depositor, where the individual author is the owner of copyright in a pictorial, graphic, or sculptural work and (i) less than five copies of the work have been published, or (ii) the work has been published in a limited edition consisting of numbered copies, the monetary value of which would make the mandatory deposit of two copies of the best edition of the work burdensome, unfair, or unreasonable.

(d) At any time after publication of a work as provided by subsection (a), the Register of Copyrights may make written demand for the required deposit on any of the persons obligated to make the deposit under subsection (a). Unless deposit is made within three months after the demand is received, the person or persons on whom the demand was made are liable—

(1) to a fine of not more than $250 for each work; and

(2) to pay into a specially designated fund in the Library of Congress the total retail price of the copies or phonorecords demanded, or, if no retail price has been fixed, the reasonable cost to the Library of Congress of acquiring them; and

(3) to pay a fine of $2,500, in addition to any fine or liability imposed under clauses (1) and (2), if such person willfully or repeatedly fails or refuses to comply with such a demand.

(e) With respect to transmission programs that have been fixed and transmitted to the public in the United States but have not been published, the Register of Copyrights shall, after consulting with the Librarian of Congress and other interested organizations and officials, establish regulations governing the acquisition, through deposit or otherwise, of copies or phonorecords of such programs for the collections of the Library of Congress.

(1) The Librarian of Congress shall be permitted, under the standards and conditions set forth in such regulations, to make a fixation of a transmission program directly from a transmission to the public, and to reproduce one copy or phonorecord from such fixation for archival purposes.

(2) Such regulations shall also provide standards and procedures by which the Register of Copyrights may make written demand upon the owner of the right of transmission in the United States, for the deposit of a copy or phonorecord of a specific transmission program. Such deposit may, at the option of the owner of the right of transmission in the United States, be accomplished by gift, by loan for purposes of reproduction, or by sale at a price not to exceed the cost of reproducing and supplying the copy or phonorecord. The regulations established under this clause shall provide reasonable periods of not less than three months for compliance with a demand, and shall allow for extensions of such periods and adjustments in the scope of the demand or the methods for fulfilling it, as reasonably warranted by the circumstances. Willful failure or refusal to comply with the conditions prescribed by such regulations shall subject the owner of the right of transmission in the United States to liability for an amount, not to exceed the cost of reproducing and supplying the copy or phonorecord in question, to be paid into a specially designated fund in the Library of Congress.

(3) Nothing in this subsection shall be construed to require the making or retention, for purposes of deposit, of any copy or phonorecord of an unpublished transmission program, the transmission of which occurs before the receipt of a specific written demand as provided by clause (2).

(4) No activity undertaken in compliance with regulations prescribed under clauses (1) or (2) of this subsection shall result in liability if intended solely to assist in the acquisition of copies or phonorecords under this subsection.

Sec. 408.   Copyright Registration in General

(a) Registration Permissive.—At any time during the subsistence of the first term of copyright in any published or unpublished work in which the copyright was secured before January 1, 1978, and during the subsistence of any copyright secured on or after that date, the owner of copyright or of any exclusive right in the work may obtain registration of the copyright claim by delivering to the Copyright Office the deposit specified by this section, together with the application and fee specified by sections 409 and 708. Such registration is not a condition of copyright protection.

(b) Deposit for Copyright Registration.—Except as provided by subsection (c), the material deposited for registration shall include—

(1) in the case of an unpublished work, one complete copy or phonorecord;

(2) in the case of a published work, two complete copies or phonorecords of the best edition;

(3) in the case of a work first published outside the United States, one complete copy or phonorecord as so published;

(4) in the case of a contribution to a collective work, one complete copy or phonorecord of the best edition of the collective work.

Copies or phonorecords deposited for the Library of Congress under section 407 may be used to satisfy the deposit provisions of this section, if they are accompanied by the prescribed application and fee, and by any additional identifying material that the Register may, by regulation, require. The Register shall also prescribe regulations establishing requirements under which copies or phonorecords acquired for the Library of Congress under subsection (e) of section 407, otherwise than by deposit, may be used to satisfy the deposit provisions of this section.

(c) Administrative Classification and Optional Deposit.—

(1) The Register of Copyrights is authorized to specify by regulation the administrative classes into which works are to be placed for purposes of deposit and registration, and the nature of the copies or phonorecords to be deposited in the various classes specified. The regulations may require or permit, for particular classes, the deposit of identifying material instead of copies or phonorecords, the deposit of only one copy or phonorecord where two would normally be required, or a single registration for a group of related works. This administrative classification of works has no significance with respect to the subject matter of copyright or the exclusive rights provided by this title.

(2) Without prejudice to the general authority provided under clause (1), the Register of Copyrights shall establish regulations specifically permitting a single registration for a group of works by the same individual author, all first published as contributions to periodicals, including newspapers, within a twelve-month period, on the basis of a single deposit, application, and registration fee, under the following conditions—

(A) if the deposit consists of one copy of the entire issue of the periodical, or of the entire section in the case of a newspaper, in which each contribution was first published; and

(B) if the application identifies each work separately, including the periodical containing it and its date of first publication.

(3) As an alternative to separate renewal registrations under subsection (a) of section 304, a single renewal registration may be made for a group of works by the same individual author, all first published as contributions to periodicals, including newspapers, upon the filing of a single application and fee, under all of the following conditions:

(A) the renewal claimant or claimants, and the basis of claim or claims under section 304(a), is the same for each of the works; and

(B) the works were all copyrighted upon their first publication, either through separate copyright notice and registration or by virtue of a general copyright notice in the periodical issue as a whole; and

(C) the renewal application and fee are received not more than twenty-eight or less than twenty-seven years after the thirty-first day of December of the calendar year in which all of the works were first published; and

(D) the renewal application identifies each work separately, including the periodical containing it and its date of first publication.

(d) Corrections and Amplifications.—The Register may also establish, by regulation, formal procedures for the filing of an application for supplementary registration, to correct an error in a copyright registration or to amplify the information given in a registration. Such application shall be accompanied by the fee provided by section 708, and shall clearly identify the registration to be corrected or amplified. The information contained in a supplementary registration augments but does not supersede that contained in the earlier registration.

(e) Published Edition of Previously Registered Work.—Registration for the first published edition of a work previously registered in unpublished form may be made even though the work as published is substantially the same as the unpublished version.

(f) Preregistration of Works Being Prepared for Commercial Distribution.—

(1) Rulemaking.—Not later than 180 days after the date of enactment of this subsection, the Register of Copyrights shall issue regulations to establish procedures for preregistration of a work that is being prepared for commercial distribution and has not been published.

(2) Class of Works.—The regulations established under paragraph (1) shall permit preregistration for any work that is in a class of works that the Register determines has had a history of infringement prior to authorized commercial distribution.

(3) Application for Registration.—Not later than 3 months after the first publication of a work preregistered under this subsection, the applicant shall submit to the Copyright Office—

(A) an application for registration of the work;

(B) a deposit; and

(C) the applicable fee.

(4) Effect of Untimely Application.—An action under this chapter for infringement of a work preregistered under this subsection, in a case in which the infringement commenced no later than 2 months after the first publication of the work, shall be dismissed if the items described in paragraph (3) are not submitted to the Copyright Office in proper form within the earlier of—

(A) 3 months after the first publication of the work; or

(B) 1 month after the copyright owner has learned of the infringement.

Sec. 409.   Application for Copyright Registration

The application for copyright registration shall be made on a form prescribed by the Register of Copyrights and shall include—

(1) the name and address of the copyright claimant;

(2) in the case of a work other than an anonymous or pseudonymous work, the name and nationality or domicile of the author or authors, and, if one or more of the authors is dead, the dates of their deaths;

(3) if the work is anonymous or pseudonymous, the nationality or domicile of the author or authors;

(4) in the case of a work made for hire, a statement to this effect;

(5) if the copyright claimant is not the author, a brief statement of how the claimant obtained ownership of the copyright;

(6) the title of the work, together with any previous or alternative titles under which the work can be identified;

(7) the year in which creation of the work was completed;

(8) if the work has been published, the date and nation of its first publication;

(9) in the case of a compilation or derivative work, an identification of any preexisting work or works that it is based on or incorporates, and a brief, general statement of the additional material covered by the copyright claim being registered; and

(10) any other information regarded by the Register of Copyrights as bearing upon the preparation or identification of the work or the existence, ownership, or duration of the copyright.

If an application is submitted for the renewed and extended term provided for in section 304(a)(3)(A) and an original term registration has not been made, the Register may request information with respect to the existence, ownership, or duration of the copyright for the original term.

Sec. 410.   Registration of Claim and Issuance of Certificate

(a) When, after examination, the Register of Copyrights determines that, in accordance with the provisions of this title, the material deposited constitutes copyrightable subject matter and that the other legal and formal requirements of this title have been met, the Register shall register the claim and issue to the applicant a certificate of registration under the seal of the Copyright Office. The certificate shall contain the information given in the application, together with the number and effective date of the registration.

(b) In any case in which the Register of Copyrights determines that, in accordance with the provisions of this title, the material deposited does not constitute copyrightable subject matter or that the claim is invalid for any other reason, the Register shall refuse registration and shall notify the applicant in writing of the reasons for such refusal.

(c) In any judicial proceedings the certificate of a registration made before or within five years after first publication of the work shall constitute prima facie evidence of the validity of the copyright and of the facts stated in the certificate. The evidentiary weight to be accorded the certificate of a registration made thereafter shall be within the discretion of the court.

(d) The effective date of a copyright registration is the day on which an application, deposit, and fee, which are later determined by the Register of Copyrights or by a court of competent jurisdiction to be acceptable for registration, have all been received in the Copyright Office.

Sec. 411.   Registration and Civil Infringement Actions

(a) Except for an action brought for violation of the rights of the author under section 106A(a), and subject to the provisions of subsection (b), no civil action for infringement of the copyright in any United States work shall be instituted until preregistration or registration of the copyright claim has been made in accordance with this title. In any case, however, where the deposit, application, and fee required for registration have been delivered to the Copyright Office in proper form and registration has been refused, the applicant is entitled to institute a civil action for infringement if notice thereof, with a copy of the complaint, is served on the Register of Copyrights. The Register may, at his or her option, become a party to the action with respect to the issue of registrability of the copyright claim by entering an appearance within sixty days after such service, but the Register's failure to become a party shall not deprive the court of jurisdiction to determine that issue.

(b)(1) A certificate of registration satisfies the requirements of this section and section 412, regardless of whether the certificate contains any inaccurate information, unless—

(A) the inaccurate information was included on the application for copyright registration with knowledge that it was inaccurate; and

(B) the inaccuracy of the information, if known, would have caused the Register of Copyrights to refuse registration.

(2) In any case in which inaccurate information described under paragraph (1) is alleged, the court shall request the Register of Copyrights to advise the court whether the inaccurate information, if known, would have caused the Register of Copyrights to refuse registration.

(3) Nothing in this subsection shall affect any rights, obligations, or requirements of a person related to information contained in a registration certificate, except for the institution of and remedies in infringement actions under this section and section 412.

(c) In the case of a work consisting of sounds, images, or both, the first fixation of which is made simultaneously with its transmission, the copyright owner may, either before or after such fixation takes place, institute an action for infringement under section 501, fully subject to the remedies provided by sections 502 through 505 and section 510, if, in accordance with requirements that the Register of Copyrights shall prescribe by regulation, the copyright owner—

(1) serves notice upon the infringer, not less than 48 hours before such fixation, identifying the work and the specific time and source of its first transmission, and declaring an intention to secure copyright in the work; and

(2) makes registration for the work, if required by subsection (a), within three months after its first transmission.

Sec. 412.   Registration as Prerequisite to Certain Remedies for Infringement

In any action under this title, other than an action brought for a violation of the rights of the author under section 106A(a), an action for infringement of the copyright of a work that has been preregistered under section 408(f) before the commencement of the infringement and that has an effective date of registration not later than the earlier of 3 months after the first publication of the work or 1 month after the copyright owner has learned of the infringement, or an action instituted under section 411(c), no award of statutory damages or of attorney's fees, as provided by sections 504 and 505, shall be made for—

(1) any infringement of copyright in an unpublished work commenced before the effective date of its registration; or

(2) any infringement of copyright commenced after first publication of the work and before the effective date of its registration, unless such registration is made within three months after the first publication of the work.

CHAPTER 5.—COPYRIGHT INFRINGEMENT AND REMEDIES

Sec.

Sec. 501.   Infringement of Copyright

(a) Anyone who violates any of the exclusive rights of the copyright owner as provided by sections 106 through 122 or of the author as provided in section 106A(a), or who imports copies or phonorecords into the United States in violation of section 602, is an infringer of the copyright or right of the author, as the case may be. For purposes of this chapter (other than section 506), any reference to copyright shall be deemed to include the rights conferred by section 106A(a). As used in this subsection, the term "anyone" includes any State, any instrumentality of a State, and any officer or employee of a State or instrumentality of a State acting in his or her official capacity. Any State, and any such instrumentality, officer, or employee, shall be subject to the provisions of this title in the same manner and to the same extent as any nongovernmental entity.

(b) The legal or beneficial owner of an exclusive right under a copyright is entitled, subject to the requirements of section 411, to institute an action for any infringement of that particular right committed while he or she is the owner of it. The court may require such owner to serve written notice of the action with a copy of the complaint upon any person shown, by the records of the Copyright Office or otherwise, to have or claim an interest in the copyright, and shall require that such notice be served upon any person whose interest is likely to be affected by a decision in the case. The court may require the joinder, and shall permit the intervention, of any person having or claiming an interest in the copyright.

(c) For any secondary transmission by a cable system that embodies a performance or a display of a work which is actionable as an act of infringement under subsection (c) of section 111, a television broadcast station holding a copyright or other license to transmit or perform the same version of that work shall, for purposes of subsection (b) of this section, be treated as a legal or beneficial owner if such secondary transmission occurs within the local service area of that television station.

(d) For any secondary transmission by a cable system that is actionable as an act of infringement pursuant to section 111(c)(3), the following shall also have standing to sue: (i) the primary transmitter whose transmission has been altered by the cable system; and (ii) any broadcast station within whose local service area the secondary transmission occurs.

(e) With respect to any secondary transmission that is made by a satellite carrier of a performance or display of a work embodied in a primary transmission and is actionable as an act of infringement under section 119(a)(5), a network station holding a copyright or other license to transmit or perform the same version of that work shall, for purposes of subsection (b) of this section, be treated as a legal or beneficial owner if such secondary transmission occurs within the local service area of that station.

(f)(1) With respect to any secondary transmission that is made by a satellite carrier of a performance or display of a work embodied in a primary transmission and is actionable as an act of infringement under section 122, a television broadcast station holding a copyright or other license to transmit or perform the same version of that work shall, for purposes of subsection (b) of this section, be treated as a legal or beneficial owner if such secondary transmission occurs within the local market of that station.

(2) A television broadcast station may file a civil action against any satellite carrier that has refused to carry television broadcast signals, as required under section 122(a)(2), to enforce that television broadcast station's rights under section 338(a) of the Communications Act of 1934 [47 U.S.C.A. § 338(a)].

Sec. 502.   Remedies for Infringement: Injunctions

(a) Any court having jurisdiction of a civil action arising under this title may, subject to the provisions of section 1498 of title 28, grant temporary and final injunctions on such terms as it may deem reasonable to prevent or restrain infringement of a copyright.

(b) Any such injunction may be served anywhere in the United States on the person enjoined; it shall be operative throughout the United States and shall be enforceable, by proceedings in contempt or otherwise, by any United States court having jurisdiction of that person. The clerk of the court granting the injunction shall, when requested by any other court in which enforcement of the injunction is sought, transmit promptly to the other court a certified copy of all the papers in the case on file in such clerk's office.

Sec. 503. Remedies for Infringement: Impounding and Disposition of Infringing Articles

(a)(1) At any time while an action under this title is pending, the court may order the impounding, on such terms as it may deem reasonable—

(A) of all copies or phonorecords claimed to have been made or used in violation of the exclusive right of the copyright owner;

(B) of all plates, molds, matrices, masters, tapes, film negatives, or other articles by means of which such copies or phonorecords may be reproduced; and

(C) of records documenting the manufacture, sale, or receipt of things involved in any such violation, provided that any records seized under this subparagraph shall be taken into the custody of the court.

(2) For impoundments of records ordered under paragraph (1)(C), the court shall enter an appropriate protective order with respect to discovery and use of any records or information that has been impounded. The protective order shall provide for appropriate procedures to ensure that confidential, private, proprietary, or privileged information contained in such records is not improperly disclosed or used.

(3) The relevant provisions of paragraphs (2) through (11) of section 34(d) of the Trademark Act (15 U.S.C. 1116(d)(2) through (11)) shall extend to any impoundment of records ordered under paragraph (1)(C) that is based upon an ex parte application, notwithstanding the provisions of rule 65 of the Federal Rules of Civil Procedure. Any references in paragraphs (2) through (11) of section 34(d) of the Trademark Act to section 32 of such Act shall be read as references to section 501 of this title, and references to use of a counterfeit mark in connection with the sale, offering for sale, or distribution of goods or services shall be read as references to infringement of a copyright.

(b) As part of a final judgment or decree, the court may order the destruction or other reasonable disposition of all copies or phonorecords found to have been made or used in violation of the copyright owner's exclusive rights, and of all plates, molds, matrices, masters, tapes, film negatives, or other articles by means of which such copies or phonorecords may be reproduced.

Sec. 504. Remedies for Infringement: Damages and Profits

(a) In General.—Except as otherwise provided by this title, an infringer of copyright is liable for either—

(1) the copyright owner's actual damages and any additional profits of the infringer, as provided by subsection (b); or

(2) statutory damages, as provided by subsection (c).

(b) Actual Damages and Profits.—The copyright owner is entitled to recover the actual damages suffered by him or her as a result of the infringement, and any profits of the infringer that are attributable to the infringement and are not taken into account in computing the actual damages. In establishing the infringer's profits, the copyright owner is required to present proof only of the infringer's gross revenue, and the infringer is required to prove his or her deductible expenses and the elements of profit attributable to factors other than the copyrighted work.

(c) Statutory Damages.—

(1) Except as provided by clause (2) of this subsection, the copyright owner may elect, at any time before final judgment is rendered, to recover, instead of actual damages and profits, an award of statutory damages for all infringements involved in the action, with respect to any one work, for which any one infringer is liable individually, or for which any two or more infringers are liable jointly and severally, in a sum of not less than $750 or more than $30,000 as the court considers just. For the purposes of this subsection, all the parts of a compilation or derivative work constitute one work.

(2) In a case where the copyright owner sustains the burden of proving, and the court finds, that infringement was committed willfully, the court in its discretion may increase the award of statutory damages to a sum of not more than $150,000. In a case where the infringer sustains the burden of proving, and the court finds, that such infringer was not aware and had no reason to believe that his or her acts constituted an infringement of copyright, the court in its discretion may reduce the award of statutory damages to a sum of not less than $200. The court shall remit statutory damages in any case where an infringer believed and had reasonable grounds for believing that his or her use of the copyrighted work was a fair use under section 107, if the infringer was: (i) an employee or agent of a nonprofit educational institution, library, or archives acting within the scope of his or her employment who, or such institution, library, or archives itself, which infringed by reproducing the work in copies or phonorecords; or (ii) a public broadcasting entity which or a person who, as a regular part of the nonprofit activities of a public broadcasting entity (as defined in section 118(f)) infringed by performing a published nondramatic literary work or by reproducing a transmission program embodying a performance of such a work.

(3)(A) In a case of infringement, it shall be a rebuttable presumption that the infringement was committed willfully for purposes of determining relief if the violator, or a person acting in concert with the violator, knowingly provided or knowingly caused to be provided materially false contact information to a domain name registrar, domain name registry, or other domain name registration authority in registering, maintaining, or renewing a domain name used in connection with the infringement.

(B) Nothing in this paragraph limits what may be considered willful infringement under this subsection.

(C) For purposes of this paragraph, the term "domain name" has the meaning given that term in section 45 of the Act entitled "An Act to provide for the registration and protection of trademarks used in commerce, to carry out the provisions of certain international conventions, and for other purposes" approved July 5, 1946 (commonly referred to as the "Trademark Act of 1946"; 15 U.S.C. 1127).

(d) Additional Damages in Certain Cases.—In any case in which the court finds that a defendant proprietor of an establishment who claims as a defense that its activities were exempt under section 110(5)

did not have reasonable grounds to believe that its use of a copyrighted work was exempt under such section, the plaintiff shall be entitled to, in addition to any award of damages under this section, an additional award of two times the amount of the license fee that the proprietor of the establishment concerned should have paid the plaintiff for such use during the preceding period of up to 3 years.

Sec. 505.   Remedies for Infringement: Costs and Attorney's Fees

In any civil action under this title, the court in its discretion may allow the recovery of full costs by or against any party other than the United States or an officer thereof. Except as otherwise provided by this title, the court may also award a reasonable attorney's fee to the prevailing party as part of the costs.

Sec. 506.   Criminal Offenses

(a) Criminal Infringement.—

(1) In General.—Any person who willfully infringes a copyright shall be punished as provided under section 2319 of title 18, if the infringement was committed—

(A) for purposes of commercial advantage or private financial gain;

(B) by the reproduction or distribution, including by electronic means, during any 180–day period, of 1 or more copies or phonorecords of 1 or more copyrighted works, which have a total retail value of more than $1,000; or

(C) by the distribution of a work being prepared for commercial distribution, by making it available on a computer network accessible to members of the public, if such person knew or should have known that the work was intended for commercial distribution.

(2) Evidence.—For purposes of this subsection, evidence of reproduction or distribution of a copyrighted work, by itself, shall not be sufficient to establish willful infringement of a copyright.

(3) Definition.—In this subsection, the term "work being prepared for commercial distribution" means—

(A) a computer program, a musical work, a motion picture or other audiovisual work, or a sound recording, if, at the time of unauthorized distribution—

(i) the copyright owner has a reasonable expectation of commercial distribution; and

(ii) the copies or phonorecords of the work have not been commercially distributed; or

(B) a motion picture, if, at the time of unauthorized distribution, the motion picture—

(i) has been made available for viewing in a motion picture exhibition facility; and

(ii) has not been made available in copies for sale to the general public in the United States in a format intended to permit viewing outside a motion picture exhibition facility.

(b) Forfeiture, Destruction, and Restitution.—Forfeiture, destruction, and restitution relating to this section shall be subject to section 2323 of title 18, to the extent provided in that section, in addition to any other similar remedies provided by law.

(c) Fraudulent Copyright Notice.—Any person who, with fraudulent intent, places on any article a notice of copyright or words of the same purport that such person knows to be false, or who, with fraudulent intent, publicly distributes or imports for public distribution any article bearing such notice or words that such person knows to be false, shall be fined not more than $2,500.

(d) Fraudulent Removal of Copyright Notice.— Any person who, with fraudulent intent, removes or alters any notice of copyright appearing on a copy of a copyrighted work shall be fined not more than $2,500.

(e) False Representation.—Any person who knowingly makes a false representation of a material fact in the application for copyright registration provided for by section 409, or in any written statement filed in connection with the application, shall be fined not more than $2,500.

(f) Rights of Attribution and Integrity.—Nothing in this section applies to infringement of the rights conferred by section 106A(a).

Sec. 507.   Limitations on Actions

(a) Criminal Proceedings.—Except as expressly provided otherwise in this title, no criminal proceeding shall be maintained under the provisions of this title unless it is commenced within five years after the cause of action arose.

(b) Civil Actions.—No civil action shall be maintained under the provisions of this title unless it is commenced within three years after the claim accrued.

Sec. 508.   Notification of Filing and Determination of Actions

(a) Within one month after the filing of any action under this title, the clerks of the courts of the United States shall send written notification to the Register of Copyrights setting forth, as far as is shown by the papers filed in the court, the names and addresses of the parties and the title, author, and registration number of each work involved in the action. If any other copyrighted work is later included in the action by amendment, answer, or other pleading, the clerk shall also send a notification concerning it to the Register within one month after the pleading is filed.

(b) Within one month after any final order or judgment is issued in the case, the clerk of the court shall notify the Register of it, sending with the notification a copy of the order or judgment together with the written opinion, if any, of the court.

(c) Upon receiving the notifications specified in this section, the Register shall make them a part of the public records of the Copyright Office.

[Sec. 509.   Repealed]

Sec. 510.   Remedies for Alteration of Programming by Cable Systems

(a) In any action filed pursuant to section 111(c)(3), the following remedies shall be available:

(1) Where an action is brought by a party identified in subsections (b) or (c) of section 501, the remedies provided by sections 502 through 505, and the remedy provided by subsection (b) of this section; and

(2) When an action is brought by a party identified in subsection (d) of section 501, the remedies provided by sections 502 and 505, together with any actual damages suffered by such party as a result of the infringement, and the remedy provided by subsection (b) of this section.

(b) In any action filed pursuant to section 111(c)(3), the court may decree that, for a period not to exceed thirty days, the cable system shall be deprived of the benefit of a statutory license for one or more distant signals carried by such cable system.

Sec. 511.   Liability of States, Instrumentalities of States, and State Officials for Infringement of Copyright

(a) In General.—Any State, any instrumentality of a State, and any officer or employee of a State or instrumentality of a State acting in his or her official capacity, shall not be immune, under the Eleventh Amendment of the Constitution of the United States or under any other doctrine of sovereign immunity, from suit in Federal court by any person, including any governmental or nongovernmental entity, for a violation of any of the exclusive rights of a copyright owner provided by sections 106 through 122, for importing copies or phonorecords in violation of section 602, or for any other violation under this title.

(b) Remedies.—In a suit described in subsection (a) for a violation described in that subsection, remedies (including remedies both at law and in equity) are available for the violation to the same extent as such remedies are available for such a violation in a suit against any public or private entity other than a State, instrumentality of a State, or officer or employee of a State acting in his or her official capacity. Such remedies include impounding and disposition of infringing articles under section 503, actual damages and profits and statutory damages under section 504, costs and attorney's fees under section 505, and the remedies provided in section 510.

Sec. 512.   Limitations on Liability Relating to Material Online

(a) Transitory Digital Network Communications.—A service provider shall not be liable for monetary relief, or, except as provided in subsection (j), for injunctive or other equitable relief, for infringement of copyright by reason of the provider's transmitting, routing, or providing connections for, material through a system or network controlled or operated by or for the service provider, or by reason of the intermediate and transient storage of that material in the course of such transmitting, routing, or providing connections, if—

(1) the transmission of the material was initiated by or at the direction of a person other than the service provider;

(2) the transmission, routing, provision of connections, or storage is carried out through an automatic technical process without selection of the material by the service provider;

(3) the service provider does not select the recipients of the material except as an automatic response to the request of another person;

(4) no copy of the material made by the service provider in the course of such intermediate or transient storage is maintained on the system or network in a manner ordinarily accessible to anyone other than anticipated recipients, and no such copy is maintained on the system or network in a manner ordinarily accessible to such anticipated recipients for a longer period than is reasonably necessary for the transmission, routing, or provision of connections; and

(5) the material is transmitted through the system or network without modification of its content.

(b) System Caching.—

(1) Limitation on Liability.—A service provider shall not be liable for monetary relief, or, except as provided in subsection (j), for injunctive or other equitable relief, for infringement of copyright by reason of the intermediate and temporary storage of material on a system or network controlled or operated by or for the service provider in a case in which—

(A) the material is made available online by a person other than the service provider;

(B) the material is transmitted from the person described in subparagraph (A) through the system or network to a person other than the person described in subparagraph (A) at the direction of that other person; and

(C) the storage is carried out through an automatic technical process for the purpose of making the material available to users of the system or network who, after the material is transmitted as described in subparagraph (B), request access to the material from the person described in subparagraph (A), if the conditions set forth in paragraph (2) are met.

(2) Conditions.—The conditions referred to in paragraph (1) are that—

(A) the material described in paragraph (1) is transmitted to the subsequent users described in paragraph (1)(C) without modification to its content from the manner in which the material was transmitted from the person described in paragraph (1)(A);

(B) the service provider described in paragraph (1) complies with rules concerning the refreshing, reloading, or other updating of the material when specified by the person making the material available online in accordance with a generally accepted industry standard data communications protocol for the system or network through which that person makes the material available, except that this subparagraph applies only if those rules are not used by the person described in paragraph (1)(A) to prevent or unreasonably impair the intermediate storage to which this subsection applies;

(C) the service provider does not interfere with the ability of technology associated with the material to return to the person described in paragraph (1)(A) the information that would have been available to that person if the material had been obtained by the subsequent users described in paragraph (1)(C) directly from that person, except that this subparagraph applies only if that technology—

(i) does not significantly interfere with the performance of the provider's system or network or with the intermediate storage of the material;

(ii) is consistent with generally accepted industry standard communications protocols; and

(iii) does not extract information from the provider's system or network other than the information that would have been available to the person described in paragraph (1)(A) if the subsequent users had gained access to the material directly from that person;

(D) if the person described in paragraph (1)(A) has in effect a condition that a person must meet prior to having access to the material, such as a condition based on payment of a fee or provision of a password or other information, the service provider permits access to the stored material in significant part only to users of its system or network that have met those conditions and only in accordance with those conditions; and

(E) if the person described in paragraph (1)(A) makes that material available online without the authorization of the copyright owner of the material, the service provider responds expeditiously to remove, or disable access to, the material that is claimed to be infringing upon notification of claimed infringement as described in subsection (c)(3), except that this subparagraph applies only if—

(i) the material has previously been removed from the originating site or access to it has been disabled, or a court has ordered that the material be removed from the originating site or that access to the material on the originating site be disabled; and

(ii) the party giving the notification includes in the notification a statement confirming that the material has been removed from the originating site or access to it has been disabled or that a court has ordered that the material be removed from the originating site or that access to the material on the originating site be disabled.

(c) Information Residing on Systems or Networks at Direction of Users.—

(1) In General.—A service provider shall not be liable for monetary relief, or, except as provided in subsection (j), for injunctive or other equitable relief, for infringement of copyright by reason of the storage at the direction of a user of material that resides on a system or network controlled or operated by or for the service provider, if the service provider—

(A)(i) does not have actual knowledge that the material or an activity using the material on the system or network is infringing;

(ii) in the absence of such actual knowledge, is not aware of facts or circumstances from which infringing activity is apparent; or

(iii) upon obtaining such knowledge or awareness, acts expeditiously to remove, or disable access to, the material;

(B) does not receive a financial benefit directly attributable to the infringing activity, in a case in which the service provider has the right and ability to control such activity; and

(C) upon notification of claimed infringement as described in paragraph (3), responds expeditiously to remove, or disable access to, the material that is claimed to be infringing or to be the subject of infringing activity.

(2) Designated Agent.—The limitations on liability established in this subsection apply to a service provider only if the service provider has designated an agent to receive notifications of claimed infringement described in paragraph (3), by making available through its service, including on its website in a location accessible to the public, and by providing to the Copyright Office, substantially the following information:

(A) the name, address, phone number, and electronic mail address of the agent.

(B) other contact information which the Register of Copyrights may deem appropriate.

The Register of Copyrights shall maintain a current directory of agents available to the public for inspection, including through the Internet, and may require payment of a fee by service providers to cover the costs of maintaining the directory.

(3) Elements of Notification.—

(A) To be effective under this subsection, a notification of claimed infringement must be a written communication provided to the designated agent of a service provider that includes substantially the following:

(i) A physical or electronic signature of a person authorized to act on behalf of the owner of an exclusive right that is allegedly infringed.

(ii) Identification of the copyrighted work claimed to have been infringed, or, if multiple copyrighted works at a single online site are covered by a single notification, a representative list of such works at that site.

(iii) Identification of the material that is claimed to be infringing or to be the subject of infringing activity and that is to be removed or access to which is to be disabled, and information reasonably sufficient to permit the service provider to locate the material.

(iv) Information reasonably sufficient to permit the service provider to contact the complaining party, such as an address, telephone number, and, if available, an electronic mail address at which the complaining party may be contacted.

(v) A statement that the complaining party has a good faith belief that use of the material in the manner complained of is not authorized by the copyright owner, its agent, or the law.

(vi) A statement that the information in the notification is accurate, and under penalty of perjury, that the complaining party is authorized to act on behalf of the owner of an exclusive right that is allegedly infringed.

(B)(i) Subject to clause (ii), a notification from a copyright owner or from a person authorized to act on behalf of the copyright owner that fails to comply substantially with the provisions of subparagraph (A) shall not be considered under paragraph (1)(A) in determining whether a service provider has actual knowledge or is aware of facts or circumstances from which infringing activity is apparent.

(ii) In a case in which the notification that is provided to the service provider's designated agent fails to comply substantially with all the provisions of subparagraph (A) but substantially complies with clauses (ii), (iii), and (iv) of subparagraph (A), clause (i) of this subparagraph applies only if the service provider promptly attempts to contact the person making the notification or takes other reasonable steps to assist in the receipt of notification that substantially complies with all the provisions of subparagraph (A).

(d) **Information Location Tools.**—A service provider shall not be liable for monetary relief, or, except as provided in subsection (j), for injunctive or other equitable relief, for infringement of copyright by reason of the provider referring or linking users to an online location containing infringing material or infringing activity, by using information location tools, including a directory, index, reference, pointer, or hypertext link, if the service provider—

(1)(A) does not have actual knowledge that the material or activity is infringing;

(B) in the absence of such actual knowledge, is not aware of facts or circumstances from which infringing activity is apparent; or

(C) upon obtaining such knowledge or awareness, acts expeditiously to remove, or disable access to, the material;

(2) does not receive a financial benefit directly attributable to the infringing activity, in a case in which the service provider has the right and ability to control such activity; and

(3) upon notification of claimed infringement as described in subsection (c)(3), responds expeditiously to remove, or disable access to, the material that is claimed to be infringing or to be the subject

of infringing activity, except that, for purposes of this paragraph, the information described in subsection (c)(3)(A)(iii) shall be identification of the reference or link, to material or activity claimed to be infringing, that is to be removed or access to which is to be disabled, and information reasonably sufficient to permit the service provider to locate that reference or link.

(e) Limitation on Liability of Nonprofit Educational Institutions.—

(1) When a public or other nonprofit institution of higher education is a service provider, and when a faculty member or graduate student who is an employee of such institution is performing a teaching or research function, for the purposes of subsections (a) and (b) such faculty member or graduate student shall be considered to be a person other than the institution, and for the purposes of subsections (c) and (d) such faculty member's or graduate student's knowledge or awareness of his or her infringing activities shall not be attributed to the institution, if—

(A) such faculty member's or graduate student's infringing activities do not involve the provision of online access to instructional materials that are or were required or recommended, within the preceding 3–year period, for a course taught at the institution by such faculty member or graduate student;

(B) the institution has not, within the preceding 3–year period, received more than two notifications described in subsection (c)(3) of claimed infringement by such faculty member or graduate student, and such notifications of claimed infringement were not actionable under subsection (f); and

(C) the institution provides to all users of its system or network informational materials that accurately describe, and promote compliance with, the laws of the United States relating to copyright.

(2) For the purposes of this subsection, the limitations on injunctive relief contained in subsections (j)(2) and (j)(3), but not those in (j)(1), shall apply.

(f) Misrepresentations.—Any person who knowingly materially misrepresents under this section—

(1) that material or activity is infringing, or

(2) that material or activity was removed or disabled by mistake or misidentification,

shall be liable for any damages, including costs and attorneys' fees, incurred by the alleged infringer, by any copyright owner or copyright owner's authorized licensee, or by a service provider, who is injured by such misrepresentation, as the result of the service provider relying upon such misrepresentation in removing or disabling access to the material or activity claimed to be infringing, or in replacing the removed material or ceasing to disable access to it

(g) Replacement of Removed or Disabled Material and Limitation on Other Liability.—

(1) No Liability for Taking Down Generally.—Subject to paragraph (2), a service provider shall not be liable to any person for any claim based on the service provider's good faith disabling of access to, or removal of, material or activity claimed to be infringing or based on facts or circumstances from which infringing activity is apparent, regardless of whether the material or activity is ultimately determined to be infringing.

(2) Exception.—Paragraph (1) shall not apply with respect to material residing at the direction of a subscriber of the service provider on a system or network controlled or operated by or for the service provider that is removed, or to which access is disabled by the service provider, pursuant to a notice provided under subsection (c)(1)(C), unless the service provider—

(A) takes reasonable steps promptly to notify the subscriber that it has removed or disabled access to the material;

(B) upon receipt of a counter notification described in paragraph (3), promptly provides the person who provided the notification under subsection (c)(1)(C) with a copy of the counter notification, and informs that person that it will replace the removed material or cease disabling access to it in 10 business days; and

(C) replaces the removed material and ceases disabling access to it not less than 10, nor more than 14, business days following receipt of the counter notice, unless its designated agent first receives notice from the person who submitted the notification under subsection (c)(1)(C) that such person has filed an action seeking a court order to restrain the subscriber from engaging in infringing activity relating to the material on the service provider's system or network.

(3) Contents of Counter Notification.—To be effective under this subsection, a counter notification must be a written communication provided to the service provider's designated agent that includes substantially the following:

(A) A physical or electronic signature of the subscriber.

(B) Identification of the material that has been removed or to which access has been disabled and the location at which the material appeared before it was removed or access to it was disabled.

(C) A statement under penalty of perjury that the subscriber has a good faith belief that the material was removed or disabled as a result of mistake or misidentification of the material to be removed or disabled.

(D) The subscriber's name, address, and telephone number, and a statement that the subscriber consents to the jurisdiction of Federal District Court for the judicial district in which the address is located, or if the subscriber's address is outside of the United States, for any judicial district in which the service provider may be found, and that the subscriber will accept service of process from the person who provided notification under subsection (c)(1)(C) or an agent of such person.

(4) Limitation on Other Liability.—A service provider's compliance with paragraph (2) shall not subject the service provider to liability for copyright infringement with respect to the material identified in the notice provided under subsection (c)(1)(C).

(h) Subpoena to Identify Infringer.—

(1) Request.—A copyright owner or a person authorized to act on the owner's behalf may request the clerk of any United States district court to issue a subpoena to a service provider for identification of an alleged infringer in accordance with this subsection.

(2) Contents of Request.—The request may be made by filing with the clerk—

(A) a copy of a notification described in subsection (c)(3)(A);

(B) a proposed subpoena; and

(C) a sworn declaration to the effect that the purpose for which the subpoena is sought is to obtain the identity of an alleged infringer and that such information will only be used for the purpose of protecting rights under this title.

(3) Contents of Subpoena.—The subpoena shall authorize and order the service provider receiving the notification and the subpoena to expeditiously disclose to the copyright owner or person authorized by the copyright owner information sufficient to identify the alleged infringer of the material described in the notification to the extent such information is available to the service provider.

(4) Basis for Granting Subpoena.—If the notification filed satisfies the provisions of subsection (c)(3)(A), the proposed subpoena is in proper form, and the accompanying declaration is properly executed, the clerk shall expeditiously issue and sign the proposed subpoena and return it to the requester for delivery to the service provider.

(5) Actions of Service Provider Receiving Subpoena.— Upon receipt of the issued subpoena, either accompanying or subsequent to the receipt of a notification described in subsection (c)(3)(A), the service provider shall expeditiously disclose to the copyright owner or person authorized by the copyright owner the information required by the subpoena, notwithstanding any other provision of law and regardless of whether the service provider responds to the notification.

(6) Rules Applicable to Subpoena.—Unless otherwise provided by this section or by applicable rules of the court, the procedure for issuance and delivery of the subpoena, and the remedies for noncompliance with the subpoena, shall be governed to the greatest extent practicable by those provisions of the Federal Rules of Civil Procedure governing the issuance, service, and enforcement of a subpoena duces tecum.

(i) Conditions for Eligibility.—

(1) Accommodation of Technology.—The limitations on liability established by this section shall apply to a service provider only if the service provider—

(A) has adopted and reasonably implemented, and informs subscribers and account holders of the service provider's system or network of, a policy that provides for the termination in appropriate circumstances of subscribers and account holders of the service provider's system or network who are repeat infringers; and

(B) accommodates and does not interfere with standard technical measures.

(2) Definition.—As used in this subsection, the term "standard technical measures" means technical measures that are used by copyright owners to identify or protect copyrighted works and—

(A) have been developed pursuant to a broad consensus of copyright owners and service providers in an open, fair, voluntary, multi-industry standards process;

(B) are available to any person on reasonable and nondiscriminatory terms; and

(C) do not impose substantial costs on service providers or substantial burdens on their systems or networks.

(j) Injunctions.—The following rules shall apply in the case of any application for an injunction under section 502 against a service provider that is not subject to monetary remedies under this section:

(1) Scope of Relief.—

(A) With respect to conduct other than that which qualifies for the limitation on remedies set forth in subsection (a), the court may grant injunctive relief with respect to a service provider only in one or more of the following forms:

(i) An order restraining the service provider from providing access to infringing material or activity residing at a particular online site on the provider's system or network.

(ii) An order restraining the service provider from providing access to a subscriber or account holder of the service provider's system or network who is engaging in infringing activity and is identified in the order, by terminating the accounts of the subscriber or account holder that are specified in the order.

(iii) Such other injunctive relief as the court may consider necessary to prevent or restrain infringement of copyrighted material specified in the order of the court at a particular online location, if such relief is the least burdensome to the service provider among the forms of relief comparably effective for that purpose.

(B) If the service provider qualifies for the limitation on remedies described in subsection (a), the court may only grant injunctive relief in one or both of the following forms:

(i) An order restraining the service provider from providing access to a subscriber or account holder of the service provider's system or network who is using the provider's service to engage in infringing activity and is identified in the order, by terminating the accounts of the subscriber or account holder that are specified in the order.

(ii) An order restraining the service provider from providing access, by taking reasonable steps specified in the order to block access, to a specific, identified, online location outside the United States.

(2) Considerations.—The court, in considering the relevant criteria for injunctive relief under applicable law, shall consider—

(A) whether such an injunction, either alone or in combination with other such injunctions issued against the same service provider under this subsection, would significantly burden either the provider or the operation of the provider's system or network;

(B) the magnitude of the harm likely to be suffered by the copyright owner in the digital network environment if steps are not taken to prevent or restrain the infringement;

(C) whether implementation of such an injunction would be technically feasible and effective, and would not interfere with access to noninfringing material at other online locations; and

(D) whether other less burdensome and comparably effective means of preventing or restraining access to the infringing material are available.

(3) Notice and Ex Parte Orders.—Injunctive relief under this subsection shall be available only after notice to the service provider and an opportunity for the service provider to appear are provided, except for orders ensuring the preservation of evidence or other orders having no material adverse effect on the operation of the service provider's communications network.

(k) Definitions.—

(1) Service Provider.—

(A) As used in subsection (a), the term "service provider" means an entity offering the transmission, routing, or providing of connections for digital online communications, between or among points specified by a user, of material of the user's choosing, without modification to the content of the material as sent or received.

(B) As used in this section, other than subsection (a), the term "service provider" means a provider of online services or network access, or the operator of facilities therefor, and includes an entity described in subparagraph (A).

(2) Monetary Relief.—As used in this section, the term "monetary relief" means damages, costs, attorneys' fees, and any other form of monetary payment.

(*l*) Other Defenses Not Affected.—The failure of a service provider's conduct to qualify for limitation of liability under this section shall not bear adversely upon the consideration of a defense by the service provider that the service provider's conduct is not infringing under this title or any other defense.

(m) Protection of Privacy.—Nothing in this section shall be construed to condition the applicability of subsections (a) through (d) on—

(1) a service provider monitoring its service or affirmatively seeking facts indicating infringing activity, except to the extent consistent with a standard technical measure complying with the provisions of subsection (i); or

(2) a service provider gaining access to, removing, or disabling access to material in cases in which such conduct is prohibited by law.

(n) Construction.—Subsections (a), (b), (c), and (d) describe separate and distinct functions for purposes of applying this section. Whether a service provider qualifies for the limitation on liability in any one of those subsections shall be based solely on the criteria in that subsection, and shall not affect a determination of whether that service provider qualifies for the limitations on liability under any other such subsection.

Sec. 513. Determination of Reasonable License Fees for Individual Proprietors

In the case of any performing rights society subject to a consent decree which provides for the determination of reasonable license rates or fees to be charged by the performing rights society, notwithstanding the provisions of that consent decree, an individual proprietor who owns or operates fewer than 7 non-publicly traded establishments in which nondramatic musical works are performed publicly and who claims that any license agreement offered by that performing rights society is unreasonable in its license rate or fee as to that individual proprietor, shall be entitled to determination of a reasonable license rate or fee as follows:

(1) The individual proprietor may commence such proceeding for determination of a reasonable license rate or fee by filing an application in the applicable district court under paragraph (2) that a rate disagreement exists and by serving a copy of the application on the performing rights society. Such proceeding shall commence in the applicable district court within 90 days after the service of such copy, except that such 90–day requirement shall be subject to the administrative requirements of the court.

(2) The proceeding under paragraph (1) shall be held, at the individual proprietor's election, in the judicial district of the district court with jurisdiction over the applicable consent decree or in that place of holding court of a district court that is the seat of the Federal circuit (other than the Court of Appeals for the Federal Circuit) in which the proprietor's establishment is located.

(3) Such proceeding shall be held before the judge of the court with jurisdiction over the consent decree governing the performing rights society. At the discretion of the court, the proceeding shall be held before a special master or magistrate judge appointed by such

judge. Should that consent decree provide for the appointment of an advisor or advisors to the court for any purpose, any such advisor shall be the special master so named by the court.

(4) In any such proceeding, the industry rate shall be presumed to have been reasonable at the time it was agreed to or determined by the court. Such presumption shall in no way affect a determination of whether the rate is being correctly applied to the individual proprietor.

(5) Pending the completion of such proceeding, the individual proprietor shall have the right to perform publicly the copyrighted musical compositions in the repertoire of the performing rights society by paying an interim license rate or fee into an interest bearing escrow account with the clerk of the court, subject to retroactive adjustment when a final rate or fee has been determined, in an amount equal to the industry rate, or, in the absence of an industry rate, the amount of the most recent license rate or fee agreed to by the parties.

(6) Any decision rendered in such proceeding by a special master or magistrate judge named under paragraph (3) shall be reviewed by the judge of the court with jurisdiction over the consent decree governing the performing rights society. Such proceeding, including such review, shall be concluded within 6 months after its commencement.

(7) Any such final determination shall be binding only as to the individual proprietor commencing the proceeding, and shall not be applicable to any other proprietor or any other performing rights society, and the performing rights society shall be relieved of any obligation of nondiscrimination among similarly situated music users that may be imposed by the consent decree governing its operations.

(8) An individual proprietor may not bring more than one proceeding provided for in this section for the determination of a reasonable license rate or fee under any license agreement with respect to any one performing rights society.

(9) For purposes of this section, the term "industry rate" means the license fee a performing rights society has agreed to with, or which has been determined by the court for, a significant segment of the music user industry to which the individual proprietor belongs.

CHAPTER 6.—IMPORTATION AND EXPORTATION

Sec.

Sec. 602.   Infringing Importation or Exportation of Copies or Phonorecords

(a) Infringing Importation or Exportation.—

(1) Importation.—Importation into the United States, without the authority of the owner of copyright under this title, of copies or phonorecords of a work that have been acquired outside the United

States is an infringement of the exclusive right to distribute copies or phonorecords under section 106, actionable under section 501.

(2) Importation or Exportation of Infringing Items.— Importation into the United States or exportation from the United States, without the authority of the owner of copyright under this title, of copies or phonorecords, the making of which either constituted an infringement of copyright, or which would have constituted an infringement of copyright if this title had been applicable, is an infringement of the exclusive right to distribute copies or phonorecords under section 106, actionable under sections 501 and 506.

(3) Exceptions.—This subsection does not apply to—

(A) importation or exportation of copies or phonorecords under the authority or for the use of the Government of the United States or of any State or political subdivision of a State, but not including copies or phonorecords for use in schools, or copies of any audiovisual work imported for purposes other than archival use;

(B) importation or exportation, for the private use of the importer or exporter and not for distribution, by any person with respect to no more than one copy or phonorecord of any one work at any one time, or by any person arriving from outside the United States or departing from the United States with respect to copies or phonorecords forming part of such person's personal baggage; or

(C) importation by or for an organization operated for scholarly, educational, or religious purposes and not for private gain, with respect to no more than one copy of an audiovisual work solely for its archival purposes, and no more than five copies or phonorecords of any other work for its library lending or archival purposes, unless the importation of such copies or phonorecords is part of an activity consisting of systematic reproduction or distribution, engaged in by such organization in violation of the provisions of section 108(g)(2).

(b) Import Prohibition.—In a case where the making of the copies or phonorecords would have constituted an infringement of copyright if this title had been applicable, their importation is prohibited. In a case where the copies or phonorecords were lawfully made, the United States Customs and Border Protection has no authority to prevent their importation. In either case, the Secretary of the Treasury is authorized to prescribe, by regulation, a procedure under which any person claiming an interest in the copyright in a particular work may, upon payment of a specified fee, be entitled to notification by United States Customs and Border Protection of the importation of articles that appear to be copies or phonorecords of the work.

Sec. 603. Importation Prohibitions: Enforcement and Disposition of Excluded Articles

(a) The Secretary of the Treasury and the United States Postal Service shall separately or jointly make regulations for the enforcement of the provisions of this title prohibiting importation.

(b) These regulations may require, as a condition for the exclusion of articles under section 602—

(1) that the person seeking exclusion obtain a court order enjoining importation of the articles; or

(2) that the person seeking exclusion furnish proof, of a specified nature and in accordance with prescribed procedures, that the copyright in which such person claims an interest is valid and that the importation would violate the prohibition in section 602; the person seeking exclusion may also be required to post a surety bond for any injury that may result if the detention or exclusion of the articles proves to be unjustified.

(c) Articles imported in violation of the importation prohibitions of this title are subject to seizure and forfeiture in the same manner as property imported in violation of the customs revenue laws. Forfeited articles shall be destroyed as directed by the Secretary of the Treasury or the court, as the case may be.

CHAPTER 7.—COPYRIGHT OFFICE

Sec.
701. The Copyright Office: General Responsibilities and Organization.
702. Copyright Office Regulations.
703. Effective Date of Actions in Copyright Office.
704. Retention and Disposition of Articles Deposited in Copyright Office.
705. Copyright Office Records: Preparation, Maintenance, Public Inspection, and Searching.
706. Copies of Copyright Office Records.
707. Copyright Office Forms and Publications.
708. Copyright Office Fees.
709. Delay in Delivery Caused by Disruption of Postal or Other Services.

Sec. 701. The Copyright Office: General Responsibilities and Organization

(a) All administrative functions and duties under this title, except as otherwise specified, are the responsibility of the Register of Copyrights as director of the Copyright Office of the Library of Congress. The Register of Copyrights, together with the subordinate officers and employees of the Copyright Office, shall be appointed by the Librarian of Congress, and shall act under the Librarian's general direction and supervision.

(b) In addition to the functions and duties set out elsewhere in this chapter, the Register of Copyrights shall perform the following functions:

(1) Advise Congress on national and international issues relating to copyright, other matters arising under this title, and related matters.

(2) Provide information and assistance to Federal departments and agencies and the Judiciary on national and international issues relating to copyright, other matters arising under this title, and related matters.

(3) Participate in meetings of international intergovernmental organizations and meetings with foreign government officials

relating to copyright, other matters arising under this title, and related matters, including as a member of United States delegations as authorized by the appropriate Executive branch authority.

(4) Conduct studies and programs regarding copyright, other matters arising under this title, and related matters, the administration of the Copyright Office, or any function vested in the Copyright Office by law, including educational programs conducted cooperatively with foreign intellectual property offices and international intergovernmental organizations.

(5) Perform such other functions as Congress may direct, or as may be appropriate in furtherance of the functions and duties specifically set forth in this title.

(c) The Register of Copyrights shall adopt a seal to be used on and after January 1, 1978, to authenticate all certified documents issued by the Copyright Office.

(d) The Register of Copyrights shall make an annual report to the Librarian of Congress of the work and accomplishments of the Copyright Office during the previous fiscal year. The annual report of the Register of Copyrights shall be published separately and as a part of the annual report of the Librarian of Congress.

(e) Except as provided by section 706(b) and the regulations issued thereunder, all actions taken by the Register of Copyrights under this title are subject to the provisions of the Administrative Procedure Act of June 11, 1946, as amended (c. 324, 60 Stat. 237, title 5, United States Code, Chapter 5, Subchapter II and Chapter 7).

(f) The Register of Copyrights shall be compensated at the rate of pay in effect for level III of the Executive Schedule under section 5314 of title 5. The Librarian of Congress shall establish not more than four positions for Associate Registers of Copyrights, in accordance with the recommendations of the Register of Copyrights. The Librarian shall make appointments to such positions after consultation with the Register of Copyrights. Each Associate Register of Copyrights shall be paid at a rate not to exceed the maximum annual rate of basic pay payable for GS–18 of the General Schedule under section 5332 of title 5.

Sec. 702.   Copyright Office Regulations

The Register of Copyrights is authorized to establish regulations not inconsistent with law for the administration of the functions and duties made the responsibility of the Register under this title. All regulations established by the Register under this title are subject to the approval of the Librarian of Congress.

Sec. 703.   Effective Date of Actions in Copyright Office

In any case in which time limits are prescribed under this title for the performance of an action in the Copyright Office, and in which the last day of the prescribed period falls on a Saturday, Sunday, holiday, or other nonbusiness day within the District of Columbia or the Federal Government, the action may be taken on the next succeeding business day, and is effective as of the date when the period expired.

Sec. 704.   Retention and Disposition of Articles Deposited in Copyright Office

(a) Upon their deposit in the Copyright Office under sections 407 and 408, all copies, phonorecords, and identifying material, including those deposited in connection with claims that have been refused registration, are the property of the United States Government.

(b) In the case of published works, all copies, phonorecords, and identifying material deposited are available to the Library of Congress for its collections, or for exchange or transfer to any other library. In the case of unpublished works, the Library is entitled, under regulations that the Register of Copyrights shall prescribe, to select any deposits for its collections or for transfer to the National Archives of the United States or to a Federal records center, as defined in section 2901 of title 44.

(c) The Register of Copyrights is authorized, for specific or general categories of works, to make a facsimile reproduction of all or any part of the material deposited under section 408, and to make such reproduction a part of the Copyright Office records of the registration, before transferring such material to the Library of Congress as provided by subsection (b), or before destroying or otherwise disposing of such material as provided by subsection (d).

(d) Deposits not selected by the Library under subsection (b), or identifying portions or reproductions of them, shall be retained under the control of the Copyright Office, including retention in Government storage facilities, for the longest period considered practicable and desirable by the Register of Copyrights and the Librarian of Congress. After that period it is within the joint discretion of the Register and the Librarian to order their destruction or other disposition; but, in the case of unpublished works, no deposit shall be knowingly or intentionally destroyed or otherwise disposed of during its term of copyright unless a facsimile reproduction of the entire deposit has been made a part of the Copyright Office records as provided by subsection (c).

(e) The depositor of copies, phonorecords, or identifying material under section 408, or the copyright owner of record, may request retention, under the control of the Copyright Office, of one or more of such articles for the full term of copyright in the work. The Register of Copyrights shall prescribe, by regulation, the conditions under which such requests are to be made and granted, and shall fix the fee to be charged under section 708(a) if the request is granted.

Sec. 705.   Copyright Office Records: Preparation, Maintenance, Public Inspection, and Searching

(a) The Register of Copyrights shall ensure that records of deposits, registrations, recordations, and other actions taken under this title are maintained, and that indexes of such records are prepared.

(b) Such records and indexes, as well as the articles deposited in connection with completed copyright registrations and retained under the control of the Copyright Office, shall be open to public inspection.

(c) Upon request and payment of the fee specified by section 708, the Copyright Office shall make a search of its public records, indexes, and deposits, and shall furnish a report of the information they disclose with respect to any particular deposits, registrations, or recorded documents.

Sec. 706.   Copies of Copyright Office Records

(a) Copies may be made of any public records or indexes of the Copyright Office; additional certificates of copyright registration and copies of any public records or indexes may be furnished upon request and payment of the fees specified by section 708.

(b) Copies or reproductions of deposited articles retained under the control of the Copyright Office shall be authorized or furnished only under the conditions specified by the Copyright Office regulations.

Sec. 707.   Copyright Office Forms and Publications

(a) Catalog of Copyright Entries.—The Register of Copyrights shall compile and publish at periodic intervals catalogs of all copyright registrations. These catalogs shall be divided into parts in accordance with the various classes of works, and the Register has discretion to determine, on the basis of practicability and usefulness, the form and frequency of publication of each particular part.

(b) Other Publications.—The Register shall furnish, free of charge upon request, application forms for copyright registration and general informational material in connection with the functions of the Copyright Office. The Register also has the authority to publish compilations of information, bibliographies, and other material he or she considers to be of value to the public.

(c) Distribution of Publications.—All publications of the Copyright Office shall be furnished to depository libraries as specified under section 1905 of title 44, and, aside from those furnished free of charge, shall be offered for sale to the public at prices based on the cost of reproduction and distribution.

Sec. 708.   Copyright Office Fees*

(a) Fees.—Fees shall be paid to the Register of Copyrights—

(1) on filing each application under section 408 for registration of a copyright claim or for a supplementary registration, including the issuance of a certificate of registration if registration is made;

(2) on filing each application for registration of a claim for renewal of a subsisting copyright under section 304(a), including the issuance of a certificate of registration if registration is made;

(3) for the issuance of a receipt for a deposit under section 407;

(4) for the recordation, as provided by section 205, of a transfer of copyright ownership or other document;

(5) for the filing, under section 115(b), of a notice of intention to obtain a compulsory license;

(6) for the recordation, under section 302(c), of a statement revealing the identity of an author of an anonymous or pseudonymous work, or for the recordation, under section 302(d), of a statement relating to the death of an author;

(7) for the issuance, under section 706, of an additional certificate of registration;

---

*   For the current fee amounts, see Copyright Office Regulations, 37 C.F.R. § 201.3, at http://copyright.gov/title37/.

(8) for the issuance of any other certification;

(9) for the making and reporting of a search as provided by section 705, and for any related services;

(10) on filing a statement of account based on secondary transmissions of primary transmissions pursuant to section 119 or 122; and

(11) on filing a statement of account based on secondary transmissions or primary transmissions pursuant to section 111.

Fees established under paragraphs (10) and (11) shall be reasonable and may not exceed one-half of the cost necessary to cover the reasonable expenses incurred by the Copyright Office for the collection and administration of the statements of account and any royalty fees deposited with such statements.

The Register is authorized to fix fees for other services, including the cost of preparing copies of Copyright Office records, whether or not such copies are certified, based on the cost of providing the service.

(b) Adjustment of Fees.—The Register of Copyrights may, by regulation, adjust the fees for the services specified in paragraphs (1) through (9) of subsection (a) in the following manner:

(1) The Register shall conduct a study of the costs incurred by the Copyright Office for the registration of claims, the recordation of documents, and the provision of services. The study shall also consider the timing of any adjustment in fees and the authority to use such fees consistent with the budget.

(2) The Register may, on the basis of the study under paragraph (1), and subject to paragraph (5), adjust fees to not more than that necessary to cover the reasonable costs incurred by the Copyright Office for the services described in paragraph (1), plus a reasonable inflation adjustment to account for any estimated increase in costs.

(3) Any fee established under paragraph (2) shall be rounded off to the nearest dollar, or for a fee less than $12, rounded off to the nearest 50 cents.

(4) Fees established under this subsection shall be fair and equitable and give due consideration to the objectives of the copyright system.

(5) If the Register determines under paragraph (2) that fees should be adjusted, the Register shall prepare a proposed fee schedule and submit the schedule with the accompanying economic analysis to the Congress. The fees proposed by the Register may be instituted after the end of 120 days after the schedule is submitted to the Congress unless, within that 120–day period, a law is enacted stating in substance that the Congress does not approve the schedule.

(c) The fees prescribed by or under this section are applicable to the United States Government and any of its agencies, employees, or officers, but the Register of Copyrights has discretion to waive the requirement of this subsection in occasional or isolated cases involving relatively small amounts.

(d)(1) Except as provided in paragraph (2), all fees received under this section shall be deposited by the Register of Copyrights in the Treasury of the United States and shall be credited to the appropriations for necessary expenses of the Copyright Office. Such fees that are collected shall remain available until expended. The Register may, in accordance with regulations that he or she shall prescribe, refund any sum paid by mistake or in excess of the fee required by this section.

(2) In the case of fees deposited against future services, the Register of Copyrights shall request the Secretary of the Treasury to invest in interest-bearing securities in the United States Treasury any portion of the fees that, as determined by the Register, is not required to meet current deposit account demands. Funds from such portion of fees shall be invested in securities that permit funds to be available to the Copyright Office at all times if they are determined to be necessary to meet current deposit account demands. Such investments shall be in public debt securities with maturities suitable to the needs of the Copyright Office, as determined by the Register of Copyrights, and bearing interest at rates determined by the Secretary of the Treasury, taking into consideration current market yields on outstanding marketable obligations of the United States of comparable maturities.

(3) The income on such investments shall be deposited in the Treasury of the United States and shall be credited to the appropriations for necessary expenses of the Copyright Office.

Sec. 709.   Delay in Delivery Caused by Disruption of Postal or Other Services

In any case in which the Register of Copyrights determines, on the basis of such evidence as the Register may by regulation require, that a deposit, application, fee, or any other material to be delivered to the Copyright Office by a particular date, would have been received in the Copyright Office in due time except for a general disruption or suspension of postal or other transportation or communications services, the actual receipt of such material in the Copyright Office within one month after the date on which the Register determines that the disruption or suspension of such services has terminated, shall be considered timely.

CHAPTER 8.—PROCEEDINGS BY COPYRIGHT ROYALTY JUDGES

Sec. 801.   Copyright Royalty Judges; Appointment and Functions

(a) Appointment.—The Librarian of Congress shall appoint 3 full-time Copyright Royalty Judges, and shall appoint 1 of the 3 as the Chief Copyright Royalty Judge. The Librarian shall make appointments to such positions after consultation with the Register of Copyrights.

(b) Functions.—Subject to the provisions of this chapter, the functions of the Copyright Royalty Judges shall be as follows:

(1) To make determinations and adjustments of reasonable terms and rates of royalty payments as provided in sections 112(e), 114, 115, 116, 118, 119, and 1004. The rates applicable under sections 114(f)(1)(B), 115, and 116 shall be calculated to achieve the following objectives:

(A) To maximize the availability of creative works to the public.

(B) To afford the copyright owner a fair return for his or her creative work and the copyright user a fair income under existing economic conditions.

(C) To reflect the relative roles of the copyright owner and the copyright user in the product made available to the public with respect to relative creative contribution, technological contribution, capital investment, cost, risk, and contribution to the opening of new markets for creative expression and media for their communication.

(D) To minimize any disruptive impact on the structure of the industries involved and on generally prevailing industry practices.

(2) To make determinations concerning the adjustment of the copyright royalty rates under section 111 solely in accordance with the following provisions:

(A) The rates established by section 111(d)(1)(B) may be adjusted to reflect—

(i) national monetary inflation or deflation; or

(ii) changes in the average rates charged cable subscribers for the basic service of providing secondary transmissions to maintain the real constant dollar level of the royalty fee per subscriber which existed as of the date of October 19, 1976, except that—

(I) if the average rates charged cable system subscribers for the basic service of providing secondary transmissions are changed so that the average rates exceed national monetary inflation, no change in the rates established by section 111(d)(1)(B) shall be permitted; and

(II) no increase in the royalty fee shall be permitted based on any reduction in the average number of distant signal equivalents per subscriber.

The Copyright Royalty Judges may consider all factors relating to the maintenance of such level of payments, including, as an extenuating factor, whether the industry has been restrained by subscriber rate regulating authorities from increasing the rates for the basic service of providing secondary transmissions.

(B) In the event that the rules and regulations of the Federal Communications Commission are amended at any time after April 15, 1976, to permit the carriage by cable systems of additional television broadcast signals beyond the local service area of the primary transmitters of such signals, the royalty rates established by section 111(d)(1)(B) may be adjusted to ensure that the rates for the additional distant signal equivalents resulting from such carriage are reasonable in the light of the changes effected by the amendment to such rules and regulations. In determining the reasonableness of rates proposed following an amendment of Federal Communications Commission rules and regulations, the Copyright Royalty Judges shall consider, among other factors, the economic impact on copyright owners and users; except that no adjustment in royalty rates shall be made under this subparagraph with respect to any distant signal equivalent or fraction thereof represented by—

> (i) carriage of any signal permitted under the rules and regulations of the Federal Communications Commission in effect on April 15, 1976, or the carriage of a signal of the same type (that is, independent, network, or noncommercial educational) substituted for such permitted signal; or

> (ii) a television broadcast signal first carried after April 15, 1976, pursuant to an individual waiver of the rules and regulations of the Federal Communications Commission, as such rules and regulations were in effect on April 15, 1976.

(C) In the event of any change in the rules and regulations of the Federal Communications Commission with respect to syndicated and sports program exclusivity after April 15, 1976, the rates established by section 111(d)(1)(B) may be adjusted to assure that such rates are reasonable in light of the changes to such rules and regulations, but any such adjustment shall apply only to the affected television broadcast signals carried on those systems affected by the change.

(D) The gross receipts limitations established by section 111(d)(1)(C) and (D) shall be adjusted to reflect national monetary inflation or deflation or changes in the average rates charged cable system subscribers for the basic service of providing secondary transmissions to maintain the real constant dollar value of the exemption provided by such section, and the royalty rate specified therein shall not be subject to adjustment.

(3)(A) To authorize the distribution, under sections 111, 119, and 1007, of those royalty fees collected under sections 111, 119, and 1005, as the case may be, to the extent that the Copyright Royalty Judges have found that the distribution of such fees is not subject to controversy.

(B) In cases where the Copyright Royalty Judges determine that controversy exists, the Copyright Royalty Judges shall determine the distribution of such fees, including partial distributions, in accordance with section 111, 119, or 1007, as the case may be.

(C) Notwithstanding section 804(b)(8), the Copyright Royalty Judges, at any time after the filing of claims under section 111, 119, or 1007, may, upon motion of one or more of the claimants and after publication in the Federal Register of a request for responses to the motion from interested claimants, make a partial distribution of such fees, if, based upon all responses received during the 30–day period beginning on the date of such publication, the Copyright Royalty Judges conclude that no claimant entitled to receive such fees has stated a reasonable objection to the partial distribution, and all such claimants—

(i) agree to the partial distribution;

(ii) sign an agreement obligating them to return any excess amounts to the extent necessary to comply with the final determination on the distribution of the fees made under subparagraph (B);

(iii) file the agreement with the Copyright Royalty Judges; and

(iv) agree that such funds are available for distribution.

(D) The Copyright Royalty Judges and any other officer or employee acting in good faith in distributing funds under subparagraph (C) shall not be held liable for the payment of any excess fees under subparagraph (C). The Copyright Royalty Judges shall, at the time the final determination is made, calculate any such excess amounts.

(4) To accept or reject royalty claims filed under sections 111, 119, and 1007, on the basis of timeliness or the failure to establish the basis for a claim.

(5) To accept or reject rate adjustment petitions as provided in section 804 and petitions to participate as provided in section 803(b)(1) and (2).

(6) To determine the status of a digital audio recording device or a digital audio interface device under sections 1002 and 1003, as provided in section 1010.

(7)(A) To adopt as a basis for statutory terms and rates or as a basis for the distribution of statutory royalty payments, an agreement concerning such matters reached among some or all of the participants in a proceeding at any time during the proceeding, except that—

(i) the Copyright Royalty Judges shall provide to those that would be bound by the terms, rates, or other determination set by any agreement in a proceeding to determine royalty rates an opportunity to comment on the agreement and shall provide to participants in the proceeding under section 803(b)(2) that would be bound by the terms, rates, or other determination set by the agreement an opportunity to comment on the agreement and object to its adoption as a basis for statutory terms and rates; and

(ii) the Copyright Royalty Judges may decline to adopt the agreement as a basis for statutory terms and rates for participants that are not parties to the agreement, if any participant described in clause (i) objects to the agreement and the Copyright Royalty Judges conclude, based on the record before them if one exists, that the agreement does not provide a reasonable basis for setting statutory terms or rates.

(B) License agreements voluntarily negotiated pursuant to section 112(e)(5), 114(f)(3), 115(c)(3)(E)(i), 116(c), or 118(b)(2) that do not result in statutory terms and rates shall not be subject to clauses (i) and (ii) of subparagraph (A).

(C) Interested parties may negotiate and agree to, and the Copyright Royalty Judges may adopt, an agreement that specifies as terms notice and recordkeeping requirements that apply in lieu of those that would otherwise apply under regulations.

(8) To perform other duties, as assigned by the Register of Copyrights within the Library of Congress, except as provided in section 802(g), at times when Copyright Royalty Judges are not engaged in performing the other duties set forth in this section.

(c) Rulings.—The Copyright Royalty Judges may make any necessary procedural or evidentiary rulings in any proceeding under this chapter and may, before commencing a proceeding under this chapter, make any such rulings that would apply to the proceedings conducted by the Copyright Royalty Judges.

(d) Administrative Support.—The Librarian of Congress shall provide the Copyright Royalty Judges with the necessary administrative services related to proceedings under this chapter.

(e) Location in Library of Congress.—The offices of the Copyright Royalty Judges and staff shall be in the Library of Congress.

(f) Effective Date of Actions.—On and after the date of the enactment of the Copyright Royalty and Distribution Reform Act of 2004, in any case in which time limits are prescribed under this title for performance of an action with or by the Copyright Royalty Judges, and in which the last day of the prescribed period falls on a Saturday, Sunday, holiday, or other nonbusiness day within the District of Columbia or the Federal Government, the action may be taken on the next succeeding business day, and is effective as of the date when the period expired.

Sec. 802.   Copyright Royalty Judgeships; Staff

(a) Qualifications of Copyright Royalty Judges.—

(1) In general.—Each Copyright Royalty Judge shall be an attorney who has at least 7 years of legal experience. The Chief Copyright Royalty Judge shall have at least 5 years of experience in adjudications, arbitrations, or court trials. Of the other 2 Copyright Royalty Judges, 1 shall have significant knowledge of copyright law, and the other shall have significant knowledge of economics. An individual may serve as a Copyright Royalty Judge only if the individual is free of any financial conflict of interest under subsection (h).

(2) Definition.—In this subsection, the term "adjudication" has the meaning given that term in section 551 of title 5, but does not include mediation.

(b) Staff.—The Chief Copyright Royalty Judge shall hire 3 full-time staff members to assist the Copyright Royalty Judges in performing their functions.

(c) Terms.—The individual first appointed as the Chief Copyright Royalty Judge shall be appointed to a term of 6 years, and of the remaining individuals first appointed as Copyright Royalty Judges, 1 shall be appointed to a term of 4 years, and the other shall be appointed to a term of 2 years. Thereafter, the terms of succeeding Copyright Royalty Judges shall each be 6 years. An individual serving as a Copyright Royalty Judge may be reappointed to subsequent terms. The term of a Copyright Royalty Judge shall begin when the term of the predecessor of that Copyright Royalty Judge ends. When the term of office of a Copyright Royalty Judge ends, the individual serving that term may continue to serve until a successor is selected.

(d) Vacancies or incapacity.—

(1) Vacancies.—If a vacancy should occur in the position of Copyright Royalty Judge, the Librarian of Congress shall act expeditiously to fill the vacancy, and may appoint an interim Copyright Royalty Judge to serve until another Copyright Royalty Judge is appointed under this section. An individual appointed to fill the vacancy occurring before the expiration of the term for which the predecessor of that individual was appointed shall be appointed for the remainder of that term.

(2) Incapacity.—In the case in which a Copyright Royalty Judge is temporarily unable to perform his or her duties, the Librarian of Congress may appoint an interim Copyright Royalty Judge to perform such duties during the period of such incapacity.

(e) Compensation.—

(1) Judges.—The Chief Copyright Royalty Judge shall receive compensation at the rate of basic pay payable for level AL–1 for administrative law judges pursuant to section 5372(b) of title 5, and each of the other two Copyright Royalty Judges shall receive compensation at the rate of basic pay payable for level AL–2 for administrative law judges pursuant to such section. The compensation of the Copyright Royalty Judges shall not be subject to any regulations adopted by the Office of Personnel Management pursuant to its authority under section 5376(b)(1) of title 5.

(2) Staff Members.—Of the staff members appointed under subsection (b)—

(A) the rate of pay of 1 staff member shall be not more than the basic rate of pay payable for level 10 of GS–15 of the General Schedule;

(B) the rate of pay of 1 staff member shall be not less than the basic rate of pay payable for GS–13 of the General Schedule and not more than the basic rate of pay payable for level 10 of GS–14 of such Schedule; and

(C) the rate of pay for the third staff member shall be not less than the basic rate of pay payable for GS–8 of the General Schedule and not more than the basic rate of pay payable for level 10 of GS–11 of such Schedule.

(3) Locality pay.—All rates of pay referred to under this subsection shall include locality pay.

(f) Independence of Copyright Royalty Judge.—

   (1) In making determinations.—

      (A) In general.—

         (i) Subject to subparagraph (B) and clause (ii) of this subparagraph, the Copyright Royalty Judges shall have full independence in making determinations concerning adjustments and determinations of copyright royalty rates and terms, the distribution of copyright royalties, the acceptance or rejection of royalty claims, rate adjustment petitions, and petitions to participate, and in issuing other rulings under this title, except that the Copyright Royalty Judges may consult with the Register of Copyrights on any matter other than a question of fact.

         (ii) One or more Copyright Royalty Judges may, or by motion to the Copyright Royalty Judges, any participant in a proceeding may, request from the Register of Copyrights an interpretation of any material questions of substantive law that relate to the construction of provisions of this title and arise in the course of the proceeding. Any request for a written interpretation shall be in writing and on the record, and reasonable provision shall be made to permit participants in the proceeding to comment on the material questions of substantive law in a manner that minimizes duplication and delay. Except as provided in subparagraph (B), the Register of Copyrights shall deliver to the Copyright Royalty Judges a written response within 14 days after the receipt of all briefs and comments from the participants. The Copyright Royalty Judges shall apply the legal interpretation embodied in the response of the Register of Copyrights if it is timely delivered, and the response shall be included in the record that accompanies the final determination. The authority under this clause shall not be construed to authorize the Register of Copyrights to provide an interpretation of questions of procedure before the Copyright Royalty Judges, the ultimate adjustments and determinations of copyright royalty rates and terms, the ultimate distribution of copyright royalties, or the acceptance or rejection of royalty claims, rate adjustment petitions, or petitions to participate in a proceeding.

      (B) Novel questions.—

         (i) In any case in which a novel material question of substantive law concerning an interpretation of those provisions of this title that are the subject of the proceeding is presented, the Copyright Royalty Judges shall request a decision of the Register of Copyrights, in writing, to resolve such novel question. Reasonable provision shall be made for comment on such request by the participants in the proceeding, in such a way as to minimize duplication and delay. The Register of Copyrights shall transmit his or her decision to the Copyright Royalty Judges within 30 days after the Register of Copyrights receives all of the briefs or comments of the participants. Such decision shall be in writing and included by the Copyright Royalty Judges in the record that accompanies their final determination. If such a decision is timely delivered to the Copyright Royalty Judges, the Copyright Royalty Judges shall apply the legal determinations embodied in the decision of the Register of Copyrights in resolving material questions of substantive law.

(ii) In clause (i), a "novel question of law" is a question of law that has not been determined in prior decisions, determinations, and rulings described in section 803(a).

(C) Consultation.—Notwithstanding the provisions of subparagraph (A), the Copyright Royalty Judges shall consult with the Register of Copyrights with respect to any determination or ruling that would require that any act be performed by the Copyright Office, and any such determination or ruling shall not be binding upon the Register of Copyrights.

(D) Review of legal conclusions by the Register of Copyrights.—The Register of Copyrights may review for legal error the resolution by the Copyright Royalty Judges of a material question of substantive law under this title that underlies or is contained in a final determination of the Copyright Royalty Judges. If the Register of Copyrights concludes, after taking into consideration the views of the participants in the proceeding, that any resolution reached by the Copyright Royalty Judges was in material error, the Register of Copyrights shall issue a written decision correcting such legal error, which shall be made part of the record of the proceeding. The Register of Copyrights shall issue such written decision not later than 60 days after the date on which the final determination by the Copyright Royalty Judges is issued. Additionally, the Register of Copyrights shall cause to be published in the Federal Register such written decision, together with a specific identification of the legal conclusion of the Copyright Royalty Judges that is determined to be erroneous. As to conclusions of substantive law involving an interpretation of the statutory provisions of this title, the decision of the Register of Copyrights shall be binding as precedent upon the Copyright Royalty Judges in subsequent proceedings under this chapter. When a decision has been rendered pursuant to this subparagraph, the Register of Copyrights may, on the basis of and in accordance with such decision, intervene as of right in any appeal of a final determination of the Copyright Royalty Judges pursuant to section 803(d) in the United States Court of Appeals for the District of Columbia Circuit. If, prior to intervening in such an appeal, the Register of Copyrights gives notification to, and undertakes to consult with, the Attorney General with respect to such intervention, and the Attorney General fails, within a reasonable period after receiving such notification, to intervene in such appeal, the Register of Copyrights may intervene in such appeal in his or her own name by any attorney designated by the Register of Copyrights for such purpose. Intervention by the Register of Copyrights in his or her own name shall not preclude the Attorney General from intervening on behalf of the United States in such an appeal as may be otherwise provided or required by law.

(E) Effect on judicial review.—Nothing in this section shall be interpreted to alter the standard applied by a court in reviewing legal determinations involving an interpretation or construction of the provisions of this title or to affect the extent to which any construction or interpretation of the provisions of this title shall be accorded deference by a reviewing court.

(2) Performance appraisals.—

(A) In general.—Notwithstanding any other provision of law or any regulation of the Library of Congress, and subject to subparagraph (B), the Copyright Royalty Judges shall not receive performance appraisals.

(B) Relating to sanction or removal.—To the extent that the Librarian of Congress adopts regulations under subsection (h) relating to the sanction or removal of a Copyright Royalty Judge and such regulations require documentation to establish the cause of such sanction or removal, the Copyright Royalty Judge may receive an appraisal related specifically to the cause of the sanction or removal.

(g) Inconsistent duties barred.—No Copyright Royalty Judge may undertake duties that conflict with his or her duties and responsibilities as a Copyright Royalty Judge.

(h) Standards of conduct.—The Librarian of Congress shall adopt regulations regarding the standards of conduct, including financial conflict of interest and restrictions against ex parte communications, which shall govern the Copyright Royalty Judges and the proceedings under this chapter.

(i) Removal or sanction.—The Librarian of Congress may sanction or remove a Copyright Royalty Judge for violation of the standards of conduct adopted under subsection (h), misconduct, neglect of duty, or any disqualifying physical or mental disability. Any such sanction or removal may be made only after notice and opportunity for a hearing, but the Librarian of Congress may suspend the Copyright Royalty Judge during the pendency of such hearing. The Librarian shall appoint an interim Copyright Royalty Judge during the period of any such suspension.

Sec. 803.   Proceedings of Copyright Royalty Judges

(a) Proceedings.—

(1) In general.—The Copyright Royalty Judges shall act in accordance with this title, and to the extent not inconsistent with this title, in accordance with subchapter II of chapter 5 of title 5, in carrying out the purposes set forth in section 801. The Copyright Royalty Judges shall act in accordance with regulations issued by the Copyright Royalty Judges and the Librarian of Congress, and on the basis of a written record, prior determinations and interpretations of the Copyright Royalty Tribunal, Librarian of Congress, the Register of Copyrights, copyright arbitration royalty panels (to the extent those determinations are not inconsistent with a decision of the Librarian of Congress or the Register of Copyrights), and the Copyright Royalty Judges (to the extent those determinations are not inconsistent with a decision of the Register of Copyrights that was timely delivered to the Copyright Royalty Judges pursuant to section 802(f)(1)(A) or (B), or with a decision of the Register of Copyrights pursuant to section 802(f)(1)(D)), under this chapter, and decisions of the court of appeals under this chapter before, on, or after the effective date of the Copyright Royalty and Distribution Reform Act of 2004.

(2) Judges acting as panel and individually.—The Copyright Royalty Judges shall preside over hearings in proceedings under this chapter en banc. The Chief Copyright Royalty Judge may designate a Copyright Royalty Judge to preside individually over such collateral and administrative proceedings, and over such proceedings under paragraphs (1) through (5) of subsection (b), as the Chief Judge considers appropriate.

(3) Determinations.—Final determinations of the Copyright Royalty Judges in proceedings under this chapter shall be made by majority vote. A Copyright Royalty Judge dissenting from the majority on any determination under this chapter may issue his or her dissenting opinion, which shall be included with the determination.

(b) Procedures.—

(1) Initiation.—

(A) Call for petitions to participate.—

(i) The Copyright Royalty Judges shall cause to be published in the Federal Register notice of commencement of proceedings under this chapter, calling for the filing of petitions to participate in a proceeding under this chapter for the purpose of making the relevant determination under section 111, 112, 114, 115, 116, 118, 119, 1004, or 1007, as the case may be—

(I) promptly upon a determination made under section 804(a);

(II) by no later than January 5 of a year specified in paragraph (2) of section 804(b) for the commencement of proceedings;

(III) by no later than January 5 of a year specified in subparagraph (A) or (B) of paragraph (3) of section 804(b) for the commencement of proceedings, or as otherwise provided in subparagraph (A) or (C) of such paragraph for the commencement of proceedings;

(IV) as provided under section 804(b)(8); or

(V) by no later than January 5 of a year specified in any other provision of section 804(b) for the filing of petitions for the commencement of proceedings, if a petition has not been filed by that date, except that the publication of notice requirement shall not apply in the case of proceedings under section 111 that are scheduled to commence in 2005.

(ii) Petitions to participate shall be filed by no later than 30 days after publication of notice of commencement of a proceeding under clause (i), except that the Copyright Royalty Judges may, for substantial good cause shown and if there is no prejudice to the participants that have already filed petitions, accept late petitions to participate at any time up to the date that is 90 days before the date on which participants in the proceeding are to file their written direct statements. Notwithstanding the preceding sentence, petitioners whose petitions are filed more than 30 days after publication of notice of commencement of a proceeding are not eligible to object to a settlement reached during the voluntary negotiation period under paragraph (3), and any objection filed by such a petitioner shall not be taken into account by the Copyright Royalty Judges.

(B) Petitions to participate. Each petition to participate in a proceeding shall describe the petitioner's interest in the subject matter of the proceeding. Parties with similar interests may file a single petition to participate.

(2) Participation in general.—Subject to paragraph (4), a person may participate in a proceeding under this chapter, including through the submission of briefs or other information, only if—

(A) that person has filed a petition to participate in accordance with paragraph (1) (either individually or as a group under paragraph (1)(B));

(B) the Copyright Royalty Judges have not determined that the petition to participate is facially invalid;

(C) the Copyright Royalty Judges have not determined, sua sponte or on the motion of another participant in the proceeding, that the person lacks a significant interest in the proceeding; and

(D) the petition to participate is accompanied by either—

(i) in a proceeding to determine royalty rates, a filing fee of $150; or

(ii) in a proceeding to determine distribution of royalty fees—

(I) a filing fee of $150; or

(II) a statement that the petitioner (individually or as a group) will not seek a distribution of more than $1000, in which case the amount distributed to the petitioner shall not exceed $1000.

(3) Voluntary negotiation period.—

(A) Commencement of proceedings.—

(i) Rate adjustment proceeding.—Promptly after the date for filing of petitions to participate in a proceeding, the Copyright Royalty Judges shall make available to all participants in the proceeding a list of such participants and shall initiate a voluntary negotiation period among the participants.

(ii) Distribution proceeding.—Promptly after the date for filing of petitions to participate in a proceeding to determine the distribution of royalties, the Copyright Royalty Judges shall make available to all participants in the proceeding a list of such participants. The initiation of a voluntary negotiation period among the participants shall be set at a time determined by the Copyright Royalty Judges.

(B) Length of proceedings.—The voluntary negotiation period initiated under subparagraph (A) shall be 3 months.

(C) Determination of subsequent proceedings.—At the close of the voluntary negotiation proceedings, the Copyright Royalty Judges shall, if further proceedings under this chapter are necessary, determine whether and to what extent paragraphs (4) and (5) will apply to the parties.

(4) Small claims procedure in distribution proceedings.—

(A) In general.—If, in a proceeding under this chapter to determine the distribution of royalties, the contested amount of a claim is $10,000 or less, the Copyright Royalty Judges shall decide the controversy on the basis of the filing of the written direct statement by the participant, the response by any opposing participant, and 1 additional response by each such party.

(B) Bad faith inflation of claim.—If the Copyright Royalty Judges determine that a participant asserts in bad faith an amount in controversy in excess of $10,000 for the purpose of avoiding a determination under the procedure set forth in subparagraph (A), the Copyright Royalty Judges shall impose a fine on that participant in an amount not to exceed the difference between the actual amount distributed and the amount asserted by the participant.

(5) Paper proceedings.—The Copyright Royalty Judges in proceedings under this chapter may decide, sua sponte or upon motion of a participant, to determine issues on the basis of the filing of the written direct statement by the participant, the response by any opposing participant, and one additional response by each such participant. Prior to making such decision to proceed on such a paper record only, the Copyright Royalty Judges shall offer to all parties to the proceeding the opportunity to comment on the decision. The procedure under this paragraph—

(A) shall be applied in cases in which there is no genuine issue of material fact, there is no need for evidentiary hearings, and all participants in the proceeding agree in writing to the procedure; and

(B) may be applied under such other circumstances as the Copyright Royalty Judges consider appropriate.

(6) Regulations.—

(A) In general.—The Copyright Royalty Judges may issue regulations to carry out their functions under this title. All regulations issued by the Copyright Royalty Judges are subject to the approval of the Librarian of Congress and are subject to judicial review pursuant to chapter 7 of title 5, except as set forth in subsection (d). Not later than 120 days after Copyright Royalty Judges or interim Copyright Royalty Judges, as the case may be, are first appointed after the enactment of the Copyright Royalty and Distribution Reform Act of 2004, such judges shall issue regulations to govern proceedings under this chapter.

(B) Interim regulations.—Until regulations are adopted under subparagraph (A), the Copyright Royalty Judges shall apply the regulations in effect under this chapter on the day before the effective date of the Copyright Royalty and Distribution Reform Act of 2004, to the extent such regulations are not inconsistent with this chapter, except that functions carried out under such regulations by the Librarian of Congress, the Register of Copyrights, or copyright arbitration royalty panels that, as of such date of enactment, are to be carried out by the Copyright Royalty Judges under this chapter, shall be carried out by the Copyright Royalty Judges under such regulations.

(C) Requirements.—Regulations issued under subparagraph (A) shall include the following:

(i) The written direct statements and written rebuttal statements of all participants in a proceeding under paragraph (2) shall be filed by a date specified by the Copyright Royalty Judges, which, in the case of written direct statements, may be not earlier than 4 months, and not later than 5 months, after the end of the voluntary negotiation period under paragraph (3). Notwithstanding the preceding sentence, the Copyright Royalty Judges may allow a participant in a proceeding to file an amended written direct statement based on new information received during the discovery process, within 15 days after the end of the discovery period specified in clause (iv).

(ii)(I) Following the submission to the Copyright Royalty Judges of written direct statements and written rebuttal statements by the participants in a proceeding under paragraph (2), the Copyright Royalty Judges, after taking into consideration the views of the participants in the proceeding, shall determine a schedule for conducting and completing discovery.

(II) In this chapter, the term "written direct statements" means witness statements, testimony, and exhibits to be presented in the proceedings, and such other information that is necessary to establish terms and rates, or the distribution of royalty payments, as the case may be, as set forth in regulations issued by the Copyright Royalty Judges.

(iii) Hearsay may be admitted in proceedings under this chapter to the extent deemed appropriate by the Copyright Royalty Judges.

(iv) Discovery in connection with written direct statements shall be permitted for a period of 60 days, except for discovery ordered by the Copyright Royalty Judges in connection with the resolution of motions, orders, and disputes pending at the end of such period. The Copyright Royalty Judges may order a discovery schedule in connection with written rebuttal statements.

(v) Any participant under paragraph (2) in a proceeding under this chapter to determine royalty rates may request of an opposing participant nonprivileged documents directly related to the written direct statement or written rebuttal statement of that participant. Any objection to such a request shall be resolved by a motion or request to compel production made to the Copyright Royalty Judges in accordance with regulations adopted by the Copyright Royalty Judges. Each motion or request to compel discovery shall be determined by the Copyright Royalty Judges, or by a Copyright Royalty Judge when permitted under subsection (a)(2). Upon such motion, the Copyright Royalty Judges may order discovery pursuant to regulations established under this paragraph.

(vi)(I) Any participant under paragraph (2) in a proceeding under this chapter to determine royalty rates may, by means of written motion or on the record, request of an opposing participant or witness other relevant information and materials if, absent the discovery sought, the Copyright Royalty Judges' resolution of the proceeding would be substantially impaired. In determining whether discovery will be granted under this clause, the Copyright Royalty Judges may consider—

(aa) whether the burden or expense of producing the requested information or materials outweighs the likely benefit, taking into account the needs and resources of the participants, the importance of the issues at stake, and the probative value of the requested information or materials in resolving such issues;

(bb) whether the requested information or materials would be unreasonably cumulative or duplicative, or are obtainable from another source that is more convenient, less burdensome, or less expensive; and

(cc) whether the participant seeking discovery has had ample opportunity by discovery in the proceeding or by other means to obtain the information sought.

(II) This clause shall not apply to any proceeding scheduled to commence after December 31, 2010.

(vii) In a proceeding under this chapter to determine royalty rates, the participants entitled to receive royalties shall collectively be permitted to take no more than 10 depositions and secure responses to no more than 25 interrogatories, and the participants obligated to pay royalties shall collectively be permitted to take no more than 10 depositions and secure responses to no more than 25 interrogatories. The Copyright Royalty Judges shall resolve any disputes among similarly aligned participants to allocate the number of depositions or interrogatories permitted under this clause.

(viii) The rules and practices in effect on the day before the effective date of the Copyright Royalty and Distribution Reform Act of 2004, relating to discovery in proceedings under this chapter to determine the distribution of royalty fees, shall continue to apply to such proceedings on and after such effective date.

(ix) In proceedings to determine royalty rates, the Copyright Royalty Judges may issue a subpoena commanding a participant or witness to appear and give testimony, or to produce and permit inspection of documents or tangible things, if the Copyright Royalty Judges' resolution of the proceeding would be substantially impaired by the absence of such testimony or production of documents or tangible things. Such subpoena shall specify with reasonable particularity the materials to be produced or the scope and nature of the required testimony. Nothing in this clause shall preclude the Copyright Royalty Judges from requesting the production by a nonparticipant of information or materials relevant to the resolution by the Copyright Royalty Judges of a material issue of fact.

(x) The Copyright Royalty Judges shall order a settlement conference among the participants in the proceeding to facilitate the presentation of offers of settlement among the participants. The settlement conference shall be held during a 21–day period following the 60–day discovery period specified in clause (iv) and shall take place outside the presence of the Copyright Royalty Judges.

(xi) No evidence, including exhibits, may be submitted in the written direct statement or written rebuttal statement of a participant without a sponsoring witness, except where the Copyright Royalty Judges have taken official notice, or in the case of incorporation by reference of past records, or for good cause shown.

(c) Determination of Copyright Royalty Judges.—

(1) Timing.—The Copyright Royalty Judges shall issue their determination in a proceeding not later than 11 months after the conclusion of the 21–day settlement conference period under subsection (b)(6)(C)(x), but, in the case of a proceeding to determine successors to rates or terms that expire on a specified date, in no event later than 15 days before the expiration of the then current statutory rates and terms.

(2) Rehearings.—

(A) In general.—The Copyright Royalty Judges may, in exceptional cases, upon motion of a participant in a proceeding under subsection (b)(2), order a rehearing, after the determination in the proceeding is issued under paragraph (1), on such matters as the Copyright Royalty Judges determine to be appropriate.

(B) Timing for filing motion.—Any motion for a rehearing under subparagraph (A) may only be filed within 15 days after the date on which the Copyright Royalty Judges deliver to the participants in the proceeding their initial determination.

(C) Participation by opposing party not required.— In any case in which a rehearing is ordered, any opposing party shall not be required to participate in the rehearing, except that nonparticipation may give rise to the limitations with respect to judicial review provided for in subsection (d)(1).

(D) No negative inference.—No negative inference shall be drawn from lack of participation in a rehearing.

(E) Continuity of rates and terms.—

(i) If the decision of the Copyright Royalty Judges on any motion for a rehearing is not rendered before the expiration of the statutory rates and terms that were previously in effect, in the case of a proceeding to determine successors to rates and terms that expire on a specified date, then—

(I) the initial determination of the Copyright Royalty Judges that is the subject of the rehearing motion shall be effective as of the day following the date on which the rates and terms that were previously in effect expire; and

(II) in the case of a proceeding under section 114(f)(1)(C) or 114(f)(2)(C), royalty rates and terms shall, for purposes of section 114(f)(4)(B), be deemed to have been set at those rates and terms contained in the initial determination of the Copyright Royalty Judges that is the subject of the rehearing motion, as of the date of that determination.

(ii) The pendency of a motion for a rehearing under this paragraph shall not relieve persons obligated to make royalty payments who would be affected by the determination on that motion from providing the statements of account and any reports of use, to the extent required, and paying the royalties required under the relevant determination or regulations.

(iii) Notwithstanding clause (ii), whenever royalties described in clause (ii) are paid to a person other than the Copyright Office, the entity designated by the Copyright

Royalty Judges to which such royalties are paid by the copyright user (and any successor thereto) shall, within 60 days after the motion for rehearing is resolved or, if the motion is granted, within 60 days after the rehearing is concluded, return any excess amounts previously paid to the extent necessary to comply with the final determination of royalty rates by the Copyright Royalty Judges. Any underpayment of royalties resulting from a rehearing shall be paid within the same period.

(3) Contents of determination.—A determination of the Copyright Royalty Judges shall be supported by the written record and shall set forth the findings of fact relied on by the Copyright Royalty Judges. Among other terms adopted in a determination, the Copyright Royalty Judges may specify notice and recordkeeping requirements of users of the copyrights at issue that apply in lieu of those that would otherwise apply under regulations.

(4) Continuing jurisdiction.—The Copyright Royalty Judges may, issue an amendment to a written determination to correct any technical or clerical errors in the determination or to modify the terms, but not the rates, of royalty payments in response to unforeseen circumstances that would frustrate the proper implementation of such determination. Such amendment shall be set forth in a written addendum to the determination that shall be distributed to the participants of the proceeding and shall be published in the Federal Register.

(5) Protective order.—The Copyright Royalty Judges may issue such orders as may be appropriate to protect confidential information, including orders excluding confidential information from the record of the determination that is published or made available to the public, except that any terms or rates of royalty payments or distributions may not be excluded.

(6) Publication of determination.—By no later than the end of the 60–day period provided in section 802(f)(1)(D), the Librarian of Congress shall cause the determination, and any corrections thereto, to be published in the Federal Register. The Librarian of Congress shall also publicize the determination and corrections in such other manner as the Librarian considers appropriate, including, but not limited to, publication on the Internet. The Librarian of Congress shall also make the determination, corrections, and the accompanying record available for public inspection and copying.

(7) Late payment.—A determination of the Copyright Royalty Judges may include terms with respect to late payment, but in no way shall such terms prevent the copyright holder from asserting other rights or remedies provided under this title.

(d) Judicial Review.—

(1) Appeal.—Any determination of the Copyright Royalty Judges under subsection (c) may, within 30 days after the publication of the determination in the Federal Register, be appealed, to the United States Court of Appeals for the District of Columbia Circuit, by any aggrieved participant in the proceeding under subsection (b)(2) who fully participated in the proceeding and who would be bound by the determination. Any participant that did not participate in a rehearing may not raise any issue that was the subject of that rehearing at any stage of judicial review of the hearing determination. If no appeal is brought within that 30–day period, the determination of the Copyright Royalty Judges shall be final, and the royalty fee or determination with respect to the distribution of fees, as the case may be, shall take effect as set forth in paragraph (2).

(2) Effect of rates.—

(A) Expiration on specified date.—When this title provides that the royalty rates and terms that were previously in effect are to expire on a specified date, any adjustment or determination by the Copyright Royalty Judges of successor rates and terms for an ensuing statutory license period shall be effective as of the day following the date of expiration of the rates and terms that were previously in effect, even if the determination of the Copyright Royalty Judges is rendered on a later date. A licensee shall be obligated to continue making payments under the rates and terms previously in effect until such time as rates and terms for the successor period are established. Whenever royalties pursuant to this section are paid to a person other than the Copyright Office, the entity designated by the Copyright Royalty Judges to which such royalties are paid by the copyright user (and any successor thereto) shall, within 60 days after the final determination of the Copyright Royalty Judges establishing rates and terms for a successor period or the exhaustion of all rehearings or appeals of such determination, if any, return any excess amounts previously paid to the extent necessary to comply with the final determination of royalty rates. Any underpayment of royalties by a copyright user shall be paid to the entity designated by the Copyright Royalty Judges within the same period.

(B) Other cases.—In cases where rates and terms have not, prior to the inception of an activity, been established for that particular activity under the relevant license, such rates and terms shall be retroactive to the inception of activity under the relevant license covered by such rates and terms. In other cases where rates and terms do not expire on a specified date, successor rates and terms shall take effect on the first day of the second month that begins after the publication of the determination of the Copyright Royalty Judges in the Federal Register, except as otherwise provided in this title, or by the Copyright Royalty Judges, or as agreed by the participants in a proceeding that would be bound by the rates and terms. Except as otherwise provided in this title, the rates and terms, to the extent applicable, shall remain in effect until such successor rates and terms become effective.

(C) Obligation to make payments.—

(i) The pendency of an appeal under this subsection shall not relieve persons obligated to make royalty payments under section 111, 112, 114, 115, 116, 118, 119, or 1003, who would be affected by the determination on appeal, from—

(I) providing the applicable statements of account and report of use; and

(II) paying the royalties required under the relevant determination or regulations.

(ii) Notwithstanding clause (i), whenever royalties described in clause (i) are paid to a person other than the Copyright Office, the entity designated by the Copyright Royalty Judges to which such royalties are paid by the copyright user (and any successor thereto) shall, within 60 days after the final resolution of the appeal, return any excess amounts previously paid (and interest thereon, if ordered pursuant to paragraph (3)) to the extent necessary to comply with the final determination of royalty rates on appeal. Any underpayment of royalties resulting from an appeal (and interest thereon, if ordered pursuant to paragraph (3)) shall be paid within the same period.

(3) Jurisdiction of court.—Section 706 of title 5 shall apply with respect to review by the court of appeals under this subsection. If the court modifies or vacates a determination of the Copyright Royalty Judges, the court may enter its own determination with respect to the amount or distribution of royalty fees and costs, and order the repayment of any excess fees, the payment of any underpaid fees, and the payment of interest pertaining respectively thereto, in accordance with its final judgment. The court may also vacate the determination of the Copyright Royalty Judges and remand the case to the Copyright Royalty Judges for further proceedings in accordance with subsection (a).

(e) Administrative matters.—

(1) Deduction of costs of Library of Congress and Copyright Office from filing fees.—

(A) Deduction from filing fees.—The Librarian of Congress may, to the extent not otherwise provided under this title, deduct from the filing fees collected under subsection (b) for a particular proceeding under this chapter the reasonable costs incurred by the Librarian of Congress, the Copyright Office, and the Copyright Royalty Judges in conducting that proceeding, other than the salaries of the Copyright Royalty Judges and the 3 staff members appointed under section 802(b).

(B) Authorization of appropriations.—There are authorized to be appropriated such sums as may be necessary to pay the costs incurred under this chapter not covered by the filing fees collected under subsection (b). All funds made available pursuant to this subparagraph shall remain available until expended.

(2) Positions required for administration of compulsory licensing.—Section 307 of the Legislative Branch Appropriations Act, 1994, shall not apply to employee positions in the Library of

Congress that are required to be filled in order to carry out section 111, 112, 114, 115, 116, 118, or 119 or chapter 10.

Sec. 804.   Institution of Proceedings

(a) Filing of petition.—With respect to proceedings referred to in paragraphs (1) and (2) of section 801(b) concerning the determination or adjustment of royalty rates as provided in sections 111, 112, 114, 115, 116, 118, 119, and 1004, during the calendar years specified in the schedule set forth in subsection (b), any owner or user of a copyrighted work whose royalty rates are specified by this title, or are established under this chapter before or after the enactment of the Copyright Royalty and Distribution Reform Act of 2004, may file a petition with the Copyright Royalty Judges declaring that the petitioner requests a determination or adjustment of the rate. The Copyright Royalty Judges shall make a determination as to whether the petitioner has such a significant interest in the royalty rate in which a determination or adjustment is requested. If the Copyright Royalty Judges determine that the petitioner has such a significant interest, the Copyright Royalty Judges shall cause notice of this determination, with the reasons for such determination, to be published in the Federal Register, together with the notice of commencement of proceedings under this chapter. With respect to proceedings under paragraph (1) of section 801(b) concerning the determination or adjustment of royalty rates as provided in sections 112 and 114, during the calendar years specified in the schedule set forth in subsection (b), the Copyright Royalty Judges shall cause notice of commencement of proceedings under this chapter to be published in the Federal Register as provided in section 803(b)(1)(A).

(b) Timing of proceedings.—

(1) Section 111 proceedings.—

(A) A petition described in subsection (a) to initiate proceedings under section 801(b)(2) concerning the adjustment of royalty rates under section 111 to which subparagraph (A) or (D) of section 801(b)(2) applies may be filed during the year 2015 and in each subsequent fifth calendar year.

(B) In order to initiate proceedings under section 801(b)(2) concerning the adjustment of royalty rates under section 111 to which subparagraph (B) or (C) of section 801(b)(2) applies, within 12 months after an event described in either of those subsections, any owner or user of a copyrighted work whose royalty rates are specified by section 111, or by a rate established under this chapter before or after the enactment of the Copyright Royalty and Distribution Reform Act of 2004, may file a petition with the Copyright Royalty Judges declaring that the petitioner requests an adjustment of the rate. The Copyright Royalty Judges shall then proceed as set forth in subsection (a) of this section. Any change in royalty rates made under this chapter pursuant to this subparagraph may be reconsidered in the year 2015, and each fifth calendar year thereafter, in accordance with the provisions in section 801(b)(2)(B) or (C), as the case may be. A petition for adjustment of rates established by section 111(d)(1)(B) as a result of a change in the rules and regulations of the Federal Communications Commission shall set forth the change on which the petition is based.

(C) Any adjustment of royalty rates under section 111 shall take effect as of the first accounting period commencing after the publication of the determination of the Copyright Royalty Judges in the Federal Register, or on such other date as is specified in that determination.

(2) Certain section 112 proceedings.—Proceedings under this chapter shall be commenced in the year 2007 to determine reasonable terms and rates of royalty payments for the activities described in section 112(e)(1) relating to the limitation on exclusive rights specified by section 114(d)(1)(C)(iv), to become effective on January 1, 2009. Such proceedings shall be repeated in each subsequent fifth calendar year.

(3) Section 114 and corresponding 112 proceedings.—

(A) For eligible nonsubscription services and new subscription services. Proceedings under this chapter shall be commenced as soon as practicable after the date of enactment of the Copyright Royalty and Distribution Reform Act of 2004 to determine reasonable terms and rates of royalty payments under sections 114 and 112 for the activities of eligible nonsubscription transmission services and new subscription services, to be effective for the period beginning on January 1, 2006, and ending on December 31, 2010. Such proceedings shall next be commenced in January 2009 to determine reasonable terms and rates of royalty payments, to become effective on January 1, 2011. Thereafter, such proceedings shall be repeated in each subsequent fifth calendar year.

(B) For preexisting subscription and satellite digital audio radio services. Proceedings under this chapter shall be commenced in January 2006 to determine reasonable terms and rates of royalty payments under sections 114 and 112 for the activities of preexisting subscription services, to be effective during the period beginning on January 1, 2008, and ending on December 31, 2012, and preexisting satellite digital audio radio services, to be effective during the period beginning on January 1, 2007, and ending on December 31, 2012. Such proceedings shall next be commenced in 2011 to determine reasonable terms and rates of royalty payments, to become effective on January 1, 2013. Thereafter, such proceedings shall be repeated in each subsequent fifth calendar year.

(C)(i) Notwithstanding any other provision of this chapter, this subparagraph shall govern proceedings commenced pursuant to section 114(f)(1)(C) and 114(f)(2)(C) concerning new types of services.

(ii) Not later than 30 days after a petition to determine rates and terms for a new type of service is filed by any copyright owner of sound recordings, or such new type of service, indicating that such new type of service is or is about to become operational, the Copyright Royalty Judges shall issue a notice for a proceeding to determine rates and terms for such service.

(iii) The proceeding shall follow the schedule set forth in subsections (b), (c), and (d) of section 803, except that—

(I) the determination shall be issued by not later than 24 months after the publication of the notice under clause (ii); and

(II) the decision shall take effect as provided in subsections (c)(2) and (d)(2) of section 803 and section 114(f)(4)(B)(ii) and (C).

(iv) The rates and terms shall remain in effect for the period set forth in section 114(f)(1)(C) or 114(f)(2)(C), as the case may be.

(4) Section 115 proceedings.—A petition described in subsection (a) to initiate proceedings under section 801(b)(1) concerning the adjustment or determination of royalty rates as provided in section 115 may be filed in the year 2006 and in each subsequent fifth calendar year, or at such other times as the parties have agreed under section 115(c)(3)(B) and (C).

(5) Section 116 proceedings.—

(A) A petition described in subsection (a) to initiate proceedings under section 801(b) concerning the determination of royalty rates and terms as provided in section 116 may be filed at any time within 1 year after negotiated licenses authorized by section 116 are terminated or expire and are not replaced by subsequent agreements.

(B) If a negotiated license authorized by section 116 is terminated or expires and is not replaced by another such license agreement which provides permission to use a quantity of musical works not substantially smaller than the quantity of such works performed on coin-operated phonorecord players during the 1–year period ending March 1, 1989, the Copyright Royalty Judges shall, upon petition filed under paragraph (1) within 1 year after such termination or expiration, commence a proceeding to promptly establish an interim royalty rate or rates for the public performance by means of a coin-operated phonorecord player of nondramatic musical works embodied in phonorecords which had been subject to the terminated or expired negotiated license agreement. Such rate or rates shall be the same as the last such rate or rates and shall remain in force until the conclusion of proceedings by the Copyright Royalty Judges, in accordance with section 803, to adjust the royalty rates applicable to such works, or until superseded by a new negotiated license agreement, as provided in section 116(b).

(6) Section 118 proceedings.—A petition described in subsection (a) to initiate proceedings under section 801(b)(1) concerning the determination of reasonable terms and rates of royalty payments as provided in section 118 may be filed in the year 2006 and in each subsequent fifth calendar year.

(7) Section 1004 proceedings.—A petition described in subsection (a) to initiate proceedings under section 801(b)(1) concerning the adjustment of reasonable royalty rates under section 1004 may be filed as provided in section 1004(a)(3).

(8) Proceedings concerning distribution of royalty fees.— With respect to proceedings under section 801(b)(3) concerning the distribution of royalty fees in certain circumstances under section 111, 119, or 1007, the Copyright Royalty Judges shall, upon a determination that a controversy exists concerning such distribution, cause to be published in the Federal Register notice of commencement of proceedings under this chapter.

Sec. 805.   General Rule for Voluntarily Negotiated Agreements

Any rates or terms under this title that—

(1) are agreed to by participants to a proceeding under section 803(b)(3),

(2) are adopted by the Copyright Royalty Judges as part of a determination under this chapter, and

(3) are in effect for a period shorter than would otherwise apply under a determination pursuant to this chapter,

shall remain in effect for such period of time as would otherwise apply under such determination, except that the Copyright Royalty Judges shall adjust the rates pursuant to the voluntary negotiations to reflect national monetary inflation during the additional period the rates remain in effect.

CHAPTER 9.—PROTECTION OF SEMICONDUCTOR CHIP PRODUCTS

(Pub.L. 98–620, 98 Stat. 3347 (1984)).

Sec.

Sec. 901.   Definitions

(a) As used in this chapter—

(1) a "semiconductor chip product" is the final or intermediate form of any product—

(A) having two or more layers of metallic, insulating, or semiconductor material, deposited or otherwise placed on, or etched away or otherwise removed from, a piece of semiconductor material in accordance with a predetermined pattern; and

(B) intended to perform electronic circuitry functions;

(2) a "mask work" is a series of related images, however fixed or encoded—

(A) having or representing the predetermined, three-dimensional pattern of metallic, insulating, or semiconductor material present or removed from the layers of a semiconductor chip product; and

(B) in which series the relation of the images to one another is that each image has the pattern of the surface of one form of the semiconductor chip product;

(3) a mask work is "fixed" in a semiconductor chip product when its embodiment in the product is sufficiently permanent or stable to permit the mask work to be perceived or reproduced from the product for a period of more than transitory duration;

(4) to "distribute" means to sell, or to lease, bail, or otherwise transfer, or to offer to sell, lease, bail, or otherwise transfer;

(5) to "commercially exploit" a mask work is to distribute to the public for commercial purposes a semiconductor chip product embodying the mask work; except that such term includes an offer to sell or transfer a semiconductor chip product only when the offer is in writing and occurs after the mask work is fixed in the semiconductor chip product;

(6) the "owner" of a mask work is the person who created the mask work, the legal representative of that person if that person is deceased or under a legal incapacity, or a party to whom all the rights under this chapter of such person or representative are transferred in accordance with section 903(b); except that, in the case of a work made within the scope of a person's employment, the owner is the employer for whom the person created the mask work or a party to whom all the rights under this chapter of the employer are transferred in accordance with section 903(b);

(7) an "innocent purchaser" is a person who purchases a semiconductor chip product in good faith and without having notice of protection with respect to the semiconductor chip product;

(8) having "notice of protection" means having actual knowledge that, or reasonable grounds to believe that, a mask work is protected under this chapter; and

(9) an "infringing semiconductor chip product" is a semiconductor chip product which is made, imported, or distributed in violation of the exclusive rights of the owner of a mask work under this chapter.

(b) For purposes of this chapter, the distribution or importation of a product incorporating a semiconductor chip product as a part thereof is a distribution or importation of that semiconductor chip product.

Sec. 902.   Subject Matter of Protection

(a)(1) Subject to the provisions of subsection (b), a mask work fixed in a semiconductor chip product, by or under the authority of the owner of the mask work, is eligible for protection under this chapter if—

(A) on the date on which the mask work is registered under section 908, or is first commercially exploited anywhere in the world, whichever occurs first, the owner of the mask work is (i) a national or domiciliary of the United States, (ii) a national, domiciliary, or sovereign authority of a foreign nation that is a party to a treaty affording protection to mask works to which the United States is also a party, or (iii) a stateless person, wherever that person may be domiciled;

(B) the mask work is first commercially exploited in the United States; or

(C) the mask work comes within the scope of a Presidential proclamation issued under paragraph (2).

(2) Whenever the President finds that a foreign nation extends, to mask works of owners who are nationals or domiciliaries of the United States protection (A) on substantially the same basis as that on which the foreign nation extends protection to mask works of its own nationals and domiciliaries and mask works first commercially exploited in that nation, or (B) on substantially the same basis as provided in this chapter, the President may by proclamation extend protection under this chapter to mask works (i) of owners who are, on the date on which the mask works are registered under section 908, or the date on which the mask works are first commercially exploited anywhere in the world, whichever occurs first, nationals, domiciliaries, or sovereign authorities of that nation, or (ii) which are first commercially exploited in that nation. The President may revise, suspend, or revoke any such proclamation or impose any conditions or limitations on protection extended under any such proclamation.

(b) Protection under this chapter shall not be available for a mask work that—

(1) is not original; or

(2) consists of designs that are staple, commonplace, or familiar in the semiconductor industry, or variations of such designs, combined in a way that, considered as a whole, is not original.

(c) In no case does protection under this chapter for a mask work extend to any idea, procedure, process, system, method of operation, concept, principle, or discovery, regardless of the form in which it is described, explained, illustrated, or embodied in such work.

Sec. 903.   Ownership, Transfer, Licensing, and Recordation

(a) The exclusive rights in a mask work subject to protection under this chapter belong to the owner of the mask work.

(b) The owner of the exclusive rights in a mask work may transfer all of those rights, or license all or less than all of those rights, by any written instrument signed by such owner or a duly authorized agent of the owner. Such rights may be transferred or licensed by operation of law, may be bequeathed by will, and may pass as personal property by the applicable laws of intestate succession.

(c)(1) Any document pertaining to a mask work may be recorded in the Copyright Office if the document filed for recordation bears the actual signature of the person who executed it, or if it is accompanied by a sworn or official certification that it is a true copy of the original, signed document. The Register of Copyrights shall, upon receipt of the document and the fee specified pursuant to section 908(d), record the document and return it with a certificate of recordation. The recordation of any transfer or license under this paragraph gives all persons constructive notice of the facts stated in the recorded document concerning the transfer or license.

(2) In any case in which conflicting transfers of the exclusive rights in a mask work are made, the transfer first executed shall be void as against a subsequent transfer which is made for a valuable consideration and without notice of the first transfer, unless the first transfer is recorded in accordance with paragraph (1) within three months after the date on which it is executed, but in no case later than the day before the date of such subsequent transfer.

(d) Mask works prepared by an officer or employee of the United States Government as part of that person's official duties are not protected under this chapter, but the United States Government is not precluded from receiving and holding exclusive rights in mask works transferred to the Government under subsection (b).

Sec. 904.   Duration of Protection

(a) The protection provided for a mask work under this chapter shall commence on the date on which the mask work is registered under section 908, or the date on which the mask work is first commercially exploited anywhere in the world, whichever occurs first.

(b) Subject to subsection (c) and the provisions of this chapter, the protection provided under this chapter to a mask work shall end ten years after the date on which such protection commences under subsection (a).

(c) All terms of protection provided in this section shall run to the end of the calendar year in which they would otherwise expire.

Sec. 905.   Exclusive Rights in Mask Works

The owner of a mask work provided protection under this chapter has the exclusive rights to do and to authorize any of the following:

(1) to reproduce the mask work by optical, electronic, or any other means;

(2) to import or distribute a semiconductor chip product in which the mask work is embodied; and

(3) to induce or knowingly to cause another person to do any of the acts described in paragraphs (1) and (2).

Sec. 906.   Limitation   on   Exclusive   Rights: Reverse Engineering; First Sale

(a) Notwithstanding the provisions of section 905, it is not an infringement of the exclusive rights of the owner of a mask work for—

(1) a person to reproduce the mask work solely for the purpose of teaching, analyzing, or evaluating the concepts or techniques embodied in the mask work or the circuitry, logic flow, or organization of components used in the mask work; or

(2) a person who performs the analysis or evaluation described in paragraph (1) to incorporate the results of such conduct in an original mask work which is made to be distributed.

(b) Notwithstanding the provisions of section 905(2), the owner of a particular semiconductor chip product made by the owner of the mask work, or by any person authorized by the owner of the mask work, may import, distribute, or otherwise dispose of or use, but not reproduce, that particular semiconductor chip product without the authority of the owner of the mask work.

Sec. 907.   Limitation   on   Exclusive   Rights: Innocent Infringement

(a) Notwithstanding any other provision of this chapter, an innocent purchaser of an infringing semiconductor chip product—

(1) shall incur no liability under this chapter with respect to the importation or distribution of units of the infringing semiconductor chip product that occurs before the innocent purchaser has notice of protection with respect to the mask work embodied in the semiconductor chip product; and

(2) shall be liable only for a reasonable royalty on each unit of the infringing semiconductor chip product that the innocent purchaser imports or distributes after having notice of protection with respect to the mask work embodied in the semiconductor chip product.

(b) The amount of the royalty referred to in subsection (a)(2) shall be determined by the court in a civil action for infringement unless the parties resolve the issue by voluntary negotiation, mediation, or binding arbitration.

(c) The immunity of an innocent purchaser from liability referred to in subsection (a)(1) and the limitation of remedies with respect to an innocent purchaser referred to in subsection (a)(2) shall extend to any person who directly or indirectly purchases an infringing semiconductor chip product from an innocent purchaser.

(d) The provisions of subsections (a), (b), and (c) apply only with respect to those units of an infringing semiconductor chip product that an innocent purchaser purchased before having notice of protection with respect to the mask work embodied in the semiconductor chip product.

Sec. 908.   Registration of Claims of Protection

(a) The owner of a mask work may apply to the Register of Copyrights for registration of a claim of protection in a mask work. Protection of a mask work under this chapter shall terminate if application for registration of a claim of protection in the mask work is not made as provided in this chapter within two years after the date on which the mask work is first commercially exploited anywhere in the world.

(b) The Register of Copyrights shall be responsible for all administrative functions and duties under this chapter. Except for section 708, the provisions of chapter 7 of this title relating to the general responsibilities, organization, regulatory authority, actions, records, and publications of the Copyright Office shall apply to this chapter, except that the Register of Copyrights may make such changes as may be necessary in applying those provisions to this chapter.

(c) The application for registration of a mask work shall be made on a form prescribed by the Register of Copyrights. Such form may require any information regarded by the Register as bearing upon the preparation or identification of the mask work, the existence or duration of protection of the mask work under this chapter, or ownership of the mask work. The application shall be accompanied by the fee set pursuant to subsection (d) and the identifying material specified pursuant to such subsection.

(d) The Register of Copyrights shall by regulation set reasonable fees for the filing of applications to register claims of protection in mask works under this chapter, and for other services relating to the administration of this chapter or the rights under this chapter, taking into consideration the cost of providing those services, the benefits of a public record, and statutory fee schedules under this title. The Register shall also specify the identifying material to be deposited in connection with the claim for registration.

(e) If the Register of Copyrights, after examining an application for registration, determines, in accordance with the provisions of this chapter, that the application relates to a mask work which is entitled to protection under this chapter, then the Register shall register the claim of protection and issue to the applicant a certificate of registration of the claim of protection under the seal of the Copyright Office. The effective date of registration of a claim of protection shall be the date on which an application, deposit of identifying material, and fee, which are determined by the Register of Copyrights or by a court of competent jurisdiction to be acceptable for registration of the claim, have all been received in the Copyright Office.

(f) In any action for infringement under this chapter, the certificate of registration of a mask work shall constitute prima facie evidence (1) of the facts stated in the certificate, and (2) that the applicant issued the certificate has met the requirements of this chapter, and the regulations issued under this chapter, with respect to the registration of claims.

(g) Any applicant for registration under this section who is dissatisfied with the refusal of the Register of Copyrights to issue a certificate of registration under this section may seek judicial review of that refusal by bringing an action for such review in an appropriate United States district court not later than sixty days after the refusal. The provisions of chapter 7 of title 5 shall apply to such judicial review. The failure of the Register of Copyrights to issue a certificate of registration within four months after an application for registration is filed shall be deemed to be a refusal to issue a certificate of registration for purposes of this subsection and section 910(b)(2), except that, upon a showing of good cause, the district court may shorten such four-month period.

Sec. 909.   Mask Work Notice

(a) The owner of a mask work provided protection under this chapter may affix notice to the mask work, and to masks and semiconductor chip products embodying the mask work, in such manner and location as to give reasonable notice of such protection. The Register of Copyrights shall prescribe by regulation, as examples, specific methods of affixation and positions of notice for purposes of this section, but these specifications shall not be considered exhaustive. The affixation of such notice is not a condition of protection under this chapter, but shall constitute prima facie evidence of notice of protection.

(b) the notice referred to in subsection (a) shall consist of—

(1) the words "mask work", the symbol *M*, or the symbol M (the letter M in a circle); and

(2) the name of the owner or owners of the mask work or an abbreviation by which the name is recognized or is generally known.

Sec. 910.   Enforcement of Exclusive Rights

(a) Except as otherwise provided in this chapter, any person who violates any of the exclusive rights of the owner of a mask work under this chapter, by conduct in or affecting commerce, shall be liable as an infringer of such rights. As used in this subsection, the term "any person" includes any State, any instrumentality of a State, and any officer or employee of a State or instrumentality of a State acting in his or her official capacity. Any State, and any such instrumentality, officer, or employee, shall be subject to the provisions of this chapter in the same manner and to the same extent as any nongovernmental entity.

(b)(1) The owner of a mask work protected under this chapter, or the exclusive licensee of all rights under this chapter with respect to the mask work, shall, after a certificate of registration of a claim of protection in that mask work has been issued under section 908, be entitled to institute a civil action for any infringement with respect to the mask work which is committed after the commencement of protection of the mask work under section 904(a).

(2) In any case in which an application for registration of a claim of protection in a mask work and the required deposit of identifying material and fee have been received in the Copyright Office in proper form and registration of the mask work has been refused, the applicant is entitled to institute a civil action for infringement under this chapter with respect to the mask work if notice of the action, together with a copy of the complaint, is served on the Register of Copyrights, in accordance with the Federal Rules of Civil Procedure. The Register may, at his or her option, become a party to the action with respect to the issue of whether the claim of protection is eligible for registration by entering an appearance within sixty days after such service, but the failure of the Register to become a party to the action shall not deprive the court of jurisdiction to determine that issue.

(c)(1) The Secretary of the Treasury and the United States Postal Service shall separately or jointly issue regulations for the enforcement of the rights set forth in section 905 with respect to importation. These regulations may require, as a condition for the exclusion of articles from the United States, that the person seeking exclusion take any one or more of the following actions:

(A) Obtain a court order enjoining, or an order of the International Trade Commission under section 337 of the Tariff Act of 1930 excluding, importation of the articles.

(B) Furnish proof that the mask work involved is protected under this chapter and that the importation of the articles would infringe the rights in the mask work under this chapter.

(C) Post a surety bond for any injury that may result if the detention or exclusion of the articles proves to be unjustified.

(2) Articles imported in violation of the rights set forth in section 905 are subject to seizure and forfeiture in the same manner as property imported in violation of the customs laws. Any such forfeited articles shall be destroyed as directed by the Secretary of the Treasury or the court, as the case may be, except that the articles may be returned to the country of export whenever it is shown to the satisfaction of the Secretary of the Treasury that the importer had no reasonable grounds for believing that his or her acts constituted a violation of the law.

Sec. 911.   Civil Actions

(a) Any court having jurisdiction of a civil action arising under this chapter may grant temporary restraining orders, preliminary injunctions, and permanent injunctions on such terms as the court may deem reasonable to prevent or restrain infringement of the exclusive rights in a mask work under this chapter.

(b) Upon finding an infringer liable, to a person entitled under section 910(b)(1) to institute a civil action, for an infringement of any exclusive right under this chapter, the court shall award such person actual damages suffered by the person as a result of the infringement. The court shall also award such person the infringer's profits that are attributable to the infringement and are not taken into account in computing the award of actual damages. In establishing the infringer's profits, such person is required to present proof only of the infringer's gross revenue, and the infringer is required to prove his or her deductible expenses and the elements of profit attributable to factors other than the mask work.

(c) At any time before final judgment is rendered, a person entitled to institute a civil action for infringement may elect, instead of actual damages and profits as provided by subsection (b), an award of statutory damages for all infringements involved in the action, with respect to any one mask work for which any one infringer is liable individually, or for which any two or more infringers are liable jointly and severally, in an amount not more than $250,000 as the court considers just.

(d) An action for infringement under this chapter shall be barred unless the action is commenced within three years after the claim accrues.

(e)(1) At any time while an action for infringement of the exclusive rights in a mask work under this chapter is pending, the court may order the impounding, on such terms as it may deem reasonable, of all semiconductor chip products, and any drawings, tapes, masks, or other products by means of which such products may be reproduced, that are claimed to have been made, imported, or used in violation of those exclusive rights. Insofar as practicable, applications for orders under this paragraph shall be heard and determined in the same manner as an application for a temporary restraining order or preliminary injunction.

(2) As part of a final judgment or decree, the court may order the destruction or other disposition of any infringing semiconductor chip products, and any masks, tapes, or other articles by means of which such products may be reproduced.

(f) In any civil action arising under this chapter, the court in its discretion may allow the recovery of full costs, including reasonable attorneys' fees, to the prevailing party.

(g)(1) Any State, any instrumentality of a State, and any officer or employee of a State or instrumentality of a State acting in his or her official capacity, shall not be immune, under the Eleventh Amendment of the Constitution of the United States or under any other doctrine of sovereign immunity, from suit in Federal court by any person, including any governmental or nongovernmental entity, for a violation of any of the exclusive rights of the owner of a mask work under this chapter, or for any other violation under this chapter.

(2) In a suit described in paragraph (1) for a violation described in that paragraph, remedies (including remedies both at law and in equity) are available for the violation to the same extent as such remedies are available for such a violation in a suit against any public or private entity other than a State, instrumentality of a State, or officer or employee of a State acting in his or her official capacity. Such remedies include actual damages and profits under subsection (b), statutory damages under subsection (c), impounding and disposition of infringing articles under subsection (e), and costs and attorney's fees under subsection (f).

Sec. 912.   **Relation to Other Laws**

(a) Nothing in this chapter shall affect any right or remedy held by any person under chapters 1 through 8 or 10 of this title, or under title 35.

(b) Except as provided in section 908(b) of this title, references to "this title" or "title 17" in chapters 1 through 8 or 10 of this title shall be deemed not to apply to this chapter.

(c) The provisions of this chapter shall preempt the laws of any State to the extent those laws provide any rights or remedies with respect to a mask work which are equivalent to those rights or remedies provided by this chapter, except that such preemption shall be effective only with respect to actions filed on or after January 1, 1986.

(d) Notwithstanding subsection (c), nothing in this chapter shall detract from any rights of a mask work owner, whether under Federal law (exclusive of this chapter) or under the common law or the statutes of a State, heretofore or hereafter declared or enacted, with respect to any mask work first commercially exploited before July 1, 1983.

Sec. 913.   **Transitional Provisions**

(a) No application for registration under section 908 may be filed, and no civil action under section 910 or other enforcement proceeding under this chapter may be instituted, until sixty days after the date of the enactment of this chapter.

(b) No monetary relief under section 911 may be granted with respect to any conduct that occurred before the date of the enactment of this chapter, except as provided in subsection (d).

(c) Subject to subsection (a), the provisions of this chapter apply to all mask works that are first commercially exploited or are registered under this chapter, or both, on or after the date of the enactment of this chapter.

(d)(1) Subject to subsection (a), protection is available under this chapter to any mask work that was first commercially exploited on or after July 1, 1983, and before the date of the enactment of this chapter, if a claim of protection in the mask work is registered in the Copyright Office before July 1, 1985, under section 908.

(2) In the case of any mask work described in paragraph (1) that is provided protection under this chapter, infringing semiconductor chip product units manufactured before the date of the enactment of this chapter may, without liability under sections 910 and 911, be imported into or distributed in the United States, or both, until two years after the date of registration of the mask work under section 908, but only if the importer or distributor, as the case may be, first pays or offers to pay the reasonable royalty referred to in section 907(a)(2) to the mask work owner, on all such units imported or distributed, or both, after the date of the enactment of this chapter.

(3) In the event that a person imports or distributes infringing semiconductor chip product units described in paragraph (2) of this subsection without first paying or offering to pay the reasonable royalty specified in such paragraph, or if the person refuses or fails to make such payment, the mask work owner shall be entitled to the relief provided in sections 910 and 911.

Sec. 914.   International Transitional Provisions

(a) Notwithstanding the conditions set forth in subparagraphs (A) and (C) of section 902(a)(1) with respect to the availability of protection under this chapter to nationals, domiciliaries, and sovereign authorities of a foreign nation, the Secretary of Commerce may, upon the petition of any person, or upon the Secretary's own motion, issue an order extending protection under this chapter to such foreign nationals, domiciliaries, and sovereign authorities if the Secretary finds—

(1) that the foreign nation is making good faith efforts and reasonable progress toward—

(A) entering into a treaty described in section 902(a)(1)(A); or

(B) enacting or implementing legislation that would be in compliance with subparagraphs (A) or (B) of section 902(a)(2); and

(2) that the nationals, domiciliaries, and sovereign authorities of the foreign nation, and persons controlled by them, are not engaged in the misappropriation, or unauthorized distribution or commercial exploitation, of mask works; and

(3) that issuing the order would promote the purposes of this chapter and international comity with respect to the protection of mask works.

(b) While an order under subsection (a) is in effect with respect to a foreign nation, no application for registration of a claim for protection in a mask work under this chapter may be denied solely because the owner of the mask work is a national, domiciliary, or sovereign authority of that foreign nation, or solely because the mask work was first commercially exploited in that foreign nation.

(c) Any order issued by the Secretary of Commerce under subsection (a) shall be effective for such period as the Secretary designates in the order, except that no such order may be effective after the date on which the authority of the Secretary of Commerce terminates under subsection (e). The effective date of any such order shall also be designated in the order. In the case of an order issued upon the petition of a person, such effective date may be no earlier than the date on which the Secretary receives such petition.

(d)(1) Any order issued under this section shall terminate if—

(A) the Secretary of Commerce finds that any of the conditions set forth in paragraphs (1), (2), and (3) of subsection (a) no longer exist; or

(B) mask works of nationals, domiciliaries, and sovereign authorities of that foreign nation or mask works first commercially exploited in that foreign nation become eligible for protection under subparagraph (A) or (C) of section 902(a)(1).

(2) Upon the termination or expiration of an order issued under this section, registrations of claims of protection in mask works made pursuant to that order shall remain valid for the period specified in section 904.

(e) The authority of the Secretary of Commerce under this section shall commence on the date of the enactment of this chapter, and shall terminate on July 1, 1995.

(f)(1) The Secretary of Commerce shall promptly notify the Register of Copyrights and the Committees on the Judiciary of the Senate and the House of Representatives of the issuance or termination of any order under this section, together with a statement of the reasons for such action. The Secretary shall also publish such notification and statement of reasons in the Federal Register.

(2) Two years after the date of the enactment of this chapter, the Secretary of Commerce, in consultation with the Register of Copyrights, shall transmit to the Committees on the Judiciary of the Senate and the House of Representatives a report on the actions taken under this section and on the current status of international recognition of mask work protection. The report shall include such recommendations for modifications of the protection accorded under this chapter to mask works owned by nationals, domiciliaries, or sovereign authorities of foreign nations as the Secretary, in consultation with the Register of Copyrights, considers would promote the purposes of this chapter and international comity with respect to mask work protection. Not later than July 1, 1994, the Secretary of Commerce, in consultation with the

Register of Copyrights, shall transmit to the Committees on the Judiciary of the Senate and the House of Representatives a report updating the matters contained in the report transmitted under the preceding sentence.

CHAPTER 10.—DIGITAL AUDIO RECORDING DEVICES AND MEDIA

(Pub.L. 102–563, 106 Stat. 4237 (1992)).

Subchapter A—Definitions

Subchapter A—Definitions

Sec. 1001. Definitions

As used in this chapter, the following terms have the following meanings:

(1) A "digital audio copied recording" is a reproduction in a digital recording format of a digital musical recording, whether that reproduction is made directly from another digital musical recording or indirectly from a transmission.

(2) A "digital audio interface device" is any machine or device that is designed specifically to communicate digital audio information and related interface data to a digital audio recording device through a nonprofessional interface.

(3) A "digital audio recording device" is any machine or device of a type commonly distributed to individuals for use by individuals, whether or not included with or as part of some other machine or device, the digital recording function of which is designed or marketed for the primary purpose of, and that is capable of, making a digital audio copied recording for private use, except for—

(A) professional model products, and

(B) dictation machines, answering machines, and other audio recording equipment that is designed and marketed primarily for the creation of sound recordings resulting from the fixation of nonmusical sounds.

(4)(A) A "digital audio recording medium" is any material object in a form commonly distributed for use by individuals, that is primarily marketed or most commonly used by consumers for the purpose of making digital audio copied recordings by use of a digital audio recording device.

(B) Such term does not include any material object—

(i) that embodies a sound recording at the time it is first distributed by the importer or manufacturer; or

(ii) that is primarily marketed and most commonly used by consumers either for the purpose of making copies of motion pictures or other audiovisual works or for the purpose of making copies of nonmusical literary works, including computer programs or data bases.

(5)(A) A "digital musical recording" is a material object—

(i) in which are fixed, in a digital recording format, only sounds, and material, statements, or instructions incidental to those fixed sounds, if any, and

(ii) from which the sounds and material can be perceived, reproduced, or otherwise communicated, either directly or with the aid of a machine or device.

(B) A "digital musical recording" does not include a material object—

(i) in which the fixed sounds consist entirely of spoken word recordings, or

(ii) in which one or more computer programs are fixed, except that a digital musical recording may contain statements or instructions constituting the fixed sounds and incidental material, and statements or instructions to be used directly or indirectly in order to bring about the perception, reproduction, or communication of the fixed sounds and incidental material.

(C) For purposes of this paragraph—

(i) a "spoken word recording" is a sound recording in which are fixed only a series of spoken words, except that the spoken words may be accompanied by incidental musical or other sounds, and

(ii) the term "incidental" means related to and relatively minor by comparison.

(6) "Distribute" means to sell, lease, or assign a product to consumers in the United States, or to sell, lease, or assign a product in the United States for ultimate transfer to consumers in the United States.

(7) An "interested copyright party" is—

(A) the owner of the exclusive right under section 106(1) of this title to reproduce a sound recording of a musical work that has been embodied in a digital musical recording or analog musical recording lawfully made under this title that has been distributed;

(B) the legal or beneficial owner of, or the person that controls, the right to reproduce in a digital musical recording or analog musical recording a musical work that has been embodied in a digital musical recording or analog musical recording lawfully made under this title that has been distributed;

(C) a featured recording artist who performs on a sound recording that has been distributed; or

(D) any association or other organization—

(i) representing persons specified in subparagraph (A), (B), or (C), or

(ii) engaged in licensing rights in musical works to music users on behalf of writers and publishers.

(8) To "manufacture" means to produce or assemble a product in the United States. A "manufacturer" is a person who manufactures.

(9) A "music publisher" is a person that is authorized to license the reproduction of a particular musical work in a sound recording.

(10) A "professional model product" is an audio recording device that is designed, manufactured, marketed, and intended for use by recording professionals in the ordinary course of a lawful business, in accordance with such requirements as the Secretary of Commerce shall establish by regulation.

(11) The term "serial copying" means the duplication in a digital format of a copyrighted musical work or sound recording from a digital reproduction of a digital musical recording. The term "digital reproduction of a digital musical recording" does not include a digital musical recording as distributed, by authority of the copyright owner, for ultimate sale to consumers.

(12) The "transfer price" of a digital audio recording device or a digital audio recording medium—

(A) is, subject to subparagraph (B)—

(i) in the case of an imported product, the actual entered value at United States Customs (exclusive of any freight, insurance, and applicable duty), and

(ii) in the case of a domestic product, the manufacturer's transfer price (FOB the manufacturer, and exclusive of any direct sales taxes or excise taxes incurred in connection with the sale); and

(B) shall, in a case in which the transferor and transferee are related entities or within a single entity, not be less than a reasonable arms-length price under the principles of the regulations adopted pursuant to section 482 of the Internal Revenue Code of 1986, or any successor provision to such section.

(13) A "writer" is the composer or lyricist of a particular musical work.

Subchapter B—Copying Controls

Sec. 1002.   Incorporation of Copying Controls

(a) **Prohibition on Importation, Manufacture, and Distribution.**—No person shall import, manufacture, or distribute any digital audio recording device or digital audio interface device that does not conform to—

(1) the Serial Copy Management System;

(2) a system that has the same functional characteristics as the Serial Copy Management System and requires that copyright and generation status information be accurately sent, received, and acted upon between devices using the system's method of serial copying regulation and devices using the Serial Copy Management System; or

(3) any other system certified by the Secretary of Commerce as prohibiting unauthorized serial copying.

(b) Development of Verification Procedure.—The Secretary of Commerce shall establish a procedure to verify, upon the petition of an interested party, that a system meets the standards set forth in subsection (a)(2).

(c) Prohibition on Circumvention of the System.—No person shall import, manufacture, or distribute any device, or offer or perform any service, the primary purpose or effect of which is to avoid, bypass, remove, deactivate, or otherwise circumvent any program or circuit which implements, in whole or in part, a system described in subsection (a).

(d) Encoding of Information on Digital Musical Recordings.—

(1) Prohibition on encoding inaccurate information.—No person shall encode a digital musical recording of a sound recording with inaccurate information relating to the category code, copyright status, or generation status of the source material for the recording.

(2) Encoding of copyright status not required.—Nothing in this chapter requires any person engaged in the importation or manufacture of digital musical recordings to encode any such digital musical recording with respect to its copyright status.

(e) Information Accompanying Transmissions in Digital Format.—Any person who transmits or otherwise communicates to the public any sound recording in digital format is not required under this chapter to transmit or otherwise communicate the information relating to the copyright status of the sound recording. Any such person who does transmit or otherwise communicate such copyright status information shall transmit or communicate such information accurately.

Subchapter C—Royalty Payments

Sec. 1003.   Obligation to Make Royalty Payments

(a) Prohibition on Importation and Manufacture.—No person shall import into and distribute, or manufacture and distribute, any digital audio recording device or digital audio recording medium unless such person records the notice specified by this section and subsequently deposits the statements of account and applicable royalty payments for such device or medium specified in section 1004.

(b) Filing of Notice.—The importer or manufacturer of any digital audio recording device or digital audio recording medium, within a product category or utilizing a technology with respect to which such manufacturer or importer has not previously filed a notice under this subsection, shall file with the Register of Copyrights a notice with respect to such device or medium, in such form and content as the Register shall prescribe by regulation.

(c) Filing of Quarterly and Annual Statements of Account.—

(1) Generally.—Any importer or manufacturer that distributes any digital audio recording device or digital audio recording medium that it manufactured or imported shall file with the Register of Copyrights, in such form and content as the Register shall prescribe by regulation, such quarterly and annual statements of account with respect to such distribution as the Register shall prescribe by regulation.

(2) Certification, verification, and confidentiality.—Each such statement shall be certified as accurate by an authorized officer or principal of the importer or manufacturer. The Register shall issue regulations to provide for the verification and audit of such statements and to protect the confidentiality of the information contained in such statements. Such regulations shall provide for the disclosure, in confidence, of such statements to interested copyright parties.

(3) Royalty payments.—Each such statement shall be accompanied by the royalty payments specified in section 1004.

Sec. 1004.   Royalty Payments

(a) Digital Audio Recording Devices.—

(1) Amount of payment.—The royalty payment due under section 1003 for each digital audio recording device imported into and distributed in the United States, or manufactured and distributed in the United States, shall be 2 percent of the transfer price. Only the first person to manufacture and distribute or import and distribute such device shall be required to pay the royalty with respect to such device.

(2) Calculation for devices distributed with other devices.—With respect to a digital audio recording device first distributed in combination with one or more devices, either as a physically integrated unit or as separate components, the royalty payment shall be calculated as follows:

(A) If the digital audio recording device and such other devices are part of a physically integrated unit, the royalty payment shall be based on the transfer price of the unit, but shall be reduced by any royalty payment made on any digital audio recording device included within the unit that was not first distributed in combination with the unit.

(B) If the digital audio recording device is not part of a physically integrated unit and substantially similar devices have been distributed separately at any time during the preceding 4 calendar quarters, the royalty payment shall be based on the average transfer price of such devices during those 4 quarters.

(C) If the digital audio recording device is not part of a physically integrated unit and substantially similar devices have not been distributed separately at any time during the preceding 4 calendar quarters, the royalty payment shall be based on a constructed price reflecting the proportional value of such device to the combination as a whole.

(3) Limits on Royalties.—Notwithstanding paragraph (1) or (2), the amount of the royalty payment for each digital audio recording device shall not be less than $1 nor more than the royalty maximum. The royalty maximum shall be $8 per device, except that in the case of a physically integrated unit containing more than 1 digital audio recording device, the royalty maximum for such unit shall be $12. During the 6th year after the effective date of this chapter, and not more than once each year thereafter, any interested copyright party may petition the Copyright Royalty Judges to increase the royalty maximum and, if more than 20 percent of the royalty payments are at the relevant royalty maximum, the Copyright Royalty Judges shall prospectively increase such royalty maximum with the goal of having no more than 10 percent of such payments at the new royalty maximum; however the amount of any such increase as a percentage of the royalty maximum shall in no event exceed the percentage increase in the Consumer Price Index during the period under review.

(b) Digital Audio Recording Media.—The royalty payment due under section 1003 for each digital audio recording medium imported into and distributed in the United States, or manufactured and distributed in the United States, shall be 3 percent of the transfer price. Only the first person to manufacture and distribute or import and distribute such medium shall be required to pay the royalty with respect to such medium.

Sec. 1005. Deposit of Royalty Payments and Deduction of Expenses

The Register of Copyrights shall receive all royalty payments deposited under this chapter and, after deducting the reasonable costs incurred by the Copyright Office under this chapter, shall deposit the balance in the Treasury of the United States as offsetting receipts, in such manner as the Secretary of the Treasury directs. All funds held by the Secretary of the Treasury shall be invested in interest-bearing United States securities for later distribution with interest under section 1007. The Register may, in the Register's discretion, 4 years after the close of any calendar year, close out the royalty payments account for that calendar year, and may treat any funds remaining in such account and any subsequent deposits that would otherwise be attributable to that calendar year as attributable to the succeeding calendar year.

Sec. 1006. Entitlement to Royalty Payments

(a) Interested Copyright Parties.—The royalty payments deposited pursuant to section 1005 shall, in accordance with the procedures specified in section 1007, be distributed to any interested copyright party—

(1) whose musical work or sound recording has been—

(A) embodied in a digital musical recording or an analog musical recording lawfully made under this title that has been distributed, and

(B) distributed in the form of digital musical recordings or analog musical recordings or disseminated to the public in transmissions, during the period to which such payments pertain; and

(2) who has filed a claim under section 1007.

(b) Allocation of Royalty Payments to Groups.—The royalty payments shall be divided into 2 funds as follows:

(1) The sound recordings fund.—66⅔ percent of the royalty payments shall be allocated to the Sound Recordings Fund. 2 ⅝ percent of the royalty payments allocated to the Sound Recordings Fund shall be placed in an escrow account managed by an independent administrator jointly appointed by the interested copyright parties described in section 1001(7)(A) and the American Federation of Musicians (or any successor entity) to be distributed to nonfeatured musicians (whether or not members of the American Federation of Musicians or any successor entity) who have performed on sound recordings distributed in the United States. 1⅜ percent of the royalty payments allocated to the Sound Recordings Fund shall be placed in an escrow account managed by an independent administrator jointly appointed by the interested copyright parties described in section 1001(7)(A) and the American Federation of Television and Radio Artists (or any successor entity) to be distributed to nonfeatured vocalists (whether or not members of the American Federation of Television and Radio Artists or any successor entity) who have performed on sound recordings distributed in the United States. 40 percent of the remaining royalty payments in the Sound Recordings Fund shall be distributed to the interested copyright parties described in section 1001(7)(C), and 60 percent of such remaining royalty payments shall be distributed to the interested copyright parties described in section 1001(7)(A).

(2) The musical works fund.—

(A) 33⅓ percent of the royalty payments shall be allocated to the Musical Works Fund for distribution to interested copyright parties described in section 1001(7)(B).

(B)(i) Music publishers shall be entitled to 50 percent of the royalty payments allocated to the Musical Works Fund.

(ii) Writers shall be entitled to the other 50 percent of the royalty payments allocated to the Musical Works Fund.

(c) Allocation of Royalty Payments Within Groups.— If all interested copyright parties within a group specified in subsection (b) do not agree on a voluntary proposal for the distribution of the royalty payments within each group, the Copyright Royalty Judges shall, pursuant to the procedures specified under section 1007(c), allocate royalty payments under this section based on the extent to which, during the relevant period—

(1) for the Sound Recordings Fund, each sound recording was distributed in the form of digital musical recordings or analog musical recordings; and

(2) for the Musical Works Fund, each musical work was distributed in the form of digital musical recordings or analog musical recordings or disseminated to the public in transmissions.

Sec. 1007. Procedures for Distributing Royalty Payments

(a) Filing of Claims and Negotiations.—

(1) Filing of Claims.—During the first two months of each calendar year, every interested copyright party seeking to receive royalty payments to which such party is entitled under section 1006 shall file with the Copyright Royalty Judges a claim for payments collected during the preceding year in such form and manner as the Copyright Royalty Judges shall prescribe by regulation.

(2) Negotiations.—Notwithstanding any provision of the antitrust laws, for purposes of this section interested copyright parties within each group specified in section 1006(b) may agree among themselves to the proportionate division of royalty payments, may lump their claims together and file them jointly or as a single claim, or may designate a common agent, including any organization described in section 1001(7)(D), to negotiate or receive payment on their behalf; except that no agreement under this subsection may modify the allocation of royalties specified in section 1006(b).

(b) Distribution of Payments in the Absence of a Dispute.—After the period established for the filing of claims under subsection (a), in each year, the Copyright Royalty Judges shall determine whether there exists a controversy concerning the distribution of royalty payments under section 1006(c). If the Copyright Royalty Judges determine that no such controversy exists, the Copyright Royalty Judges shall, within 30 days after such determination, authorize the distribution of the royalty payments as set forth in the agreements regarding the distribution of royalty payments entered into pursuant to subsection (a). The Librarian of Congress shall, before such royalty payments are distributed, deduct the reasonable administrative cost incurred under this section.

(c) Resolution of Disputes.—If the Copyright Royalty Judges find the existence of a controversy, the Copyright Royalty Judges shall, pursuant to chapter 8 of this title, conduct a proceeding to determine the distribution of royalty payments. During the pendency of such a proceeding, the Copyright Royalty Judges shall withhold from distribution an amount sufficient to satisfy all claims with respect to which a controversy exists, but shall, to the extent feasible, authorize the distribution of any amounts that are not in controversy. The Librarian of Congress shall, before such royalty payments are distributed, deduct the reasonable administrative costs incurred under this section.

Subchapter D—Prohibition on Certain Infringement Actions, Remedies, and Arbitration

Sec. 1008. Prohibition on Certain Infringement Actions

No action may be brought under this title alleging infringement of copyright based on the manufacture, importation, or distribution of a digital audio recording device, a digital audio recording medium, an analog recording device, or an analog recording medium, or based on the noncommercial use by a consumer of such a device or medium for making digital musical recordings or analog musical recordings.

Sec. 1009.   Civil Remedies

(a) Civil Actions.—Any interested copyright party injured by a violation of section 1002 or 1003 may bring a civil action in an appropriate United States district court against any person for such violation.

(b) Other Civil Actions.—Any person injured by a violation of this chapter may bring a civil action in an appropriate United States district court for actual damages incurred as a result of such violation.

(c) Powers of the Court.—In an action brought under subsection (a), the court—

(1) may grant temporary and permanent injunctions on such terms as it deems reasonable to prevent or restrain such violation;

(2) in the case of a violation of section 1002, or in the case of an injury resulting from a failure to make royalty payments required by section 1003, shall award damages under subsection (d);

(3) in its discretion may allow the recovery of costs by or against any party other than the United States or an officer thereof; and

(4) in its discretion may award a reasonable attorney's fee to the prevailing party.

(d) Award of Damages.—

(1) Damages for section 1002 or 1003 violations.—

(A) Actual damages.—

(i) In an action brought under subsection (a), if the court finds that a violation of section 1002 or 1003 has occurred, the court shall award to the complaining party its actual damages if the complaining party elects such damages at any time before final judgment is entered.

(ii) In the case of section 1003, actual damages shall constitute the royalty payments that should have been paid under section 1004 and deposited under section 1005. In such a case, the court, in its discretion, may award an additional amount of not to exceed 50 percent of the actual damages.

(B) Statutory damages for section 1002 violations.—

(i) **Device.**—A complaining party may recover an award of statutory damages for each violation of section 1002(a) or (c) in the sum of not more than $2,500 per device involved in such violation or per device on which a service prohibited by section 1002(c) has been performed, as the court considers just.

(ii) **Digital musical recording.**—A complaining party may recover an award of statutory damages for each violation of section 1002(d) in the sum of not more than $25 per digital musical recording involved in such violation, as the court considers just.

(iii) **Transmission.**—A complaining party may recover an award of damages for each transmission or communication that violates section 1002(e) in the sum of not more than $10,000, as the court considers just.

(2) **Repeated violations.**—In any case in which the court finds that a person has violated section 1002 or 1003 within 3 years after a final judgment against that person for another such violation was entered, the court may increase the award of damages to not more than double the amounts that would otherwise be awarded under paragraph (1), as the court considers just.

(3) **Innocent violations of section 1002.**—The court in its discretion may reduce the total award of damages against a person violating section 1002 to a sum of not less than $250 in any case in which the court finds that the violator was not aware and had no reason to believe that its acts constituted a violation of section 1002.

(e) **Payment of Damages.**—Any award of damages under subsection (d) shall be deposited with the Register pursuant to section 1005 for distribution to interested copyright parties as though such funds were royalty payments made pursuant to section 1003.

(f) **Impounding of Articles.**—At any time while an action under subsection (a) is pending, the court may order the impounding, on such terms as it deems reasonable, of any digital audio recording device, digital musical recording, or device specified in section 1002(c) that is in the custody or control of the alleged violator and that the court has reasonable cause to believe does not comply with, or was involved in a violation of, section 1002.

(g) **Remedial Modification and Destruction of Articles.**—In an action brought under subsection (a), the court may, as part of a final judgment or decree finding a violation of section 1002, order the remedial modification or the destruction of any digital audio recording device, digital musical recording, or device specified in section 1002(c) that

(1) does not comply with, or was involved in a violation of, section 1002, and

(2) is in the custody or control of the violator or has been impounded under subsection (f).

Sec. 1010.   Determination of Certain Disputes

(a) **Scope of determination.**—Before the date of first distribution in the United States of a digital audio recording device or a digital audio interface device, any party manufacturing, importing, or distributing such device, and any interested copyright party may mutually agree to petition the Copyright Royalty Judges to determine whether such device is subject to section 1002, or the basis on which royalty payments for such device are to be made under section 1003.

(b) **Initiation of proceedings.**—The parties under subsection (a) shall file the petition with the Copyright Royalty Judges requesting the commencement of a proceeding. Within 2 weeks after receiving such a petition, the Chief Copyright Royalty Judge shall cause notice to be published in the Federal Register of the initiation of the proceeding.

(c) **Stay of judicial proceedings.**—Any civil action brought under section 1009 against a party to a proceeding under this section shall, on application of one of the parties to the proceeding, be stayed until completion of the proceeding.

 (d) Proceeding.—The Copyright Royalty Judges shall conduct a proceeding with respect to the matter concerned, in accordance with such procedures as the Copyright Royalty Judges may adopt. The Copyright Royalty Judges shall act on the basis of a fully documented written record. Any party to the proceeding may submit relevant information and proposals to the Copyright Royalty Judges. The parties to the proceeding shall each bear their respective costs of participation.

 (e) Judicial review.—Any determination of the Copyright Royalty Judges under subsection (d) may be appealed, by a party to the proceeding, in accordance with section 803(d) of this title. The pendency of an appeal under this subsection shall not stay the determination of the Copyright Royalty Judges. If the court modifies the determination of the Copyright Royalty Judges, the court shall have jurisdiction to enter its own decision in accordance with its final judgment. The court may further vacate the determination of the Copyright Royalty Judges and remand the case for proceedings as provided in this section.

CHAPTER 11.—SOUND RECORDINGS AND MUSIC VIDEOS

Sec.
1101. Unauthorized Fixation and Trafficking in Sound Recordings and Music Videos.

Sec. 1101. Unauthorized Fixation and Trafficking in Sound Recordings and Music Videos

 (a) Unauthorized Acts.—Anyone who, without the consent of the performer or performers involved—

  (1) fixes the sounds or sounds and images of a live musical performance in a copy or phonorecord, or reproduces copies or phonorecords of such a performance from an unauthorized fixation,

  (2) transmits or otherwise communicates to the public the sounds or sounds and images of a live musical performance, or

  (3) distributes or offers to distribute, sells or offers to sell, rents or offers to rent, or traffics in any copy or phonorecord fixed as described in paragraph (1), regardless of whether the fixations occurred in the United States,

shall be subject to the remedies provided in sections 502 through 505, to the same extent as an infringer of copyright.

 (b) Definition.—As used in this section, the term "traffic in" means transport, transfer, or otherwise dispose of, to another, as consideration for anything of value, or make or obtain control of with intent to transport, transfer, or dispose of.

 (c) Applicability.—This section shall apply to any act or acts that occur on or after the date of the enactment of the Uruguay Round Agreements Act.

 (d) State Law Not Preempted.—Nothing in this section may be construed to annul or limit any rights or remedies under the common law or statutes of any State.

CHAPTER 12.—COPYRIGHT PROTECTION AND MANAGEMENT SYSTEMS

(Pub.L. 105–304, 112 Stat. 2863 (1998)).

Sec.

Sec. 1201.   Circumvention of Copyright Protection Systems

(a) Violations Regarding Circumvention of Technological Measures.—

(1)(A) No person shall circumvent a technological measure that effectively controls access to a work protected under this title. The prohibition contained in the preceding sentence shall take effect at the end of the 2–year period beginning on the date of the enactment of this chapter.

(B) The prohibition contained in subparagraph (A) shall not apply to persons who are users of a copyrighted work which is in a particular class of works, if such persons are, or are likely to be in the succeeding 3–year period, adversely affected by virtue of such prohibition in their ability to make noninfringing uses of that particular class of works under this title, as determined under subparagraph (C).

(C) During the 2–year period described in subparagraph (A), and during each succeeding 3–year period, the Librarian of Congress, upon the recommendation of the Register of Copyrights, who shall consult with the Assistant Secretary for Communications and Information of the Department of Commerce and report and comment on his or her views in making such recommendation, shall make the determination in a rulemaking proceeding for purposes of subparagraph (B) of whether persons who are users of a copyrighted work are, or are likely to be in the succeeding 3–year period, adversely affected by the prohibition under subparagraph (A) in their ability to make noninfringing uses under this title of a particular class of copyrighted works. In conducting such rulemaking, the Librarian shall examine—

(i) the availability for use of copyrighted works;

(ii) the availability for use of works for nonprofit archival, preservation, and educational purposes;

(iii) the impact that the prohibition on the circumvention of technological measures applied to copyrighted works has on criticism, comment, news reporting, teaching, scholarship, or research;

(iv) the effect of circumvention of technological measures on the market for or value of copyrighted works; and

(v) such other factors as the Librarian considers appropriate.

(D) The Librarian shall publish any class of copyrighted works for which the Librarian has determined, pursuant to the rulemaking conducted under subparagraph (C), that noninfringing uses by persons who are users of a copyrighted work are, or are likely to be, adversely affected, and the prohibition contained in subparagraph (A) shall not apply to such users with respect to such class of works for the ensuing 3–year period.

(E) Neither the exception under subparagraph (B) from the applicability of the prohibition contained in subparagraph (A), nor any determination made in a rulemaking conducted under subparagraph (C), may be used as a defense in any action to enforce any provision of this title other than this paragraph.

(2) No person shall manufacture, import, offer to the public, provide, or otherwise traffic in any technology, product, service, device, component, or part thereof, that—

(A) is primarily designed or produced for the purpose of circumventing a technological measure that effectively controls access to a work protected under this title;

(B) has only limited commercially significant purpose or use other than to circumvent a technological measure that effectively controls access to a work protected under this title; or

(C) is marketed by that person or another acting in concert with that person with that person's knowledge for use in circumventing a technological measure that effectively controls access to a work protected under this title.

(3) As used in this subsection—

(A) to "circumvent a technological measure" means to descramble a scrambled work, to decrypt an encrypted work, or otherwise to avoid, bypass, remove, deactivate, or impair a technological measure, without the authority of the copyright owner; and

(B) a technological measure "effectively controls access to a work" if the measure, in the ordinary course of its operation, requires the application of information, or a process or a treatment, with the authority of the copyright owner, to gain access to the work.

(b) Additional Violations.—

(1) No person shall manufacture, import, offer to the public, provide, or otherwise traffic in any technology, product, service, device, component, or part thereof, that—

(A) is primarily designed or produced for the purpose of circumventing protection afforded by a technological measure that effectively protects a right of a copyright owner under this title in a work or a portion thereof;

(B) has only limited commercially significant purpose or use other than to circumvent protection afforded by a technological measure that effectively protects a right of a copyright owner under this title in a work or a portion thereof; or

(C) is marketed by that person or another acting in concert with that person with that person's knowledge for use in circumventing protection afforded by a technological measure that effectively protects a right of a copyright owner under this title in a work or a portion thereof.

(2) As used in this subsection—

(A) to "circumvent protection afforded by a technological measure" means avoiding, bypassing, removing, deactivating, or otherwise impairing a technological measure; and

(B) a technological measure "effectively protects a right of a copyright owner under this title" if the measure, in the ordinary course of its operation, prevents, restricts, or otherwise limits the exercise of a right of a copyright owner under this title.

(c) Other Rights, Etc., Not Affected.—

(1) Nothing in this section shall affect rights, remedies, limitations, or defenses to copyright infringement, including fair use, under this title.

(2) Nothing in this section shall enlarge or diminish vicarious or contributory liability for copyright infringement in connection with any technology, product, service, device, component, or part thereof.

(3) Nothing in this section shall require that the design of, or design and selection of parts and components for, a consumer electronics, telecommunications, or computing product provide for a response to any particular technological measure, so long as such part or component, or the product in which such part or component is integrated, does not otherwise fall within the prohibitions of subsection (a)(2) or (b)(1).

(4) Nothing in this section shall enlarge or diminish any rights of free speech or the press for activities using consumer electronics, telecommunications, or computing products.

(d) Exemption for Nonprofit Libraries, Archives, and Educational Institutions.—

(1) A nonprofit library, archives, or educational institution which gains access to a commercially exploited copyrighted work solely in order to make a good faith determination of whether to acquire a copy of that work for the sole purpose of engaging in conduct permitted under this title shall not be in violation of subsection (a)(1)(A). A copy of a work to which access has been gained under this paragraph—

(A) may not be retained longer than necessary to make such good faith determination; and

(B) may not be used for any other purpose.

(2) The exemption made available under paragraph (1) shall only apply with respect to a work when an identical copy of that work is not reasonably available in another form.

(3) A nonprofit library, archives, or educational institution that willfully for the purpose of commercial advantage or financial gain violates paragraph (1)—

(A) shall, for the first offense, be subject to the civil remedies under section 1203; and

(B) shall, for repeated or subsequent offenses, in addition to the civil remedies under section 1203, forfeit the exemption provided under paragraph (1).

(4) This subsection may not be used as a defense to a claim under subsection (a)(2) or (b), nor may this subsection permit a nonprofit library, archives, or educational institution to manufacture, import, offer to the public, provide, or otherwise traffic in any technology, product, service, component, or part thereof, which circumvents a technological measure.

(5) In order for a library or archives to qualify for the exemption under this subsection, the collections of that library or archives shall be—

(A) open to the public; or

(B) available not only to researchers affiliated with the library or archives or with the institution of which it is a part, but also to other persons doing research in a specialized field.

(e) Law Enforcement, Intelligence, and Other Government Activities.—This section does not prohibit any lawfully authorized investigative, protective, information security, or intelligence activity of an officer, agent, or employee of the United States, a State, or a political subdivision of a State, or a person acting pursuant to a contract with the United States, a State, or a political subdivision of a State. For purposes of this subsection, the term "information security" means activities carried out in order to identify and address the vulnerabilities of a government computer, computer system, or computer network.

(f) Reverse Engineering.—

(1) Notwithstanding the provisions of subsection (a)(1)(A), a person who has lawfully obtained the right to use a copy of a computer program may circumvent a technological measure that effectively controls access to a particular portion of that program for the sole purpose of identifying and analyzing those elements of the program that are necessary to achieve interoperability of an independently created computer program with other programs, and that have not previously been readily available to the person engaging in the circumvention, to the extent any such acts of identification and analysis do not constitute infringement under this title.

(2) Notwithstanding the provisions of subsections (a)(2) and (b), a person may develop and employ technological means to circumvent a technological measure, or to circumvent protection afforded by a technological measure, in order to enable the identification and analysis under paragraph (1), or for the purpose of enabling interoperability of an independently created computer program with other programs, if such means are necessary to achieve such interoperability, to the extent that doing so does not constitute infringement under this title.

(3) The information acquired through the acts permitted under paragraph (1), and the means permitted under paragraph (2), may

be made available to others if the person referred to in paragraph (1) or (2), as the case may be, provides such information or means solely for the purpose of enabling interoperability of an independently created computer program with other programs, and to the extent that doing so does not constitute infringement under this title or violate applicable law other than this section.

(4) For purposes of this subsection, the term "interoperability" means the ability of computer programs to exchange information, and of such programs mutually to use the information which has been exchanged.

(g) Encryption Research.—

    (1) Definitions.—For purposes of this subsection—

      (A) the term "encryption research" means activities necessary to identify and analyze flaws and vulnerabilities of encryption technologies applied to copyrighted works, if these activities are conducted to advance the state of knowledge in the field of encryption technology or to assist in the development of encryption products; and

      (B) the term "encryption technology" means the scrambling and descrambling of information using mathematical formulas or algorithms.

    (2) Permissible Acts of Encryption Research.—Notwithstanding the provisions of subsection (a)(1)(A), it is not a violation of that subsection for a person to circumvent a technological measure as applied to a copy, phonorecord, performance, or display of a published work in the course of an act of good faith encryption research if—

      (A) the person lawfully obtained the encrypted copy, phonorecord, performance, or display of the published work;

      (B) such act is necessary to conduct such encryption research;

      (C) the person made a good faith effort to obtain authorization before the circumvention; and

      (D) such act does not constitute infringement under this title or a violation of applicable law other than this section, including section 1030 of title 18 and those provisions of title 18 amended by the Computer Fraud and Abuse Act of 1986.

    (3) Factors in Determining Exemption.—In determining whether a person factors to be considered shall include—

      (A) whether the information derived from the encryption research was disseminated, and if so, whether it was disseminated in a manner reasonably calculated to advance the state of knowledge or development of encryption technology, versus whether it was disseminated in a manner that facilitates infringement under this title or a violation of applicable law other than this section including a violation of privacy or breach of security;

(B) whether the person is engaged in a legitimate course of study, is employed, or is appropriately trained or experienced, in the field of encryption technology; and

(C) whether the person provides the copyright owner of the work to which the technological measure is applied with notice of the findings and documentation of the research, and the time when such notice is provided.

(4) Use of Technological Means for Research Activities.—Notwithstanding the provisions of subsection (a)(2), it is not a violation of that subsection for a person to—

(A) develop and employ technological means to circumvent a technological measure for the sole purpose of that person performing the acts of good faith encryption research described in paragraph (2); and

(B) provide the technological means to another person with whom he or she is working collaboratively for the purpose of conducting the acts of good faith encryption research described in paragraph (2) or for the purpose of having that other person verify his or her acts of good faith encryption research described in paragraph (2).

(5) Report to Congress.—Not later than 1 year after the date of the enactment of this chapter, the Register of Copyrights and the Assistant Secretary for Communications and Information of the Department of Commerce shall jointly report to the Congress on the effect this subsection has had on—

(A) encryption research and the development of encryption technology;

(B) the adequacy and effectiveness of technological measures designed to protect copyrighted works; and

(C) protection of copyright owners against the unauthorized access to their encrypted copyrighted works.

The report shall include legislative recommendations, if any.

(h) Exceptions Regarding Minors.—In applying subsection (a) to a component or part, the court may consider the necessity for its intended and actual incorporation in a technology, product, service, or device, which—

(1) does not itself violate the provisions of this title; and

(2) has the sole purpose to prevent the access of minors to material on the Internet.

(i) Protection of Personally Identifying Information.—

(1) Circumvention Permitted.—Notwithstanding the provisions of subsection (a)(1)(A), it is not a violation of that subsection for a person to circumvent a technological measure that effectively controls access to a work protected under this title, if—

(A) the technological measure, or the work it protects, contains the capability of collecting or disseminating personally identifying information reflecting the online activities of a natural person who seeks to gain access to the work protected;

(B) in the normal course of its operation, the technological measure, or the work it protects, collects or disseminates personally identifying information about the person who seeks to gain access to the work protected, without providing conspicuous notice of such collection or dissemination to such person, and without providing such person with the capability to prevent or restrict such collection or dissemination;

(C) the act of circumvention has the sole effect of identifying and disabling the capability described in subparagraph (A), and has no other effect on the ability of any person to gain access to any work; and

(D) the act of circumvention is carried out solely for the purpose of preventing the collection or dissemination of personally identifying information about a natural person who seeks to gain access to the work protected, and is not in violation of any other law.

(2) Inapplicability to Certain Technological Measures.— This subsection does not apply to a technological measure, or a work it protects, that does not collect or disseminate personally identifying information and that is disclosed to a user as not having or using such capability.

(j) Security Testing.—

(1) Definition.—For purposes of this subsection, the term "security testing" means accessing a computer network, solely for the purpose of good faith testing, investigating, or correcting, a security flaw or vulnerability, with the authorization of the owner or operator of such computer, computer system, or computer network.

(2) Permissible Acts of Security Testing.—Notwithstanding the provisions of subsection (a)(1)(A), it is not a violation of that subsection for a person to engage in an act of security testing, if such act does not constitute infringement under this title or a violation of applicable law other than this section, including section 1030 of title 18 and those provisions of title 18 amended by the Computer Fraud and Abuse Act of 1986.

(3) Factors in Determining Exemption.—In determining whether a person qualifies for the exemption under paragraph (2), the factors to be considered shall include—

(A) whether the information derived from the security testing was used solely to promote the security of the owner or operator of such computer, computer system or computer network, or shared directly with the developer of such computer, computer system, or computer network; and

(B) whether the information derived from the security testing was used or maintained in a manner that does not facilitate infringement under this title or a violation of applicable law other than this section, including a violation of privacy or breach of security.

(4) Use of Technological Means for Security Testing.— Notwithstanding the provisions of subsection (a)(2), it is not a violation of that subsection for a person to develop, produce, distribute or employ technological means for the sole purpose of performing the acts of security testing described in subsection (2), provided such technological means does not otherwise violate section (a)(2).

(k) Certain Analog Devices and Certain Technological Measures.—

(1) Certain Analog Devices.—

(A) Effective 18 months after the date of the enactment of this chapter, no person shall manufacture, import, offer to the public, provide or otherwise traffic in any—

(i) VHS format analog video cassette recorder unless such recorder conforms to the automatic gain control copy control technology;

(ii) 8mm format analog video cassette camcorder unless such camcorder conforms to the automatic gain control technology;

(iii) Beta format analog video cassette recorder, unless such recorder conforms to the automatic gain control copy control technology, except that this requirement shall not apply until there are 1,000 Beta format analog video cassette recorders sold in the United States in any one calendar year after the date of the enactment of this chapter;

(iv) 8mm format analog video cassette recorder that is not an analog video cassette camcorder, unless such recorder conforms to the automatic gain control copy control technology, except that this requirement shall not apply until there are 20,000 such recorders sold in the United States in any one calendar year after the date of the enactment of this chapter; or

(v) analog video cassette recorder that records using an NTSC format video input and that is not otherwise covered under clauses (i) through (iv), unless such device conforms to the automatic gain control copy control technology.

(B) Effective on the date of the enactment of this chapter, no person shall manufacture, import, offer to the public, provide or otherwise traffic in—

(i) any VHS format analog video cassette recorder or any 8mm format analog video cassette recorder if the design of the model of such recorder has been modified after such date of enactment so that a model of recorder that previously conformed to the automatic gain control copy control technology no longer conforms to such technology; or

(ii) any VHS format analog video cassette recorder, or any 8mm format analog video cassette recorder that is not an 8mm analog video cassette camcorder, if the design of the model of such recorder has been modified after such date of enactment so that a model of recorder that previously conformed to the four-line colorstripe copy control technology no longer conforms to such technology.

Manufacturers that have not previously manufactured or sold a VHS format analog video cassette recorder, or an 8mm format analog cassette recorder, shall be required to conform to the four-line colorstripe copy control technology in the initial model of any such recorder manufactured after the date of the enactment of this chapter, and thereafter to continue conforming to the four-line colorstripe copy control technology. For purposes of this subparagraph, an analog video cassette recorder "conforms to" the four-line colorstripe copy control technology if it records a signal that, when played back by the playback function of that recorder in the normal viewing mode, exhibits, on a reference display device, a display containing distracting visible lines through portions of the viewable picture.

(2) Certain Encoding Restrictions.—No person shall apply the automatic gain control copy control technology or colorstripe copy control technology to prevent or limit consumer copying except such copying—

(A) of a single transmission, or specified group of transmissions, of live events or of audiovisual works for which a member of the public has exercised choice in selecting the transmissions, including the content of the transmissions or the time of receipt of such transmissions, or both, and as to which such member is charged a separate fee for each such transmission or specified group of transmissions;

(B) from a copy of a transmission of a live event or an audiovisual work if such transmission is provided by a channel or service where payment is made by a member of the public for such channel or service in the form of a subscription fee that entitles the member of the public to receive all of the programming contained in such channel or service;

(C) from a physical medium containing one or more prerecorded audiovisual works; or

(D) from a copy of a transmission described in subparagraph (A) or from a copy made from a physical medium described in subparagraph (C).

In the event that a transmission meets both the conditions set forth in subparagraph (A) and those set forth in subparagraph (B), the transmission shall be treated as a transmission described in subparagraph (A).

(3) Inapplicability.—This subsection shall not—

(A) require any analog video cassette camcorder to conform to the automatic gain control copy control technology with respect to any video signal received through a camera lens;

(B) apply to the manufacture, importation, offer for sale, provision of, or other trafficking in, any professional analog video cassette recorder; or

(C) apply to the offer for sale or provision of, or other trafficking in, any previously owned analog video cassette recorder, if such recorder was legally manufactured and sold when new and not subsequently modified in violation of paragraph (1)(B).

(4) Definitions.—For purposes of this subsection:

(A) An "analog video cassette recorder" means a device that records, or a device that includes a function that records, on electromagnetic tape in an analog format the electronic impulses produced by the video and audio portions of a television program, motion picture, or other form of audiovisual work.

(B) An "analog video cassette camcorder" means an analog video cassette recorder that contains a recording function that operates through a camera lens and through a video input that may be connected with a television or other video playback device.

(C) An analog video cassette recorder "conforms" to the automatic gain control copy control technology if it—

(i) detects one or more of the elements of such technology and does not record the motion picture or transmission protected by such technology; or

(ii) records a signal that, when played back, exhibits a meaningfully distorted or degraded display.

(D) The term "professional analog video cassette recorder" means an analog video cassette recorder that is designed, manufactured, marketed, and intended for use by a person who regularly employs such a device for a lawful business or industrial use, including making, performing, displaying, distributing, or transmitting copies of motion pictures on a commercial scale.

(E) The terms "VHS format", "8mm format", "Beta format", "automatic gain control copy control technology", "colorstripe copy control technology", "four-line version of the colorstripe copy control technology", and "NTSC" have the meanings that are commonly understood in the consumer electronics and motion picture industries as of the date of the enactment of this chapter.

(5) Violations.—Any violation of paragraph (1) of this subsection shall be treated as a violation of subsection (b)(1) of this section. Any violation of paragraph (2) of this subsection shall be deemed an "act of circumvention" for the purposes of section 1203(c)(3)(A) of this chapter.

Sec. 1202.   Integrity of Copyright Management Information

(a) False Copyright Management Information.—No person shall knowingly and with the intent to induce, enable, facilitate, or conceal infringement—

(1) provide copyright management information that is false, or

(2) distribute or import for distribution copyright management information that is false.

(b) Removal or Alteration of Copyright Management Information.—No person shall, without the authority of the copyright owner or the law—

(1) intentionally remove or alter any copyright management information,

(2) distribute or import for distribution copyright management information knowing that the copyright management information has been removed or altered without authority of the copyright owner or the law, or

(3) distribute, import for distribution, or publicly perform works, copies of works, or phonorecords, knowing that copyright management information has been removed or altered without authority of the copyright owner or the law,

knowing, or, with respect to civil remedies under section 1203, having reasonable grounds to know, that it will induce, enable, facilitate, or conceal an infringement of any right under this title.

(c) Definition.—As used in this section, the term "copyright management information" means any of the following information conveyed in connection with copies or phonorecords of a work or performances or displays of a work, including in digital form, except that such term does not include any personally identifying information about a user of a work or of a copy, phonorecord, performance, or display of a work:

(1) The title and other information identifying the work, including the information set forth on a notice of copyright.

(2) The name of, and other identifying information about, the author of a work.

(3) The name of, and other identifying information about, the copyright owner of the work, including the information set forth in a notice of copyright.

(4) With the exception of public performances of works by radio and television broadcast stations, the name of, and other identifying information about, a performer whose performance is fixed in a work other than an audiovisual work.

(5) With the exception of public performances of works by radio and television broadcast stations, in the case of an audiovisual work, the name of, and other identifying information about, a writer, performer, or director who is credited in the audiovisual work.

(6) Terms and conditions for use of the work.

(7) Identifying numbers or symbols referring to such information or links to such information.

(8) Such other information as the Register of Copyrights may prescribe by regulation, except that the Register of Copyrights may not require the provision of any information concerning the user of a copyrighted work.

(d) Law Enforcement, Intelligence, and Other Government Activities.—This section does not prohibit any lawfully authorized investigative, protective, information security, or intelligence activity of an officer, agent, or employee of the United States, a State, or a political subdivision of a State, or a person acting pursuant to a contract with the United States, a State, or a political subdivision of a State. For purposes of this subsection, the term "information security" means activities carried out in order to identify and address the vulnerabilities of a government computer, computer system, or computer network.

(e) Limitations on Liability.—

(1) Analog Transmissions.—In the case of an analog transmission, a person who is making transmissions in its capacity as a broadcast station, or as a cable system, or someone who provides programming to such station or system, shall not be liable for a violation of subsection (b) if—

(A) avoiding the activity that constitutes such violation is not technically feasible or would create an undue financial hardship on such person; and

(B) such person did not intend, by engaging in such activity, to induce, enable, facilitate, or conceal infringement of a right under this title.

(2) Digital Transmissions.—

(A) If a digital transmission standard for the placement of copyright management information for a category of works is set in a voluntary, consensus standard-setting process involving a representative cross-section of broadcast stations or cable systems and copyright owners of a category of works that are intended for public performance by such stations or systems, a person identified in paragraph (1) shall not be liable for a violation of subsection (b) with respect to the particular copyright management information addressed by such standard if—

(i) the placement of such information by someone other than such person is not in accordance with such standard; and

(ii) the activity that constitutes such violation is not intended to induce, enable, facilitate, or conceal infringement of a right under this title.

(B) Until a digital transmission standard has been set pursuant to subparagraph (A) with respect to the placement of copyright management information for a category of works, a person identified in paragraph (1) shall not be liable for a violation of subsection (b) with respect to such copyright management information, if the activity that constitutes such violation is not intended to induce, enable, facilitate, or conceal infringement of a right under this title, and if—

(i) the transmission of such information by such person would result in a perceptible visual or aural degradation of the digital signal; or

(ii) the transmission of such information by such person would conflict with—

(I) an applicable government regulation relating to transmission of information in a digital signal;

(II) an applicable industry-wide standard relating to the transmission of information in a digital signal that was adopted by a voluntary consensus standards body prior to the effective date of this chapter; or

(III) an applicable industry-wide standard relating to the transmission of information in a digital signal that was adopted in a voluntary, consensus standards-setting process open to participation by a representative cross-section of broadcast stations or cable systems and copyright owners of a category of works that are intended for public performance by such stations or systems.

(3) **Definitions.**—As used in this subsection—

(A) the term "broadcast station" has the meaning given that term in section 3 of the Communications Act of 1934 (47 U.S.C. 153); and

(B) the term "cable system" has the meaning given that term in section 602 of the Communications Act of 1934 (47 U.S.C. 522).

Sec. 1203.   Civil Remedies

(a) **Civil Actions.**—Any person injured by a violation of section 1201 or 1202 may bring a civil action in an appropriate United States district court for such violation.

(b) **Powers of the Court.**—In an action brought under subsection (a), the court—

(1) may grant temporary and permanent injunctions on such terms as it deems reasonable to prevent or restrain a violation, but in no event shall impose a prior restraint on free speech or the press protected under the 1st amendment to the Constitution;

(2) at any time while an action is pending, may order the impounding, on such terms as it deems reasonable, of any device or product that is in the custody or control of the alleged violator and that the court has reasonable cause to believe was involved in a violation;

(3) may award damages under subsection (c);

(4) in its discretion may allow the recovery of costs by or against any party other than the United States or an officer thereof;

(5) in its discretion may award reasonable attorney's fees to the prevailing party; and

(6) may, as part of a final judgment or decree finding a violation, order the remedial modification or the destruction of any device or product involved in the violation that is in the custody or control of the violator or has been impounded under paragraph (2).

(c) **Award of Damages.**—

(1) In General.—Except as otherwise provided in this title, a person committing a violation of section 1201 or 1202 is liable for either—

(A) the actual damages and any additional profits of the violator, as provided in paragraph (2), or

(B) statutory damages, as provided in paragraph (3).

(2) Actual Damages.—The court shall award to the complaining party the actual damages suffered by the party as a result of the violation, and any profits of the violator that are attributable to the violation and are not taken into account in computing the actual damages, if the complaining party elects such damages at any time before final judgment is entered.

(3) Statutory Damages.—

(A) At any time before final judgment is entered, a complaining party may elect to recover an award of statutory damages for each violation of section 1201 in the sum of not less than $200 or more than $2,500 per act of circumvention, device, product, component, offer, or performance of service, as the court considers just.

(B) At any time before final judgment is entered, a complaining party may elect to recover an award of statutory damages for each violation of section 1202 in the sum of not less than $2,500 or more than $25,000.

(4) Repeated Violations.—In any case in which the injured party sustains the burden of proving, and the court finds, that a person has violated section 1201 or 1202 within 3 years after a final judgment was entered against the person for another such violation, the court may increase the award of damages up to triple the amount that would otherwise be awarded, as the court considers just.

(5) Innocent Violations.—

(A) In General.—The court in its discretion may reduce or remit the total award of damages in any case in which the violator sustains the burden of proving, and the court finds, that the violator was not aware and had no reason to believe that its acts constituted a violation.

(B) Nonprofit Library, Archives, Educational Institutions, or Public Broadcasting Entities.—

(i) **Definition.**—In this subparagraph, the term "public broadcasting entity" has the meaning given such term under section 118(f).

(ii) **In general.**—In the case of a nonprofit library, archives, educational institution, or public broadcasting entity, the court shall remit damages in any case in which the library, archives, educational institution, or public broadcasting entity sustains the burden of proving, and the court finds, that the library, archives, educational institution, or public broadcasting entity was not aware and had no reason to believe that its acts constituted a violation.

Sec. 1204.   Criminal Offenses and Penalties

(a) In General.—Any person who violates section 1201 or 1202 willfully and for purposes of commercial advantage or private financial gain—

> (1) shall be fined not more than $500,000 or imprisoned for not more than 5 years, or both, for the first offense; and

> (2) shall be fined not more than $1,000,000 or imprisoned for not more than 10 years, or both, for any subsequent offense.

(b) Limitation for Nonprofit Library, Archives, Educational Institution, or Public Broadcasting Entity.—Subsection (a) shall not apply to a nonprofit library, archives, educational institution, or public broadcasting entity (as defined under section 118(f)).

(c) Statute of Limitations.—No criminal proceeding shall be brought under this section unless such proceeding is commenced within 5 years after the cause of action arose.

Sec. 1205.   Savings Clause

Nothing in this chapter abrogates, diminishes, or weakens the provisions of, nor provides any defense or element of mitigation in a criminal prosecution or civil action under, any Federal or State law that prevents the violation of the privacy of an individual in connection with the individual's use of the Internet.

CHAPTER 13.—PROTECTION OF ORIGINAL DESIGNS

(Pub.L. 105–304, 112 Stat. 2905 (1998)).

Sec. 1301.   Designs Protected

(a) Designs Protected.—

(1) In General.—The designer or other owner of an original design of a useful article which makes the article attractive or distinctive in appearance to the purchasing or using public may secure the protection provided by this chapter upon complying with and subject to this chapter.

(2) Vessel features.—The design of a vessel hull, deck, or combination of a hull and deck, including a plug or mold, is subject to protection under this chapter, notwithstanding section 1302(4).

(3) Exceptions.—Department of Defense rights in a registered design under this chapter, including the right to build to such registered design, shall be determined solely by operation of section 2320 of title 10 or by the instrument under which the design was developed for the United States Government.

(b) Definitions.—For the purpose of this chapter, the following terms have the following meanings:

(1) A design is "original" if it is the result of the designer's creative endeavor that provides a distinguishable variation over prior work pertaining to similar articles which is more than merely trivial and has not been copied from another source.

(2) A "useful article" is a vessel hull or deck, including a plug or mold, which in normal use has an intrinsic utilitarian function that is not merely to portray the appearance of the article or to convey information. An article which normally is part of a useful article shall be deemed to be a useful article.

(3) A "vessel" is a craft—

(A) that is designed and capable of independently steering a course on or through water through its own means of propulsion; and

(B) that is designed and capable of carrying and transporting one or more passengers.

(4) A "hull" is the exterior frame or body of a vessel, exclusive of the deck, superstructure, masts, sails, yards, rigging, hardware, fixtures, and other attachments.

(5) A "plug" means a device or model used to make a mold for the purpose of exact duplication, regardless of whether the device or model has an intrinsic utilitarian function that is not only to portray the appearance of the product or to convey information.

(6) A "mold" means a matrix or form in which a substance for material is used, regardless of whether the matrix or form has an intrinsic utilitarian function that is not only to portray the appearance of the product or to convey information.

(7) A "deck" is the horizontal surface of a vessel that covers the hull, including exterior cabin and cockpit surfaces, and exclusive of masts, sails, yards, rigging, hardware, fixtures, and other attachments.

Sec. 1302.   Designs not Subject to Protection

Protection under this chapter shall not be available for a design that is—

(1) not original;

(2) staple or commonplace, such as a standard geometric figure, a familiar symbol, an emblem, or a motif, or another shape, pattern, or configuration which has become standard, common, prevalent, or ordinary;

(3) different from a design excluded by paragraph (2) only in insignificant details or in elements which are variants commonly used in the relevant trades;

(4) dictated solely by a utilitarian function of the article that embodies it; or

(5) embodied in a useful article that was made public by the designer or owner in the United States or a foreign country more than 2 years before the date of the application for registration under this chapter.

Sec. 1303.   Revisions, Adaptations, and Rearrangements

Protection for a design under this chapter shall be available notwithstanding the employment in the design of subject matter excluded from protection under section 1302 if the design is a substantial revision, adaptation, or rearrangement of such subject matter. Such protection shall be independent of any subsisting protection in subject matter employed in the design, and shall not be construed as securing any right to subject matter excluded from protection under this chapter or as extending any subsisting protection under this chapter.

Sec. 1304.   Commencement of Protection

The protection provided for a design under this chapter shall commence upon the earlier of the date of publication of the registration under section 1313(a) or the date the design is first made public as defined by section 1310(b).

Sec. 1305.   Term of Protection

(a) In General.—Subject to subsection (b), the protection provided under this chapter for a design shall continue for a term of 10 years beginning on the date of the commencement of protection under section 1304.

(b) Expiration.—All terms of protection provided in this section shall run to the end of the calendar year in which they would otherwise expire.

(c) Termination of Rights.—Upon expiration or termination of protection in a particular design under this chapter, all rights under this chapter in the design shall terminate, regardless of the number of different articles in which the design may have been used during the term of its protection.

Sec. 1306.   Design Notice

(a) Contents of Design Notice.—

(1) Whenever any design for which protection is sought under this chapter is made public under section 1310(b), the owner of the design shall, subject to the provisions of section 1307, mark it or have it marked legibly with a design notice consisting of—

(A) the words "Protected Design", the abbreviation "Prot'd Des.", or the letter "D" with a circle, or the symbol " *D* ";

(B) the year of the date on which protection for the design commenced; and

(C) the name of the owner, an abbreviation by which the name can be recognized, or a generally accepted alternative designation of the owner.

Any distinctive identification of the owner may be used for purposes of subparagraph (C) if it has been recorded by the Administrator before the design marked with such identification is registered.

(2) After registration, the registration number may be used instead of the elements specified in subparagraphs (B) and (C) of paragraph (1).

(b) Location of Notice.—The design notice shall be so located and applied as to give reasonable notice of design protection while the useful article embodying the design is passing through its normal channels of commerce.

(c) Subsequent Removal of Notice.—When the owner of a design has complied with the provisions of this section, protection under this chapter shall not be affected by the removal, destruction, or obliteration by others of the design notice on an article.

Sec. 1307.   Effect of Omission of Notice

(a) Actions with Notice.—Except as provided in subsection (b), the omission of the notice prescribed in section 1306 shall not cause loss of the protection under this chapter or prevent recovery for infringement under this chapter against any person who, after receiving written notice of the design protection, begins an undertaking leading to infringement under this chapter.

(b) Actions Without Notice.—The omission of the notice prescribed in section 1306 shall prevent any recovery under section 1323 against a person who began an undertaking leading to infringement under this chapter before receiving written notice of the design protection. No injunction shall be issued under this chapter with respect to such undertaking unless the owner of the design reimburses that person for any reasonable expenditure or contractual obligation in connection with such undertaking that was incurred before receiving written notice of the design protection, as the court in its discretion directs. The burden of providing written notice of design protection shall be on the owner of the design.

Sec. 1308.   Exclusive Rights

The owner of a design protected under this chapter has the exclusive right to—

(1) make, have made, or import, for sale or for use in trade, any useful article embodying that design; and

(2) sell or distribute for sale or for use in trade any useful article embodying that design.

Sec. 1309.   Infringement

(a) **Acts of Infringement.**—Except as provided in subsection (b), it shall be infringement of the exclusive rights in a design protected under this chapter for any person, without the consent of the owner of the design, within the United States and during the term of such protection, to—

(1) make, have made, or import, for sale or for use in trade, any infringing article as defined in subsection (e); or

(2) sell or distribute for sale or for use in trade any such infringing article.

(b) **Acts of Sellers and Distributors.**—A seller or distributor of an infringing article who did not make or import the article shall be deemed to have infringed on a design protected under this chapter only if that person—

(1) induced or acted in collusion with a manufacturer to make, or an importer to import such article, except that merely purchasing or giving an order to purchase such article in the ordinary course of business shall not of itself constitute such inducement or collusion; or

(2) refused or failed, upon the request of the owner of the design, to make a prompt and full disclosure of that person's source of such article, and that person orders or reorders such article after receiving notice by registered or certified mail of the protection subsisting in the design.

(c) **Acts Without Knowledge.**—It shall not be infringement under this section to make, have made, import, sell, or distribute, any article embodying a design which was created without knowledge that a design was protected under this chapter and was copied from such protected design.

(d) **Acts in Ordinary Course of Business.**—A person who incorporates into that person's product of manufacture an infringing article acquired from others in the ordinary course of business, or who, without knowledge of the protected design embodied in an infringing article, makes or processes the infringing article for the account of another person in the ordinary course of business, shall not be deemed to have infringed the rights in that design under this chapter except under a condition contained in paragraph (1) or (2) of subsection (b). Accepting an order or reorder from the source of the infringing article shall be deemed ordering or reordering within the meaning of subsection (b)(2).

(e) **Infringing Article Defined.**—As used in this section, an "infringing article" is any article the design of which has been copied from a design protected under this chapter, without the consent of the owner of the protected design. An infringing article is not an illustration or picture of a protected design in an advertisement, book, periodical, newspaper, photograph, broadcast, motion picture, or similar medium. A design shall not be deemed to have been copied from a protected design if it is original and not substantially similar in appearance to a protected design.

(f) **Establishing Originality.**—The party to any action or proceeding under this chapter who alleges rights under this chapter in a design shall have the burden of establishing the design's originality whenever the opposing party introduces an earlier work which is identical to such design, or so similar as to make prima facie showing that such design was copied from such work.

(g) **Reproduction for Teaching or Analysis.**—It is not an infringement of the exclusive rights of a design owner for a person to reproduce the design in a useful article or in any other form solely for the purpose of teaching, analyzing, or evaluating the appearance, concepts, or techniques embodied in the design, or the function of the useful article embodying the design.

Sec. 1310.   Application for Registration

(a) **Time Limit for Application for Registration.**—Protection under this chapter shall be lost if application for registration of the design is not made within 2 years after the date on which the design is first made public.

(b) **When Design is Made Public.**—A design is made public when an existing useful article embodying the design is anywhere publicly exhibited, publicly distributed, or offered for sale or sold to the public by the owner of the design or with the owner's consent.

(c) **Application by Owner of Design.**—Application for registration may be made by the owner of the design.

(d) **Contents of Application.**—The application for registration shall be made to the Administrator and shall state—

(1) the name and address of the designer or designers of the design;

(2) the name and address of the owner if different from the designer;

(3) the specific name of the useful article embodying the design;

(4) the date, if any, that the design was first made public, if such date was earlier than the date of the application;

(5) affirmation that the design has been fixed in a useful article; and

(6) such other information as may be required by the Administrator.

The application for registration may include a description setting forth the salient features of the design, but the absence of such a description shall not prevent registration under this chapter.

(e) **Sworn Statement.**—The application for registration shall be accompanied by a statement under oath by the applicant or the applicant's duly authorized agent or representative, setting forth, to the best of the applicant's knowledge and belief—

    (1) that the design is original and was created by the designer or designers named in the application;

    (2) that the design has not previously been registered on behalf of the applicant or the applicant's predecessor in title; and

    (3) that the applicant is the person entitled to protection and to registration under this chapter.

If the design has been made public with the design notice prescribed in section 1306, the statement shall also describe the exact form and position of the design notice

(f) Effect of Errors.—

    (1) Error in any statement or assertion as to the utility of the useful article named in the application under this section, the design of which is sought to be registered, shall not affect the protection secured under this chapter.

    (2) Errors in omitting a joint designer or in naming an alleged joint designer shall not affect the validity of the registration, or the actual ownership or the protection of the design, unless it is shown that the error occurred with deceptive intent.

(g) Design Made in Scope of Employment.—In a case in which the design was made within the regular scope of the designer's employment and individual authorship of the design is difficult or impossible to ascribe and the application so states, the name and address of the employer for whom the design was made may be stated instead of that of the individual designer.

(h) Pictorial Representation of Design.—The application for registration shall be accompanied by two copies of a drawing or other pictorial representation of the useful article embodying the design, having one or more views, adequate to show the design, in a form and style suitable for reproduction, which shall be deemed a part of the application.

(i) Design in More Than One Useful Article.—If the distinguishing elements of a design are in substantially the same form in different useful articles, the design shall be protected as to all such useful articles when protected as to one of them, but not more than one registration shall be required for the design.

(j) Application for More Than One Design.—More than one design may be included in the same application under such conditions as may be prescribed by the Administrator. For each design included in an application the fee prescribed for a single design shall be paid.

Sec. 1311. Benefit of Earlier Filing Date in Foreign Country

An application for registration of a design filed in the United States by any person who has, or whose legal representative or predecessor or successor in title has, previously filed an application for registration of the same design in a foreign country which extends to designs of owners who are citizens of the United States, or to applications filed under this chapter, similar protection to that provided under this chapter shall have that same effect as if filed in the United States on the date on which the application was first filed in such foreign country, if the application in the United States is filed within 6 months after the earliest date on which any such foreign application was filed.

Sec. 1312.   Oaths and Acknowledgments

(a) In General.—Oaths and acknowledgments required by this chapter—

(1) may be made—

(A) before any person in the United States authorized by law to administer oaths; or

(B) when made in a foreign country, before any diplomatic or consular officer of the United States authorized to administer oaths, or before any official authorized to administer oaths in the foreign country concerned, whose authority shall be proved by a certificate of a diplomatic or consular officer of the United States; and

(2) shall be valid if they comply with the laws of the State or country where made.

(b) Written Declaration in Lieu of Oath.—

(1) The Administrator may by rule prescribe that any document which is to be filed under this chapter in the Office of the Administrator and which is required by any law, rule, or other regulation to be under oath, may be subscribed to by a written declaration in such form as the Administrator may prescribe, and such declaration shall be in lieu of the oath otherwise required.

(2) Whenever a written declaration under paragraph (1) is used, the document containing the declaration shall state that willful false statements are punishable by fine or imprisonment, or both, pursuant to section 1001 of title 18, and may jeopardize the validity of the application or document or a registration resulting therefrom.

Sec. 1313.   Examination of Application and Issue or Refusal of Registration

(a) Determination of Registrability of Design; Registration.— Upon the filing of an application for registration in proper form under section 1310, and upon payment of the fee prescribed under section 1316, the Administrator shall determine whether or not the application relates to a design which on its face appears to be subject to protection under this chapter, and, if so, the Register shall register the design. Registration under this subsection shall be announced by publication. The date of registration shall be the date of publication.

(b) Refusal to Register; Reconsideration.—If, in the judgment of the Administrator, the application for registration relates to a design which on its face is not subject to protection under this chapter, the Administrator shall send to the applicant a notice of refusal to register and the grounds for the refusal. Within 3 months after the date on which the notice of refusal is sent, the applicant may, by written request, seek reconsideration of the application. After consideration of such a request, the Administrator shall either register the design or send to the applicant a notice of final refusal to register.

(c) Application to Cancel Registration.—Any person who believes he or she is or will be damaged by a registration under this chapter may, upon payment of the prescribed fee, apply to the Administrator at any time to cancel the registration on the ground that the design is not subject to protection under this chapter, stating the reasons for the request. Upon receipt of an application for cancellation, the Administrator shall send to the owner of the design, as shown in the records of the Office of the Administrator, a notice of the application, and the owner shall have a period of 3 months after the date on which such notice is mailed in which to present arguments to the Administrator for support of the validity of the registration. The Administrator shall also have the authority to establish, by regulation, conditions under which the opposing parties may appear and be heard in support of their arguments. If, after the periods provided for the presentation of arguments have expired, the Administrator determines that the applicant for cancellation has established that the design is not subject to protection under this chapter, the Administrator shall order the registration stricken from the record. Cancellation under this subsection shall be announced by publication, and notice of the Administrator's final determination with respect to any application for cancellation shall be sent to the applicant and to the owner of record. Costs of the cancellation procedure under this subsection shall be borne by the nonprevailing party or parties, and the Administrator shall have the authority to assess and collect such costs.

Sec. 1314.   Certification of Registration

Certificates of registration shall be issued in the name of the United States under the seal of the Office of the Administrator and shall be recorded in the official records of the Office. The certificate shall state the name of the useful article, the date of filing of the application, the date of registration, and the date the design was made public, if earlier than the date of filing of the application, and shall contain a reproduction of the drawing or other pictorial representation of the design. If a description of the salient features of the design appears in the application, the description shall also appear in the certificate. A certificate of registration shall be admitted in any court as prima facie evidence of the facts stated in the certificate.

Sec. 1315.   Publication of Announcements and Indexes

(a) Publications of the Administrator.—The Administrator shall publish lists and indexes of registered designs and cancellations of designs and may also publish the drawings or other pictorial representations of registered designs for sale or other distribution.

(b) File of Representatives of Registered Designs.—The Administrator shall establish and maintain a file of the drawings or other pictorial representations of registered designs. The file shall be available for use by the public under such conditions as the Administrator may prescribe.

Sec. 1316.   Fees

The Administrator shall by regulation set reasonable fees for the filing of applications to register designs under this chapter and for other services relating to the administration of this chapter, taking into consideration the cost of providing these services and the benefit of a public record.

Sec. 1317.   Regulations

The Administrator may establish regulations for the administration of this chapter.

Sec. 1318.   Copies of Records

Upon payment of the prescribed fee, any person may obtain a certified copy of any official record of the Office of the Administrator that relates to this chapter. That copy shall be admissible in evidence with the same effect as the original.

Sec. 1319.   Correction of Errors in Certificates

The Administrator may, by a certificate of correction under seal, correct any error in a registration incurred through the fault of the Office, or, upon payment of the required fee, any error of a clerical or typographical nature occurring in good faith but not through the fault of the Office. Such registration, together with the certificate, shall thereafter have the same effect as if it had been originally issued in such corrected form.

Sec. 1320.   Ownership and Transfer

(a) Property Right in Design.—The property right in a design subject to protection under this chapter shall vest in the designer, the legal representatives of a deceased designer or of one under legal incapacity, the employer for whom the designer created the design in the case of a design made within the regular scope of the designer's employment, or a person to whom the rights of the designer or of such employer have been transferred. The person in whom the property right is vested shall be considered the owner of the design.

(b) Transfer of Property Right.—The property right in a registered design, or a design for which an application for registration has been or may be filed, may be assigned, granted, conveyed, or mortgaged by an instrument in writing, signed by the owner, or may be bequeathed by will.

(c) Oath or Acknowledgment of Transfer.—An oath or acknowledgment under section 1312 shall be prima facie evidence of the execution of an assignment, grant, conveyance, or mortgage under subsection (b).

(d) Recordation of Transfer.—An assignment, grant, conveyance, or mortgage under subsection (b) shall be void as against any subsequent purchaser or mortgagee for a valuable consideration, unless it is recorded in the Office of the Administrator within 3 months after its date of execution or before the date of such subsequent purchase or mortgage.

Sec. 1321.   Remedy for Infringement

(a) In General.—The owner of a design is entitled, after issuance of a certificate of registration of the design under this chapter, to institute an action for any infringement of the design.

(b) Review of Refusal to Register.—

(1) Subject to paragraph (2), the owner of a design may seek judicial review of a final refusal of the Administrator to register the

design under this chapter by bringing a civil action, and may in the same action, if the court adjudges the design subject to protection under this chapter, enforce the rights in that design under this chapter.

(2) The owner of a design may seek judicial review under this section if—

(A) the owner has previously duly filed and prosecuted to final refusal an application in proper form for registration of the design;

(B) the owner causes a copy of the complaint in the action to be delivered to the Administrator within 10 days after the commencement of the action; and

(C) the defendant has committed acts in respect to the design which would constitute infringement with respect to a design protected under this chapter.

(c) Administrator as Party to Action.—The Administrator may, at the Administrator's option, become a party to the action with respect to the issue of registrability of the design claim by entering an appearance within 60 days after being served with the complaint, but the failure of the Administrator to become a party shall not deprive the court of jurisdiction to determine that issue.

(d) Use of Arbitration to Resolve Dispute.—The parties to an infringement dispute under this chapter, within such time as may be specified by the Administrator by regulation, may determine the dispute, or any aspect of the dispute, by arbitration. Arbitration shall be governed by title 9. The parties shall give notice of any arbitration award to the Administrator, and such award shall, as between the parties to the arbitration, be dispositive of the issues to which it relates. The arbitration award shall be unenforceable until such notice is given. Nothing in this subsection shall preclude the Administrator from determining whether a design is subject to registration in a cancellation proceeding under section 1313(c).

Sec. 1322.   Injunctions

(a) In General.—A court having jurisdiction over actions under this chapter may grant injunctions in accordance with the principles of equity to prevent infringement of a design under this chapter, including, in its discretion, prompt relief by temporary restraining orders and preliminary injunctions.

(b) Damages for Injunctive Relief Wrongfully Obtained.—A seller or distributor who suffers damage by reason of injunctive relief wrongfully obtained under this section has a cause of action against the applicant for such injunctive relief and may recover such relief as may be appropriate, including damages for lost profits, cost of materials, loss of good will, and punitive damages in instances where the injunctive relief was sought in bad faith, and, unless the court finds extenuating circumstances, reasonable attorney's fees.

Sec. 1323.   Recovery for Infringement

(a) Damages.—Upon a finding for the claimant in an action for infringement under this chapter, the court shall award the claimant damages adequate to compensate for the infringement. In addition, the court may increase the damages to such amount, not exceeding $50,000 or $1 per copy, whichever is greater, as the court determines to be just. The damages awarded shall constitute compensation and not a penalty. The court may receive expert testimony as an aid to the determination of damages.

(b) Infringer's Profits.—As an alternative to the remedies provided in subsection (a), the court may award the claimant the infringer's profits resulting from the sale of the copies if the court finds that the infringer's sales are reasonably related to the use of the claimant's design. In such a case, the claimant shall be required to prove only the amount of the infringer's sales and the infringer shall be required to prove its expenses against such sales.

(c) Statute of Limitations.—No recovery under subsection (a) or (b) shall be had for any infringement committed more than 3 years before the date on which the complaint is filed.

(d) Attorney's Fees.—In an action for infringement under this chapter, the court may award reasonable attorney's fees to the prevailing party.

(e) Disposition of Infringing and Other Articles.—The court may order that all infringing articles, and any plates, molds, patterns, models, or other means specifically adapted for making the articles, be delivered up for destruction or other disposition as the court may direct.

Sec. 1324. Power of Court Over Registration

In any action involving the protection of a design under this chapter, the court, when appropriate, may order registration of a design under this chapter or the cancellation of such a registration. Any such order shall be certified by the court to the Administrator, who shall make an appropriate entry upon the record.

Sec. 1325. Liability for Action on Registration Fraudulently Obtained

Any person who brings an action for infringement knowing that registration of the design was obtained by a false or fraudulent representation materially affecting the rights under this chapter, shall be liable in the sum of $10,000, or such part of that amount as the court may determine. That am amount shall be to compensate the defendant and shall be charged against the plaintiff and paid to the defendant, in addition to such costs and attorney's fees of the defendant as may be assessed by the court.

Sec. 1326. Penalty for False Marking

(a) In General.—Whoever, for the purpose of deceiving the public, marks upon, applies to, or uses in advertising in connection with an article made, used, distributed, or sold, a design which is not protected under this chapter, a design notice specified in section 1306, or any other words or symbols importing that the design is protected under this chapter, knowing that the design is not so protected, shall pay a civil fine of not more than $500 for each such offense.

(b) Suit by Private Persons.—Any person may sue for the penalty established by subsection (a), in which event one-half of the penalty shall be awarded to the person suing and the remainder shall be awarded to the United States.

Sec. 1327.   Penalty for False Representation

Whoever knowingly makes a false representation materially affecting the rights obtainable under this chapter for the purpose of obtaining registration of a design under this chapter shall pay a penalty of not less than $500 and not more than $1,000, and any rights or privileges that individual may have in the design under this chapter shall be forfeited.

Sec. 1328.   Enforcement by Treasury and Postal Service

(a) Regulations.—The Secretary of the Treasury and the United States Postal Service shall separately or jointly issue regulations for the enforcement of the rights set forth in section 1308 with respect to importation. Such regulations may require, as a condition for the exclusion of articles from the United States, that the person seeking exclusion take any one or more of the following actions:

(1) Obtain a court order enjoining, or an order of the International Trade Commission under section 337 of the Tariff Act of 1930 excluding, importation of the articles.

(2) Furnish proof that the design involved is protected under this chapter and that the importation of the articles would infringe the rights in the design under this chapter.

(3) Post a surety bond for any injury that may result if the detention or exclusion of the articles proves to be unjustified.

(b) Seizure and Forfeiture.—Articles imported in violation of the rights set forth in section 1308 are subject to seizure and forfeiture in the same manner as property imported in violation of the customs laws. Any such forfeited articles shall be destroyed as directed by the Secretary of the Treasury or the court, as the case may be, except that the articles may be returned to the country of export whenever it is shown to the satisfaction of the Secretary of the Treasury that the importer had no reasonable grounds for believing that his or her acts constituted a violation of the law.

Sec. 1329.   Relation to Design Patent Law

The issuance of a design patent under title 35, United States Code, for an original design for an article of manufacture shall terminate any protection of the original design under this chapter.

Sec. 1330.   Common Law and Other Rights Unaffected

Nothing in this chapter shall annul or limit—

(1) common law or other rights or remedies, if any, available to or held by any person with respect to a design which has not been registered under this chapter; or

(2) any right under the trademark laws or any right protected against unfair competition.

Sec. 1331.   Administrator; Office of the Administrator

In this chapter, the "Administrator" is the Register of Copyrights, and the "Office of the Administrator" and the "Office" refer to the Copyright Office of the Library of Congress.

Sec. 1332.   No Retroactive Effect

Protection under this chapter shall not be available for any design that has been made public under section 1310(b) before the effective date of this chapter.

APPENDIX B

THE 1909 COPYRIGHT ACT (EXCERPTS)

CHAPTER 1—REGISTRATION OF COPYRIGHTS

§ 1.   Exclusive Rights as to Copyrighted Works.—Any person entitled thereto, upon complying with the provisions of this title, shall have the exclusive right:

(a) To print, reprint, publish, copy, and vend the copyrighted work;

(b) To translate the copyrighted work into other languages or dialects, or make any other version thereof, if it be a literary work; to dramatize it if it be a nondramatic work; to convert it into a novel or other nondramatic work if it be a drama; to arrange or adapt it if it be a musical work; to complete, execute, and finish it if it be a model or design for a work of art;

(c) To deliver, authorize the delivery of, read, or present the copyrighted work in public for profit if it be a lecture, sermon, address or similar production, or other nondramatic literary work; to make or procure the making of any transcription or record thereof by or from which, in whole or in part, it may in any manner or by any method be exhibited, delivered, presented, produced, or reproduced; and to play or perform it in public for profit, and to exhibit, represent, produce, or reproduce it in any manner or by any method whatsoever. The damages for the infringement by broadcast of any work referred to in this subsection shall not exceed the sum of $100 where the infringing broadcaster shows that he was not aware that he was infringing and that such infringement could not have been reasonably foreseen; and

(d) To perform or represent the copyrighted work publicly if it be a drama or, if it be a dramatic work and not reproduced in copies for sale, to vend any manuscript or any record whatsoever thereof; to make or to procure the making of any transcription or record thereof by or from which, in whole or in part, it may in any manner or by any method be exhibited, performed, represented, produced, or reproduced; and to exhibit, perform, represent, produce, or reproduce it in any manner or by any method whatsoever; and

(e) To perform the copyrighted work publicly for profit if it be a musical composition; and for the purpose of public performance for profit, and for the purposes set forth in subsection (a) hereof, to make any arrangement or setting of it or of the melody of it in any system of notation or any form of record in which the thought of an author may be recorded and from which it may be read or reproduced: *Provided,* That the provisions of this title, so far as they secure copyright controlling the parts of instruments serving to reproduce mechanically the musical work, shall include only compositions published and copyrighted after July 1, 1909, and shall not include the works of a foreign author or composer unless the foreign state or nation of which such author or composer is a citizen or subject grants, either by treaty, convention, agreement, or law, to citizens of the United States similar rights. And as a condition of extending the copyrighted control to such mechanical reproductions, that whenever the owner of a musical copyright has used or permitted or knowingly acquiesced in the use of the copyrighted work upon the parts of instruments serving to reproduce mechanically the musical work, any other person may make similar use of the copyrighted work upon the payment to the copyright proprietor of a royalty of 2 cents on each such part manufactured, to be paid by the manufacturer thereof; and the copyright proprietor may require, and if so the manufacturer shall furnish, a report under oath on the 20th day of each month on the number of parts of instruments manufactured during the previous month serving to reproduce mechanically said musical work, and royalties shall be due on the parts manufactured during any month upon the 20th of the next succeeding month. The payment of the royalty provided for by this section shall free the articles or devices for which such royalty has been paid from further contribution to the copyright except in case of public performance for profit. It shall be the duty of the copyright owner, if he uses the musical composition himself for the manufacture of parts of instruments serving to reproduce mechanically the musical work, or licenses others to do so, to file notice thereof, accompanied by a recording fee, in the copyright office, and any failure to file such notice shall be a complete defense to any suit, action, or proceeding for any infringement of such copyright.

In case of failure of such manufacturer to pay to the copyright proprietor within thirty days after demand in writing the full sum of royalties due at said rate at the date of such demand, the court may award taxable costs to the plaintiff and a reasonable counsel fee, and the court may, in its discretion, enter judgment therein for any sum in addition over the amount found to be due as royalty in accordance with the terms of this title, not exceeding three times such amount.

The reproduction or rendition of a musical composition by or upon coin-operated machines shall not be deemed a public performance for profit unless a fee is charged for admission to the place where such reproduction or rendition occurs.

(f) To reproduce and distribute to the public by sale or other transfer of ownership, or by rental, lease, or lending, reproductions of the copyrighted work if it be a sound recording: *Provided,* That the exclusive right of the owner of a copyright in a sound recording to reproduce it is limited to the right to duplicate the sound recording in a tangible form that directly or indirectly recaptures the actual sounds fixed in the recording: *Provided further,* That this right does not extend to the making or duplication of another sound recording that is an independent fixation of other sounds, even though such sounds imitate or simulate those in the copyrighted sound recording; or to reproductions made by transmitting organizations exclusively for their own use.

§ 2. Rights of Author or Proprietor of Unpublished Work.— Nothing in this title shall be construed to annul or limit the right of the author or proprietor of an unpublished work, at common law or in equity, to prevent the copying, publication, or use of such unpublished work without his consent, and to obtain damages therefor.

§ 3. Protection of Component Parts of Work Copyrighted; Composite Works or Periodicals.—The copyright provided by this title shall protect all the copyrightable component parts of the work copyrighted, and all matter therein in which copyright is already subsisting, but without extending the duration or scope of such copyright. The copyright upon composite works or periodicals shall give to the proprietor thereof all the rights in respect thereto which he would have if each part were individually copyrighted under this title.

§ 4. All Writings of Author Included.—The works for which copyright may be secured under this title shall include all the writings of an author.

§ 5. Classification of Works for Registration.—The application for registration shall specify to which of the following classes the work in which copyright is claimed belongs:

(a) Books, including composite and cyclopedic works, directories, gazetteers, and other compilations.

(b) Periodicals, including newspapers.

(c) Lectures, sermons, addresses (prepared for oral delivery).

(d) Dramatic or dramatico-musical compositions.

(e) Musical compositions.

(f) Maps.

(g) Works of art; models or designs for works of art.

(h) Reproductions of a work of art.

(i) Drawings or plastic works of a scientific or technical character.

(j) Photographs.

(k) Prints and pictorial illustrations including prints or labels used for articles of merchandise.

(*l*) Motion-picture photoplays.

(m) Motion pictures other than photoplays.

(n) Sound recordings.

The above specifications shall not be held to limit the subject matter of copyright as defined in section 4 of this title, nor shall any error in classification invalidate or impair the copyright protection secured under this title.

* * * *

§ 7. Copyright on Compilations of Works in Public Domain or of Copyrighted Works; Subsisting Copyrights Not Affected.

—Compilations or abridgements, adaptations, arrangements, dramatizations, translations, or other versions of works in the public domain or of copyrighted works when produced with the consent of the proprietor of the copyright in such works, or works republished with new matter, shall be regarded as new works subject to copyright under the provisions of this title; but the publication of any such new works shall not affect the force or validity of any subsisting copyright upon the matter employed or any part thereof, or be construed to imply an exclusive right to such use of the original works, or to secure or extend copyright in such original works.

* * * *

§ 9. Authors or Proprietors, Entitled; Aliens.

—The author or proprietor of any work made the subject of copyright by this title, or his executors, administrators, or assigns, shall have copyright for such work under the conditions and for the terms specified in this title: *Provided, however,* That the copyright secured by this title shall extend to the work of an author or proprietor who is a citizen or subject of a foreign state or nation only under the conditions described in subsections (a), (b), or (c) below:

(a) When an alien author or proprietor shall be domiciled within the United States at the time of the first publication of his work; or

(b) When the foreign state or nation of which such author or proprietor is a citizen or subject grants, either by treaty, convention, agreement, or law, to citizens of the United States the benefit of copyright on substantially the same basis as to its own citizens, or copyright protection, substantially equal to the protection secured to such foreign author under this title or by treaty; or when such foreign state or nation is a party to an international agreement which provides for reciprocity in the granting of copyright, by the terms of which agreement the United States may, at its pleasure, become a party thereto.

The existence of the reciprocal conditions aforesaid shall be determined by the President of the United States, by proclamation made from time to time, as the purposes of this title may require: *Provided,* That whenever the President shall find that the authors, copyright owners, or proprietors of works first produced or published abroad and subject to copyright or to renewal of copyright under the laws of the United States, including works subject to ad interim copyright, are or may have been temporarily unable to comply with the conditions and formalities prescribed with respect to such works by the copyright laws of the United States, because of the disruption or suspension of facilities essential for such compliance, he may by proclamation grant such extension of time as he may deem appropriate for the fulfillment of such conditions or formalities by authors, copyright owners, or proprietors who are citizens of the United States or who are nationals of countries which accord substantially equal treatment in this respect to authors, copyright owners, or proprietors who are citizens of the United States: *Provided further,* That no liability shall attach under this title for lawful uses made or acts done prior to the effective date of such proclamation in connection with such works, or in respect to the continuance for one year subsequent to such date of any business undertaking or enterprise lawfully undertaken prior to such date involving expenditure or contractual obligation in connection with the exploitation, production, reproduction, circulation, or performance of any such work.

The President may at any time terminate any proclamation authorized herein or any part thereof or suspend or extend its operation for such period or periods of time as in his judgment the interests of the United States may require.

(c) When the Universal Copyright Convention, signed at Geneva on September 6, 1952, shall be in force between the United States of America and the foreign state or nation of which such author is a citizen or subject, or in which the work was first published. Any work to which copyright is extended pursuant to this subsection shall be exempt from the following provisions of this title: (1) The requirement in section 1(e) that a foreign state or nation must grant to United States citizens mechanical reproduction rights similar to those specified therein; (2) the obligatory deposit requirements of the first sentence of section 13; (3) the provisions of sections 14, 16, 17, and 18; (4) the import prohibitions of section 107, to the extent that they are related to the manufacturing requirements of section 16; and (5) the requirements of sections 19 and 20: *Provided, however,* That such exemptions shall apply only if from the time of first publication all the copies of the work published with the authority of the author or other copyright proprietor shall bear the symbol © accompanied by the name of the copyright proprietor and the year of first publication placed in such manner and location as to give reasonable notice of claim of copyright.

Upon the coming into force of the Universal Copyright Convention in a foreign state or nation as hereinbefore provided, every book or periodical of a citizen or subject thereof in which ad interim copyright was subsisting on the effective date of said coming into force shall have copyright for twenty-eight years from the date of first publication abroad without the necessity of complying with the further formalities specified in section 23 of this title.

The provisions of this subsection shall not be extended to works of an author who is a citizen of, or domiciled in the United States of America regardless of place of first publication, or to works first published in the United States.

§ 10.   Publication of Work With Notice.—Any person entitled thereto by this title may secure copyright for his work by publication thereof with the notice of copyright required by this title; and such notice shall be affixed to each copy thereof published or offered for sale in the United States by authority of the copyright proprietor, except in the case of books seeking ad interim protection under section 22 of this title.

§ 11.   Registration of Claim and Issuance of Certificate.— Such person may obtain registration of his claim to copyright by complying with the provisions of this title, including the deposit of copies, and upon such compliance the Register of Copyrights shall issue to him the certificates provided for in section 209 of this title.

§ 12.   Works Not Reproduced for Sale.—Copyright may also be had of the works of an author, of which copies are not reproduced for sale, by the deposit, with claim of copyright, of one complete copy of such work if it be a lecture or similar production or a dramatic, musical, or dramatico-musical composition; of a title and description, with one print taken from each scene or act, if the work be a motion-picture photoplay; of a photographic print if the work be a photograph; of a title and description, with not less than two prints taken from different sections of a complete motion picture, if the work be a motion picture other than a photoplay; or of a photograph or other identifying reproduction thereof, if it be a work of art or a plastic work or drawing. But the privilege of registration of copyright secured hereunder shall not exempt the copyright proprietor from the deposit of copies, under sections 13 and 14 of this title, where the work is later reproduced in copies for sale.

§ 13.   Deposit of Copies After Publication; Action or Proceeding for Infringement.—After copyright has been secured by publication of the work with the notice of copyright as provided in section 10 of this title, there shall be promptly deposited in the Copyright Office or in the mail addressed to the Register of Copyrights, Washington, District of Columbia, two complete copies of the best edition thereof then published, or if the work is by an author who is a citizen or subject of a foreign state or nation and has been published in a foreign country, one complete copy of the best edition then published in such foreign country, which copies or copy, if the work be a book or periodical, shall have been produced in accordance with the manufacturing provisions specified in section 16 of this title; or if such work be a contribution to a periodical, for which contribution special registration is requested, one copy of the issue or issues containing such contribution; or if the work belongs to a class specified in subsections (g), (h), (i) or (k) of section 5 of this title, and if the Register of Copyrights determines that it is impracticable to deposit copies because of their size, weight, fragility, or monetary value he may permit the deposit of photographs or other identifying reproductions in lieu of copies of the work as published under such rules and regulations as he may prescribe with the approval of the Librarian of Congress; or if the work is not reproduced in copies for sale there shall be deposited the copy, print, photograph, or other identifying reproduction provided by section 12 of this title, such copies or copy, print, photograph, or other reproduction to be accompanied in each case by a claim of copyright. No action or proceeding shall be maintained for infringement of copyright in any work until the provisions of this title with respect to the deposit of copies and registration of such work shall have been complied with.

§ 14.   Same; Failure to Deposit; Demand; Penalty.—Should the copies called for by section 13 of this title not be promptly deposited as provided in this title, the Register of Copyrights may at any time after the publication of the work, upon actual notice, require the proprietor of the copyright to deposit them, and after the said demand shall have been made, in default of the deposit of copies of the work within three months from any part of the United States, except an outlying territorial possession of the United States, or within six months from any outlying territorial possession of the United States, or from any foreign country, the proprietor of the copyright shall be liable to a fine of $100 and to pay to the Library of Congress twice the amount of the retail price of the best edition of the work, and the copyright shall become void.

* * * *

§ 19.   Notice; Form.—The notice of copyright required by section 10 of this title shall consist either of the word "Copyright", the abbreviation "Copr.", or the symbol ©, accompanied by the name of the copyright proprietor, and if the work be a printed literary, musical, or dramatic work, the notice shall include also the year in which the copyright was secured by publication. In the case, however, of copies of works specified in subsections (f) to (k), inclusive, of section 5 of this title, the notice may consist of the letter C enclosed within a circle, thus ©, accompanied by the initials, monogram, mark, or symbol of the copyright proprietor: *Provided,* That on some accessible portion of such copies or of the margin, back, permanent base, or pedestal, or of the substance on which such copies shall be mounted, his name shall appear. But in the case of works in which copyright was subsisting on July 1, 1909, the notice of copyright may be either in one of the forms prescribed herein or may consist of the following words: "Entered according to Act of Congress, in the year ___, by A.B., and in the office of the Librarian of Congress, at Washington, D.C.," or, at his option the word "Copyright", together with the year the copyright was entered and the name of the party by whom it was taken out; thus, "Copyright, 19__, by A.B."

In the case of reproductions of works specified in subsection (n) of section 5 of this title, the notice shall consist of the symbol P (the letter P in a circle), the year of first publication of the sound recording, and the name of the owner of copyright in the sound recording, or an abbreviation by which the name can be recognized, or a generally known alternative designation of the owner: *Provided,* That if the producer of the sound recording is named on the labels or containers of the reproduction, and if no other name appears in conjunction with the notice, his name shall be considered a part of the notice.

§ 20.   Same; Place of Application of; One Notice in Each Volume or Number of Newspaper or Periodical.—The notice of copyright shall be applied, in the case of a book or other printed publication, upon its title page or the page immediately following, or if a periodical either upon the title page or upon the first page of text of each separate number or under the title heading, or if a musical work either upon its title page or the first page of music, or if a sound recording on the surface of reproductions thereof or on the label or container in such manner and location as to give reasonable notice of the claim of copyright. One notice of copyright in each volume or in each number of a newspaper or periodical published shall suffice.

§ 21.   Same; Effect of Accidental Omission From Copy or Copies.—Where the copyright proprietor has sought to comply with the provisions of this title with respect to notice, the omission by accident or mistake of the prescribed notice from a particular copy or copies shall not invalidate the copyright or prevent recovery for infringement against any person who, after actual notice of the copyright, begins an undertaking to infringe it, but shall prevent the recovery of damages against an innocent infringer who has been misled by the omission of the notice; and in a suit for infringement no permanent injunction shall be had unless the copyright proprietor shall reimburse to the innocent infringer his reasonable outlay innocently incurred if the court, in its discretion, shall so direct.

* * * *

§ 24.   Duration, Renewal and Extension.—The copyright secured by this title shall endure for twenty-eight years from the date of first publication, whether the copyrighted work bears the author's true name or is published anonymously or under an assumed name: *Provided,* That in the case of any posthumous work or of any periodical, cyclopedic, or other composite work upon which the copyright was originally secured by the proprietor thereof, or of any work copyrighted by a corporate body (otherwise than as assignee or licensee of the individual author) or by an employer for whom such work is made for hire, the proprietor of such copyright shall be entitled to a renewal and extension of the copyright in such work for the further term of twenty-eight years when application for such renewal and extension shall have been made to the copyright office and duly registered therein within one year prior to the expiration of the original term of copyright: *And provided further,* That in the case of any other copyrighted work, including a contribution by an individual author to a periodical or to a cyclopedic or other composite work, the author of such work, if still living, or the widow, widower, or children of the author, if the author be not living, or if such author, widow, widower or children be not living, then the author's executors, or in the absence of a will, his next of kin shall be entitled to a renewal and extension of the copyright in such work for a further term of twenty-eight years when application for such renewal and extension shall have been made to the copyright office and duly registered therein within one year prior to the expiration of the original term of copyright: *And provided further,* That in default of the registration of such application for renewal and extension, the copyright in any work shall determine at the expiration of twenty-eight years from first publication.

* * * *

§ 26.   Terms Defined.—In the interpretation and construction of this title "the date of publication" shall in the case of a work of which copies are reproduced for sale or distribution be held to be the earliest date when copies of the first authorized edition were placed on sale, sold, or publicly distributed by the proprietor of the copyright or under his authority, and the word "author" shall include an employer in the case of works made for hire.

For the purposes of this section and sections 10, 11, 13, 14, 21, 101, 106, 109, 209, 215, but not for any other purpose, a reproduction of a work described in subsection 5(n) shall be considered to be a copy thereof. "Sound recordings" are works that result from the fixation of a series of musical, spoken, or other sounds, but not including the sounds accompanying a motion picture. "Reproductions of sound recordings" are material objects in which sounds other than those accompanying a motion picture are fixed by any method now known or later developed, and from which the sounds can be perceived, reproduced, or otherwise communicated, either directly or with the aid of a machine or device, and include the "parts of instruments serving to reproduce mechanically the musical work", "mechanical reproductions", and "interchangeable parts, such as discs or tapes for use in mechanical music-producing machines" referred to in sections 1(e) and 101(e) of this title.

§ 27.   Copyright Distinct From Property in Object Copyrighted; Effect of Sale of Object, and of Assignment of Copyright.—The copyright is distinct from the property in the material object copyrighted, and the sale or conveyance, by gift or otherwise, of the material object shall not of itself constitute a transfer of the copyright, nor shall the assignment of the copyright constitute a transfer of the title to the material object; but nothing in this title shall be deemed to forbid, prevent, or restrict the transfer of any copy of a copyrighted work the possession of which has been lawfully obtained.

§ 28.   Assignments and Bequests.—Copyright secured under this title or previous copyright laws of the United States may be assigned, granted, or mortgaged by an instrument in writing signed by the proprietor of the copyright, or may be bequeathed by will.

* * * *

§ 30.   Same; Record.—Every assignment of copyright shall be recorded in the copyright office within three calendar months after its execution in the United States or within six calendar months after its execution without the limits of the United States, in default of which it shall be void as against any subsequent purchaser or mortgagee for a valuable consideration, without notice, whose assignment has been duly recorded.

§ 31.   Same; Certificate of Record.—The Register of Copyrights shall, upon payment of the prescribed fee, record such assignment, and shall return it to the sender with a certificate of record attached under seal of the copyright office, and upon the payment of the fee prescribed by this title he shall furnish to any person requesting the same a certified copy thereof under the said seal.

§ 32.   Same; Use of Name of Assignee in Notice.—When an assignment of the copyright in a specified book or other work has been recorded the assignee may substitute his name for that of the assignor in the statutory notice of copyright prescribed by this title.

CHAPTER 2—INFRINGEMENT PROCEEDINGS

Sec.
§ 101.   Infringement.
    (a) Injunction.
    (b) Damages and profits; amount; other remedies.
§ 104.   Willful infringement for profit.

§ 101.   Infringement.—If any person shall infringe the copyright in any work protected under the copyright laws of the United States such person shall be liable:

(a) Injunction.—To an injunction restraining such infringement;

(b) Damages and Profits; Amount; Other Remedies.—To pay to the copyright proprietor such damages as the copyright proprietor may have suffered due to the infringement, as well as all the profits which the infringer shall have made from such infringement, and in proving profits the plaintiff shall be required to prove sales only, and the defendant shall be required to prove every element of cost which he claims, or in lieu of actual damages and profits, such damages as to the court shall appear to be just, and in assessing such damages the court may, in its discretion, allow the amounts as hereinafter stated, but in case of a newspaper reproduction of a copyrighted photograph, such damages shall not exceed the sum of $200 nor be less than the sum of $50, and in the case of the infringement of an undramatized or nondramatic work by means of motion pictures, where the infringer shall show that he was not aware that he was infringing, and that such infringement could not have been reasonably foreseen, such damages shall not exceed the sum of $100; and in the case of an infringement of a copyrighted dramatic or dramatico-musical work by a maker of motion pictures and his agencies for distribution thereof to exhibitors, where such infringer shows that he was not aware that he was infringing a copyrighted work, and that such infringements could not reasonably have been foreseen, the entire sum of such damages recoverable by the copyright proprietor from such infringing maker and his agencies for the distribution to exhibitors of such infringing motion picture shall not exceed the sum of $5,000 nor be less than $250, and such damages shall in no other case exceed the sum of $5,000 nor be less than the sum of $250, and shall not be regarded as a penalty. But the foregoing exceptions shall not deprive the copyright proprietor of any other remedy given him under this law, nor shall the limitation as to the amount of recovery apply to infringements occurring after the actual notice to a defendant, either by service of process in a suit or other written notice served upon him. . . .

* * * *

§ 104.   Willful Infringement for Profit.—(a) Except as provided in subsection (b), any person who willfully and for profit shall infringe any copyright secured by this title, or who shall knowingly and willfully aid or abet such infringement, shall be deemed guilty of a misdemeanor, and upon conviction thereof shall be punished by imprisonment for not exceeding one year or by a fine of not less than $100 nor more than $1,000, or both, in the discretion of the court: *Provided, however,* That nothing in this title shall be so construed as to prevent the performance of religious or secular works such as oratorios, cantatas, masses, or octavo choruses by public schools, church choirs, or vocal societies, rented, borrowed, or obtained from some public library, public school, church choir, school choir, or vocal society, provided the performance is given for charitable or educational purposes and not for profit.

(b) Any person who willfully and for profit shall infringe any copyright provided by section 1(f) of this title, or who should knowingly and willfully aid or abet such infringement, shall be fined not more than $25,000 or imprisoned not more than one year, or both, for the first offense and shall be fined not more than $50,000 or imprisoned not more than two years, or both for any subsequent offense.

* * * *

APPENDIX C

REGULATIONS OF THE U.S. COPYRIGHT OFFICE

The current text of the regulations of the U.S. Copyright Office, codified at Chapter II of Title 37 of the Code of Federal Regulations, is available online at http://www.copyright.gov/title37/. The current text of the regulations of the Copyright Royalty Board, including the rates and terms for statutory licenses, codified at Chapter III of Title 37 of the Code of Federal Regulations, is available online at http://www.loc.gov/crb/laws/title37/.

BERNE CONVENTION FOR THE PROTECTION OF LITERARY AND ARTISTIC WORKS

(Paris Text 1971, Excerpts)

The countries of the Union, being equally animated by the desire to protect, in as effective and uniform a manner as possible, the rights of authors in their literary and artistic works,

Recognising the importance of the work of the Revision Conference held at Stockholm in 1967,

Having resolved to revise the Act adopted by the Stockholm Conference, while maintaining without change Article 1 to 20 and 22 to 26 of that Act.

Consequently, the undersigned Plenipotentiaries, having presented their full powers, recognised as in good and due form, have agreed as follows:

Article 1

The countries to which this Convention applies constitute a Union for the protection of the rights of authors in their literary and artistic works.

Article 2

(1) The expression "literary and artistic works" shall include every production in the literary, scientific and artistic domain, whatever may be the mode or form of its expression, such as books, pamphlets and other writings; lectures, addresses, sermons and other works of the same nature; dramatic or dramatico-musical works; choreographic works and entertainments in dumb show; musical compositions with or without words; cinematographic works to which are assimilated works expressed by a process analogous to cinematography; works of drawing, painting, architecture, sculpture, engraving and lithography; photographic works to which are assimilated works expressed by a process analogous to photography; works of applied art; illustrations, maps, plans, sketches and three-dimensional works relative to geography, topography, architecture or science.

(2) It shall, however, be a matter for legislation in the countries of the Union to prescribe that works in general or any specified categories of works shall not be protected unless they have been fixed in some material form.

(3) Translations, adaptations, arrangements of music and other alterations of a literary or artistic work shall be protected as original works without prejudice to the copyright in the original work.

(4) It shall be a matter for legislation in the countries of the Union to determine the protection to be granted to official texts of a legislative, administrative and legal nature, and to official translations of such texts.

(5) Collections of literary or artistic works such as encyclopaedias and anthologies which, by reason of the selection and arrangement of their contents, constitute intellectual creations shall be protected as such, without prejudice to the copyright in each of the works forming part of such collections.

(6) The works mentioned in this Article shall enjoy protection in all countries of the Union. This protection shall operate for the benefit of the author and his successors in title.

(7) Subject to the provisions of Article 7(4) of this Convention, it shall be a matter for legislation in the countries of the Union to determine the extent of the application of their laws to works of applied art and industrial designs and models, as well as the conditions under which such works, designs and models shall be protected. Works protected in the country of origin solely as designs and models shall be entitled in another country of the Union only to such special protection as is granted in that country to designs and models; however, if no such special protection is granted in that country, such works shall be protected as artistic works.

(8) The protection of this Convention shall not apply to news of the day or to miscellaneous facts having the character of mere items of press information.

Article 2bis

(1) It shall be a matter for legislation in the countries of the Union to exclude, wholly or in part, from the protection provided by the preceding Article political speeches and speeches delivered in the course of legal proceedings.

(2) It shall also be a matter for legislation in the countries of the Union to determine the conditions under which lectures, addresses and other works of the same nature which are delivered in public may be reproduced by the press, broadcast, communicated to the public by wire and made the subject of public communication as envisaged in Article 11bis (1) of this Convention, when such use is justified by the informatory purpose.

(3) Nevertheless, the author shall enjoy the exclusive right of making a collection of his works mentioned in the preceding paragraphs.

Article 3

(1) The protection of this Convention shall apply to:

(a) authors who are nationals of one of the countries of the Union, for their works, whether published or not;

(b) authors who are not nationals of one of the countries of the Union, for their works first published in one of those countries, or simultaneously in a country outside the Union and in a country of the Union.

(2) Authors who are not nationals of one of the countries of the Union but who have their habitual residence in one of them shall, for the purposes of this Convention, be assimilated to nationals of that country.

(3) The expression "published works" means works published with the consent of their authors, whatever may be the means of manufacture of the copies, provided that the availability of such copies has been such as to satisfy the reasonable requirements of the public, having regard to the nature of the work. The performance of a dramatic, dramatico-musical, cinematographic or musical work, the public recitation of a literary work, the communication by wire or the broadcasting of literary or artistic works, the exhibition of a work of art and the construction of a work of architecture shall not constitute publication.

(4) A work shall be considered as having been published simultaneously in several countries if it has been published in two or more countries within thirty days of its first publication.

Article 4

The protection of this Convention shall apply, even if the conditions of Article 3 are not fulfilled, to:

(a) authors of cinematographic works the maker of which has his headquarters or habitual residence in one of the countries of the Union;

(b) authors of works of architecture erected in a country of the Union or of other artistic works incorporated in a building or other structure located in a country of the Union.

Article 5

(1) Authors shall enjoy, in respect of works for which they are protected under this Convention, in countries of the Union other than the country of origin, the rights which their respective laws do now or may hereafter grant to their nationals, as well as the rights specially granted by this Convention.

(2) The enjoyment and the exercise of these rights shall not be subject to any formality; such enjoyment and such exercise shall be independent of the existence of protection in the country of origin of the work. Consequently, apart from the provisions of this Convention, the extent of protection, as well as the means of redress afforded to the author to protect his rights, shall be governed exclusively by the laws of the country where protection is claimed.

(3) Protection in the country of origin is governed by domestic law. However, when the author is not a national of the country of origin of the work for which he is protected under this Convention, he shall enjoy in that country the same rights as national authors.

(4) The country of origin shall be considered to be:

(a) in the case of works first published in a country of the Union, that country; in the case of works published simultaneously in several countries of the Union which grant different terms of protection, the country whose legislation grants the shortest term of protection;

(b) in the case of works published simultaneously in a country outside the Union and in a country of the Union, the latter country;

(c) in the case of unpublished works or of works first published in a country outside the Union, without simultaneous publication in a country of the Union, the country of the Union of which the author is a national, provided that:

(i) when these are cinematographic works the maker of which has his headquarters or his habitual residence in a country of the Union, the country of origin shall be that country, and

(ii) when these are works of architecture erected in a country of the Union or other artistic works incorporated in a building or other structure located in a country of the Union, the country of origin shall be that country.

Article 6

(1) Where any country outside the Union fails to protect in an adequate manner the works of authors who are nationals of one of the countries of the Union, the latter country may restrict the protection given to the works of authors who are, at the date of the first publication thereof, nationals of the other country and are not habitually resident in one of the countries of the Union. If the country of first publication avails itself of this right, the other countries of the Union shall not be required to grant to works thus subjected to special treatment a wider protection than that granted to them in the country of first publication.

(2) No restrictions introduced by virtue of the preceding paragraph shall affect the rights which an author may have acquired in respect of a work published in a country of the Union before such restrictions were put into force.

(3) The countries of the Union which restrict the grant of copyright in accordance with this Article shall give notice thereof to the Director General of the World Intellectual Property Organisation (hereinafter designated as "the Director General") by a written declaration specifying the countries in regard to which protection is restricted, and the restrictions to which rights of authors who are nationals of those countries are subjected. The Director General shall immediately communicate this declaration to all the countries of the Union.

Article 6bis

(1) Independently of the author's economic rights, and even after the transfer of the said rights, the author shall have the right to claim authorship of the work and to object to any distortion, mutilation or other modification of, or other derogatory action in relation to, the said work, which would be prejudicial to his honour or reputation.

(2) The rights granted to the author in accordance with the preceding paragraph shall, after his death, be maintained, at least until the expiry of the economic rights, and shall be exercisable by the persons or institutions authorized by the legislation of the country where protection is claimed. However, those countries whose legislation, at the moment of their ratification of or accession to this Act, does not provide for the protection after the death of the author of all the rights set out in the preceding paragraph may provide that some of these rights may, after his death, cease to be maintained.

(3) The means of redress for safeguarding the rights granted by this Article shall be governed by the legislation of the country where protection is claimed.

Article 7

(1) The term of protection granted by this Convention shall be the life of the author and fifty years after his death.

(2) However, in the case of cinematographic works, the countries of the Union may provide that the term of protection shall expire fifty years after the work has been made available to the public with the consent of the author, or, failing such an event within fifty years from the making of such a work, fifty years after the making.

(3) In the case of anonymous or pseudonymous works, the terms of protection granted by this Convention shall expire fifty years after the work has been lawfully made available to the public. However, when the pseudonym adopted by the author leaves no doubt as to his identity, the term of protection shall be that provided in paragraph (1). If the author of an anonymous or pseudonymous work discloses his identity during the above-mentioned period, the term of protection applicable shall be that provided in paragraph (1). The countries of the Union shall not be required to protect anonymous or pseudonymous works in respect of which it is reasonable to presume that their author has been dead for fifty years.

(4) It shall be a matter for legislation in the countries of the Union to determine the term of protection of photographic works and that of works of applied art in so far as they are protected as artistic works; however, this term shall last at least until the end of a period of twenty-five years from the making of such a work.

(5) The term of protection subsequent to the death of the author and the terms provided by paragraphs (2), (3) and (4) shall run from the date of death or of the event referred to in those paragraphs, but such terms shall always be deemed to begin on the first of January of the year following the death or such event.

(6) The countries of the Union may grant a term of protection in excess of those provided by the preceding paragraphs.

(7) Those countries of the Union bound by the Rome Act of this Convention which grant, in their national legislation in force at the time of signature of the present Act, shorter terms of protection than those provided for in the preceding paragraphs shall have the right to maintain such terms when ratifying or acceding to the present Act.

(8) In any case, the term shall be governed by the legislation of the country where protection is claimed; however, unless the legislation of that country otherwise provides, the term shall not exceed the term fixed in the country of origin of the work.

Article 7bis

The provisions of the preceding Article shall also apply in the case of a work of joint authorship, provided that the terms measured from the death of the author shall be calculated from the death of the last surviving author.

Article 8

Authors of literary and artistic works protected by this Convention shall enjoy the exclusive right of making and of authorising the translation of their works throughout the term of protection of their rights in the original works.

Article 9

(1) Authors of literary and artistic works protected by this Convention shall have the exclusive right of authorising the reproduction of these works, in any manner or form.

(2) It shall be a matter for legislation in the countries of the Union to permit the reproduction of such works in certain special cases, provided that such reproduction does not conflict with a normal exploitation of the work and does not unreasonably prejudice the legitimate interests of the author.

(3) Any sound or visual recording shall be considered as a reproduction for the purposes of this Convention.

Article 10

(1) It shall be permissible to make quotations from a work which has already been lawfully made available to the public, provided that their making is compatible with fair practice, and their extent does not exceed that justified by the purpose, including quotations from newspaper articles and periodicals in the form of press summaries.

(2) It shall be a matter for legislation in the countries of the Union, and for special agreements existing or to be concluded between them, to permit the utilisation, to the extent justified by the purpose, of literary or artistic works by way of illustration in publications, broadcasts or sound or visual recordings for teaching, provided such utilisation is compatible with fair practice.

(3) Where use is made of works in accordance with the preceding paragraphs of this Article, mention shall be made of the source, and of the name of the author if it appears thereon.

Article 10bis

(1) It shall be a matter for legislation in the countries of the Union to permit the reproduction by the press, the broadcasting or the communication to the public by wire of articles published in newspapers or periodicals on current economic, political or religious topics, and of broadcast works of the same character, in cases in which the reproduction, broadcasting or such communication thereof is not expressly reserved. Nevertheless, the source must always be clearly indicated; the legal consequences of a breach of this obligation shall be determined by the legislation of the country where protection is claimed.

(2) It shall also be a matter for legislation in the countries of the Union to determine the conditions under which, for the purpose of reporting current events by means of photography, cinematography, broadcasting or communication to the public by wire, literary or artistic works seen or heard in the course of the event may, to the extent justified by the informatory purpose, be reproduced and made available to the public.

Article 11

(1) Authors of dramatic, dramatico-musical and musical works shall enjoy the exclusive right of authorising:

(i) the public performance of their works, including such public performance by any means or process;

(ii) any communication to the public of the performance of their works.

(2) Authors of dramatic or dramatico-musical works shall enjoy, during the full term of their rights in the original works, the same rights with respect to translations thereof.

Article 11bis

(1) Authors of literary and artistic works shall enjoy the exclusive right of authorising:

(i) the broadcasting of their works or the communication thereof to the public by any other means of wireless diffusion of signs, sounds or images;

(ii) any communication to the public by wire or by rebroadcasting of the broadcast of the work, when this communication is made by an organisation other than the original one;

(iii) the public communication by loudspeaker or any other analogous instrument transmitting, by signs, sounds or images, the broadcast of the work.

(2) It shall be a matter for legislation in the countries of the Union to determine the conditions under which the rights mentioned in the preceding paragraph may be exercised, but these conditions shall apply only in the countries where they have been prescribed. They shall not in any circumstances be prejudicial to the moral rights of the author, nor to his right to obtain equitable remuneration which, in the absence of agreement, shall be fixed by competent authority.

(3) In the absence of any contrary stipulation, permission granted in accordance with paragraph (1) of this Article shall not imply permission to record, by means of instruments recording sounds or images, the work broadcast. It shall, however, be a matter for legislation in the countries of the Union to determine the regulations for ephemeral recordings made by a broadcasting organisation by means of its own facilities and used for its own broadcasts. The preservation of these recordings in official archives may, on the ground of their exceptional documentary character, be authorised by such legislation.

Article 11ter

(1) Authors of literary works shall enjoy the exclusive right of authorising:

(i) the public recitation of their words, including such public recitation by any means or process;

(ii) any communication to the public of the recitation of their works.

(2) Authors of literary works shall enjoy, during the full term of their rights in the original works, the same rights with respect to translations thereof.

Article 12

Authors of literary or artistic works shall enjoy the exclusive right of authorising adaptations, arrangements and other alterations of their works.

Article 13

(1) Each country of the Union may impose for itself reservations and conditions on the exclusive right granted to the author of a musical work and to the author of any words, the recording of which together with the musical work has already been authorised by the latter, to authorise the sound recording of that musical work, together with such words, if any; but all such reservations and conditions shall apply only in the countries which have imposed them and shall not, in any circumstances, be prejudicial to the rights of these authors to obtain equitable remuneration which, in the absence of agreement, shall be fixed by competent authority.

(2) Recordings of musical works made in a country of the Union in accordance with Article 13(3) of the Conventions signed at Rome on 2 June 1928, and at Brussels on 26 June 1948, may be reproduced in that country without the permission of the author of the musical work until a date two years after that country becomes bound by this Act.

(3) Recordings made in accordance with paragraphs (1) and (2) of this Article and imported without permission from the parties concerned into a country where they are treated as infringing recordings shall be liable to seizure.

Article 14

(1) Authors of literary or artistic works shall have the exclusive right of authorising:

(i) the cinematographic adaptation and reproduction of these works, and the distribution of the works thus adapted or reproduced;

(ii) the public performance and communication to the public by wire of the works thus adapted or reproduced.

(2) The adaptation into any other artistic form of a cinematographic production derived from literary or artistic works shall, without prejudice to the authorisation of the author of the cinematographic production, remain subject to the authorisation of the authors of the original works.

(3) The provisions of Article 13(1) shall not apply.

*Article 14*bis

(1) Without prejudice to the copyright in any work which may have been adapted or reproduced, a cinematographic work shall be protected as an original work. The owner of copyright in a cinematographic work shall enjoy the same rights as the author of an original work, including the rights referred to in the preceding Article.

(2)(a) Ownership of copyright in a cinematographic work shall be a matter for legislation in a country where protection is claimed.

(b) However, in the countries of the Union which, by legislation, include among the owners of copyright in a cinematographic work authors who have brought contributions to the making of the work, such authors, if they have undertaken to bring such contributions, may not, in the absence of any contrary or special stipulation, object to the reproduction, distribution, public performance, communication to the public by wire, broadcasting or any other communication to the public, or to the subtitling or dubbing of texts, of the work.

(c) The question whether or not the form of the undertaking referred to above should, for the application of the preceding subparagraph (b), be in a written agreement or a written act of the same effect shall be a matter for the legislation of the country where the maker of the cinematographic work has his headquarters or habitual residence. However, it shall be a matter for the legislation of the country of the Union where protection is claimed to provide that the said undertaking shall be in a written agreement or a written act of the same effect. The countries whose legislation so provides shall notify the Director General by means of a written declaration, which will be immediately communicated by him to all the other countries of the Union.

(d) By "contrary or special stipulation" is meant any restrictive condition which is relevant to the aforesaid undertaking.

(3) Unless the national legislation provides to the contrary, the provisions of paragraph (2)(b) above shall not be applicable to authors of scenarios, dialogues and musical works created for the making of the cinematographic work, or to the principal director thereof. However, those countries of the Union whose legislation does not contain rules providing for the application of the said paragraph (2)(b) to such director shall notify the Director General by means of a written declaration, which will be immediately communicated by him to all the other countries of the Union.

Article 14ter

(1) The author, or after his death the persons or institutions authorised by national legislation, shall, with respect to original works of art and original manuscripts of writers and composers, enjoy the inalienable right to an interest in any sale of the work subsequent to the first transfer by the author of the work.

(2) The protection provided by the preceding paragraph may be claimed in a country of the Union only if legislation in the country to which the author belongs so permits, and to the extent permitted by the country where this protection is claimed.

(3) The procedure for collection and the amounts shall be matters for determination by national legislation.

Article 15

(1) In order that the author of a literary or artistic work protected by this Convention shall, in the absence of proof to the contrary, be regarded as such, and consequently be entitled to institute infringement proceedings in the countries of the Union, it shall be sufficient for his name to appear on the work in the usual manner. This paragraph shall be applicable even if this name is a pseudonym, where the pseudonym adopted by the author leaves no doubt as to his identity.

(2) The person or body corporate whose name appears on a cinematographic work in the usual manner shall, in the absence of proof to the contrary, be presumed to be the maker of the said work.

(3) In the case of anonymous and pseudonymous works, other than those referred to in paragraph (1) above, the publisher whose name appears on the work shall, in the absence of proof to the contrary, be deemed to represent the author, and in this capacity he shall be entitled

to protect and enforce the author's rights. The provisions of this paragraph shall cease to apply when the author reveals his identity and establishes his claim to authorship of the work.

(4)(a) In the case of unpublished works where the identity of the author is unknown, but where there is every ground to presume that he is a national of a country of the Union, it shall be a matter for legislation in that country to designate the competent authority which shall represent the author and shall be entitled to protect and enforce his rights in the countries of the Union.

(b) Countries of the Union which makes such designation under the terms of this provision shall notify the Director General by means of a written declaration giving full information concerning the authority thus designated. The Director General shall at once communicate this declaration to all other countries of the Union.

Article 16

(1) Infringing copies of a work shall be liable to seizure in any country of the Union where the work enjoys legal protection.

(2) The provisions of the preceding paragraph shall also apply to reproductions coming from a country where the work is not protected, or has ceased to be protected.

(3) The seizure shall take place in accordance with the legislation of each country.

Article 17

The provisions of this Convention cannot in any way affect the right of the Government of each country of the Union to permit, to control, or to prohibit, by legislation or regulation, the circulation, presentation, or exhibition of any work or production in regard to which the competent authority may find it necessary to exercise that right.

Article 18

(1) This Convention shall apply to all works which, at the moment of its coming into force, have not yet fallen into the public domain in the country of origin through the expiry of the term of protection.

(2) If, however, through the expiry of the term of protection which was previously granted, a work has fallen into the public domain of the country where protection is claimed, that work shall not be protected anew.

(3) The application of this principle shall be subject to any provisions contained in special conventions to that effect existing or to be concluded between countries of the Union. In the absence of such provisions, the respective countries shall determine, each in so far as it is concerned, the conditions of application of this principle.

(4) The preceding provisions shall also apply in the case of new accessions to the Union and to cases in which protection is extended by the application of Article 7 or by the abandonment of reservations.

Article 19

The provisions of this Convention shall not preclude the making of a claim to the benefit of any greater protection which may be granted by legislation in a country of the Union.

Article 20

The Governments of the countries of the Union reserve the right to enter into special agreements among themselves, in so far as such agreements grant to authors more extensive rights than those granted by the Convention, or contain other provisions not contrary to this Convention. The provisions of existing agreements which satisfy these conditions shall remain applicable.

* * * *

Article 33

(1) Any dispute between two or more countries of the Union concerning the interpretation or application of this Convention, not settled by negotiation, may, by any one of the countries concerned, be brought before the International Court of Justice by application in conformity with the Statute of the Court, unless the countries concerned agree on some other method of settlement. The country bringing the dispute before the Court shall inform the International Bureau; the International Bureau shall bring the matter to the attention of the other countries of the Union.

(2) Each country may, at the time it signs this Act or deposits its instrument of ratification or accession, declare that it does not consider itself bound by the provisions of paragraph (1). With regard to any dispute between such country and any other country of the Union, the provisions of paragraph (1) shall not apply.

(3) Any country having made a declaration in accordance with the provisions of paragraph (2) may, at any time, withdraw its declaration by notification addressed to the Director General.

* * * *

Article 36

(1) Any country party to this Convention undertakes to adopt, in accordance with its constitution, the measures necessary to ensure the application of this Convention.

(2) It is understood that, at the time a country becomes bound by this Convention, it will be in a position under its domestic law to give effect to the provisions of this Convention.

* * * *

APPENDIX E

UNIVERSAL COPYRIGHT CONVENTION, AS REVISED AT PARIS, 1971 (EXCERPTS)

The Contracting States,

Moved by the desire to ensure in all countries copyright protection of literary, scientific and artistic works,

Convinced that a system of copyright protection appropriate to all nations of the world and expressed in a universal convention, additional to, and without impairing international systems already in force, will ensure respect for the rights of the individual and encourage the development of literature, the sciences and the arts,

Persuaded that such a universal copyright system will facilitate a wider dissemination of works of the human mind and increase international understanding,

Have resolved to revise the Universal Copyright Convention as signed at Geneva on 6 September 1952 (hereinafter called "the 1952 Convention"), and consequently,

Have agreed as follows:

Article I

Each Contracting State undertakes to provide for the adequate and effective protection of the rights of authors and other copyright proprietors in literary, scientific and artistic works, including writings, musical, dramatic and cinematographic works, and paintings, engravings and sculpture.

Article II

1. Published works of nationals of any Contracting State and works first published in that State shall enjoy in each other Contracting State the same protection as that other State accords to works of its nationals first published in its own territory, as well as the protection specially granted by this Convention.

2. Unpublished works of nationals of each Contracting State shall enjoy in each other Contracting State the same protection as that other State accords to unpublished works of its own nationals, as well as the protection specially granted by this Convention.

3. For the purpose of this Convention any Contracting State may, by domestic legislation, assimilate to its own nationals any person domiciled in that State.

Article III

1. Any Contracting State which, under its domestic law, requires as a condition of copyright, compliance with formalities such as deposit, registration, notice, notarial certificates, payment of fees or manufacture

or publication in that Contracting State, shall regard these requirements as satisfied with respect to all works protected in accordance with this Convention and first published outside its territory and the author of which is not one of its nationals, if from the time of the first publication all the copies of the work published with the authority of the author or other copyright proprietor bear the symbol © accompanied by the name of the copyright proprietor and the year of first publication placed in such manner and location as to give reasonable notice of claim of copyright.

2.   The provisions of paragraph 1 shall not preclude any Contracting State from requiring formalities or other conditions for the acquisition and enjoyment of copyright in respect of works first published in its territory or works of its nationals wherever published.

3.   The provisions of paragraph 1 shall not preclude any Contracting State from providing that a person seeking judicial relief must, in bringing the action, comply with procedural requirements, such as that the complainant must appear through domestic counsel or that the complainant must deposit with the court or an administrative office, or both, a copy of the work involved in the litigation; provided that failure to comply with such requirements shall not affect the validity of the copyright, nor shall any such requirement be imposed upon a national of another Contracting State if such requirement is not imposed on nationals of the State in which protection is claimed.

4.   In each Contracting State there shall be legal means of protecting without formalities the unpublished works of nationals of other Contracting States.

5.   If a Contracting State grants protection for more than one term of copyright and the first term is for a period longer than one of the minimum periods prescribed in Article IV, such State shall not be required to comply with the provisions of paragraph 1 of this Article in respect of the second or any subsequent term of copyright.

Article IV

1.   The duration of protection of a work shall be governed, in accordance with the provisions of Article II and this Article, by the law of the Contracting State in which protection is claimed.

2.   (a) The term of protection for works protected under this Convention shall not be less than the life of the author and twenty-five years after his death. However, any Contracting State which, on the effective date of this Convention in that State, has limited this term for certain classes of works to a period computed from the first publication of the work, shall be entitled to maintain these exceptions and to extend them to other classes of works. For all these classes the term of protection shall not be less than twenty-five years from the date of first publication.

(b) Any Contracting State which, upon the effective date of this Convention in that State, does not compute the term of protection upon the basis of the life of the author, shall be entitled to compute the term of protection from the date of the first publication of the work or from its registration prior to publication, as the case may be, provided the term of protection shall not be less than twenty-five years from the date of first publication or from its registration prior to publication, as the case may be.

(c) If the legislation of a Contracting State grants two or more successive terms of protection, the duration of the first term shall not be less than one of the minimum periods specified in sub-paragraphs (a) and (b).

3. The provisions of paragraph 2 shall not apply to photographic works or to works of applied art; provided, however, that the term of protection in those Contracting States which protect photographic works, or works of applied art in so far as they are protected as artistic works, shall not be less than ten years for each of said classes of works.

4. (a) No Contracting State shall be obliged to grant protection to a work for a period longer than that fixed for the class of works to which the work in question belongs, in the case of unpublished works by the law of the Contracting State of which the author is a national, and in the case of published works by the law of the Contracting State in which the work has been first published.

(b) For the purposes of the application of sub-paragraph (a), if the law of any Contracting State grants two or more successive terms of protection, the period of protection of that State shall be considered to be the aggregate of those terms. However, if a specified work is not protected by such State during the second or any subsequent term for any reason, the other Contracting States shall not be obliged to protect it during the second or any subsequent term.

5. For the purposes of the application of paragraph 4, the work of a national of a Contracting State, first published in a non-Contracting State, shall be treated as though first published in the Contracting State of which the author is a national.

6. For the purposes of the application of paragraph 4, in case of simultaneous publication in two or more Contracting States, the work shall be treated as though first published in the State which affords the shortest term; any work published in two or more Contracting States within thirty days of its first publication shall be considered as having been published simultaneously in said Contracting States.

Article IVbis

1. The rights referred to in Article I shall include the basic rights ensuring the author's economic interests, including the exclusive right to authorize reproduction by any means, public performance and broadcasting. The provisions of this Article shall extend to works protected under this Convention either in their original form or in any form recognizably derived from the original.

2. However, any Contracting State may, by its domestic legislation, make exceptions that do not conflict with the spirit and provisions of this Convention, to the rights mentioned in paragraph 1 of this Article. Any State whose legislation so provides, shall nevertheless accord a reasonable degree of effective protection to each of the rights to which exception has been made.

Article V

1. The rights referred to in Article I shall include the exclusive right of the author to make, publish and authorize the making and publication of translations of works protected under this Convention.

2. However, any Contracting State may, by its domestic legislation, restrict the right of translation of writings, but only subject to the following provisions:

(a) If, after the expiration of a period of seven years from the date of the first publication of a writing, a translation of such writing has not been published in a language in general use in the Contracting State, by the owner of the right of translation or with his authorization, any national of such Contracting State may obtain a non-exclusive licence from the competent authority thereof to translate the work into that language and publish the work so translated.

(b) Such national shall in accordance with the procedure of the State concerned, establish either that he has requested, and been denied, authorization by the proprietor of the right to make and publish the translation, or that, after due diligence on his part, he was unable to find the owner of the right. A licence may also be granted on the same conditions if all previous editions of a translation in a language in general use in the Contracting State are out of print.

(c) If the owner of the right of translation cannot be found, then the applicant for a licence shall send copies of his application to the publisher whose name appears on the work and, if the nationality of the owner of the right of translation is known, to the diplomatic or consular representative of the State of which such owner is a national, or to the organization which may have been designated by the government of that State. The licence shall not be granted before the expiration of a period of two months from the date of the dispatch of the copies of the application.

(d) Due provision shall be made by domestic legislation to ensure to the owner of the right of translation a compensation which is just and conforms to international standards, to ensure payment and transmittal of such compensation, and to ensure a correct translation of the work.

(e) The original title and the name of the author of the work shall be printed on all copies of the published translation. The licence shall be valid only for publication of the translation in the territory of the Contracting State where it has been applied for. Copies so published may be imported and sold in another Contracting State if a language in general use in such other State is the same language as that into which the work has been so translated, and if the domestic law in such other State makes provision for such licences and does not prohibit such importation and sale. Where the foregoing conditions do not exist, the importation and sale of such copies in a Contracting State shall be governed by its domestic law and its agreements. The licence shall not be transferred by the licencee.

(f) The licence shall not be granted when the author has withdrawn from circulation all copies of the work.

* * * *

Article VI

"Publication", as used in this Convention, means the reproduction in tangible form and the general distribution to the public of copies of a work from which it can be read or otherwise visually perceived.

Article VII

This Convention shall not apply to works or rights in works which, at the effective date of this Convention in a Contracting State where protection is claimed, are permanently in the public domain in the said Contracting State.

* * * *

Article X

1.   Each Contracting State undertakes to adopt, in accordance with its Constitution, such measures as are necessary to ensure the application of this Convention.

2.   It is understood that at the date this Convention comes into force in respect of any State, that State must be in a position under its domestic law to give effect to the terms of this Convention.

* * * *

Article XVII

1.   This Convention shall not in any way affect the provisions of the Berne Convention for the Protection of Literary and Artistic Works or membership in the Union created by that Convention.

2.   In application of the foregoing paragraph, a declaration has been annexed to the present Article. This declaration is an integral part of this Convention for the States bound by the Berne Convention on 1 January 1951, or which have or may become bound to it at a later date. The signature of this Convention by such States shall also constitute signature of the said declaration, and ratification, acceptance or accession by such States shall include the declaration, as well as this Convention.

Article XVIII

This Convention shall not abrogate multilateral or bilateral copyright conventions or arrangements that are or may be in effect exclusively between two or more American Republics. In the event of any difference either between the provisions of such existing conventions or arrangements and the provisions of this Convention, or between the provisions of this Convention and those of any new convention or arrangement which may be formulated between two or more American Republics after this Convention comes into force, the convention or arrangement most recently formulated shall prevail between the parties thereto. Rights in works acquired in any Contracting State under existing conventions or arrangements before the date this Convention comes into force in such State shall not be affected.

Article XIX

This Convention shall not abrogate multilateral or bilateral conventions or arrangements in effect between two or more Contracting States. In the event of any difference between the provisions of such existing conventions or arrangements and the provisions of this Convention, the provisions of this Convention shall prevail. Rights in works acquired in any Contracting State under existing conventions or arrangements before the date on which this Convention comes into force in such State shall not be affected. Nothing in this Article shall affect the provisions of Articles XVII and XVIII.

Article XX

Reservations to this Convention shall not be permitted.

Appendix Declaration Relating to Article XVII

The States which are members of the International Union for the Protection of Literary and Artistic Works (hereinafter called "the Berne Union") and which are signatories to this Convention,

Desiring to reinforce their mutual relations on the basis of the said Union and to avoid any conflict which might result from the co-existence of the Berne Convention and the Universal Copyright Convention,

Recognizing the temporary need of some States to adjust their level of copyright protection in accordance with their stage of cultural, social and economic development,

Have, by common agreement, accepted the terms of the following declaration:

(a) Except as provided by paragraph (b), works which, according to the Berne Convention, have as their country of origin a country which has withdrawn from the Berne Union after 1 January 1951, shall not be protected by the Universal Copyright Convention in the countries of the Berne Union;

(b) Where a Contracting State is regarded as a developing country in conformity with the established practice of the General Assembly of the United Nations, and has deposited with the Director-General of the United Nations Educational, Scientific and Cultural Organization, at the time of its withdrawal from the Berne Union, a notification to the effect that it regards itself as a developing country, the provisions of paragraph (a) shall not be applicable as long as such State may avail itself of the exceptions provided for by this Convention in accordance with Article V^{bis};

(c) The Universal Copyright Convention shall not be applicable to the relationships among countries of the Berne Union in so far as it relates to the protection of works having as their country of origin, within the meaning of the Berne Convention, a country of the Berne Union.

AGREEMENT ON TRADE-RELATED ASPECTS OF INTELLECTUAL PROPERTY RIGHTS (EXCERPTS)

MTN/FA II–A1C

Members,

Desiring to reduce distortions and impediments to international trade, and taking into account the need to promote effective and adequate protection of intellectual property rights, and to ensure that measures and procedures to enforce intellectual property rights do not themselves become barriers to legitimate trade;

Recognizing, to this end, the need for new rules and disciplines concerning:

(a) the applicability of the basic principles of the GATT 1994 and of relevant international intellectual property agreements or conventions;

(b) the provision of adequate standards and principles concerning the availability, scope and use of trade-related intellectual property rights;

(c) the provision of effective and appropriate means for the enforcement of trade-related intellectual property rights, taking into account differences in national legal systems;

(d) the provision of effective and expeditious procedures for the multilateral prevention and settlement of disputes between governments; and

(e) transitional arrangements aiming at the fullest participation in the results of the negotiations;

Recognizing the need for a multilateral framework of principles, rules and disciplines dealing with international trade in counterfeit goods;

Recognizing that intellectual property rights are private rights;

Recognizing the underlying public policy objectives of national systems for the protection of intellectual property, including development and technological objectives;

Recognizing also the special needs of the least-developed country Members in respect of maximum flexibility in the domestic implementation of laws and regulations in order to enable them to create a sound and viable technological base;

Emphasizing the importance of reducing tensions by reaching strengthened commitments to resolve disputes on trade-related intellectual property issues through multilateral procedures;

Desiring to establish a mutually supportive relationship between the WTO and the World Intellectual Property Organization (WIPO) as well as other relevant international organizations;

Hereby agree as follows:

PART I—GENERAL PROVISIONS AND BASIC PRINCIPLES

Article 1

Nature and Scope of Obligations

1.   Members shall give effect to the provisions of this Agreement. Members may, but shall not be obliged to, implement in their domestic law more extensive protection than is required by this Agreement, provided that such protection does not contravene the provisions of this Agreement. Members shall be free to determine the appropriate method of implementing the provisions of this Agreement within their own legal system and practice.

2.   For the purposes of this Agreement, the term "intellectual property" refers to all categories of intellectual property that are the subject of Sections 1 to 7 of Part II.

3.   Members shall accord the treatment provided for in this Agreement to the nationals of other Members.[1] In respect for the relevant intellectual property right, the nationals of other Members shall be understood as those natural or legal persons that would meet the criteria for eligibility for protection provided for in the Paris Convention (1967), the Berne Convention (1971), the Rome Convention and the Treaty on Intellectual Property in Respect of Integrated Circuits, were all Members of the WTO members of those conventions.[2] Any Member availing itself of the possibilities provided in paragraph 3 of Article 5 or paragraph 2 of Article 6 of the Rome Convention shall make a notification as foreseen in those provisions to the Council for Trade-Related Aspects of Intellectual Property Rights.

Article 2

Intellectual Property Conventions

* * * *

2.   Nothing in Parts I to IV of this Agreement shall derogate from existing obligations that Members may have to each other under the Paris Convention, the Berne Convention, the Rome Convention and the Treaty on Intellectual Property in Respect of Integrated Circuits.

---

[1]   When "nationals" are referred to in this Agreement, they shall be deemed, in the case of a separate customs territory Member of the WTO, to mean persons, natural or legal, who are domiciled or who have a real and effective industrial or commercial establishment in that customs territory.

[2]   In this Agreement, "Paris Convention" refers to the Paris Convention for the Protection of Industrial Property; "Paris Convention (1967)" refers to the Stockholm Act of this Convention of 14 July 1967. "Berne Convention" refers to the Berne Convention for the Protection of Literary and Artistic Works; "Berne Convention (1971)" refers to the Paris Act of this Convention of 24 July 1971. "Rome Convention" refers to the International Convention for the Protection of Performers, Producers of Phonograms and Broadcasting Organizations, adopted at Rome on 26 October 1961. "Treaty on Intellectual Property in Respect of Integrated Circuits" (IPIC Treaty) refers to the Treaty on Intellectual Property in Respect of Integrated Circuits, adopted at Washington on 26 May 1989.

Article 3

National Treatment

1.   Each Member shall accord to the nationals of other Members treatment no less favourable than that it accords to its own nationals with regard to the protection[3] of intellectual property, subject to the exceptions already provided in, respectively, the Paris Convention (1967), the Berne Convention (1971), the Rome Convention and the Treaty on Intellectual Property in Respect of Integrated Circuits. In respect of performers, producers of phonograms and broadcasting organizations, this obligation only applies in respect of the rights provided under this Agreement. Any Member availing itself of the possibilities provided in Article 6 of the Berne Convention and paragraph 1(b) of Article 16 of the Rome Convention shall make a notification as foreseen in those provisions to the Council for Trade-Related Aspects of Intellectual Property Rights.

2.   Members may avail themselves of the exceptions permitted under paragraph 1 above in relation to judicial and administrative procedures, including the designation of an address for service or the appointment of an agent within the jurisdiction of a Member, only where such exceptions are necessary to secure compliance with laws and regulations which are not inconsistent with the provisions of this Agreement and where such practices are not applied in a manner which would constitute a disguised restriction on trade.

Article 4

Most-Favoured-Nation Treatment

With regard to the protection of intellectual property, any advantage, favour, privilege or immunity granted by a Member to the nationals of any other country shall be accorded immediately and unconditionally to the nationals of all other Members. Exempted from this obligation are any advantage, favour, privilege or immunity accorded by a Member:

(a) deriving from international agreements on judicial assistance and law enforcement of a general nature and not particularly confined to the protection of intellectual property;

(b) granted in accordance with the provisions of the Berne Convention (1971) or the Rome Convention authorizing that the treatment accorded be a function not of national treatment but of the treatment accorded in another country;

(c) in respect of the rights of performers, producers of phonograms and broadcasting organizations not provided under this Agreement;

(d) deriving from international agreements related to the protection of intellectual property which entered into force prior to the entry into force of the Agreement Establishing the WTO, provided that such agreements are notified to the Council for Trade-Related Aspects of

---

[3]   For the purposes of Articles 3 and 4 of this Agreement, "protection" shall include matters affecting the availability, acquisition, scope, maintenance and enforcement of intellectual property rights as well as those matters affecting the use of intellectual property rights specifically addressed in this Agreement.

Intellectual Property Rights and do not constitute an arbitrary or unjustifiable discrimination against nationals of other Members.

Article 5

Multilateral Agreements on Acquisition or Maintenance of Protection

The obligations under Articles 3 and 4 above do not apply to procedures provided in multilateral agreements concluded under the auspices of the World Intellectual Property Organization relating to the acquisition or maintenance of intellectual property rights.

Article 6

Exhaustion

For the purposes of dispute settlement under this Agreement, subject to the provisions of Articles 3 and 4 above nothing in this Agreement shall be used to address the issue of the exhaustion of intellectual property rights.

Article 7

Objectives

The protection and enforcement of intellectual property rights should contribute to the promotion of technological innovation and to the transfer and dissemination of technology, to the mutual advantage of producers and users of technological knowledge and in a manner conducive to social and economic welfare, and to a balance of rights and obligations.

Article 8

Principles

1.   Members may, in formulating or amending their national laws and regulations, adopt measures necessary to protect public health and nutrition, and to promote the public interest in sectors of vital importance to their socio-economic and technological development, provided that such measures are consistent with the provisions of this Agreement.

2.   Appropriate measures, provided that they are consistent with the provisions of this Agreement, may be used to prevent the abuse of intellectual property rights by right holders or the resort to practices which unreasonably restrain trade or adversely affect the international transfer of technology.

PART II—STANDARDS CONCERNING THE AVAILABILITY, SCOPE AND USE OF INTELLECTUAL PROPERTY RIGHTS

Section 1:

Copyright and Related Rights

Article 9

Relation to Berne Convention

1.   Members shall comply with Articles 1–21 and the Appendix of the Berne Convention (1971). However, Members shall not have rights

or obligations under this Agreement in respect of the rights conferred under Article 6*bis* of that Convention or of the rights derived therefrom.

2.   Copyright protection shall extend to expressions and not to ideas, procedures, methods of operation or mathematical concepts as such.

Article 10

Computer Programs and Compilations of Data

1.   Computer programs, whether in source or object code, shall be protected as literary works under the Berne Convention (1971).

2.   Compilations of data or other material, whether in machine readable or other form, which by reason of the selection or arrangement of their contents constitute intellectual creations shall be protected as such. Such protection, which shall not extend to the data or material itself, shall be without prejudice to any copyright subsisting in the data or material itself.

Article 11

Rental Rights

In respect of at least computer programs and cinematographic works, a Member shall provide authors and their successors in title the right to authorize or to prohibit the commercial rental to the public of originals or copies of their copyright works. A Member shall be excepted from this obligation in respect of cinematographic works unless such rental has led to widespread copying of such works which is materially impairing the exclusive right of reproduction conferred in that Member on authors and their successors in title. In respect of computer programs, this obligation does not apply to rentals where the program itself is not the essential object of the rental.

Article 12

Term of Protection

Whenever the term of protection of a work, other than a photographic work or a work of applied art, is calculated on a basis other than the life of a natural person, such term shall be no less than fifty years from the end of the calendar year of authorized publication, or, failing such authorized publication within fifty years from the making of the work, fifty years from the end of the calendar year of making.

Article 13

Limitations and Exceptions

Members shall confine limitations or exceptions to exclusive rights to certain special cases which do not conflict with a normal exploitation of the work and do not unreasonably prejudice the legitimate interests of the right holder.

Article 14

Protection of Performers, Producers of Phonograms (Sound Recordings) and Broadcasting Organizations

1.   In respect of a fixation of their performance on a phonogram, performers shall have the possibility of preventing the following acts when undertaken without their authorization: the fixation of their

unfixed performance and the reproduction of such fixation. Performers shall also have the possibility of preventing the following acts when undertaken without their authorization: the broadcasting by wireless means and the communication to the public of their live performance.

2.   Producers of phonograms shall enjoy the right to authorize or prohibit the direct or indirect reproduction of their phonograms.

3.   Broadcasting organizations shall have the right to prohibit the following acts when undertaken without their authorization: the fixation, the reproduction of fixations, and the rebroadcasting by wireless means of broadcasts, as well as the communication to the public of television broadcasts of the same. Where Members do not grant such rights to broadcasting organizations, they shall provide owners of copyright in the subject matter of broadcasts with the possibility of preventing the above acts, subject to the provisions of the Berne Convention (1971).

4.   The provisions of Article 11 in respect of computer programs shall apply *mutatis mutandis* to producers of phonograms and any other right holders in phonograms as determined in domestic law. If, on the date of the Ministerial Meeting concluding the Uruguay Round of Multilateral Trade Negotiations, a Member has in force a system of equitable remuneration of right holders in respect of the rental of phonograms, it may maintain such system provided that the commercial rental of phonograms is not giving rise to the material impairment of the exclusive rights of reproduction of right holders.

5.   The term of the protection available under this Agreement to performers and producers of phonograms shall last at least until the end of a period of fifty years computed from the end of the calendar year in which the fixation was made or the performance took place. The term of protection granted pursuant to paragraph 3 above shall last for at least twenty years from the end of the calendar year in which the broadcast took place.

6.   Any Member may, in relation to the rights conferred under paragraphs 1–3 above, provide for conditions, limitations, exceptions and reservations to the extent permitted by the Rome Convention. However, the provisions of Article 18 of the Berne Convention (1971) shall also apply, *mutatis mutandis,* to the rights of performers and producers of phonograms in phonograms.

PART III—ENFORCEMENT OF INTELLECTUAL PROPERTY RIGHTS

Section 1:

General Obligations

Article 41

1.   Members shall ensure that enforcement procedures as specified in this Part are available under their law so as to permit effective action against any act of infringement of intellectual property rights covered by this Agreement, including expeditious remedies to prevent infringements and remedies which constitute a deterrent to further infringements. These procedures shall be applied in such a manner as to avoid the creation of barriers to legitimate trade and to provide for safeguards against their abuse.

2.   Procedures concerning the enforcement of intellectual property rights shall be fair and equitable. They shall not be unnecessarily complicated or costly, or entail unreasonable time-limits or unwarranted delays.

3.   Decisions on the merits of a case shall preferably be in writing and reasoned. They shall be made available at least to the parties to the proceeding without undue delay. Decisions on the merits of a case shall be based only on evidence in respect of which parties were offered the opportunity to be heard.

4.   Parties to a proceeding shall have an opportunity for review by a judicial authority of final administrative decisions and, subject to jurisdictional provisions in a Member's law concerning the importance of a case, of at least the legal aspects of initial judicial decisions on the merits of a case. However, there shall be no obligation to provide an opportunity for review of acquittals in criminal cases.

5.   It is understood that this Part does not create any obligation to put in place a judicial system for the enforcement of intellectual property rights distinct from that for the enforcement of law in general, nor does it affect the capacity of Members to enforce their law in general. Nothing in this Part creates any obligation with respect to the distribution of resources as between enforcement of intellectual property rights and the enforcement of law in general.

Section 2:

Civil and Administrative Procedures and Remedies

. . .

Article 44

Injunctions

1.   The judicial authorities shall have the authority to order a party to desist from an infringement, inter alia to prevent the entry into the channels of commerce in their jurisdiction of imported goods that involve the infringement of an intellectual property right, immediately after customs clearance of such goods. Members are not obliged to accord such authority in respect of protected subject matter acquired or ordered by a person prior to knowing or having reasonable grounds to know that dealing in such subject matter would entail the infringement of an intellectual property right.

2.   Notwithstanding the other provisions of this Part and provided that the provisions of Part II specifically addressing use by governments, or by third parties authorized by a government, without the authorization of the right holder are complied with, Members may limit the remedies available against such use to payment of remuneration in accordance with subparagraph (h) of Article 31. In other cases, the remedies under this Part shall apply or, where these remedies are inconsistent with a Member's law, declaratory judgments and adequate compensation shall be available.

Article 45

Damages

1.   The judicial authorities shall have the authority to order the infringer to pay the right holder damages adequate to compensate for the

injury the right holder has suffered because of an infringement of that person's intellectual property right by an infringer who knowingly, or with reasonable grounds to know, engaged in infringing activity.

2.   The judicial authorities shall also have the authority to order the infringer to pay the right holder expenses, which may include appropriate attorney's fees. In appropriate cases, Members may authorize the judicial authorities to order recovery of profits and/or payment of pre-established damages even where the infringer did not knowingly, or with reasonable grounds to know, engage in infringing activity.

APPENDIX G

WORLD INTELLECTUAL PROPERTY ORGANIZATION COPYRIGHT TREATY (EXCERPTS)

(Geneva 1996)

CRNR/DC/94

Preamble

The Contracting Parties,

Desiring to develop and maintain the protection of the rights of authors in their literary and artistic works in a manner as effective and uniform as possible,

Recognizing the need to introduce new international rules and clarify the interpretation of certain existing rules in order to provide adequate solutions to the questions raised by new economic, social, cultural and technological developments,

Recognizing the profound impact of the development and convergence of information and communication technologies on the creation and use of literary and artistic works,

Emphasizing the outstanding significance of copyright protection as an incentive for literary and artistic creation,

Recognizing the need to maintain a balance between the rights of authors and the larger public interest, particularly education, research and access to information, as reflected in the Berne Convention,

Have agreed as follows:

Article 1

Relation to the Berne Convention

(1) This Treaty is a special agreement within the meaning of Article 20 of the Berne Convention for the Protection of Literary and Artistic Works, as regards Contracting Parties that are countries of the Union established by that Convention. This Treaty shall not have any connection with treaties other than the Berne Convention, nor shall it prejudice any rights and obligations under any other treaties.

(2) Nothing in this Treaty shall derogate from existing obligations that Contracting Parties have to each other under the Berne Convention for the Protection of Literary and Artistic Works.

(3) Hereinafter, "Berne Convention" shall refer to the Paris Act of July 24, 1971 of the Berne Convention for the Protection of Literary and Artistic Works.

(4) Contracting Parties shall comply with Articles 1 to 21 and the Appendix of the Berne Convention.[1]

Article 2

Scope of Copyright Protection

Copyright protection extends to expressions and not to ideas, procedures, methods of operation or mathematical concepts as such.

Article 3

Application of Articles 2 to 6 of the Berne Convention

Contracting Parties shall apply *mutatis mutandis* the provisions of Articles 2 to 6 of the Berne Convention in respect of the protection provided for in this Treaty.[2]

Article 4

Computer Programs

Computer programs are protected as literary works within the meaning of Article 2 of the Berne Convention. Such protection applies to computer programs, whatever may be the mode or form of their expression.[3]

Article 5

Compilations of Data (Databases)

Compilations of data or other material, in any form, which by reason of the selection or arrangement of their contents constitute intellectual creations, are protected as such. This protection does not extend to the data or the material itself and is without prejudice to any copyright subsisting in the data or material contained in the compilation.[4]

---

[1] **Agreed statement concerning Article 1(4):** The reproduction right, as set out in Article 9 of the Berne Convention, and the exceptions permitted thereunder, fully apply in the digital environment, in particular to the use of works in digital form. It is understood that the storage of a protected work in digital form in an electronic medium constitutes a reproduction within the meaning of Article 9 of the Berne Convention.

[2] **Agreed statement concerning Article 3:** It is understood that in applying Article 3 of this Treaty, the expression "country of the Union" in Articles 2 to 6 of the Berne Convention will be read as if it were a reference to a Contracting Party to this Treaty, in the application of those Berne Articles in respect of protection provided for in this Treaty. It is also understood that the expression "country outside the Union" in those Articles in the Berne Convention will, in the same circumstances, be read as if it were a reference to a country that is not a Contracting Party to this Treaty, and that "this Convention" in Articles 2(8), 2*bis*(2), 3, 4 and 5 of the Berne Convention will be read as if it were a reference to the Berne Convention and this Treaty. Finally, it is understood that a reference in Articles 3 to 6 of the Berne Convention to a "national of one of the countries of the Union" will, when these Articles are applied to this Treaty, mean, in regard to an intergovernmental organization that is a Contracting Party to this Treaty, a national of one of the countries that is member of that organization.

[3] **Agreed statement concerning Article 4:** The scope of protection for computer programs under Article 4 of this Treaty, read with Article 2, is consistent with Article 2 of the Berne Convention and on a par with the relevant provisions of the TRIPS Agreement.

[4] **Agreed statement concerning Article 5:** The scope of protection for compilations of data (databases) under Article 5 of this Treaty, read with Article 2, is consistent with Article 2 of the Berne Convention and on a par with the relevant provisions of the TRIPS Agreement.

Article 6

Right of Distribution

(1) Authors of literary and artistic works shall enjoy the exclusive right of authorizing the making available to the public of the original and copies of their works through sale or other transfer of ownership.

(2) Nothing in this Treaty shall affect the freedom of Contracting Parties to determine the conditions, if any, under which the exhaustion of the right in paragraph (1) applies after the first sale or other transfer of ownership of the original or a copy of the work with the authorization of the author.[5]

Article 7

Right of Rental

(1) Authors of

(i) computer programs;

(ii) cinematographic works; and

(iii) works embodied in phonograms, as determined in the national law of Contracting Parties, shall enjoy the exclusive right of authorizing commercial rental to the public of the originals or copies of their works.

(2) Paragraph (1) shall not apply

(i) in the case of computer programs, where the program itself is not the essential object of the rental; and

(ii) in the case of cinematographic works, unless such commercial rental has led to widespread copying of such works materially impairing the exclusive right of reproduction.

(3) Notwithstanding the provisions of paragraph (1), a Contracting Party that, on April 15, 1994, had and continues to have in force a system of equitable remuneration of authors for the rental of copies of their works embodied in phonograms may maintain that system provided that the commercial rental of works embodied in phonograms is not giving rise to the material impairment of the exclusive right of reproduction of authors.[6] [7]

---

[5] **Agreed statement concerning Articles 6 and 7:** As used in these Articles, the expressions "copies" and "original and copies," being subject to the right of distribution and the right of rental under the said Articles, refer exclusively to fixed copies that can be put into circulation as tangible objects.

[6] **Agreed statement concerning Articles 6 and 7:** As used in these Articles, the expressions "copies" and "original and copies," being subject to the right of distribution and the right of rental under the said Articles, refer exclusively to fixed copies that can be put into circulation as tangible objects.

[7] **Agreed statement concerning Article 7:** It is understood that the obligation under Article 7(1) does not require a Contracting Party to provide an exclusive right of commercial rental to authors who, under that Contracting Party's law, are not granted rights in respect of phonograms. It is understood that this obligation is consistent with Article 14(4) of the TRIPS Agreement.

Article 8

Right of Communication to the Public

Without prejudice to the provisions of Articles 11(1)(ii), 11bis(1)(i) and (ii), 11ter(1)(ii), 14(1)(ii) and 14bis(1) of the Berne Convention, authors of literary and artistic works shall enjoy the exclusive right of authorizing any communication to the public of their works, by wire or wireless means, including the making available to the public of their works in such a way that members of the public may access these works from a place and at a time individually chosen by them.[8]

Article 9

Duration of the Protection of Photographic Works

In respect of photographic works, the Contracting Parties shall not apply the provisions of Article 7(4) of the Berne Convention.

Article 10

Limitations and Exceptions

(1) Contracting Parties may, in their national legislation, provide for limitations of or exceptions to the rights granted to authors of literary and artistic works under this Treaty in certain special cases that do not conflict with a normal exploitation of the work and do not unreasonably prejudice the legitimate interests of the author.

(2) Contracting Parties shall, when applying the Berne Convention, confine any limitations of or exceptions to rights provided for therein to certain special cases that do not conflict with a normal exploitation of the work and do not unreasonably prejudice the legitimate interests of the author.[9]

Article 11

Obligations concerning Technological Measures

Contracting Parties shall provide adequate legal protection and effective legal remedies against the circumvention of effective technological measures that are used by authors in connection with the exercise of their rights under this Treaty or the Berne Convention and that restrict acts, in respect of their works, which are not authorized by the authors concerned or permitted by law.

---

[8] **Agreed statement concerning Article 8:** It is understood that the mere provision of physical facilities for enabling or making a communication does not in itself amount to communication within the meaning of this Treaty or the Berne Convention. It is further understood that nothing in Article 8 precludes a Contracting Party from applying Article 11*bis*(2).

[9] **Agreed statement concerning Article 10:** It is understood that the provisions of Article 10 permit Contracting Parties to carry forward and appropriately extend into the digital environment limitations and exceptions in their national laws which have been considered acceptable under the Berne Convention. Similarly, these provisions should be understood to permit Contracting Parties to devise new exceptions and limitations that are appropriate in the digital network environment.

It is also understood that Article 10(2) neither reduces nor extends the scope of applicability of the limitations and exceptions permitted by the Berne Convention.

Article 12

Obligations concerning Rights Management Information

(1) Contracting Parties shall provide adequate and effective legal remedies against any person knowingly performing any of the following acts knowing, or with respect to civil remedies having reasonable grounds to know, that it will induce, enable, facilitate or conceal an infringement of any right covered by this Treaty or the Berne Convention:

(i) to remove or alter any electronic rights management information without authority;

(ii) to distribute, import for distribution, broadcast or communicate to the public, without authority, works or copies of works knowing that electronic rights management information has been removed or altered without authority.

(2) As used in this Article, "rights management information" means information which identifies the work, the author of the work, the owner of any right in the work, or information about the terms and conditions of use of the work, and any numbers or codes that represent such information, when any of these items of information is attached to a copy of a work or appears in connection with the communication of a work to the public.[10]

Article 13

Application in Time

Contracting Parties shall apply the provisions of Article 18 of the Berne Convention to all protection provided for in this Treaty.

Article 14

Provisions on Enforcement of Rights

(1) Contracting Parties undertake to adopt, in accordance with their legal systems, the measures necessary to ensure the application of this Treaty.

(2) Contracting Parties shall ensure that enforcement procedures are available under their law so as to permit effective action against any act of infringement of rights covered by this Treaty, including expeditious remedies to prevent infringements and remedies which constitute a deterrent to further infringements.

* * * *

Article 22

No Reservations to the Treaty

No reservation to this Treaty shall be admitted.

* * * *

---

[10] **Agreed statement concerning Article 12:** It is understood that the reference to "infringement of any right covered by this Treaty or the Berne Convention" includes both exclusive rights and rights of remuneration.

It is further understood that Contracting Parties will not rely on this Article to devise or implement rights management systems that would have the effect of imposing formalities which are not permitted under the Berne Convention or this Treaty, prohibiting the free movement of goods or impeding the enjoyment of rights under this Treaty.

APPENDIX H

WORLD INTELLECTUAL PROPERTY ORGANIZATION PERFORMANCES AND PHONOGRAMS TREATY (EXCERPTS)

(Geneva 1996)

CRNR/DC/95

Preamble

The Contracting Parties,

Desiring to develop and maintain the protection of the rights of performers and producers of phonograms in a manner as effective and uniform as possible,

Recognizing the need to introduce new international rules in order to provide adequate solutions to the questions raised by economic, social, cultural and technological developments,

Recognizing the profound impact of the development and convergence of information and communication technologies on the production and use of performances and phonograms,

Recognizing the need to maintain a balance between the rights of performers and producers of phonograms and the larger public interest, particularly education, research and access to information,

Have agreed as follows:

CHAPTER I—GENERAL PROVISIONS

Article 1

Relation to Other Conventions

(1) Nothing in this Treaty shall derogate from existing obligations that Contracting Parties have to each other under the International Convention for the Protection of Performers, Producers of Phonograms and Broadcasting Organizations done in Rome, October 26, 1961 (hereinafter the "Rome Convention").

(2) Protection granted under this Treaty shall leave intact and shall in no way affect the protection of copyright in literary and artistic works. Consequently, no provision of this Treaty may be interpreted as prejudicing such protection.[1]

---

[1] **Agreed statement concerning Article 1(2):** It is understood that Article 1(2) clarifies the relationship between rights in phonograms under this Treaty and copyright in works embodied in the phonograms. In cases where authorization is needed from both the author of a work embodied in the phonogram and a performer or producer owning rights in the phonogram,

(3) This Treaty shall not have any connection with, nor shall it prejudice any rights and obligations under, any other treaties.

Article 2

Definitions

For the purposes of this Treaty:

(a) "performers" are actors, singers, musicians, dancers, and other persons who act, sing, deliver, declaim, play in, interpret, or otherwise perform literary or artistic works or expressions of folklore;

(b) "phonogram" means the fixation of the sounds of a performance or of other sounds, or of a representation of sounds, other than in the form of a fixation incorporated in a cinematographic or other audiovisual work;[2]

(c) "fixation" means the embodiment of sounds, or of the representations thereof, from which they can be perceived, reproduced or communicated through a device;

(d) "producer of a phonogram" means the person, or the legal entity, who or which takes the initiative and has the responsibility for the first fixation of the sounds of a performance or other sounds, or the representations of sounds;

(e) "publication" of a fixed performance or a phonogram means the offering of copies of the fixed performance or the phonogram to the public, with the consent of the rightholder, and provided that copies are offered to the public in reasonable quantity;[3]

(f) "broadcasting" means the transmission by wireless means for public reception of sounds or of images and sounds or of the representations thereof; such transmission by satellite is also "broadcasting"; transmission of encrypted signals is "broadcasting" where the means for decrypting are provided to the public by the broadcasting organization or with its consent;

(g) "communication to the public" of a performance or a phonogram means the transmission to the public by any medium, otherwise than by broadcasting, of sounds of a performance or the sounds or the representations of sounds fixed in a phonogram. For the purposes of Article 15, "communication to the public" includes making the sounds or representations of sounds fixed in a phonogram audible to the public.

---

the need for the authorization of the author does not cease to exist because the authorization of the performer or producer is also required, and vice versa.

It is further understood that nothing in Article 1(2) precludes a Contracting Party from providing exclusive rights to a performer or producer of phonograms beyond those required to be provided under this Treaty.

[2] **Agreed statement concerning Article 2(b):** It is understood that the definition of phonogram provided in Article 2(b) does not suggest that rights in the phonogram are in any way affected through their incorporation into a cinematographic or other audiovisual work.

[3] **Agreed statement concerning Articles 2(e), 8, 9, 12 and 13:** As used in these Articles, the expressions "copies" and "original and copies," being subject to the right of distribution and the right of rental under the said Articles, refer exclusively to fixed copies that can be put into circulation as tangible objects.

Article 3

Beneficiaries of Protection under this Treaty

(1) Contracting Parties shall accord the protection provided under this Treaty to the performers and producers of phonograms who are nationals of other Contracting Parties.

(2) The nationals of other Contracting Parties shall be understood to be those performers or producers of phonograms who would meet the criteria for eligibility for protection provided under the Rome Convention, were all the Contracting Parties to this Treaty Contracting States of that Convention. In respect of these criteria of eligibility, Contracting Parties shall apply the relevant definitions in Article 2 of this Treaty.[4]

(3) Any Contracting Party availing itself of the possibilities provided in Article 5(3) of the Rome Convention or, for the purposes of Article 5 of the same Convention, Article 17 thereof shall make a notification as foreseen in those provisions to the Director General of the World Intellectual Property Organization (WIPO).[5]

Article 4

National Treatment

(1) Each Contracting Party shall accord to nationals of other Contracting Parties, as defined in Article 3(2), the treatment it accords to its own nationals with regard to the exclusive rights specifically granted in this Treaty, and to the right to equitable remuneration provided for in Article 15 of this Treaty.

(2) The obligation provided for in paragraph (1) does not apply to the extent that another Contracting Party makes use of the reservations permitted by Article 15(3) of this Treaty.

CHAPTER II—RIGHTS OF PERFORMERS

Article 5

Moral Rights of Performers

(1) Independently of a performer's economic rights, and even after the transfer of those rights, the performer shall, as regards his live aural performances or performances fixed in phonograms, have the right to claim to be identified as the performer of his performances, except where omission is dictated by the manner of the use of the performance, and to object to any distortion, mutilation or other modification of his performances that would be prejudicial to his reputation.

(2) The rights granted to a performer in accordance with paragraph (1) shall, after his death, be maintained, at least until the expiry of the economic rights, and shall be exercisable by the persons or institutions authorized by the legislation of the Contracting Party where protection is claimed. However, those Contracting Parties whose legislation, at the moment of their ratification of or accession to this Treaty, does not

---

[4]   **Agreed statement concerning Article 3(2):** For the application of Article 3(2), it is understood that fixation means the finalization of the master tape ("bande-mère").

[5]   **Agreed statement concerning Article 3:** It is understood that the reference in Articles 5(a) and 16(a)(iv) of the Rome Convention to "national of another Contracting State" will, when applied to this Treaty, mean, in regard to an intergovernmental organization that is a Contracting Party to this Treaty, a national of one of the countries that is a member of that organization.

provide for protection after the death of the performer of all rights set out in the preceding paragraph may provide that some of these rights will, after his death, cease to be maintained.

(3) The means of redress for safeguarding the rights granted under this Article shall be governed by the legislation of the Contracting Party where protection is claimed.

Article 6

Economic Rights of Performers in their Unfixed Performances

Performers shall enjoy the exclusive right of authorizing, as regards their performances:

(i) the broadcasting and communication to the public of their unfixed performances except where the performance is already a broadcast performance; and

(ii) the fixation of their unfixed performances.

Article 7

Right of Reproduction

Performers shall enjoy the exclusive right of authorizing the direct or indirect reproduction of their performances fixed in phonograms, in any manner or form.[6]

Article 8

Right of Distribution

(1) Performers shall enjoy the exclusive right of authorizing the making available to the public of the original and copies of their performances fixed in phonograms through sale or other transfer of ownership.

(2) Nothing in this Treaty shall affect the freedom of Contracting Parties to determine the conditions, if any, under which the exhaustion of the right in paragraph (1) applies after the first sale or other transfer of ownership of the original or a copy of the fixed performance with the authorization of the performer.[7]

Article 9

Right of Rental

(1) Performers shall enjoy the exclusive right of authorizing the commercial rental to the public of the original and copies of their performances fixed in phonograms as determined in the national law of Contracting Parties, even after distribution of them by, or pursuant to, authorization by the performer.

---

[6] **Agreed statement concerning Articles 7, 11 and 16:** The reproduction right, as set out in Articles 7 and 11, and the exceptions permitted thereunder through Article 16, fully apply in the digital environment, in particular to the use of performances and phonograms in digital form. It is understood that the storage of a protected performance or phonogram in digital form in an electronic medium constitutes a reproduction within the meaning of these Articles.

[7] **Agreed statement concerning Articles 2(e), 8, 9, 12 and 13:** As used in these Articles, the expressions "copies" and "original and copies," being subject to the right of distribution and the right of rental under the said Articles, refer exclusively to fixed copies that can be put into circulation as tangible objects.

(2) Notwithstanding the provisions of paragraph (1), a Contracting Party that, on April 15, 1994, had and continues to have in force a system of equitable remuneration of performers for the rental of copies of their performances fixed in phonograms, may maintain that system provided that the commercial rental of phonograms is not giving rise to the material impairment of the exclusive right of reproduction of performers.[8]

Article 10

Right of Making Available of Fixed Performances

Performers shall enjoy the exclusive right of authorizing the making available to the public of their performances fixed in phonograms, by wire or wireless means, in such a way that members of the public may access them from a place and at a time individually chosen by them.

CHAPTER III—RIGHTS OF PRODUCERS OF PHONOGRAMS

Article 11

Right of Reproduction

Producers of phonograms shall enjoy the exclusive right of authorizing the direct or indirect reproduction of their phonograms, in any manner or form.[9]

Article 12

Right of Distribution

(1) Producers of phonograms shall enjoy the exclusive right of authorizing the making available to the public of the original and copies of their phonograms through sale or other transfer of ownership.

(2) Nothing in this Treaty shall affect the freedom of Contracting Parties to determine the conditions, if any, under which the exhaustion of the right in paragraph (1) applies after the first sale or other transfer of ownership of the original or a copy of the phonogram with the authorization of the producer of the phonogram.[10]

Article 13

Right of Rental

(1) Producers of phonograms shall enjoy the exclusive right of authorizing the commercial rental to the public of the original and copies of their phonograms, even after distribution of them by or pursuant to authorization by the producer.

---

[8] **Agreed statement concerning Articles 2(e), 8, 9, 12 and 13:** As used in these Articles, the expressions "copies" and "original and copies," being subject to the right of distribution and the right of rental under the said Articles, refer exclusively to fixed copies that can be put into circulation as tangible objects.

[9] **Agreed statement concerning Articles 7, 11 and 16:** The reproduction right, as set out in Articles 7 and 11, and the exceptions permitted thereunder through Article 16, fully apply in the digital environment, in particular to the use of performances and phonograms in digital form. It is understood that the storage of a protected performance or phonogram in digital form in an electronic medium constitutes a reproduction within the meaning of these Articles.

[10] **Agreed statement concerning Articles 2(e), 8, 9, 12 and 13:** As used in these Articles, the expressions "copies" and "original and copies," being subject to the right of distribution and the right of rental under the said Articles, refer exclusively to fixed copies that can be put into circulation as tangible objects.

(2) Notwithstanding the provisions of paragraph (1), a Contracting Party that, on April 15, 1994, had and continues to have in force a system of equitable remuneration of producers of phonograms for the rental of copies of their phonograms, may maintain that system provided that the commercial rental of phonograms is not giving rise to the material impairment of the exclusive rights of reproduction of producers of phonograms.[11]

Article 14

Right of Making Available of Phonograms

Producers of phonograms shall enjoy the exclusive right of authorizing the making available to the public of their phonograms, by wire or wireless means, in such a way that members of the public may access them from a place and at a time individually chosen by them.

CHAPTER IV—COMMON PROVISIONS

Article 15

Right to Remuneration for Broadcasting and Communication to the Public

(1) Performers and producers of phonograms shall enjoy the right to a single equitable remuneration for the direct or indirect use of phonograms published for commercial purposes for broadcasting or for any communication to the public.

(2) Contracting Parties may establish in their national legislation that the single equitable remuneration shall be claimed from the user by the performer or by the producer of a phonogram or by both. Contracting Parties may enact national legislation that, in the absence of an agreement between the performer and the producer of a phonogram, sets the terms according to which performers and producers of phonograms shall share the single equitable remuneration.

(3) Any Contracting Party may in a notification deposited with the Director General of WIPO, declare that it will apply the provisions of paragraph (1) only in respect of certain uses, or that it will limit their application in some other way, or that it will not apply these provisions at all.

(4) For the purposes of this Article, phonograms made available to the public by wire or wireless means in such a way that members of the public may access them from a place and at a time individually chosen by them shall be considered as if they had been published for commercial purposes.[12] [13]

---

[11] **Agreed statement concerning Articles 2(e), 8, 9, 12 and 13:** As used in these Articles, the expressions "copies" and "original and copies," being subject to the right of distribution and the right of rental under the said Articles, refer exclusively to fixed copies that can be put into circulation as tangible objects.

[12] **Agreed statement concerning Article 15:** It is understood that Article 15 does not represent a complete resolution of the level of rights of broadcasting and communication to the public that should be enjoyed by performers and phonogram producers in the digital age. Delegations were unable to achieve consensus on differing proposals for aspects of exclusivity to be provided in certain circumstances or for rights to be provided without the possibility of reservations, and have therefore left the issue to future resolution.

[13] **Agreed statement concerning Article 15:** It is understood that Article 15 does not prevent the granting of the right conferred by this Article to performers of folklore and producers

Article 16

Limitations and Exceptions

(1) Contracting Parties may, in their national legislation, provide for the same kinds of limitations or exceptions with regard to the protection of performers and producers of phonograms as they provide for, in their national legislation, in connection with the protection of copyright in literary and artistic works.

(2) Contracting Parties shall confine any limitations of or exceptions to rights provided for in this Treaty to certain special cases which do not conflict with a normal exploitation of the performance or phonogram and do not unreasonably prejudice the legitimate interests of the performer or of the producer of the phonogram.[14] [15]

Article 17

Term of Protection

(1) The term of protection to be granted to performers under this Treaty shall last, at least, until the end of a period of 50 years computed from the end of the year in which the performance was fixed in a phonogram.

(2) The term of protection to be granted to producers of phonograms under this Treaty shall last, at least, until the end of a period of 50 years computed from the end of the year in which the phonogram was published, or failing such publication within 50 years from fixation of the phonogram, 50 years from the end of the year in which the fixation was made.

Article 18

Obligations concerning Technological Measures

Contracting Parties shall provide adequate legal protection and effective legal remedies against the circumvention of effective technological measures that are used by performers or producers of phonograms in connection with the exercise of their rights under this Treaty and that restrict acts, in respect of their performances or

---

of phonograms recording folklore where such phonograms have not been published for commercial gain.

[14] **Agreed statement concerning Articles 7, 11 and 16:** The reproduction right, as set out in Articles 7 and 11, and the exceptions permitted thereunder through Article 16, fully apply in the digital environment, in particular to the use of performances and phonograms in digital form. It is understood that the storage of a protected performance or phonogram in digital form in an electronic medium constitutes a reproduction within the meaning of these Articles.

[15] **Agreed statement concerning Article 16:** The agreed statement concerning Article 10 (on Limitations and Exceptions) of the WIPO Copyright Treaty is applicable *mutatis mutandis* also to Article 16 (on Limitations and Exceptions) of the WIPO Performances and Phonograms Treaty. [The text of the agreed statement concerning Article 10 of the WCT reads as follows:

It is understood that the provisions of Article 10 permit Contracting Parties to carry forward and appropriately extend into the digital environment limitations and exceptions in their national laws which have been considered acceptable under the Berne Convention. Similarly, these provisions should be understood to permit Contracting Parties to devise new exceptions and limitations that are appropriate in the digital network environment.

It is also understood that Article 10(2) neither reduces nor extends the scope of applicability of the limitations and exceptions permitted by the Berne Convention.]

phonograms, which are not authorized by the performers or the producers of phonograms concerned or permitted by law.

Article 19

Obligations concerning Rights Management Information

(1) Contracting Parties shall provide adequate and effective legal remedies against any person knowingly performing any of the following acts knowing, or with respect to civil remedies having reasonable grounds to know, that it will induce, enable, facilitate or conceal an infringement of any right covered by this Treaty:

(i) to remove or alter any electronic rights management information without authority;

(ii) to distribute, import for distribution, broadcast, communicate or make available to the public, without authority, performances, copies of fixed performances or phonograms knowing that electronic rights management information has been removed or altered without authority.

(2) As used in this Article, "rights management information" means information which identifies the performer, the performance of the performer, the producer of the phonogram, the phonogram, the owner of any right in the performance or phonogram, or information about the terms and conditions of use of the performance or phonogram, and any numbers or codes that represent such information, when any of these items of information is attached to a copy of a fixed performance or a phonogram or appears in connection with the communication or making available of a fixed performance or a phonogram to the public.[16]

Article 20

Formalities

The enjoyment and exercise of the rights provided for in this Treaty shall not be subject to any formality.

Article 21

Reservations

Subject to the provisions of Article 15(3), no reservations to this Treaty shall be permitted.

---

[16] **Agreed statement concerning Article 19:** The agreed statement concerning Article 12 (on Obligations concerning Rights Management Information) of the WIPO Copyright Treaty is applicable *mutatis mutandis* also to Article 19 (on Obligations concerning Rights Management Information) of the WIPO Performances and Phonograms Treaty.

[The agreed statement concerning Article 12 of the WIPO Copyright Treaty reads as follows:

It is understood that the reference to "infringement of any right covered by this Treaty or the Berne Convention" includes both exclusive rights and rights of remuneration.

It is further understood that Contracting Parties will not rely on this Article to devise or implement rights management systems that would have the effect of imposing formalities which are not permitted under the Berne Convention or this Treaty, prohibiting the free movement of goods or impeding the enjoyment of rights under this Treaty.]

Article 22

Application in Time

(1) Contracting Parties shall apply the provisions of Article 18 of the Berne Convention, *mutatis mutandis*, to the rights of performers and producers of phonograms provided for in this Treaty.

(2) Notwithstanding paragraph (1), a Contracting Party may limit the application of Article 5 of this Treaty to performances which occurred after the entry into force of this Treaty for that Party.

Article 23

Provisions on Enforcement of Rights

(1) Contracting Parties undertake to adopt, in accordance with their legal systems, the measures necessary to ensure the application of this Treaty.

(2) Contracting Parties shall ensure that enforcement procedures are available under their law so as to permit effective action against any act of infringement of rights covered by this Treaty, including expeditious remedies to prevent infringements and remedies which constitute a deterrent to further infringements.

* * * *